INDIRECT DISCRIMINATION

A Case Study into the Development of the Legal Concept of Indirect Discrimination under EC Law

CHRISTA TOBLER

INSTITUUT VOOR
RECHTSWETENSCHAPPELIJK
ONDERZOEK

intersentia

Antwerpen – Oxford

Distribution for the UK:
Hart Publishing
Salter's Boat Yard
Folly Bridge
Abingdon Road
Oxford OX1 4LB
UK
Tel: + 44 1865 24 55 33
Fax: + 44 1865 79 48 82

Distribution for Switzerland and Germany:
Schulthess Verlag
Zwingliplatz 2
CH-8022 Zürich
Switzerland
Tel: + 41 1 251 93 36
Fax: + 41 1 261 63 94

Distribution for North America:
Gaunt Inc.
Gaunt Building
3011 Gulf Drive
Holmes Beach
Florida 34217-2199
USA
Tel: + 1 941 778 5211
Fax: + 1 941 778 5252

Distribution for other countries:
Intersentia Publishers
Groenstraat 31
2640 Mortsel
Belgium
Tel: + 32 3 680 15 50
Fax: + 32 3 658 71 21

Indirect Discrimination
Christa Tobler

© 2005 Intersentia
Antwerpen – Oxford
http://www.intersentia.be

ISBN 90-5095-458-8
D/2005/7849/51
NUR 825

The concept of discrimination must be interpreted on the basis of factual criteria. A purely theoretical idea is not sufficient.
(The Commission in *Sotgiu*, 1974)

Nothing is more fascinating and at the same time more deceptive than equality, and justice is often based on inequality; all this is well known.
(Advocate General Lagrange in *Italian Refrigerators*, 1963)

FOREWORD

This book is an updated and restructured version of a habilitation thesis submitted in the summer of 2003 to the Law Faculty of the University of Basel, Switzerland. In German speaking Switzerland, the habilitation is a prerequisite for eligibility for what are termed ordinary professorships. Under the traditional habilitation system, a candidate must first submit a written thesis on a topic of personal expertise. Once such a thesis has been approved, a candidate must present and defend an oral address in a separate subject area. The habilitation thesis and oral presentation together determine the range of subjects which the candiate will be entitled to teach once the habilitation procedure has been successfully completed (the so-called venia legendi). In my case, the written habilitation thesis concerned the development of the legal concept of indirect discrimination under both EC law and Swiss sex equality law. The oral presentation addressed the liberalization of the Swiss electricity market.

In Switzerland, habilitation theses are published only after successful completion of the habilitation procedure. I am grateful to the Law Faculty of Basel University and in particular to Prof. Anne Peters for their support and help throughout this rigorous procedure. I am also very grateful to Prof. Ingeborg Schwenzer whose efforts enabled me to come to Basel from The Netherlands where I was living and working at a time when I had no formal links with any Swiss university. Without her assistance, in all likelihood I would not have undertaken my habilitation in Basel nor served in my present capacity at the University's Europe Institute.

As originally submitted, my habilitation thesis was written in English. Also written in English, this book presents to the greater public-at-large those aspects of my thesis which specifically concern EC law. However, in the near future I intend to publish the chapter that deals specifically with Swiss law in a German language version. Since English is not my mother tongue, I enlisted the assistance of a native speaker to perform the various tasks involved in the language editing of this present publication. I have enjoyed the support of Sylvester (Danny) Ryan who dedicates himself to helping non-native English speakers express themselves in law. Indeed, his grounding in both language and EC law contributed significantly to my efforts to express myself clearly in this book. For that I am truly grateful to him.

When I undertook the study of law in Switzerland in the early 1980s, EC law was not a well established part of the university legal curriculum. In fact, I only began my formal study of EC law during the academic year 1993/1994 as a participant of The Leiden LL.M. Programme in EC Law. That same academic year I also gained a thorough grounding in equality and discrimination law through courses offered by the (then in existence) Department on Women and the Law (afdeling vrouw en recht) of the Law Faculty of Leiden University. The coursework that I was privileged to take in Leiden laid the groundwork for the analyses which I have undertaken in this book. Thus, I would like to express my heartfelt thanks to all my Leiden teachers, but particularly to Prof. Rikki Holtmaat (Professor of International Non-Discrimination Law at the Leiden Law Faculty), Dr. Bob Lane (of Edinburgh University and my teacher in the important Basic Course of the Leiden LL.M. Programme) and Prof. Piet Jan Slot (Director of the Europa Institute of the Leiden Law Faculty). After the completion of my LL.M. studies at Leiden, Prof. Slot enabled me to return to the Europa Institute and to work for The Leiden LL.M. Programme in EC Law. I have benefitted enormously from my continued close association with Leiden, particularly with regard to my knowledge of EC law. In the framework of my position with Leiden University, the work done for this present study was part of the E.M. Meijers Institute's research programme 'Securing the rule of law in a world of multilevel jurisdiction: coherence, institutional principles and fundamental rights' and, more specifically, of the sub-programme 'The protection of fundamental rights in an integrating Europe'.

Finally, my education, my habilitation and the publication of this book would not have been possible without the love, care and continued support of family and friends, particularly of my parents, Ruth and Theophil Tobler-Pulfer, and of my partner, Jacques Beglinger. They have been and continue to be a blessing to me. It is to them that I dedicate this book – though in the case of my mother, I must do so 'in loving memory'.

Basel and Leiden, March 2005

Christa Tobler

TABLE OF CONTENTS

ABBREVIATIONS

AG	Advocate General
AJP	Aktuelle Juristische Praxis
Art.	Article
BRK	Zeitschrift für Bank- und Kapitalmarktrecht
CDE	Cahiers de droit européen
CEDAW	Convention on the Elimination of All Forms of Discrimination against Women
CML Rev	Common Market Law Review
DM	Deutsche Mark (German Mark; former German currency)
ECHR	European Convention on Human Rights (European Convention for the Protection of Human Rights and Fundamental Freedoms)
EC	European Community
ECHR	European Convention on Human Rights
ECJ	European Court of Justice (Court of Justice of the European Communities)
ECSC	European Coal and Steel Community
EEC	European Economic Community
e.g.	exempli gratia (for example)
EL Rev	European Law Review
EU	European Union
EuGH	Europäischer Gerichtshof (Court of Justice of the European Communities)
EuGRZ	Europäische Grundrechte-Zeitschrift
EWS	Zeitschrift für europäisches Wirtschafts- und Steuerrecht
GATT	General Agreement on Trade and Tariffs
I.C.R.	Industrial Court Reports (UK)
i.e.	id est (that is)
ISO	International Organization for Standardization
ILJ	Industrial Law Journal
LL.M.	Master of Laws

MJ	Maastricht Journal of European and Comparative Law
NJB	Nederlands Juristenblad
NJW	Neue Juristische Wochenschrift
NTER	Nederlands tijdschrift voor Europees recht
n.y.r.	not yet reported
OJ	Official Journal of the European Union
PCIJ	Permanent Court of International Justice
RdA	Recht der Arbeit
R & R	Tijdschrift voor Rechtstheorie en Rechtsphilosophie
RTDE	Revue trimestrielle de droit européen
Rt. Hon.	Right Honorable (Government Minister in the UK)
S.C.R.	Supreme Court Reports (Canada)
SDA	Sex Discrimination Act (UK)
SEW	Sociaal-economische wetgeving
SR	Systematische Sammlung (systematic collection of Swiss Federal law)
StR	Steuer Revue
TvC	Tijdschrift voor Consumentenrecht
UK	United Kingdom of Great Britain and Northern Ireland
USA	United States of America
WTO	World Trade Organisation
ZeuP	Zeitschrift für Europäisches Privatrecht
ZvglRwiss	Zeitschrift für vergleichende Rechtswissenschaft

PART ONE:
INTRODUCTION AND BACKGROUND

This study concerns the development of the legal concept of indirect discrimination under EC law. Essentially, this study asks why the concept was originally needed, what it meant then and means today, and whether it is still necessary. The first part introduces the subject and explains the methodology of the research (below A.). Next, this study discusses several fundamental legal concepts that provide a background for the later analysis of the concept of indirect discrimination (below B.). The introductory part concludes with remarks on the historical precursors of the legal concept of indirect discrimination in EC law (below C.).

A. SUBJECT AND METHODOLOGY OF THE STUDY

I. ON THE SUBJECT

1. INTRODUCING INDIRECT DISCRIMINATION

The prohibition against discrimination in EC law has not always included *indirect* discrimination. Originally, EC law prohibited only what is now termed direct discrimination, that is discrimination caused by express reliance on grounds prohibited by law as the basis for disadvantageous treatment. Under EC law, only later was the legal concept of indirect discrimination created by the Court of Justice *through its case law*, a phenomenon that has been called 'a remarkable example of judicial creativity' (Barnard & Hepple).[1] Garrone[2] has tried to capture the general meaning of this case law-based concept in the following way:[3]

> 'The use of apparently neutral criteria may [...] lead to discrimination which is then termed indirect discrimination. Such discrimination is presumed to exist if a measure predominantly disadvantages persons who are members of a group that is protected against the use of a criterion prohibited as regards other persons – in this case there is an indirect distinction; this indirect distinction is discriminatory unless the contrary is proven. Such proof may be brought in two ways: a) the measure at issue does not lead to inequality because similar situations are treated similarly or different situations are treated differently, without taking into account in any way the prohibited criterion; b) the measure does not lead to discrimination in the strict sense, because it aims at a legitimate objective and is proportionate in that regard. Obviously, an objective may be legitimate only if it has nothing to do with the prohibited criterion.'[4]

---

[1] Barnard & Hepple 1999, p. 400. Similarly, Hernu 2003, p. 268, speaks of 'le fruit d'une construction prétorienne'.

[2] Garrone 1994, p. 448.

[3] Garrone's definition will be revisited in the context of the conclusions on the EC law part of the study, see below Part 2, A.IV.5.a.

[4] Translation provided by the present writer. The original French text reads: '[L]'emploi de critères en apparence neutres peut [...] conduire à une discrimination, qualifiée alors de discrimination indirecte. Cette discrimination est présumée dès qu'une mesure nuit davantage aux personnes membres d'un groupe protégé contre emploi d'un critère prohibé qu'aux autres personnes – il y a alors distinction indirecte; cette distinction indirecte est discriminatoire, à moins que la preuve du

More recently, other *legal definitions* of indirect discrimination have developed. For example, in Art. 2(2) of the Revised Second Equal Treatment Directive,[5] which deals with sex equality in employment, indirect discrimination is defined as relating to the situation 'where an apparently neutral provision, criterion or practice would put persons of one sex at a particular disadvantage compared with persons of the other sex, unless that provision, criterion or practice is objectively justified by a legitimate aim, and the means of achieving that aim are appropriate and necessary'.

In the light of these various definitions, the determination of whether or not indirect discrimination exists in a particular case is characterised by *two basic elements*, one relating to the nature of the prohibited measure and one to legitimacy of any justification:[6]

– The nature of the prohibited measure: indirect discrimination is *caused in an indirect way*, namely through a measure that on its face is not based on an explicitly prohibited discriminatory ground. In spite of its formal neutrality, the measure predominantly disadvantages persons (or objects) protected by an explicit non-discrimination provision (resulting in a so-called disparate effect or disparate impact).

– Justification: reliance on an apparently neutral ground with a disparate impact is prohibited unless there is *objective justification*. This requires that the measure is taken in the interest of a legitimate aim and that the measure is proportionate.

2. WHY A STUDY ON INDIRECT DISCRIMINATION?

The importance of the concept of indirect discrimination is often emphasised in academic writing (e.g. Sjerps:[7] 'the most promising aspect of non-discrimination law', Senden:[8] 'the corner stone of EC equality law', Lundström:[9] 'of fundamental and growing importance in anti-discrimination legislation'). As with all types of discrimination law, the legal prohibition against indirect discrimination is intended to operate in the practice of everyday life, rather than remaining a merely scholarly or theoretical

---

contraire ne soit apportée. Cette preuve peut être fournie de deux manières: a) la mesure en cause ne constitue pas une inégalité, car elle traite de façon similaire des situations similaires ou de façon différente des situations différentes, sans tenir nullement compte du critère prohibé; b) la mesure ne constitue pas une discrimination au sens étroit, car elle vise un objectif légitime et lui est proportionnée. Un objectif ne peut évidemment être légitime que s'il n'y a rien à faire avec le critère prohibé.'

5   Directive 2002/73/EC, 2002 L 269/15.
6   On the question whether this element concerns justification in the proper sense of the word or rather an issue of causation, see below Part 2, A.IV.3.e.
7   Sjerps 1994, p. 87.
8   Senden 1996, p. 158.
9   Lundström 2001, p. 143

notion. However, as Prechal[10] notes, even though the concept's development in EC law began in the late 1960s, it is still neither generally understood nor accepted – and, sometimes, not even acknowledged. In addition, its application can raise difficult questions even for specialists in anti-discrimination law. Against this background, there is *a genuine need for a better understanding* of the meaning of the legal concept of indirect discrimination and its proper place in the EC legal order. Studying it, therefore, is more than merely an academic exercise.

> The comments made by the news magazine The Economist[11] on a decision of a UK labour tribunal serves as an example of the lack of knowledge about, and understanding of, the concept of indirect discrimination among the general public and illustrates that difficult legal issues may arise in that context. This case, decided under national law, concerned the appointment by the UK Lord Chancellor, Lord Irvine, of a personal friend as his special adviser. A female solicitor complained, arguing that the Lord Chancellor's restricting the search to those personally known to him amounted to sex discrimination prohibited under national law. The labour tribunal to which she turned agreed. Noting that the Lord Chancellor had more male than female personal friends (he himself had declared this to be so), the tribunal stated that in such circumstances the appointment on the basis of personal knowledge will result in consideration of more men rather than women. In other words, limiting the search for a special advisor to the Lord Chancellor's own circle had a disproportionate negative impact on women. The Economist thought the court's finding of sex discrimination rather peculiar, arguing that '[i]n fact, the real discrimination in this case was not on grounds of sex, but against anyone who was not a friend of the Lord Chancellor'. Further comments concerned possible justification as well as the scope of the non-discrimination legislation in question (in particular the argument that a much more promising case might have been brought against Prime Minister Tony Blair for appointing Lord Irvine in the first place, given that the latter was made Lord Chancellor because of his being Mr Blair's old friend and patron).

3. A STUDY ON EC LAW

As is indicated by this study's title, this research focuses on *EC law*. Within that framework, the analysis is not limited to a specific field of EC law. Because the development of the concept of indirect discrimination in various areas of EC law is interconnected, it would be a mistake to limit the analysis to a particular discriminatory ground in an isolated way. Thus, the study provides *a broad analysis in various areas of EC law.*[12] Though the study limits itself to EC law, it is important to keep in mind that this legal order exists in a broader framework of international law. Both

---

[10]   Prechal 2004, pp. 535 subs.
[11]   The Economist of November 20th 1999, p. 54: 'Derry's friends'.
[12]   Regarding the specific fields that are covered, see later in this part, B.V.1.

international trade law (in particular of the Word Trade Organization (WTO)),[13] and human rights law (in particular the Council of Europe's Convention on Human Rights (ECHR)[14] and the United Nations' human rights law) are relevant to EC law. Bieback[15] has underlined the need for a broader study of the concept of indirect discrimination in today's public international law. However, that is not the aim of this present study which will touch upon public international law only briefly in the context of the broader historical background of the concept of indirect discrimination as relevant to EC law.[16]

> An example of an indirect discrimination approach in *international trade law* is found in the WTO rules concerning the internal taxation of goods, whose thrust is comparable to Art. 90 EC.[17] Fauchald[18] mentions 'implicit discrimination' and explains: '[T]here is no doubt that taxes may affect domestic and imported products differently even if they do not explicitly distinguish between them, and that such tax arrangements may violate Articles I and III of GATT 1994. [...] The essential feature of implicit discrimination is that the differential treatment of products is based on circumstances that are related to products as such, and not to the origin of the products.'[19]
>
> Regarding *human rights law*, statements to the effect that the prohibition of discrimination includes indirect discrimination are increasingly made in academic writing (regarding Art. 14 ECHR, e.g. Steiner,[20] Grief,[21] Waddington & Hendriks,[22] Gerards;[23] regarding the Convention on the Elimination of All Forms of Discrimination against Women (CEDAW),[24]

---

[13]   Before the existence of the WTO, all Member States were members of the GATT. Now the EC itself is a member. In terms of substance, important EC law provisions are modelled after GATT law; e.g. Mortelmans 1997, p. 186, regarding Art. 30 EC and Art. XX of the GATT. Generally on the relationship between EU and WTO trade law, e.g. Weiler 2000.

[14]   Art. 6(2) EU specifically refers to the 'fundamental rights, as guaranteed by the European Convention for the Protection of Human Rights and Fundamental Freedoms signed in Rome on 4 November 1950' that the Union shall respect. On the relationship between EU/EC law and ECHR law, e.g. Krüger & Polakiewicz 2001.

[15]   Bieback 1997, p. 15.

[16]   See later in this part, C.I.

[17]   Regarding Art. 90 EC, see further below Part 2, A.I.4.a. More generally, e.g. Barnard 2004, p. 31.

[18]   Fauchald 1998, pp. 161, 215 and 219.

[19]   Implicit discrimination should be distinguished from 'discrimination de facto', a term used for instance by Cottier & Mavroidis 2000, p. 4 (namely in contrast to 'discrimination de jure') which seems to correspond to what in EC law is termed substantive or material equality (see later in this part, B.II.2., and Verhoosel 2002, p. 21).

[20]   Steiner 1999, p. 348.

[21]   Grief 2002, at HR/6 subs.

[22]   Waddington & Hendriks 2002, p. 420.

[23]   Gerards 2002, p. 114.

[24]   On the relationship between EC law and the CEDAW, e.g. Gaspard 2003, also Holtmaat 2003 (CEDAW), p. 172.

e.g. Loenen,[25] Kägi-Diener,[26] König;[27] regarding the International Convention on the Elimination of All Forms of Racial Discrimination (CERD), e.g. Banton;[28] regarding human rights law in general, e.g. Hausammann).[29] For a long time, the European Court of Human Rights avoided the term though it accepted the concept in substance.[30] More recently, the Court stated in *Hoogendijk v. The Netherlands:*[31] '[W]here an applicant is able to show, on the basis of undisputed official statistics, the existence of a prima facie indication that a specific rule – although formulated in a neutral manner – in fact affects a clearly higher percentage of women than men, it is for the respondent Government to show that this is the result of objective factors unrelated to any discrimination on grounds of sex. If the onus of demonstrating that a difference in impact for men and women is not in practice discriminatory does not shift to the respondent Government, it will be in practice extremely difficult to prove *indirect discrimination*.' (Emphasis added.)

4. THE TWO MAIN RESEARCH QUESTIONS

Within the legal framework just described, this present study examines why the legal concept of indirect discrimination was originally needed, what it meant then and means today, how it can be distinguished from other concepts and whether it is still needed, given developments in EC law. These examinations are carried out through *two main research questions*, concerning, first, the development of the concept itself and, second, its place today in EC law.

a. The development of the legal concept of indirect discrimination

The first question requires little explanation. It simply examines the process of development of the legal concept of indirect discrimination and the issues raised in the course of that development. Most of the present study devoted to this question is essentially an exercise in legal history based on a detailed analysis of, first and foremost, the Court of Justice's indirect discrimination case law as handed down since

---

[25] Loenen 1996 (Inclusion), p. 23.
[26] Kägi-Diener 2001, p. 253.
[27] König 2004, p. 26.
[28] Banton 1996, p. 66.
[29] Hausammann 2002, p. 100.
[30] The Court has repeatedly held that discrimination can arise through 'measures whose object or result is to prejudice' protected persons (e.g. *Marckx v. Belgium*, application no. 6833/74, judgment of 13 June 1979, Publ. ECHR Series A Volume 31, para. 40). More recently, the Court also speaks of 'disproportionately prejudicial effects on a particular group' that may be considered as discriminatory notwithstanding the fact that the measure is not specifically directed or aimed at that group (e.g. *Hugh Jordan v. UK*, application no. 24746/94, judgment of 4 May 2001, para. 154). However, the test set up by the Court in this context is very hard to meet, see Gerards 2002, p. 115.
[31] *Hoogendijk v. The Netherlands*, application no. 58641/00, decision of 6 January 2005. The national legislation at issue in this case had an EC law background.

the late 1960s. The analysis of the *case law-based concept* will show that the two fundamental features of the concept – namely the recognition of the possibility that discrimination can be of an indirect nature and the element of objective justification – neither developed simultaneously nor in the same way in various areas of EC law. In addition, a wide variety of questions and problems calling for discussion have arisen in the course of this development. The adoption of the more recent *legal definitions* seems to complicate matters further given that some of them are inconsistent either with each other or with the case law definition. Ultimately, the question to be addressed is whether the concept of indirect discrimination, as defined today in EC law, is able to serve the purposes for which it was 'invented' or, rather, whether it should be improved.

b. The place of the concept in today's EC law

The *second research question* requires somewhat more explanation. Ultimately, it asks whether the concept of indirect discrimination is still necessary in EC law. The answer depends upon the existence of alternatives that might take its place. Accordingly, the concept of indirect discrimination remains more important in those areas of EC law where discrimination is the only type of infringement, for instance in social law. The situation is different in EC free movement law which prohibits not only (direct and indirect) discrimination but also what in this study is termed *restrictions in a wider sense.* The fact that it is sometimes difficult to draw the dividing line between these various concepts, particularly between indirect discrimination and restrictions in a wider sense, has led to debates about whether and to what extent a distinction between the various concepts is still necessary or useful, especially in light of possible justifications. This discussion is particularly fuelled by seemingly sweeping statements on justification such as in the Portuguese *Golden Shares* case[32] (para. 48) and in *Bacardi*[33] (para. 32) where the Court explained that free movement rights may be limited by national rules justified by reasons mentioned in the Treaty or for overriding requirements of the general interest. As Drijber[34] has pointed out, such statements must be read in their specific context. At least on the conceptual level, the Portuguese *Golden Shares* case shows that it is still necessary to distinguish between different forms of infringement under free movement law. This case also raises some other issues that are relevant to the second research question of this present study.

The *Golden Shares* cases concerned national systems granting the State certain prerogatives to intervene in the share structure and the management of privatised

---

[32]   Case C-367/98, *ECR* I-4731; the other *Golden Shares* cases are: Case C-483/99, *ECR* I-4781; Case C-503/99, *ECR* I-4809; Case C-463/00, *ECR* I-4581, and Case C-98/01, *ECR* I-4641.

[33]   Case C-429/02, judgment of 13 July 2004, n.y.r.

[34]   Drijber 2002, p. 238.

undertakings in strategically important areas, such as the energy sector. Considering such prerogatives incompatible with EC law, the Commission instituted enforcement proceedings against a number of Member States. The Court focused on the rules on free movement of capital (Art. 56 subs. EC)[35] and within that framework examined first the restrictive nature of the contested measures and, then, the issue of justification. In contrast to other *Golden Shares* cases, the Portuguese case involved two different types of measures, one expressly based on nationality (the law made it possible to limit the access of foreigners to the capital of undertakings in the process of being privatised so that they could hold only a certain number of shares), the other applicable regardless of nationality (namely the requirement of prior authorization for the sale of shares to other parties). The Court explicitly distinguished between these measures and examined them in turn (*Commission v Portugal*, para. 39 subs.). The Court quoted the Commission's Communication on intra-EU investment[36] which distinguishes between discriminatory and non-discriminatory measures in terms of both the nature of the measure and the justification available in such cases. The Court did not contradict that distinction but rather confirmed it through its approach in the Portuguese case (a fact that is noted only in some academic literature).[37]

Specifically, the Court held that the *limitations imposed on foreigners* involve 'unequal treatment of nationals of other Member States and restrict[s] the free movement of capital', in other words, a prohibited discrimination. Because the Portuguese Government had not pleaded any justification in this context, the Court did not need to elaborate on the possibility of justifications which are potentially available in cases involving discriminatory measures. However, earlier in the judgment the Court quoted the Commission which had distinguished between categories of justification according to which 'discriminatory measures' can only be justified on the basis of express derogation grounds provided by the Treaty (Art. 58 EC), whilst 'non-discriminatory measures' can be justified both on these grounds as well as on general interest grounds; *Commission v Portugal*, para. 24 and 27). The Court examined the *authorization requirement* in that latter context, recalling that the Treaty lays down a general prohibition on restrictions on the movement of capital which goes beyond the mere elimination of unequal treatment on grounds of nationality. The Court noted that a prior authorization requirement constitutes such a restriction, making it necessary 'to consider whether, and on what basis, that restriction may be justified' (*Commission v Portugal*, para. 46). The Court acknowledged that certain concerns may justify the retention by the Member States of a degree of influence within undertakings that were initially public and subsequently privatised, where those undertakings are active in fields involving the provision of strategic services or services in the public interest. The

---

[35] The Commission had also raised complaints regarding the freedom of establishment (Art. 43 EC).
[36] Communication on certain legal aspects concerning intra-EU investment, *OJ* 1997 C 220/15.
[37] Compare Bayer 2002, p. 2289; Ruge 2002, p. 422; Grundmann & Möslein 2002, p. 761, footnote 28, and p. 763; Mortelmans 2002, p. 345; Schutte-Feenstra 2002, p. 275; Szyszczak 2002, p. 273; Fleischer 2003, p. 495; Krause 2002, p. 2748, and Ebke 2002, p. 336.cz

Court noted, however, that those concerns cannot entitle Member States to plead their own systems of property ownership, referred to in Article 222 of the Treaty, by way of justification for such obstacles to the exercise of the freedoms provided for by the Treaty. To this, the Court added (*Commission v Portugal*, para. 48):[38] 'The free movement of capital, as a fundamental principle of the Treaty, may be restricted only by national rules which are justified by reasons referred to in Article 73d(1) of the Treaty or by overriding requirements of the general interest and which are applicable to all persons and undertakings pursuing an activity in the territory of the host Member State. Furthermore, in order to be so justified, the national legislation must be suitable for securing the objective which it pursues and must not go beyond what it necessary in order to attain it, so as to accord with the principle of proportionality'.[39]

Although the Portuguese *Golden Shares* case appears to confirm the need to distinguish between different types of infringements, it also raises questions about *the place of the legal concept of indirect discrimination* in the framework of Art. 56 EC. Indirect discrimination is mentioned neither in the Commission's Communication nor in the Court's judgment referring to that Communication. Opposing discriminatory and non-discriminatory measures, the Commission simply defined the former as 'those applied exclusively to investors from another EU Member State' and the latter as 'those applied to nationals and other EU investors alike'. The fact that this latter category is termed 'non-discriminatory', rather than 'indistinctly applicable' or 'formally neutral', could be taken to indicate that it does not include indirect discrimination. This would, however, be puzzling in view of the fact that measures indirectly discriminating on grounds of nationality are indeed applied to nationals and foreigners alike. In fact, this study's main part[40] will demonstrate that thus far the Court has never made an explicit finding of indirect discrimination in the area of free movement of capital, even though some cases could be analysed in that framework.[41]

---

[38] For that last statement, see also Case C-483/99, [2002] *ECR* I-4781 (para. 45), Case C-503/99, [2002] *ECR* I-4809 (para. 45), Case C-463/00, [2003] *ECR* I-4581 (para. 68). In the fifth *Golden Shares* case, there is no such statement since no argument relating to justification had been raised; see Case C-98/01, [2003] *ECR* I-4641 (para. 49).

[39] Mortelmans 2002, p. 345, notes that the Court's reference to justification in the general interest was, in fact, not necessary in the context of the first three *Golden Shares* cases, since the justifications relied on by the French and Belgian Governments could be examined in the light of the express derogation provision of Art. 58 EC and the justification relied on by the Portuguese Government was not acceptable anyway since it was purely economic (on this latter issue, see below Part 2, A.IV.3.c). Mortelmans thought that the Court's remarks on general interest justification might prove useful in future golden shares cases. However, the later Spanish case also concerned public security (see para. 71), and the UK case did not raise the issue of justification at all (see para. 49).

[40] See below Part 2, A.4.m.

[41] Although further examples will be discussed in this study's main part, one case dealing with the issue of golden shares deserves brief mention at this point. *Commission v Italy* (Case C-58/99, *ECR* I-3811) involved a rule prohibiting all professional persons lawfully pursuing their activities in other Member States or recently established in Italy from performing certain tasks. Though the Commission, AG Mischo or the Court did not analyse the case in this framework, it can easily be argued that criteria

This type of situation raises a number of questions that will be discussed in the context of the second research question, in particular: first, is it at all possible to make a clear distinction between the various concepts, both in terms of the nature of the prohibited measures and in terms of possible justifications, and second, is it useful to do so from a practical perspective? Alternatively, would it be possible to abandon certain or even all such distinctions in favour of a more limited number of concepts of even of a single and simpler standard? If so, how likely is the Court of Justice to adopt such an approach?

II. ON METHOD

Having set out the research questions and their implications, the next step is to explain the research method and the study's structure.

1. A LEGAL AND CONCEPTUAL ANALYSIS ESSENTIALLY BASED ON CASE LAW

The method used in academic research, obviously, depends on its subject matter. Wentholt[42] notes that the concept of equality (and, therefore, also that of discrimination) can be studied either on a theoretical and philosophical level (normative analysis) or on the level of its practical legal meaning (legal analysis). This present study focuses on that latter one in that it aims to provide a *legal analysis* of the concept of indirect discrimination in the context of its historical development. In contrast, it does not aim to provide a normative examination of the meanings of equality and discrimination nor examine the place of indirect discrimination in such a framework.[43]

The study focuses on the development of the notion of indirect discrimination from a purely legal concept, into what will be termed the *indirect discrimination formula*. Thus, the focus concerns the general definition of indirect discrimination rather than the details of every conceivable application in practice. Others have

---

specifying professionals 'lawfully pursuing their activities in another Member State' or 'recently established in Italy', whilst formally neutral in terms of nationality, tend to disadvantage foreigners in particular, because it is most often foreigners who will find themselves in such situations.

[42] Wentholt 1996, pp. 142 and 143.

[43] Therefore, it suffices to note that academic views on this issue differ and to give some examples: Morris 1995, p. 228, sees indirect discrimination law as an effort to compensate individuals for wrongs (rather than as an effort to award them distributive benefits); McCrudden 1985, pp. 82 subs., puts it in the context of redistributive justice (see also Gardner 1989, p. 4; Kyriazis 1990, p. 86; Barbera 1994, p. 4; Somek 2001, p. 187) and Bieback 1997, p. 38, considers it a liberal concept of procedural justice in the classical sense.

performed detailed and valuable studies in that regard which will be relied on where necessary for present purposes.

Finally, for the very reason that in EC law the concept of indirect discrimination was developed through the Court of Justice's case law, this present study is set up as *a case study*. In this regard, particular emphasis is put on the cases, the arguments made in their context and the precise wording used by the Court in formulating its considerations and findings. In addition, this study can be read on two levels. Thus, the text of the study has been divided into regular and small print sections. For understanding the flow of the argument, it is sufficient to read the main text in regular print. The more detailed explanations and the quotes in the small print paragraphs are intended to allow the reader to understand the broader context and to consult the original formulations.

2. A NOTE ON MATERIALS, LANGUAGE AND REFERENCE TO EC LAW PROVISIONS

In the framework just described, the research for this study involved a large number of decisions by the Court of Justice and of academic comments on them.[44] The number of such comments is so large that choices had to be made, limiting the materials under consideration. Other limitations resulted from the lack of availability of certain pieces in the libraries consulted,[45] and naturally, the present writer's language abilities also imposed certain limits. Most of the literature drawn from for this study has been written in the English, Dutch or German languages, though some of it was in French, Italian and Spanish. The language version of all the forms of EC legislation and as well as the case law cited in this study is English.

This study employs various forms to refer to specific EC law provisions, depending upon the period of time to which each relates (i.e. pre- and post-Maastricht and, within the latter category, pre- and post-Amsterdam). In principle, the study follows the system suggested by the Court of Justice,[46] though a derogation is made in relation to Art. 141(1) and (2) EC, the Treaty provision on equal pay for men and women that plays an essential role in the context of indirect sex discrimination. Here, the ordinary

---

[44] A list of case notes is provided by the Court of Justice in its *Notes. Références de doctrine aux arrêts de la court de Justice et du Tribunal de première instance des Communautés européennes*, available at the following internet site: http://www.curia.eu.int/en/recdoc/notes/index.htm.

[45] Essentially the university libraries of Leiden (the Netherlands), Basel, Zurich and Berne (all in Switzerland) as well as the library of the European University Institute at Florence (Italy).

[46] See the Note on the citation of articles of the Treaties in the publications of the Court of Justice and the Court of First Instance, *OJ* 1999 C 246/1; also to be found at the site http://www.curia.eu.int/en/jurisp/renum.htm.

reference system is used rather than the more complicated exception rule formulated by the Court.

In the Court's system, references such as 'Art. 1 of the EEC Treaty' refer to the Treaty's pre-Maastricht version (when the name of the Community was 'European Economic Community', EEC), references such as 'Art. 1 of the EC Treaty' relate to the post-Maastricht but pre-Amsterdam version and references such as 'Art. 1 EC' to the consolidated[47] Amsterdam version of the EC Treaty (with the Maastricht version, the name of the Community changed into the simple 'European Community', EC) and to the Nice Treaty[48] (which is the version now in force). In this present study, the general reference 'of the Treaty' includes all pre-Amsterdam versions.

According to the Court, references to provisions of the Treaty's social chapter should be followed by the general remark 'Articles 117 to 120 of the EC Treaty have been replaced by Articles 136 EC to 143 EC', rather than by a reference to the former numbering of the specific provision at issue. The reason for this is the fact that during the course of the revision of Amsterdam Arts. 117-120 were replaced *en bloc* as a consequence of the integration of the former Social Agreement[49] and that, as a result, the former provisions are hardly recognisable in the new text of the social chapter. However, Art. 141 EC is an exception in that its first two sections are easily recognisable as an amended version of the former Art. 119 of the EC Treaty. Therefore, it seems simpler to refer to them in the same way as other Treaty provisions ('Art. 119 of the EC Treaty (now, after amendment, Art. 141(1) and (2) EC)' and 'Art. 141(1) and (2) EC (formerly Art. 119 of the EC Treaty)', respectively), rather than by using the somewhat cumbersome reference suggested by the Court.

---

[47] The Amsterdam revision of the EU and EC Treaties led to a cleaning up and renumbering of the Treaty provisions, the result of which is referred to as the 'consolidated versions' of the Amsterdam Treaties. The consolidated version of the EC Treaty is published in *OJ* 1999 C 246/1 p. 173. The so-called Amsterdam Draft Treaty (version indicating the changes before renumbering), important because its numbering is used in conversion tables, can be found in *OJ* 1997 C 340/1.

[48] For the text of the Treaty of Nice, see *OJ* 2001 C 80/1. For the consolidated version of the EC Treaty in the Nice version, see *OJ* 2002 C 325/01. The Nice Treaty has been in force since 1 February 2003.

[49] The Social Agreement was concluded by eleven of the then twelve Member States; the UK abstained. It was based on the Social Protocol which was attached to the Treaty on the occasion of the revision of Maastricht (*OJ* 1992 C 191/90). The background for this was the UK's resistance to secondary law on social law issues which made the adoption of such law impossible under a legislative procedure requiring unanimity (Arts. 100 and 235 of the EC Treaty). In the Social Protocol, the twelve Member States agreed that eleven of them (all except the UK) were entitled to move forward in the area of social law. This was an early instance of variable geometry (Europe with different speeds). It was reversed by the integration of the provisions of the Social Agreement into the Treaty which became possible when the UK, under its new Labour government, gave up its former resistance against social law made on the level of the Community; see Tobler 2000 (Sex Equality Law).

3. SET-UP OF THE STUDY

The study is divided into three major parts. *Part 1* continues by introducing a number of fundamental legal notions that form the theoretical background for the later analyses on indirect discrimination. This part also serves as an independent, general introduction to the legal concepts of equality and discrimination particularly relevant to EC law. Further, the introductory part briefly discusses the historical precursors of the legal concept of indirect discrimination as it is known today in EC law.

Part 2 presents detailed and extensive analyses of the historical development of the concept of indirect discrimination in EC law. Beginning with the *case law-based concept*, Part 2 first discusses the recognition that discrimination may have an indirect nature and then examines the development of the element of objective justification. This is followed by a discussion of a number of other related issues. Next, Part 2 examines the development of the more recent *legal definitions* of indirect discrimination and compares them to the case law-based definitions.

Part 3 deals with conceptual distinctions which exist in EC law between direct and indirect discrimination on the one hand and, in the specific context of free movement law, between indirect discrimination and restrictions in a wider sense on the other hand. Bringing together the study's most important findings, Part 3 provides suggestions for an improved definition of indirect discrimination and for sharper lines of demarcation between the various concepts. It also examines whether it would be possible to abandon the distinctions between the various concepts altogether and to adopt an approach which relies on one single and more simple standard instead. Finally, Part 3 also assesses whether such an approach is likely to be embraced by the Court of Justice.

B. PARAMETERS

I. INTRODUCTORY REMARKS

The following remarks introduce several fundamental legal concepts that form the background necessary for the later analysis relating to indirect discrimination. Since indirect discrimination is a specific form of discrimination and, as such, inescapably linked to equality, equality and discrimination are the most important parameters with regard to this study. Again, the aim of this present study is not to contribute to the *normative* examination of the meaning of equality and, thus, to explore in depth the many meanings of this concept – which have been described as deeply contested, puzzled, ever-evasive and relating to eternal issues (e.g. Lacey,[50] Kravaritou,[51] Holtmaat,[52] Harms,[53] Dworkin).[54] Rather, the following sections simply introduce a number of *legal concepts* of equality (below II.) and discrimination (below III.) in variations that are relevant for the purposes of this study. The concept of restrictions in a wider sense due to its relevance in EC free movement law is also examined because of this concept's importance in the context of the distinctions under EC law between indirect discrimination and other concepts (IV.). Given the need for these parameters, a further section explains the nature of an equality or non-discrimination provision, thereby setting out those areas of EC law that are to be discussed and those to be omitted (below V.). Sub-part B. concludes with a summary of the most important points concerning these parameters (below VI.).

By way of a general introduction, the relevance to the legal concept of indirect discrimination of the parameters discussed below can be set out briefly as follows:
– In the framework of most legal orders, including EC law, indirect discrimination is normally discussed in the context of *equality in the law*, a concept that relates to the law's substance, rather than only to its application (which is the focus of equality before the law).
– The concept of indirect discrimination is linked to a particular interpretation of legal equality that requires that *likes be treated alike and unalikes unalike*, according

---

[50] Lacey 1987, p. 413.
[51] Kravaritou 1994, p. 227.
[52] Holtmaat 1999 (Eeuwige kwesties).
[53] Harms 2000, p. 105.
[54] Dworkin 2000, p. 2.

to their differences. Under alternative approaches, this concept may be less relevant or even altogether irrelevant.

- The concept of indirect discrimination is said to be related to *substantive* rather than formal equality because it is effect-oriented.
- In view of its aims, indirect discrimination is sometimes linked to *equality of opportunity*, according to which prospects and experiences in life ought not to vary because of arbitrary criteria such as sex, race or handicap.
- Given the factual background of many indirect discrimination cases, in particular in the area of social law, the legal concept of indirect discrimination is also said to be meant to apply to situations involving *structural discrimination*, that is, disadvantage caused through structural, systemic or institutional aspects of a society.
- The legal concept of indirect discrimination has been developed in order to complement the more straightforward concept of *direct discrimination* which involves disadvantage caused through explicit (or, depending on the interpretation, at least obvious) reliance on a prohibited discriminatory ground.
- In early EC case law, the Court of Justice distinguished between discrimination in form and in substance. The question of how this distinction relates to indirect discrimination is debated in academic writing.
- The role which the legal concept of indirect discrimination can play in the context of *openly worded provisions*, that is, in non-discrimination provisions that do not mention discriminatory grounds at all or that provide an open list of such grounds as mere examples, depends notably on the justification test.
- The contemporary definition of indirect discrimination contains the element of *objective justification*. In academic writing, it is debated whether this is an issue of justification in the strict sense of the word ('there is discrimination but it can be justified') or rather an issue of causation (meaning that in cases involving legitimate justification, there is no discrimination in the first place because the cause for the disadvantage is something different from the prohibited ground).
- Particularly with regard to indirect discrimination, issues of *justification are often confused with issues of comparability*, though from a conceptual point of view the latter concern an earlier level of the analysis.
- All legal discussions of discrimination should be considered in the light of the contrasting concept of *factual discrimination* which relates to practices that, though not legally prohibited, may appear discriminatory on the basis of different, extra-legal standards.
- In EC free movement law, the concept of indirect discrimination must be recognised as distinct from not only that of direct discrimination but also that of *restrictions in a wider sense* (those measures which, though formally neutral, are liable to hamper or to render less attractive the exercise of free movement rights).

The distinction between the concepts of indirect discrimination and restrictions in a wider sense is particularly difficult to identify.

These points will be revisited during the following discussions on equality and discrimination. Thus, a fuller treatment of the legal concept of indirect discrimination will be developed over the course of this study.

II. EQUALITY

Equality has been variously called the myth of the 20th century,[55] the pivotal issue of the 21st century,[56] but also the endangered species of political ideas.[57] As a *legal concept,* it appears in a number of forms. Discussed below are equality before and in the law, formal and substantive equality, as well as equality of opportunity. This is followed by some remarks on the function of equality in EC law.

1. EQUALITY BEFORE THE LAW AND IN THE LAW

a. The concepts

Arguably, the two most basic notions of equality are equality before the law and equality in the law.[58] Vierdag's[59] seminal study on the concept of discrimination in international law, which discusses them in a particularly helpful manner, points out that *equality before the law* means the same application of the law to everybody regardless of the content of the law. Equality in that sense does not relate to the substantive legal differentiations made by the law (e.g. in an apartheid system, between persons of different race), it merely requires the same application of the law to all persons (e.g. the same application of the apartheid system to all citizens, whatever their race). Vierdag in this context quotes Kelsen, according to whom this understanding of equality requires nothing in addition to the general principle, present in all law, of the lawfulness of the application of the law. Accordingly, equality before the law can be described as a predominantly technical principle. In the present writer's analysis, the famous *Yick Wo and Wo Lee*[60] case, decided by the U.S. Supreme Court in 1886

---

[55] Apollis 1980, p. 73.
[56] MacKinnon 2001, p. vi.
[57] Dworkin 2000, p. 1.
[58] The terminology may differ. Alkema & Rop 2002, p. 31, for example, speak of 'equality through the law'.
[59] Vierdag 1973, pp. 16 subs.
[60] *Yick Wo v. Hopkins* and *Wo Lee v. Hopkins,* 118 U.S. 356 (1886).

concerning an unequal application of law on the basis of race of an in itself non-discriminatory rule, provides an example.

The case concerned two Chinese men active in a laundry business in California for more than twenty years. Under the applicable legislation, persons wishing to engage in that activity in San Francisco needed to obtain the consent of the board of supervisors, except if the laundry was located in a building constructed either of brick or stone. Almost all of San Francisco's laundries, including Mr Wo's and Mr Lee's business locations, were made of wood. Messrs Wo and Lee were put in prison when they carried on with their activities after their licences had not been renewed. In court, they argued that the refusal to renew their licences constituted a 'system of oppression to one kind of men, and favoritism to all others', maintaining that the Californian rules were 'void by reason of their administration, operating unequally [...], – an unjust and illegal discrimination [...] which, though not made expressly by the ordinances, is made possible by them' (*Yick Wo and Wo Lee*, p. 358 and 369). The Supreme Court agreed, finding that the board responsible for the licences had denied the applications for renewal to more than 200 Chinese persons while granting the renewal to all non-Chinese persons except for one. Judge Matthews explained (*Yick Wo and Wo Lee*, p. 373 and 374): '[...] an administration directed so exclusively against a particular class of persons as to warrant and require the conclusion that, whatever may have been the intent of the ordinances as adopted, they are applied by the public authorities charged with their administration, and thus representing the state itself, with a mind so unequal and oppressive as to amount to a practical denial by the state of that equal protection of the laws which is secured to the petitioners, as to all other persons, by the broad an benign provisions of the fourteenth amendment to the constitution of the United States. Though the law itself be fair on its face, and impartial in appearance, yet, if it is applied and administered by public authority with an evil eye and unequal hand, so as practically to make unjust and illegal discriminations between persons in similar circumstances, material to their rights, the denial of equal justice is within the prohibitions of the constitution. [...] the conclusion cannot be resisted that no reason for it exists except hostility to the race and nationality to which the petitioners belong.'

In such a case, the discrimination does not result from the relevant provision itself (requiring a renewal of the permit), but rather from how it is applied. As Manolkidis[61] notes, the *Yick Wo and Wo Lee* case involved discriminatory intent on the part of the San Francisco city administration which was inferred from a consistent practice of refusing applications for laundry permits from Chinese applicants while accepting almost every Caucasian petitioner. In other words, a truly neutral rule was applied in a non-neutral way so as to lead, in fact, to racial discrimination. This constitutes discrimination on the level of equality *before* the law, rather than equality in the law and, in that context, is direct discrimination.[62] There would have been a *prima facie* case of *indirect discrimination* as related to equality *in* the law if the race-neutral differentiation ground mentioned in the law (namely the

---

[61]   Manolkidis 1997, p. 83.
[62]   Though MacKinnon 2001, pp. 69 subs., mentions the case in the context of disparate impact (see later in this part, C.II.).

material from which buildings were made), had disadvantaged Chinese persons in particular, due to the fact that the operators of wooden laundry buildings were usually Chinese. (However, this was not the case in San Francisco.)

Today, the equality debate focuses mainly on *equality in the law* which concerns the character of legal differentiations of the law's content (for example, the differences in treatment under the apartheid system), or, in essence, with the system itself. Equality in the law involves the notion *suum cuique tribuere* (to grant each person his or her due). According to Vierdag, equality in the law aims to bring about equality of social conditions. However, this goal may require different treatment of various parties,[63] though in Vierdag's view same treatment must still prevail in so far as there are no relevant inequalities to be taken into account. Because of its focus on the substantive nature of a given measure, indirect discrimination is usually regarded as related to equality in the law rather than to equality before the law.

b. *Equality in the law: an 'Aristotelian' notion*

i. The Aristotelian formula

In the Western world, the legal concept of equality has traditionally been interpreted[64] on the basis of the writings by the Greek philosopher Aristotle (384-322 B.C.)[65] which are understood as meaning that justice requires that things that are like should be treated alike, while things that are unalike should be treated unalike in proportion to their unalikeness. In such a framework, equality is a necessary corollary[66] of justice.

> According to Tridimas,[67] Aristotle considered equality and justice as synonymous. In contrast, Powers[68] argues that Aristotle simply quoted a 'general opinion' which he personally refuted. Whatever the correct interpretation, MacKinnon[69] is correct in noting that for the purposes of 'real life', what Aristotle thought or meant is less important than what has actually been made of his thinking – hence the use of the term 'Aristotelian' in this present study when referring to the principle that likes should be treated alike and unalikes differently.

---

[63] McKean 1983, p. 286, speaks about relative equality, i.e. 'different treatment proportionate to concrete individual circumstances'.

[64] This includes both national and public international law; see Plender 1995, p. 63.

[65] See in particular Aristotle 1980, V (a more recent English translation is Aristotle 2000).

[66] In the context of sex equality (but not necessarily limited to it), Ley 1993 argues that the other necessary corollary of justice is recognition (i.e. respect for and recognition of plaintiffs as persons brave enough to fight for justice).

[67] Tridimas 1999, p. 40, footnote 1.

[68] Powers 1996, p. 130.

[69] MacKinnon 2001, p. 4. On the link of equality and justice in Aristotle's work, see also von Leyden 1985 and Gardner 1996.

According to a well-known shorthand, the benchmark for legal equality is 'to treat likes alike and unalikes unalike, according to the difference'. Vierdag[70] explains the meaning of this as follows: '[I]f equal treatment is accorded to equals the result is equal social conditions; if equal treatment is accorded to unequals the result is unequal social conditions; likewise if unequal treatment is accorded to equals the result is unequal social conditions; if unequal treatment is accorded to equals, then, depending on the factual unequalness and the character of the treatment: the inequality as to the social conditions has increased, has become wider, or the inequality as to the social conditions is compensated, a certain levelling has come about.' To explain the Aristotelian formula's general and widespread acceptance, Vierdag[71] points to its ambiguous and formal nature. The latter element indicates that equality in itself cannot determine the nature of the treatment in question, whilst it is precisely on the nature of the treatment that its result depends. The former, ambiguity, refers to the dual character of the equality formula: equality can mean either treating likes alike or treating unalikes unalike ('Gleichheit bedeutet einmal: jedem das Gleiche, einmal: jedem das Seine.'; Salomon, as quoted by Vierdag).

This inevitably leads to the questions: 'What is alike?' and 'What is unalike or different?' Vierdag observes that absolute equality in the sense of alikeness or sameness can only exist between abstract notions, such as exist in mathematics. Elsewhere, the plurality of objects and of situations always and necessarily entails some difference, in that even identical objects still differ as to their respective places. Equality is, therefore, a relative notion, an abstraction involving more or fewer differences. Against this background, the element of 'alikeness' in the Aristotelian formula in practice translates into the 'similarly situated requirement', or the requirement of *comparability of situation* (More,[72] Plötscher).[73] Börner[74] explains that the question of alikeness requires two intellectual steps, one logical, and the other axiological. The logical step involves an assessment of sameness and difference, and the axiological step involves a value judgment concerning the relevance of the sameness or the difference found in the specific context at issue.[75] Vierdag notes that since law is a system of abstractions and differentiations, a dilemma results as to whether aspects of equality or aspects of inequality should prevail. As a matter of choice and of will, this issue depends on whether one wants to stress the attributes which are different or, rather, those which are in common. There are no logical or legal limits regarding the capacity of human judgment to ignore, to recognize or to introduce inequalities on whatever grounds.

---

[70] Vierdag 1973, p. 13.
[71] Idem, at pp. 8 subs.
[72] More 1993, p. 48.
[73] Plötscher 2003, p. 42, speaks of 'Identität als Einssein'.
[74] Börner 1973, pp. 51 subs.
[75] In contrast, according to Zuleeg 1992, p. 478, the first step is not strictly logical and both steps can fall together.

MacKinnon's[76] finding, made in the framework of U.S. law, that the status of not being similarly situated 'can be created by Congress as well as God, biology, and the market', is particularly telling in this context.

ii. Aristotelian equality – An empty shell?

The characteristics of the Aristotelian equality formula have inspired much critical analysis. A particularly well-known example is provided by Westen who has called the Aristotelian notion of equality 'empty' and even 'patently absurd'.[77]

> Westen[78] explains: 'Just as no category of 'like' people exists in nature, neither do categories of 'like' treatment exist; treatments can be alike only in reference to some moral rule. [...] So there it is: equality is entirely '[c]ircular'. [...] Equality is an empty vessel with no substantive moral content of its own. Without moral standards, equality remains meaningless. [...] Equality is an undeniable and unchangeable moral truth because it is a simple tautology.' In Westen's view, equality should be abandoned as an explanatory norm and replaced by a discourse on rights. This is based on two propositions, namely: '(1) that statements of equality logically entail (and necessarily collapse into) simpler statements of rights; and (2) that the additional step of transforming simple statements of rights into statements of equality not only involves unnecessary work but also engenders profound conceptual confusion.' According to Westen, '[e]quality will cease to mystify – and cease to skew moral and political discourse – when people come to realise that it is an empty form having no substantive content of its own. That will occur as soon as people realize that every moral and legal argument can be framed in the form of an argument for equality. People will then answer arguments for equality by making counter-arguments for equality. Or simpler still, they will see that they can do without equality altogether.' In the USA, Westen's views engendered a lively academic debate on the usefulness of the legal concept of equality.[79]

In spite of such criticism, Western societies appear to be reluctant to let go of an Aristotelian understanding of equality. They seem to agree with Steindorff,[80] according to whom the concept of equality can be made relevant by rendering it concrete. However, the fact remains that in doing so legal orders tend to rely on principles and

---

[76] MacKinnon 2001, p. 247.
[77] According to Westerman 2000, p. 115, the argument goes back to views expressed by the legal philosopher Hans Kelsen. Also Chavret 1969, p. 1, spoke about Aristotelian equality as 'a relatively trivial and uninteresting affair'.
[78] Westen 1982, pp. 442 and 596, see also Westen 1990. Westen's argument has been variously reiterated, e.g. Harms 2000, pp. 106 subs. For further examples, see Gerards 2002, p. 9, footnote 9.
[79] E.g. the following comments and Westen's answers: Burton 1981/82, Westen 1981/82, Chemerinsky 1983, D'Amato 1983, Westen 1983 (The Meaning of Equality), Greenawalt 1983, Westen 1983 (To Lure the Tarantula).
[80] Steindorff 1965, p. 59. See also Barnard 1998, p. 363.

views valid at a particular point in time in the mainstream of their societies, thereby making the concept's meaning dependent on the context in which it is applied. Against this background, Westerman[81] has argued that both the interpretation of the principle of equality as an empty shell and that as a not yet perfected form of the ideal of substantive equality[82] are misleading. Instead, she proposes to regard the principle as a heuristic device, i.e. 'a way to find arguments, a vantage-point (*topos*), from which the various conflicting justifications can be assessed'.

> Westerman explains: 'The principle is not an empty shell, because it generates reasons and arguments that could not have been found without the principle. Neither is the principle an expression of just one overriding aim, but a way to develop and to assess various and conflicting aims. The development of the principle of equality over the years has shown that the principle has acquired a dynamism of its own. It is not only a means to solve problems, but generates new problems as well. Or it generates problems that did not exist in the first place. The principle of equality not only meets old needs, but creates new possibilities as well. Therefore, it is dangerous to fix one of a set of definite goals. Such a strategy would narrow down its wide array of new possibilities and turn the principle into the empty shell it never was.'

c. The Aristotelian approach in EC law

In the European Communities, it became clear early on that the legal concept of equality underlying these legal orders is based on an Aristotelian understanding. As More[83] observes, the starting point for this approach can be found in the law of the (now expired) European Coal and Steel Community (ECSC).[84]

> As an early indication, More mentions *Hauts Fourneaux de Chasse*[85] (p. 230) concerning discrimination allegedly caused through the application of a uniform equalization rate to ferrous scrap of foreign and domestic origin. The Court found that it was 'conceivable that a uniform rate may have different effects' but that there was not 'sufficient legal proof that the application of a uniform rate constituted discrimination'. Wouters[86] points to *Fonderies de Pont-à-Mousson*[87] (at p. 231) where the Court held that discrimination results from 'dissimilar treatment of comparable situations'. A further early example from ECSC law is *Klöckner-Werke*[88] (at p. 345) where the Court stated: 'For the High Authority to be accused of discrimination it must be shown to have treated like cases differently, thereby subjecting

---

81   Westerman 2000, pp. 122 subs.
82   See later in this part, B.II.2.
83   More 1993, p. 53.
84   See Europäische Kommission 2002.
85   Case 15/57, [1957-1958] *ECR* 211.
86   Wouters 1999, p. 102.
87   Case 14/59, [1959] *ECR* 215.
88   Joined Cases 17 and 20/61, [1962] *ECR* 325.

some to disadvantages as opposed to others, without such differentiation being justified by the existence of substantive objective differences'.

In EC law, the seminal decision is *Italian refrigerators*,[89] a customs case decided in 1963 that concerned the import of very cheap refrigerators from Italy into France for which the Commission had authorised the French Republic to impose a special import tax should Italy not itself agree to impose such a tax upon export.[90] Italy asked the Court to annul the Commission decision, arguing in particular that it infringed the Treaty's general non-discrimination provision, then Art. 7 of the EEC Treaty (later Art. 6 of the EC Treaty, now Art. 12 EC). According to Italy, the decision discriminated against Italian products because the special tax was not imposed on all imports alike. The Commission countered by pointing out that Italian refrigerators were cheaper by far than refrigerators imported from any other Member State. It argued that in a situation where difficulties are created exclusively by imports from one Member State, there would in fact be discrimination if the protective measures extended to importers from other Member States as well. The Commission emphasised that the principle of non-discrimination in EC law is based not only on procedural criteria but also on substantive criteria and that discrimination 'could also be caused if different situations were treated in the same manner' (*Italian Refrigerators*, p. 172). Both AG Lagrange and the Court agreed, the latter holding that discrimination could result from 'treating either similar situations differently or different situations identically' (*Italian Refrigerators*, pp. 190 and under pp. 177 subs., respectively).

> The AG observed: 'It is well known first that the principle of non-discrimination has a double aspect, both positive and negative; discrimination consists both in treating different situations in the same way and in treating comparable situations in different ways [...]. [E]quality in fact may involve the necessity of different treatment in order to attain a result which establishes an equilibrium between different situations. [...] It is thus that I gladly support the distinction proposed by the honourable representative of the Commission during the oral procedure between what he called discrimination in form and discrimination in substance.' The Court found that '[t]he different treatment of non-comparable situations does not lead automatically to the conclusion that there is discrimination. An appearance of discrimination in form may therefore correspond in fact to an absence of discrimination in substance. Discrimination in substance would consist in treating either similar situations differently or different situations identically. [... D]iscrimination [...] might just as well take the form of dissimilar situations being treated identically [...].'
> The Court's reliance on the Aristotelian formula has *variously been confirmed in other EC law contexts*, for instance in *Sermide*[91] (para. 28), where the Court held that the non-

---

[89] Case 13/63, [1963] *ECR* 165.
[90] The basis for this was Art. 226 of the EEC Treaty, a provision that dealt with intervention measures during the transitional period and that now is repealed.
[91] Case 106/83, [1984] *ECR* 4209.

discrimination principle under Art. 40(3) of the EEC Treaty (agricultural law) requires that 'comparable situations must not be treated differently and different situations must not be treated in the same way unless such treatment is objectively justified' (in the context of sex equality, e.g. *Airola*,[92] para. 10, and *Hill and Stapleton*,[93] para. 22).

In EC law, as elsewhere, as a precondition for equal treatment, alikeness has come to be viewed as being *similarly situated (comparable)*, as opposed to being absolutely the same. In his opinion in the *Ruckdeschel* case (p. 1779), AG Capotorti explained this point in the following manner: 'Clearly the concept of comparability of situations does not mean that they should be exactly alike. Comparability must be determined against the background of competition [...] and in each case in the light of the objectives of the measure at issue; it is principally in the light of those objectives that it is possible to determine whether certain differences existing between undertakings are sufficient to make it impossible to treat them as comparable cases and, in consequence, to subject them to different treatment [...].' Dourado[94] speaks of 'substantially comparable situations'. As will be seen later, only in very exceptional cases is the Court willing to move away from an understanding of equality that is not based on comparability.[95]

The requirement of comparability is not usually expressly mentioned in EC law but is simply presumed as inherent in equality and non-discrimination provisions. However, with regard to the principle of equal pay for men and women, Art. 141(1) and (2) EC and Art. 1 of the Equal Pay Directive[96] explicitly refer to 'equal work' and 'work of equal value'.[97] According to Kentridge,[98] this can be explained by the fact that the concept of work of equal value is designed to facilitate pay equality between men and women in a labour market which has tended to segregate them informally into different types of job. If the Directive did not specifically use the term 'work of equal value', then situations involving work that is not the same or not similar but nevertheless of equal value might not be recognised as comparable. As a consequence, important areas of employment would be left untouched.

---

92   Case 21/74, [1975] *ECR* 221; see More 1993, p. 55.
93   Case C-243/95, [1998] *ECR* I-3739.
94   Dourado 2002, p. 152.
95   See later in this part, B.III.3.c.
96   Directive 75/117/EEC, *OJ* 1975 L 45/19.
97   Art. 119 of the EEC Treaty only mentioned equal work, whilst work of equal value was at the time only mentioned in the Equal Pay Directive (Art. 1). The Court of Justice in *Jenkins* (Case 96/80, [1981] *ECR* 911, para. 22) held that this Directive does not change the scope of Art. 119 which in effect meant that the right to equal pay for work of equal value was supposed to be part of Art. 119 itself. Through the Amsterdam revision, the words 'or work of equal value' were inserted into what then became Art. 141(1) EC.
98   Kentridge 1994, p. 201.

2. FORMAL AND SUBSTANTIVE EQUALITY

a. The concepts

Within the framework of equality in the law, a distinction is often made between formal and substantive equality.[99] Wentholt[100] explains that a *formal*[101] equality *approach* focuses on the first part of the Aristotelian equality formula, the basic assumption being one of sameness of subjects of law: 'Men and women, 'white' and 'black' people, abled and disabled, etc. [...] must be treated equally.' It is said that formal equality concerns consistency more than substance, since it is satisfied whether the parties are treated equally well or equally badly – equally bad treatment is, nonetheless, equal treatment (Fredman,[102] Möstl,[103] Christensen,[104] Norberg,[105] Foubert).[106] Hepple, Choussey & Choudhury[107] also note that this appearance of neutrality is deceptive in that a value judgment is required to choose whether to insist on a levelling up or to permit a levelling down. Further, formal equality focuses on discrimination that can be identified based on the mere appearance or form of a measure, that is, distinctions that are explicitly based on prohibited grounds of differentiation. Accordingly, discrimination in that framework can only take the form of direct discrimination. Such an approach thereby disregards the consequences of a given treatment in terms of its effect and, consequently, also the possibility that discrimination might be caused through application of a criterion that is formally neutral in appearance but not in its effect (in other words, indirect discrimination).

Formal equality differs from the concept of *substantive equality* (sometimes referred to as equality of results, also de facto, material or relative equality). With regard to substantive equality, the decisive question is whether a ground for differentiation – whether or not explicitly prohibited – results in prohibited discrimination (Fredman).[108] The concept of substantive equality recognizes the fact that discrimination can be either of a direct or of an indirect nature. The general equality maxim underlying a substantive equality approach is the full Aristotelian formula, including

---

[99] According to some, the distinction between formal and substantive equality coincides with that between equality before and equality in the law; compare Vierdag 1973, p. 16; McKean 1983, p. 286; Tridimas 1992, p. 23.

[100] Wentholt 2000, p. 44.

[101] Again, the terminology may differ. Barrett 2004, p. 121, for example, speaks of 'absolute or mathematical equality'. He uses the term 'formal equality' for an understanding that is based on the full Aristotelian formula.

[102] Fredman 1996, pp. 7 subs.

[103] Möstl 2002, p. 329.

[104] Christensen 2001, p. 32.

[105] Norberg 2001, p. 72.

[106] Foubert 2002, p. 21.

[107] Hepple, Choussey & Choudhury 2000, p. 27.

[108] Fredman 2002, pp. 11 subs.

---

its second part ('treating likes alike' *AND* 'treating unalikes unalike'; Vierdag).[109] In the framework of such an approach, differential treatment of unalikes is positively demanded, rather than either prohibited or merely tolerated. This approach is in line with the view that law 'should take account of the social effects of legal rules and decisions' (Koopmans).[110] Accordingly, Hervey & Shaw[111] in the context of sex equality law insist that substantive equality take account 'of women's difference of situation, however this is constructed: biologically, socially, economically, culturally, historically'. Loenen[112] speaks of substantive equality as a right to inclusion. Given the relevance of the full Aristotelian equality formula, the central issues of a substantive notion of equality are the comparability of situations and the appropriate treatment of differences. According to Loenen,[113] these issues lead to two sets of questions. First: Are there relevant differences? And: How are they determined? Second: What kind of treatment is required to achieve substantive equality? And: What is the underlying idea or norm on which the treatment is to be determined? Loenen adds that positive acknowledgement of difference often requires new legal measures. She concludes that, to achieve substantive equality in law, the major role is for the legislator, rather than for the courts.

b. In EC law

In practice, the equality concept within a given legal order usually reflects a mixture of formal and substantive elements. EC law provides such an example.

i. A formal starting point

Even though EC equality law is based in principle on an Aristotelian understanding of the term, in practice there is a *stronger emphasis on the first part of the formula* ('treating alikes alike') and, thereby, on formal equality. Thus, in concrete equality provisions the starting point is invariably that of equal treatment, unequal treatment being construed as an exception to the rule (e.g. Arts. 43 and 50 EC, the Second Equal Treatment Directive).[114]

---

[109] Vierdag 1973, p. 8. – According to some authors, substantive equality may be understood as encompassing various notions of equality, such as equality of result and equality of opportunity; see Barnard & Hepple 2000, p. 564 subs.

[110] Koopmans 1975, p. 240. In a more general context, see also Trakman 1994, p. 27, according to whom 'in order for constitutional rights to be effective for all citizens, they should be considered in relation to their substantive nature and effect'.

[111] Hervey & Shaw 1998, p. 114.

[112] Loenen 1995 (Substantive equality).

[113] Idem, pp. 195 and 198; also Loenen 1992, p. 24.

[114] Directive 76/207/EEC, *OJ* 1976 L 39/40, as amended.

In many cases, this results directly from the wording of an equality or non-discrimination provision. Art. 43(3) EC (freedom of establishment) and Art. 50 EC (concerning free movement of services) serve as examples: both provide for access to the market 'under the same conditions as' those applicable to the host State's own nationals. In the area of social law, the best-known example is the Second Equal Treatment Directive where equal treatment is even mentioned in the Directive's title. Art. 2, the Directive's central provision, first provides for the principle of equal treatment but then makes allowance for different treatment in certain, exceptional cases. According to Wentholt,[115] this structure 'shows that equal treatment is the norm, with even preferential treatment constructed as an exception to it'. Indeed, the Court stated in *Dekker*[116] (para. 20, in relation to the original version of the Directive) 'that Article 2(2), (3) and (4) of the Directive provide for exceptions to the principle of equal treatment set out in Article 2(1)'. Wentholt observes that this differs from the more general understanding of equality in EC law where preferential treatment is seen as part of the concept of substantive equality and as necessary for its achievement. Wentholt concludes that 'the concrete legal norm fundamentally differs from the principle as seen on the abstract level'.

In the same vein, the Court of Justice in its case law tends to rely on a finding of non-comparability only in order to state that the unequal treatment complained of is not discriminatory, without thereafter examining the adequacy of the treatment in view of the possibility of discrimination caused through same treatment (e.g. *Scholten Honig*).[117]

In *Scholten Honig* the Court began by explaining that the prohibition of discrimination in what is now Art. 34(2) EC (agricultural law) 'is merely a specific enunciation of the general principle of equality [...]. That principle requires that similar situations shall not be treated differently unless the differentiation is objectively justified.' The Court then went on to examine whether or not the products at issue, namely isoglucose and other products of the starch industry, were comparable. It found that this was not the case and simply concluded that the difference in treatment at issue did not constitute discrimination (para. 26 subs.; on the Court's formal approach in the context of Art. 34(2) EC, see also Plötscher).[118]

In contrast, cases where the Court clearly found discrimination caused through same treatment of non-comparable situations are quite rare (*Merida*,[119] possibly also *Spain v Commission*).[120] As a consequence of the emphasis on formal equality in EC law,

---

[115]   Wentholt 1996, p. 147.
[116]   Case C-177/88, *ECR* [1990] I-3941.
[117]   Joined Cases 103 and 145/77, [1978] *ECR* 2037.
[118]   Plötscher 2003, p. 91.
[119]   Case C-400/02, judgment of 16 September 2004, n.y.r.
[120]   Case C-304/01, judgment of 9 September 2004, n.y.r., concerning alleged discrimination through different treatment under the general equality principle. The Court held that the situations were not comparable (para. 34) and then proceeded to examine 'the justification of the difference in treatment' (para. 35 subs.). In contrast, Spain seemed to argue that there was justification for same treatment.

indirect discrimination is usually put in that particular context as well, though, as the Court's decision in the *Merida* case seems to indicate, it can also play a role in a framework where equality requires unequal treatment. This point is further discussed in this study's main part.[121]

ii. Substantive equality in EC law

Though there are no explicit references to substantive equality in the provisions of *written EC equality law,* traces of that notion can nevertheless be discerned. For example, elements of a substantive equality approach are found in the 'exceptions' of the Second Equal Treatment Directive[122] on the protection of women with regard to pregnancy and maternity and on positive action (regarding positive action, see also Art. 141(4) EC). These reflect, to some extent, the need to take into account factual differences between men and women. Another example involves the duty of employers to make reasonable accommodations for persons with disabilities (Art. 5 of the General Framework Directive,[123] Art. 1d(4) of the Staff Regulations).[124] This can be interpreted as a duty to actively take account of the characteristics of handicapped persons (compare Jolls).[125]

In the *case law,* prior to 1998 there were no references to substantive equality even though the concept had been raised repeatedly before the Court of Justice in earlier cases. The first such case was *Birds Eye Walls.*[126]

> The case concerned a supplementary occupational pension which the employer paid to employees who for reasons of ill health were forced to give up their work before reaching the standard retirement age. The aim of the scheme was to make up for the loss of income which workers suffered from early retirement, in order to grant them an income equivalent to that which they would have received through a State pension and a full occupational pension had they been able to continue to work (so-called 'bridging pension'). A further aim was to place women and men on an equal footing, taking into account that the retirement age for women and men differed (60 years for women and 65 years for men). As a consequence, the bridging pension paid to women above the age of 60 was reduced in view of their state pensions while that of men, who did not receive a state pension at this age, continued at an unreduced rate. Ms Roberts, the plaintiff in the national proceedings,

---

[121] See below Part 2, A.IV.2.b.ii.

[122] Directive 76/207/EEC, *OJ* 1976 L 39/40 (as amended).

[123] Directive 2000/78/EC, *OJ* 2000 L 303/16.

[124] Regulation 259/68/EEC, Euratom, ECSC, *OJ* 1968 L 56/1 (as amended). For a consolidated text incorporating the numerous amendments, see http://www.europa.eu.int/comm/dgs/person-nel_administration/statut/tocen100.pdf.

[125] Jolls 2000, p. 231. According to Jolls, an accommodation requirement or mandate is 'a requirement that employers take special steps in response to the distinctive needs of particular, identifiable demographic groups of workers'; see also Jolls 2001, p. 648, and later in this part, B.II.3.c.

[126] Case C-132/92, [1993] *ECR* I-5579.

complained that the system involved sex discrimination. According to the Commission, the system ultimately did not discriminate on grounds of sex because the employer was 'attempting to achieve substantive equality between the sexes by compensating for an inequality arising from the difference in pensionable ages in a particular set of circumstances where such inequality would cause considerable hardship' (*Birds Eye Walls*, para. 15; the Commission did not mention formal equality).[127] The Court, whilst agreeing that the case did not involve discrimination, did not refer to substantive equality but simply found that the cases were not comparable (*Birds Eye Walls*, para. 17-23).[128]

Similar arguments were made by a number of Advocates General, notably AG Tesauro who in a number of cases pleaded fervently for a substantive equality approach (*Habermann-Beltermann*,[129] point 11 of the AG's opinion; *Webb*,[130] point 8 of the AG's opinion; *Kalanke*,[131] points 7 subs. of the AG's opinion; *P. v S.*,[132] point 19 of the AG's opinion). Later, AG Tesauro was joined by a number of his colleagues (e.g. AG La Pergola in *Gerster*,[133] point 41 of the AG's opinion; AG Ruiz-Jarabo Colomer in *Larsson*,[134] point 28 of the AG's opinion, and in *Thibault*,[135] point 19 subs. of the AG's opinion; AG Saggio in *Badeck*,[136] point. 26 and 27 of the AG's opinion, and AG Alber in *Lommers*,[137] point 88 of the AG's opinion).

The most extensive remarks by AG Tesauro on this issue are found in *Kalanke* where he argued that sections 2 to 4 of Art. 2 of the Second Equal Treatment Directive (in its original version),[138] rather than providing genuine derogations from the prohibition of discrimination on grounds of sex, aim at ensuring that the principle of equal treatment is effective by authorizing such inequalities as are necessary. According to the AG, the reasoning underlying such provisions is that of substantive equality which 'necessitates taking account of the existing inequalities which arise because a person belongs to a particular class of persons or to a particular social group; it enables and requires the unequal, detrimental effects which

---

[127] In later cases, the two concepts are contrasted to each other; e.g. *Blanchard*, para. 90 (Case T-368/94, [1996] *ECR* II-41, IA-1, II-1).

[128] This approach has been heavily criticised by academic commentators. Hervey & Shaw 1998, p. 60, remark that the Court's consideration of pension cases 'often seems to take place in isolation from the economic realities of pensions and old-age benefit for women, where women suffer manifold minimum threshold and access problems'.

[129] Case C-421/92, [1994] *ECR* I-1657. The case concerned night work by a pregnant woman.

[130] Case C-32/93, [1994] *ECR* I-3567. The case concerned the dismissal of a pregnant worker due to her pregnancy.

[131] Case C-450/93, [1995] *ECR* I-305. The case concerned the acceptability of positive action under Art. 2(4) of the Second Equal Treatment Directive.

[132] Case C-13/94, [1996] *ECR* I-2143. The case concerned the dismissal of a transsexual person due to gender reassignment; point 19 of the AG's opinion; see further below Part 3, A.III.3.b.

[133] Case C-1/95, [1997] *ECR* I-5253.

[134] Case C-400/95, [1997] *ECR* I-2757.

[135] Case C-136/95, [1998] *ECR* I-2011.

[136] Case C-158/97, [2000] *ECR* I-1875.

[137] Case C-476/99, [2002] *ECR* I-2891.

[138] Directive 76/207/EEC, *OJ* 1976 L 39/40.

those inequalities have on the members of the group in question to be eliminated or, in any event, neutralized by means of specific measures. Unlike the principle of formal equality, which precludes basing unequal treatment of individuals on certain differentiating factors, such as sex, the principle of substantive equality refers to a positive concept by basing itself precisely on the relevance of those different factors themselves in order to legitimize an unequal right, which is to be used in order to achieve equality as between persons who are regarded not as neutral but having regard to their differences. In the final analysis, the principal of substantive equality complements the principle of formal equality and authorizes only such deviations from that principle as are justified by the end which they seek to achieve, that of securing actual equality. The ultimate objective is therefore the same: securing equality as between persons.'[139]

Considering that neither formal nor substantive equality were mentioned in the EC law at issue in these cases, it is interesting to consider why AG Tesauro dwelt upon those concepts. The present writer suspects that he drew upon his Italian background. In Italy, formal and substantive equality has long been a subject of academic discourse (e.g. Romanoli[140] and, in the specific context of sex equality law e.g. Ballestero,[141] Gianformaggio).[142] The term even appears in the text of the Italian law on positive actions (Art. 1(1)).[143]

In *Thibault*,[144] a case decided in 1998, for the first time the Court referred to substantive equality by stating that the result pursued by the Second Equal Treatment Directive (in its original version)[145] 'is substantive, not formal, equality' (para. 26; later confirmed in *Mahlburg*,[146] para. 28).

> *Thibault* concerned rules under a collective national labour agreement according to which an employee was entitled to a special salary increase if the result of the assessment of his or her work and conduct had been positive. This assessment had to be carried out if the employee had been present at work for at least six months of the relevant year. During the year 1983, Ms Thibault was absent from work for some seven months due to illness and pregnancy. Consequently, her employer refused the assessment and, consequently, Ms Thibault was not eligible for the salary increase. Without the pregnancy leave (a maximum of 28 weeks under French law), Ms Thibault would have fulfilled the six months requirement. The case raised questions concerning the legality of such a regime under Art. 2(3)

---

[139] Though it should be added that AG Tesauro's approach to the *Kalanke* case failed to reflect a truly substantive equality approach; e.g. Tobler 1997, p. 105.

[140] Romanoli 1973.

[141] Ballestero 1994.

[142] Gianformaggio 1996.

[143] Legge 10 Aprile 1991, n. 125, Azioni positive per la realizzazione della parità uomo-donna nel lavoro, Gazzetta ufficiale 15 April 1991, n. 88. Art. 1(1) reads: 'Le disposizioni contenute nella presente legge hanno lo scopo di favorire l'occupazione femminile e di realizzare l'uguaglianza sostanziale tra uomini e donne nel lavoro, al fine di rimuovere gli ostacoli che di fatto impediscono la realizzazione di pari opportunità.'

[144] Case C-136/95, [1998] *ECR* I-2011.

[145] Directive 76/207/EEC, *OJ* 1976 L 39/40.

[146] Case C-207/98, [2000] *ECR* I-549.

of the Second Equal Treatment Directive. AG Ruiz-Jarabo Colomer, referring to substantive equality, argued in favour of different treatment for different situations. The Court explained (*Thibault*, para. 26): 'The conferral of such rights, recognised by the Directive, is intended to ensure implementation of the principle of equal treatment for men and women regarding both access to employment (Article 3(1)) and working conditions (Article 5(1)). Therefore, the exercise of the rights conferred on women under Article 2(3) cannot be the subject of unfavourable treatment regarding their access to employment or their working conditions. In that light, the result pursued by the Directive is substantive, not formal, equality.'

The term *substantive equality* also appears in *Badeck*[147] (para. 31 and 32) and *Abrahamsson*[148] (para. 47 and 48) in the context of criteria used to evaluate the qualifications of a candidate for a particular job. Against that background, AG Alber in his opinion on *Griesmar*[149] (point 82) concluded that the Court had held that the principle of equal treatment aims at substantive, not formal, equality (see also Tridimas).[150] However, it should be noted that this case law concerns very specific issues arising in only one area of Community law (sex equality). Future case law will have to show whether the Court is willing to explicitly make similar statements in a broader context. In Shaw's[151] analysis, the Court has thus far merely flirted with a more substantive concept of equality in its interpretations of the legal concept of discrimination. Finally, whilst the term substantive equality does not appear at all in written EC law and only rarely in case law, other expressions which appear to be related can be found in EC legislation, namely *full equality in practice* (Art. 141(4) EC) and *equality in fact and in law* (the preamble of Regulation 1612/68).[152] As will be seen in this study's main part,[153] the Court has linked the latter expression to the distinction between direct and indirect discrimination.

3. EQUALITY OF OPPORTUNITY

a. The concept

Another conception of equality, also relevant in the context of indirect discrimination, is *equality of opportunity,* sometimes contrasted to equality of treatment (Lanquetin).[154]

---

[147]   Case C-158/97, *ECR* I-1875.
[148]   Case C-407/98, [2000] *ECR* I-5539.
[149]   Case C-366/99, [2001] *ECR* I-9383.
[150]   Tridimas 1999, p. 40.
[151]   Shaw 2001, p. 126.
[152]   Regulation 1612/68/EEC, *OJ* English Special Edition 1968 L 257/2, p. 475 (as amended).
[153]   See below Part 2, A.I.2.c.
[154]   Lanquetin 1996 (Egalité des chances), p. 497. For the origins of equality of opportunity as a legal term in international law, see p. 495.

This concept is perceived as steering a middle ground between formal equality and substantive equality (Fredman).[155] Equality of opportunity has been described as the proverbial 'level playing field' (Sohrab),[156] the 'recognition of the rights of social categories' (Vogel-Polsky)[157] and as 'a broad principle that the chances and experiences which life offers to individuals ought not to vary because of the arbitrary criterion of a person's being male rather than female, white rather than black, or able-bodied rather than disabled' (Ellis).[158] Some authors distinguish between a formal and a substantive understanding (e.g. Jacobs,[159] Koggel,[160] Strauss,[161] Fredman).[162] According to Jacobs,[163] *formal equality of opportunity* requires 'that everyone has the same legal rights of access to all advantaged social positions and offices and that these positions and offices be open to talents in the sense that they are to be distributed to those able and willing to strive for them'. In contrast, *substantive equality of opportunity* refers to the idea that 'those who are at the same level of talent and ability, and have the same willingness to use them, should have the same prospects of success regardless of their initial place in the social system'. It should be noted that the latter formulation does not automatically lead to equality of outcome (or results) since the outcome depends on the number of persons who actually take the advantage of the opportunities provided (Tobler).[164] A substantive understanding of equality of opportunity may include positive obligations: that is, not just a duty for the public authority to eliminate discrimination from its activities but also 'to act positively to promote equality of opportunity and good relations between different groups through all its policy making and in carrying out all its activities' (McCrudden).[165]

b. In EC law

In EC law, equality of opportunity can be seen as the underlying general idea of many areas of the law (e.g. the references in *Deutsche Tierzüchter*,[166] para. 160, in the context of public procurement under the TACIS Regulation,[167] and by AG Alber in *Lehtonen*,[168] point 65 of the AG's opinion, in the context of free movement of workers). In addition,

---

[155] Fredman 2002, p. 14.
[156] Sohrab 1994, p. 31.
[157] Vogel-Polsky 1990, p. 4.
[158] Ellis 1997, p. 173.
[159] Jacobs 1994, p. 64.
[160] Koggel 1994, pp. 44 subs.
[161] Strauss 1998, p. 52.
[162] Fredman 2002, pp. 11 subs.
[163] Jacobs 1994, p. 64.
[164] Tobler 1997, p. 102.
[165] McCrudden 2003, p. 13.
[166] Case T-145/98, [2000] *ECR* II-387.
[167] Regulation 1279/96/EC, Euratom, *OJ* 1996 L 165/1 (no longer in force).
[168] Case C-176/96, [2000] *ECR* I-2681.

the term 'equality of opportunity' also appears in written EC law, in the context of positive action, though only in the original version of Art. 2(4) of the Second Equal Treatment Directive[169] (but neither in Art. 6(3) of the former Social Agreement[170] nor in the more recent provisions concerning positive action, Art. 2(8) of the Revised Equal Treatment Directive[171] and Art. 141(4) EC).

> According to Art. 2(4) of the Second Equal Treatment Directive in its original version, the Directive 'shall be without prejudice to measures to promote equal opportunity for men and women, in particular by removing existing inequalities which affect women's opportunities in the areas referred to in Article 1(1)'. In contrast, the parallel provision in the Social Agreement, Art. 6(3), made reference to 'measures providing for specific advantages'.[172] Today, Art. 141(4) EC and Art. 2(8) of the Revised Equal Treatment Directive refer to 'full equality in practice between men and women in working life' (see also Art. 1(d)(2) of the Staff Regulations,[173] Art. 5 of the Race Directive[174] and Art. 7 of the General Framework Directive).[175] In academic writing, it has been argued that this, together with other changes of the Treaty adopted in the Amsterdam revision, should prompt the Court to take a more positive attitude towards positive action measures (e.g. Fenwick,[176] Tobler,[177] with further references). This is notably also the opinion of the EFTA Court (*EFTA Surveillance Authority v Norway*,[178] para. 56 and 57).

Case law elaborating on the legal meaning of the aim of 'promoting equal opportunities' as mentioned in the original version of Art. 2(4) of the Second Equal Treatment Directive appeared in the 1990s only, first in the *Kalanke*[179] case. That case law seems to indicate that the meaning of equality of opportunity in EC sex equality law is somewhere between the definitions of formal and substantive equality of opportunity

---

[169] Directive 76/207/EEC, *OJ* 1976 L 39/40.
[170] *OJ* 1992 C 191/90.
[171] Directive 2002/73, *OJ* 2002 L 269/15.
[172] The only case ever decided in that context is *Griesmar* (Case C-366/99, [2001] *ECR* I-9383); see Tobler 2002 (Rechtsgelijkheid)..
[173] Regulation 259/68/EEC, Euratom, ECSC, *OJ* 1968 L 56/1 (as amended). For a consolidated text, see http://www.europa.eu.int/comm/dgs/personnel_administration/statut/tocen100.pdf.
[174] Directive 2000/43/EC, *OJ* 2000 L 180/22.
[175] Directive 2000/78/EC, *OJ* 2000 L 303/16.
[176] Fenwick 1998, p. 515.
[177] Tobler 2003, pp. 82 subs.
[178] Case E-1/02, [2003] *EFTA Court Reports* 1. The Court was unable to apply such an approach in that particular case due to the fact that EEA sex equality law does not include the provisions introduced into the Treaty through the Amsterdam revision. Also, the homogeneity principle would have restricted its application; see Tobler 2004, p. 258.
[179] Case C-450/93, [1995] *ECR* I-305. In *Hofmann* (Case 184/83, [1988] *ECR* 6315), the Court had merely touched upon the provision without specifying the precise meaning of the term 'equality of opportunity'. Yet an earlier case concerned positive action in the context of Staff law and, therefore, relied on the unwritten general sex equality principle rather than the Directive; namely *Delauche* (Case 111/86, [1987] *ECR* 5345).

according to Jacobs. The concept is clearly *not limited to equal starting positions*, even though that seemed to be implied in *Kalanke* (para. 23) where the Court stated in an *obiter dictum* that a national positive action measure must not 'substitute for equality of opportunity as envisaged in Article 2(4) the result which is only to be arrived at by providing such equality of opportunity'. In *Badeck* (para. 52),[180] the Court held that reserving training places for women irrespective of candidates' qualifications can be acceptable and that such a measure 'forms part of a restricted concept of equality of opportunity'. This statement, later repeated in *Lommers*[181] (para. 32 subs. and 38), must be read as a *post scriptum* to *Kalanke* clarifying that equality of result is not totally eclipsed by the concept of equality of opportunity in EC sex equality law (Tobler).[182] At the same time, it is also clear that – as opposed to the United Nations Women's Convention (CEDAW)[183] – so far EC law only permits positive action but does not actively require it. In that sense, there is no full equality of opportunity as understood by McCrudden.[184]

c. Specifically: positive equality obligations in EC law

McCrudden describes proactive promotion of equality of opportunity between particular groups as requiring not only steps to eliminate discrimination but also positive action to promote equality and to combat discrimination. In recent years, elements of *positive equality obligations* have appeared in written EC law, first on the level of the EC Treaty and later also in secondary law. On the Treaty level, the Amsterdam revision added 'equality between men and women' to the list of Community tasks in Art. 2 EC and introduced Art. 3(2) EC providing that '[i]n all the activities referred to in this Article, the Community shall aim to eliminate inequalities, and to promote equality, between men and women' (compare also the first sentence of Art. 23 of the Charter of Fundamental Rights).[185] On the level of secondary law, a similar obligation can be found in Art. 1(a) of the Revised Second

---

[180] Case C-158/97, [2000] *ECR* I-1875. There is no such statement in the earlier case *Marshall* where the Court for the first time found that that a certain type of measure is in line with EC law (Case C-409/95, [1997] *ECR* I-6363).

[181] Case C-476/99, [2002] *ECR* I-2891.

[182] Tobler 2003, p. 75.

[183] Under Art. 4(1) CEDAW, which forms the broader background to EC sex equality law, positive action ('temporary special measures') can be a matter of a *positive duty*; see General recommendation No. 25, on article 4, paragraph 1, of the Convention on the Elimination of All Forms of Discrimination against Women, on temporary special measures, para. 7; http://www.un.org/womenwatch/daw/cedaw/recommendations.htm; Mulder 1999, Cook 2003, Tobler 2003, p. 71.

[184] McCrudden 2003, pp. 8 subs.

[185] *OJ* 2000 C 364/01. In the Charter of Fundamental Rights of the Union which forms the second part of the EU Constitutional Treaty, see the first sentence of Art. II-83; Treaty establishing a Constitution for Europe, *OJ* 2004 C 310.

Equal Treatment Directive.[186] Another example, Art. 5 of the General Framework Directive[187] obliges employers to actively provide for reasonable accommodation for disabled people. Academic writing has emphasised that such positive obligations go beyond the traditional prohibitions of (sex) discrimination in EC law (e.g. Koukoulis-Spiliotopoulos,[188] Epiney & Freiermuth Abt,[189] Prechal,[190] Pirstner-Ebner,[191] Meyer,[192] the von der Groeben & Schwarze Commentary).[193]

4. SOME REMARKS ON THE FUNCTION OF EQUALITY IN EC LAW

Before turning to the concept of discrimination, some brief remarks shall be made on the function of equality in EC law. In the context where the equality principle forms one of the essential theoretical foundations of the European Communities, and in the broader sense of the whole idea of European integration (Emiliou),[194] two different perspectives are usually distinguished, one economic and one social (Schiek).[195]

a. The economic (competition) perspective

In spite of its remarkable development in a variety of other directions, Community law largely remains economic law. As a consequence, there is what Fredman[196] calls a particularly symbiotic relationship between equality and economic concerns. In the 1960s, Steindorff[197] called non-discrimination 'an instrument of the economic constitution in the common market'. Today, Tridimas[198] still speaks of equality as the keystone of economic integration. Within that framework, the *main focus is on competition*. AG Tesauro expressed this idea in the following manner (*Assurances du Crédit*,[199] point 11 of the AG's opinion): 'Community legislation chiefly concerns economic situations and activities. If, in this field, different rules are laid down for similar situations, the result is not merely inequality before the law, but also, and

---

[186] Directive 2002/73/EC, *OJ* 2002 L 269/15.
[187] Directive 2000/78/EC, *OJ* 2000 L 303/16.
[188] Koukoulis-Spiliotopoulos 2001, pp. 26 subs.
[189] Epiney & Freiermuth Abt 2003, p. 42.
[190] Prechal 2004, pp. 538 and 541.
[191] Pirstner-Ebner 2004, p. 206.
[192] Meyer 2002, p. 27.
[193] Von der Groeben & Schwarze Commentary, n. 11 subs. Ad Art. 3 EC.
[194] Emiliou 1996, p. 148.
[195] Schiek 2000, p. 34.
[196] Fredman 2002, p. 24.
[197] Steindorff 1965, p. 2.
[198] Tridimas 1999, pp. 45 subs.
[199] Case C-63/89, [1991] *ECR* I-1799.

inevitably, distortions of competition which are absolutely irreconcilable with the fundamental philosophy of the common market'. Colin & Sinkondo[200] note that non-discrimination is a prerequisite for real and healthy competition. In the specific context of agricultural law, Barents[201] explains that 'the application of the equality principle in the agricultural sector depends on the existence of an actual or potential competitive relation between agricultural products. [...] If the equality rule is interpreted and applied in this way, the inevitable result is that any modification of a competitive relation between products by a Community measure amounts to discrimination. As a consequence, the non-discrimination rule imposes on the Community a prohibition on the distortion of competition.' These views are confirmed by the Court's case law (e.g. *SNUPAT*,[202] p. 143; *Social Housing*, para. 15).[203]

> In *SNUPAT*, a coal and steel case, the Court stated that 'there may be considered as discriminatory in principle, and accordingly, prohibited by the Treaty, *inter alia*, measures or interventions [...] which are calculated, by substantially increasing differences in production costs otherwise than through changes in productivity, to give rise to an appreciable disequilibrium in the competitive position of the undertakings concerned. In other words, any intervention attempting to distort or actually distorting competition artificially and significantly must be regarded as discriminatory and incompatible with the Treaty [...].' In the EC law case *Social Housing*, the Court explained that equal treatment of foreign workers with regard to housing is necessary in the interest of 'complete equality of competition'.

According to Bernard,[204] the principle of equality in the case law of the Court on economic policy in the first instance appears to impose a duty on the Community legislator not to distort competition. In such a context, equality is not a goal in itself but rather *serves as an instrument* with regard to the aim of establishing and making the common market functional. De Búrca[205] speaks of 'the instrumental role of equality' (see also Malmstedt,[206] Wouters,[207] Bell).[208]

An economic perspective of equality is not limited to economic law in a strict sense but can also *play a role in social law*. Norberg[209] points to the general parallels between

---

[200]   Colin & Sinkondo 1993, p. 38.
[201]   Barents 1994 (Agricultural Law), pp. 334 subs.
[202]   Joined Cases 32 and 33/58, [1959] *ECR* 127.
[203]   Case 63/86, [1988] *ECR* 29.
[204]   Bernard 1996, pp. 79 subs.
[205]   De Búrca 1997, pp. 14, 23 subs. and 30. According to this author, the Court has moved from an equal treatment approach towards an approach aiming at achieving market unity. More 1999, p. 524, considers it safer to describe this new approach as merely complementing the equal treatment approach.
[206]   Malmstedt 2001.
[207]   Wouters 2001, pp. 310 subs.
[208]   Bell 2002, p. 36.
[209]   Norberg 2001, p. 71.

social non-discrimination law and competition law, explaining that both of them 'are enacted in order to prevent groups or companies that have achieved a powerful position in the market from closing that market and blocking the entrance of more competent competitors who might challenge their position. The one they want to shut out is unfavourably treated in comparison with the members inside the group. This is the core meaning of the legal concept of discrimination'. As for specific links between EC social law and economic and competition issues, it is widely accepted that the only social law provision of a substantive nature in the Treaty itself, Art. 119 of the EEC Treaty (now Art. 141(1) and (2) EC), on equal pay for men and women, was originally written into the Treaty for economic reasons (Imbrechts,[210] Barnard,[211] Hepple,[212] Kenner,[213] O'Leary).[214]

> Having domestic legislation regarding equal pay, France insisted on including the provision in the Treaty. France feared that it would otherwise suffer a competitive disadvantage vis-à-vis the other Member States: employers would be encouraged to practice a form of social dumping, avoiding doing business or setting up companies in France due to the expense resulting from domestic equal pay provisions. As Imbrechts explains, '[c]e n'est ni un souci de protection de la femme, ni des exigences d'une saine politique sociale qui ont inspiré les auteurs du traité mais bien le souci de garantir l'égalité des conditions de concurrence des différentes industries des pays membres'. However, more recently the Court stated in Schröder[215] (para. 57) that the economic aim pursued by Art. 141 EC 'is secondary to the social aim pursued by the same provision, which constitutes the expression of a fundamental human right'. McCrudden[216] in this context speaks of a move from one function to another.

Further, by far the largest part of EC social law has been secondary law for which there was no specific legal basis provision (that is, a provision specifically allowing for the adoption of social law) at the time of its adoption. Rather, such legislation was adopted on the basis of provisions enabling the Community to legislate in the interest of the common market (Arts. 100 and 235 of the EEC Treaty, now 94 and 308 EC; see Tobler).[217] More[218] observes that when the Community sought to expand its competencies into the field of social law, it could only do so by demonstrating the economic need for such actions, that is, by showing that such matters directly affected the

---

[210] Imbrechts 1986, p. 232. According to Imbrechts, the oldest trace of the principle of equal pay can be found in the preamble to part VIII as well as in Art. 427 of the Treaty of Versailles concluded in 1919.
[211] Barnard 1996 (Economic Objectives).
[212] Hepple 1996, pp. 241 subs.
[213] Kenner 2003, pp. 458 subs.
[214] O'Leary 2002, pp. 139 subs.
[215] Case C-50/96, [2000] ECR I-743.
[216] McCrudden 2003, p. 12.
[217] Tobler 2000 (Sex Equality Law), pp. 143 subs.
[218] More 1996, p. 265.

competitive conditions within the Community market. Though no longer predominant, the economic aspect of non-discrimination law in the area of EC social law and human rights continues to have a presence, at least as a side effect. Further, this economic argument has been extended to other grounds of discrimination for which there is much more recent EC legislation, adopted on the basis of Art. 13 EC (the Race Directive[219] and the General Framework Directive).[220]

> Though their preambles emphasise these Directives' human rights background, the economic argument still arises. Thus, when the British House of Lords assessed the proposals for these Directives, it did so not only in terms of the human rights perspective but also stated that 'the proposals are likely to facilitate free movement, to limit unfair competition, and to enhance the success of the single market'.[221] In the context of the Race Directive, McInerny[222] points to the reference in the preamble to *economic* and social cohesion objectives as well as to references in the Commission's Explanatory Memorandum to economic integration, whose alternative rationale is also patent in the Impact Assessment Form.

b. The social (human rights or solidarity) perspective

Prohibitions of discrimination on grounds such as sex, sexual orientation, race and religion are part of the larger body of human rights law. In such a context, equality can be conceived of as an independent Community goal in its own right (Barnard:[223] 'a societal goal, a general aspirational principle of citizenship and a free-standing, fundamental right'; de Búrca:[224] 'an autonomous value forming a central part of the Community's goals'). Thus, Bernard[225] explains that the existence of an area such as sex equality law is not satisfactorily explained through an economic rationale only in that sex equality is concerned with the effect of certain treatment on victims and, therefore, based on the 'harm principle'. This view is also reflected in the slogan that 'Women's Rights are Human Rights', created by the United Nations' World Conference on Human Rights held in Vienna in 1993. Within the framework of EC law, this approach is confirmed by the case law of the Court of Justice which has long emphasised the social goals of the equal pay principle (*Defrenne II*,[226] *Defrenne III*,[227] *Schröder*).[228]

---

[219] Directive 2000/43/EC, *OJ* 2000 L 180/22.
[220] Directive 2000/78/EC, *OJ* 2000 L 303/16.
[221] House of Lords 2000 (EU proposals).
[222] McInerny 2000, p. 322.
[223] Barnard 1998, p. 372.
[224] De Búrca 1997, p. 30.
[225] Bernard 1996, pp. 83 and 86.
[226] Case 43/75, [1976] *ECR* 455.
[227] Case 149/77, [1978] *ECR* 1365.
[228] Case C-50/96, [2001] *ECR* I-9383.

In *Defrenne II* (para. 12), the Court explained that Art. 119 of the EEC Treaty (now Art. 141(1) and (2) EC) serves the double aim of serving both economic and social goals (as is indeed confirmed by the provision's place in the Treaty's social chapter). In *Defrenne III*, (para. 27), the Court stated that 'there can be no doubt that the elimination of discrimination based on the sex forms part of those fundamental rights' (meaning the fundamental rights which the Community must ensure). More recently, the Court held that the economic aim pursued by Art. 141 EC 'is secondary to the social aim pursued by the same provision, which constitutes the expression of a fundamental human right' (*Schröder*, para. 57). This statement is usually welcomed. Kenner, for example, speaks about a paradigm shift which provides a basis for a more fundamental appraisal of the economic bias in the Court's sex equality jurisprudence. In contrast, Beaumont[229] asks: 'Why is it more important for social reasons to prevent sex discrimination than it is for economic reasons to prevent companies in some countries from gaining an unfair advantage by not having to pay women the same as men? [...] Is the right to a job not just as important as the right not be sexually discriminated against?'

Regarding the more recent discriminatory grounds of racial or ethnic origin, religion or belief, disability, age and sexual orientation, Bell[230] has argued that the legal basis provision on which they rest might be perceived as concrete evidence of a social citizenship model, in that Art. 13 EC is not a Treaty provision that depends on the establishment of an economic rationale in terms of market integration but rather one that allows for the independent pursuit by the Union of specific social objectives.

Finally, social aspects may also be inherent in *economic law*, though here they are of a less obvious nature.[231] In his writings about the basics of economic law, Van Gerven[232] emphasises the importance of solidarity, based on the argument that equality in the economic context needs to be understood as being framed by the terms of liberty and solidarity.[233] Together, they form the triad of liberty, equality and solidarity (in which Van Gerven sees a modernised version of the French Revolution's slogan of 'égalité, liberté, fraternité').[234] These values must be respected both in vertical (State

---

[229]   Beaumont 2002, pp. 160/161.

[230]   Bell 2002, pp. 121 subs., also 190 subs.

[231]   Compare also Currall 1990, p. 21, according to whom the Court turned certain free movement rights 'into a kind of human rights'.

[232]   Van Gerven 1971, pp. 404 subs., and Van Gerven 1975, p. 303. – See also Colin & Sinkondo 1993, p. 47, and Zacher 2002, 153 subs.

[233]   Solidarity as an underlying principle of economic law should be distinguished from the constitutional principle of solidarity as suggested by Xuereb 2002, p. 647. According to this author, solidarity should be a legal principle which 'would apply wherever a proposed Community measure was required and proportionate to the need to act in the general interest (so that the principles of subsidiarity and proportionality were satisfied) but where the impact on one or more Member States was unequal or disproportionate because particularly burdensome, and would oblige the 'Community' to make provision for the abatement of this hardship or otherwise 'exempt' such Member'.

[234]   This slogan can still be found in Art. 2 of the French Constitution as the official motto of the French Republic. In this broader framework, another modernised version has been suggested by French feminists according to whom the component *fraternité* should be replaced by that of *parité*; e.g. Gaspard, Servan-Schreiber & Le Gall 1992, Tobler 2001 (Parité), with further references.

– citizens) and horizontal (citizens – citizens) relationships. According to Van Gerven, equality in the latter context is desirable for at least two reasons, namely the protection of one's person and the guarantee of a sufficient degree of competition. Equality in the economic context can, therefore, be defined as the protection of the economically weaker party against the unlimited freedom of the economically stronger party.

III. DISCRIMINATION

1. INTRODUCTORY REMARKS

The concepts of equality and discrimination are intrinsically linked. The Court of Justice usually acknowledges this link by stating that a given non-discrimination provision is merely a specific enunciation of the Community's general equality principle (e.g. *Ruckdeschel,*[235] para. 7, regarding Art. 34(2) EC; see also point 3 of AG Lagrange's opinion; compare Plender).[236] In academic writing, there is consensus that the existence of discrimination entails an absence of equality. However, opinions differ as to the precise nature of that link. According to McKean,[237] non-discrimination is simply a negative way of stating the principle of equality, a view which implies that equality does not go any further than non-discrimination. In contrast, Barnard[238] argues that equality goes further in that it imposes more positive obligations. Others state that whatever the correct answer might be to this question on a theoretical level, it is irrelevant in the specific context of EC law since the Court of Justice uses the terms interchangeably (Mohn,[239] Tridimas,[240] Barrett;[241] in the Court's case law, see *Europe Chemi-Con,*[242] para. 33).

In EC law, discrimination has traditionally been a fundamental concept, especially with regard to the establishment of the common market which forms its historical nucleus. Numhauser-Henning[243] appropriately notes that 'the ECJ's case law on non-discrimination, which is built on Article 6 (now Art. 12(1) EC) and Art. 119 (now Art. 141 EC) in the Treaty of Rome, may be said to form a normative core in Community

---

[235]   Joined Cases 117/76 and 16/77, [1977] *ECR* 1753.
[236]   Plender 1995, p. 65.
[237]   McKean 1983, p. 287.
[238]   Barnard 1998, pp. 353 and 363.
[239]   Mohn 1990, p. 3.
[240]   Tridimas 1999, p. 42.
[241]   Barrett 2004, p. 130.
[242]   Case C-422/02 P, judgment of 27 January 2005, n.y.r. In this anti-dumping case, the Court stated that 'it matters little whether the principle […] is described as the 'principle of equal treatment' or the 'principle of non-discrimination'. They are simply two labels for a single general principle of Community law, which prohibits both treating similar situations differently and treating different situations in the same way unless there are objective reasons for such treatment […].'
[243]   Numhauser-Henning 2001 (Introduction), p. 21.

law'. The following sections of this study begin by focusing on the concept of discrimination as such and then turn to important forms through which non-discrimination provisions are expressed, particularly in the context of EC law. Thereafter, a number of specific aspects of discrimination and justification are discussed. As will be seen in this study's main part,[244] the relationship between these two ideas is debated, in particular in relation to indirect discrimination. For reasons that will be explained later, the present discussion treats discrimination and its justification as distinct notions (rather than conceiving of justification as inherent in the concept of discrimination).

2. THE GENERAL CONCEPT OF DISCRIMINATION

Academic writers sometimes bemoan the *lack of a uniform definition* of discrimination (e.g. Hilson,[245] in the context of EC free movement law). Indeed, the legal concept of discrimination is rarely defined in a general sense[246] in written law, though some UN human rights Conventions with their broad definitions are notable exceptions (e.g. Art. 1 CEDAW; Holtmaat).[247]

> Under Art. 1 CEDAW, discrimination within the meaning of the Convention means 'any distinction, exclusion or restriction made on the basis of sex which has the effect or purpose of impairing or nullifying the recognition, enjoyment or exercise by women, irrespective of their marital status, on a basis of equality of men and women, of human rights and fundamental freedoms in the political, economic, social, cultural, civil or any other field.'

According to Ermacora,[248] the legal concept of discrimination is derived from U.S. law[249] but acquired a clearer meaning only through the law of the United Nations where it stands for arbitrary treatment, that is, treatment for which there is no legitimate reason. In such a framework, discrimination in a general sense means 'unjustified disadvantageous treatment'. Somewhat more specifically, Ellis[250] explains that there are two basic constituent elements of all forms of discrimination, namely adverse impact and causation ('some sort of adverse impact on their victims and a prohibited

---

[244] See below Part 2, A.IV.3.e.
[245] Hilson 1999, p. 448.
[246] The definitions in the EC Directives adopted on the basis of Art. 13 EC are not general in that sense but deal with the *specific* forms of direct and indirect discrimination in EC law, see below Part 2, B.
[247] Holtmaat 2003 (CEDAW), pp. 168 subs.
[248] Ermacora 1971, p. 7.
[249] According to Plötscher 2003, p. 28, the legal concept of discrimination originated in the 19th century in U.S. competition law.
[250] Ellis 1994 (Definition of Discrimination), p. 565.

classification underlying that impact'). Vierdag[251] gives the following general definition: 'We start by saying that discrimination occurs when the equality or inequality of treatment results from a 'wrong' judgment as to the relevance or irrelevance of the various human attributes that are taken into account. Therefore, discrimination will be provisionally defined as 'wrongly equal, or wrongly unequal treatment'.' He then clarifies the element 'wrongly equal treatment' as meaning that 'discrimination occurs when in a legal system an inequality is introduced in the enjoyment of a certain right, or in a duty, while there is no sufficient connection between the inequality upon which the legal inequality is based, and the right or duty in which this inequality is made'. 'Wrongly equal treatment' means 'discrimination which occurs when in a legal system no inequality is introduced in the enjoyment of a certain right, or in a duty, and as a result thereof no sufficient connection exists between the unequalness of the subjects treated and the right or the duty.'

Whilst under Vierdag's definition discrimination can be caused both by different and same treatment, some authors generally describe it as *different treatment only*[252] (e.g. Loenen:[253] 'ongerechtvaardigd onderscheid'; Epiney:[254] 'eine irgendwie ausge-staltete unterschiedliche Behandlung'; Plötscher:[255] 'ganz allgemein die Ungleich-behandlung vergleichbarer Tatbestände'; in a more general context, also Christen-sen).[256] Strictly speaking, such a narrow definition can apply only where equality is not fully based on the Aristotelian formula but where an emphasis is put on same treatment. Such is the case not only in the Netherlands' constitutional law where equality is expressly defined as equal treatment with regard to comparable cases (Art. 1 of the Constitution)[257] but also in the written EC law, as discussed previously. Accordingly, Gerards[258] notes that the term discrimination in EC law means unjustified different treatment. Holtmaat[259] and Alkema & Rop[260] argue that in such systems not every form of unequal treatment that conflicts with the law should be understood as discrimination but that the latter term should be reserved to certain severe types of unequal treatment which need to be examined in a strict legal framework, in particular in relation to justification.

---

[251]   Vierdag 1973, pp. 60/61.
[252]   Foubert 2002, p. 31, in this context suggests the terms 'discrimination *sensu lato*' to refer to both versions and 'discrimination *stricto sensu*' for unequal treatment of equal cases.
[253]   Loenen 1998, p. 34.
[254]   Epiney 1995, p. 19.
[255]   Plötscher 2003, p. 33.
[256]   Christensen 2001, p. 32.
[257]   Art. 1 of the Dutch Constitution states that all persons in the Netherlands shall be treated equally in equal situations: 'Allen die zich in Nederland bevinden, worden in gelijke gevallen gelijk behandeld. Discriminatie wegen godsdienst, levensovertuiging, politieke gezindheid, ras, geslacht of op welke grond dan ook, is niet toegestaan.'
[258]   Gerards 2002, p. 221, footnote 1.
[259]   Holtmaat 2002, in particular pp. 170 subs.; also Holtmaat 2003 (Stop de uitholling).
[260]   Alkema & Rop 2002, pp. 37 subs.

Alkema & Rop and Holtmaat plead in favour of a distinction between discrimination in the strict sense (discrimination in a pejorative sense) and discrimination in a neutral sense (unlawful unequal treatment). The former concerns instances of systematic subordination of groups of persons because of important characteristics that determine their identity, whereas the latter concern other cases where the law prescribes equal treatment. Discrimination in the strict sense is characterised by three factors, namely 1) one group in society has the power of excluding or stigmatising another group; 2) the exclusion of the powerless group is (all)pervasive, that is, it is not limited to one given sphere; and 3) the characteristic by which the classification or exclusion takes place is fundamental to a person's or a group's understanding of self (identity) and cannot be discarded based on one's own free will (immutability). According to Holtmaat, discrimination on grounds of sex and race[261] are examples of discrimination in this strict sense (so-called 'suspect criteria').[262] An example of the less strict category of unequal treatment is provided by disadvantageous treatment on grounds of the type of employment contract (part-time work, fixed-term work, and the like). According to Alkema & Rop, this category also includes characteristics that are not absolute but merely temporary or subject to change, such as age and nationality.

3. COMPARABILITY AS A PRECONDITION FOR A FINDING OF DISCRIMINATION

a. The importance of comparability

As mentioned earlier,[263] comparability is of central importance in the framework of an Aristotelian understanding of equality, and in particular in a legal order such as EC law where the main focus is on same treatment or formal equality. In such a context, comparability is also a precondition for a finding of (direct or indirect) discrimination. Fredman[264] aptly refers to 'the threshold question of when two individuals are relevantly alike'. Sex-based job segregation provides an example for the problems that can arise in that context.

Sex-based job segregation with different levels of pay means that comparators of the opposite sex are simply missing. As a consequence, to begin with, all forms of analysis of discrimination are excluded, unless it can be proven that there is work of equal value which is better paid in the case of male workers (which is a particularly complicated issue in the

---

[261] Obviously, given the medical possibilities existing today, immutability in these cases means immutability in principle only.

[262] The term is derived from U.S. law. A similar distinction is also made by the European Court of Human Rights under the European Convention on Human Rights; compare Fredman 2002, p. 117.

[263] See earlier in this part, B.II.b.

[264] Fredman 2002, p. 7.

context of indirect sex discrimination).[265] This has been called a fundamental shortcoming of a comparative approach (Fredman,[266] Hepple).[267]

The situation differs where discrimination is only one possible form of infringement of the law, as is the case in EC free movement law. Here, lack of comparability is not necessarily the end of the matter because an alternative concept of restrictions in a wider sense is not based on comparability.[268] Its practical significance is illustrated in cases such as *Schindler*[269] and *Corsica Ferries France II*.[270]

Messrs Schindler were accused of having infringed British law on lotteries by sending envelopes containing invitations to participate in the German *Süddeutsche Klassenlotterie* from the Netherlands to the UK. Under UK law, small lotteries as well as chance games were permitted but large lotteries were prohibited. The Schindlers as well as the Commission argued that this legislation was 'in fact discriminatory' because it provided indirect protection to the British undertakings engaging in the operation of small lotteries and chance games. The argument was rejected by both the AG and the Court. AG Gulman suggested that the contested rules should be assessed in the framework of a restriction-based approach (*Schindler*, point 65 subs. of the AG's opinion). The Court agreed. It explicitly rejected the plea of indirect discrimination on grounds of nationality and explained that the distinction made between big and small lotteries concerned non-comparable situations (*Schindler*, para. 43 subs.) – an assessment that was criticised by Schroeder[271] but apparently accepted by other commentators (e.g. Gormley,[272] Stein).[273]

Corsica Ferries France II concerned the duty of shipping companies in the Italian ports of Genoa and La Spezia to avail themselves of the mooring services of Italian companies holding exclusive rights with regard to those services. However, at La Spezia only operators of vessels whose gross tonnage exceeded 500 were obliged to use the mooring services. Corsica Ferries France complained of an infringement of the Community law on free movement of services (Art. 49 EC and Art. 9 of Regulation 4055/86).[274] In particular, the company argued that more national than non-national transport undertakings escaped the obligation to use the mooring services in La Spezia. AG Fennelly acknowledged that the rules at issue seemed to be indirectly discriminatory but immediately added that Corsica Ferries France could not rely on any such discrimination because its proper comparators were Italian transport undertakings using vessels of analogous size which were treated in precisely the same way. According to the AG, the situation differed from that in *Corsica*

---

[265]   See further below Part 2, A.IV.2.f.
[266]   Fredman 2002, pp. 9 subs.
[267]   Hepple 1996, p. 248 (also 241).
[268]   See later in this part, B.IV., also Part 3, B.
[269]   Case C-275/92, [1994] *ECR* I-1039.
[270]   Case C-266/96, [1998] *ECR* I-3949.
[271]   Schroeder 1994, p. 376.
[272]   Gormley 1994, p. 652.
[273]   Stein 1994, p. 315.
[274]   Regulation 4055/86/EEC, *OJ* 1986, L 378/1 (as amended).

Ferries Italia[275] where indirect discrimination had been found (*Corsica Ferries France II*, points 35 subs. of the AG's opinion). The Court expressly followed this reasoning and ruled out the possibility of a finding of discrimination. Instead, the Court assessed the case in the framework of a restriction-based approach (*Corsica Ferries France II*, para. 57 subs.).

b. The assessment of comparability in EC law

As Fredman[276] notes, 'the choice of comparator itself requires a complex value judgment as to which of the myriad differences between any two individuals are relevant and which are irrelevant. The choice of the relevant characteristics is often itself determinative of the outcome'. Within a framework based on an Aristotelian understanding of equality, the finding that there is no discrimination due to lack of comparability is not problematic as long as the assessment in that regard is appropriate and accurate. However, it has been noted that in EC case law *a questionable use of comparability* as a means to decide on potential indirect discrimination cases seems to be on the rise (Drijber & Prechal).[277] In such cases, the suspicion may arise that the Court avoids delicate questions regarding the nature of the alleged discrimination and its justifiability by concentrating on comparability instead and, more specifically, by assessing the comparability of the situations at issue in a problematic way. In the context of free movement law, the Court's decision in the case *Schumacker*[278] is a case in point. In the context of sex equality, *Helmig*[279] is sometimes discussed in this framework (e.g. Veldman,[280] Drijber & Prechal,[281] Schiek,[282] Barnard & Hepple[283] – though in the present writer's analysis, the Court's focus was rather on the existence of a difference in treatment). There are also cases which present a different situation, in that a proper analysis of comparability would have helped to avoid problematic or vague statements by the Court on the nature of the alleged infringement. In the present writer's view, the sex equality case *Schnorbus*[284] is a prime example. In free movement law, *Dafeki*[285] is illustrative. All of these cases will be discussed in this study's main part.[286]

---

[275] Case C-18/93, [1994] *ECR* I-1783; see below Part 2, A.I.4.k.
[276] Fredman 2002, p. 98.
[277] Drijber & Prechal 1997, p. 163.
[278] Case C-279/93, [1995] *ECR* I-225.
[279] Joined Cases C-399/92, C-409/92, C-425/92, C-34/93, C-50/93 & C-78/93, [1994] *ECR* I-5727.
[280] Veldman 1996, p. 36.
[281] Drijber & Prechal 1997, p. 137.
[282] Schiek 1997, p. 178.
[283] Barnard & Hepple 2000, p. 570.
[284] Case C-79/99, [2000] *ECR* I-10997.
[285] Case C-336/94, [1997] *ECR* I-6761.
[286] Regarding *Schumacker* and *Helmig*, see below Part 2, A.IV.4.c, regarding *Schnorbus*, Part 3, A.II.2.c, and regarding *Dafeki*, Part 3, B.II.3.b.

c. Exceptions where comparability is not a precondition in EC law

Because of the pitfalls inherent in comparability issues, some authors have argued that comparability should not be decisive to a finding of discrimination, be it in particularly grave cases (e.g. Holtmaat[287] regarding what this author calls discrimination in the strict sense) or more generally (e.g. Gerards).[288] In EC law there are some, if only a few, cases where comparability is not a precondition for a finding of discrimination, notably those concerning discrimination on grounds of pregnancy (though even this point is disputed) and discrimination in the form of harassment.

i. Pregnancy discrimination

In early EC case law on *discrimination on grounds of pregnancy*, some arguments made before the European Court of Justice were similar to the reasoning reflected in well known and much criticised early U.S. and Canadian case law on that issue (*Geduldig v. Aiello*,[289] *General Electric Co. v Gilbert et al.*,[290] *Bliss v. Attorney General of Canada*).[291]

> In *Geduldig v. Aiello*, the U.S. Supreme Court found that there was no sex discrimination when a State insurance scheme provided that certain disabilities attributable to normal pregnancy were not compensable. The Court acknowledged that only women can become pregnant, thereby implying that it is only women who will suffer from a rule such as that at issue. However, it also pointed out that '[t]he lack of identity between the excluded disability and gender as such under this insurance program becomes clear upon the most cursory analysis. The program divides potential recipients into two groups – pregnant women and non-pregnant persons. While the first group is exclusively female, the second includes members of both sexes. The fiscal and actuarial benefits of the program thus accrue to members of both sexes.' (*Geduldig v. Aiello*, p. 497). From this, the Court concluded that the exclusion of pregnant women from the benefits in question was merely the result of a restriction of the insurance scheme to a limited number of risks which was acceptable for, among others, financial reasons; it was not the result of sex discrimination. In *General Electric Co. v. Gilbert et al.* (p. 136) the Court held that 'we have here no question of excluding a disease or disability comparable in all other respects to covered diseases or disabilities and yet confined to the members of one race or sex. Pregnancy is, of course, confined to women, but it is in other ways significantly different from the typical covered disease or disability.' The Court refused to consider maternity benefits to be sex-related based on the argument that not all female workers will become, or even can become,

---

287   Holtmaat 2003, See earlier in this part, B.III.2.

288   Gerards 2002, in particular p. 667 subs.

289   *Geduldig v. Aiello*, 417 U.S. 484 (1974). This case was decided under the Equal Protection Clause of the Fourteenth Amendment to the U.S. Federal Constitution.

290   *General Electric Co. v. Gilbert et al.*, 429 U.S. 125 (1976). This case was decided under Title VII of the Civil Rights Act of 1964.

291   *Bliss v. Attorney General of Canada* [1979] 1 S.C.R. 183.

pregnant. Similarly, in the Canadian Supreme Court decision *Bliss*, Justice Richie stated that if the provision at issue treated unemployed pregnant women differently from other unemployed persons, be they male or female, 'it is, it seems to me, because they are pregnant and not because they are women'.

The approach reflected in these cases has been severely criticised for its one-sided standard. Mahoney[292] speaks about the 'the bizarre conclusion that discrimination on the basis of pregnancy did not amount to discrimination on the basis of sex' and MacKinnon[293] asks: 'Must pregnancy be covered because it disables women or may it be excluded because it cannot disable men?' (see also Fredman,[294] Foubert).[295]

On the level of U.S. Federal legislation, the above case law was later remedied through the Pregnancy Discrimination Act of 1978 which explicitly provides that '[t]he terms 'because of sex' or 'on the basis of sex' include, but are not limited to, because of or on the basis of pregnancy, childbirth, or related medical condition' (see Loenen).[296] In *CalFed*,[297] the U.S. Supreme Court upheld this Act as constitutional. However, as far as U.S. Federal constitutional law is concerned, *Geduldig v Aiello* still stands (MacKinnon).[298] In Canada, *Bliss v. Attorney General of Canada* was later overruled by *Brooks v. Canada Safeway Ltd.*[299]

In the EC law case *Dekker*,[300] the UK Government argued that the Second Equal Treatment Directive (in its original version)[301] required that a woman not be rejected for a particular post on grounds that she is or will become unable to work if a man would have been rejected on the same grounds. This argument was not surprising given the importance of the issue of comparability in EC law. After all, in *Macarthys*[302] the Court had held that a finding of sex discrimination requires an actual (as opposed to a merely hypothetical) comparator. However, in the context of pregnancy, the Court did not agree with the UK Government's argument but rather held that the absence of male candidates who could be compared to the woman in question cannot affect the finding of sex discrimination (*Dekker*, para. 17). Accordingly, when the Court in *Webb*[303] (para. 25) specified that 'pregnancy is not in any way comparable with a

---

[292] Mahoney 1992, p. 767.
[293] MacKinnon 1979, p. 111; see also MacKinnon 2001, pp. 247 subs. and 396 subs.
[294] Fredman 2002, p. 99.
[295] Foubert 2002, pp. 301 subs.
[296] Loenen 1992, p. 90.
[297] *California Federal Savings and Loan Association v. Guerra*, 479 US 272 (1986); usually referred to as *CalFed*.
[298] MacKinnon 2001, pp. 252 and 392.
[299] *Brooks v. Canada Safeway Ltd.* [1989] 1 S.C.R. 1219.
[300] Case C-177/88, [1990] *ECR* I-3941.
[301] Directive 76/207/EEC, *OJ* 1976 L 39/40.
[302] Case 129/79, [1980] *ECR* 1275.
[303] Case C-32/93, [1994] *ECR* I-3567. Bamforth 1993, pp. 874 subs., mentions that before the British court the applicant had argued that the application of the 'but for' test would also lead to a finding of direct discrimination. The origins of the 'but for' test can be found in Anglo-Saxon law on non-contractual liability where it is used in order to prove the causality of an act with regard to the damage sustained: the damage would not have been caused but for the act in question; therefore the act is

pathological condition, and even less so with unavailability for work on non-medical grounds', this did not exclude a finding of sex discrimination but, on the contrary, served to support the above statement in *Dekker*. The Court's approach in these cases is usually understood as *doing away with the requirement of a male comparator* in the specific context of pregnancy discrimination (see Foubert).[304] It was largely welcomed (e.g. Fredman,[305] Hoskins,[306] Moore,[307] Prechal,[308] Boch,[309] McGlynn;[310] Shaw[311] even speaks about a major reconceptualization of the notions of discrimination and equal treatment). In contrast, authors such as Ellis[312] and Wintemute[313] have challenged the Court's approach, arguing that an element of comparability is important to the component of disadvantageous treatment as a matter of principle and, thus, also in cases of discrimination on grounds of pregnancy (see also Honeyball).[314] However, as Mancini & O'Leary[315] point out, it is difficult to see where the Court would begin to find a comparator when it comes to pregnancy and maternity. In the present writer's view, the Court's approach is, therefore, entirely appropriate.

ii. Discrimination through harassment

Another example under EC law of discrimination that is not comparison-based involves harassment. For example, Art. 2(3) of the General Framework Directive[316] provides: 'Harassment shall be deemed to be discrimination within the meaning of paragraph 1, when an unwanted conduct related to racial or ethnic origin takes place with the purpose or effect of violating the dignity of a person and of creating an intimidating, hostile, degrading, humiliating or offensive environment. In this context,

---

to be considered the cause for the damage; see Gimeno Verdejo & Rojes I Pujol 1999, p. 214. In the present writer's analysis, cases such as *Grant* (Case C-249/96, [1998] *ECR* I-621) show that the Court of Justice does not rely on this test; see Tobler 2001 (Same-Sex Couples), pp. 278 subs.

[304] According to some, the Court actually tried to find a comparator for a pregnant worker, but eventually recognized the uniqueness of pregnancy and the impossibility of comparing pregnancy to any other physical condition; Foubert 2002, p. 150, with further references. Others argue that the Court did not eliminate the comparison element but only shifted the emphasis by concentrating on the equality of men and women as workers rather than as persons of different sex. In this interpretation, the Court held that the fact that a worker is pregnant is not enough to differentiate her from other, non-pregnant workers; Carracciolo di Torella & Masselot 2001, pp. 243 and 246.

[305] Fredman 1992, p. 122.
[306] Hoskins 1994, pp. 229 subs.
[307] Moore 1994, pp. 657/658.
[308] Prechal 1991, p. 666.
[309] Boch 1998, p. 181.
[310] McGlynn 2001, p. 208.
[311] Shaw 1991, p. 319.
[312] Ellis 1994 (Definition of Discrimination), p. 571, and Ellis 1998, pp. 204 subs.
[313] Wintemute 1998, pp. 25 subs.
[314] Honeyball 2000, pp. 47 subs.
[315] Mancini & O'Leary 1999, p. 338.
[316] Directive 2000/78/EC, *OJ* 2000 L 303/16.

the concept of harassment may be defined in accordance with the national laws and practice of the Member States.' (see also Art. 2(3) of the Race Directive[317] and Art. 2(3) of the Revised Second Equal Treatment Directive).[318] This is a new type of discrimination, the special feature of which is that it is not based on an Aristotelian understanding of equality. Accordingly, Kenner[319] speaks about a radical shift in the Community's concept of discrimination (see also Epiney & Freiermuth Abt).[320]

> The recognition of harassment as a form of discrimination reflects an alternative and more modern approach to discrimination which embraces a theory developed by the U.S. scholar MacKinnon. This radical theory denies both the need and the usefulness of a requirement of comparability for a discrimination analysis because the deepest problems of sex inequality will not find women similarly situated to men. Instead, it defines discrimination as systematic disadvantage of social groups based on their domination by other groups (hence the theory's names 'inequality approach' and later 'dominance approach'). Accordingly, the only question for sex equality litigation is whether a given policy or practice integrally contributes to the maintenance of an underclass or a deprived position because of gender status (see in particular MacKinnon 1978, 1982, 1983, 1987, 1991). This approach allowed MacKinnon to conclude that sexual harassment must be conceived of as a form of sex discrimination, independently of any requirement of comparability. MacKinnon's theory has not only been instrumental for changes in U.S. law in relation to sexual harassment, it has also influenced the adoption of the above EC law provisions on harassment (compare Tobler).[321] However, Driessen-Reilly & Driessen[322] argue that still more legislation is needed because under existing EC law the prohibition does not cover the bulk of harassment situations, those which comprise bullying and mobbing for reasons other than discrimination (see also Holtmaat).[323]

4. IMPORTANT FORMS OF NON-DISCRIMINATION PROVISIONS

The following sections introduce a number of important forms which non-discrimination provisions may take, particularly in EC law. These are, first, open and closed provisions and, second, symmetric and asymmetric provisions. The former are of particular interest in the context of indirect discrimination; the latter are of more general importance.

---

[317] Directive 2000/43/EC, *OJ* 2000 L 180/22.
[318] Directive 2002/73, *OJ* 2002 L 269/15.
[319] Kenner 2003, pp. 406 and 408 subs.
[320] Epiney & Freiermuth Abt 2003, pp. 127 subs.
[321] Tobler 2002 (MacKinnon), p. 961.
[322] Driessen-Reilly & Driessen 2003, pp. 502 subs.
[323] Holtmaat 2004 (Seksuele intimidatie).

a. Open and closed non-discrimination provisions

Non-discrimination provisions can be worded either in an open or in a closed way (Bayefsky,[324] Plötscher).[325] A provision is *of a closed nature* when it contains an exhaustive list of prohibited discriminatory grounds. In such a framework, there are only limited possibilities for bringing a case involving a ground that is not explicitly prohibited within the application field of the law. One such possibility involves a broad interpretation of an express discriminatory ground in such a way that it includes the ground in question. Fredman[326] speaks of the 'stretching of existing categories' and Bell[327] uses the term 'submerging'. In EC law, the case *P. v S.*[328] provides an example where such a strategy succeeded. Here the Court was prepared to include discrimination on grounds of gender reassignment (transsexuality), which is not explicitly prohibited under EC law, into the existing category of discrimination on grounds of sex. The other possibility for bringing a case involving a ground that is not explicitly prohibited within the application field of the law is to rely on the concept of indirect discrimination, as discussed in this study.

In contrast, *openly worded provisions* do not provide for an exhaustive list of discriminatory grounds. Such provisions can take two forms. First, they may *omit any mention of specific discriminatory grounds* ('open-textured equality guarantees', in the terminology of Fredman).[329] EC law provides several such examples, including, in particular, the unwritten general principle of equality, which provides the basis for all explicit EC equality law and which generally requires that 'similar situations shall not be treated differently unless differentiation is objectively justified' (*Ruckdeschel,*[330] para. 7). According to the Grabitz & Hilf Commentary,[331] this principle is concerned with all possible criteria though strictly speaking, the principle does not depend on any criteria at all. That is why it should be distinguished from general non-discrimination principles that focus on particular discriminatory grounds, such as the general principle of non-discrimination on grounds of *sex*, recognised by the Court in cases such as *Defrenne III*[332] and *Rinke.*[333] Other examples of openly worded non-discrimina-

---

[324]   Bayefsky 1990, pp. 5 subs.
[325]   Plötscher 2003, p. 44, speaks of general and special prohibitions of discrimination *(allgemeine und besondere Diskriminierungsverbote).*
[326]   Fredman 2002, pp. 68 subs.
[327]   Bell 2002, p. 110.
[328]   Case C-13/94, [1996] *ECR* I-2143; see further Part 3, A.III.3.b.
[329]   Fredman 2002, p. 67.
[330]   Joined Cases 117/76 and 16/77, [1977] *ECR* 1753.
[331]   Grabitz & Hilf Commentary (as of 1989), n. 6 ad Art. 6 of the EC Treaty.
[332]   Case 149/77, [1978] *ECR* 1365.
[333]   Case C-25/02, judgment of 9 September 2003, n.y.r.

tion provisions in EC law are Art. 34(2) EC (*Sermide*, para. 28)[334] and Art. 42 of the Second Company Law Directive.[335]

Art. 34(2) EC has to be seen against the background of Art. 34(1) EC which mentions three possible forms of common market organisation for the field of agriculture, namely common rules on competition, compulsory coordination of the various national market organisations and European market organisations (the latter usually referred to as Common Market Organisations). Regarding the latter, Art. 34(2) EC provides: 'The common organisation shall be limited to pursuit of the objectives set out in Article 33 and shall exclude any discrimination between producers or consumers within the Community.' The Court explained in *Sermide* that under that provision, 'comparable situations must not be treated differently and different situations must not be treated in the same way unless such treatment is objectively justified'. As Plötscher[336] notes, Art. 34(2) EC is structurally identical with the general equality principle. Art. 42 of the Second Company Law Directive provides: 'For the purposes of the implementation of Directive member states' laws shall ensure equal treatment of all shareholders who are in the same position.'

Alternatively, openly worded provisions may *list a number of specific grounds in a non-exhaustive manner* ('limitative enumeration' or 'enuntiative provisions', according to Asscher-Vonk).[337] Such provisions are particularly common in public international law. In EC law, Art. 21(1) of the Charter of Fundamental Rights[338] is framed in this manner.

Some examples are:
1) Art. 2 of the United Nations' Universal Declaration on Human Rights which provides: 'Everyone is entitled to all the rights and freedoms set forth in this declaration, *without distinction of any kind, such as* race, colour, sex, language, religion, political, or other opinion, national or social origin, property, birth or other status [...].' (Emphasis added.);
2) Art. 14 of the European Convention on Human Rights according to which '[t]he enjoyment of the rights and freedoms set forth in this Convention shall be secured without discrimination on *any ground such as* sex, race, colour, language, religion, political or other opinion, national or social origin, association with a national minority, property, birth or other status' (emphasis added);

---

[334]   Case 106/83, [1984] *ECR* 4209.
[335]   Directive 77/91/EEC, *OJ* 1977 L 26/1 (as amended).
[336]   Plötscher 2003, p. 37.
[337]   Asscher-Vonk 1997, p. 281. This author uses the term in relation to Art. 13 EC. Authors such as Whittle rightly emphasised early on that Art. 13 EC (then Art. 6A of the Draft Amsterdam Treaty) is a legal basis provision and not a substantive provision; Whittle 1998, p. 53. However, the distinction between open and closed provisions can also be used in that particular context.
[338]   Charter of Fundamental Rights of the European Union, *OJ* 2000 C 364/1. The Charter currently does not have the standing of legislation; see Commission Communication on the legal nature of the Charter of Fundamental Rights of the EU, COM(2000) 644 fin., point 4 subs.

3) Art. 21(1) of the EU Charter of Fundamental Rights under which '[a]ny discrimination based on *any ground such as* sex, race, colour, ethnic or social origin, genetic features, language, religion or belief, political or any other opinion, membership of a national minority, property, birth, disability, age or sexual orientation shall be prohibited' (emphasis added). In the Charter of Fundamental Rights of the Union which forms the second part of the EU Constitutional Treaty, this is now Art. II-81(1).[339]

Hepple, Choussey & Choudhury[340] argue that an approach that specifies particular grounds to the exclusion of others treats discrimination as atomised, focusing on particular specific characteristics. In contrast, open-ended non-discrimination provisions regard all forms of arbitrary discrimination as inter-connected. For purposes of this present study, the distinction between the different types of provisions raises the question whether and to what extent there is a need for the concept of indirect discrimination in cases of openly framed provisions. This point will be discussed in the study's main part.[341]

b. Symmetric and asymmetric non-discrimination provisions

A second distinction exists between symmetric and asymmetric non-discrimination provisions. Most provisions are of a *symmetric* nature in the sense that they protect all groups or situations concerned by the relevant discriminatory ground (for instance, in the case of sex discrimination, men as well as women). Some authors even apply the notion of non-discrimination provisions solely to symmetrical provisions (Hintersteininger),[342] though this approach seems to be exceptional. In this present study, it is used in both situations. A provision is *asymmetric* if it prohibits discrimination against only a certain specified group or situation. In practice, this means that the prohibited discrimination can arise only in relation to that group or situation. In EC law, the Directives on Part-Time Work Directive[343] and on Fixed-Term Work[344] as well as Art. 90(1) EC provide examples. Sometimes, the non-discrimination

---

[339] Treaty establishing a Constitution for Europe, *OJ* 2004 C 310. In the framework of the Constitutional Treaty, the Charter of Fundamental Rights will be binding law. The provisions of the Charter are addressed to the institutions, bodies and agencies of the Union with due regard for the principle of subsidiarity, and to the Member States though in that case only when they are implementing Union law (Art. II-111).

[340] Hepple, Choussey & Choudhury 2000, p. 42.

[341] See below Part 2.A.IV.2.c.

[342] Hintersteininger 1999, p. 22. For example, the author calls the asymmetrical prohibition of Art. 90 EC a prohibition of worse treatment (*Schlechterstellungsverbot*).

[343] Directive 97/81/EC, *OJ* 1998 L 14/9 (as amended).

[344] Directive 1999/70/, *OJ* 1999 L 175/43.

provisions in the area of free movement are also included in this category (De Schutter,[345] Plötscher,[346] less explicitly also Stampe).[347]

The Part-Time Work Directive specifically prohibits discrimination against part-time workers (rather than more generally, discrimination on grounds of working time). Clause 4(1) of the framework agreement on part-time work concluded by the European Social Partners, which forms the substantive part of the Directive, provides: 'In respect of employment conditions, part-time workers shall not be treated in a less favourable manner than comparable full-time workers solely because they work part time unless different treatment is justified on objective grounds.' Clause 4(1) of the Fixed-Term Work Directive is worded in the same manner. Similarly, Art. 90(1) EC, containing a prohibition that complements the Treaty title on free movement of goods, protects products only of *other* Member States (rather than more generally prohibiting discrimination on grounds of the origin of the products). In the framework of free movement law, Art. 39 EC, for example, prohibits discrimination on grounds of nationality only with regard to foreigners (though this has been interpreted by the Court as meaning persons who have exercised their free movement rights, thereby including nationals of the Member State at issue; *Singh*).[348] This raises the issue of reverse discrimination (e.g. *Saunders*),[349] a problem that is usually seen as an issue of *scope* (in the sense that free movement provisions relate to situations with a cross-border element only; see further e.g. Epiney,[350] Poiares Maduro)[351] but sometimes also of comparability (Plender).[352]

An asymmetric approach is sometimes urged in the context of social law, in view of the asymmetrical nature of the discrimination. For example, it is *women* who, historically, have been the typical victims of sex discrimination, rather than men. An asymmetrical approach is, therefore, considered to be essential to the effectiveness of non-discrimination legislation (e.g. Hanau & Preis,[353] Fredman,[354] Loenen,[355]

---

[345] De Schutter 1999, p. 37.
[346] Plötscher 2003, pp. 80 and 161.
[347] Stampe 2001, p. 80.
[348] Case C-370/90, [1992] *ECR* I-4265. Martin 1998, p. 617, concludes that the Court in fact recognises a new non-discrimination criterion not mentioned in the Treaty, namely that of whether or not a person has exercised his or her free movement rights.
[349] Case 175/78, [1979] *ECR* 1129.
[350] Epiney 1995.
[351] Poiares Maduro 2000.
[352] Plender 1995, pp. 73 subs.
[353] Hanau & Preis 1988, p. 206.
[354] Fredman 1992, p. 125.
[355] Loenen 1999, pp. 199 subs.

Wentholt,[356] Prechal,[357] Steiner,[358] Refaeil & Siegwart,[359] Tobler,[360] Burri,[361] Hervey,[362] Stampe).[363] In this area of EC law, it is well known that significant sex equality cases have been brought by men (e.g. *Barber*).[364] Apart from some exceptions as mentioned above, EC law usually reflects a symmetric approach, though an asymmetrical element can be found in Declaration 28,[365] adopted in the framework of the Treaty of Amsterdam concerning what is now Art. 141(4) EC on positive action. The Declaration provides: 'When adopting measures referred to in Article 119(4) of the Treaty establishing the European Community, Member States should, in the first instance, aim at improving the situation of women in working life.'

5. SPECIFIC NOTIONS OF DISCRIMINATION

a. Introductory remarks

The following sections discuss a number of specific concepts of discrimination that are important for the purposes of this present study. These include direct, indirect, structural and factual discrimination, as well as discrimination in form and in substance. Other notions, sometimes found in academic writing, are not discussed because they are not relevant to EC law as interpreted by the Court of Justice (the Calliess & Ruffert Commentary;[366] of course, this does not rule out the possibility that EC law can be analysed in terms of such distinctions).

Some examples are:
1) Open and covert direct discrimination ('offene und verdeckte Diskriminierung') as described by Arioli.[367] According to Arioli, direct discrimination is open when sex is used directly as a differentiation criterion, and it is covert where the differentiation criterion is not sex specific, but the relevant requirement can in fact be fulfilled only by one sex;

---

[356] Wentholt 1996, p. 149.
[357] Prechal 1993, p. 97. Prechal notes in this context that 'the prohibition of indirect discrimination should be rather considered as a remedy to treat some of the symptoms th[a]n as an instrument getting to the root of the problem'.
[358] Steiner 1999, p. 319.
[359] Refaeil & Siegwart 1997, p. 7.
[360] Tobler 1999, p. 401.
[361] Burri 2000, p. 147.
[362] Hervey 1996, pp. 406 subs.
[363] Stampe 2001, pp. 128 subs.
[364] Case C-262/88, [1990] *ECR* I-1889.
[365] Declaration on Art. 119(4) of the Treaty establishing the European Community, *OJ* 1997 C 340/136.
[366] Calliess & Ruffert Commentary 2002, n. 39 ad Art. 141 EC.
[367] Arioli 1992, p. 52.

2) Covert direct discrimination, discrimination due to prejudice, and statistical discrimination are each regarded as specific expressions of direct discrimination by Christensen.[368] The first of these is described as the case where an employer does not, as a matter of principle, wish to hire women or foreigners and, therefore, formulates certain conditions which these groups of persons are characteristically unable to comply with and for which there is no other rational basis. Discrimination due to prejudice involves the erroneous perception by an employer that members of the group against which he or she discriminates lack necessary qualities or qualifications. Finally, statistical discrimination exists where the allocator of resources knows that a significant proportion of people belonging to a group with easily establishable characteristics do not satisfy the norm applied by him or her, and where he or she, therefore, excludes everybody who belongs to this group, including the few members who do satisfy the norm;

3) Covert and indirect discrimination ('verdeckte und mittelbare Diskriminierung') as distinguished by Wisskirchen[369] and Blomeyer.[370] In this view, covert discrimination is based on a differentiation criterion that is not sex itself, but describes sex in a sufficiently clear manner, making this a 'sex-specific' criterion. Covert discrimination is intentional since it refers to cases where the discriminator wants to discriminate on the basis of sex but is hindered in doing so by the prohibition of such discrimination and therefore intentionally and consciously wishes to circumvent the prohibition. In contrast, indirect discrimination involves a sex-neutral criterion, and does not depend upon the intention behind the criterion;

4) Transparent and non-transparent discrimination ('doorzichtige en ondoorzichtige discriminatie'), a distinction suggested by Veldman[371] in the context of sex discrimination in relation to pay. Whilst transparent discrimination results from reliance on a directly or indirectly discriminatory criterion, non-transparent discrimination is based on different practices and can be identified only on the basis of a statistical analysis and, more specifically, probability calculations. (It would seem that non-transparent discrimination is a form of structural discrimination.);

5) Indirect and hidden discrimination ('indirekte und versteckte Diskriminierung') as referred to by the von der Groeben & Schwarze Commentary.[372] Under this view, indirect discrimination relates to side aspects of establishment ('Begleitumstände des Niederlassungsvorganges') rather than directly to the access to or the exercise of a profession. Hidden discriminations are caused by criteria which are fulfilled almost automatically by the nationals of the relevant State but cause difficulties to foreigners.

b. Direct and indirect discrimination

The most important distinction for the purposes of this present study is that between direct and indirect discrimination. It has potential relevance wherever a legal order

---

[368] Christensen 2001, pp. 39 subs.
[369] Wisskirchen 1994, p. 72.
[370] Blomeyer 1994, pp. 17/18.
[371] Veldman 1995, pp. 296 subs.
[372] Von der Groeben & Schwarze Commentary 2004, n. 72 ad Art. 43 EC.

prohibits discrimination on specific grounds, and particularly where the list of explicitly mentioned grounds is a closed one (Gerards).[373]

i. Direct discrimination

Direct discrimination is *explicitly or obviously based on a prohibited ground*. Accordingly, Kapteyn & VerLoren van Themaat[374] speak about 'visible discrimination'. Because of its obvious character, it is possible to conceive of it as intentional and objectively disadvantageous (Barbera),[375] though proof of intent is not necessary for a finding of direct discrimination (in the context of EC law, *Dekker*, para. 22).[376] The concept of direct discrimination usually also covers cases of reliance on a ground that is linked in an indissoluble way to a prohibited discriminatory ground (e.g. pregnancy and biological maternity as linked to sex, though this point is sometimes debated).[377] A classic example of direct discrimination is unequal hourly pay for men and women for the same work.

> An historical illustration of this practice, still common in some parts of the world, is provided by Elizabeth von Arnim (1866-1941)[378] in her autobiographical novel 'Elizabeth and her German garden'. The author describes the pay practice for hired hands on her husband's farm in the following way: '[T]hey [meaning the men] get a mark and a half to two marks a day and as many potatoes as they can eat. The women get less, not because they work less, but because they are women and must not be encouraged.'

The term *direct discrimination* did not originally appear in the wording of EC law. The reason for this is simply that no other identified notions existed at the time; discrimination was understood to mean what later was termed direct discrimination (McCrudden).[379] Eventually, in the context of sex discrimination, the Court explained that whether there is direct or indirect discrimination 'depends on whether the fundamental reason for the refusal of employment is one which applies without distinction to workers of either sex or, conversely, whether it applies exclusively to one sex' (*Dekker*, para. 10). The latter situation embodies direct discrimination. As Julén[380] observes, this was the *first definition* of direct discrimination in EC law as such. Meanwhile, a new generation of EC non-discrimination Directives provides legal

---

[373]   Gerards 2002, p. 13.
[374]   Kapteyn & VerLoren van Themaat 2003, p. 588.
[375]   Barbera 1994, p. 55.
[376]   Case C-177/88, [1990] I-3941.
[377]   See earlier in this part, B.III.3.c.i.
[378]   Von Arnim Elizabeth, *Elizabeth and her German garden*, London: Virago Press 1985, p. 75.
[379]   McCrudden 1982, p. 336.
[380]   Julén 2001, p. 179.

definitions (e.g. the General Framework Directive[381] and the Race Directive[382] as well as the Revised Second Equal Treatment Directive).[383]

> Art. 2(2)(a) of the General Framework Directive states that 'direct discrimination shall be taken to occur where one person is treated less favourably than another is, has been or would be treated in a comparable situation, on any of the grounds referred to in Article 1'. Art. 2(2)(a) of the Race Directive is worded in the same manner. Art.1(2) of the Revised Second Equal Treatment Directive defines direct discrimination as relating to the situation 'where one person is treated less favourably on grounds of sex than another is, has been or would be treated in a comparable situation'.

Finally, what constitutes direct discrimination in a particular legal order depends on the scope of its non-discrimination rules, which develops over time. This will be discussed later, in the context of factual discrimination.[384]

ii. Indirect discrimination

As already noted at the beginning of this present study, the concept of indirect discrimination is intended to deal with *seemingly neutral differentiation criteria with a disproportionate impact* or effect upon a group (or object) that is protected by an explicit prohibition of discrimination (e.g. O'Donovan & Szyszczak,[385] Loenen,[386] Wentholt).[387] The need for recognition of the legal concept of indirect discrimination arose because, in the words of Bell,[388] 'as states and employers become more aware of the penalties for unlawful discrimination, overt prejudice migrates into more covert forms of discrimination'. This point is illustrated by the fact patterns of cases such as the important EC law case *Jenkins*[389] and the landmark case under U.S. law, *Griggs v. Duke Power Co.*[390]

> *Jenkins* concerned an employer who used to pay female workers less than male workers (direct sex discrimination). Following the UK's accession to the Community, the employer changed its practice in order to avoid falling under the new prohibition of pay discrimination on grounds of sex. Subsequently, the same wages were paid to men and women, but 10% less to part-time workers than to full-time workers. Similarly, *Griggs v. Duke Power*

---

[381] Directive 2000/78/EC, *OJ* 2000 L 303/16.
[382] Directive 2000/43/EC, *OJ* 2000 L 180/22.
[383] Directive 2002/73/EC, *OJ* 2002 L 269/15.
[384] See later in this part, B.III.5.e.
[385] O'Donovan & Szyszczak 1988, p. 67.
[386] Loenen 1999, p. 195.
[387] Wentholt 2000, p. 54.
[388] Bell 2001, p. 659.
[389] Case 96/80, [1981] *ECR* 911, see further below Part 2, A.I.4.h.
[390] *Griggs v. Duke Power Co.*, 401 U.S. 424 (1971); see later in this part, C.II.1.b.

Co. involved an employer who used to discriminate openly on grounds of race but changed its policy upon adoption of the Civil Rights Act of 1964. The new system, based on school diplomas and intelligence tests, was seemingly race-neutral but had a disparate impact upon black persons due to the inferior quality of their education in formerly segregated schools.

Against this background, it has been argued that a prohibition merely of direct discrimination amounts to an invitation to rely instead on indirectly discriminatory measures. Lundström,[391] for example, calls the prohibition of mere direct sex discrimination 'a blunt, inadequate instrument for achieving true equality between the sexes with a real content as regards both the distribution of power and the distribution of good things in a society'. As De Schutter[392] points out, it must necessarily be accompanied by a prohibition against indirectly discriminatory measures, lest the former remain a purely illusory promise of equality.

The definition of indirect discrimination focuses on the *treatment of groups* (though the remedies still concern the individual; Lacey;[393] see further McCrudden).[394] For example, in situations where it is usually women who perform part-time work,[395] worse treatment of part-time workers than of full-time workers will have a disparate impact on women. Whether the use of a formally neutral criterion leads to indirect discrimination depends on the *factual circumstances* of the case. These may change over time. Thus, if similar percentages of men and women engage in part-time work, there can be no finding of indirect sex discrimination in this context. De Schutter[396] aptly refers to the 'caractère toujours provisoire, rebus sic stantibus' of a finding of indirect discrimination. At the same time, it is also possible that a law might explicitly prohibit reliance on a ground which thus far has been recognised as relevant in the context of indirect discrimination based only on a different ground, thereby moving from indirect to direct discrimination. In EC law, the criterion of part-time work has 'migrated' in this way into specific legislation on that matter, namely the Part-Time Work Directive.[397] Sjerps[398] speaks of 'indirect discrimination as a stepping-stone'.

> The Part-Time Work Directive explicitly prohibits discrimination against part-time workers. This means that within the field of application of this Directive, discrimination on grounds of working time to the disadvantage of part-time workers constitutes direct discrimination (though the prohibition is of a rather weak nature due to the open justification possibi-

---

[391] Lundström 2001, p. 145.
[392] De Schutter 1999, pp. 14/15.
[393] Lacey 1992, p. 102.
[394] McCrudden 2001, p. 255.
[395] For the social and economic background of this phenomenon, see Eckart 1998, Tobler 1999; also Schmidt 1995, pp. 39 subs. On part-time work, see further below Part 2, A.I 4.h.
[396] De Schutter 1999, p. 21/22.
[397] Directive 97/81/EC, *OJ* 1998 L 14/9 (as amended).
[398] Sjerps 1999, pp. 241 subs.

lities).[399] Though they are not specifically mentioned in the Directive, both direct and indirect discrimination are conceivable. As an example, Burri[400] mentions the case where workers are granted the opportunity to follow courses during their working time without at the same time reducing the workload of the workers in relation to their time at work. Sjerps' remark on indirect discrimination as a stepping-stone concerns Dutch law where discrimination on grounds of part-time work was explicitly outlawed earlier than under EC law. Similarly, Wentholt[401] notes that in Dutch law the concept of indirect discrimination was effective in outlawing 'new' types of discrimination, thereby making it possible to change the legal reaction to societal behaviour that is deemed 'socially unjust'.

In most European national legal orders (with the exception of the UK and Ireland),[402] the concept of indirect discrimination was *introduced as a result of EC law* (Prechal,[403] Holtmaat & Loenen).[404] In countries such as France, Spain, Germany and most of the new Member States, the concept was, in fact, entirely new. Not all of these states found the concept easy to comprehend. For example, when Germany implemented the Second Equal Treatment Directive (in its original version)[405] the Government did not distinguish between direct and indirect discrimination and did not include the criteria of marital and family status[406] explicitly mentioned in Art. 2 of the Directive into the German implementing law. Colneric[407] considers the acceptance of the concept of indirect discrimination under German law the most important practical change in her country's equality law.

iii. Discrimination *sui generis* prohibited under EC law?

Finally, it should be noted that whilst direct and indirect discrimination used to be the only two relevant categories of discrimination under EC law, it may well be that legislative developments will lead to the eventual recognition of types of discrimination that cannot be analysed in this framework. According to Waddington & Hendriks,[408] breach of an employer's duty to provide for reasonable accommodation for employees

---

[399]   See further below Part 3, II.2.c.i.
[400]   Burri 2000, p. 375.
[401]   Wentholt 2000, p. 60.
[402]   See later in this part, C.III.
[403]   Prechal 2004, pp. 535 subs.
[404]   Holtmaat & Loenen 1997, p. 33, in relation to Dutch law.
[405]   Directive 76/207/EEC, *OJ* 1976 L 39/40.
[406]   See Gesetzesentwurf der Bundesregierung über die Gleichbehandlung von Männern und Frauen am Arbeitsplatz und über die Erhaltung von Ansprüchen bei Betriebsübergang (Arbeitsrechtliches EG-Anpassungsgesetz), *RdA* 1980, 52-55.
[407]   Colneric 1996, p. 233.
[408]   Waddingtom & Hendriks 2002, pp. 405 subs. and 423 subs.

with handicaps under Art. 5 of the General Framework Directive[409] provides an example.

> Waddington & Hendriks argue that the failure to provide such accommodation amounts to a prohibited discrimination falling outside the categories of direct and indirect discrimination (discrimination *sui generis*). In these authors' view, a finding of *direct* discrimination on grounds of handicap would require an approach similar to that applied by the Court of Justice in *Dekker*[410] in relation to discrimination on grounds of pregnancy, where the Court in effect disposed of the requirement of a male comparator.[411] As far as *indirect* discrimination on grounds of handicap is concerned, Waddington & Hendriks point to the difficulties involved in assigning an appropriate comparator. The authors explain: 'Different from direct and indirect discrimination, reasonable accommodation discrimination typically emerges in response to the failure to make an adaptation to ensure equal opportunities and commonly does not follow from differentiation on a forbidden or seemingly neutral ground – a distinction which is sometimes difficult to apply with respect to groups in need of adaptations. Reasonable accommodation discrimination is also different from direct and indirect discrimination given that a disadvantage is not necessarily experienced by all or most members of a particular group, but is [...] experienced on the individual level, depending on both individual and environmental factors. Reasonable accommodation discrimination therefore requires a different approach to do justice to the particularities of an individual in a given situation – or, as was held by the Canadian Supreme Court, 'Accommodation ensures that each person is assessed according to his or her personal abilities rather than presumed group characteristics'.'

In making their argument regarding discrimination, Waddington & Hendriks refer to the statement in Art. 5 of the Directive that the obligation to provide reasonable accommodation is necessary in order to guarantee compliance with the principle of equal treatment. However, it should be noted that failure to provide reasonable accommodation is not mentioned as a form of discrimination in Art. 2 of the Directive. Most likely, the interpretation suggested by Waddington & Hendriks has to be seen against the background of UK non-discrimination legislation regarding handicap which is explicit on this point.[412] Though EC law may not explicitly regard the breach of the duty to provide reasonable accommodation as a specific type of discrimination, it is certainly possible to speak about discrimination in a broader sense, for example by drawing parallels to other types of discrimination (as is done by Jolls[413] in the context of U.S. law when she argues that, in particular circumstances, antidiscri-

---

[409]   Directive 2000/78/EC, *OJ* 2000 L 303/16.
[410]   Case C-177/88, [1990] I-3941.
[411]   See earlier in this part, B.III.3.c.
[412]   See also below Part 2, B.III.2.b.
[413]   Jolls 2000 and 2001.

mination and accommodation are identical) or to positive action (as is done by Prechal[414] according to whom accommodation is a form of positive action).

c. Structural discrimination

On the theoretical level, a further important concept is that of *structural (institutional or systemic) discrimination*. Though this concept does not explicitly appear in EC law, it is nevertheless relevant in the context of this present study because, in the context of social law in particular, indirect discrimination is said to have been 'invented in order to cater for the situation of institutional discrimination' (Ellis).[415] Compared to direct and indirect discrimination, the term 'structural discrimination' refers to a type of discrimination with a *much more complex* nature. Structural discrimination arises from deeply rooted views, opinions and value judgments relied on in a given society or from societal, cultural, economic patterns and structures (see in particular McCrudden[416] in his seminal article on structural race discrimination; also Barbera,[417] Heinze,[418] Lanquetin,[419] Holtmaat).[420] Structural discrimination concerns the 'consequences of a set of institutions if that set could have been selected differently or may be altered in the future by us acting as a collective body' (Somek).[421] Hepple, Choussey & Choudhury[422] refer to the widely quoted definition in the 'Stephen Lawrence Inquiry' carried out in the UK in the context of racism, according to which institutional racism is:

'[T]he collective failure of an organisation to provide an appropriate and professional service to people because of their colour, culture or ethnic origin. It can be seen or detected in processes, attitudes and behaviour which amount to discrimination through unwitting prejudice, ignorance, thoughtlessness and racist stereotyping which disadvantage minority ethnic people. It persists because of the failure of the organisation openly and adequately to recognise and address the existence and causes by policy, example and leadership. Without recognition and action to eliminate such racism it can prevail as part of the ethos or culture of the organisation. It is a corrosive disease.'

---

[414]   Prechal 2004, p. 538.
[415]   Ellis 1994 (Definition of Discrimination), p. 572.
[416]   McCrudden 1982, p. 345.
[417]   Barbera 1994, p. 49.
[418]   Heinze 1994, p. 227.
[419]   Lanquetin 1996 (La preuve), p. 495.
[420]   Holtmaat 1996 (Alle dingen), pp. 126/127, also Holtmaat 2001 (Gender).
[421]   Somek 2001, p. 180.
[422]   Hepple, Choussey & Choudhury 2000, p. 15.

Accordingly, structural discrimination often occurs independently of individuals' intentions or even awareness, even of its very victims' (e.g. Crosby,[423] McGinley,[424] Somek).[425] As Lacey[426] puts it, 'much institutional discrimination is or is seen as normal, usual behaviour'. A well-known example is sex-specific job segregation which often has negative consequences for women (Holtmaat,[427] Vogel-Polsky).[428] Other examples are the notorious lack of sufficient accessible public toilets for persons with handicaps, and more generally of public toilets for women (Edwards & McKie).[429]

> The sex-specific segregation of work concerns in particular the notoriously low pay for work considered to be typically women's work, but also the presumption traditionally underlying labour law rules that a typical worker works life-long and full-time (a labour pattern typical of male workers which does not apply to many women). As for the lack of sufficient accessible toilets for persons with a handicap, the British Toilet Association[430] has pointed out that providing no public toilets at all (rather than toilets not accessible for everyone) is not considered discrimination on grounds of disability under the EC General Framework Directive.[431]

The fact that structural discrimination is even more hidden than indirect discrimination makes this form extremely difficult to address, particularly through the legal system. In addition to the prohibition against indirect discrimination, the main instruments in this context are positive action and, more generally, positive duties to promote equality.[432] Structural discrimination does not usually appear in non-discrimination legislation as such. The duty of 'social engineering' in Art. 5 CEDAW provides a notable exception.

> Art. 5 CEDAW addresses the problem by describing it and, further, by obliging the Signatory States to engage in what is often referred to as social engineering: 'States Parties shall take all appropriate measures: (a) To modify the social and cultural patterns of conduct of men and women, with a view to achieving the elimination of prejudices and customary and all other practices which are based on the idea of the inferiority or the superiority of either of the sexes or on stereotyped roles for men and women; (b) To ensure that family education includes a proper understanding of maternity as a social function and the recognition of the common responsibility of men and women in the upbringing and development of their

---

[423]   Crosby 1996.
[424]   McGinley 2000.
[425]   Somek 2001, p. 180.
[426]   Lacey 1987, p. 418.
[427]   Holtmaat 1989, pp. 483/484.
[428]   Vogel-Polsky 1998.
[429]   Edwards & McKie 1996.
[430]   As reported by The Economist of August 17th 2002, p. 30: 'Public toilets. Bog standards.'
[431]   Directive 2000/78/EC, OJ 200 0 L 303/16.
[432]   See earlier in this part, B.II.3.c.

children, it being understood that the interest of the children is the primordial consideration in all cases.' The United Nations Human Rights Fact Sheet No. 22[433] explains: 'The importance of the Convention on the Elimination of All Forms of Discrimination against Women lies in the fact that it adds new, substantive provisions to the other instruments which also deal with equality and non-discrimination. Article 5 recognizes that, even if women's legal equality is guaranteed and special measures are taken to promote their de facto equality, another level of change is necessary for women's true equality. States should strive to remove the social, cultural and traditional patterns which perpetuate gender-role stereotypes and to create an overall framework in society that promotes the realization of women's full rights.' (See also Holtmaat 2004 (Towards Different Law).)

d. Specifically in EC law: discrimination in form and in substance

Two additional conceptions of discrimination that appear in the Court of Justice's early case law are *discrimination in form and in substance*. In the *Italian Refrigerators*[434] case (para. 4, p. 177), the Court stated that '[t]he different treatment of non-comparable situations does not lead automatically to the conclusion that there is discrimination. An appearance of discrimination in form may therefore correspond in fact to an absence of discrimination in substance. Discrimination in substance would consist in treating either similar situations differently or different situations identically. [... D]iscrimination [...] might just as well take the form of dissimilar situations being treated identically [...].' This study's main part[435] will show that the term *discrimination in substance* has sometimes been used synonymously with that of indirect discrimination. However, in the present writer's opinion this practice is certainly not in line with the Court's use of terminology as just quoted, which clearly concerns a different phenomenon – though how precisely, is debated.[436] According to Timmermans,[437] substantive discrimination refers to same treatment of different cases (equal treatment of unalikes), which implies that formal discrimination refers to different treatment of same cases (unequal treatment of likes). Voogsgeerd[438] suggests that the concept of substantive discrimination is useful for the purposes of the common market and free movement law in the EC where it focuses purely on the prohibited effect (meaning that all legal or factual differences that cannot be objectively justified are within its wide scope). In contrast, according to Rating[439] it may not even have been the Court's

---

[433] Human Rights Fact Sheet No. 22, published by the Centre for Human Rights, United Nations Office at Geneva.
[434] Case 13/63, [1963] *ECR* 165.
[435] See below Part 2, IV.2.b.i.
[436] Though according to Hernu 2003, p. 256, the Court's statements constitute 'un enoncé remarquable par sa simplicité et sa clareté'.
[437] Timmermans 1982, pp. subs.
[438] Voogsgeerd 2000, pp. 69 subs.
[439] Rating 1994, p. 54.

intention to define a new form of discrimination in *Italian Refrigerators*, but only to underline the need for a pragmatic approach. The present writer suspects that, beside confirming the Aristotelian framework of equality and non-discrimination in EC law, the idea behind the Court's distinction was to underline that the mere fact of same treatment is not in itself sufficient to conclude that there is no discrimination and, *vice versa*, that different treatment is not sufficient in itself for a finding of actual discrimination. Rather, such a finding depends on whether the case involves comparable or non-comparable situations. Viewed in this way, discrimination in substance consists of treating either similar situations differently or different situations identically (Wouters,[440] Waelbroeck,[441] Drijber & Prechal).[442] However, today the debate on the correct interpretation may be moot because the Court no longer uses these terms. Thus, in *Schumacker*[443] (para. 30) the Court simply referred to settled case law according to which 'discrimination can arise only through the application of different rules to comparable situations or the application of the same rule to different situations',[444] without mentioning discrimination in form or in substance.

e. Factual discrimination

i. The concept

A final, though *non-legal notion of discrimination* that needs mention is that of *factual discrimination*. Bamforth[445] emphasises the importance of an extra-legal concept as necessary in order to provide an independent criterion for assessing the result of applying particular interpretations of a legal concept. According to this author, there exists a tendency whereby lawyers, in particular, lose sight of this point and understand discrimination only in a strictly legal sense. This tendency is dangerous because it can obscure the fact that the law exists to serve social goals and that these goals can also be served by extra-legal devices. It is, therefore, important to recognize that a situation which does not involve discrimination in the legal sense may still involve factual discrimination according to other standards (see also Schefer).[446] Obviously, appropriate examples depend on the existence of such standards and, thus, often raise issues for debate. This is illustrated by the political discussions concerning different pension ages for men and women.

---

[440] Wouters 1999, p. 104, and Wouters 2001, pp. 313 subs.
[441] Waelbroeck 1983, pp. 1336 subs.
[442] Drijber & Prechal 1997, p. 124.
[443] Case C-279/93, [1995] *ECR* I-225.
[444] This formula is consistently used in the Court's case law, recently e.g. *Rieser* (Case C-157/02, judgment of 5 February 2004, n.y.r., para. 39, in the context of transport law) and *Alabaster* (Case C-147/02, judgment of 30 March 2004, n.y.r., para. 45, in the context of sex equality law).
[445] Bamforth 1996, p. 58.
[446] Schefer 2002, p. 479.

In EC law, at least for the time being, a difference in treatment of the sexes with respect to their pension ages is explicitly made possible by the social security Directives (Art. 7(a) of the Third Equal Treatment Directive[447] and Art. 9(a) of the Fourth Equal Treatment Directive)[448] within their field of application (though not in relation to equal pay as covered by Art. 141(1) and (2) EC; see the *Barber* case law).[449] Whilst some consider this a discriminatory arrangement, others think that a lower pension age for women is appropriate in view of structural disadvantages faced by women in every day life, such as multiple burdens, generally lower wages and tax regimes disencouraging paid work for married women. Similar issues arise in the context of night-work and military service (e.g. Schiek,[450] Hoppe,[451] Bigler-Eggenberger.[452] Klett).[453]

In some cases, the problem may eventually be settled by the adoption of new legislation which, partially or wholly, converts what has been thus far recognized as only factual discrimination into a legally recognised form of discrimination. In EC law, the long planned legislation on free movement of services in the field of transport provides an example.

Under Art. 51(1) EC, transport is excluded from the application of the general Treaty rules on free movement of services. Instead, freedom of movement was to be granted through specific secondary legislation (Art. 80(2) EC). No such legislation was in force at the time when *Corsica Ferries France I*[454] arose, a case concerning free movement in the field of maritime transport. Thus, a finding of (indirect) discrimination on grounds of nationality was excluded and the discrimination complained of could be of only a factual nature. The situation changed with the adoption of Regulation 4055/86[455] which, in the later case *Corsica Ferries Italia*,[456] made a finding of (indirect) discrimination possible on grounds of nationality.

ii. The relevance of the law's limited field of application

As is evident from the example of free movement of services in EC transport law, just mentioned, a finding of nothing more than factual discrimination often results from

---

[447] Directive 79/7/EEC, *OJ* 1979 L 6/24.
[448] Directive 86/378/EEC, *OJ* 1986 L 225/40 (as amended).
[449] *Barber* (Case C-262/88, [1990] *ECR* I-1889) and of the later case law notably *Moroni* (Case C-110/91, [1993] *ECR* I-6591).
[450] Schiek 1992, pp. 12 subs. Regarding night-work in EC law, see in particular *Stoeckel* (Case C-345/89, [1991] *ECR* I-4047), confirmed in *Commission v France* (Case C-197/96, [1997] *ECR* I-1489); also *Levy* (Case C-158/91, [1993] ECR I-4287).
[451] Hoppe 2002, p. 82.
[452] Bigler-Eggenberger 2003, p. 326, in the context of Swiss law.
[453] Klett 2004, p. 139, in the context of Swiss law.
[454] Case C-49/89, [1989] *ECR* I-4441.
[455] Regulation 4055/86/EEC, *OJ* 1986, L 378/1 (as amended).
[456] Case C-18/93, [1994] *ECR* I-1783, see further below Part 2, A.I.4.k.ii.

the *limited field of application of the existing legislation*. As Rust[457] aptly states, the scope of non-discrimination legislation acts like the eye of a needle[458] which has to be passed through before the discrimination allegedly arising in a particular case can be addressed in substance. If a concrete case does not fall within the field of application of a non-discrimination provision, that provision is simply irrelevant from a legal point of view, however blatant the discrimination may be in factual terms. This is especially true in EC law where much of the non-discrimination law is rather limited in scope.[459] Further, wide variations in the scope of the various provisions necessitate precise distinctions between various kinds of discrimination. This situation in itself is difficult, and it also causes problems in the context of multiple (cumulative or intersectional) discrimination (Fredman,[460] Bell).[461]

> The term 'multiple (cumulative or intersectional) discrimination' relates to the fact that some individuals experience discrimination based on more than one ground. For instance, black women are subject to racism and sexism, as well as bearing a 'third burden', namely that of discrimination against black men. Fredman explains that such discrimination is not fully described by simply adding two kinds of discrimination together. She notes that the existing legal framework of the EC contains no mechanism for dealing with such cross currents, though multiple discrimination against women is mentioned in the preamble to the Race Directive[462] (consideration 14, in the context of the Community's task under Art. 3(2) EC to eliminate inequalities and to promote equality between men and women). Fredman therefore advocates a single harmonised statute which includes all relevant discriminatory grounds and does not necessitate harsh distinctions between them.

An additional problem arises in cases where the Court of Justice assesses the already limited scope of the law in a restricted, problematic or unsatisfactory manner. In many cases, the Court has been generous, in line with the generally applied principle that the basis for fundamental rights must be interpreted widely (e.g. *Lawrie-Blum*,[463] para. 17). However, this is not always the case. Thus, the Court's decision in the sex equality case *Meyers*[464] contrasts favourably with the approach in *Jackson and Cresswell*.[465]

---

[457] Rust 1997, p. 149.
[458] See the biblical comparison with the likeliness of a rich person to get into the kingdom of God; Matthew 19, 24, Mark 10, 25 and Luke 18, 25.
[459] See also below, Part 2, B.IV.2.
[460] Fredman 2002, pp. 70 and 83 subs., see also Fredman 2001, p. 158.
[461] Bell 2002, pp. 114 subs.
[462] Directive 2000/43/EC, *OJ* 2000 L 180/22.
[463] Case 66/85, [1986] *ECR* 2121.
[464] Case C-116/94, [1995] *ECR* I-2131.
[465] Joined Cases C-63/91 and C-64/91, [1992] *ECR* I-4737.

Ms Meyers complained about indirect sex discrimination caused by the refusal to let her deduct child-care costs from her gross income in order to qualify for a family credit, an income-related benefit intended to supplement the income of low-paid workers who are responsible for a child. The Court found that this type of benefit falls within the material scope of the Third Equal Treatment Directive[466] (*Meyers*, para. 16 subs.). In contrast, Ms Jackson and Ms Cresswell were less fortunate. Their case concerned a statutory social security scheme providing for income support. An unemployed single mother and an unemployed divorced mother respectively, the plaintiffs wished to deduct child-minding expenses from their income, in order to lower their income and thereby increase the benefit due to them. However, according to the relevant rules, child-minding expenses were not deductible from earnings from part-time work or from allowances paid during certain types of vocational training. The plaintiffs argued that they were suffering indirect sex discrimination prohibited by Community law. This raised questions regarding the scope of the Second[467] and the Third Equal Treatment Directives. The Court held that neither Directive covered the case. Regarding the Third Directive, the problem was one of the Directive's material scope since 'a benefit, if it is to fall within the scope of Directive 79/7, must constitute the whole or part of a statutory scheme providing protection against one of the specified risks or a form of social assistance having the same objective' (*Jackson and Cresswell*, para. 15). As far as the Second Directive is concerned, the Court found that neither Ms Jackson nor Ms Cresswell fell within the Directive's personal scope since they were not workers within the meaning of the Directive (*Jackson and Cresswell*, para. 28). As a result, a case of quite clear factual indirect sex discrimination – as AG van Gerven remarked, 'lone parents, mainly women, suffer *de facto* unequal treatment compared with married parents or parents otherwise living together' (*Jackson and Cresswell*, point 37 of the AG's opinion) – was not found to involve discrimination in law. The AG's opinion shows that the outcome could have been different (*Jackson and Cresswell*, point 15 subs. and 23 subs. of the opinion).

iii. In particular: limited number and reach of discriminatory grounds

Of particular importance in the context of factual discrimination is, of course, the number and the reach of the discriminatory grounds mentioned in the law. These may develop over time. Regarding the *number of legally recognised discriminatory grounds*, Timmermans[468] in 1982 identified three broad categories. The first and most important concerned nationality, relevant notably in the context of free movement. A second category included a variety of other types, such as discrimination in the context of competition law. The third category was that of discrimination on grounds of sex. Since then, to these have been added the group of grounds mentioned in Art. 13 EC, introduced through the Amsterdam Treaty revision, namely race or ethnic origin,

---

[466]   Directive 79/7/EEC, *OJ* 1979 L 6/24.
[467]   Directive 76/207/EEC, *OJ* 1976 L 39/40 (in its original version).
[468]   Timmermans 1982, p. 429.

religion or belief, disability, age, and sexual orientation.[469] Over time, the list of grounds relevant in the framework of EC law may develop further, for example as a consequence of technical and scientific changes that cause new types of discrimination to come into existence (e.g. discrimination on grounds of genetic features,[470] as mentioned in Art. 21 of the Charter of Fundamental Rights).[471] Against this background, some academic writers point to the proliferation of the equality principle, and some warn that the ever widening range of discriminatory grounds will ultimately make equality law less effective (e.g. Witteveen,[472] Alkema & Rop,[473] Holtmaat).[474]

Within a limited list of discriminatory grounds, their *substantive reach* is of fundamental importance. As has already been mentioned, under EC law it was possible to argue that discrimination on grounds of gender reassignment is included in the category of sex.[475] In contrast, such an approach did not succeed in the case of discrimination on grounds of homosexuality (*Grant*),[476] where only after the adoption of specific secondary legislation (in the form of the General Framework Directive)[477] was some legal recognition granted (and only to a limited extent) to this type of factual discrimination. As Bell[478] states: 'Discrimination against lesbian women and gay men has a long history, but the construction of their maltreatment as *discrimination*, and therefore unacceptable behaviour, is more recent.'

---

[469] As the example of secondary legislation on sex discrimination shows, the lack of a specific legal basis provision under the former state of Community law is not per se an explanation for the fact that there was no legislation on other types of discrimination before the new Art. 13 Directives; see Tobler 2000 (Sex Equality Law), pp. 143/144. As in that area, the Treaty's general legal basis provisions (formerly Arts. 100, 100a and 235 of the EC Treaty, now Arts. 94, 95 and 308 EC) could have been relied on. Therefore, Clapham & Weiler 1993, p. 28, rightly note that the reason why the Community did not take such action is lack of political will.

[470] Hepple, Choussey & Choudhury 2000, p. 47, describe genetic discrimination 'as the different treatment of individuals and their family based on having symptoms of a genetic disease'. The Economist reported in 2001 that in the USA there were already court cases involving such discrimination (The Economist of April 4th 2001, p. 19: 'The politics of genes. America's next ethical war').

[471] Charter of Fundamental Rights of the European Union, *OJ* 2000 C 364/1. In the Charter of Fundamental Rights of the Union which forms the second part of the EU Constitutional Treaty, this is Art. II-81(1); Treaty establishing a Constitution for Europe, *OJ* 2004 C 310.

[472] Witteveen 2000.

[473] Alkema & Rop 2002, p. 51.

[474] Holtmaat 2002, pp. 163 subs.; also Holtmaat 2003 (Stop de uitholling).

[475] See earlier in this part B.III.4.a, further below Part 3, A.III.3.b.

[476] Case C-249/96, [1998] *ECR* I-621; see further below Part 3, A.III.3.b.

[477] Directive 2000/78/EC, *OJ* 2000 L 303/16.

[478] Bell 2002, p. 89.

6. JUSTIFICATION FOR DISCRIMINATION

a. The concept

If a situation is found to involve (direct or indirect) discrimination in the sense described thus far, such a finding does not automatically ensure that the act or rule causing such discrimination is prohibited. It is merely a *prima facie* finding due to the fact that *it may be possible to justify derogations* from the prohibition against discrimination. In the framework of an Aristotelian equality approach, justification in the strict sense of the word ('justification proper') can be pursued through one of two possibilities: in the interest of issues of special importance either to distinguish between two situations even though they are comparable or not to distinguish between two situations even though they are different. In such cases, discrimination exists in principle but is made acceptable as a result of the weighing of conflicting interests, namely of non-discrimination on the one hand and of a concern unrelated to it on the other (e.g. the protection of public health, public security and public policy under Art. 39(3) EC). Leader[479] speaks of 'cross-cutting reasons for discrimination'. The possibility of justification always threatens the effectiveness of non-discrimination law which is why it has been called an inevitable evil (Mortelmans).[480] As far as *indirect* discrimination is concerned, a debate is taking place in academic writing as to whether objective justification concerns justification proper in the sense described above, or whether it is rather a matter of causation. Opinions are also divided on the question as to whether or not the justification possibilities differ with respect to cases of direct and indirect discrimination. Both issues will be discussed in the study's main part.[481]

b. Derogations in form or in substance?

Whether a given ground framed in terms of a derogation from the prohibition against discrimination is indeed a derogation *in terms of its substance* may be subject to dispute (e.g. Foubert;[482] compare also Jarass).[483] In the framework of EC law, before the Court of Justice the point was first made by AG Darmon in relation to Art. 2(4) of the Second Equal Treatment Directive (in its original version)[484] which allows positive action measures (*Hofmann*,[485] point 9 of the AG's opinion). This point was later taken up and elaborated upon by AG Saggio arguing that positive action is a matter of ensuring

---

[479]   Leader 1996, pp. 111 subs.
[480]   Mortelmans 1997, p. 183.
[481]   See below Part 2, A.IV.3.e and Part 3, A.II.2, respectively.
[482]   Foubert 2002, pp. 39 subs.
[483]   Jarass 2000 (Unified Approach), pp. 155 subs.
[484]   Directive 76/207/EEC, *OJ* 1976 L 39/40; see already earlier in this part, B.II.3.b.
[485]   Case 184/83, [1984] *ECR* 3047.

equality in the actual conditions of employment (*Badeck*,[486] points 26 and 27 of the AG's opinion).

> AG Saggio in *Badeck* explained that 'it is true that the legality of such measures depends on whether the positive action can be reconciled with the general principle of non-discrimination, it is equally true, as various learned writers have often pointed out, that the principle of non-discrimination, designed – for the purposes of the present case – to ensure equal treatment for employees, and the principle of equal opportunity – on which positive action is based -, designed to ensure equality in the actual conditions of employees, or in other words the principles of formal and substantive equality, are not completely at odds: if substantive equality can be achieved by measures that are, by their very nature, discriminatory, then such measures are in fact pursuing the same objective as the first principle, but with the additional twist that the legislature finds itself obliged to remedy a situation where some sections of the population face a real difficulty which cannot be addressed by applying the general principle of non-discrimination. If we follow this line of reasoning, we may come to doubt whether substantive equality is the exception to the rule of formal equality or, in other words, whether the provisions on which positive action is based – in this case Article 119(4) of the EC Treaty[487] and Article 2(4) of the Directive – are in the nature of exceptions and must therefore be interpreted strictly. I therefore consider that there is nothing, at Community level, to prevent a national legislature from adopting positive measures that actually reinstate the group at which they are aimed in cases where the group in question, that is to say women, are in a particularly difficult situation and where the mere guarantee of equal treatment and observance of the (negative) principle of non-discrimination by the State authorities does not adequately protect their position. Such measures may therefore be designed not merely to guarantee women an equal opportunity at the starting-point by creating the conditions to enable them to compete on an equal footing for each particular post, but to have a real effect on their social integration by giving them actual priority in appointment and promotion.'

The Court, however, continues to insist that Art. 2(4) of the Second Equal Treatment Directive is indeed an exception (*Lommers*,[488] para. 39) and, thus, to perceive positive action in favour of women as a form of discrimination against men, if only in a *prima facie* form ('discriminatory in appearance').[489] The Court's case law demonstrates that such 'discrimination' can be either direct (e.g. *Kalanke*,[490] *Marschall*,[491] *Lommers*)[492]

---

486   Case C-158/97, [2000] *ECR* I-1875.
487   This numbering refers to the so-called Draft Amsterdam Treaty, see *OJ* 1997 C 340/1.
488   Case C-476/99, [2002] *ECR* I-2891.
489   In the present writer's view, this is contrary to the CEDAW; Tobler 2003, p. 71.
490   Case C-450/93, [1995] *ECR* I-3051. This case concerned a sex-specific rule, namely that women had to be given precedence in appointment and promotion over equally well qualified male candidates in the case of underrepresentation. Note, however, that according to Fredman 1999, p. 206, *Kalanke* involved a measure 'aimed at a problem which, from the UK or US perspective, looks like a classic indirect discrimination or disparate impact scenario'.
491   Case C-409/95, [1997] *ECR* I-6363.
492   Case C-476/99, [2002] *ECR* I-2891.

or indirect (see the Court's remarks in *Badeck*,[493] para. 32, and *Abrahamsson*,[494] para. 47 and 48; Numhauser-Henning,[495] Barnard,[496] Hervey).[497]

> Regarding *indirect* discrimination in particular, the Court in *Badeck* mentioned the criteria for the assessment of given candidate's qualifications, relevant under the contested regulation of the German *Land* of Hesse. According to these rules, capabilities and experience acquired by carrying out family responsibilities were to be taken into account in so far as they were of importance for the suitability, performance and capability of candidates, whereas seniority, age and the date of last promotion were to be taken into account only in so far as they were of importance for the same purposes. Family status or income of the partner is immaterial, and part-time work, leave and delays in completing training as a result of looking after children or dependants in need of care must not be granted a negative effect. Though the legitimacy of these criteria was not challenged, the Court nevertheless stated: 'Such criteria, although formulated in terms which are neutral as regards sex and thus capable of benefiting men too, in general favour women. They are manifestly intended to lead to an equality which is substantive rather than formal, by reducing the inequalities which may occur in practice in social life.' Similarly, the Court remarked in *Abrahamsson* that 'it is legitimate for the purposes of that assessment for certain positive and negative criteria to be taken into account which, although formulated in terms which are neutral as regards sex and thus capable of benefiting men too, in general favour women. [...] The clear aim of such criteria is to achieve substantive, rather than formal, equality by reducing de facto inequalities which may arise in society and, thus, in accordance with Article 141(4) EC, to prevent or compensate for disadvantages in the professional career of persons belonging to the under-represented sex.'

Mutatis mutandis, similar questions regarding the proper nature of provisions framed in terms of derogations also arise in the context of other interests, such as the protection of women with regard to pregnancy and maternity.[498]

c. Absolutely and relatively worded provisions

In EC law, some discrimination provisions are *worded in an absolute way* in the sense that they do not mention any justification possibilities (e.g. Art. 12(1) EC, Art. 90(1) EC). In contrast, others explicitly mention grounds for derogation (so-called textual

---

[493] Case C-158/97, [2000] *ECR* I-1875.
[494] Case C-407/98, [2000] *ECR* I-5539.
[495] Numhauser-Henning 2001 (Swedish Sex Equality Law), p. 123.
[496] Barnard 2000, p. 251.
[497] Hervey 2002, p. 119.
[498] Compare earlier in this part, B.II.2.b.ii, in the context of substantive equality. However, see also Foubert's plea in favour of a justification approach. According to this author, if pregnancy is seen as a relevant difference which allows different treatment, there is a risk that the link with the principle of equality is destroyed; Foubert 2002, p. 42.

or statutory derogations)[499] which are, therefore, said to be framed in a relative manner (e.g. Arts. 39(3), 46 and 55 EC in conjunction with Art. 46 EC regarding public policy, public security and public health, as fleshed out in Directive 64/221).[500] A given provision's nature regarding justification may be debated, for instance due to changes of the law over time. In EC law, the principle of equal pay for men and women provides such an example.

> In its original version expressed in the Treaty (Art. 119 of the EEC Treaty), the principle of equal pay for men and women was clearly worded in an absolute manner. It has been argued that this situation changed with the adoption of the Social Agreement[501] whose Art. 6(3) generally allowed for 'measures providing for specific advantages in order to prevent or compensate for disadvantages in their [women's] professional careers'. Thus, in *Griesmar*[502] (para. 60), the applicant claimed that through this provision 'an entire novelty' had been introduced, namely 'the possibility of discrimination, not in regard to equal treatment, but in regard to equal pay'. (By discrimination he clearly meant justification.) The Court did not rule on this issue as it found Art. 6(3) to be inapplicable. As a result of the integration of the Social Agreement into the Treaty, the amended version of Art. 119 now contains a provision on positive action (Art. 141(4) EC). Opinions differ on whether or not this makes Art. 141 EC a relatively worded provision. The Schwarze[503] and Calliess & Ruffert Commentaries[504] as well as Meyer[505] regard it as a derogation but Barnard & Hepple[506] disagree because Art. 141(4) EC is 'framed as essential to the achievement of 'full equality' in practice, that is substantive equality'.

The (substantive) question as to whether the (usually limited) justification catalogues in EC law can be expanded and whether a possibility of justification even exists in the case of provisions not mentioning any derogations will be discussed in the study's main part.[507]

d. Justification and scope

Jarass[508] has emphasised the importance of clearly distinguishing between issues of scope on the one hand and issues of justification on the other, both on the conceptual level and on the level of the practical analysis of a given case. First, there is an im-

---

[499] 'Benannte Ausnahmen' in the terminology of Jarass 2000 (Elemente), p. 716.
[500] Directive 64/221, *OJ* English Special Edition 1964, No. 850/64, p. 117.
[501] See *OJ* 1992 C 191/90.
[502] Case C-366/99, [2001] *ECR* I-9383.
[503] Schwarze Commentary 2000, n. 54 ad Art. 141 EC.
[504] Calliess & Ruffert Commentary 2002, n. 80 subs. ad Art. 141 EC.
[505] Meyer 2002, p. 155.
[506] Barnard & Hepple 2000, p. 576.
[507] See below Part 3, A.II.2. Accordingly, the terms absolute and relative as used in the present context merely concern the *wording* of a particular provision and not its substantive content.
[508] Jarass 2000 (Elemente), p. 717, also Jarass 1995, p. 221 subs.

portant role for the principle of proportionality in the context of justifications but not in that of scope. Second, an important difference exists with regard to the requisite burden of proof. Where there is no reversal of the burden of proof (that is, for those situations falling outside the reach of the Burden of Proof Directive,[509] of the non-discrimination Directives adopted under Art. 13 EC[510] and of case law such as *Danfoss*),[511] generally speaking, the plaintiff bears the burden of proof for establishing that a given difference in treatment falls within the field of application of a given provision. In contrast, the burden of proof for justification lies with the defendant. Further, the scope of a non-discrimination provision is an issue that must be assessed well before that of justification can even be raised (Wentholt).[512]

An example of mixing issues of scope and of justification through a problematic use of terminology is provided by the GTE[513] Commentary where the question of whether a given case concerns discrimination on grounds of sex or rather discrimination on some other ground was discussed under the heading of justification ('Rechtfertigungsgründe für ein Klagebehren wegen Lohndiskriminierung') However, case law such as *P. v S.*[514] (concerning discrimination on grounds of gender reassignment) does not concern the question whether sex discrimination can be justified but rather the question of the reach (scope) of the prohibition of sex discrimination (Hoppe;[515] compare also Kenner).[516]

e. *Justification and objective differences (comparability)*

Apollis[517] generally remarks that the Court of Justice's case law concerning justification is characterised 'by a singular lack of precision and sometimes even coherence'. That certainly appears true with regard to the Court's use of terminology. The term 'justification' does not always refer to 'justification proper' but instead is used in the context of the issue of comparability. This use is confusing because, from a conceptual point of view, a finding of *comparability is a prerequisite* for equal treatment and hence also for a finding of the discrimination resulting from unequal treatment. As such, it differs from the cross-cutting reasons that constitute justification proper and that must be examined only after a *prima facie* finding of discrimination has been made. *Ruckdeschel*[518] is a case in point.

---

509   Directive 97/80/EC, *OJ* 1998 L 14/6 (as amended).
510   Directive 2000/43/EC, *OJ* 2000 L 180/22; Directive 2000/78/EC, *OJ* 2000 L 303/16, and Directive 2004/113/EC, *OJ* 2004 L 373/37.
511   Case 109/88, [1989] *ECR* 3199.
512   Wentholt 1990, p. 76.
513   GTE Commentary 1997, n. 55 subs. ad Art. 119 of the EC Treaty.
514   Case C-13/94, [1996] *ECR* I-2143.
515   Hoppe 2002, p. 80; see below Part 3, A.III.2.b.
516   Kenner 2003, p. 439 (in the context of discrimination on grounds of sexual identity).
517   Apollis 1980, p. 81.
518   Joined Cases 117/76 and 16/77, [1977] *ECR* 1753.

Ruckdeschel concerned the revision of the Common Market Organization regarding cereals through which a certain production refund was maintained solely for the processing of maize into starch, but abolished for the processing of maize into so-called *Quellmehl*. According to AG Capotorti, the Court's case law established that 'differentiation based on objective criteria is permissible but any unjustified difference of treatment constitutes discrimination' (opinion of the AG, p. 1778 subs.). The Court stated that the products 'must be treated in the same manner unless differentiation is objectively justified' and then explained that the fundamental principle of equality 'requires that similar situations shall not be treated differently unless differentiation is objectively justified' (para. 7-9). The Court found that no proof had been brought forward for the Commission's and the Council's allegations that the two products were no longer comparable since *Quellmehl* was now used to a large extent for animal feed rather than for human consumption.

The issue of comparability acquires particular importance in cases where no grounds exist for justification because in those cases only the argument of non-comparability presents any possibility of avoiding a finding that different treatment constitutes discrimination. Cases such as *Abdoulaye*[519] and *Österreichischer Gewerkschaftsbund, Gewerkschaft der Privatangestellten*[520] illustrate this point.

Abdoulaye concerned the absolutely framed[521] principle of equal pay for men and women (now Art. 141(1) and (2) EC and the First Equal Treatment Directive).[522] In spite of the existence of different treatment of men and women regarding their pay, the Court denied the existence of sex discrimination on the basis of the non-comparability of the situations of men and women in the relevant context. The payment at issue was a special benefit for recent mothers. The Court emphasised that '[t]he principle of equal pay enshrined in Article 119 of the Treaty, like the general principle of non-discrimination of which it is a particular expression, presupposes that male and female workers whom it covers are in comparable situations' (*Abdoulaye*, para. 16).

Österreichischer Gewerkschaftsbund, Gewerkschaft der Privatangestellten concerned the calculation of a termination payment by taking into account as 'length of service' the duration of military (or an equivalent civilian) service which was performed usually by men, but not the duration of parental leave, taken usually by women. According to the applicant, this system of calculation amounted to indirect sex discrimination prohibited under the equal pay principle (Art. 141(1) and (2) EC). The Court, however, agreed with the respondent that the two situations were not comparable since parental leave is taken voluntarily and is governed by the individual interests of the worker, whilst military and civilian service correspond to a civic obligation imposed in the public interest. According to the Court, the voluntary nature of parental leave 'is not lost because of difficulties in

---

[519] Case C-218/98, [1999] *ECR* I-5723.
[520] Case C-220/02, judgment of 8 June 2004, n.y.r.
[521] On the debate whether Art. 141(4) EC forms a derogation to that principle, see earlier in this part, B.III.6.c.
[522] Directive 75/117/EEC, *OJ* 1975 L 45/19.

finding appropriate structures for looking after a very young child, however regrettable such a situation may be' (*Österreichischer Gewerkschaftsbund, Gewerkschaft der Privatangestellten,* para. 60).

IV. RESTRICTIONS IN A WIDER SENSE

1. THE CONCEPT

Under the Court's case law, EC free movement law not only prohibits direct and indirect discrimination but also *restrictions in a wider sense*. Originally, the Treaty provisions on restrictions to free movement were interpreted by the Court as prohibiting only discrimination, conceived of as what is today termed direct discrimination and only later deemed to include indirect discrimination, as discussed in this study. Eventually, the range of possible infringements was further widened so as to include what in this study is termed restrictions in a wider sense (see in particular Behrens;[523] further e.g. Mattera,[524] Drijber & Prechal,[525] Kingreen,[526] Keunen,[527] Johnson & O'Keeffe,[528] Everling,[529] Roth,[530] Martin).[531] A measure constitutes a restriction in this sense 'where that measure, even though it is applicable without discrimination on grounds of nationality, is liable to hamper or to render less attractive the exercise by Community nationals, including those of the Member State which enacted the measure, of fundamental freedoms guaranteed by the Treaty' (*Kraus,*[532] para. 32). Restrictions in a wider sense are prohibited unless they can be justified by the general interest (*Gebhard,*[533] para. 37).

> Against the background of the Court's case law, Handoll[534] distinguishes three broad types of restrictions namely, first, national obstacles which contradict the very right of the free movement asserted (e.g. national provisions in the field of services that effectively require establishment, such as those at issue in the *French Tourist Guides* case),[535] secondly, obstacles that otherwise impinge on the economic activity itself (e.g. national requirements regarding

---

[523] Behrens 1992, pp. 155 subs.
[524] Mattera 1993, p. 65.
[525] Drijber & Prechal 1997, p. 124.
[526] Kingreen 1999, pp. 38 subs.
[527] Keunen 2001, pp. 339 subs.
[528] Johnson & O'Keeffe 1994.
[529] Everling 1997.
[530] Roth 1997.
[531] Martin 1998.
[532] Case C-19/92, [1993] *ECR* I-1663.
[533] Case C-55/94, [1995] *ECR* I-4165.
[534] Handoll 1995, para. 6.18.
[535] Case C-154/89, [1991] *ECR* I-659.

professional qualifications that do not take account of knowledge and qualifications already acquired by the person concerned in another Member State, such as in *Clinical Biological Laboratories*)[536] and, thirdly, other obstacles that do not directly relate to the economic activity itself or to its exercise, but in a more general way hinder free movement (e.g. national requirements regarding driving licences which may have an effect on a person's economic activities, such as in *Choquet*).[537]

2. DEVELOPMENT AND RELEVANCE IN THE CONTEXT OF THIS PRESENT STUDY

The restriction-based approach was first developed in the context of free movement of services (*Van Binsbergen*)[538] and from there extended to other areas of Community law. Doubts lingered longest in the area of free movement of persons,[539] and particularly regarding the free movement of workers where the wording of Art. 48(2) of the EEC Treaty (now Art. 39(2) EC) related to discrimination only. Those doubts were eventually alleviated by the Court's ruling in the *Bosman* case[540] (para. 92 subs.), though criticism persists with regard to this development (e.g. Daniele).[541] More recently, the relevance of the restriction-based approach was confirmed in the context of the free movement of capital in the *Golden Shares* cases (e.g. *Commission v Portugal*,[542] para. 44) and the free movement of workers in relation to taxation (e.g. *De Groot*,[543] para. 78 subs.)[544].

Behrens[545] has emphasised the fundamental importance of the development of the concept of restrictions in a wider sense. According to this author, it not only indicates a move from non-discrimination to non-restriction but also from the 'import state principle' to the 'home state principle', from a freedom for producers to a freedom

---

[536]   Case 221/85, [1987] *ECR* 719.

[537]   Case 16/78, [1978] *ECR* 2293.

[538]   Case 33/74, [1974] *ECR* 1299; see further below Part 3, B.I.2.a.i.

[539]   Compare the different interpretations of the Court's decision in *Stanton* (Case 143/87, [1988] *ECR* 3877; see also the parallel case *Wolf* (Joined Cases 154 and 155/87, [1988] *ECR* 3897) by Garrone 1994, pp. 436 subs., and by Kaldellis 2001, p. 32.

[540]   Case C-415/93, [1995] *ECR* I-4921. On the development in the area of free movement of persons, see AG Lenz' analysis of the case law previous to *Bosman*, at point 165 subs. of the AG's opinion; further e.g. Moitinho de Almeida 1994.

[541]   Daniele 1997, p. 195.

[542]   Case C-367/98, [2002] *ECR* I-4731.

[543]   Case C-385/00, [2002] *ECR* I-11819.

[544]   According to Breitenmoser 2003, p. 1165, this is a new development as far as direct taxation is concerned. However, it should be noted that *De Groot* was not the first case where the Court applied a restriction-based approach in the context of direct taxation. Rather, the same approach can already be observed in *Bachmann* (Case C-204/90, [1992] *ECR* I-249, para. 31-33), though here in the context of free movement of services rather than that of free movement of workers.

[545]   Behrens 1992, pp. 155 subs.

for consumers and from a privilege for foreigners to equality of competition. As indicated at the very beginning of this study, the concept of restrictions in this wider sense is relevant for present purposes because of its seemingly close relationship to indirect discrimination, particularly in view of the shared possibility of open justification. In fact, it will be demonstrated that this concept was developed against the background of fact patterns that might also be analysed in the framework of indirect discrimination. In more recent cases, the Court's reasoning sometimes seems to oscillate between the two concepts, and there are even cases where, although the Court was explicitly urged to specify the nature of the infringement at issue, the Court quite obviously dodged the question. This raises the question of where to establish the dividing line between the two concepts. This question will be discussed in the study's main part.[546]

V. WHAT IS AN EQUALITY OR NON-DISCRIMINATION RULE FOR THE PRESENT PURPOSES?

Against the background of the discussion of important parameters (above), the following sections explain the nature of an equality (or non-discrimination) rule for the purposes of this present study. These sections will indicate which areas of EC law are relevant to the analysis in the study's main part as well as which will be excluded from the examination. Further, several analytical tools for analysing such provisions will be proposed.

1. RELEVANT TYPES OF RULES

a. Only substantive rules directly prohibiting discrimination

A first point – perhaps a rather obvious one – is that *only substantive provisions* on equality and discrimination which in themselves prohibit discrimination are relevant in the present context. In addition to written provisions, these also include the unwritten general equality principle as well as the unwritten general principle of non-discrimination on grounds of sex, both recognised by the Court as fundamental principles of Community law (e.g. see *Ruckdeschel*[547] and *Rinke*,[548] respectively). Excluded are both the legal basis provisions as relevant in the context of non-

---

[546] See below Part 3, B.
[547] Joined Cases 117/76 and 16/77, [1977] *ECR* 1753; see Tridimas 1999, pp. 40 subs.
[548] Case C-25/02, judgment of 9 September 2003, n.y.r.

discrimination (Arts. 12(2) and 13 EC as well as the legal basis provision in specific parts of the Treaty, such as Art. 40 EC) and the programmatic provisions which are not in themselves framed as prohibitions against discrimination (e.g. Arts. 2, 3(2) and 137 EC).[549]

> To label provisions such as Art. 2 and 3(2) EC as *programmatic* does not mean that they have no legal effect but merely that they are not in themselves discrimination provisions within the meaning of this present study (Meyer,[550] with further references). For example, AG Stix-Hackl argued in her opinion on *Dory*[551] (points 68 and 105) that reference could be made to Art. 3(2) EC in the interpretation of secondary law and that, accordingly, national measures might be 'amenable to some extent to a review of content by reference to the aims of Article 3(2) EC, at least where the subject matter concerns one of the fields referred to in Article 3(1) EC'. Some authors even consider that Art. 3(2) EC established a new and general prohibition of discrimination for the whole spectrum of EC law (e.g. the von der Groeben & Schwarze Commentary;[552] apparently the view is based on the assumption that only the second part of Art. 3(2) EC is related specifically to sex equality. As Meyer[553] points out, that view may rely on the provision's wording in German which is open to more than one interpretation.)

b. Only equality and non-discrimination provisions in a strict sense

i. Included provisions and areas of law

Not all provisions found to be related to equality or discrimination by the Court, or analysed by academic commentators in that context, are considered non-discrimination provisions for the purposes of this present study which adheres to a strict or technical approach. Within this framework, equality and non-discrimination rules are *comparison-based* and *do not themselves define the level of treatment* that is required in the interest of legal equality. In other words, such rules require (or prohibit) comparatively equal or unequal treatment without defining the level of that treatment. These include, notably, the Treaty rules on free movement of persons (workers and establishment, including social security as related to free movement of persons), services and capital. In this present study, these are at the centre of attention as far as *economic law* is concerned. In addition, several specific areas are considered, namely public procurement, direct taxation and transport. This examination will also include Art. 90(1) EC on the discriminatory taxation of goods and Art. 34(2) EC on agricul-

---

[549] For an overview on equality provisions in a broad sense in EC law see Wouters 2001, pp. 303 subs.
[550] Meyer 2002, pp. 25 subs.
[551] Case C-186/01, [2003] *ECR* I-2479.
[552] Von der Groeben & Schwarze Commentary 2004, n. 11 and 12 ad Art. 3 EC.
[553] Meyer 2002, p. 28.

tural goods.[554] In the context of *social law*, a particular emphasis is placed on sex equality for the simple reason that because the relevant legislation has existed for so long, a large body of case law has developed creating a situation which differs from that involving more recent legislation related to other fields of EC law.

ii. Not the basic Treaty provisions on free movement of goods

The most important set of provisions which do not fulfil the above conditions[555] are those involving the *free movement of goods*. Arts. 25, 28 and 29 EC prescribe a specific kind of treatment, namely that of refraining from imposing customs duties and quantitative restrictions (Lyons;[556] also Martin).[557] For that reason, they are not discussed in this study. Further, for reasons of consistency, Art. 31 EC which is, in fact, framed in terms of discrimination, will not be addressed by this study.

> Art. 31 EC prohibits discriminatory State monopolies of a commercial character ('no discrimination regarding the conditions under which goods are procured and marketed [...] between nationals of Member States'). A case decided by the EFTA Court in the framework of EEA law illustrates that indirect discrimination may play a role in this context. *EFTA Surveillance Authority v Norway*[558] concerned the Norwegian State retail alcohol monopoly which required that alcoholic beverages with an alcohol content between 2,5 and 4,75% be sold through State monopoly outlets, with the exception of beer with the same alcohol content. This type of beer was usually domestically produced. The Court first confirmed that the two categories of beverages are products in competition (*EFTA Surveillance Authority v Norway*, para. 39). It then held that the Norwegian retail system 'constitutes discrimination within the meaning of Article 16 of the EEA Agreement' (*EFTA Surveillance Authority v Norway*, para. 42). The Court did not mention indirect discrimina-

---

[554] Though related to free movement of goods in terms of substance, these provisions are different from the basic provisions in the Treaty title on free movement of goods which are excluded from the ambit of this study (see immediately below, in the following section). The difference in approach between these categories corresponds to a difference in nature of their issues. Thus, customs duties are by their very nature obstacles to trade and as such prohibited. The situation differs with regard to internal taxation provisions which, however, can become obstacles if imposed in a discriminatory or protective manner.

[555] Possibly, the right to set up agencies, branches or subsidiaries under Art. 43 EC can also be seen in that context, though it is sometimes mentioned in the context of indirect discrimination, e.g. Eberhartinger 1997, p. 47. In the present writer's analysis, it can be argued on the basis of *Klopp* (Case 107/83, [1984] *ECR* 2971, para. 18 subs.) that in relation to agencies, branches and subsidiaries the Treaty provides not only for the right to set them up under the same conditions as are applicable to nationals of the State in question, but also for a free standing right that is subject only to the observance of the professional rules of conduct (prudential supervision). According to Schneider 1996, p. 514, the Court filled Art. 43 EC with substantive meaning (though this statement is made in the context of the development of restrictions in a wider sense).

[556] Lyons 2001, p. 29.

[557] Martin 1998, p. 267.

[558] Case E-9/00, [2002] *EFTA Court Reports* 72.

tion but this is what it must have meant in view, particularly, of its general statement that Art. 16 prohibits discrimination in law and in fact (*EFTA Surveillance Authority v Norway*, para. 36, with further references).

The exclusion of the Treaty title on free movement of goods from the analysis in this present study is, of course, not intended to deny that its provisions and its related case law contain certain elements of discrimination (in particular, consider the last sentence of Art. 30 EC and *Keck*)[559] and that, more generally, *the term discrimination has traditionally been used in this context* also by the Court (e.g. *Commission v Luxembourg and Belgium*,[560] p. 432; *Irish Souvenirs*,[561] para. 14; *Pistre*,[562] para. 51; *Guimont*,[563] para. 20). Although AG Gand in his opinion on the *Diamantarbeiders*[564] case (p. 230) explained that discrimination is not a condition *sine qua non* in the context of import restrictions,[565] some authors insist that it remains the essential characteristic of the provisions on free movement of goods.[566] Thus, not surprisingly, *indirect discrimination* is also mentioned in this context. According to some authors, certain cases decided by the Court of Justice are in fact indirect discrimination cases, or at least related closely to that concept in terms of their structure (e.g. Barnard,[567] Bernard,[568] Norberg,[569] Hakenberg,[570] Plötscher).[571]

> According to Barnard, Art. 28 EC is underpinned by notions of non-discrimination and therefore outlaws both direct and indirect discrimination. In Barnard's view, an import restriction caused by an indistinctly (or equally) applicable measure 'is, in essence, indirect discrimination'. Similarly, Bernard has raised the question as to whether '*Cassis de Dijon*

---

559   Joined Cases C-267/91 and C-268/91, [1993] *ECR* I-6097.
560   Joined Cases 2/62 and 3/62, [1962] *ECR* 425.
561   Case 113/80, [1981] *ECR* 1625.
562   Joined Cases C-321 to 325/94, [1997] *ECR* I-2343.
563   Case C-448/98, [2000] *ECR* I-10663.
564   Joined Cases 2/69 and 3/69, [1969] *ECR* 211. See GTE Commentary 1997, n. 43 ad Art. 30 of the EC Treaty; Grabitz & Hilf Commentary (as of 1989), n. 3 ad Art. 28 EC; Jarass 2000 (Elemente), p. 709.
565   The approach is different under Art. 29 EC (export rules) in that here the Court explicitly requires a 'difference in treatment', see *Groenveld* (Case 15/79, [1979] *ECR* 3409), para. 7. This has been criticised by, among others, Oliver 1999, p. 803, who suggests that the language of the *Groenveld* test should 'be reworded so as to cover any measure which has the object or the effect of treating exports less favourably than goods intended for the domestic market'.
566   Marenco 1984, pp. 314 subs., is probably the best known example (see also Défalque 1987, p. 481, and Hilson 1999, p. 447). Views differ on whether and to what extent *Keck* (Joined Cases C-267/91 and C-268/91, [1993] *ECR* I-6097, para. 16) confirmed Marenco's view. For examples, see de Búrca 1997, pp. 21 subs.; Bernard 1998, pp. 14; also Oliver 2003, para. 6.48 and 6.54 subs., and Eeckhout 2000, pp. 191 subs.
567   Barnard 1996, pp. 70 and 74.
568   Idem, pp. 82 and 93.
569   Norberg 2001, p. 73.
570   Hakenberg 2000, p. 95.
571   Plötscher 2003, pp. 171 and 182 subs.

[can] be explained in terms of indirect discrimination', based on the understanding that the Court's concept of mandatory requirements can be seen as simply a by-product of the concept of indirect discrimination. Norberg goes so far as to assert that *Cassis de Dijon* is 'the leading case on indirect discrimination in the field of free movement of goods'. In this author's analysis, the indirect sex discrimination case *Jenkins*[572] merely exemplified an application by the Court of the same principles in different contexts. Hakenberg calls the *Reinheitsgebot*[573] case a typical example of hidden discrimination. Plötscher refers to cases such as *Commission v Belgium*,[574] *Wallonian Waste*,[575] *Bluhme*,[576] *Aragonesa*[577] and *Du Pont de Nemours*.[578]

According to Oliver & Roth,[579] recent case law 'indicates that the Court seems to be ready to take the criterion of *de facto* discrimination seriously'. However, the Court itself thus far has never used the term *indirect discrimination* in the context of Art. 28 EC, not even in *Centro-Com*[580] which is referred to by Streinz & Leible[581] as a concrete example of indirect discrimination under the *Keck*[582] approach. Both the EFTA Court (*Fatgún*,[583] para. 38) and the Court of Justice (*Karner*,[584] para. 20) explicitly mentioned overt or direct discrimination, which seems to imply that there might also be cases involving covert or indirect discrimination. However, the Court chose to speak more generally of rules 'applied without distinction to national and imported products and thus likely to constitute a potential impediment to intra-Community trade covered by Article 28 EC'.

In *Centro-Com*, an Italian company brought an action against the Bank of England for refusing Barclays Bank, London, authorization to transfer, from a Yugoslav account to Centro-Com, sums needed to pay for medical products exported from Italy to Montenegro. The Bank of England first agreed to authorize the debiting of Yugoslav accounts in payment for exports made for medical and humanitarian purposes. After reports of abuse the Bank changed its policy and decided to authorize debiting only where the exports were made from the UK. The Dutch Government and the Commission argued that this amounted to indirect discrimination on grounds of nationality prohibited by what was then Art. 6 of the Treaty

---

[572] Case 96/80, [1981] *ECR* 911; see further below Part 2, A.I.4.h and II.3.a.
[573] Case 178/84, [1987] *ECR* 1227.
[574] Case 155/82, [1983] *ECR* 531.
[575] Case C-2/90, [1992] *ECR* I-4431.
[576] Case C-67/97, [1998] *ECR* I-8033.
[577] Joined Cases C-1/90 and 176/90, [1991] *ECR* I-4151.
[578] Case C-21/88, [1990] *ECR* I-889. – In academic writing, see further e.g. Epiney 1995, pp. 38 subs., especially 47 subs.; Heselhaus 2001, p. 462; Scott 2002, pp. 275 subs.
[579] Oliver & Roth 2004, p. 416.
[580] Case C-124/95, [1997] *ECR* I-81.
[581] Streinz & Leible 2000, p. 462.
[582] Joined Cases C-267/91 and C-268/91, [1993] *ECR* I-6097.
[583] Case E-5/98, [1999] *EFTA Court Reports* 51.
[584] Case C-71/02, judgment of 25 March 2004, n.y.r.

(now Art. 12 EC). The Court, rather than assessing the case in the light of Art. 6, followed the approach suggested by AG Jacobs and found that the restriction on the payment at issue was equivalent to a quantitative restriction of the export of goods (Art. 28 EC). The Court did not mention indirect discrimination in that context (*Centro-Com*, para. 41).

Fatgún involved the award of a public works contract regarding the delivery and installation of roof elements for a school building (public procurement). In the negotiations with Fatgún, which was the company submitting the lowest tender, the authorities required the use of roof elements produced in Iceland. Fatgún lost the contract as a consequence of the fact that it used roof elements imported from Norway. The Supreme Court of Iceland asked the EFTA Court for an advisory opinion (an indirect action corresponding, in principle, to the preliminary ruling in EC law) on the question as to whether a clause requiring the purchase of products from Iceland is permissible under the EEA Agreement. The EFTA Court found 'overt discrimination' prohibited under Arts. 11 and 13 EEA (which correspond in terms of substance to Arts. 28 and 30 EC).

In *Karner*, the Court of Justice stated generally that the principle that Art. 28 EC cannot be considered inapplicable merely because all the facts of the specific case before the national court are confined to a single Member State, 'has been upheld by the Court not only in cases where the national rule in question gave raise to direct discrimination against goods imported from other Member States [...], but also in situations where the national rule applied without distinction to national and imported products and was thus likely to constitute a potential impediment to intra-Community trade covered by Article 28 EC.' As an example of the latter category, the Court mentioned *Guimont*.[585]

Regardless of further development in the Court's language, for present purposes it is decisive that when the term *discrimination* is used in the context of Art. 23 subs. EC, it has a much broader meaning than that used in this study. For example, according to Jarass[586] the rules on free movement of goods concern, 'as a starting point, all measures regulating goods crossing intra-Community borders more strictly than goods circulating within a Member State' (see further e.g. Colin & Sinkondo,[587] de Búrca,[588] Shuibhne,[589] Plötscher).[590]

---

[585]   Case C-448/98, [2000] *ECR* I-10663. This case concerned the sale of cheese under the name of 'Emmenthal'. Under French rules Emmenthal was a product characterised, among other things, by a hard, dry rind. The Court spoke about a national rule 'adopted in the absence of common or harmonised rules and applicable without distinction to national products and to products imported from other Member States' (para. 27).

[586]   Jarass 2000 (Unified Approach), pp. 145/146.

[587]   Colin & Sinkondo 1993, p. at 37.

[588]   De Búrca 2002, pp. 184 and 186 subs.

[589]   Shuibne 2002, pp. 408 subs.

[590]   Plötscher 2003, pp. 162 subs.

iii. Not competition law

The analysis in this study also *excludes the Treaty rules on competition*. Non-discrimination is certainly relevant in the context of competition law on a general level[591] as well as in the framework of certain specific provisions, such as Arts. 81(1)(d), 82(c) – though in this latter case not explicitly[592] – and 87(2)(a) EC. However, the set-up of Arts. 81, 82 and 87 EC reflects the fact that the aim of the EC competition rules reaches far beyond mere equal treatment (Martin,[593] Plötscher).[594] Because of this wider framework, it is often not necessary in concrete cases to rely on the concept of discrimination.

> Thus, Plötscher notes that in Art. 82 cases involving differentiations on the basis of nationality or residence, the Commission as well as the Court regularly rely on the general clause of Art. 82(1) EC, rather than make a finding of discrimination under Art. 82(c) EC which then requires a clarification of the relationship between that provision and Art. 12(1) EC. It should be noted, however, that more recently the Court of First Instance has made an express link between competition rules and Art. 12(1) EC in the *Thermenhotel* case (para. 114 subs.).[595] The Court explained that Art. 12(1) EC did not lend itself to be applied independently in this particular action, due to the existence of the competition rules in the EC Treaty which cover discrimination with reference to the geography and sector of the market under consideration.

2. ANALYTICAL TOOLS FOR ANALYSING NON-DISCRIMINATION AND EQUALITY PROVISIONS

The analyses carried out in this study are based on the assumption that a typical equality or non-discrimination provision contains *certain characteristic elements*. These are a consequence of the fact that equality in the Aristotelian sense is a relative concept. Provisions such as 'the right to equality is guaranteed' or 'discrimination is prohibited' are meaningless in themselves because they lack necessary points of reference. In Bobbio's[596] words: 'L'égalité, d'accord, mais entre qui, en quoi et sur quel critère?' In order to be workable, an equality or non-discrimination provision needs clarifying elements. In academic writing, a number of rather general elements are distinguished, including most often an objective element (i.e. the existence of a distinction, exclusion

---

[591] On the link between equality and competition, see earlier in this part, B.II.4.
[592] E.g. Goyder 2003, p. 322, who observes that discrimination on grounds of nationality may be treated as an abusive practice under Art. 82 EC.
[593] Martin 1998, p. 271.
[594] Plötscher 2003, p. 95.
[595] Case T-158/99, judgment of 13 January 2004, n.y.r.
[596] Bobbio 1996, p. 24.

or preference), a subjective element (the basis on which the distinction, exclusion or preference is made), an element of effect (the nullifying or impairing of equality of opportunity or of equal treatment) and, possibly, an element of justification (Nielsen;[597] see also Jarass,[598] Kingreen).[599] Wherever useful for purposes of this present study, the following somewhat more specific *catalogue of elements* will be relied on:

- The *type* of the provision (henceforth referred to as the *provision*): depending on its wording, it can be either an equality provision or a non-discrimination provision. In the first case, the provision's wording refers to 'equality', 'same treatment', 'same conditions' and the like (e.g. Arts. 43 and 50 EC) and in the second case to 'discrimination', 'less favourable treatment', 'dissimilar conditions' and the like (e.g. Arts. 12 and 34(2) EC). In the specific context of EC law, this distinction is of a merely formal nature; it does not appear to have consequences on the level of substance.[600]

- The *object* of equality or discrimination: that is, the persons, objects or situations to whose treatment the prescribed equality/forbidden discrimination refers (To whom or to what does equality or discrimination apply? Henceforth: the *object*). In principle, the object needs to be distinguished from the persons who may invoke the provision, though they may be the same in specific contexts.

- The *ground* for equal treatment or non-discrimination: that is, the focus point of equality and non-discrimination (On what basis is the equality or discrimination based? Henceforth: the *ground*). This is the crucial element for the purposes of indirect discrimination as discussed in this study.

- The persons *protected* by the provision: that is, the persons who can invoke the provision (Who is supposed to be granted equality or freedom from discrimination? Henceforth, the *protected*). In many cases, this is the same as the object of equality or discrimination.

- The persons *obliged* by the provisions: that is, addressee of the norm or the person who has to observe the provision by granting equality or avoiding discrimination (Who is obliged to ensure equality or to desist from discriminatory behaviour? Henceforth, the *obliged*).

Art. 75(1) EC, a non-discrimination provision from the area of transport law, is a rare example that contains almost all of the above elements. More often, one or more

---

[597] Nielsen 1990, p. 830.
[598] Jarass 1995, pp. 214 subs.
[599] Kingreen 1999, pp. 74 subs.
[600] Compare Plötscher 2003, pp. 33 subs, with further references.

elements are missing,[601] though even in that case they may still be relevant under the Court's case law (e.g. the issue of horizontal direct effect of certain Treaty provisions).

> Art. 75(1) reads: 'In the case of transport within the Community, discrimination which takes the form of carriers charging different rates and imposing different conditions for the carriage of the same goods over the same transport links on grounds of the country of origin or of destination of the goods in question shall be abolished.' This provision is framed in terms of non-discrimination (provision); it concerns rates and conditions for the carriage of goods within the Community (object); the prohibited criteria for discrimination are the country of origin and the destination of the goods in question (ground) and the obligation of non-discrimination rests upon the carrier of the goods (obliged). The only element not expressly mentioned is that of the persons protected. However, it is clear from the other elements that these must be the persons for whom the transport is undertaken.
> With regard to what it what is today Arts. 39, 49 and 141(1) EC, the provisions' wording would appear to refer solely to the Member States as the designated obliged entities. However, the Court held that the category of the obliged also includes private persons (*Walrave and Koch*,[602] *Angonese*,[603] *Defrenne II*).[604]

VI. SUMMARY OF THE MOST IMPORTANT POINTS

The following paragraphs revisit a number of legal concepts that are of fundamental importance for this study's further analysis, namely equality, discrimination and restrictions in a wider sense.

1. EQUALITY

A first and important distinction is that between *equality before the law*, which concerns only the application of the law, whatever its content, and *equality in the law*, which is concerned with law's substance. The legal concept of indirect discrimination is normally seen as relevant in the latter context. In EC law, equality in the law has traditionally been interpreted as requiring 'to treat likes alike and unalikes unalike, according to the difference', based on the writings of the Greek philosopher Aristotle. Equality in that sense is a relative concept that requires an examination into the

---

[601]   Zuleeg 1992, p. 473, mentions a view according to which a provision is only then properly a non-discrimination provision if it lists discrimination criteria (in that sense now Plötscher 2003, p. 318, point 2). However, Zuleeg notes that this is not applicable in the framework of the EC Treaty.
[602]   Case 36/74, [1974] *ECR* 1405.
[603]   Case C-281/98, [2000] *ECR* I-4139.
[604]   Case 43/75, [1976] *ECR* 455.

question of whether any two given situations are comparable for the purpose of the issue at hand (the 'similarly situated requirement'). Within the framework of the Aristotelian equality formula, comparability is always the first issue to be examined. Its outcome will determine whether equality requires same or different treatment. Though, according to the Court equality in EC law is to be interpreted in an Aristotelian sense, written equality and non-discrimination law place *a strong emphasis on the formula's first part* and, thereby, on equal treatment. Indirect discrimination is usually examined in this context.

Particularly important for present purposes is the distinction *between formal and substantive equality*. Formal equality is based on an assumption of sameness of the subjects under the law and mandates equal treatment towards all. In contrast, a substantive equality approach recognises that there may be differences that are relevant in the framework of the non-discrimination analysis. Substantive equality focuses on the outcome rather than on the mere form of a given treatment. EC law reflects a mixture of both formal and substantive elements. Though the term *substantive equality* does not appear in the written law, it is now mentioned in the Court's case law. Because of its focus on the effect of apparently neutral measures, the prohibition of indirect discrimination is often linked to the concept of substantive equality. The Court in that context sometimes uses the phrase 'equality in fact and in law'.

Indirect discrimination is also said to serve the goal of *equality of opportunity* according to which the opportunities and experiences which life offers ought not to vary because of arbitrary criteria. In the Court of Justice's case law, the concept is not limited to equal starting positions but also includes results-oriented elements (substantive interpretation, as opposed to formal interpretation).

2. DISCRIMINATION

As far as discrimination is concerned, three legal concepts in particular are relevant for the present purposes. These obviously include *indirect discrimination*, that is discrimination caused through an apparently neutral rule or measure. The concept was developed in contrast to that of *direct discrimination*, which denotes unfavourable treatment through measures that are explicitly or obviously based on a discriminatory ground prohibited by the law. Further, indirect discrimination is sometimes said to be a means to address instances of *structural discrimination,* meaning disadvantages arising from deeply rooted views, opinions and value judgments relied on in a given society or from societal, cultural, economic patterns and structures.

Discrimination provisions can take various forms. Of these, the distinction between open and closed wording is most relevant in the context of indirect discrimination. A provision is *worded in a closed manner* if it provides for an exhaustive list of discriminatory criteria. In such a case, there are two possibilities for finding discrimination in the face of a differentiation criterion that is not directly prohibited. One is to include the ground in question in the interpretation of an explicitly prohibited ground, and the other is to rely on the concept of indirect discrimination. A provision *is worded in an open fashion* if it either mentions no discriminatory grounds whatsoever or merely a non-exhaustive list of examples. This raises the question of to what extent the concept of indirect discrimination is relevant in such a context.

EC law often provides for possible *justifications* for discrimination. Justification in its proper sense relates to possibilities available in the interest of issues of special importance to distinguish between two situations even though they are comparable or not to distinguish between two situations even though they are different. Justification in that sense concerns 'cross-cutting reasons for discrimination'. Unfortunately, the issue involving justification is often confused with that of comparability. With regard to the legal concept of indirect discrimination, objective justification is part of its very definition. Views differ as to whether it concerns justification proper or rather an issue of causation.

3.   RESTRICTIONS IN A WIDER SENSE

A legal concept separate from discrimination, but still important in the present context for purposes of setting workable boundaries between complex legal concepts, is that of *restrictions in a wider sense,* relevant to EC law on free movement. This term denotes a measure which, even though applicable without distinction on grounds of nationality, is liable to hamper or to render less attractive the exercise by Community nationals of fundamental freedoms guaranteed by the Treaty. Like that of indirect discrimination, the definition of restrictions in a wider sense includes an element of open justification possibilities.

C. HISTORICAL PRECURSORS OF THE CONCEPT OF INDIRECT DISCRIMINATION

Plender[605] observes that equality is not a creature of the Community but rather 'an adopted infant, originating in national and public international law'. Similarly, first traces of the legal concept of *indirect discrimination* can be found in public international law (below I.). Because of its influence in Europe, U.S. law is particularly important (below II.). Briefly mentioned are also UK and Irish law which were the first to introduce legal definitions of indirect discrimination in Europe (below III.). Finally, the coal and steel case *Geitling*[606] is examined since here the Court of Justice first used the term 'indirect discrimination', though in a sense the Court's use there differs from that discussed in this study (below IV).

I. HISTORIC ORIGINS IN PUBLIC INTERNATIONAL LAW

According to Govers,[607] the terms 'direct' and 'indirect discrimination' were used for the first time in the *Déclaration des Droits Internationaux de l'Homme*, issued by the *Institut de Droit International* in 1929. Art. 5 of the Declaration stated: 'L'égalité prévue ne devra pas être nominal, mais effective. Elle exclue toute discrimination directe ou indirecte.' According to Schindler,[608] the concept of indirect discrimination was also present in international treaties of that era, based on references to 'equality in law and in fact'. For example, Art. 8 of the Treaty on the protection of Polish minorities of 1919, provided that Polish minorities 'shall enjoy the same treatment and security in law and in fact as the other Polish nationals'. Schindler even argued that indirect discrimination was also prohibited in the absence of such references because it constituted an abuse of the law. Both Govers and Schindler perceived traces of the concept of indirect discrimination in early case law of the Permanent Court of International Justice. They mention three pre-Second World War decisions, namely

---

[605] Plender 1995, p. 60.
[606] Case 2/56, [1957/1958] *ECR* 3.
[607] Govers 1981, p. 20.
[608] Schindler 1957, p. 143.

German settlers in Poland,[609] *Polish minorities in Dantzig,*[610] and *Minority schools in Albania*[611] (though these authors do not entirely agree as far as the relevance of this last case is concerned). In all of these cases the Permanent Court of International Justice, faced with formally neutral rules, emphasised the importance of equality both in law and in fact.

> *German settlers in Poland* was decided under Art. 8 of the Polish Minority Treaty. It concerned disadvantageous treatment of German minorities in Poland through a law that was worded neutrally with regard to what was then conceived of as race. The Court explained: 'The facts that no racial discrimination appears in the text of the law [...] and that in a few instances the law applies to non-German Polish nationals who took as purchasers from original holders of German race, make no substantial difference. Art. 8 is designed to meet precisely such complaints as are made in the present case. There must be equality in fact as well as ostensible legal equality in the sense of the absence of discrimination in the words of the law.'
>
> *Polish minorities in Dantzig* concerned Art. 104(5) of the Treaty of Versailles which provided for the conclusion of a Treaty between Poland and Germany aimed at preventing 'any discrimination within the Free City to the detriment of the citizens of Poland and other persons of Polish origin or speech'. The Court held: 'It should be remarked [...] that the prohibition against discrimination in order to be effective, must ensure the absence of discrimination in fact as well as in law. A measure which in terms is of general application, but in fact is directed against Polish nationals and other persons of Polish origin or speech, constitutes a violation of the prohibition.'
>
> *Minority schools in Albania* involved the first sentence of Art. 5 of the 'Albanian Declaration' of 2 October 1921 which provided for 'the same treatment and security in law and in fact' of Albanian nationals who belong to racial, linguistic, or religious minorities as that for other Albanians. Greek minorities in Albania ran their own private schools which enabled religion-based education. They were closed down in the framework of measures taken in 1933 in order to close 'private schools of all categories'. This measure affected mainly minority schools. The Court stated: 'Equality in law precludes discrimination of any kind; whereas equality in fact may involve the necessity of different treatment in order to attain a result which establishes an equilibrium between different situations. It is easy to imagine cases in which equality of treatment of the majority and of the minority, whose situations and requirements are different, would result in inequality in fact; treatment of this description would run counter to the first sentence of the first paragraph of article 5. The equality between members of the majority and of the minority must be an effective, genuine equality; that is the meaning of the provision.' These statements were made in the context of the *general* section of Art. 5 (rather than in relation to the part specifically mentioning

---

609   [1923] *PCIJ* 3 (10 September 1923).
610   [1932] *PCIJ* 1 (4 February 1932).
611   [1935] *PCIJ* 1 (6 April 1935).

the right to maintain schools and educational establishments; compare the different comments made by Govers,[612] Loenen[613] and Schindler).[614]

II. THE 'DISPARATE IMPACT' DOCTRINE IN U.S. LAW

In U.S. law the concept of indirect discrimination, usually[615] referred to as *disparate (or adverse) impact* (as opposed to disparate treatment), can be found comparatively early (Curtin).[616] Though its main source is Supreme Court case law relating to Title VII (employment discrimination section) of the Civil Rights Act 1964, early traces of the concept can also be found in other contexts.

1. INTRODUCTION THROUGH CASE LAW

a. Early indications

A number of early U.S. cases have been interpreted as pointing in the direction of recognising disparate impact, though none of them have acquired the status of a landmark case. According to Gerards,[617] the earliest relevant case is *Wilson v. Lane*,[618] decided in 1939 by the U.S. Supreme Court under the Equal Protection Clause. In this case, the Court held that the Fourteenth Amendment to the Federal Constitution 'nullifies sophisticated as well as simple-minded modes of discrimination'. Schindler[619] refers to the *Oyama* decision of 1948,[620] concerning compatibility of the California Alien Land Law with the Equal Protection Clause, where the Supreme Court stated that it had to examine 'not merely whether [...] rights have been denied in express terms, but also whether they have been denied in substance and effect'. Also interesting is *Local 189, Papermakers v. the United States*,[621] decided in 1969, where the Fifth Circuit Court of Appeals held that reliance on a standard neutral on its face is no

---

612 Govers 1981, p. 20.
613 Loenen 1998, p. 24; Veldman 1995, p. 176.
614 Schindler 1957, p. 146.
615 Seeland 1982, p. 295, speaks of 'individual discrimination' and 'organizational discrimination'.
616 Curtin 1989, p. 235.
617 Gerards 2002, pp. at 370 subs.
618 *Wilson v. Lane*, 307 U.S. 268 (1939).
619 Schindler 1957, p. 145.
620 *Oyama v. California*, 332 U.S. 633 (1948).
621 *Local 189, United Papermakers and Paperworkers v. the United States*, 416 F.2d 980 (5th Cir. 1969). See also the important precedent *Quarles v. Philip Morris*, 179 F. Supp 505 (E.D. VA. 1968) which, however, did not contain such wording.

defence under Title VII of the Civil Rights Act when the effect of the standard is to lock the victims of racial prejudice into an inferior position. A final example, *Gaston County v. United States*[622] of 1969, was later described as involving a measure that 'would abridge the right to vote indirectly on account of race' (Chief Justice Burger in the landmark case *Griggs v. Duke Power Co.*,[623] discussed immediately below), though the decision itself is not quite that explicit.

> *Lane v. Wilson* concerned new rules on the registration for elections in Oklahoma according to which all persons already registered in 1914 did not need not to reregister, but others had to within twelve days. This clearly disadvantaged African Americans who had not been entitled to vote in 1914. Gerards points out that it was clear that the legislator was in fact quite aware of the disparate effect of its new rules. The Court held that the Fourteenth Amendment 'nullifies sophisticated as well as simple-minded modes of discrimination. It hits onerous procedural requirements which effectively handicap exercise of the franchise by the colored race although the abstract right to vote may remain unrestricted as to race'.
> *Oyama* concerned a Japanese ineligible for American citizenship who bought land for his minor son, an American citizen. Under Californian law at the time, aliens ineligible for American citizenship were forbidden to acquire, own, lease or transfer agricultural property in the state, and intent to prevent or avoid the law was presumed whenever an ineligible alien bought land for a transfer to a citizen or eligible alien. The Supreme Court observed that '[i]n approaching cases, such as this one, in which federal constitutional rights are asserted, it is incumbent on us to inquire not merely whether those rights have been denied in express terms, but also whether they have been denied in substance and effect'.
> *Local 189, Papermakers v. the United States* concerned a Southern papermill that used to be segregated on the basis of race and which changed its system in such a way that racial integration was achieved in some progression lines only. In particular, black employees were lower on the integrated progression ladders than white employees (who were often many years their junior in terms of total length of service with the company). Against that background, basing promotion on the basis of seniority obviously disadvantaged blacks. McCrudden[624] discusses the case in the context of institutional discrimination.
> *Gaston County v. United States* concerned voter registration under the Voting Rights Act of 1965 which had suspended any test or device which acted as a prerequisite to registering to vote. This Act also applied to the North Carolina literacy test. Gaston County in North Carolina brought an action for reinstatement of the test, claiming that its use did not discriminate on grounds of race. The Supreme Court explained that 'it is appropriate for a Court to consider whether a literacy or educational requirement has the "effect of denying ... the right to vote on account of race or color" because the State or subdivision which seeks to impose the requirement has maintained separate and inferior schools for its negro residents who are now of voting age'. In view of Gaston County's segregated school system, the Court found that it was only reasonable to infer that among black children fewer will

---

[622] *Gaston County v. United States*, 395 U.S. 285 (1969).
[623] *Griggs v. Duke Power Co.*, 401 U.S. 424 (1971).
[624] McCrudden 1982, p. 328.

achieve any given degree of literacy than will their better-educated contemporaries. Accordingly, the Court found that an 'impartial' administration of the literacy test would serve only to perpetuate the existing inequities in a different form.

b. The landmark case: Griggs v. Duke Power Co.

Usually, *Griggs v. Duke Power Co.*,[625] decided in 1971, is mentioned as the decisive (and often as the first) case on disparate impact (e.g. O'Donovan & Szyszczak,[626] Blom,[627] Blomeyer,[628] Wisskirchen,[629] Bieback,[630] Bartlett & Harris,[631] Selmi,[632] Steiner,[633] Stampe,[634] Fredman,[635] Waddington & Hendriks,[636] Jolls).[637] In this case, the U.S. Supreme Court not only recognised an indirect form of discrimination but also indicated the *raison d'être* of the disparate impact doctrine. *Griggs* concerned racial discrimination as prohibited under section 703(a) of Title VII of the Civil Rights Act 1964. The plaintiffs challenged the requirement of a high school diploma or the passing of intelligence tests as a condition of employment in or of transfer to jobs at the Duke Power Company plant. Since the requirement was not directed at measuring the ability to learn to perform a job, it was found to be unlawful by the Supreme Court even though the contested rule was formally neutral in terms of race. Writing for the Court, Chief Justice Burger explained that the objective of the enactment of Title VII was 'to achieve equality of employment opportunities and remove barriers that have operated in the past to favor an identifiable group of white employees over other employees. Under the Act, practices, procedures, or tests neutral on their face, and even neutral in terms of intent, cannot be maintained if they operate to 'freeze' the status quo of prior discriminatory employment practices.' The Chief Justice continued – famously – that Congress did not intend 'to provide equality of opportunity merely in the sense of the fabled offer of milk to the stork and the fox',[638] but rather that 'the vessel in

---

[625]   *Griggs v. Duke Power Co.*, 401 U.S. 424 (1971).
[626]   O'Donovan & Szyszczak 1988, p. 97.
[627]   Blom 1992, p. 44.
[628]   Blomeyer 1994, p. 97.
[629]   Wisskirchen 1994, pp. 20 and 29 subs.
[630]   Bieback 1997, p. 20.
[631]   Bartlett & Harris 1998, p. 166.
[632]   Selmi 1999, p. 214.
[633]   Steiner 1999, p. 177.
[634]   Stampe 2001, p. 46.
[635]   Fredman 2002, p. 106.
[636]   Waddingtom & Hendriks 2002, p. 407, footnote 14.
[637]   Jolls 2001, p. 652.
[638]   This refers to a fable by Aesop (6th century before Christ) about a fox who invites a *crane* to dinner and serves soup in a shallow dish, making it impossible for the guest to eat. When the crane invites the fox for dinner in return, the fox finds the food served in a tall jar with a narrow neck (see Aesop.34 Halm). – The crane became a *stork* (and thus an animal with an even longer beak) only in later (Latin) versions of the fable (see Phaedrus I, 26).

which the milk is proffered be one all seekers can use. The Act proscribes not only overt discrimination, but also practices that are fair in form, but discriminatory in operation. The touchstone is business necessity. If an employment practice which operates to exclude Negroes cannot be shown to be related to job performance, the practice is prohibited.'

The parallels between the inclusion into the prohibition of discrimination also of 'practices that are fair in form, but discriminatory in operation' and indirect discrimination as understood in Europe are clear. In fact, *Griggs* was *very influential in European social law* where it led to the first legal definition of indirect discrimination in the UK and, indirectly, Ireland.[639] In the framework of EC law, *Griggs* was relied on before the Court of Justice in the important sex equality law case *Jenkins*[640] and prominently mentioned in the AG's opinion in that case. Returning to U.S. law, it is important to note that the *disparate impact approach is restricted to a particular legal realm*, namely employment law under the Civil Rights Act. In *Washington v. Davis*,[641] the Court held that in the context of constitutional claims under the Equal Protection Clause of the Fourteenth Amendment to the Federal Constitution, intent was a necessary element (McCrudden,[642] MacKinnon).[643] According to Loenen,[644] the far-reaching potential of the disparate impact doctrine seems to have been a major reason for this limitation. Accordingly, the disparate impact doctrine does not reflect a universal approach in all areas of U.S. law.

2. INTRODUCING A LEGAL DEFINITION THROUGH THE CIVIL RIGHTS ACT 1991

In the field of employment law under the Civil Rights Act, the U.S. Supreme Court later made it considerably easier for businesses to justify policies with a disparate impact, having found that a mere economic justification was sufficient. The Court also held that statistical evidence of racial imbalance was not, in itself, sufficient to show *prima facie* disparate impact; rather, the victim had to be able to point to a particular employment practice in that context (*Wards Cove*).[645] Reactions to this approach led to the adoption of the Civil Rights Act of 1991 which in Section 703 for the first time included a statutory definition of adverse impact in U.S. law:

---

[639] See later in this part, C.III.
[640] Case 96/80, [1981] *ECR* 911. See further below, Part 2, A.I.4.h. and A.II.3.
[641] *Washington v. Davis*, 426 U.S. 229 (1976).
[642] McCrudden 1982, p. 336.
[643] MacKinnon 2001, pp. 102 subs.
[644] Loenen 1999, p. 200; also Sedler 1999, pp. 94 subs.
[645] *Wards Cove Packing Co. v. Atonio*, 460 U.S. 642 (1989).

'(A) An unlawful employment practice based on disparate impact is established under this title only if (i) a complaining party demonstrates that a respondent uses a particular employment practice that causes a disparate impact on the basis of color, religion, sex or national origin and the respondent fails to demonstrate that the challenged practice is job related for the position in question and consistent with business necessity; [...].'

Congress in Section 701 explicitly added a description of the term 'business necessity' which was meant to codify the meaning as used in *Griggs* and to overrule *Wards Cove*. Business necessity is described as meaning '(A) in the case of employment practices involving selection [...], the practice or group of practices must bear a significant relationship to successful performance of the job; or (B) in the case of employment practices that do not involve selection, the practice or group of practices must bear a significant relationship to a significant business objective of the employer'. Section 701 further states that demonstrable evidence is required for these purposes. As Selmi[646] explains, the new legal definition 'explicitly included the disparate impact theory safely within the scope of Title VII, an essential protection given the substantial possibility that the Supreme Court may have eliminated the theory altogether if given the opportunity'. However, Selmi also notes that disparate impact cases in the U.S. are notoriously expensive and time-consuming and that, therefore, few cases have actually been brought under the new law.

III. EUROPEAN PRECURSORS: UK AND IRISH LAW

The U.S. disparate impact doctrine led to the first legal definition of indirect discrimination in Europe in the UK Sex Discrimination Act (SDA) 1975. Previous UK anti-discrimination legislation had concerned itself only with direct discrimination and the Government did not originally intend to include a prohibition on indirect discrimination within the SDA. However, before the publication of the bill, Secretary of State Roy Jenkins visited the USA where he learned about *Griggs v. Duke Power Co.*[647] This led to a moving away from a discrimination test necessarily based on intent (McCrudden,[648] Pannick,[649] McColgan).[650] Section 1(1) SDA provides:

'A person discriminates against a woman in any circumstances relevant for the purposes of any provision of this Act if – (a) on the ground of her sex he treats her less favourably

---

[646] Selmi 1999, pp. 215 subs.
[647] *Griggs v. Duke Power Co.*, 401 U.S. 424 (1971).
[648] McCrudden 1982, pp. 336 subs.
[649] Pannick 1985, p. 39.
[650] McGolgan 2000, pp. 66/67. On the influence of the U.S. disparate impact doctrine on UK law see also Szyszczak 1981, p. 678; McCrudden 1982, pp. 329 subs.; O'Donovan & Szyszczak 1988, p. 98; Curtin 1989, p. 236; Barbera 1994, p. 55, and Bieback 1997, pp. 21 and 122.

than he treats or would treat a man, or (b) he applies to her a requirement or condition which applies or would apply equally to a man but – (i) which is such that the proportion of women who can comply with it is considerably smaller than the proportion of men who can comply with it, and (ii) which he cannot show to be justifiable irrespective of the sex of the person to whom it is applied, and (iii) which is to her detriment because she cannot comply with it.'

Though there are important similarities, McCrudden[651] observes that the SDA did not accurately copy the U.S. approach since 'disparate effect 'and 'present unfavourable effects of past intentional discrimination', distinguished by the U.S. courts under Title VII, were subsumed into Section 1(1)(b) SDA.[652] The UK definition in the SDA was the precursor for another early legal definition of indirect sex discrimination in Europe, namely that in the Irish Employment Equality Act 1977 (Curtin).[653] Section 2(c) of that Act provided:[654]

'For the purposes of this Act, discrimination shall be taken to occur in any of the following cases: [...] (c) where because of his sex or marital status a person is obliged to comply with a requirement, relating to employment of membership of a body, which is not an essential requirement for such employment or membership and in respect of which the proportion of persons of the other sex or (as the case may be) of a different marital status but of the same sex able to comply is higher.'

On the level of the European Community, the UK definition would later be relied on before the Court of Justice in the important sex equality case *Jenkins*.[655]

IV. THE FIRST EXPLICIT REFERENCE IN THE LAW OF THE EUROPEAN COMMUNITIES: *GEITLING*

The first explicit reference by the Court of Justice to indirect discrimination occurred in *Geitling*,[656] a case decided in 1957 under the law of the (since expired) European Coal and Steel Community. However, the following discussion will show that the term as it is used in this case differs from today's understanding of indirect discrimination.

---

[651] McCrudden 1977, p. 242; McCrudden 1982, p. 346.

[652] A further legal definition of indirect discrimination can be found in Section 1(1)(b) of the UK Race Relations Act 1976. McCrudden explains that here there is no requirement that past discrimination is shown.

[653] Curtin 1989, p. 236. On indirect sex discrimination under Irish law, see also Callender & Meenan 1994, pp. 24 subs.

[654] The Employment Equality Act 1977 is no longer in force. Today, the relevant legislation consists of the Employment Equality Act 1998-2004 and the Equal Status Act 2000-2004.

[655] Case 96/80, [1981] *ECR* 911; see below Part 2, A.I.4.h.

[656] Case 2/56, [1957/1958] *ECR* 3.

The case involved a decision by producers of Ruhr coal to restructure their existing modes of sale by dividing their then existing cartel into three independent selling agencies called Geitling, Präsident and Mausegatt. The Geitling cartel applied for authorization from the ECSC High Authority which accepted most of its arrangements on the grounds that they would improve the distribution of fuels and that they were necessary to ensure profitable sales, stable employment and regular supplies. However, according to the High Authority parts of the agreement went beyond that purpose, in particular the possibility that Geitling wholesale customers might obtain a right to direct supplies involving price discounts under the following conditions: 1) the trader sold within the Common Market a minimum of 75,000 metric tons of fuel from the producer basins of the Community, 2) of that total, at least 40,000 metric tons were sold within the trader's sales area, and 3) of these, at least 25,000 metric tons originated from the three selling agencies for Ruhr coal and of these at least half from Geitling. According to the High Authority, the supplementary requirement that 12,500 metric tons had to be purchased from the Ruhr agencies led to unequal treatment of wholesalers and other producers, thereby infringing Art. 4(b) of the Coal and Steel Treaty.[657]

Geitling brought an action for annulment against this decision, arguing that discrimination on the same economic level is 'impossible at law' and that 'the clause at issue does not encourage the customers to distinguish between the different producers, but between one particular kind of coal, Ruhr coal, and other kinds'. According to Geitling, the advantages obtained from that distinction arose from natural conditions, and the failure to exploit them would amount to discrimination to the detriment of the two other selling agencies for Ruhr coal (*Geitling*, p. 14). AG Roemer was not convinced. Pointing to Art. 60(1) of the Coal and Steel Treaty which gives an example of discrimination on the same economic level in the form of local price reductions, the AG explained that the purpose of such reductions is to encourage the purchasers situated in the area in question to give preference to the relevant producer, thereby indirectly leading to discrimination between competing producers. Differentiation at the same economic level cannot be but indirect. Regarding the case at hand, AG Roemer noted that 'the members of the Geitling selling agency credit *their* wholesalers with tonnages purchased from *certain* other agencies, thereby favouring those specific agencies'. Thus, he concluded that there was discrimination between producers. He also found discrimination between consumers (traders) resulting from the difference in treatment according to whether or not they purchased a certain amount of fuel from Geitling and/or Mausegatt and Präsident (*Geitling*, points VII.2.

---

[657] Art. 4(b) provides: 'The following are recognized to be incompatible with the common market for coal and steel, and are, therefore, abolished and prohibited within the Community in the manner set forth in the present Treaty: [...] (b) measures or practices discriminating among producers, among buyers or among consumers, specifically as concerns prices, delivery terms and transportation rates, as well as measures or practices which hamper the buyer in the free choice of his supplier [...].'

and 4. of the AG's opinion). The Court agreed and found discrimination between consumers and between producers. In the Court's considerations, the term 'indirect discrimination' appears in the latter context where the Court held (*Geitling*, p. 21): 'The effect of the clause [at] issue is that the applicants take into account purchases made by wholesalers from two other given agencies, whereas the same competition should exist between the said agencies and the applicants as exists between the latter and the other producers of the Community, whose sales the said applicants do not take into account. That method of proceeding constitutes indirect discrimination in that it encourages the purchases towards a preference for obtaining supplies from the producers of Ruhr coal, to the detriment of the remaining producers of the Community.'

The Court did not define the new concept of indirect discrimination. In the present writer's analysis, its meaning is different from indirect discrimination as understood in this present study. In particular, the term 'indirect discrimination' is not used in relation to the differentiation ground applied by the Geitling cartel (namely the origin of the products sold by the traders)[658] but instead refers to the fact that different treatment of consumers indirectly led to a difference in treatment of the producers. According to Rating,[659] this would today be termed direct discrimination. In terms of the structural elements proposed earlier,[660] the indirect nature of such discrimination relates to the persons affected by the non-discrimination rule ('the protected'). Therefore, *Geitling* is not an indirect discrimination case and, therefore, not a precursor of the Court's indirect discrimination case law as examined in this study. Nevertheless, the two situations share an aspect, namely the fact that the Court recognised discrimination caused in a rather obscure manner. In that sense, the Court's approach to such situations is in both cases based on the concern to look behind the mere form of a measure in order to find out about its actual effect ('substance prevails over form').[661]

---

[658]   It should be noted that Art. 4(b) of the ECSC Treaty does not mention a discrimination criterion. This differs from Art. 60(1) regarding pricing practices which might also have been relevant but was not relied on in *Geitling*: 'Pricing practices contrary to the provisions of Articles 2, 3 and 4 are prohibited, particularly: [...] discriminatory practices involving the application by a seller within the single market of unequal conditions to comparable transactions, especially according to the nationality of the buyer.'

[659]   Rating 1994, p. 54.

[660]   See earlier in this part, B.V.2.

[661]   For indirect discrimination, see further below Part 2, A.III.2.

PART TWO:
THE DEVELOPMENT OF THE LEGAL CONCEPT OF INDIRECT DISCRIMINATION IN EC LAW

This study's second part examines how the legal concept of indirect discrimination came into existence in EC law and the issues that arose in this context. It begins with in-depth analyses of the case law on which the concept's early development is based (which is still relevant in important areas of EC law; below A.). Thereafter, it turns to the much more recent legal definitions (below B.).

A. THE DEVELOPMENT THROUGH CASE LAW

The analyses of the development of the *case law-based definition* of the legal concept of indirect discrimination proceeds in two steps, each corresponding to the two basic aspects of the concept of indirect discrimination as they developed sequentially through the Court's case law – namely: first, the recognition by the Court of the potentially indirect nature of discrimination (first part of the indirect discrimination formula, below I.) and, second, the element of objective justification (second part of the indirect discrimination formula, below II.). Afterwards, a discussion of particular findings regarding the case law-based definition follows (below III. and IV.).

I. RECOGNITION OF THE POSSIBILITY THAT DISCRIMINATION CAN BE OF AN INDIRECT NATURE

1. INTRODUCTORY REMARKS

In a first step, the Court recognised that discrimination can occur not only through explicit and obvious reliance on prohibited grounds of differentiation but also through reliance on grounds which appear to be neutral. The following analyses of the Court's case law proceeds in a chronological manner beginning with discrimination on grounds of nationality in the area of free movement of workers and then in a number of areas where other types of discrimination are relevant. Such a broad approach affords discussion of important cases and identification of several relevant issues. These analyses illustrate that the particular nature of any given area may influence the development of a concept such as that of indirect discrimination.

> In the order of their appearance, the areas (and discriminatory grounds) discussed below are:
> - Free movement of workers (discrimination on grounds of nationality);
> - Staff law (sex discrimination);
> - Internal taxation of goods (discrimination based on the origin of the products);
> - Freedom of establishment (discrimination on grounds of nationality);

- Agriculture and, more specifically, fisheries (discrimination between fishing vessels flying the flag of a Member State and registered in the Community Territory);
- Social security law (discrimination on grounds of nationality);
- Procedural law, as an example taken from the wide field of application of Art. 12(1) EC (discrimination on grounds of nationality);
- Employment law outside staff law (sex discrimination in the context of equal pay);
- Free movement of services (discrimination on grounds of nationality);[662]
- Free movement of transport services (discrimination on grounds of nationality);
- Free movement of capital (under the old regime: discrimination based on the nationality or the place of residence of the parties or the place where capital is invested; under the new regime: discrimination on grounds of nationality);[663]
- Public procurement, as examined under the general free movement rules (discrimination on grounds of nationality);
- Income taxation, as examined under the general free movement rules (discrimination on grounds of nationality).

The present analyses focus on the Court's case law from 1969 to the present. However, the earliest traces of a recognition in EC law that discrimination can result from reliance on apparently neutral grounds can be found in the General Programmes on free movement in the areas of establishment[664] and services[665] of 1961 where reference is made to 'requirements that are applicable irrespective of nationality but have the effect of exclusively or principally excluding foreigners'. Later, the Court interpreted this as indirect discrimination on grounds of nationality.[666] Similarly, the second part of Art. 3(1) of Regulation 1612/68[667] states that provisions of national law shall not apply 'where, though applicable irrespective of nationality, their exclusive or principle aim or effect is to keep nationals of other Member States away from the employment offered'. However, the Court's earliest statements on indirect discrimination were made independently of such texts.[668] For the purposes of the following analyses, it is, therefore, appropriate to stress case law. The main findings of these analyses will be as follows:

- Three foundational cases from the late 1960s and the early 1970s introduced the concept of indirect discrimination into EC law, namely *Ugliola*,[669] *Sotgiu*[670] (both

---

662   Regarding the question which grounds are prohibited in relation to free movement of services, see later in this part, A.I.4.j.
663   On the relevance of discrimination even under the new regime, see later in this part, A.I.4.m.
664   General Programme for the abolition of restrictions on freedom of establishment, *OJ* English Special Edition, Second Series, IX, p. 7.
665   General Programme for the abolition of restrictions on freedom to provide services; *OJ* English Special Edition, Second Series, IX, p. 3.
666   See later in this part, A.I.2.c.
667   Regulation 1612/68/EEC, *OJ* English Special Edition 1968 L 257/2, p. 475 (as amended).
668   In *Sotgiu* (Case 152/73, [1974] *ECR* 153), the Court referred to the preamble of Regulation 1612/68 where equality in law and in fact is mentioned, but not to Art. 3(1); see later in this part, A.I.2.c.
669   Case 15/69, [1969] *ECR* 363.
670   Case 152/73, [1974] *ECR* 153.

concerning free movement of workers) and *Sabbatini*[671] (concerning sex equality in Staff law). Providing a general description of, and indicating the *raison d'être* for the new concept, *Sotgiu* became a landmark case in respect of indirect discrimination on grounds of nationality.

- In the field of sex equality law outside Staff law, the Court initially caused confusion by distinguishing between 'direct and overt discrimination' and 'indirect and disguised discrimination' in a context that did not concern the substantive nature of discrimination but rather the scope of the direct effect of the equal pay principle (*Defrenne II*).[672]
- *Defrenne II* also appears to provide several fleeting indications that indirect sex discrimination might be understood as a substantive concept. However, *Jenkins*[673] and *Bilka*[674] were more explicit, the latter emerging as the landmark case for indirect sex discrimination. None of these decisions makes reference to precedents from economic law.
- Over time, the Court recognised the relevance of the new concept to an ever broader range of areas and prohibitions against discrimination. Many of these cases raise difficult issues, for instance, concerning the relationship of indirect discrimination to other concepts in EC law.
- The first case on free movement of services, *Seco*,[675] reflects a broader understanding of the concept of indirect discrimination than previously recognized. This can be explained by the fact that *Seco* concerned a situation involving double regulation (that is, a situation where the national legal orders of two Member States apply simultaneously). Such cases would later be assessed by the Court in the framework of the concept of restrictions in a wider sense, rather than that of indirect discrimination.
- In some specific areas, the concept of indirect discrimination developed along more individual lines. With regard to transport and direct taxation, this new concept did not appear until much later due to features particular to these areas of law. Regarding public procurement, liberalising secondary law appears to make the concept of indirect discrimination unnecessary but is, in fact, not relied on by the Court. Finally, regarding the free movement of capital, the term *discrimination* appeared in the case law only quite recently, and to this day there are no explicit references to indirect discrimination.

---

[671]   Case 20/71, [1972] *ECR* 345.
[672]   Case 43/75, [1976] *ECR* 455.
[673]   Case 96/80, [1981] *ECR* 911.
[674]   Case 170/84, [1986] *ECR* 1607.
[675]   Joined Cases 62/81 and 63/81, [1982] *ECR* 223.

2. THE FOUNDATIONAL CASES: INTRODUCING THE IDEA OF INDIRECT DISCRIMINATION

a. Free movement of workers: Ugliola

i. The case

The first decision where the Court of Justice referred to indirect discrimination in the context of EEC law[676] was *Ugliola*[677] in 1969. Mr Ugliola, an Italian national living and working in Germany, was unable to benefit from a rule according to which military service was to be taken into account for the purposes of the calculation of employees' length of service in employment. Only service performed in Germany was taken into account. Mr Ugliola, who had performed military service in Italy, claimed that limiting benefits *on the basis of the place where the service was performed* amounted to discrimination on grounds of nationality. The German Government countered by arguing that the criterion relied on did not involve nationality but rather the place where military service had been performed. The Government reasoned that such a rule benefited both nationals and foreigners who did their military service in the German army alike. A German citizen who performed his military service for another Member State did not benefit from these special measures either. According to the Government, a different approach would indirectly underwrite the defence budget of other Member States.[678] A request for a preliminary ruling resulted, relating to the interpretation of the Regulations 38/64/EEC[679] and 1612/68/EEC.[680]

Both AG Gand and the Court agreed with Mr Ugliola. The AG pointed out that the contested rule was 'not based expressly on nationality, but on the call-up for service which is itself based on nationality' and concluded that it ran counter to the very purpose of the free movement rules (*Ugliola*, p. 375). The Court first noted that the fulfilment of an obligation for military service is liable to affect a migrant worker's conditions of employment in another Member State and that the nature of the consequences of military service remain essentially the same whether the worker is called up by the State of employment (host State) or by the State of nationality. In

---

[676] Regarding the Court's reference to indirect discrimination in the coal and steel case *Geitling* (Case 2/56, [1957/1958] *ECR* 3), see above Part 1, C.IV.

[677] Case 15/69, [1969] *ECR* 363.

[678] In the light of more recent case law concerning rules relating to the national armies, in particular *Sirdar* (Case C-273/97, [1999] *ECR* I-7403), *Kreil* (Case C-285/98, [2000] *ECR* I-69) and *Dory* (Case C-186/01, [2003] *ECR* I-2479), it is interesting to note that the German Government's first (and unsuccessful) argument was that the matter *fell outside the scope of Community law* since it was part of military rather than of labour law. Similarly, the employer claimed that the case concerned public law rather than labour law (*Ugliola*, p. 365 and 367). The Court did not accept these arguments.

[679] Regulation 38/64/EEC, *OJ* No. 62 of 17 April 1964, p. 965 (no longer in force).

[680] Regulation 1612/68/EEC, *OJ* English Special Edition 1968 L 257/2, p. 475 (as amended).

answer to the specific question referred, the Court held that Member States may not derogate from the equality of treatment prescribed by Art. 48 of the EEC Treaty (now Art. 39 EC) 'by indirectly introducing discrimination in favour of their own nationals alone' (*Ugliola*, para. 6).

> Specifically, AG Gand thought that, at first sight, Germany's argument regarding the effect of the German rule 'may appear attractive'. However, he found it unconvincing for two reasons. First, he pointed out that the performance of military service in the army of the State other than that of which one is a national is a hypothesis which even the Government of Germany considered to be somewhat theoretical. Second, the AG explained that the treatment at issue 'is, perhaps, not based expressly on nationality, but on the call-up for service, which is itself based on nationality. In fact, the provision in question only benefits German citizens and although it is quite justifiable within the sphere of German legislation, the very purpose of the regulation on freedom of movement is precisely to abolish such privileges.'
>
> The Court explained (*Ugliola*, para. 6 and 7): 'Apart from the cases expressly referred to in paragraph (3), Article 48 of the Treaty does not allow Member States to make any exceptions to the equality of treatment and protection required by the Treaty for all workers within the Community by indirectly introducing discrimination in favour of their own nationals alone based upon obligations for military service. Consequently, as[681] a rule of national law protecting workers from the unfavourable consequences, as regards conditions of work and employment in an undertaking, arising out of the absence through obligations for military service must also be applied to the nationals of other Member States employed in the territory of the State in question who are subject to military service in their country of origin. Therefore, the abovementioned provisions entitle a migrant worker who is a national of a Member State and who has had to interrupt his employment with an undertaking in another Member State in order to fulfil his obligations for military service in the country of which he is a national, to have the period of his military service taken into account in the calculation of his seniority in that undertaking, to the extent to which the periods of military service in the country of employment are also taken into account for the benefit of national workers.'

ii. Comments

The Court's reference to 'indirectly introduced discrimination' in *Ugliola* clearly relates to reliance on a formally neutral ground of differentiation (the place of performance of military service) and, thereby, to the most decisive element of the indirect discrimination formula (Craig & de Búrca).[682] Though this was a new development in the Court's case law, apparently it was perceived as neither problematic nor parti-

---

[681]   The wording of this sentence corresponds to that printed in the English version of the European Court Reports. The French version indicates that the word 'as' should be omitted.

[682]   Craig & de Búrca 2003, p. 716.

cularly noteworthy at the time. Thus, Napoletano[683] simply quotes the Court and comments that it interpreted Art. 48 of the EEC Treaty correctly. In today's academic writing, *Ugliola* is rarely even cited as the first indirect discrimination decision in EEC law (e.g. Rating,[684] Loenen,[685] Adobati,[686] Kapteyn & VerLoren van Themaat,[687] Schweitzer & Hummer,[688] the von der Groeben & Schwarze Commentary,[689] the Calliess & Ruffert Commentary,[690] Weatherill & Beaumont,[691] Borchardt).[692] Academic comments tend to focus on the issue of *comparability* rather than on the nature of the discrimination at issue (e.g. Wyatt,[693] Schimana,[694] Riegel).[695] In fact, the Court itself does not even mention *Ugliola* in later decisions involving indirect discrimination on grounds of nationality.[696]

Clearly, *Ugliola* is *not recognized as a landmark case*. There may be various reasons for this. First, the Court did not opt for the indirect discrimination approach based upon a *conceptual* analysis of the differences between two concepts of discrimination (namely direct and indirect discrimination). Rather, the reference to 'indirectly introduced discrimination' appears to be an *almost casual remark* made in the context of a separate issue, namely that of justification.[697] Second, whilst *Ugliola* involved a formally neutral measure, the ground of differentiation relied on necessarily and obviously had discriminatory effects in that only German (male) citizens were called to military service under German law and the group benefiting from the rule consisted of only German citizens ('discrimination in favour of their own nationals alone'). In

---

[683] Napoletano 1972, p. 694.

[684] Rating 1994, p. 54.

[685] Loenen 1998, p. 47.

[686] Adobati 1995, p. 112, footnote 48.

[687] Kapteyn & VerLoren van Themaat 2003, p. 588.

[688] Schweitzer & Hummer 1996, p. 354, n. 1157.

[689] Von der Groeben & Schwarze Commentary 2004, n. 13 ad Art. 39 EC.

[690] Calliess & Ruffert Commentary 2002, n. 46 ad Art. 39 EC.

[691] Weatherill & Beaumont 1999, p. 632, mention the case, but do not put it in the context of indirect discrimination.

[692] Borchardt 2002, p. 311, n. 702.

[693] Wyatt 1981, p. 44. Wyatt interprets the Court's ruling as meaning that a failure to assimilate acts outside the territory of a Member State with acts within '*may* amount to discrimination where the acts are truly comparable'.

[694] Schimana 1978, p. 1018. This author argues that military service performed in Germany and elsewhere are two distinct matters which should be treated differently. Comparability in the present context would require the comparability of the different Member States' legislation on worker's protection in the context of military service.

[695] Riegel 1978, pp. 1422/1423. Though this author criticises Schimana's point that comparability would require comparability of the different Member States' legislation on worker's protection in the context of military service, he agrees that the situations at issue in *Ugliola* were not comparable.

[696] It would seem that the case is referred to in this context only once, namely by AG Lenz in his opinion on *Allué I* (Case 33/88, [1989] *ECR* 1591), point 15 of the AG's opinion.

[697] See later in this part, A.II.2.a.

the words of Wyatt & Dashwood,[698] the case concerned a ground that, 'although theoretically applicable to nationals and non-nationals alike, will in practice be fulfilled
only by nationals'. Reliance on the place of performance of military service had, therefore, the *same effect as explicit reliance on nationality* would have had.[699] Finally, a
finding of discrimination under such circumstances should not have been surprising
given that Art. 3(1) of Regulation 1612/68[700] explicitly refers to provisions of national
law applicable irrespective of nationality whose exclusive or principal aim or effect
is to keep nationals of other Member States away from the employment offered.
Though, the Court did not refer to this provision. Whatever the influence of the particular features of the specific case, *Ugliola* is undoubtedly important for present purposes because it marks the starting point of the Court's case law on indirect discrimination.

b. The general principle of non-discrimination on grounds of sex: Sabbatini

The next relevant case is *Sabbatini*,[701] a sex equality case decided in 1972 under
Community Staff law where the Court took the same approach as in *Ugliola*,[702] though
in less explicit terms.

i. The case

Sabbatini concerned a refusal by the European Parliament to continue to grant an
expatriation allowance to a female official because, after her marriage, she was no
longer the head of her household. The refusal was based on Art. 4(3) of Annex VII
to the Staff Regulations[703] according to which an official marrying a person who at the
date of marriage did not qualify for the allowance 'shall forfeit the right to expatriation
allowance unless that official thereby becomes a head of household'. The application
of Art. 1(3) of the same Annex usually resulted in a married male official being deemed
the head of household. In Ms Sabbatini's view, reliance on such a criterion amounted
to prohibited discrimination. The European Parliament disagreed, arguing that 'the
institution and the concept of head of household [...] create no discrimination
whatsoever between the sexes; they entail not the superiority of one spouse over the
other, but the management of matters of family concern by one of the spouses rather
than the other' (*Sabbatini*, p. 349). In contrast, AG Roemer noted that even though

---

[698] Wyatt & Dashwood 2000, p. 401.
[699] See further below Part 3, A.II.2.c.
[700] Regulation 1612/68/EEC, *OJ* English Special Edition 1968 L 257/2, p. 475 (as amended).
[701] Case 20/71, [1972] *ECR* 363. See also the parallel case *Chollet* (Case 32/71, [1972] *ECR* 363.), decided on the same day as *Sabbatini*.
[702] Case 15/69, [1969] *ECR* 363.
[703] Regulation 259/68/EEC, Euratom, ECSC, *OJ* 1968 L 56/1 (meanwhile amended).

the contested rule did not distinguish between male and female officials, it nevertheless manifestly drew a distinction between the sexes since the status of head of household was determined according to sex (*Sabbatini*, p. 356 of the AG's opinion).[704] The Court found in favour of Ms Sabbatini, holding that the Staff Regulations may not treat officials differently according to sex and that, in making such a distinction, the Staff Regulations, in fact, created a difference of treatment between male and female officials (*Sabbatini*, para. 5 subs.).

> The Court explained that although Art. 4(3) of Annex VII 'does not of itself create any difference of treatment as between the sexes, it must however be examined in conjunction with Article 1(3) of the same Annex, which provides that the term 'head of household' normally refers to a married male official, whereas a married female official is considered to be head of household only in exceptional circumstances, in particular in cases of invalidity or serious illness of the husband. It is thus clear that the provision the validity of which is contested does in fact create a difference of treatment as between male and female officials inasmuch as it renders the retention of the expatriation allowance conditional upon the acquisition of the status of head of household within the meaning of the Staff Regulations. [...T]he Staff Regulations cannot [...] treat officials differently according to whether they are male of female, since termination of the status of expatriate must be dependent for both male and female officials on uniform criteria, irrespective of sex. Consequently, by rendering the retention of the allowance subject to the acquisition of the status of 'head of household' – as it is defined in Article 1 (3) – the Staff Regulations have created an arbitrary difference of treatment between officials.'

ii. Comments

Sabbatini is the first case where the Court, in substance though not in its wording, found indirect sex discrimination (Rating).[705] The case displays certain rather obvious parallels with *Ugliola*:[706] both cases concerned formally neutral measures and in both cases the starting point for the Court's finding was the factual effect of the measure in question, rather than its formal appearance. (This latter point is clearly demonstrated by the way in which the Court in *Sabbatini* contrasted the mere appearance of Art. 4(3) with its effect in connection with Art. 1(3)). Further, in both cases the disparate effect of the apparently neutral rule was caused by legislation (in *Ugliola*, by a national law providing for the obligation of men to perform military service in their country of origin; in *Sabbatini* by the Staff law provision usually deeming the husband to be the head of household). At the same time, the novelty of the Court's approach was perhaps more apparent in *Sabbatini* since there it was not *exclusively*

---

[704]   At the same time, the AG thought that the system was justified; see later in this part, A.II.2.a.ii.
[705]   Rating 1994, p. 56.
[706]   Case 15/69, [1969] *ECR* 363.

but merely *predominantly* men who benefited from the contested rule. This is typical of situations involving indirect discrimination[707] which, as Plötscher[708] observes, are characterised by a loosening of the strength of the required link of the disadvantage with the prohibited discrimination criterion.

However, *Sabbatini* raises questions regarding the *basis* for the Court's findings of indirect sex discrimination. At the time, Staff law contained no equality provision whatsoever. In making her argument, Ms Sabbatini relied both on an alleged general principle of law prohibiting any discrimination on grounds of sex and also, more particularly, on the principle of equal pay for men and women guaranteed by what was then Art. 119 of the EEC Treaty (now, after amendment, Art. 141(1) and (2) EC). Pointing out that no such general principle existed in the laws of the Member States, AG Roemer seemed to suggest the need to apply only Art. 119 (*Sabbatini*, point 2 of the AG's opinion). The Court's judgment is not clear on that point, nor is the decision in the later Staff case *Airola*[709] which also concerned indirect sex discrimination. Commentators thought that the Court relied on an *unwritten general principle of non-discrimination specifically on grounds of sex* (Massaro,[710] Streil).[711] Such an approach was later confirmed by the Court in *Defrenne III*[712] (para. 29; e.g. Ellis,[713] Rating,[714] also Gori).[715] For present purposes, the Court's focus on sex as a prohibited discrima-tory

---

[707] Though, it has been noted that the Court, confronted with similar situations in later cases, was not always equally consistent in its approach, e.g. *De Angelis* (Case 246/83, [1985] *ECR* 1253). This case concerned a residence requirement according to which the allowance was to be paid only if the official, during the five years ending six months before he or she entered the service, did not habitually reside (or carry on his or her main occupation) within the European territory of the country concerned. Ms De Angelis argued that the application of this requirement discriminated against married women because they might be legally bound to accompany their husbands wherever they established their residence. However, the Court agreed with AG Darmon who did not find discrimination (*De Angelis*, p. 1257 and para. 18). According to Ellis 1998, p. 185, the AG's remarks have 'a disturbingly unperceptive quality' and the judgment shows a lack of sensitivity as to what is truly adverse to a greater number of women than men.

[708] Plötscher 2003, p. 55.

[709] Case 21/74, [1975] *ECR* 221.

[710] Massaro 1976, pp. 530/531.

[711] Streil 1975, p. 322.

[712] Case 149/77, [1978] *ECR* 1365.

[713] Ellis 1998, pp. 183 subs.

[714] Rating 1994, pp. 56 subs.

[715] Gori 1985, pp. 9 subs. – More recently, the Court confirmed that relationship in a more general context, stating that under the general principle of non-discrimination on grounds of sex 'compliance with the prohibition of indirect discrimination on grounds of sex is a condition governing the legality of all measures adopted by the Community institutions', *Rinke* (Case C-25/02, judgment of 9 September 2003, n.y.r.), para. 28. It should be noted that under the Court's case law, the general principle of non-discrimination on grounds of sex is particularly relevant in the context of actions by the Community *institutions* but much less so when the compatibility of Member State law with EC law is at issue. In *Defrenne III* (Case 149/77, [1978] *ECR* 1365), to which the Court referred in *Rinke*, the recognition of such a fundamental right did not allow Ms Gabrielle Defrenne to rely on Community law in relation to a matter (namely dismissal) for which, at the time, there was no specific

ground explains the relevance of the concept of indirect discrimination in cases such as *Sabbatini* and *Airola*.[716]

Finally, though the approach in *Sabbatini* was, in principle, the same as that in *Ugliola*, the Court's terminology was less explicit in *Sabbatini* than in the earlier case (*Ugliola*: 'indirectly introducing discrimination'; *Sabbatini*: 'in fact creating a difference between male and female officials'). In the context of sex equality, the term 'indirect discrimination' appeared for the first time in *Airola*[717] (p. 225), in the submissions of the Commission (which also spoke about '*de facto* discrimination'). The Court, itself, used the term for the first time in the Staff law case *De Angelis*[718] (para. 18).

c) *Sotgiu, a landmark case on discrimination on grounds of nationality*

The third foundational case in the context of the introduction of the idea of indirect discrimination into EC law, the landmark case *Sotgiu*[719] of 1974, is in many ways more explicit than its predecessor in the area of free movement of workers, *Ugliola*.[720] In *Sotgiu*, the Court not only applied an indirect discrimination approach but also for

---

716   written EEC sex equality law (*Defrenne III*, para. 30 subs.). Gori 1985, p. 14, agrees that the notion of pay, however broadly interpreted by the Court, must have limits; see also Ellis 1998, pp. 188 subs. Compare also *Prais* (Case 130/75, [1976] *ECR* 1589), in the context of freedom of religion; Mohn 1990, pp. 24 subs.). In *Prais* (para. 10), the Court referred to freedom of religion as embodied in the European Convention on Human Rights and thus part of the fundamental rights recognised in Community law. Though the Court did not use such language, *Prais* can be read as a case involving (potential) *indirect* discrimination on grounds of religion, caused through the decision to hold a recruitment competition on a Friday which was a Jewish holiday.

717   Case 21/74, [1975] *ECR* 221. In that case, the application of an indirect discrimination approach is particularly interesting because it can be seen as leading to *an inroad into an area of national competence*, if only for the purposes of Community Staff law. The case concerned the concept of nationality which, under the rules of Public International Law, belongs to the sphere of national competence (*Micheletti*, Case C-369/90, [1992] *ECR* I-423, para. 10; Hall 1995, pp. 15 subs.; Del Valle Galvez 2003, pp. 210 subs.). *Airola* concerned the entitlement to an expatriation allowance which was granted only to officials who 'are not and have never been nationals of the State in whose territory the place where they are employed is situated'. The Court held that the concept of 'nationals' must be interpreted in such a way as to avoid any unwarranted difference of treatment between male and female officials in comparable situations. Such a difference in treatment would result from an interpretation of the concept of nationals as also including the nationality which was imposed by law on a female official by virtue of her marriage and which she was unable to renounce (*Airola*, para. 10 and 11). Streil 1975, p. 322, notes that the Court opted for a limited Community concept of nationality for the special purposes of the Staff law provision in question (see also Schermers 1975, p. 519). However, the Court's approach was limited by the express reason that the wife had no possibility of renouncing the new nationality. This was decisive for *Van den Broek* (Case 37/74, [1975] *ECR* 235), decided on the same day as *Airola*, where the Court refused to find (indirect) sex discrimination.

718   Case 246/83, [1985] *ECR* 1253.
719   Case 152/73, [1974] *ECR* 153.
720   Case 15/69, [1969] *ECR* 363.

the first time gave a *general* description of that phenomenon. In addition, the Court explained the *raison d'être* for the new legal concept.

i. The case

Mr Sotgiu, an Italian employee of the German Federal Postal Services, received a separation allowance because he was employed away from home (his family lived in Italy). Following a revision of the relevant legislation, a distinction was made between two categories of workers. Those who had already lived in Germany at the time of their initial employment were entitled to an allowance of 10 DM per day, whilst those whose residence at that time had been situated abroad received only 7,50 DM. Mr Sotgiu fell within the latter category. He brought an action, claiming that reliance on a worker's residence at the time of initial employment leads to discrimination on grounds of nationality prohibited by Regulation 1612/68.[721] The German Government countered by arguing that no prohibited difference in treatment existed in that the contested rules merely took account of differences in the factual circumstances of workers. Both German and foreign workers living in Germany at the time of recruitment received the allowance only if they were prepared to transfer their residence to their place of work. Foreign workers whose home was abroad did not have to fulfil this condition. The Italian Government supported Mr Sotgiu, arguing that the criterion based upon the place of recruitment might make it possible to circumvent the prohibition against discrimination on grounds of nationality while in fact substantially leading to such discrimination (*Sotgiu*, p. 160/161). Similarly, the Commission referred to 'the problem of hidden or indirect discrimination' (*Sotgiu*, p. 160/161). AG Mayras agreed, asking emphatically whether it was not necessary in such cases to go beyond mere appearances and consider hidden or disguised forms of discrimination (*Sotgiu*, p. 174).

> Specifically, the Italian Government argued that 'the spirit and aim of Art. 7 of Regulation No 1612/68 involve a prohibition on treating workers differently according to the place of recruitment if the latter is situated within the Community. The criterion of the place of recruitment might make it possible to circumvent the prohibition on discrimination based on nationality: in fact workers recruited abroad are normally of foreign nationality and a criterion of differentiation based on place of recruitment of the worker would lead substantially to discrimination against non-national Community workers. Such a criterion is contrary to the principle of freedom of movement.' The Commission stated: 'The concepts of discrimination and of nationality must be interpreted on the basis of factual criteria. A purely theoretical idea is not sufficient. Rules based on other criteria such as residence abroad, language, place of birth, descent or performance of military service in the country may in fact conceal discrimination on the basis of nationality. Such would be the case in particular if the application of certain criteria of differentiation were to result, in all cases

---

[721] Regulation No 1612/68/EEC, *OJ* English Special Edition 1968 L 257/2 (as amended).

or in the vast majority of cases, in foreigners alone being affected without any objective justification.'

AG Mayras noted that under Art. 48(2) of the EEC Treaty (now Art. 39(2) EC) and under Art. 7 of Regulation 1612/68 'discrimination may be hidden or disguised. This is the case in particular when a national law or national rules, without referring to nationality, make the grant of payments or advantages linked to employment dependent upon criteria pertaining for example to descent, place of birth or normal residence on the national territory in such a way that enjoyment of the these advantages is in fact reserved for nationals and cannot, with certain exceptions, apply to workers who are nationals of other Member States. Must we not', he asked, 'in such cases, going beyond appearances, condemn a violation of equality of treatment which may be compared with a true misuse of powers within the meaning of Community law?' The AG considered that the criterion based upon residence can be discriminatory in this sense since 'a violation of the equality of treatment envisaged by Article 48(2) of the Treaty and Article 7(1) of Regulation No 1612/68 may result from national rules which make a distinction, as far as concerns conditions of work, based not on nationality but on the place of residence of the worker at the time of his appointment, provided that such rules do in fact result in unfavourable discrimination against workers who are nationals of other Member States by comparison with national workers' (*Sotgiu*, p. 174).

The Court ruled in Mr Sotgiu's favour, stating that the Community rules regarding equality of treatment forbid 'not only overt discrimination by reason of nationality, but also all covert forms of discrimination which, by the application of other criteria of differentiation, lead in fact to the same result'. The Court added that such an interpretation is necessary in order to ensure the effectiveness of equality of treatment which is fundamental to the Community (*Sotgiu*, para. 11 and 12).

> The Court explained: 'The rules regarding equality of treatment, both in the Treaty and in Article 7 of Regulation No 1612/68, forbid not only overt discrimination by reason of nationality, but also all covert forms of discrimination which, by the application of other criteria of differentiation, lead in fact to the same result. This interpretation, which is necessary to ensure the effective working of one of the fundamental principles of the Community, is explicitly recognized by the fifth recital of the preamble to Regulation No 1612/68 which requires that equality of treatment of workers shall be ensured 'in fact and in law'. It may therefore be that criteria such as place of origin or residence of a worker may, according to the circumstances, be tantamount, as regards their practical effect, to discrimination on the grounds of nationality, such as is prohibited by the Treaty and the Regulation. However, this would not be the case with a separation allowance the conditions of allotment and rules for the payment of which took account of objective differences which the situation of workers may involve according to whether their residence, at the time [of] their taking up a given post, is within the territory of the State in question or abroad.' In the operative part of the judgment, the Court stated: 'The taking into consideration, as a criterion for the grant of a separation allowance, of the fact that a worker has his residence in the territory of another Member State may, according to the circumstances, constitute discrimination

forbidden by Article 7 (1) and (4) of Regulation No 1612/68. This is not the case however if the scheme relating to such an allowance takes account of objective differences in the situation of workers according to whether their residence at the time when they take up employment is within the territory of the State concerned or abroad.'

ii. Comments

The relevance of the *Sotgiu* decision in the present context is obvious. Three aspects in particular should be emphasised at this stage of these analyses: 1) the recognition by the Court that discrimination may be of an indirect nature, 2) the general nature of the Court's description of this phenomenon, and 3) the fact that the Court indicated the reason for its approach (the Court's remarks concerning objective differences will be discussed later).[722] As for the first of these aspects, the recognition by the Court that discrimination may be of an *indirect nature* was not new but rather had already been made in the *Ugliola*[723] and *Sabbatini*[724] cases. Nevertheless, two elements are noteworthy in that context. First, the effect of the contested ground of differentiation in *Sotgiu* is comparable to that at issue in *Sabbatini* in that it only *predominantly* disadvantaged foreigners (rather than *exclusively* as in *Ugliola*). In other words, the Court's general description of covert (indirect) discrimination as a form of discrimination which in fact 'leads to the *same* result' as overt (direct) discrimination, is not, strictly speaking, accurate. Second, the Court's use of terminology should be noted. In the submissions to the Court, a number of different expressions were used, including in particular 'hidden or disguised forms of discrimination', 'indirect discrimination', 'would lead substantially to discrimination', 'in fact result in unfavourable discrimination' and 'tantamount, as regards their practical effect, to discrimination'. By its own reference to 'all covert forms of discrimination', the Court coined a term which it would use regularly thereafter, though later alongside other expressions such as indirect discrimination.

The second aspect of the ruling is particularly important: in *Sotgiu*, for the first time[725] the Court provided *a general definition* of the indirect nature of the discrimination at issue. According to the Court's definition, which was not limited to the specific area of free movement of workers ('the rules regarding equality of treatment, both in the Treaty and in Article 7 of Regulation No 1612/68'), indirect discrimination includes

---

[722] See later in this part, A.II.2.b.
[723] Case 15/69, [1969] *ECR* 363; see earlier in this part, A.I.2.a.
[724] Case 20/71, [1972] *ECR* 345; see earlier in this part, A.I.2.b.
[725] According to Plender 1995, p. 69, the Court in *Sotgiu* 'restated its well-known proposition that the rules regarding equality of treatment [...] forbid not only overt discrimination by reason of nationality but also all covert forms of discrimination which, by the application of other criteria of differentiation, lead in fact to the same result'. However, whilst it is true that the Court confirmed the indirect discrimination approach as applied in earlier cases, there had thus far been *no general description* of that phenomenon that could have been restated.

'all covert forms of discrimination which, by the application of other criteria of
differentiation, lead in fact to the same result'. This reflects, first of all, the fact that
the concept of indirect discrimination is *effect-oriented*. What matters is not whether
the ground of differentiation is discriminatory on its face but rather whether its effects
actually amount to discrimination based on a prohibited ground. This is in line with
the Commission's suggestion of an interpretation of the prohibition against discrimination on the basis of factual, rather than theoretical, criteria. The Court's definition
also provides a clear answer to AG Mayras' question whether the Court must go
beyond appearances and take into consideration hidden or disguised forms of
discrimination. The answer, a resounding 'yes', reflects a principle that is of general
importance in EC law, namely that substance prevails over form.[726]

The third important aspect of the *Sotgiu* decision is the fact that the Court indicates
the reasons for its approach, namely the concern for the effectiveness of the law. According to the Court, the interpretation followed is necessary to ensure the effectiveness
of equality as a fundamental principle of Community law. The Court found a basis
for this in a consideration in the preamble of Regulation 1612/68[727] which states that
'the right of freedom of movement, in order that it may be exercised, by objective
standards, in freedom and dignity, requires that equality of treatment shall be ensured
in fact and in law' (emphasis added).[728] This corresponds to the Italian Government's
argument regarding the prevention of potential circumventions of the prohibition
against discrimination.

Given these striking features, it is surprising that the *Sotgiu* decision generated so
very few case notes and that in them there is virtually no discussion of the issue of
indirect discrimination (Wyatt,[729] Tizzano).[730] Nowadays, *Sotgiu* is regularly cited as
a landmark decision in academic writing (e.g. the Mégret Commentary,[731] Beaumont
& Weatherill,[732] the Schwarze Commentary,[733] the Geiger Commentary,[734] the Calliess

---

[726]   An approach based on this principle can be observed in the Court's case law in many different
        contexts. An example is provided by *Grimaldi* (Case C-322/88, [1989] *ECR* 4407, para. 14) where
        the Court, in the context of direct effect, stated that 'the choice of form cannot alter the nature of
        a measure'. A legislative example is the reference to 'decisions in the form of a regulation' in Art.
        230 EC concerning the action for annulment.
[727]   Regulation 1612/68/EEC, *OJ* English Special Edition 1968 L 257/2, p. 475 (as amended).
[728]   Interestingly, the Court did not refer to Art. 3(1) of the same Regulation.
[729]   Wyatt 1975, pp. 62/63.
[730]   Tizzano 1974, pp. 210-211.
[731]   Mégret Commentary (as of 1972), p. 13, n. 8.
[732]   Weatherill & Beaumont 1999, p. 632. In the earlier edition of their textbook (Weatherill & Beaumont
        1995, p. 551), these authors put the case in the context of a Member State's duty 'to apply its rules
        in a manner that reflects the migrant's objectively different situation' which rather evokes the notion
        of discrimination in substance (see above Part 1, B.III.5.d).
[733]   Schwarze Commentary 2000, n. 36 ad Art. 39 EC.
[734]   Geiger Commentary 2000, n. 15 ad Art. 39 EC; see also n. 8 ad Art. 12(1) EC.

& Ruffert Commentary,[735] the von der Groeben & Schwarze Commentary).[736] Indeed, as will be seen below, the Court has regularly referred to *Sotgiu* as a landmark decision when applying the concept of indirect discrimination in other areas, though notably only with regard to areas within the sphere of economic law and to the exclusion of social law and, in particular, sex equality law.

d. An interim conclusion (I)

The Court's decisions in the three foundational cases, namely *Ugliola*[737] (decided in 1969), *Sabbatini*[738] (decided in 1972) and the landmark case of *Sotgiu*[739] (decided in 1974), introduced into EC law the idea that discrimination may be of an indirect nature, based on an apparently neutral criterion of differentiation. In *Ugliola*, the Court stated that the Member States may not derogate from the equality of treatment required by the Treaty for workers 'by indirectly introducing discrimination in favour of their own nationals alone'. The fact that the Court's statements in *Sotgiu* are both more explicit and more encompassing explains why this case has become the landmark case for indirect discrimination, specifically, *on grounds of nationality* (and more generally in the area of economic law). By using the term *covert discrimination*, the Court confirmed that discrimination may occur indirectly. The Court also provided a general description of that phenomenon: 'all covert forms of discrimination which, by the application of other criteria of differentiation, lead in fact to the same result'. Under this definition, the legal concept of indirect discrimination is effect-oriented and based on the principle that substance prevails over form. The Court has also explained the reasons for this approach, namely its concern for the effectiveness of equality law. The aim is to prevent the circumvention of the prohibition against discrimination.

The first indirect *sex discrimination* case, *Sabbatini*, was decided after *Ugliola* but before *Sotgiu*. Though the language in *Sabbatini* is not very explicit, the Court's approach is clearly the same as in *Ugliola* which, however, is not cited as a precedent. Unlike *Ugliola*, *Sabbatini* concerned a measure whose effect was not the same as that which results from direct discrimination in that it merely disadvantaged predominantly one group while favouring another (disparate effect, as in *Sotgiu*). Though the Court's terminology is far from uniform, it is clear that all of the above cases concern the *same phenomenon*. Discrimination can occur not only through obvious and express reliance on a prohibited discriminatory ground but also through the use of an apparently neutral criterion that has a disparate effect in terms of a prohibited ground. Finally,

---

[735]   Calliess & Ruffert Commentary 2002, n. 46 ad Art. 39 EC.
[736]   Von der Groeben & Schwarze Commentary 2004, n. 13 ad Art. 30 EC.
[737]   Case 15/69, [1969] *ECR* 363.
[738]   Case 20/71, [1972] *ECR* 345.
[739]   Case 152/73, [1974] *ECR* 153.

it is interesting to note that the public international law precursors on indirect discrimination, mentioned in the introduction to this present study,[740] do not appear to have played any role in the context of the three foundational cases introducing the concept into the EC legal order.

3. A COMPLICATED BUT NECESSARY EXCURSION: THE *DEFRENNE II* DISTINCTION IN RELATION TO DIRECT EFFECT

Defrenne II,[741] decided under what was then Art. 119 of the EEC Treaty (equal pay for men and women; now, after amendment, Art. 141(1) and (2) EC), is relevant for present purposes because of its explicit references to *indirect discrimination* which at the time caused considerable confusion (and, at times, still does so today).

a. The case

Defrenne II concerned the different retirement ages imposed by the Belgian airline Sabena on air stewardesses and male cabin stewards. When Ms Defrenne's employment contract was automatically terminated upon her reaching the age forty, she complained of unequal treatment on grounds of sex and brought an action for compensation for the loss she had suffered in terms of salary, termination allowance and pension. Her complaints led to three important preliminary rulings by the Court of Justice.[742] The main issue of the second of these was whether or not Art. 119 was directly effective, that is, capable of being relied on by individuals before national courts in the face of conflicting national law.[743] AG Trabucchi suggested that Art. 119 could be directly effective only in so far as its explicit wording was concerned, namely in relation to equal pay for equal work, as opposed to equal pay for work of equal value (which at that time was not mentioned in Art. 119 but was nevertheless part of it).[744] The

---

[740] See above Part 1, C.

[741] Case 43/75, [1976] *ECR* 455.

[742] Case 80/70, [1976] *ECR* 455 (*Defrenne I*), Case 43/75, [1976] *ECR* 455 (*Defrenne II*) and Case 149/77, [1978] *ECR* 1365 (*Defrenne III*).

[743] The essential criteria for an EC law provision to be directly effective are that it is clear and precise as well as unconditional and that it leaves no legislative discretion to the Member States. In essence, these conditions go back to the landmark case on direct effect of Treaty provisions, *Van Gend en Loos* (Case 26/62, [1963] *ECR* 1).

[744] Work of equal value was mentioned in the Equal Pay Directive (Directive 75/117/EEC, *OJ* 1975 L 45/19). In *Jenkins* (Case 96/80, [1981] *ECR* 911, para. 22), the Court held that this Directive does not change the content nor the scope of Art. 119 EC which in effect means that the right to equal pay for work of equal value was supposed to be part of Art. 119 itself. Since the Amsterdam revision, the wording of Art. 141 EC explicitly includes work of equal value.

Court agreed with AG Trabucchi that a distinction had to be made, namely 'between, first, direct and overt discrimination which may be identified solely with the aid of the criteria based on equal work and equal pay referred to by the article in question, and secondly, indirect and disguised discrimination which can only be identified by reference to more explicit implementing provisions of a Community or national character' (*Defrenne II*, para. 18).

Specifically, the AG explained (*Defrenne II*, p. 486 and 487): '[A]s regards the abolition, in connexion with pay, of all discrimination based on sex, Article 119 imposes an obligation which is clear, precise and unconditional. It must, however, be emphasized that Article 119 does not provide for, or rather does not always necessarily provide for, all possible implications of the principle of equal pay for men and women in its fullest sense. The application of the principle to the situations other than those referred to in the aforesaid article (cases where 'the same work', namely identical work, is performed) lies, without doubt, outside the context in which the question of the direct applicability of the rules can arise and more properly falls within the field of social policy the definition and application of which primarily depend on the initiative and coordinating action of the Community executive and of the Member States. [...] Apart from cases where work which is not identical has to be established as being of equal value, which could undoubtedly give rise to fairly complicated assessments on the part, in the first place, of the legislature, the application of Article 119 does not necessarily require the adoption of implementing legislation in circumstances (which, in this case, are exclusively the concern of the court making the reference) where work which is undoubtedly identical is differently rewarded on grounds of sex.'

The Court held (*Defrenne II*, para. 18 and 19): 'For the purpose of the implementation of these provisions a distinction must be drawn within the whole area of application of Article 119 between, first, direct and overt discrimination which may be identified solely with the aid of the criteria based on equal work and equal pay referred to by the article in question, and secondly, indirect and disguised discrimination which can only be identified by reference to more explicit implementing provisions of a Community or national character. It is impossible not to recognize that the complete implementation of the aim pursued by Article 119, by means of the elimination of all discrimination, direct or indirect, between men and women workers, not only as regards individual undertakings but also entire branches of industry and even of the economic system as a whole, may in certain cases involve the elaboration of criteria whose implementation necessitates the taking of appropriate measures at Community and national level.' As an example of the category in which direct effect is possible, the Court referred to cases where the discrimination both has its origin either in legislative provisions or in collective labour agreements and also may be detected on the basis of a purely legal analysis of the situation. According to the Court, in such a situation the national court is in a position to establish all the facts which enable it to decide whether a woman worker is receiving lower pay than a male worker performing the same tasks. Therefore, '[i]n such a situation, at least, Article 119 is directly applicable and may thus give rise to individual rights which the courts must protect' (*Defrenne II*, para. 24). The Court summarised its findings on this point as follows (*Defrenne II*, para. 40): 'The reply to the first question must therefore be that the principle of equal pay contained in

Article 119 may be relied upon before the national courts and that these courts have a duty to ensure the protection of the rights which this provision vests in individuals, in particular as regards those types of discrimination arising directly from legislative provisions or collective labour agreement, as well as in cases in which men and women receive unequal pay for equal work which is carried out in the same establishment of service, whether private or public.'

The expression 'indirect discrimination' appears again later in the decision where the Court limited the temporal effect of its ruling.[745] Referring to a Resolution adopted by the Member States concerning equal pay,[746] the Court noted that '[u]nder the terms of that Resolution all discrimination, both direct and indirect, was to have been completely eliminated by 31 December 1964' (*Defrenne II*, para. 48). It added that the Equal Pay Directive 'was intended to encourage the proper implementation of Article 119 by means of a series of measures to be taken on the national level, in order, in particular, to eliminate indirect forms of discrimination' (*Defrenne II*, para. 60).

b. Comments

i. Para. 18: 'indirect discrimination' as related to direct effect

As is evident from the above, the distinction made by the Court in para. 18 of the *Defrenne II* decision between 'direct and overt discrimination', on the one hand, and 'indirect and disguised discrimination', on the other hand, concerned the question under what circumstances Art. 119 of the EEC Treaty could be regarded as *directly effective*. At the time, this was a delicate issue since neither the Commission nor the Member States believed that Art. 119 had direct effect (Craig & de Búrca).[747] Not surprisingly, the Court's finding of direct effect (and especially horizontal direct effect) was severely criticised.[748] However, the Court qualified its finding by ruling that the conditions for direct effect were fulfilled only in the case of 'direct and overt discrimination' but not in that of 'indirect and disguised discrimination'. This distinction, later confirmed in *Macarthys*[749] and *Worringham*,[750] caused considerable

---

[745] The Court decided that the direct effect of Art. 119 could not be relied on in order to support claims concerning pay periods prior to the date of the decision, except with regard to those workers who had already brought legal proceedings or made an equivalent claim (*Defrenne II*, para. 75).

[746] Resolution concerning the harmonization of rates of pay for men and women, published in the Bulletin of the EEC 1962, no 1, p. 7 (this page reference concerns the Dutch version as the present writer was unable to find the English version in the Bulletin which begins with the year 1968).

[747] Craig & de Búrca 2003, p. 188; see also Blomeyer 1994, p. 119.

[748] E.g. VerLoren van Themaat 1997, though this view was not shared by all commentators, e.g. Van Gerven 1977.

[749] Case 129/79, *ECR* 1275.

[750] Case 69/80, [1981] *ECR* 767, though here only in substance but not in terminology (and thus different from what Steiner 1999, p. 129, seems to say).

confusion (e.g. Du Pré,[751] Crisham,[752] Rating,[753] Martin).[754] In particular, it was unclear whether the Court's statements also referred to a substantive concept of indirect discrimination, such as defined in *Sotgiu*.[755] Following *Defrenne II*, AG Warner repeatedly complained about what he considered confusing and unnecessary language by the Court (*Jenkins*,[756] p. 938 of the AG's opinion, *Worringham*, p. 803 of the AG's opinion).

> In *Jenkins*, AG Warner pointed to differences between the French and the English language versions of the Court's decision: 'The confusion has mostly arisen from the English texts of the relevant judgments of the Court, where in particular the terms 'overt', on the one hand, and 'disguised', on the other, are each used, in relation to discrimination, to connote what in my opinion are different notions. If one examines the French texts of those judgments, one sees that the Court has consistently used the terms 'dissimulées' in expressing the dichotomy in the *Sotgiu, Commission v Ireland* and *Toia* cases, whilst in the *second Defrenne* case and in *Macarthys v Smith* it used the contrasting phrases 'directes et ouvertes' and 'indirectes et déguisées'. Nonetheless, it does not, with respect, seem to me that the latter phrase, however one renders it in English, is appropriate to describe those kinds of discrimination as regards which Article 119 does not have direct effect. Article 119 is, in my opinion, more accurately described as not having direct effect where a court cannot apply its provisions by reference to the simple criteria that those provisions themselves lay down and where, consequently, implementing legislation, either Community or national, is necessary to lay down the relevant criteria. It would, if I may respectfully say so, be helpful if, in the judgment in this case, or perhaps in the judgment *Worringham v Lloyds Bank*, your Lordships were to clarify that point.'
>
> The AG repeated his criticism in his opinion on the *Worringham* case: 'I understand, of course, that Art. 119 has direct effect in some areas and not in others; [...] What puzzles me is why the concepts of 'direct and overt' discrimination as distinct from 'indirect and disguised' discrimination should be relevant in that connexion. We are all familiar with the cases in this Court that establish that covert discrimination is just as much discrimination as overt discrimination [here, the AG referred to *Sotgiu*]. In none of those cases, however, was it suggested, or could it sensibly have been suggested, that the distinction between overt and covert discrimination affected the question whether the relevant provision of Community law had direct effect or not. In the present case, there is nothing indirect, covert or disguised about the different treatment of men and women under Lloyd's Bank's pension arrangements.'

---

[751] Du Pré 1976, p. 580.
[752] Crisham 1977, p. 111.
[753] Rating 1994, p. 59.
[754] Martin 1998, p. 306.
[755] Case 152/73, [1974] *ECR* 153, discussed earlier in this part, A.I.2.c.
[756] Case 96/80, [1981] *ECR* 911, discussed later in this part, A.I.4.h.

In hindsight, clearly the Court's statements in para. 18 of the *Defrenne II* judgment
concern a different matter from that of direct or indirect reliance on a prohibited
discriminatory ground. Ellis[757] explains that the distinction which the Court seems
to have been making was simply between discrimination which can be identified
without any need for further explanatory legislation and that which cannot. AG
VerLoren van Themaat later used the expressions 'discrimination directly ascertainable
by the courts' and 'discrimination not directly ascertainable by the Courts' (*Burton,*[758]
point 2.6 in the AG's opinion). Similarly, the UK Government and AG Geelhoed referred to *Defrenne II* as the source for the claim that the direct effect of Article 141 EC
is limited to those cases in which courts 'can detect discrimination on the basis of a
(purely) legal analysis' (*Lawrence,*[759] points 37 and 53 of the AG's opinion). It has been
suggested that the *Defrenne II* distinction could also be applied to other areas of law
(Wyatt,[760] regarding Art. 90 EC concerning the internal taxation of goods). However,
the Court itself eventually abandoned this confusing use of terminology in relation
to direct effect. The judgment usually cited in that context is *Jenkins*[761] (the von der
Groeben & Schwarze Commentary,[762] the Calliess & Ruffert Commentary,[763] Craig
& de Búrca),[764] though in the present writer's analysis *Murphy*[765] is better authority.

> It is submitted that in *Jenkins*, the Court's statements still implied a distinction dependent
> upon whether or not Community or national measures were to be relied on in order to
> establish a difference in pay. That confusion continued after that judgment is evident from
> the questions raised in that regard by the later *Bilka*[766] case. In *Murphy*, the Court held that
> '[i]n so far as it is established that the difference in wage levels in question is based on
> discrimination on grounds of sex, Article 119 of the EEC Treaty is directly applicable in
> the sense that the workers concerned may rely on it in legal proceedings in order to obtain
> equal pay within the meaning of the provision and in the sense that national courts or
> tribunals must take it into account as a constituent part of Community law' (*Murphy*, para.
> 11). Here, the *Defrenne II* distinction is no longer mentioned (nevertheless, AG van Gerven
> later brought up this distinction in his opinion in *Ten Oever,*[767] at point 3).

---

[757] Ellis 1998, p. 112; see also Blomeyer 1994, pp. 55 subs.
[758] Case 19/81, [1982] *ECR* 554.
[759] Case C-320/00, [2002] *ECR* I-7325.
[760] Wyatt 1980, p. 379. Wyatt argues that Art. 90(1) EC should be understood as involving direct and
overt discrimination within the meaning of the *Defrenne* line of cases (in other words, it would be
directly effective) and Art. 90(2) EC would concern indirect and disguised discrimination (in other
words, it would not be directly effective). According to Wyatt, the latter lacks a precise reference point
and poses difficulties for national courts arising from economic factors involved in the analysis.
[761] Discussed later in this part, A.I.4.h.
[762] Von der Groeben & Schwarze Commentary 2004, n. 230 ad Art. 141 EC and Protocol no. 17.
[763] Calliess & Ruffert Commentary 2002, n. 5 ad Art. 141 EC.
[764] Craig & de Búrca 2003, p. 853.
[765] Case 157/86, [1988] *ECR* 673.
[766] Case 170/84, [1986] *ECR* 1607; see later in this part, A.I.4.h.
[767] Case C-109/91, [1993] *ECR* I-4879.

ii. Para. 19, 48 and 60: a trace of a substantive notion of indirect discrimination

In contrast to para. 18, arguably the Court's references to 'indirect discrimination' in para. 19, 48 and 60 of the *Defrenne II* judgment were made in a different context from direct effect (para. 19: 'the elimination of all discrimination, direct or indirect'; para. 48: 'all discrimination, both direct and indirect, was to have been completely eliminated'; para. 60: 'to eliminate indirect forms of discrimination'; see Du Pré,[768] in relation to para. 48). This is noteworthy because the Equal Pay Resolution,[769] to which the Court referred in that context, mentions neither direct nor indirect discrimination.[770] However, given the modest position of these references, as well as the fact that *Defrenne II* itself concerned direct[771] pay discrimination, these can be no more than general and rather fleeting remarks which, unsurprisingly, tend to be overlooked in academic writing. The fact that the later decisions *Jenkins*[772] and *Bilka*[773] are far more explicit explains why they receive greater attention in the context of a substantive notion of indirect sex discrimination.

c. An interim conclusion (II)

The conclusion to be drawn is that in *Defrenne II*[774] the term 'indirect discrimination' appears to be used in two distinct contexts, one concerning the direct effect of Art. 119 of the EEC Treaty and the other concerning the substantive nature of discrimination. *Defrenne II* is best known for having raised the former issue. Though the Court eventually discontinued its use of such terminology as 'direct and overt discrimination' and 'indirect and disguised discrimination' in relation to direct effect, confusion persists to some degree. Some commentators still fail to distinguish between the issues of direct effect on the one hand and indirect discrimination in a substantive sense on the other hand (e.g. the Calliess & Ruffert Commentary,[775] the Mégret Commentary,[776]

---

[768] Du Pré 1976, p. 580.

[769] Resolution concerning the harmonization of rates of pay for men and women, published in the Bulletin of the EEC 1962, no 1, p. 7. (Again, this page reference concerns the Dutch version as the present writer was unable to find the English version in the Bulletin which begins with the year 1968 only.)

[770] Indirect discrimination is explicitly mentioned in other documents, such as the Commission reports on the situation in the Member States regarding Art. 119; Commission Documents SEC (73) 3000 fin. and SEC (70) 2338 fin.

[771] For that reason, the von der Groeben & Schwarze Commentary call the case *'eine historische Reminiszenz'*; n. 452 ad Art. 141 EC and Protocol no. 17.

[772] Case 96/80, [1981] *ECR* 911.

[773] Case 170/84, [1986] *ECR* 1607; for both cases, see later in this part, A.I.4.h.

[774] Case 43/75, [1976] *ECR* 455.

[775] Calliess & Ruffert Commentary 2002, n. 5 ad Art. 141 EC.

[776] Mégret Commentary (as of 1972), p. 123, n. 52.

De Schutter,[777] Wouters,[778] the von der Groeben & Schwarze Commentary).[779] Perhaps such confusion results from the fact that *Defrenne II* is still the landmark case with regard to the direct effect (and, in particular, horizontal direct effect) of the Treaty's equal pay provision (e.g. *Lawrence*, para. 13).[780] Situations where some aspects of a judgment are no longer 'good law' are apt to result in persistent misunderstandings.

4. APPLICATION OF THE CONCEPT IN AN ENLARGING CONTEXT

The cases discussed thus far have concerned only a limited number of areas of Community law (namely free movement of workers as well as labour law involving both Staff law and EC labour law which, in turn, binds the Member States) and of only certain types of discrimination (namely discrimination on grounds of nationality and of sex). Over time, the Court has recognised the potentially indirect nature of discrimination in other contexts. This development is examined chronologically in the Court's case law.

a. Internal taxation of goods

i. Preliminary remarks

Art. 90 EC (formerly Art. 95 of the Treaty) deals with barriers to the import of goods caused by taxation imposed by Member States. The provision's first section prohibits *discrimination* through different levels of taxation for products from other Member States that are similar to domestically produced goods, to the disadvantage of the former (discrimination on grounds of the origin of the goods). The second section prohibits *indirect protection* of domestically produced goods through differential taxation of goods that though not similar are nevertheless in competition.[781] Against the background of an Aristotelian understanding of equality, only the former situation concerns discrimination in the strict sense of the word (though some appear to take a different view, e.g. Stampe).[782]

---

[777] De Schutter 1999, p. 35.
[778] Wouters 1999, p. 103, footnote 46.
[779] Von der Groeben & Schwarze Commentary 2004, n. 230 ad Art. 141 EC and Protocol no. 17; though more accurate n. 455.
[780] Case C-320/00, [2002] *ECR* I-7325.
[781] This interpretation is not apparent from the wording of Art. 90(2) EC itself but results from case law; see *Co-Frutta* (Case 193/85, [1987] *ECR* 2085), para. 19.
[782] Stampe 2001, p. 75.

In the framework of an Aristotelian approach to equality, non-discrimination, as a right to equal treatment (first part of the equality formula), presupposes the comparability of situations.[783] Art. 90(2) EC concerns non-comparable products. Weatherill & Beaumont[784] helpfully explain: 'The two paragraphs of Article 90 (ex 95) are in this sense distinct. Under paragraph (1) products, being similar, must be taxed at similar levels. Under paragraph (2) products are competing rather than similar. The Treaty requires that protection be eliminated. In practical application that means that differences in taxation must reflect objective differences in the nature of the product, or, at least, such differences must be so insubstantial as to involve no protective consequences.'

Discrimination under Art. 90(1) EC has been described as a situation 'where the taxation on the imported product and that on the similar domestic product are calculated in a different manner on the basis of different criteria which lead, if only in certain cases, to higher taxation imposed on the imported product' (Quigley).[785] Academic literature generally recognises that this prohibition includes *indirect* discrimination, though by using different terminology (e.g. Demaret:[786] 'formal or material discrimination'; Easson:[787] 'formal and 'effective discrimination'). In this context, as an important preliminary point, a distinction needs to be made between the direct or indirect *imposition* of taxation, on the one hand, and the direct or indirect *discrimination* that may occur in this context, on the other hand. It is important to note that the words 'directly or indirectly' used in Art. 90(1) EC refer not to the discrimination ground from which they are to be distinguished, but rather to the imposition of the taxation of the goods (in the terms of the structural elements proposed in the introduction:[788] the *object* of non-discrimination), as were at issue, for example, in *Schöttle & Söhne*[789] (the Mégret[790] Commentary, the Geiger Commentary)[791] and, possibly, *Marsala*[792] (discussed below).

Schöttle & Söhne concerned a charge imposed on the international transport of goods by road according to the distance covered within the national territory and to the weight of the goods in question. The Court held that the taxation of the carriage of goods has an immediate effect on the cost of national and imported products and, therefore, consisted of 'taxation imposed indirectly on products within the meaning of Art. 95 [of the Treaty]'.

---

783 See above Part 1, B.II.1.b.
784 Weatherill & Beaumont 1999, p. 483.
785 Quigley 1997, p. 278.
786 Demaret 2000, p. 175.
787 Easson 1993, p. 61.
788 See above Part 1, B.V.2.
789 Case 20/76, [1977] *ECR* 247.
790 Mégret Commentary (as of 1972), n. 17bis ad Arts. 95-99.
791 Geiger Commentary 2000, n. 7 ad Art. 90 EC, where the case is mentioned in the context of the field of application of Art. 90(1) EC.
792 Case 277/83, [1985] *ECR* 2049.

Consequently, the tax had to be applied in a manner which would not discriminate against imported products (*Schöttle & Söhne*, para. 15 and 16). According to the Calliess & Ruffert Commentary,[793] this case involved indirect discrimination.

ii. Indirect discrimination: a general statement in *Steinike & Weinlig*

The earliest[794] explicit mention of indirect discrimination in the context of the internal taxation of goods is found in *Steinike & Weinlig*[795] in 1977 where the Court explained that 'the objective of Article 95 is to abolish direct or indirect discrimination against imported products' (para. 30).[796] However, this merely general statement made no link to the specific case at hand,[797] and, further, the Court did not explain what it meant by the various terms used. The absence of legal comment indicates that academic writers of the time were not surprised by the Court's reference to indirect discrimination (e.g. Barents,[798] Dashwood,[799] Tinnion;[800] see also X).[801] This is very different matter from that of *direct* taxation (which will be discussed later).[802] Today's commentators do not seem to find such references particularly challenging either (e.g. Demaret,[803] Easson,[804] Quigley,[805] Lyon).[806] In fact, such an explicit reference to 'indirect discrimination' can also be found in Art. 18 of the EEC – Austrian Free Trade

---

[793] Calliess & Ruffert Commentary 2002, n. 13 ad Art. 90 EC.

[794] Calliess & Ruffert (idem) mention two earlier cases as involving indirect discrimination, namely *Commission v Belgium* (Case 77/69, [1970] *ECR* 237) and *FOR* (Case 54/72, [1973] *ECR* 193). However, in both cases, the different tax treatment was immediately based on the origin of the goods, which excludes indirect discrimination. *Commission v Belgium* involved the use of different tax bases dependent on whether the wood in question was produced domestically or imported. In the *FOR* case, an operation which with regard to a domestic product constituted a single transaction for tax purposes was broken down into two distinct and, therefore, separately taxable operations in the case of foreign products.

[795] Case 78/76, [1977] *ECR* 595.

[796] Compare also the later *Regenerated Petroleum Products* (Case 21/79, [1980] *ECR* 1), para. 16.

[797] *Steinike & Weinlig* concerned a charge levied by the German authorities on the processing of concentrates from citrus fruit, such as those imported by the company Steinike und Weinlig from Italy as well as various third countries into Germany. The charge consisted of a contribution required from all processing companies and intended to finance a fund intended to promote the sale and export of products of the German agricultural, food, and forestry industries. The Court held that there is no discrimination where internal taxation on their being processed into more elaborate products applies to domestic products and to previously imported products without any distinction of rate, basis or assessment or detailed rules for the levying thereof being made between them by reason of their origin (para. 30).

[798] Barents 1977.

[799] Dashwood 1977.

[800] Tinnion 1977.

[801] X 1978 (Steinike & Weinlig).

[802] See later in this part, A.I.5.b.

[803] Demaret 2000, p. 175.

[804] Easson 1993, p. 61.

[805] Quigley 1997, p. 276.

[806] Lyons 2001, p. 33.

Agreement of 1972[807] which provided that the Contracting Parties 'shall refrain from any measure or practice of an internal fiscal nature establishing, whether directly or indirectly, discrimination between the products of one Contracting Party and like products originating in the territory of the other Contradicting Party'. But in contrast to Art. 90(1) EC, the words 'directly or indirectly' in this provision refer to the *discrimination*, and not to the imposition of tax. This indicates that the legal concept of indirect discrimination was already both familiar and undisputed in relation to the internal taxation of goods and helps to explain why its application to the interpretation of Treaty law was not deemed revolutionary.

iii. In search of application in concrete cases

Although *general* remarks on indirect discrimination in the context of Art. 90(1) EC are easy to find, it is far more difficult to identify instances of its *actual application*. The difficulty generally[808] lies in the fact that the Court does often not specify whether a given case involves discrimination prohibited under Art. 90(1) EC, or rather protection prohibited under Art. 90(2) EC. The *Spirits cases*[809] and *Humblot*[810] are examples.

> The so-called *Spirits cases* of 1980 concerned national taxation systems favouring particular categories of alcoholic products that tended to be traditional domestic products. In three of them, the Court found a breach of Art. 95. However, in what Weatherill & Beaumont

---

[807] Free Trade Agreement between the EEC and Austria, concluded and approved in the name of the Community by Regulation 2836/72, OJ English Special Edition 1972, L 300/3.

[808] Some academic writers refer to cases which clearly do not involve indirect discrimination. Vanistendael 1994, p. 309, cites *Hauptzollamt Flensburg* (Case 38/82, [1983] *ECR* 1271) which concerned a national tax advantage that depended upon whether the spirits were distilled by cooperatives consisting of a group of small-scale farmers. The Court held that 'such a requirement does not in fact constitute a specifically national condition but may be met by undertakings in all Member States provided that it is understood as referring to groups of the same economic and social groups as those envisaged by the national law' (*Hauptzollamt Flensburg*, para. 15). A further condition required that the spirits taxed at the lower rate must be produced from the raw materials specified in the national provisions (fruit, berries, wine, wine lees, must, roots or their residues). Again, the Court observed that such raw materials are also produced in other Member States and that, consequently, the national provisions do not prescribe a condition which only domestic products are capable of fulfilling (*Hauptzollamt Flensburg*, para. 17). The Court's conclusion therefore was that a tax advantage granted under the conditions described does not lead to discrimination. Weatherill & Beaumont 1999, p. 479, cite *French Natural Sweet Wines* (Case 196/85, [1987] *ECR* 1597) which concerned a preferential tax scheme that was confined to those liqueur wines whose production was 'traditional and customary'. The Court found that there was no evidence of giving preference to French wines at the expense of wines from other Member States (*French Natural Sweet Wines*, para. 10).

[809] The terms is usually used in relation to a group of cases decided in 1980, in particular *Commission v Denmark* (Case 171/78, [1980] *ECR* 447), *Commission v France* (Case 168/78, [1980] *ECR* 347), *Commission v Italy* (Case 169/78, [1980] *ECR* 385) and *Commission v UK* (Case 170/78 [1980] *ECR* 417 and [1983] *ECR* 2265). See also *Commission v Greece* (Case C-230/89, [1991] *ECR* I-1909).

[810] Case 112/84, [1985] *ECR* 1367.

(in an early edition of their text-book)[811] called 'a rather cavalier approach to the distinction
between the two paragraphs in Article 95', the Court did not specify whether the products
in question were similar (section 1 of Art. 95) or dissimilar but still in competition (section
2 of Art. 95). In other words, the Court did not specify whether the cases involved discrimination or protectionism. According to the Court, the national tax systems contained 'incon-
testable discriminatory or protective characteristics' (*Commission v Denmark*, para. 36; see
also *Commission v Italy*, para. 35 and *Commission v France*, para. 41). The same kind of
approach is also reflected in the more recent 'spirits' case *Commission v Greece*. Under the
national taxation system, a value added tax of 36% had to be paid on a supply of a certain
group of spirits (namely whisky, gin, vodka, run, tequila, arak and tafia), while a rate of 16%
applied to another group (among which there were ouzo, brandy and liqueurs). The
Commission deemed the two groups of products comparable. Given that the first group
was produced abroad and the second group usually in Greece, the Commission argued that
the case involved discriminatory taxation based upon the origin of the goods. The Court
agreed that there was an infringement of Art. 95 of the Treaty but left open whether this
concerned section 1 or section 2 (*Commission v Greece*, para. 10). According to one comment,[812] a finding of an infringement was inevitable. Indeed, but one still wonders which
type of infringement?[813]

Humblot concerned national law according to which cars rated at 16 CV or less where
subject to an annual differential tax which increased progressively and uniformly with the
power rating. Cars rated higher were subject to a special tax levied at a single rate almost
five times higher than the highest rate of the differential tax. The Court explained that
'[a]lthough the system embodies no formal distinction based on the origin of the products
it manifestly exhibits *discriminatory or protective* features contrary to Article 95, since the
power rating determining liability to the special tax has been fixed at a level such that only
imported cars, in particular from other Member States, are subject to the special tax whereas
all cars of domestic manufacture are liable to the distinctly more advantageous differential
tax' (*Humblot*, para. 14; emphasis added). Again, the Court left open whether or not the
products were comparable for the purposes of Art. 90 EC (Terra & Wattel).[814] Farmer &
Lyal[815] generally speak of an indirect conflict with the principle of equal treatment whereas
others argue more specifically that if the infringement constituted discrimination, it must
have been indirect (Craig & de Búrca,[816] Steiner & Woods).[817]

---

[811]   Weatherill & Beaumont 1995, p. 410. In the more recent edition of the text-book, this remark cannot
        be found any longer, see Weatherill & Beaumont 1999, pp. 480 and 483.
[812]   E.K. 1991, p. 1751.
[813]   Some writers speak of indirect (or factual) discrimination; e.g. Ohler 1997, p. 108; the Léger
        Commentary, n. 33 ad Art. 90 EC. – Generally on the Court's alcohol cases, see Rodrigues Iglesias
        2000; also Priebe 1984.
[814]   Terra & Wattel 2001, p. 9.
[815]   Farmer & Lyal 1994, p. 47.
[816]   Craig & de Búrca 2003, p. 594.
[817]   Steiner & Woods 2003, p. 210.

Arguably, *Marsala*[818] provides an example of an application of an indirect discrimination approach. In this case, the Court clearly identified the *discriminatory* nature of the measure in question (in other words, the goods in question were comparable) though made no mention of *indirect* discrimination. *Marsala* concerned Italian legislation on the taxation of wine alcohol. Basically, the same rates applied to the manufacturing of nationally produced wine alcohol and to foreign-produced wine alcohol. However, a reduction was granted with respect to the manufacture of alcohol distilled from wine used in the manufacture of liqueur wines which qualify for the designation 'Marsala', a beverage made exclusively in Italy (more specifically, in Western Sicily; see p. 2050 of AG Gordon Slynn's opinion), where it amounted to over 90% of domestically produced liqueur wines with a registered designation of origin. The Court noted that liqueur wines constitute a range of homogeneous products with similar characteristics and similar properties which meet the same needs from the point of view of consumers (in other words, the products were similar within the meaning of what was then Art. 95 (1) of the EEC Treaty). The Court further observed that 'foreign liqueur wines can never be called Marsala and can therefore never qualify for the tax advantage granted in respect of Marsala', that 'no imported liqueur wine can ever qualify for the preferential treatment accorded to Marsala and that imported liqueur wines accordingly suffer discrimination' (*Marsala*, para. 13 and 15). The Court did not mention the term 'indirect discrimination' at this point though it later confirmed generally 'the purpose of the first paragraph of Article 95, which is to eliminate all forms of direct or indirect discrimination' (*Marsala*, para. 17). Easson[819] argues that the discrimination found by the Court was clearly of an indirect nature because 'the advantage could effectively be claimed only by wines produced in Sicily'. If so, it should be noted that this was indirect discrimination caused by what appears to have been the *indirect imposition* of taxes: the tax benefit enjoyed by Marsala did not concern the taxation of Marsala itself but was a production benefit in a wider sense, made possible through the availability of a cheaper ingredient thanks to a tax benefit which occurred on the level of the production of this very ingredient. The reduction of the tax to be paid for wine alcohol in an indirect way led to a benefit only for a domestically produced good (namely Marsala) and to the detriment of similar foreign liqueurs (as well as of similar domestically produced liqueurs, though that aspect is not relevant in the framework of legislation relating to trade between the Member States).

---

[818]   Case 277/83, [1985] *ECR* 2049.
[819]   Easson 1993, p. 61, footnote 144.

b. Freedom of establishment

In the area of freedom of establishment (Art. 43 EC), the development was similar to
that of the internal taxation of goods in the sense that a general statement on indirect
discrimination occurred early but cases reflecting an actual application are more
difficult to come by.

i. A general statement in *Thieffry*

An initial *statement of a general nature* appears in *Thieffry*,[820] a decision handed down
in 1977. The case concerned a Belgian national holding a doctorate in Belgian law who
first practised as an attorney-at-law at the Brussels Bar and later established himself
in Paris. There, Mr Thieffry obtained a French certificate for the profession of
advocate; his Belgian degree was recognised as equivalent to a licentiate's degree under
French law. Nonetheless, Mr Thieffry's application to take the necessary oath to register
for practical training was rejected on the grounds that he held neither a licentiate's
nor a doctor's degree in French law. Mr Thieffry claimed that this constituted 'discrimination exercised in relation to the nationality of diplomas' and that 'discrimination
based on the criterion of nationality must be rejected, whether it is applied to the
person himself or whether it takes the form of a national law demanding a national
diploma' (*Thieffry*, p. 768/769). Both the Commission and AG Mayras identified this
as a claim of indirect discrimination on grounds of nationality in the context of the
freedom of establishment (*Thieffry*, p. 773 and 793). The Court generally remarked
that 'in the General Programme for the abolition of restrictions on freedom of
establishment the Council proposed to eliminate not only overt discrimination, but
also any form of disguised discrimination' (*Thieffry*, para. 13)[821] but then decided the
case in a different conceptual framework, that of restrictions in a wider sense.[822] Given
the Court's explicit wording, it is obviously correct to characterize this general statement as a recognition of the potentially indirect nature of discrimination as applied
to the area of freedom of establishment (the Hailbronner Commentary).[823]

Title III of the General Programme[824] listed a number of restrictions that were to be
eliminated. After a list of what today would be termed as direct discrimination (using

---

[820] Case 71/76, [1977] *ECR* 765. See later also *Lopez Brea* (Joined Cases C-330/90 and C-331/90, [1992]
ECR I-323), para. 13. Stadlmeier 1995, p. 23, even considers that were it not for the missing element
of mandatory requirements, the statements could be seen as the origin of a uniform concept of the
prohibition of restrictions in a wider sense rather than only of discriminations.

[821] See already earlier in this part, A.I.1.

[822] See further below Part 3, B.II.2.a.ii.

[823] Hailbronner, Klein, Magiera & Müller-Graff Commentary 1998, n. 8 ad Art. 52 of the EC Treaty.

[824] General Programme for the abolition of restrictions on freedom of establishment, *OJ* English Special
Edition, Second Series, IX, p. 7.

expressions such as 'treating him differently from nationals of the State concerned' and 'provisions and practices which, in respect of foreign nationals only'), there are references to requirements that are applicable irrespective of nationality but have the effect of exclusively or principally excluding foreigners. In the Establishment Programme, this is worded as follows: 'Any requirements imposed [...] in respect of the taking up or pursuit of an activity as a self-employed person where, although applicable irrespective of nationality, their effect is exclusively or principally to hinder the taking up or pursuit of such activity by foreign nationals.' (In the General Programme on services,[825] the relevant passage is worded in the same manner). In *Thieffry* (para. 13 and 14), the Court explained: 'In the General Programme for the abolition of restrictions on freedom of establishment [...], the Council proposed to eliminate not only overt discrimination, but also any form of disguised discrimination, by designing in Title III (B) as restrictions which are to be eliminated, 'any requirements imposed, pursuant to any provision laid by any law, regulation or administrative action or in consequence of any administrative practice, in respect of the taking up or pursuit of an activity as a self-employed person where, although applicable irrespective of nationality, their effect is exclusively or principally to hinder the taking up or pursuit of such activity by foreign nationals' [...]. In the context of the abolition of restrictions on freedom of establishment, that programme provides useful guidance for the implementation of the relevant provisions of the Treaty.'

ii. Concrete application: *Data-processing contracts*

However, it is difficult to find *early cases of actual application* of an indirect discrimination approach in the context of freedom of establishment.[826] In the present writer's analysis, the first[827] case that clearly reflects an indirect discrimination approach was decided only in 1989, namely *Data-processing contracts*.[828] This case concerned Italian legislation providing that only those companies in which all or a majority of their shares were either directly or indirectly in Italian public or State ownership were

---

[825] General Programme for the abolition of restrictions on freedom to provide services; *OJ* English Special Edition, Second Series, IX, p. 3.

[826] AG Lenz mentioned indirect discrimination in his opinion on the *Clinical biological laboratories* case (Case 221/85, [1987] *ECR* 719, point 31 of the opinion) but then dismissed it in view of lack of evidence. After a general reference to the prohibition of 'any discrimination', the Court held that the national legislation in question did not permit the conclusion that it was adopted for discriminatory purposes or that it produced discriminatory effects (*Clinical biological laboratories*, para. 11); see further Boutard Labarde 1988, pp. 510-511, and Craig & de Búrca 2003, p. 783.

[827] The von der Groeben & Schwarze Commentary lists the earlier case *Avoir fiscal* (Case 270/83, [1986] *ECR* 273) in the context of indirect discrimination (n. 129 ad Vorbemerkung zu den Artikeln 90-93). In this case, AG Mancini mentioned *Sotgiu* (Case 152/73, [1974] *ECR* 153) when referring to the Commission's argument that the discrimination at issue 'is admittedly not explicit, in point of fact it is well hidden' (*Avoir fiscal*, point 10 of the AG's conclusion). The Court made no such reference but simply stated in a general way that 'any discrimination' is prohibited (*Avoir fiscal*, notably para. 13 and 14). *Avoir fiscal* itself concerned *direct* discrimination on grounds of nationality; see later in this part, A.I.5.b.i.

[828] Case C-3/88, [1989] *ECR* 4035. This case also concerned the freedom to provide services.

allowed to conclude contracts with the Italian State for the development of data-processing systems. Indirect discrimination on grounds of nationality[829] was explicitly mentioned by AG Mischo who countered the Italian Government's argument that no distinction on the basis of nationality was made. He pointed out that such an argument might only work on a formal level because the legislation violated the prohibition against indirect discrimination: whilst not all Italian companies were treated more favourably than foreign companies, all companies receiving favourable treatment under the legislation were Italian (*Data-processing contracts*, point 6 subs. of the AG's opinion). The Court, contrasting 'overt discrimination' and 'any form of disguised discrimination', agreed (*Data-processing contracts*, para. 8 and 9). Given the Court's explicit language, *Data-processing contracts* concerns, beyond any doubt, indirect discrimination applied to the area of freedom of establishment (e.g. Dahlgaard Dingel,[830] Fernández Martín,[831] Sanfilippo,[832] X).[833]

> The Court held: 'According to the Court's case law the principle of equal treatment, of which Articles 52 and 59 of the Treaty embody specific instances, prohibits not only overt discrimination by reason of nationality but also all covert forms of discrimination which, by the application of other criteria of differentiation, lead in fact to the same result [...]. Although the law and decree-laws in issue apply without distinction to all companies, whether of Italian or foreign nationality, they essentially favour Italian companies. As the Commission has pointed out, without being contradicted by the Italian Government, there are at present no data-processing companies from other Member States all or the majority of whose shares are in Italian public ownership.'

c.   An interim conclusion (III)

The two areas just examined, namely the internal taxation of goods (Art. 90 EC) and freedom of establishment (Art. 43 EC), have in common that general statements on the relevance of indirect discrimination can be found early on in the Court's case law and that these statements are not accompanied by further explanations. In both areas it is difficult to find early cases where the concept of indirect discrimination was actually and explicitly applied. This is in sharp contrast to other areas of EC law where the Court not only explicitly stated the relevance of the legal notion of indirect (covert) discrimination but also explained what this term means and why the concept is

---

[829]   According to Art. 48 EC, companies or firms formed in accordance with the law of a Member State and having their registered office, central administration or place of business within the Community shall, for the purposes of freedom of establishment, be treated in the same way as natural persons who are nationals of Member States. This means in effect that residence is for companies what nationality is for natural persons.

[830]   Dahlgaard Dingel 1999, p. 164, footnote 5.

[831]   Fernández Martín 1996, p. 9.

[832]   Sanfilippo 1990, p. 422.

[833]   X 1990, p. 113.

necessary (e.g. *Sotgiu*,[834] in the context of free movement of workers). The Court's use of terminology in relation to the legal concept of indirect discrimination is still not uniform but, nevertheless, is explicit and clear ('direct and indirect discrimination' in the context of Art. 90 EC, 'any form of disguised discrimination' and 'covert discrimination' in the context of Art. 43 EC).

d. Agricultural law

i. Preliminary remarks

Chronologically speaking, with regard to ECJ cases on indirect discrimination, the next area of law is agricultural law. The Treaty provisions on this issue (Arts. 32 subs. EC) provide a framework for the Common Agricultural Policy (CAP) which is put into practice through secondary law adopted on the basis of Arts. 34(1) and 37 EC. Gencarelli[835] observes that agricultural law now constitutes a complete and coherent subsystem in the framework of EC law whose secondary law generates more than 50% of all of the EC's derived legislation. As far as discrimination is concerned, the Treaty in Art. 34(2) EC (originally Art. 40(3) of the EEC Treaty) states that EC secondary law must not discriminate between producers nor between consumers (though the Court has interpreted this provision as including other groups of economic agents also subject to Community agricultural law; the von der Groeben & Schwarze Commentary).[836] A difference in treatment in relation to *products* is relevant in so far as it leads to different treatment of these concerned persons (Plötscher).[837] Usher[838] observes that non-discrimination is perhaps the most important legal principle expressed by the Treaty in relation to common agricultural organisations. The discussion below demonstrates that the case law on the specific non-discrimination provisions in secondary law confirms the relevance of the concept of indirect discrimination also in the field of agricultural law.

ii. Sea Fisheries: the case

The first, and for present purposes particularly illustrative case from the area of agriculture is *Sea Fisheries*.[839] At issue was Art. 2(1) of Regulation 101/76[840] which

---

[834] Case 152/73, [1974] *ECR* 153.
[835] Gencarelli 2001, p. 657.
[836] Von der Groeben & Schwarze Commentary 2004, n. 59 ad Art. 34 EC.
[837] Plötscher 2003, p. 86. The author speaks about a subcategory of Art. 34(2) EC. However, in the framework used in this study, this situation is rather comparable to the type of indirectly caused discrimination at issue in *Geitling* (Case 2/56, [1957/1958] *ECR* 3); see above Part 1, C.IV.
[838] Usher 2001, p. 40.
[839] Case 61/77, [1978] *ECR* 417.
[840] Regulation 101/76/EEC, *OJ* 1976 L 20/19 (no longer in force).

mandated equal treatment of Member States through 'equal conditions of access and use of the fishing grounds for all vessels flying the flag of a Member State and registered in the Community territory'. In 1976, the Council adopted the so-called Hague Resolution in which the Member States agreed to extend, by concerted action, the limits of their fishing zones to 200 miles off their North Sea and North Atlantic coasts. In this context, the Community planned to set up a common system for the conservation and management of fishery resources, a matter considered particularly urgent by Ireland who made it clear that, in the absence of an early agreement on this issue, she would adopt unilateral interim measures. When the adoption of the common system proved time-consuming, Ireland adopted rules that made it an offence to enter into, remain and fish in certain parts of the Irish fishery zone. However, Ireland created an exemption for sea fishing boats not exceeding 33 metres in registered length or having a main engine or engines not exceeding a total of 1,100 brake horse-power. In the Commission's view, Ireland's different treatment of fishing vessels according to their length and strength of engine infringed Community law in that the Irish fishing fleet was composed almost exclusively of small inshore fishing boats which qualified for the exemption, whereas the fleets of other countries did not. In addition, the prohibition applied to a large area of the open Atlantic most of which was substantially nearer to Ireland than to ports of other Member States. Given the fact that smaller boats are usually less able to travel long distances in bad weather or to stay at sea for long periods, the Irish rules in fact favoured boats based in Ireland. Of the Irish fleet, a mere 0,19% was negatively affected (merely 2 out of 1100 Irish boats did not qualify for the exemption, and one of them had normally not fished in the area in question) whilst all of the Dutch fleet normally operating in the waters concerned, and 25% of the French fleet were affected (the UK fleet was not affected at all). The Commission, therefore, accused Ireland of engaging in what it called discrimination in substance, caused by treating different situations in an identical way. Before the Court of Justice, both the Dutch Government and AG Reischl emphasised that the effect of the contested measure had to be taken into consideration, rather than only its formal content. In this context, the AG explicitly referred to the indirect discrimination case *Sotgiu*.[841] The Court agreed and noted that although under the Accession Treaty Ireland was in principle competent to take appropriate conservation measures,[842] these had to conform to the requirements of Community law. Explicitly referring to *Sotgiu* and the prohibition against covert discrimination, the Court concluded that the Irish measures were contrary to both Art. 7 of the EEC Treaty (now Art. 12 EC) and Art. 2(1) of Regulation 101/76.

---

[841] Case 152/73, [1974] *ECR* 153.

[842] Otherwise, the Community competence in the area of fisheries is an exclusive one; *Sea Fisheries*, para. 56 subs.

Specifically, the Dutch Government stressed that 'the essential point is the effect of those measures. Article 2(1) of Regulation 101/76 indicates 'shall not lead to' differences in treatment of other Member States. The measures in question must therefore be assessed primarily on their material effect and not simply on their formal presentation' (*Sea Fisheries*, p. 429). AG Reischl agreed. Referring to *Sotgiu*, he explained that 'the ascertainable effects and not technical legal trappings are decisive' (*Sea Fisheries*, p. 464). As the effect of the measures in question was considerably different on the various Member States, the AG found it 'impossible to doubt that the Irish measures led to discrimination against the French and Netherlands fishing fleets in relation to the Irish fishing fleet and in addition to detect a difference in treatment if the examination is limited to the other Member States, with the exception of Ireland' (*Sea Fisheries*, p. 466). The Court held (*Sea Fisheries*, para. 78 and 79): 'As the Court has had occasion to declare in other contexts, in particular in its judgment of 12 February 1974 in Case 152/73, *Sotgiu v Deutsche Bundespost* [1974] ECR 153 the rules regarding equality of treatment enshrined in Community law forbid not only discrimination by reason of nationality but also all covert forms of discrimination which, by the application of other criteria of differentiation, lead in fact to the same result. This certainly applies in the case of the criteria employed in the contested measures the effect of which is to keep out of Irish waters a substantial proportion of the fishing fleets of other Member States which have traditionally fished in those areas whereas under the same measures no comparable obligation is imposed on Irelands own nationals.'

iii. Comments

The statements by the Court in *Sea Fisheries* are so clear that they require little comment as far as the recognition of the potentially indirect nature of discrimination in the area of agricultural law is concerned. *Sea Fisheries* simply confirms the indirect discrimination approach of earlier cases (V.C.)[843] in the context of a particularly illustrative example (the Mégret Commentary).[844] According to Winkel & van Borries,[845] this case contributed substantially to the development of the concept of indirect discrimination and paved the way for its application wherever discrimination is forbidden. However, it raises the question of the *relationship* of the Court's finding of indirect discrimination in the context of specific secondary agricultural law *with Art. 34(2) EC*. For example, Barents[846] links the Court's findings in *Sea Fisheries* to that provision. In contrast, Gerards[847] argues that indirect discrimination is not an issue in the context of Art. 34(2) EC because this provision is openly formulated. In the present writer's view, *Sea Fisheries* clearly concerned a specific non-discriminatory provision set up in specific secondary law for a specific subcategory of agricultural law,

---

[843] V.C. 1979, p. 928.
[844] Mégret Commentary (as of 1972), p. 47 n. 68.
[845] Winkel & van Borries 1978, p. 498.
[846] Barents 1994 (Agricultural Law), p. 333.
[847] Gerards 2002, p. 239.

rather than directly implicating Art. 34(2) EC which simply supplies a general background of such legislation. The relevance of the concept of indirect discrimination
in the context of openly worded non-discrimination provisions will be discussed
later.[848]

Another conceptual issue of a more general nature arises in that the Court found
indirect discrimination whilst the Commission alleged the existence of *discrimination
in substance*,[849] caused by treating different situations in an identical way. According
to Timmermans,[850] these are very similar concepts which in the specific case of *Sea
Fisheries* amounted to the same thing in that the discrimination was caused in two
ways: first, by differentiating according to the size of the fishing vessels which in effect
imposed different treatment according to nationality[851] (indirect discrimination) and
second, through treating non-comparable fleets equally (the Dutch and the French
fishing fleets on the one hand and the Irish fleet on the other hand amounting to
discrimination in substance; see also Scovazzi).[852] Veldman,[853] however, disagrees and
argues that the Court in *Sea Fisheries* considered the fleets comparable. Again, this issue
will be further discussed later.[854]

e. Social security in the context of free movement

i. Preliminary remarks

The next area under consideration is social security law, a field for which the European
Community lacks the requisite competence to compel harmonization (or positive
integration) but where prohibitions of discrimination on grounds of nationality and
on grounds of sex (negative integration)[855] exist. Such prohibitions can be found in
the Third,[856] Fourth[857] and Fifth[858] Equal Treatment Directives, discussed later under
the more general heading of sex discrimination.[859] The following analyses focus on
discrimination on grounds of nationality as prohibited by Community law coordina-

---

[848] See later in this part, A.IV.2.c.
[849] See above, Part 1, B.III.5.d.
[850] Timmermans 1978, p. 587.
[851] Timmermans refers here to Art. 7 of the Treaty (now Art. 12(1) EC), rather than to the prohibition
of discrimination under the Fisheries Regulation.
[852] Scovazzi 1979, p. 64.
[853] Veldman 1995, pp. 162 and 163.
[854] See later in this part, A.IV.2.b.i.
[855] On the terms negative and positive integration as coined by the Dutch economist Jan Tinbergen,
see Kapteyn & VerLoren van Themaat 2003, p. 97.
[856] Directive 79/7/EEC, *OJ* 1979 L 6/24.
[857] Directive 86/378/EEC, *OJ* 1986 L 225/40 (as amended).
[858] Directive 86/613/EEC, *OJ* 1986 L 359/56.
[859] See later in this part, A.I.4.h.iv.

ting[860] the national social security systems, based on Art. 41 EC (which is situated amongst the provisions on free movement of workers). Authors such as Pennings[861] and Keunen[862] emphasise that equal treatment in relation to nationality is fundamental to coordination schemes. For a long time, the basic measure adopted in this context was Regulation 1408/71.[863] In its original version, the link with equal treatment in relation to nationality was evident even in the choice of its legal bases which, beside Arts. 51 (now Art. 41 EC) and 2 (now Art. 2 EC), also included Art. 7 of the EEC Treaty (later Art. 6 of the EC Treaty, now Art. 12 EC). Later, the link became less obvious in that the legal basis is now merely Arts. 51 and 235 of the Treaty (meanwhile Arts. 41 and 308 EC).[864] Particularly important for present purposes is Art. 3(1) of Regulation 1408/71 which explicitly prohibited discrimination on grounds of nationality[865] (the Regulation has recently been replaced by Regulation 2004/883[866] where Art. 4 provides for the right to equal treatment on grounds of nationality in relation to benefits and obligations).[867] Due to the limited scope of the Community's coordinating of social security law, the prohibition *in Art. 7(2) of Regulation 1612/68*[868] against discrimination on grounds of nationality in relation to social advantages is also relevant in the context of social security (Pennings,[869] Keunen).[870] Having been previously discussed in the context of *Sotgiu*,[871] this point needs no further explanation.

---

860 On the difference between harmonization and coordination see Pennings 2003, p. 7 subs.; GTE Commentary 1997, n. 41 subs. ad Art. 51 of the EC Treaty, and Keunen 2001, pp. 301 subs.

861 Pennings 2003, p. 10.

862 Keunen 2001, p. 19.

863 Regulation 1408/71/EEC, *OJ* English Special Edition 1971(II) L 149/2, p. 416 (as amended).

864 Art. 235 was added in order to make it possible to extend the Regulation's field of application to the self-employed.

865 Art. 3(1) reads: 'Subject to the special provisions of the Regulation, persons resident in the territory of one of the Member States to whom this Regulation applies shall be subject to the same obligations and enjoy the same benefits under the legislation of any Member State as the nationals of that State.'

866 Regulation 883/2004/EC, *OJ* 2004 L 166/1; see Annex 3 of the Commission's Communication on Updating and simplifying the Community acquis, COM(2003) 71, which in turn is based on the Commission's Better Regulation Initiative of the year 2002, COM(2002) 278. According to Art. 91, the new Regulation shall apply from the date of entry into force of the Implementing Regulation provided for by Art. 89.

867 Art. 4 of the new Regulation provides: 'Unless otherwise provided for by this Regulation, persons to whom this Regulation applies shall enjoy the same benefits and be subject to the same obligations under the legislation of any Member State as the nationals thereof.'

868 Regulation 1612/68/EEC, *OJ* English Special Edition 1968 L 257/2, p. 475 (as amended).

869 Pennings 2003, pp. 129 subs. The Commission proposal for a revision of Regulation 1612/68 of 1989 provided for explicit mention of social security in Art. 7(1) ('with respect to health, safety and hygiene, and with respect to remuneration, dismissal, social security [...]'; Proposal for a European Parliament and Council Regulation amending Council Regulation (EEC) No 1612/68 on freedom of movement for workers within the Community, *OJ* 1998 C 344/9, meanwhile withdrawn, see COM(2004) 542 (01).

870 Keunen 2001, pp. 329 subs.

871 Case 152/73, [1974] *ECR* 153; see earlier in this part, A.I.2.c.

ii. A general statement: *Kenny*

Although not very explicitly, the Court made a general statement on indirect discrimination on grounds of nationality in *Kenny*,[872] decided in 1978, the same year as *Sea Fisheries*.[873] There, the Court recalled that social security law falls within the competence of the Member States which are free to set conditions in so far as these apply without discrimination regarding their own or foreign EC nationals. The Court added that '[i]t would be otherwise if the conditions for the acquisition or retention of the right were defined in such a way that they could in fact be fulfilled only by nationals or if the conditions for loss or suspension of the right were defined in such a way that they would in fact more easily be satisfied by nationals of other Member States than by those of the State of the competent institution' (*Kenny*, para. 16/17). Obviously, this refers to indirect discrimination on grounds of nationality (e.g. the GTE Commentary),[874] though the Court does not use that term. In *Kenny*, as far as the present writer can see, the facts at issue did not raise any suspicion of indirect discrimination.[875]

iii. The Court's case law: *Palermo-Toia*

An apt example of the application of an indirect discrimination approach in the context of coordinating social security law is found in *Palermo-Toia*[876] of 1979. French legislation provided for an old-age benefit for *women of insufficient means* if they had reared at least five children. Additional conditions demanded that such a woman was married to an employed person and that both she and her children were of French nationality. The refusal of the benefit to Ms Palermo-Toia (an Italian), due to the fact that some of her children were of foreign nationality, raised questions relating to Art. 3(1) of Regulation 1408/71. The Commission pointed to the prohibition against indirect discrimination on grounds of nationality (*Palermo-Toia*, p. 2650 subs.). AG Warner agreed and explicitly referred to *Sotgiu*[877] and *Sea Fisheries*[878] (*Palermo-Toia*, p. 2659).[879] The Court quoted in substance earlier case law, though without citing any

---

[872] Case 1/78, [1978] *ECR* 1489.
[873] Case 61/77, [1978] *ECR* 417, see also the related case *Schonenberg* (Case 88/77, [1978] *ECR* 473).
[874] GTE Commentary 1997, n. 78 ad Art. 51 of the EC Treaty.
[875] Mr Kenny, an Irish national residing in the UK, applied for a sickness benefit with regard to medical treatment he had received in Ireland while being imprisoned there. The benefit was refused to him because persons undergoing imprisonment were disqualified under the scheme for the period of such imprisonment. This was independent of any element that might have had a particular effect in terms of nationality.
[876] Case 237/78, [1979] *ECR* 2645.
[877] Case 152/73, [1974] *ECR* 153.
[878] Case 61/77, [1978] *ECR* 417.
[879] The Commission had referred to two different cases which, however, were not decided in the framework of indirect discrimination, namely *Maris* (Case 55/77, [1977] *ECR* 2327) and *Choquet* (Case 16/78, [1978] *ECR* 2293; see below Part 3, B.I.2.a.iii).

of the cases themselves. Not surprisingly, the Court found that a condition concerning the nationality of the children leads to a disguised form of discrimination on grounds of nationality (*Palermo-Toia*, para. 12-14).

> The Commission considered: 'The arguments in favour of a negative answer are in the first place that, in form, the condition concerning the nationality of the applicant's children applies equally to French nationals and to foreigners. Secondly, it is one of the objective conditions giving entitlement to the benefit. Thirdly, to the extent to which the condition is objectively justified having regard to the nature and purpose of the benefit, there cannot be any discrimination, since that concept presupposes an *arbitrary* difference in treatment. The objective justification is the fact that the objective condition is due to a consideration of demographic policy. The argument in favour of an affirmative answer is that the prohibition on discrimination, contained in Article 3 (1) of Regulation No 1408/71 does not apply solely to discrimination in form but also to discrimination in substance or indirect discrimination, that is to say that provisions which lay down requirements applicable both to a State's own nationals and to foreigners, but which in reality are more difficult for foreigners to satisfy [...]. The effect of the condition concerning the nationality of the children varies according as a French national or a national of another Community State is involved. That condition is more easily satisfied by a French mother.'
>
> The Court explained that the provisions in Art. 3(1) of the Regulation 'prohibit not only patent discrimination, based on the nationality of the beneficiaries of social security schemes, but also all disguised forms of discrimination which, by the application of other distinguishing criteria, lead in fact to the same result. A condition concerning the nationality of the children, such as that imposed by the applicable French legislation, is capable of leading in fact to the result that a mother of foreign nationality may benefit from the allowance only in exceptional cases. In particular she will be at a disadvantage in relation to mothers who are nationals of the State of residence when the nationality of the children depends in principle on that of the parents under the legislation of the country of origin and of the country of residence, as is the case with the Italian and French legislation in this regard. Therefore the condition concerning the nationality of the children must be regarded as indirect discrimination, unless it was justified by objective differences.'

Like *Sea Fisheries*, *Palermo-Toia* is very clear: the Court's decision simply confirms the relevance of the indirect discrimination approach in the specific context of coordinating social security legislation relating to workers (Pennings).[880] It is a logical continuation of the Court's earlier case law on free movement of workers, which should not be surprising given the particular link between these two areas of Community law. Notably, this application concerns a different type of law, namely *coordinating* Community law. As the Austrian Government's arguments in the recent

---

[880]   Pennings 2003, p. 121.

Öztürk[881] case demonstrate, the Member States do not always find it easy to accept the fundamental importance not only of direct but also of *indirect* discrimination on grounds of nationality in this particular context. Finally, as does *Sea Fisheries*,[882] *Palermo-Toia* raises the issue of the relationship between indirect discrimination and discrimination in substance. Here, the Commission explicitly equated the two notions by referring to 'discrimination in substance or indirect discrimination'. Again, this issue will be revisited later.[883]

f. Indirect discrimination in the context of Art. 12(1) EC (general prohibition of discrimination on grounds of nationality)

i. Preliminary remarks

Both in *Sea Fisheries*[884] and *Kenny*,[885] the *(prima facie)* case for indirect discrimination on grounds of nationality found by the Court was linked not only to the specific prohibitions of discrimination on grounds of nationality relevant in the particular context but also to the general[886] provision of Art. 12 EC (originally Art. 7 of the EEC Treaty, later Art. 6 of the EC Treaty). Being general in nature, Art. 12 covers an extremely diverse spectrum of issues.[887] Below, rather than discussing each of these

---

[881]   Case C-373/02, judgment of 28 April 2004, n.y.r., para. 42: 'According to the Austrian Government, Article 3(1) of Decision 3/80 does not prohibit a refusal to take account of periods in which unemployment benefits are paid in another Member State for the purposes of determining entitlement to an early retirement pension. The result of taking the opposite view would be that all coordinating measures forming part of national social security schemes, such as the rule on the aggregation of insurance periods, would be regarded as measures intended to combat covert discrimination.' As expected, the Court did not accept that view but rather confirmed the relevance of the prohibition of indirect discrimination on grounds of nationality in the context of national social security law. Decision 3/80 seeks to coordinate the social security systems of the Member States with a view to giving Turkish workers who are or have been employed in one or more Member States of the Community and the family members and survivors of such workers the right to benefits in the traditional branches of social security (Decision No 3/80 on the application of the social security schemes of the Member States of the European Communities to Turkish workers and members of their families, OJ 1983 C 110/60).

[882]   Case 61/77, [1978] *ECR* 417.

[883]   See later in this part, A.IV.2.b.

[884]   Case 61/77, [1978] *ECR* 417; see earlier in this part, A.I.4.d.

[885]   Case 1/78, [1978] *ECR* 1489; see earlier in this part, A.I.4.e.

[886]   Contrary to what is sometimes claimed in academic writing (e.g. Plötscher 2003, p. 101), the use of the term 'general' in this context is not confusing if it is remembered that it concerns first and foremost the provision's exceptionally wide scope (rather than the range of relevant discriminatory grounds).

[887]   Under the Court's case law, this scope seems to be ever increasing, in particular in the context of EU citizenship (Arts. 17 EU subs.), as is evidenced by cases such as *Hayes and Hayes* (Case C-323/95, [1997] *ECR* I-1711; concerning civil procedure), *Grzelczyk* (Case C-184/99, [2001] *ECR* I-6193; concerning minimum subsistence allowances). In *Bidar* (Case C-209/03, judgment of 15 March 2005, n.y.r., para. 31), a case concerning student loans, the Court stated that '[t]o assess the scope of

---

individual categories, this analysis focuses on the first indirect discrimination case in which Art. 12(1) EC was at issue by itself, rather than in combination with other more specific provisions. By 1976, Bleckmann[888] had already argued that the prohibition on grounds of nationality of what was then Art. 7 of the EEC Treaty also includes indirect (hidden) discrimination. But, he also observed that clarity was lacking in that regard. Notably, he did not cite a single case as an example. In the present writer's analysis, the first[889] such case dates from 1980.

ii. Boussac

Boussac[890] concerned a matter of German civil procedure law regarding the type of proceedings available for the recovery of debts. After a revision in the law, it was no longer possible to use the so-called *Mahnverfahren*, an especially simple and expeditious summary procedure formerly applicable against a debtor established in Germany for debts expressed in foreign currency. Newly introduced data-processing techniques could only be used for debts expressed in the national currency. However, the law did allow for the use of the *Mahnverfahren* in cases involving debts expressed in foreign currency if they were subject to the Brussels Convention.[891] These rules barred Boussac, a French company, from using the *Mahnverfahren* when it tried to recover a debt expressed in French francs from Ms Gerstenmeier, a client living in Germany. Boussac claimed that these rules constituted covert discrimination on grounds of nationality, prohibited under Art. 7 of the EEC Treaty. In contrast, Germany argued that there was no 'actual discrimination', as the restriction stemmed from the need for adequate procedural organization. In its view, equal treatment was guaranteed by the fact that decisions of foreign courts were enforceable in Germany regardless of the currency at issue. The Commission believed there was no serious evidence of discrimination based on nationality as the rules 'do not in fact take into account the nationality of the parties but draw a distinction solely on the basis of objective criteria such as the debtor's residence and the currency in which the debt at issue is expressed' (*Boussac*, p. 3430 subs.). AG Mayras, agreeing with Boussac, explained that legislation of the kind at issue 'is clearly not a series of overtly, or to use another word, directly

---

888 application of the Treaty within the meaning of Art. 12 EC, that article must be read in conjunction with the provisions of the Treaty on citizenship of the Union'. More generally, see already O'Leary 1997; outside Art. 18 EC, e.g. *Ricordi* (Case C-360/00, [2002] *ECR* I-5089; concerning copyright).

888 Bleckman 1976, p. 477.

889 Some commentators mention much later decisions only, e.g. the Calliess & Ruffert Commentary 2002, n. 38 ad Art. 12(1) EC). On the other hand, the Geiger Commentary generally mentions *Sotgiu* which did not concern Art. 12 EC; Geiger Commentary 2000, n. 8 ad Art. 12(1) EC.

890 Case 22/80, [1980] *ECR* 3427.

891 Convention of 27 September 1968 on jurisdiction and enforcement of judgments in civil and commercial matters, *OJ* 1998 C 27/1 (meanwhile replaced by Regulation 44/2001/EC, *OJ* 2001 L 12/1, as amended).

discriminatory rules'. If there was any form of discrimination at all, it could only be indirect which he thought likely in the light of *Sotgiu*.[892] The AG further stated that '[w]ith regard to indirect and covert discrimination it seems to me in fact that account must also be taken of the practical effects of the rules which are criticized', and in this particular case, he considered such effects negligible and, therefore, legally irrelevant (*Boussac*, p. 3443 subs.). The Court, however, did not deal with his arguments,[893] simply stating that Art. 7 prohibits both overt and covert discrimination and repeating in this context the description of the latter phenomenon as expressed in *Sotgiu* (though, again, without explicitly citing that case). The Court then held that '[t]here is no doubt that a national law which subjects access to the courts to conditions relating to the currency in which debts are expressed might in fact place creditors established in the other Member States in a less favourable position than creditors established on national territory and thus constitute a barrier to trade in the common market which would principally affect the nationals of the other Member States' (*Boussac*, para. 9 and 10).

Like *Sea Fisheries*[894] and *Palermo-Toia*,[895] *Boussac* clearly speaks for itself: it confirms the applicability of the indirect discrimination approach in the specific context of Art. 12(1) EC and at the same time provides an illustrative application of that approach (e.g. Schockweiler,[896] the Mégret Commentary,[897] the von der Groeben & Schwarze Commentary).[898] If the decision is, nevertheless, special, this is because of the Court's approach to justification which will be discussed later.[899]

g. An interim conclusion (IV)

Sea Fisheries,[900] *Palermo-Toia*,[901] and *Boussac*[902] share a common feature in that in each the Court repeated its decisive statements made in the landmark case of *Sotgiu*[903] (though actually citing that case only in *Sea Fisheries*), including its description of the phenomenon of indirect discrimination as relating to 'all forms of discrimination which, by the application of other distinguishing criteria, lead in fact to the same result'. The three cases provide particularly clear illustrations of what indirect ('covert'

---

892   Case 152/73, [1974] *ECR* 153.
893   On *de minimis* arguments, see later in this part, A.IV.2.d.i.
894   Case 61/77, [1978] *ECR* 417.
895   Case 237/78, [1979] *ECR* 2645.
896   Schockweiler 1991, p. 6.
897   Mégret Commentary (as of 1972), p. 47 n. 68.
898   Von der Groeben & Schwarze Commentary 2004, n. 4 ad Art. 12 EC.
899   See later in this part, A.II.2.c.
900   Case 61/77, [1978] *ECR* 417.
901   Case 237/78, [1979] *ECR* 2645.
902   Case 22/80, [1980] *ECR* 3427.
903   Case 152/73, [1974] *ECR* 153.

or 'disguised') discrimination on grounds of nationality can mean in practice and in diverse contexts. Importantly, the three cases show that by the late 1970s the indirect discrimination approach as described in *Sotgiu* was firmly established in a number of core areas of EC economic law, in particular in the area of the free movement of persons.

h. Sex equality law outside staff law: Art. 119 of the EEC Treaty and the Equal Treatment Directives

i. Preliminary remarks

After *Boussac*,[904] the next two cases relevant to the development of the concept of indirect discrimination in EC law concern sex equality, more specifically Art. 119 of the EEC Treaty on equal pay for men and women. Unlike the Equal Treatment Directives concerning other employment issues that were adopted in the 1970s and 1980s,[905] neither Art. 119 of the Treaty nor the Equal Pay Directive[906] mention indirect discrimination (and neither do Art. 141(1) and (2) EC which now replace Art. 119).[907] The relevance of that concept in the context of equal pay is, therefore, entirely based on case law. The Court's decision in the *Jenkins*[908] case of 1981 is usually regarded as the starting point, but it should be recalled that first traces of a substantive notion of indirect sex discrimination already appeared in *Defrenne II*[909] in 1976. *Jenkins* is important because it was more specific and because it provided a first application of the indirect discrimination approach in EC sex equality law outside of Staff law. Significantly, the fact that *Jenkins* lacked clarity explains why the later *Bilka*[910] case emerged as the landmark case of this area of law. Both cases involved disadvantageous treatment of part-time workers which has become the classic example of indirect sex discrimination. Below, they are discussed in turn.

ii. Jenkins: the case

Jenkins[911] concerned an employer, Kingsgate, who used to pay women employees at a lower rate than men but later switched to a pay practice based on working time. As

---

[904]   Case 22/80, [1980] *ECR* 3427.
[905]   See later in this section, under iv.
[906]   Directive 75/117/EEC, *OJ* 1975 L 45/19.
[907]   See, however, the definitions in Art. 2 of the proposed Recasting Directive; Proposal for a Directive on the implementation of the principle of equal opportunities and equal treatment of men and women in matters of employment and occupation, COM(2004) 279.
[908]   Case 96/80, [1981] *ECR* 911.
[909]   Case 43/75, [1976] *ECR* 455; discussed earlier in this part, A.I.3.
[910]   Case 170/84, [1986] *ECR* 1607.
[911]   Case 96/80, [1981] *ECR* 911.

a part-time worker, Ms Jenkins was paid 10% less than full-time workers performing
the same work. Faced with the accusation that this was discriminatory under EC law,
Kingsgate argued that the pay practice was based on considerations other than sex and,
further, that the practice was instituted for good business reasons (namely to
discourage absenteeism and ensure fuller use of machinery, thereby encouraging
greater productivity). Ms Jenkins, referring to the U.S. landmark case on disparate
impact, *Griggs v. Duke Power Co.*,[912] maintained that the prohibition of sex discrimination under EC law covered 'not merely practices which are intended to discriminate
but equally those which are discriminatory in their effect'. Ms Jenkins also commented
on the terminology used in U.S., UK[913] and EC law, pointing out that the American
term 'adverse impact' corresponded to the notion of 'indirect discrimination' as used
in U.K. legislation, and insisted that this notion should not be confused with the
'indirect and disguised discrimination' described by the Court in *Defrenne II*[914] as
falling outside the scope of the direct effect of Art. 119. Like Ms Jenkins, AG Warner
considered the Griggs approach appropriate, pointing out that it would accord with
a familiar line of authority of the Court, including, in particular, *Sotgiu.*[915] He argued
that there was no reason for applying a different approach in the context of sex discrimination (*Jenkins*, opinion of the AG, p. 935 subs.).

> Specifically, Ms Jenkins argued that the aim of Art. 119 would be frustrated by a pay practice
> effectively confining the equal pay principle to full-time workers. She pointed out that by
> far the majority of part-time workers in the Community were women and that in the United
> Kingdom in particular the proportion of women in part-time work was even greater than
> in the other Member States, due mainly to family obligations. Ms Jenkins drew a parallel
> to the U.S. Supreme Court's *Griggs* decision, maintaining that 'what must be prohibited
> are not merely practices which are intended to discriminate, but equally those which are
> discriminatory in their effect, irrespective of the intentions of their authors. [...T]he prin-
> ciple of equal pay is violated not only where an employer intends to discriminate against
> a woman on grounds of sex but also where the effect of his policy on pay is to discriminate
> against her on such grounds. If a condition or requirement which must be met in order
> to obtain equal pay for equal work operates so as to exclude women and cannot be shown
> to have a manifest relationship to the services involved, the application of such a condition
> or requirement must be considered to be contrary to the principle of equal pay.' (*Jenkins*,
> p. 915 and 917).

> AG Warner began by emphasising that 'Article 119 is concerned, and concerned only, with
> discrimination 'based on sex' and is not concerned with discrimination based on any other
> criterion'. He remarked that discrimination between full-time and part-time workers is not
> necessarily discrimination between men and women. The AG mentioned the case where

---

[912]   *Griggs v. Duke Power Co.*, 401 U.S. 424 (1971); see above Part 1, C.II.1.b.
[913]   See above Part 1, C.III.
[914]   Case 43/75, [1976] *ECR* 455.
[915]   Case 152/73, [1974] *ECR* 153.

the part-time workers are predominantly or exclusively men and where the same is true of the full-time workers. As far as the alleged discrimination on grounds of sex was concerned, the AG thought that the '*Griggs* approach' advocated by Ms Jenkins was correct, in spite of possible difficulties in monitoring it (a point also made by the Commission). He explained that '[i]t is the only approach that reconciles the need to prevent discrimination against women disguised as differentiation between full-time workers with the need to prevent injustice to an employer who differentiates between full-time and part-time workers for sound reasons unconnected with their sex'. The AG drew 'considerable comfort' from the fact that his conclusion accorded with the conclusions of the U.S. Supreme Court in such cases as *Griggs*. He added that he drew 'similar comfort from the fact that that conclusion accords with a familiar line of authority in this Court', referring notably to *Sotgiu* and concluded: 'I can see no reason for applying a different principle to sex discrimination.'

The Court agreed that in a case such as that of Ms Jenkins the difference in treatment, although presented as a difference based on weekly working hours, may in reality constitute an indirect way of reducing the level of pay of part-time workers because they are exclusively or predominantly women. The Court explained that it is decisive whether a considerably smaller percentage of women than of men perform the minimum number of weekly working hours required in order to be able to claim the full-time hourly rate of pay. In such cases, the inequality in pay is contrary to Article 119 of the Treaty unless it can be explained by factors other than discrimination based on sex (*Jenkins*, para. 13-15).

The Court began by recalling that the pay differences prohibited by Art. 119 of the Treaty are exclusively those based on the difference of the sex of the workers. It agreed that the fact that part-time work is paid at an hourly rate lower than pay for full-time work does not *per se* amount to prohibited discrimination. It then continued: '[...] if it is established that a considerably smaller percentage of women than of men perform the minimum number of weekly working hours required in order to be able to claim the full-time hourly rate of pay, the inequality in pay will be contrary to Article 119 of the Treaty where, regard being had to the difficulties encountered by women in arranging to work that minimum number of hours per week, the pay policy of the undertaking in question cannot be explained by factors other than discrimination based on sex. Where the hourly rate of pay differs according to whether the work is part-time or full-time it is for the national courts to decide in each individual case whether, regard being had to the facts of the case, its history and the employer's intention, a pay policy such as that which is at issue in the main proceedings although represented as a difference based on weekly working hours is or is not in reality discrimination based on the sex of the worker. The reply to the first three questions must therefore be that a difference in pay between full-time workers and part-time workers does not amount to discrimination prohibited by Article 119 of the Treaty unless it is in reality merely an indirect way of reducing the level of pay of part-time workers on the grounds that that group of workers is composed exclusively or predominantly of women.'

iii. Comments

Though the Court in *Jenkins* did not use the words *indirect, covert* or *disguised* discrimination, clearly it applied an indirect discrimination approach (e.g. the Mégret Commentary,[916] Ellis,[917] Blomeyer,[918] Stampe,[919] the von der Groeben & Schwarze Commentary,[920] O'Leary).[921] However, in spite of parallels with other areas of EC law – concerning discrimination both on grounds of sex (namely in the context of Staff law) and on grounds of nationality –, the Court did not refer to any EC law precedents.[922] Nor did it mention the U.S. case *Griggs v. Duke Power Co.*,[923] though some authors suspect that it was, nevertheless, inspired by that case (e.g. Kyriazis,[924] Burri).[925] As for the Court's description of indirect sex discrimination caused through the differentiation criterion of working time, it should be noted that it included the case both where the part-time workers are exclusively women (*mutatis mutandis,* the situation in *Ugliola*)[926] and where they are merely predominantly women (the situations in *Sotgiu*[927] and *Sabbatini*).[928] Importantly, the Court's statements in *Jenkins* contained an element that was missing in indirect discrimination cases from other areas of EC law, namely the possibility of explaining the contested measure with factors other than discrimination based on sex (this will be discussed later, in the context of objective justification).[929]

A further noteworthy element lies in the fact that in the context of indirect sex discrimination caused by reliance on working time the Court explicitly acknowledged 'the difficulties encountered by women in arranging to work that minimum number of hours per week'. As AG van Gerven later put it, in doing so the Court took 'account of an inequality stemming from a sociological phenomenon', namely the traditional division of roles among heterosexual couples (*Jackson and Cresswell*,[930] point 20 of the AG's opinion). Indeed, the problem underlying indirect sex discrimination in social law is often one of *structural discrimination*.[931] In the words of von Prondzynsky &

---

[916]   Mégret Commentary (as of 1972), p. 126, n. 54.
[917]   Ellis 1998, p. 112.
[918]   Blomeyer 1994, p. 63.
[919]   Stampe 2001, p. 92.
[920]   Von der Groeben & Schwarze Commentary 2004, n. 456 ad Art. 141 EC and Protocol no. 17.
[921]   O'Leary 2002, p. 143.
[922]   Nor did it otherwise place its approach in the broader context of EC law, such as the free movement of goods, mentioned by Norberg in the context of *Jenkins*. According to Norberg 2001, p. 73, *Jenkins* involved simply the application by the Court of the principles set up in *Cassis de Dijon* (Case 120/78, [1979] *ECR* 649) in a different context; see further above Part 1, B.V.1.b.ii.
[923]   *Griggs v. Duke Power Co.*, 401 U.S. 424 (1971).
[924]   Kyriazis 1990, p. 94.
[925]   Burri 2000, p. 115.
[926]   Case 15/69, [1969] *ECR* 363.
[927]   Case 152/73, [1974] *ECR* 153.
[928]   Case 20/71, [1972] *ECR* 345. – See further below, Part 3, A.II.2.
[929]   See later in this part, A.II.3.b.
[930]   Joined Cases C-63/91 and C-64/91, [1992] *ECR* I-4737.
[931]   On this term, see above Part 1, B.II.5.c.

Richards,[932] 'indirect discrimination is a structural problem, connected with the structures of the labour market and society'. Obviously, the 'substance prevails over form' approach which characterises the concept of indirect discrimination in EC law acquires special meaning in such a context. Against this background, academic writers sometimes argue that the concept of indirect discrimination in EC law should be seen as a means to actively combat the underlying structural discrimination (e.g. Ellis:[933] 'invented in order to cater for the situation of institutionalised discrimination'). However, it would seem that the link with structural discrimination was stronger in the U.S. Supreme Court's landmark case law on disparate impact, *Griggs v. Duke Power Co.*,[934] than in the Court of Justice's case law on indirect discrimination in EC social (sex equality) law in that the Supreme Court much more explicitly criticised the problems related to the underlying reasons for the indirect discrimination at issue.[935]

Not surprisingly, *Jenkins* was handed down after the adoption of the Second Equal Treatment Directive[936] with its first explicit prohibition of indirect sex discrimination. However, given the lack of a legal definition at that time, the Court's decision was all the more important as far as the *meaning of the concept* of indirect sex discrimination and *the modalities of its application* were concerned. In that regard, *Jenkins* was far from clear, to the point of being called 'enigmatic, to say the least' (Szyszczak)[937] and even 'totally ambiguous' (Barrett,[938] see also Kyriazis,[939] Rating).[940] First, the Court did not clarify the relationship between the indirect discrimination approach and the statements in *Defrenne II* on the reach of the direct effect of the equal pay principle. Arguments brought forward in the context of the later *Bilka*[941] case (which will be discussed in the following section) show that uncertainties persisted. Second, the Court did not give a *general* description of the phenomenon of indirect sex discrimination, comparable to that in *Sotgiu*[942] in the context of indirect discrimination on grounds of nationality. According to Rating,[943] the Court, in fact, carefully avoided such a definition. Blom[944] even thinks that the Court in *Jenkins* was rather hesitant in accepting the relevance of the prohibition of indirect discrimination in the context of the equal pay principle at all. Thirdly, academic commentators struggled to understand the Court's

---

932   Von Prondzynsky & Richards 1995, p. 122.
933   Ellis 1994 (Definition of Discrimination), p. 572, and Ellis 1998, pp. 122 and 186.
934   *Griggs v. Duke Power Co.*, 401 U.S. 424 (1971); see above Part 1, C.II.1.b.
935   The strong link with structural or institutional discrimination in the U.S. Supreme Court's case law has been emphasised by McCrudden 1982, pp. 329 subs.
936   Directive 76/207/EEC, *OJ* 1976, L 39/40 (in its original version).
937   Szyszczak 1981, p. 679.
938   Barrett 1981, p. 189.
939   Kyriazis 1990, pp. 94 subs.
940   Rating 1994, p. 66.
941   Case 170/84, [1986] *ECR* 1607.
942   Case 152/73, [1974] *ECR* 153.
943   Rating 1994, p. 66.
944   Blom 1992, p. 15.

reference to the employer's intent. Szyszczak[945] argued that if intent is relevant, 'the European Court of Justice has misunderstood the concept of indirect discrimination since the criterion of indirect discrimination is that intent is irrelevant – it is the *effects* which are important'. Others simply wondered what the Court could have meant by mentioning intent (e.g. Barrett,[946] Plender,[947] and Crisham).[948]

> Barrett saw two possible interpretations. One is that 'the difference between part-time and full-time working is capable of constituting a material difference, provided that the employer has a genuine business-related *motive* for making the distinction, other than the *desire* to discriminate against women' (emphasis added). Should this be correct, then the only purpose for establishing the adverse impact of the differential treatment of women would be to shift the burden of proof on the employer. The second interpretation according to Barrett was that the difference between part-time and full-time working is capable of constituting a material difference, but only if the employer proves that it is objectively necessary to achieve some business-related purpose. Plender suggested that the Court's reference to the employer's subjective intentions and to the objective justification for his or her conduct 'may, perhaps, be reconciled if it is observed that both elements may play a part in the shifting of the burden of proof in the course of trial before the national judge. An employer who has adopted a facially neutral criterion, which is discriminatory in effect, might be able to defend himself in an action based on Art. 119 by showing that his policy was objectively justified; but it might then be open to the employee to rebut the employer's case by showing that his subjective intent was discriminatory.'

In fact, when the *Jenkins* case returned to the national court, its president found the Court of Justice's ruling so unclear that he applied his own re-interpretation of national law, holding that unintentional indirect discrimination against part-time female workers was contrary to the British Equal Pay Act, even if (possibly) not unlawful under EC law (Barnard & Hepple).[949]

iii. *Bilka*: the case

Like *Jenkins*,[950] *Bilka*[951] involved lower pay for part-time work than for full-time work. The case concerned a supplementary occupational pension scheme[952] which allowed

---

[945]   Szyszczak 1981, p. 680.
[946]   Barrett 1981, pp. 177 and 184/185.
[947]   Plender 1982, pp. 650 subs.
[948]   Crisham 1981, p. 605.
[949]   Barnard & Hepple 1999, p. 401.
[950]   Case 96/80, [1981] *ECR* 911.
[951]   Case 170/84, [1986] *ECR* 1607.
[952]   Held by the Court to be covered by the term 'pay'; *Bilka* (para. 10 subs.). This approach would later play an important role in the *Barber* case (Case C-262/88, [1990] *ECR* I-1889) where the Court held that (contracted-out) occupational pensions concern pay and which eventually led to the revision of the Fourth Equal Treatment Directive (Directive 96/97/EC, *OJ* 1997 L 46/20, as amended).

participation by part-time employees only if they had worked full-time for at least 15 years out of a total period of 20 years. Bilka employed predominantly women, and more than 90% of its part-time work force were women. According to Ms Weber von Hartz, *Jenkins* implied that no distinction should be made between direct and indirect discrimination with regard to the illegality of a certain course of action. As had Ms Jenkins, she pointed to the societal function of part-time work. She further pointed out that such practices consolidate the traditional division of roles between men and women without making women economically independent. It is, she said, a manifestation of the conflict inherent in the situation faced by women: home and family on the one hand, employment on the other. The national court asked the Court of Justice explicitly whether a case like that of Ms Weber von Hartz involves indirect sex discrimination (*Bilka*, para. 8): 'May there be an infringement of Article 119 of the EEC Treaty in the form of 'indirect discrimination' where a department store which employs predominantly women excludes part-time employees from benefits under its occupational pension scheme although such exclusion affects disproportionately more women than men?'

The arguments made before the Court illustrate the *degree of insecurity* still existing at that time concerning the meaning of *Jenkins* and its relationship with *Defrenne II*.[953] The Government of the United Kingdom maintained that the application of Art. 119 to cases of indirect discrimination was excluded because of the issue of intent. In contrast, the Commission thought that the absence of discriminatory intent on the employer's part does not prevent a finding of indirect discrimination. Regarding the relationship with *Defrenne II*, the Commission thought that *Jenkins* seemed to add 'a distinction between discrimination which can be judicially identified without further assistance and discrimination which can be identified only by reference to more precise criteria laid down by Community or national law'. The Commission added that it considered the terms covert discrimination and indirect discrimination 'not particularly useful in defining the scope of the principles laid down by the Court in previous cases' (*Bilka*, point 11 subs. of the AG's opinion). Even AG Darmon seemed to struggle interpreting the national court's questions as asking 'in essence whether that judgment [meaning *Jenkins*] refers only to 'disguised' discrimination, which is thus intentional, or if it may also apply to 'indirect' discrimination, that is to say purely objective discrimination. In that case there would be discrimination where because of women's traditional family responsibilities they were *in fact* excluded from entitlement to benefits' (*Bilka*, point 4 of the AG's opinion). The terminological ambiguity at issue culminated in the AG's question whether 'the indirect discrimination described by the Bundesarbeitsgericht [is not] in fact direct discrimination within the meaning of the judgment in the second *Defrenne* case'.

---

[953]   Case 43/75, [1976] *ECR* 455.

In its judgment, the Court of Justice avoided the *Defrenne II* terminology, even when rephrasing the national court's question. According to the Court, the national court wished to learn 'whether a staff policy pursued by a department store company excluding part-time employees from an occupational pension scheme constitutes discrimination contrary to Art. 119 where that exclusion affects a far greater number of women than men' (*Bilka*, para. 24). In answering that question, the Court simply stated that the *Bilka* case was comparable to *Jenkins* and that, therefore, the conclusion reached there was also valid in the present case (*Bilka*, para. 28). It then proceeded to restate its general findings in *Jenkins*, though without mentioning the employer's intent (*Bilka*, para. 29-31).

> The Court held: 'If therefore, it should be found that a much lower proportion of women than of men work full time, the exclusion of part-time workers from the occupational pension scheme would be contrary to Article 119 of the Treaty where, taking into account the difficulties encountered by women workers in working full-time, that measure could not be explained by factors which exclude any discrimination on grounds of sex. However, if the undertaking is able to show that its pay practice may be explained by objectively justified factors unrelated to any discrimination on grounds of sex there is no breach of Article 119. The answer to the first question referred by the national court must therefore be that Article 119 of the EEC Treaty is infringed by a department store company which excludes part-time employees from its occupational pension scheme, where that exclusion affects a far greater number of women than men, unless the undertaking shows that the exclusion is based on objectively justified factors unrelated to any discrimination on grounds of sex.'

iv. Comments

Commentators interpreted the lack of any express[954] reference in *Bilka* to the employer's intent as confirming the irrelevance of that element, in line with the approach taken by the U.S. Supreme Court in *Griggs v. Duke Power Co.*[955] (Ellis,[956] with further references).[957] Thus, by clarifying *Jenkins*, *Bilka* quickly became *the landmark case* with regard to indirect sex discrimination. According to Rating,[958] the Court for the first time provided a definition of indirect sex discrimination in the true sense of

---

[954] Though according to Heide 1999, p. 397, *Bilka* 'explicitly acknowledged that no intention of discrimination was required'.

[955] *Griggs v. Duke Power Co.*, 401 U.S. 424 (1971). Here, Chief Justice Burger explained that 'good intent or absence of discriminatory intent does not redeem employment procedures or testing mechanisms that operate as 'built-in headwinds' for minority groups and are unrelated to measuring job capability'. However, as indicated earlier, this is true only with regard to statutory prohibitions against discrimination; see above Part 1, C.II.

[956] Ellis 1998, p. 114.

[957] As regards the relationship to the *Defrenne II* distinction, final clarification would be brought about through *Murphy* (Case 157/86, [1988] *ECR* 673), as mentioned earlier in this part, A.I.3.

[958] Rating 1994, p. 71.

the word. However, as far as the indirect discrimination formula's first part (the discrimination's indirect nature) is concerned[959] and except for the issue of the employer's intent, the differences between *Jenkins* and *Bilka* are insignificant. Neither of them provides a *general* definition of indirect sex discrimination. Rather, they give a description of what is meant in the context of the specific case of indirect sex discrimination caused through reliance on the criterion of working time. Also, both cases concerned only one very specific issue involving sex equality, namely equal pay.[960] Nevertheless, *Bilka* has been interpreted as stating a general test on indirect sex discrimination that has since been applied in the context of employment issues other than pay. In fact, this so-called 'Bilka test' has been restated only in more general terms in much later case law (*Seymour-Smith*).[961] Notably, in both cases the Court avoided an express reference to 'indirect discrimination', even though this term appeared in the national court's question in *Bilka* and even though the Court itself had already used it in the framework of Community Staff law.[962] Possibly, this avoidance of more explicit language was due to the confusion caused by the terminology used in *Defrenne II*[963] (as has already been noted, that issue was not clarified by *Bilka* but only through later case law). Finally, it should once again be recalled that both *Jenkins* and *Bilka* concerned EC sex equality legislation that did not provide for an explicit prohibition of indirect discrimination. Sex equality legislation other than concerning pay contains such explicit prohibitions. In such cases, the recognition of the concept of indirect discrimination as such is, obviously, far less spectacular (*Kirshammer-Hack*,[964] in the context of the Second Equal Treatment Directive in its original version,[965] concerning access to employment, vocational training and promotion, and working conditions; *Teuling*,[966] in the context of the Third Equal Treatment Directive,[967] concerning statutory social security; and *Jørgensen*,[968] in the context of the Fifth Equal Treatment Directive,[969] concerning self-employed women).

---

[959]   Objective justification will be discussed later in this part, II.3.

[960]   On the application of the concept of indirect discrimination in the even more specific context of cases involving unequal pay for work that is allegedly of equal value, see later in this part, A.IV.2.f.

[961]   *Seymour-Smith* (Case C-167/97, [1999] *ECR* I-623), para. 15; see later in this part, A.III.1.a.ii.

[962]   See later in this part, III.1.c.

[963]   Case 43/75, [1976] *ECR* 455; see earlier in this part, A.I.3.

[964]   Case C-189/91, [1993] *ECR* I-6185.

[965]   Directive 76/207/EEC, *OJ* 1976, L 39/40.

[966]   Case 30/85, [1987] *ECR* 2497.

[967]   Directive 79/7/EEC, *OJ* 1979 L 6/24.

[968]   Case C-226/98, [2000] *ECR* I-2447.

[969]   Directive 86/613/EEC, *OJ* 1986 L 359/56.

In the first[970] relevant case under the Second Equal Treatment Directive, *Kirshammer-Hack*, AG Darmon recommended explicitly that 'the Court should consider that its case-law on indirect discrimination on the basis of Article 119 extends to directives enacted in order to apply that provision. The same should therefore apply to Directive 76/207/EEC.' The Court agreed (*Kirshammer-Hack*, para. 22). In the area of social security, the first indirect discrimination case was *Teuling* where the Court held that it is 'clear from the very words of Art. 4 (1) that increases [meaning increases in the calculation of benefits under a social security scheme due in respect of a spouse or for dependents] are prohibited if they are directly or indirectly based on the sex of the beneficiary' (*Teuling*, para. 12; see further Ellis[971] and Whiteford).[972] *Jørgensen*, the first indirect discrimination case under the Fifth Equal Treatment Directive, was at the same time the first case ever to be decided by the Court in the framework of that Directive.

i. An interim conclusion (V)

In conclusion, after rather fleeting indications in *Defrenne II*[973] that may be relevant for present purposes, the Court in *Jenkins*[974] and *Bilka*[975] clearly confirmed that sex discrimination can be of an indirect nature in the sense that it can be caused through reliance on an apparently neutral differentiation ground. *Bilka* became the landmark case notably because it did not repeat the confusing reference to the employer's intent found in *Jenkins*. According to *Bilka*, indirect sex discrimination exists when a significantly lower proportion of women than of men work full time and if the measure cannot be explained by factors which exclude any discrimination on grounds of sex. This has been understood as implying a more general test regarding indirect sex discrimination (the 'Bilka test') which is not limited to the specific case of discrimination caused in the context of working time or of equal pay. In both *Jenkins* and *Bilka*, the Court avoided the expression 'indirect discrimination' perhaps due to the use of the same term in the different context of direct effect found in *Defrenne II*. Surprisingly, the Court in *Jenkins* did not refer to any EC legal precedents, whether they be drawn from Staff law (which also concerned sex discrimination) or from other areas such as free movement of workers. Neither did the Court mention the U.S. landmark case on disparate impact, *Griggs v. Duke Power Co.*[976] nor the UK concept of indirect discrimination with its early legal definition of indirect sex discrimination. While the

---

[970]   According to Fuchsloch 1995, p. 43, the first indirect discrimination case outside the area of equal pay was *Marshall I* (Case 152/84, [1986] *ECR* 723). However, that case concerned the dismissal of a woman upon her reaching the pension age which was set differently for men and women. This is an example of direct sex discrimination (*Marshall I*, para. 38).

[971]   Ellis 1998, pp. 272 subs. and 295.

[972]   Whiteford 1997, pp. 99 subs. and 115 subs.

[973]   Case 43/75, [1976] *ECR* 455.

[974]   Case 96/80, [1981] *ECR* 911.

[975]   Case 170/84, [1986] *ECR* 1607.

[976]   *Griggs v. Duke Power Co.*, 401 U.S. 424 (1971); see above Part 1, C.II.

Court, in substance, clearly built on earlier case law (at least as far as the recognition of the potentially indirect nature of the prohibited discrimination is concerned)[977] and most likely also was influenced by other legal orders, the wording of the *Jenkins* judgment gives the impression that the Court 'reinvented' the indirect discrimination approach in the context of EC sex equality law.

j. Free movement of services

i. Preliminary remarks

Compared to the complex development in the area of sex equality law, it is easier to identify the first decision reflecting an indirect discrimination approach in the law on free movement of services. This is clearly *Seco*,[978] a case decided in 1982. However, in terms of its factual situation this case is not a typical indirect discrimination case. As a preliminary point, it should be noted that there seems to be some uncertainty with regard to the *grounds leading to direct discrimination* in the area of the free movement of services. In the Treaty, reference to nationality is made in Art. 50 EC in the context of the right to equal treatment ('under the same conditions as are imposed by that State on its own nationals'), whilst residence is referred to in Art. 49 EC in the context of restrictions ('restrictions in respect of nationals of Member States who are established in a State of the Community other than that of the person for whom the services is intended').[979] In *Van Binsbergen*[980] (para. 10), the Court stated generally that '[t]he restrictions to be abolished [...] include all requirements imposed on the person providing the service by reason in particular of his nationality or of the fact that he does not habitually reside in the State where the service is provided, which do not apply to persons established within the national territory' (see also *Debauve*,[981] para. 13). In *Van Wesemael*[982] (para. 27) the Court spoke of 'all discrimination against the person providing the service by reason of his nationality or the fact that he is established in a Member State other than in which the service is to be provided' (see also the EFTA Court in *EFTA Surveillance Authority v Iceland*,[983] para. 28.)[984] More recently, in *Wolff*

---

[977] Again, the conceptually new element in *Jenkins* and *Bilka*, namely justification, will be discussed later in this part, II.3.b.

[978] Joined Cases 62/81 and 63/81, [1982] *ECR* 223.

[979] In contrast, Art. 54 EC, a transitional provision, mentions 'distinctions on grounds of nationality or residence'.

[980] Case 33/74, [1974] *ECR* 1299.

[981] Case 52/79, [1980] *ECR* 833.

[982] Joined Cases 110/78 and 111/78, [1979] *ECR* 35.

[983] Case E-1/03, [2003] *EFTA Court Reports* 143.

[984] According to the EFTA Court, Art. 36 EEA (which corresponds to Art. 49 EC) 'requires [...] the elimination of all discrimination based on nationality or place of residence'. In contrast, the Norberg, Hökborg, Johansson, Eliasson & Dedichem Commentary 1993, p. 448, mentions only discrimination on the basis of nationality.

& Müller[985] (para. 31, with further references), the Court held that according to settled case law, Art. 49 EC 'requires not only the elimination of all discrimination on grounds of *nationality* against providers of services who are established in another Member State' but also of restrictions in a wider sense. (Emphasis added.)

This issue is debated in academic writing. According to some, in the area of free movement of services the Treaty prohibits discrimination on grounds of both nationality and residence as direct discrimination (e.g. Wyatt & Dashwood,[986] the Mégret Commentary,[987] Garrone,[988] Martin,[989] Handoll,[990] Hintersteininger,[991] Jarass,[992] Plötscher,[993] O'Leary & Fernández Martín,[994] Barnard).[995] Some others mention nationality only when speaking about discrimination (e.g. the Calliess & Ruffert Commentary,[996] the Geiger Commentary,[997] Breitenmoser & Husheer,[998] Herdegen).[999] According to the von der Groeben & Schwarze Commentary,[1000] the wording of Art. 49 EC should be understood as referring to the provision's scope rather than to its substance (meaning that EU nationals of other Member States are entitled to the provision's legal protection only if they are resident in another Member States because, only then, is there the necessary international element). The present writer agrees with the logic of those who emphasise the differences between wordings of the provisions. Such a view explains why reliance on a residence criterion infringes Art. 49 but that this infringement can only be characterized either as indirect discrimination or as a restriction in a wider sense (Colin & Sinkondo).[1001] Accordingly, one may logically draw a parallel with the law on the freedom of establishment where reliance on the place of establishment of a company leads to direct discrimination (Art. 48 EC). Thus, the factual circumstances of a given case would determine whether the use of a residence criterion leads to direct discrimination (in the case of companies) or rather to indirect discrimination (in the case of natural persons).

---

[985] Case C-60/03, judgment of 12 October 2004, n.y.r.
[986] Wyatt & Dashwood 2000, p. at 474.
[987] Mégret Commentary (as of 1972), p. 65, n. 22.
[988] Garrone 1994, p. 437.
[989] Martin 1994, p. 96.
[990] Handoll 1995, para. 5:20.
[991] Hintersteininger 1999, p. 14.
[992] Jarass 2000 (Unified Approach), p. 145.
[993] Plötscher 2003, pp. 142 subs.
[994] O'Leary & Fernández Martín 2002, p. 164.
[995] Barnard 2004, p. 347.
[996] Calliess & Ruffert Commentary 2002, n. 36 ad Art. 50 EC.
[997] Geiger Commentary 2000, n. 9 ad Art. 50 EC.
[998] Breitenmoser & Husheer 2002, p. 455, n. 989.
[999] Herdegen 2003, p. 261, n. 324.
[1000] Von der Groeben & Schwarze Commentary 2004, n. 12 subs. ad Art. 49 EC.
[1001] Colin & Sinkondo 1993, p. 43.

ii. The *Seco* case

Seco[1002] concerned a Luxembourg law which allowed the employment of foreign nationals temporarily resident in Luxembourg only on the condition that the workers were insured under the national old age and health scheme. Whilst foreign workers were eligible for exemption from their share of insurance contributions in order to avoid double insurance, the same was not possible in relation to the employer's share and, thus, resulted in a double burden for the employer. The French companies Seco and Giral were faced with that difficulty when employing foreign workers in Luxembourg who were already insured in France. They claimed that they were 'discriminated against, at least indirectly, owing to the cumulative application of two bodies of social security legislation' (*Seco*, p. 228). The Commission agreed that the situation involved discrimination, though apparently based on a rather broad understanding of that concept which included all restrictions, even if applied irrespective of nationality. In contrast, AG VerLoren van Themaat, though first considering discrimination in substance, thought that a case such as *Seco* involved a '*de facto* restriction' (*Seco*, p. 231 and 242 subs.).

> The Commission considered that Art. 59 of the Treaty 'entails an outright prohibition of all discrimination against a supplier of services based on his nationality or on the fact that he is established in a Member State other than that in which the service is provided. It provides for the abolition of all requirements imposed on the supplier of services which are likely to prohibit or otherwise hinder his activities. Only exceptionally and in the case of certain services of a special nature may a Member State impose on the [service] supplier certain specific requirements based on the public interest and applying to all persons established in that State, provided that the reason for those requirements is the application of professional trade rules justified by the public interest and applying to all persons established in the State. [... E]ven if the restriction imposed arises from a provision which applies irrespective of nationality, it is a form of discrimination which is prohibited under Article 59 of the Treaty.'
>
> AG VerLoren van Themaat explained that, given the identical treatment of domestic and foreign employers, there was no question of any 'discrimination in form' and then proceeded to examine the case from the perspective of 'discrimination in substance stemming from the equal treatment of situations which are not in fact the same'. However, in the AG's analysis, the case at hand did not in fact involve this type of discrimination but rather 'a *de facto* restriction on the provision of services due to the double payment of contributions', in the sense of 'provisions or practices which, in respect of foreign nationals only, "make the provision of services more costly through taxation or other financial burdens" as referred to in Section A (e) of Title III of the General Programme'. According to the AG, this type of restriction could 'be regarded as prohibited on the basis of the rationale of the aforesaid provision of the General Programme'.

[1002]   Joined Cases 62/81 and 63/81, [1982] *ECR* 223.

It would seem that, in form, the Court agreed with the two companies but, in essence, also with the Commission. It recalled the prohibition of indirect (covert) discrimination as based on earlier case law (though without explicitly referring to any precedent) and held that rules of the type at issue lead to such discrimination because employers established in other Member States had to bear a heavier burden than did domestic employers (*Seco*, para. 8 and 9).

> The Court stated: 'Thus [Arts. 59 and 60 of the EEC Treaty, now Arts. 49 and 50 EC] prohibit not only overt discrimination based on nationality of the person providing a service but also all forms of covert discrimination which, although based on criteria which appear to be neutral, in practice lead to the same result. Such is the case with national legislation of the kind in question when the obligation to pay the employer's share of social security contributions imposed on persons providing services within the national territory is extended to employers established in another Member State who are already liable under the legislation of that State for similar contributions in respect of the same workers and the same periods of employment. In such a case the legislation of the State in which the service is provided proves in economic terms to be more onerous for employers established in another Member State, who in fact have to bear a heavier burden than those established within the national territory.'

iii. Comments

Given its explicit wording, not surprisingly *Seco* is frequently cited as the Court's first indirect discrimination ruling in the area of free movement of services (e.g. the Mégret[1003] and Calliess & Ruffert[1004] Commentaries; Martin).[1005] However, this case presents an unusual fact pattern. The problems complained of in *Seco* resulted from the fact that foreign employers were subject to two legal orders which made the Luxembourg requirements more burdensome for foreign employers than for national employers. The issue, therefore, involves double burdens caused through double regulation. This differs from traditional indirect discrimination cases where the groups to be compared are subject only to one regime, for instance as in *Rush Portuguesa*[1006] – a case that is interesting for present purposes because, like *Seco*, it concerned the employment by a company for the purposes of the provision of services in another Member State.

> *Rush Portuguesa* involved a subcontract entered into between a Portuguese company and a French company to carry out certain tasks involved in the construction of a railway line in France. Having brought Portuguese workers to France, the Portuguese company

---

[1003] Mégret Commentary (as of 1972), p. 66, n. 23.
[1004] Calliess & Ruffert Commentary 2002, n. 37 ad Art. 50 EC.
[1005] Martin 1994, p. 97.
[1006] Case C-113/89, [1990] I-1417.

confronted French legal requirements that foreign workers be recruited only through a French office and that such workers possess French work permits.[1007] AG van Gerven emphasized the fact that this matter did not involve double regulation (point 11 of the AG's opinion). Although the Court's finding of (indirect) discrimination makes perfect sense in such a framework, it has been severely criticized by Rodière[1008] ('motifs inadmissibles', 'on pense rêver').

The Court's explanations for its finding of indirect discrimination in *Seco* are noteworthy. As Timmermans[1009] observes, the Court relied on a somewhat *different definition* of indirect discrimination than in its earlier case law. In *Sotgiu*,[1010] it spoke of reliance on 'other criteria of differentiation', whereas in *Seco* it referred only to 'criteria which appear to be neutral' without mentioning a difference in treatment. One might indeed argue that *Seco* did not involve different treatment in a strict sense: there was undeniably equal treatment under the Luxembourg law alone but a different and unequal effect on nationals and foreigners resulted solely due to the added impact of the legal order of another Member State which also regulated the matter. This might explain why the Court used a slightly modified definition of indirect discrimination: it did not apply the traditional test (negative effect *predominantly* for foreigners) but simply stated that the application of the Luxembourg legislation to foreign employers (quite independent of their number) proved 'more onerous in economic terms' because they 'in fact had to bear a heavier burden'. In substance, this would seem to correspond to the broad definition of discrimination relied on by the Commission.

Two plausible lines of reasoning can help make better sense of *Seco* which is certainly not a typical indirect discrimination case. First, double burden cases typically involve a *difference in situation*: whilst domestic companies are merely subject to one legal order, foreign companies may be subject to two legal orders. Seen in this way, AG VerLoren van Themaat's examination of the case in terms of discrimination in substance[1011] makes good sense (see also Voogsgeerd).[1012] Following a similar line of reasoning, Timmermans[1013] suggests that *Seco* be viewed as a case involving equal treatment of unequals. In his view, the decision to examine the case in the framework of indirect discrimination relied on a matter of terminology rather than of substance. The second plausible explanation involves viewing *Seco* in the context of the concept

---

[1007] In this case, the fact that the legal position of the *employers as service providers* was at issue, and not that of their employees, was of particular relevance because the case occurred at a time when, due to the accession of Portugal to the EEC, the Community rules on free movement of services were in full force whilst the applicability of the rules on free movement of workers had been delayed until 1 January 1993; compare Gormley 1992, p. 67.

[1008] Rodière 1990, p. 637.

[1009] Timmermans 1983, p. 318.

[1010] Case 152/73, [1974] *ECR* 153.

[1011] See above Part 1, B.III.5.d.

[1012] Voogsgeerd 2000, p. 70.

[1013] Timmermans 1982, pp. 317/318.

of *restrictions in a wider sense*,[1014] as was apparently suggested by AG VerLoren van
Themaat's reference to 'a *de facto* restriction' in the context of the General Programme
on services.[1015] Indeed, the Court itself has since repeatedly referred to *Seco* in that
context. In addition, the Court no longer applies the indirect discrimination approach
in double regulation cases. It will be argued later in this study that this change may
be related to the Court's (more general) statement that difficulties arising from the
legal regime in *another* Member State shall not be deemed as leading to discrimination.[1016] More importantly, such a reading also indicates that the Court has not pursued the somewhat broader definition of indirect discrimination that appears to flow
from *Seco*.

k. Transport law

i. Preliminary remarks

Though by their nature transport services are indeed services within the meaning of
the Treaty, nonetheless transport services are excluded from the application of the
Treaty's general rules on services by virtue of Art. 51(1) EC. Thus, free movement in
this area must be ensured through secondary legislation based on the special title on
transport (Arts. 70 subs. EC). This title contains several rather specific provisions
relating to discrimination (e.g. Arts. 72, 75(1) and 76 EC). Unlike the Treaty title on
agriculture,[1017] the transport title does not contain any *general* reference to non-
discrimination. Thus, such equality and can be found only *in the specific secondary
legislation* adopted for the various sub-fields of transport (road, rail and inland
waterway, based on Art. 71 EC, as well as air and maritime transport, based on Art.
80(2) EC). Such legislation was not adopted for a long time (see the famous *Transport
Policy* ruling of 1985),[1018] during which findings of legally prohibited discrimina

---

[1014] See above Part 1, B.IV.

[1015] General Programme for the abolition of restrictions on freedom to provide services; *OJ* English
Special Edition, Second Series, IX, p. 3.

[1016] See below Part 3, B.IV.2.

[1017] See earlier in this part, A.I.4.d.

[1018] Case 13/83, [1985] *ECR* 1513. Even though the Commission had presented numerous proposals,
the Council adopted only minimal measures which failed to meet the requirements of the Common
Market. The European Parliament repeatedly called upon the Council in this context, but to no avail.
Eventually, Parliament brought an action for failure to act which led to the *Transport Policy* ruling.
In this judgment, the Court acknowledged the absence of a Common Transport Policy, but refused
to accept the Dutch Government's argument that, in such circumstances, the Treaty's general
provisions on free movement of services became directly effective upon the expiry of the transitional
period as well as for the area of transport (*Transport Policy*, para. 59-63.) Instead, the Court upheld
the Parliament's view that the Council was obliged to act by adopting legislation providing for the
freedom to provide services; its discretion in setting up the Common Transport Policy concerned
only the means employed to obtain the prescribed result. The Court therefore found that the Council
had failed to fulfil its obligations under the Treaty (*Transport Policy*, para. 49-51 and 64-68). It is

tion were not possible despite the fact that factual discriminations undeniably existed, as already noted.[1019] As in the area of sex equality,[1020] early non-discrimination provisions in transport law did not mention *indirect* discrimination, and only later was explicit legislation adopted in that regard (e.g. Art. 6(3) of Regulation 3118/93 on road *cabotage* (goods),[1021] Art. 7(b) of Directive 93/89 on road taxes,[1022] as applied in the *Brenner Maut*[1023] case). In the absence of such later and explicit provisions, the concept of indirect discrimination had to be introduced through the Court's case law.

ii. *Corsica Ferries Italia*: the case

The first relevant case, *Corsica Ferries Italia*,[1024] was decided under Regulation 4055/86[1025] whose Art. 1(1) prohibits discrimination on grounds of nationality in the field of maritime transport. The case concerned charges to be paid by operators of ships for piloting services for entry into the port of Genoa. Such charges differed depending upon whether or not the vessel was operated by an undertaking authorized to engage in maritime *cabotage* (that is, in transport between ports located within the same country). Under Italian law, only vessels flying the Italian flag were able to obtain

---

only after this judgment which, in the words of Greaves 2000, p. 12, provided 'a gentle warning' (!), that the Council adopted the measures necessary to set up a Common Transport policy providing for the principle of free movement of services in this field. – In the area of freedom of establishment, the Court was willing to find direct applicability of the Treaty's non-discrimination provision (*Reyners*, Case 2/74, [1974] *ECR* 631, para. 25/26). The difference lies in the fact that there is no such substantive provision in the transport title and consequently had to be introduced through the secondary legislation in question.

[1019] See above Part 1, B.III.5.e.

[1020] See above Part 2, A.I.2.b and 4.h.

[1021] Regulation 3118/93/EEC, *OJ* 1993 L 279/1 (as amended). Art. 6(3) provides: 'The provisions referred to in paragraph 1 shall be applied to non-resident transport operators on the same conditions as those which that Member State imposes on its own nationals, so as to prevent any open or hidden discrimination on grounds of nationality or place of establishment.' The provisions referred to in this section are national provisions regarding rates and conditions in the area governing the transport contract, weights and dimensions of road vehicles, requirements relating to the carriage of certain categories of goods, in particular dangerous goods, perishable foodstuffs, live animals, driving and rest time and value added tax (VAT) on transport services.

[1022] Directive 93/89/EEC, *OJ* 1993 L 279/32 (no longer in force). Art. 7(b) provided that 'tolls and charges may not discriminate, directly or indirectly, on the grounds of the nationality of the haulier or of origin or destination of the vehicle'.

[1023] Case C-205/98, [2000] *ECR* I-7367. The case concerned a change in the Austrian tariff rules for the use of the Brenner motorway which were found to indirectly discriminate on grounds of nationality since, on the whole, the increases affected only vehicles with more than three axles, a category in which foreign-registered vehicles very largely predominated.

[1024] Case C-18/93, [1994] *ECR* I-1783.

[1025] Regulation 4055/86/EEC, *OJ* 1986, L 378/1 (as amended). Art. 1(1) provides: 'Freedom to provide maritime services between Member States and between Member States and third countries shall apply in respect of nationals of Member States who are established in a Member State other than that of the person for whom the services are intended.'

such permission. The company Corsica Ferries, though established under Italian law, operated ferries flying the Panamanian flag and therefore did not qualify for the lower tariffs. Before the Court of Justice, the Commission argued that the contested condition constitutes 'covert discrimination based on nationality' since, 'generally speaking, vessels flying the Italian flag belong to Italian nationals or companies, whilst nationals or companies of other Member States do not generally operate with vessels flying the Italian flag'. AG Van Gerven agreed – adding, however, that a finding of an infringement of Community law could also have been reached solely on the basis of the earlier *Corsica Ferries France I*[1026] decision (*Corsica Ferries Italia*, para. 24 of the AG's opinion). The Court explicitly found indirect discrimination on grounds of nationality (*Corsica Ferries Italia*, para. 32, 33 and 35).

> The Court noted that 'the system gives preferential treatment to vessels permitted to engage in maritime cabotage, in other words, those flying the Italian flag' and continued: 'Such a system indirectly discriminates between economic operators according to their nationality, since vessels flying the national flag are generally operated by national economic operators, whereas transport undertakings from other Member States as a rule do not operate ships registered in the State applying that system. [...] It follows that Article 1(1) of Regulation 4055/86 prohibits a Member State from applying different tariffs for identical piloting services, depending on whether or not an undertaking, even one from that Member State, which provides maritime transport services between that Member State and another Member State, operates a vessel authorized to engage in maritime cabotage, which is reserved to vessels flying the flag of that State.'

iii. Comments

Although *Corsica Ferries Italia* is the first indirect discrimination case both in the field of maritime transport and in Community transport law in general, academic comments often give the impression that it was neither surprising nor even particularly noteworthy. In fact, indirect discrimination is not even discussed in the case notes available to the present writer (Slot,[1027] X).[1028] Asked for an explanation, Slot stated that he thought the point too obvious to mention at the time. Such a comment might indicate that by the time when *Corsica Ferries Italia* was decided – which is comparatively late because of the slow development of the secondary law – the concept of indirect discrimination was so well established that its application in yet another area of Community law no longer attracted attention. In addition, explicit prohibitions of indirect discrimination were already established legislatively for other sub-areas of

---

[1026] Case C-49/89, [1989] *ECR* I-4441.
[1027] Slot 1995 (SEW) and (CML Rev).
[1028] X 1995, pp. 373/374.

transport law. In all, the concept of indirect discrimination was not altogether new even in EC transport law.

Other aspects of *Corsica Ferries Italia* are important to note. First, the discriminatory effect of the contested distinction resulted from *two cumulative factors:* 1) only vessels flying the Italian flag were allowed to engage in *cabotage* and 2) these vessels were usually operated by Italian firms (presumably because of perceived disadvantages of operating under the Italian flag in the eyes of foreign operators).[1029] In other words, such a situation might be termed 'doubly indirect discrimination'[1030] in that two steps were necessary in order to arrive at the finding of indirect discrimination on grounds of nationality. As such, the discrimination was more indirect – even more remote – than in 'ordinary' indirect discrimination cases. For the final finding, however, such a complicated set of factors made no difference in that 'doubly indirect discrimination' is just as prohibited as the 'ordinary', more simple kind (for a similar set of facts, compare *Brenner Maut*,[1031] para. 63). Secondly, as AG van Gerven argued, an indirect discrimination approach was *not necessary* in the *Corsica Ferries Italia* case in order to justify a finding of an infringement. Instead, it would have been possible to rely on the concept of 'discrimination between persons providing transport services between a port situated in the national territory and a port situated in another Member State of the Community and persons providing transport services between two ports situated in the national territory', as mentioned by the Court in *Corsica Ferries France I*[1032]

[1029] Again, the explanation given upon enquiry by Slot.

[1030] On another type of 'doubly indirect discrimination', see for example Christa Tobler, 'Die doppelt-indirekte Diskriminierung der erwerbstätigen Frau am Beispiel der Gartenzwerge' (unpublished text, on file with the author).

[1031] Case C-205/98, [2000] *ECR* I-7367. In this case, the Court stated that, 'for the purposes of establishing the existence of discrimination indirectly based on the nationality of hauliers, the registration of vehicles constitutes, as the rules on the carriage of goods by road in the European Union stand at present, a valid criterion in so far as vehicles registered in a Member State are, as a rule, operated by economic operators of the same Member State'. The Court in this context explicitly referred to *Corsica Ferries Italia* ('see, *mutatis mutandis*, in relation to vessels flying the national flag, the judgment in *Corsica Ferries,* cited above, paragraph 33').

[1032] Case C-49/89, [1989] *ECR* I-4441. This case concerned French rules on a charge to be borne by ship owners on all passengers of the ship when embarking or disembarking at a Corsica port. At the same time, in respect to services provided between Corsica and France, the charge was payable only upon embarkation. The company Corsica Ferries France claimed that this constituted 'discrimination on geographical grounds', arguing that '[t]he Treaty prohibits not merely discrimination on grounds of nationality [...], but all forms of discrimination based on the localization of an economic activity which hinder the establishment of a unified economic area' (*Corsica Ferries France I*, p. 4444). As was noted earlier, the Court did not find an infringement because Regulation 4055/86 had not yet entered into force. However, before presenting this conclusion, the Court stated that rules of the type at issue 'may constitute a restriction on freedom to provide services within the Community within the meaning of the first paragraph of Article 59 of the EEC Treaty in so far as it discriminates between persons providing transport services between a port situated in national territory and a port situated in another Member State of the Community and persons providing transport services between two ports situated in national territory' (*Corsica Ferries France I*, para. 7).

(para. 7). Apparently, the AG regarded the Italian rule as a form of discrimination *sui generis*, relevant in the specific context of maritime transport law and distinct from indirect discrimination on grounds of nationality. However, the Court in *Corsica Ferries Italia* did not opt for such a 'specific' approach but preferred to use the occasion in order to confirm the relevance of the concept of indirect discrimination in EC transport law.

Finally, it is noteworthy that the legal concept of indirect discrimination as reflected in *Corsica Ferries Italia* made its appearance in EC transport law *almost simultaneously with that of restrictions in a wider sense*.[1033] This latter approach, which was developed later than that of indirect discrimination, is reflected in *Corsica Ferries France II*,[1034] a case decided in the same year as *Corsica Ferries Italia*. Again, this coincidence appears to result from the slow development of EC transport law which brought non-discrimination provisions in existence only at a time when the concept of restrictions in a wider sense was equally well established in the broader framework of EC law. The dividing line between the two concepts will be discussed later in the study.[1035]

l. An interim conclusion (VI)

Both *Seco*[1036] and *Corsica Ferries Italia*[1037] concerned the free movement of services, the first as guaranteed under the Treaty's general rules and the second as provided for by secondary transport law. In both cases, the Court not only recognised that discrimination can be of an indirect nature but also unequivocally and explicitly spoke about indirect discrimination. In terms of principle, therefore, these cases are clear and simple. Given the prior history of the concept of indirect discrimination in EC law, these cases are not surprising. The slow development of the relevant secondary law explains why the concept was particularly late to emerge in EC transport law. In addition, the two cases are characterised by certain features related to their specific fact patterns. *Corsica Ferries Italia* involved *doubly indirect discrimination*, that is a situation where two subsequent and cumulative steps were necessary in order to identify the disparate effect of the measure. The Court's decision makes clear that for a finding of indirect discrimination it does not matter how remote the link with nationality is in terms of numbers of steps in identifying the effect of the contested measure, provided such a link can indeed be shown. *Seco*'s special feature lies in the fact that it is a *double regulation* case. A finding of indirect discrimination in such a context requires a broader understanding of the concept than is found in more traditional cases in that it does not require different treatment. *Seco*, indeed, reflects

---

[1033] See above Part 1, B.IV.
[1034] Case C-266/96, [1998] *ECR* I-3949.
[1035] See below Part 3, B.
[1036] Joined Cases 62/81 and 63/81, [1982] *ECR* 223.
[1037] Case C-18/93, [1994] *ECR* I-1783.

this broader understanding. However, that fact that more recent double regulation cases are consistently examined in the framework of the prohibition of restrictions in a wider sense, rather than that of indirect discrimination, indicates that the Court later abandoned the broader approach reflected in *Seco* and returned to the more traditional interpretation.

m. What about free movement of capital?

i. Preliminary remarks

The fact that *no (explicit) indirect discrimination decisions*[1038] have yet been issued concerning the area of free movement of capital (Barnard)[1039] explains why this study has yet to discuss this important area of EC law. According to some commentators, the Treaty rules on free movement of capital are constructed as mere prohibitions of restrictions (e.g. Plötscher).[1040] However, this is certainly not true with regard to the original version of these rules, and even today, although the Treaty no longer explicitly mentions discrimination as such, there are still elements which are related to discrimination. As for the *original Treaty provision,* Art. 67(1) of the EEC Treaty expressly prohibited both restrictions and discriminations (namely those based on the nationality or the place of residence of the parties and the place where the capital is invested).[1041] The von der Groeben & Schwarze Commentary[1042] explains that originally discrimination was expressly mentioned because of its importance as a specific form of the prohibited restrictions (also Schön,[1043] with further references). Due to its somewhat vague wording, Art. 67(1) was not by itself capable of have direct effect (*Casati,*[1044] para. 8 subs.). Thus, *secondary law* was necessary. The most important[1045] measure in that context was Directive 88/361,[1046] under whose Art. 1 the Member States were obliged to 'abolish restrictions on movements of capital taking place between persons resident in Member States'. This provision was held to be directly effective

---

[1038] See already above Part 1, A.I.4.b.

[1039] Barnard 2004, p. 467.

[1040] Plötscher 2003, p. 142, footnote 218.

[1041] Art. 67(1) provided: 'During the transitional period and to the extent necessary to ensure the proper functioning of the market, Member States shall progressively abolish between themselves all restrictions on the movement of capital belonging to persons resident in Member States and any discrimination based on the nationality or on the place of residences of the parties or on the place where such capital is invested.'

[1042] Von der Groeben & Schwarze Commentary 2004, n. 8 ad Vorbemerkungen Arts. 56-60 EC.

[1043] Schön 1997, p. at 755.

[1044] Case 203/80, [1981] *ECR* 2595,

[1045] Earlier Directives were the First and the Second Directive for the implementation of Article 67 of the Treaty, *OJ* English Special Edition 1959-1962, p. 49, and *OJ* English Special Edition 1963-1964, p. 5, respectively. They did not contain a provision directly prohibiting restrictions to free movement.

[1046] Directive 88/361/EEC, *OJ* 1988 L 178/5.

(*Bordessa*)[1047] and as such was of much greater practical value than was the very Treaty provision which it fleshed out. For present purposes, it is important to note that this Directive was *not framed in terms of discrimination* but only mentioned restrictions. Lelakis[1048] at the time stated that the Directive prohibited not only 'explicit restrictions' but also a host of 'measures of equivalent effect' – that is, not only measures completely blocking free movement but also those merely capable of hindering or making less attractive such movement. According to the Commission, discriminatory measures were intended to be covered (the Mégret Commentary).[1049]

Subsequently, the *Treaty of Maastricht* brought a new regime, replacing the original Treaty provisions with Arts. 73a-73h of the EC Treaty (effective as of 1 January 1994).[1050] Art. 73b, replacing the former Art. 67 (and remaining unchanged after the Amsterdam revision, except for its number which is now Art. 56 EC), provides for full freedom of movement (even in relation to third countries) and is directly effective (*Sanz de Lera*).[1051] Like Art. 1 of Directive 88/361, Art. 56 EC *does not mention discrimination* but merely restrictions.[1052] In academic writing, some authors do not mention discrimination at all (e.g. the Schwarze Commentary),[1053] whilst others explain that the prohibition against discrimination is automatically covered under the wider concept of general restrictions (e.g. the old edition of Kapteyn & VerLoren van Themaat,[1054] Schön,[1055] Hintersteininger).[1056] The Commission in a Communication of 1997 explicitly mentioned discriminatory and non-discriminatory restrictions (with regard to nationality).[1057]

However, for a long time the Court did not assess capital cases at all in terms of discrimination at all but rather spoke merely about restrictions.[1058] Explicit findings

---

[1047] Joined Cases C-358 and C-416/93, [1995] *ECR* I-361.
[1048] Lelakis 1991, p. 48.
[1049] Mégret Commentary (as of 1972), p. 175, n. 23.
[1050] That was the time of entry into the second phase of Economic and Monetary Union (Art. 109e(1) of the EC Treaty).
[1051] Joined Cases C-163/94, C-165/94 and C-250/94, [1995] *ECR* I-4821.
[1052] Discrimination is mentioned the context of derogations only, Art. 58(3) EC. To that extent, the situation is similar to that of free movement of goods under Art. 28 and 30 EC; see above Part 1, B.V.1.b.ii.
[1053] Schwarze Commentary 2000, n. 16 subs. ad Art. 56 EC.
[1054] Kapteyn & VerLoren van Themaat 1995, p. 442.
[1055] Schön 1997, p. 755.
[1056] Hintersteininger 1999, p. 75.
[1057] Communication of the Commission on certain legal aspects concerning intra-EU investment, *OJ* 1997 C 220/15. In point 3, it is stated: 'The relevant Treaty provisions governing the freedom of capital movements are enshrined in Articles 73b and ff. In particular, Article 73b of the Treaty provides that 'all restrictions on the movement of capital between Member States shall be prohibited`. This means that all restrictions, both those of a discriminatory (i.e. applied only to other EU investors) and those of a non-discriminatory character (i.e. applied to nationals and to other EU investors alike) are not allowed.'
[1058] Though according to Barnard 1004, p. 470, it was not until the *Golden Shares* cases (see above Part 1, A.4.b) that the Court fully embraced the formula for restrictions in a wider sense.

of discrimination are quite recent and inevitably involve instances of blatant *direct* discrimination on grounds of nationality (e.g. *Konle*,[1059] para. 23 and 24; *Albore*,[1060] para. 16 and 17; compare also *Commission v Portugal*,[1061] discussed earlier).

> *Konle* concerned Austrian legislation on the acquisition of buildings which treated Austrian and foreign nationals differently by imposing certain conditions only on foreign buyers. The Court held that the Austrian law 'which exempts only Austrian nationals from having to obtain authorization before acquiring a plot of land which is built on and thus from having to demonstrate, to that end, that the planned acquisition will not be used to establish a secondary residence, creates a discriminatory restriction against nationals of other Member States in respect of capital movements between Member States. Such discrimination is prohibited by Article 73b of the Treaty, unless it is justified on grounds permitted by the Treaty.'
>
> The situation in *Albore* was similar where the Court held that in so far as the Italian law exempts only Italian nationals from the requirement of obtaining a prior authorization to buy property in certain parts of the national territory, that law 'imposes on nationals of the other Member States a discriminatory restriction on capital movements between Member States [...]. Such discrimination is prohibited by Article 73b of the Treaty unless it is justified on grounds permitted by the Treaty.'

According to the Callies & Ruffert Commentary,[1062] cases involving infringements of the rules on free movement of capital usually also involve an element of *indirect discrimination*. However, thus far this term appears only in general statements by the Court regarding the duties of the Member States in the context of direct taxation (as relevant in the context of free movement of capital). Thus, in *Commission v France*[1063] (para. 21) the Court reiterated its well known statement that 'although direct taxation falls within the competence of the Member States, they must exercise that competence consistently with Community law and therefore avoid any overt or covert discrimination by reason of nationality' but, this time, in the context of free movement of capital (the Court refers to *De Groot*[1064] and *Schilling and Fleck-Schilling*,[1065] both concerning free movement of workers). Although the Court of Justice has thus far made no actual findings of indirect discrimination in the context of free movement of capital, nevertheless cases exist which, if analysed in the framework of discrimination, might be seen in that context. Below, two such examples are discussed, *Svensson and*

[1059]   Case C-302/97, [1999] *ECR* I-3099.
[1060]   Case C-423/98, [2000] *ECR* I-5965.
[1061]   Case C-367/98, [2002] *ECR* I-4731.
[1062]   Calliess & Ruffert Commentary 2002, n. 52 ad Art. 56 EC.
[1063]   Case C-334/02, judgment of 4 March 2004, n.y.r.
[1064]   Case C-385/00, [2002] *ECR* I-11819.
[1065]   Case C-209/01, judgment of 13 November 2003, n.y.r.

Gustavsson,[1066] decided under the old regime, and *Trummer and Mayer*,[1067] decided under the new regime.

ii.   Under the old regime: the example of *Svensson and Gustavsson*

Svensson and Gustavsson[1068] concerned the entitlement to a housing subsidy under Luxembourg law granted on the condition that the loan intended to finance the construction, acquisition or improvement of housing which was to benefit from the subsidy had been obtained from a credit institution approved in Luxembourg. AG Elmer considered that the case concerned the free movement of services rather than the free movement of capital. He spoke of national rules 'which involve an indirect difference in treatment between the competitive positions of domestic and foreign undertakings as a result of a requirement of establishment' (*Svensson and Gustavsson*, point 18 of the AG's opinion). The Court found an infringement under both sets of rules. In the context of services, the Court spoke of – unspecified – discrimination (*Svensson and Gustavsson*, para. 11), and in that of capital the Court merely referred to an obstacle 'liable to dissuade those concerned from approaching banks established in another Member State and therefore [to] constitute an obstacle to free movements of capital such as bank loans' (*Svensson and Gustavsson*, para. 10).

According to Hatzopoulos,[1069] the Court's finding of twin violations under two different areas of free movement law reflects the intention to ensure that the judgment remained valid for cases covered by the future regime on free movement of capital. (At the time when the preliminary reference in *Svensson and Gustavsson* was made, the entry into force of the Treaty of Maastricht was imminent). In addition, it can be argued that the Court made a deliberate choice in differentiating between the approaches for each of the two areas – finding an obstacle, rather than an instance of discrimination, in the context of free movement of capital – especially given that the same differentiation ground was at issue in both contexts. The reasons behind that choice remain unclear. As Sideed[1070] notes, the ruling contains hardly any legal analysis of Art. 1 of Directive 88/361.[1071] Given the nature of the differentiation ground at issue (namely obtaining the loan from a credit institution approved in Luxembourg – that is, the place where the capital is obtained), the Court's finding of discrimination on grounds of nationality in the context of free movement of *services* must be understood as relating to *indirect* discrimination. As a matter of logic, the same result could have

---

[1066]   Case C-484/93, [1995] *ECR* I-3955.
[1067]   Case C-222/97, [1999] *ECR* I-1661.
[1068]   Case C-484/93, [1995] *ECR* I-3955.
[1069]   Hatzopoulos 1996, p. 579.
[1070]   Sideek 1999, p. 84.
[1071]   Directive 88/361/EEC, *OJ* 1988 L 178/5. Art. 1 provided: 'Member States shall abolish restrictions on movements of capital taking place between persons resident in Member States'.

been expected had Directive 88/361 been applied in a discrimination framework: after all, the discriminatory grounds listed in Art. 67(1) of the EEC Treaty included nationality but did not specify the origin of capital.

Although the Court of Justice preferred not even to mention discrimination in *Svensson and Gustavsson* in the context of free movement of capital, interestingly its approach in the more recent EEA law case *Ospelt*[1072] differs. The case concerns Art. 40 EEA which can be compared to Art. 67(1) of the EEC Treaty as far as its wording is concerned in relation to the targeted infringements.[1073] In the *Ospelt* case, the Court expressly mentioned discrimination, though not *indirect* discrimination, the concept mentioned by AG Geelhoed (though in a different legal context from that of free movement of capital).[1074] Similarly, the EFTA Court in the earlier *Íslandsbanki-FBA*[1075] case mentioned discrimination in a general manner but did not specify indirect discrimination. As with *Svensson and Gustavsson*, it can be argued that this EEA law case can be analysed in terms of indirect discrimination on grounds of nationality.

> *Ospelt* involved an Austrian regional law for the trade in agricultural property containing a prior authorization requirement. In principle, the authorization was granted only if it was consistent with the preservation of an effective agricultural community and if the acquirer him- or herself cultivated the plot as part of an agricultural establishment and had his or her place of residence there. Ms Ospelt was refused authorization for selling land situated in Austria to a Family Foundation established in Liechtenstein. The national court's question concerned the interpretation of *EC law* (namely Arts. 12 EC and 56 EC subs.), but the Court of Justice examined the questions in the light of the relevant *EEA law* (which, again, corresponds to the old EC law regime). Indirect discrimination on the basis of nationality was examined by AG Geelhoed (*Ospelt*, points 127 and 128 of the AG's opinion) but the Court of Justice did not follow that line of reasoning. Rather, it began by stating that the EEA rules on free movement of capital prohibit 'restrictions on the movement of capital and discrimination' (*Ospelt*, para. 28) and then held that the national measures of the type in question amount to *prima facie* restrictions, and in the case of the authorization requirement possibly even to (direct) discrimination against nationals of the EFTA States participating in the EEA. Regarding the residence requirement in particular, the Court found that the law did not distinguish between Austrian nationals and foreigners. As a restriction, the Court found the residence requirement to be disproportionate (*Ospelt*, para. 37 subs.).

[1072] Case C-452/01, judgment of 23 September 2003, n.y.r.

[1073] Art. 40 EEA is similar to Art. 67(1) of the EEC Treaty but does not suffer from the limitations which prevented that provision from being directly effective. It provides: 'Within the framework of the provisions of this Agreement, there shall be no restrictions between the Contracting Parties on the movement of capital belonging to persons resident in EC Member States or EFTA States and no discrimination based on the nationality or on the place of residence of the parties or on the place where such capital is invested. Annex XII contains the provisions necessary to implement this Article.'

[1074] Concerning free movement of capital, see Schneider 2003, p. 385.

[1075] Case E-1/00, [2000-2001] *EFTA Court Reports* 8.

Íslandsbanki-FBA concerned Icelandic legislation under which State guarantees were available for banks, credit funds, financial institutions and the like in return for the payment of a guarantee fee. The fees payable on foreign loans amounted to 0,0625% every three months on the average outstanding principal of assessable obligations, while the guarantee fees payable on domestic loans were equal to 0,0375%. The EFTA Court noted that the principle of non-discrimination mentioned in Art. 4 EEA (which corresponds to Art. 12 EC) has been given effect in the field of free movement of capital by Art. 40 EEA (*Íslandsbanki-FBA*, para. 36). As for the case at hand, it found that '[n]ational provisions such as those at issue in the main proceedings provide for an inherent difference in the treatment of loans from foreign lenders and loans from domestic lenders' and that '[a]ll other terms being equal, that difference will render foreign loans more expensive than domestic ones. Such differentiated treatment may dissuade borrowers from approaching lenders established in another EEA State'. The Court concluded that provisions such as those at issue constitute a restriction on the free movement of capital (*Íslandsbanki-FBA*, para. 25 and 26).

iii. Under the new regime: *Trummer and Mayer*

Under the new regime, *Trummer and Mayer*[1076] serves as an example of a case that, if analysed in a framework of discrimination, can be deemed to involve indirect discrimination on grounds of nationality. The case concerned a rule allowing registration of a mortgage only if expressed in the national currency. The Court held because such a condition makes mortgages less attractive and potentially more expensive, it is a restriction in principle prohibited under Article 73b of the EC Treaty (*Trummer and Mayer*, para. 26-28).

Mr Mayer, a resident of Germany, sold Mr Trummer, a resident of Austria, a share in the ownership of a property in Austria for a sum denominated in German marks. The parties agreed that a mortgage should be created to secure the payment of the purchase price. The Austrian authorities allowed the registration of the sale but refused to register the agreement regarding the mortgage. Under Austrian law, such mortgages could be registered only if expressed in Austrian schillings or by reference to the price in gold. Having found that the creation of a mortgage to secure a debt payable in the currency of another Member State is covered by Art. 73(b) EC,[1077] the Court stated: 'The effect of national rules such as those at issue in the main proceedings is to weaken the link between the debt to be secured, payable in the currency of another Member State, and the mortgage, whose value may, as a result of subsequent currency exchange fluctuations, come to be lower than that of the debt to be secured. This can only reduce the effectiveness of such a security, and thus its

---

[1076]   Case C-222/97, [1999] *ECR* I-1661.

[1077]   The Court of Justice interpreted the transaction in question as a liquidation of an investment in real property within the meaning of the old Capital Directive (Directive 88/361/EEC, *OJ* 1988 L 178/5). Formally, this Directive was obsolete due to a newer version of the Treaty provisions. When the Court under the new regime still refers to this Directive, it is merely because the Treaty does not define the term capital; see Landsmeer 2000, pp. 198 subs.

attractiveness. Consequently, those rules are liable to dissuade the parties concerned from denominating a debt in the currency of another Member State, and may thus deprive them of a right which constitutes a component element of the free movement of capital and payments [...]. Furthermore, the rules at issue may well cause the contracting parties to incur additional costs, by requiring them, purely for the purposes of registering the mortgage, to value the debt in the national currency and, as the case may be, formally to record that currency conversion. In those circumstances, an obligation to have recourse to the national currency for the purposes of creating a mortgage must be regarded, in principle, as a restriction on the movement of capital within the meaning of Article 73b of the Treaty.'

As with *Svensson and Gustavsson*,[1078] it may be argued that the condition at issue in *Trummer and Mayer*, namely that the security must be expressed in the national currency, constitutes *prima facie* indirect discrimination on grounds of nationality. After all, foreign investors are more likely to wish to register mortgages expressed in a foreign currency than nationals of the Member State concerned. The Court, however, opted for a different approach. Rather than focusing on the question of whether there was unequal treatment, it simply pointed to the reduction of the attractiveness of the security to foreigners and spoke of a restriction. Landsmeer[1079] emphasises the broad reach of such an approach and notes that it might be explained by the fact that capital is much more sensitive to barriers and regulations than are other areas.

n. An interim conclusion (VII)

Apparently, in the context of the free movement of capital as interpreted by the Court of Justice, indirect discrimination thus far has remained *a merely theoretical notion*. As far as the old regime is concerned, an early edition of the GTE[1080] Commentary, noting that the differentiation grounds that are most relevant in practice were explicitly mentioned in the Treaty, indicates that indirect discrimination could not have been very relevant in practice, even had the Court applied a discrimination-based analysis. As it was, the Court generally preferred to find (unspecified) restrictions rather than discrimination. Meanwhile, cases such as *Konle*,[1081] *Albore*[1082] and *Commission v Portugal*[1083] confirm that the prohibition in Art. 56 EC against all restrictions of movement of capital includes the prohibition of discrimination on grounds of nationality and that the Court is ready to use the term at least in blatant cases. In the framework of EEA law – which corresponds to the old EC regime in that it explicitly mentions restrictions and discrimination –, both the EFTA Court and the Court of Justice have recognised the relevance of the concept of discrimination, though here, too, there are

---

[1078]   Case C-484/93, [1995] *ECR* I-3955.
[1079]   Landsmeer 2000, pp. 198 subs.
[1080]   GTE Commentary 1991, 1991, n. 16 ad Art. 67 of the EEC Treaty.
[1081]   Case C-302/97, [1999] I-3099.
[1082]   Case C-423/98, [2000] *ECR* I-5965.
[1083]   Case C-367/98, [2002] *ECR* I-4731.

as yet no explicit findings of *indirect* discrimination. Whether the express recognition of the concept of discrimination as such in the context of EC law will eventually bring about actual and explicit findings of indirect discrimination remains to be seen. Commenting on *Konle* and *Albore*, Peers[1084] has argued that it may be best to limit the discrimination-based approach to cases involving obvious instances of direct discrimination (on grounds of nationality). But even if so, it would most likely only be discrimination on grounds of *nationality*, to the exclusion of the other discriminatory grounds that were mentioned in Art. 67 of the EEC Treaty (namely the place of residence of the parties and the place where the capital is invested; compare, however, the Lenz & Borchardt Commentary).[1085] For situations where EC law on the free movement of capital does not mention any discriminatory grounds, the focus on discrimination on grounds of nationality can easily be explained by the existence of Art. 12 EC. This focus also explains why in a case like *Barbier*,[1086] which involved different treatment based on residence, the applicants as well as AG Mischo argued that there actually was *indirect* discrimination based on nationality (*Barbier*, point 71 of the AG's opinion; the Court found a restriction).

5. APPLICATION OF THE GENERAL RULES IN TWO SPECIFIC CONTEXTS

As part of this study's examination of the emergence of the first part of the indirect discrimination formula through various areas of EC law, the following sections will look at public procurement and direct taxation. Both areas are unusual in that neither is addressed by any specific Treaty titles or chapters. However, with regard to public procurement a substantial body of secondary law exists. The following discussion will show that the concept of indirect discrimination was introduced into both areas through *general* Treaty rules on free movement.

a. Public procurement

i. Preliminary remarks

In the framework of the substantial body of secondary law on public procurement that has been adopted over time,[1087] two types of Directives can be distinguished, namely

---

[1084] Peers 2002, p. 344.
[1085] According to the Lenz & Borchardt Commentary 2003, n. 17 ad Art. 56 EC, the prohibition of discrimination relates not only to nationality but also to the parties' residence and the place of investment.
[1086] Case C-364/01, judgment of 11 December 2003, n.y.r.
[1087] For a useful overview of the Directives presently in force, see http://europa.eu.int/comm/internal_market/publicprocurement/legislation_en.htm#current.

those aimed at the liberalization of the public procurement markets and those aimed at the coordination of the procedures for the award of public contracts. The *coordination Directives* (recently recast)[1088] apply only under certain conditions which notably include the financial value of the contract. They contain provisions on the suitability of potential contractors and on the quality of contracts under consideration during the selection process. Though there are no discrimination provisions in these Directives, the Court observed in *Concordia Bus*[1089] (para. 81) that 'the duty to observe the principle of equal treatment lies at the very heart of the public procurement directives, which are intended in particular to promote the development of effective competition in the fields to which they apply and which lay down criteria for the award of contracts which are intended to ensure such competition'[1090] (see also Sundberg-Weitman[1091] and AG Tesauro in his opinion on *Commission v Denmark*,[1092] point 17). Neither *liberalising Directives* 70/32[1093] nor 71/304[1094] explicitly mention discrimination, but they each contain a list of restrictions which has been described as covering 'a number of forms of (overt or not so overt) discrimination' (Winter).[1095] Thus, Art. 3(1)(c) of Directive 71/304 specifically mentions restrictions 'existing by reason of provisions or practices which, although applicable irrespective of nationality, nonetheless hinder exclusively or principally the professional trade or trade activities of nationals of other Member States'. In this context, Sundberg-Weitman[1096] speaks about indirect discrimination but given the provision's explicit wording that label is, in fact, not even necessary. Despite the availability of such grounds, the following discussion of the Court's case law will show that the legal concept of indirect discrimination was introduced into EC public procurement law on the basis not of secondary law but rather of the Treaty's general free movement provisions.

[1088] In March 2004, the European Parliament and the Council adopted two Directives on the coordination of the procedures for the award of public contracts which are intended to replace the various Directives now in existence, namely Directive 2004/17/EC, *OJ* 2004 L 134/1, and Directive 2004/18/EC, *OJ* 2004 L 134/114; see Knauff 2004 and Arrowsmith 2004. Recasting of this legislation is based on the Commission's initiative of Updating and simplifying the Community acquis, COM(2003) 71 (see the reference to public procurement in Annex 3), which in turn is based on the Commission's Better Regulation Initiative of the year 2002, COM(2002) 278.

[1089] Case C-513/99, *ECR* [2002] I-7213.

[1090] On the link between equality and competition, see above Part 1, B.II.4.

[1091] Sundberg-Weitman 1997, p. 223; see also Arrowsmith 2002, p. 3-24, at 3.

[1092] Case C-243/89, [1993] *ECR* I-3353.

[1093] Directive 70/32/EEC on the provision of goods to the State, to local authorities and other official bodies, *OJ* 1970 L 13/1.

[1094] Directive 71/304/EEC, *OJ* 1971 L 185/1.

[1095] Winter 1991, p. 744.

[1096] Sundberg-Weitman 1977, p. 724.

ii. *Beentjes*: the case

In the first[1097] relevant case, *Beentjes*,[1098] the plaintiff's tender was rejected because its
work force did not include a certain percentage of formerly long-term unemployed
persons who were subsequently employed through the regional employment office.
Beentjes complained of an infringement of the Coordination Directive on public works
(then Directive 71/305).[1099] Before the Court, indirect discrimination was mentioned
by the Italian Government which argued that the provisions of the Directive 'seek to
give undertakings in the Community equal access to the activities in question without
any overt or disguised discrimination' (*Beentjes*, p. 4642). The Court held that in
principle it was possible to require the employment of long-term unemployed persons
in a public procurement procedure.[1100] It added, however, that the Member States must
comply with all relevant provisions of Community law, in particular those on free
movement. In that context, the Court specifically pointed out that 'the obligation to
employ long-term unemployed persons could *inter alia* infringe the prohibition of
discrimination on grounds of nationality laid down in the second paragraph of Article
7 of the Treaty if it became apparent that such a condition could be satisfied only by
tenderers from the State concerned or indeed that tenderers from other Member States

---

[1097] According to Greenwood 1984, pp. 51/52, *Transporoute* (Case 76/81, [1982] *ECR* 417) is an even
earlier example. However, the Court did not mention discrimination in this case. The case concerned
a Belgian company that was not awarded a contract because it was not in possession of an establishment permit issued by the Luxembourg Government. The Court held that to make the provision
of services in one Member State conditional upon the possession of an establishment permit in the
host Member State would deprive Art. 59 of all useful effect, the purpose of this provision being
precisely to abolish restrictions on the freedom to provide services by persons who are not established
in the State in which the service is to be provided (*Transporoute*, para. 14). Further, as the case
involved a company, the differentiation criterion at issue (namely the requirement of an establishment
permit which meant that company had to be resident in Luxembourg) would have led to direct
discrimination (see above Part 2, A.I.4.j).

[1098] Case 31/87, [1988] *ECR* 4635.

[1099] Directive 71/305/EEC, *OJ* 1971 L 185/5 (no longer in force).

[1100] The Court indicated that this was due to the fact that the Directive does not lay down a uniform and
exhaustive body of Community rules. Following *Beentjes*, the place of acceptable social criteria in
the procurement procedure was not clear and much debated; e.g. Tobler 2000 (Women's Clauses),
pp. 624 subs., with further references. In *Commission v France* (Case C-225/98, [2000] *ECR* I-7445),
para. 49 subs., the Court specified that they are additional award criteria which effectively means
that award criteria can be based on considerations other than the lowest price or the 'most
economically advantageous offer' (which are the only elements mentioned in the Directive). See also
the interpretative communication of the Commission on the Community law applicable to public
procurement and the possibilities for integrating social considerations into public procurement,
COM(2001) 566 fin., further *Concordia Bus* (Case C-513/99, [2002] *ECR* I-7213) and *Wienstrom*
(Case C-448/01, judgment of 4 December 2003, n.y.r.). Bovis 2002, p. 1050, speaks of public
procurement as a policy instrument; see also Charro 2002, pp. 185 subs. In the new legislation, non-
economic criteria relating to the performance of the contract are explicitly mentioned; Art. 38 of
Directive 2004/17/EC, *OJ* 2004 L 134/1, and Art. 26 of Directive 2004/18/EC, *OJ* 2004 L 134/114;
see Odendahl 2004. More generally, McCrudden 2004.

would have difficulty in complying with it' (*Beentjes*, para. 30). In the judgment's operative part, the Court stated that '[t]he condition relating to the employment of long-term unemployed persons is compatible with the directive if it has no direct or indirect discriminatory effect on tenderers from other Member States of the Community'.

iii. Comments

The Court's statements clearly confirm the relevance of the concept of indirect discrimination in the area of public procurement (Lauria),[1101] though *not in the context of the specific secondary law on that subject* but rather in the context of the Treaty provisions on free movement and discrimination on grounds of nationality. The present writer would therefore disagree with Scott[1102] who claims that *Beentjes* 'is concerned with Member State compliance with a public procurement directive and not with the Treaty' (and questions why the case should be seen as an indirect discrimination case). Some academic writing pointed out that the liberalising Directive 71/304,[1103] whilst formally still in force, had lost all practical relevance due to the Court's recourse to directly effective Treaty rules (Pijnacker-Hordijk & Van der Bend,[1104] Winter).[1105] The reasons for this are unclear. Given that public procurement cases involve vertical relationships (namely between the State and enterprises), the lack of horizontal direct effect in the case of Directives[1106] cannot have been the reason.[1107] Again, for present purposes, the Court's reliance on the general rules is noteworthy because an indirect discrimination approach would not have been necessary in the context of the liberalising secondary legislation. Instead, the Court could simply have relied on the wording of Art. 3(1)(c) of Directive 71/304, without having to explain the specific nature of the infringement. With regard to the specific case of *Beentjes*, the Court left the actual application of the indirect discrimination approach to the national court (in contrast to the later *Data-processing contracts*[1108] case where the Court itself decided the issue). The majority of commentators agree that *Beentjes* indeed involved indirect discrimination on grounds of nationality. Arguing that there would be no discrimina-

---

[1101] Lauria 1998, p. 32.
[1102] Scott 2002, p. 282.
[1103] Directive 71/304/EEC, *OJ* 1971 L 185/1.
[1104] Pijnacker Hordijk & Van der Bend 1999, p. 16.
[1105] Winter 1991, p. 744.
[1106] See *Marshall I* (Case 152/84, [1986] *ECR* 723), para. 48, confirmed by *Faccini Dori* (Case C-91/92, [1994] *ECR* I-3325), para. 20.
[1107] Otherwise the situation could have been compared to that regarding Art. 141(1) and (2) EC and the Equal Pay Directive (Directive 75/117/EEC, *OJ* 1975 L 45/19) where the Court circumvented the problem caused by the lack of horizontal direct effect of the Directive by holding that the Directive did not add to the Treaty provision, see *Jenkins* (Case 96/80, [1981] *ECR* 911), para. 22.
[1108] Case C-3/88, [1989] *ECR* 4035; see earlier in this part, A.I.4.b.ii. Otherwise, this case reflects the same approach, namely reliance on Treaty provisions rather than on specific liberalising law.

tion if the unemployed persons could be registered in any other Member State,
Pijnacker Hordijk & Van de Bend[1109] point to the fact that the unemployed persons
had to be registered with a regional, and therefore a Dutch, unemployment office (see
also Van de Meent[1110] and Gormley,[1111] who speaks about 'a blatant local-grab
measure').[1112]

b. Direct (income) taxation

i. Preliminary remarks

A second example of a specific area where the concept of indirect discrimination
emerged through the application of general free movement rules is direct (income)
taxation. As in the case of public procurement, no Treaty title or chapter specifically
deals with this issue.[1113] The difference lies in the fact that there is little specific
secondary law in the field of direct taxation[1114] (Vanistendael,[1115] von Bahr).[1116] In areas
not covered by such legislation, the general rules on free movement are relevant insofar
as taxation measures have an impact in the field at issue (Wathelet).[1117] In the particular
context of income taxation of migrant workers and self-employed persons, the non-
discrimination principle is explicitly set out in Art. 7(2) of Regulation 1612/68[1118] (right
to equal treatment in relation to social and tax benefits). However, the concept of
indirect discrimination appeared only quite recently in the EC case law on direct taxation. Though in contrast to EC transport law,[1119] in the area of direct taxation legislative
development was not particularly slow and, thus, cannot explain the relatively late
appearance of this concept. Indeed, the free movement provisions had existed for

---

[1109] Pijnacker Hordijk & Van de Bend 1999, p. 1999, at 237.
[1110] Van de Meent 1995, p. 148. Though the author does not explicitly speak about indirect discrimination, it is clear from this statement that this is what he means.
[1111] Gormley 1992, p. 67.
[1112] In contrast, Fierstra 1990, p. 78, finds the issue difficult to decide. He argues that the analysis would
have to include the treatment both of the contractors and of their employees. Such an encompassing
analysis might raise complex questions relating to the nature of the infringement, similar to the
'avoidance' cases that will be discussed later; see below Part 3, B.IV.4.
[1113] Art. 293 EC is not a substantive provision; it simply obliges the Member States to enter into negotiations, in so far as necessary, concerning the problem of double taxation (among other matters).
[1114] Some harmonisation exists in particular in the field of company law; e.g. Directive 90/434/EEC, *OJ*
1990 L 225/1 (so-called (Taxation) Merger Directive; as amended), and Directive 90/435/EEC, *OJ*
1990 L 225/6 (so-called Parent-Subsidiary Directive, as amended). There is now also the Directive
2003/48, *OJ* 2003 L 157/38 (as amended). See generally Van Raad 2004, second volume.
[1115] Vanistendael 1994, pp. 293 subs.
[1116] Von Bahr 2003, p. 433.
[1117] Wathelet 2002, pp. 1 subs.
[1118] Regulation 1612/68/EEC, *OJ* English Special Edition 1968 L 257/2, p. 475 (as amended).
[1119] See earlier in this part, A.I.4.k.

decades before the first taxation case, *Avoir fiscal*,[1120] was decided by the Court of Justice in 1986. Given national politics and other sensitive factors, taxation was a particularly delicate matter (compare Wouters[1121] who warned against a mechanical application of the Court's free movement case law in the area of direct taxation).

> For present purposes, *Avoir fiscal* is notably *not an indirect* discrimination case, though at the time such a claim was argued by the Commission (*Avoir fiscal*, p. 289, para. 7 and 11) and though the case is mentioned in that context by Farmer.[1122] *Avoir fiscal* involved a residence criterion applied to companies (namely in the form of a national provision denying imputation credits to branches of foreign companies while such credits were granted to domestic companies). Van Raad[1123] at the time emphasised that because the case concerned companies, it raised the issue of direct discrimination. He referred to *Sotgiu*[1124] and suggested that a broadened interpretation of Art. 7 of the Treaty (now Art. 12 EC) applied to the income taxation of both aliens and non-residents 'would substantially expand the legal arsenal of a resident in one EC State who derives income from another EC State in which he is taxed less favourably than a resident of the latter State in otherwise equal circumstances'.

Below, two indirect discrimination rulings are discussed, namely *Biehl*[1125] and *Commerzbank*.[1126] Whilst the former concerned the differentiation ground of habitual residence, the latter involved fiscal or tax residence. These two distinct notions have to be carefully differentiated. Habitual residence refers to a person's place of residence in the ordinary sense of the word. In contrast, fiscal residence is a specific tax law term which denotes a person's residence as defined by tax law and which does not necessarily coincide with his or her habitual residence (Brian & McIntyre).[1127] The discussion will show that the Court's finding of indirect discrimination in the context of tax residence was perceived as far more revolutionary than its corresponding judgment regarding habitual residence.

ii. Habitual residence in *Biehl*: the case

The first indirect discrimination case in the area of direct taxation, *Biehl*,[1128] decided in 1990, concerned a Luxembourg rule according to which a worker was able to get a refund for over-deducted taxes only if he or she had been resident in Luxembourg

---

[1120] Case 270/83, [1986] *ECR* 273.
[1121] Wouters 1994, p. 183.
[1122] Farmer 1995, p. 310.
[1123] Van Raad 1986, pp. 41 and 46.
[1124] Case 152/73, [1974] *ECR* 153.
[1125] Case C-175/88, [1990] *ECR* I-1779.
[1126] Case C-330/91, [1993] *ECR* I-4017.
[1127] Brian & McIntyre 1995, pp. 21 subs.
[1128] Case C-175/88, [1990] *ECR* I-1779.

during an entire tax year. Mr Biehl, a German national who, after having worked for a number of years in Luxembourg, moved to Germany during the course of the tax year in question, argued that such a condition constitutes indirect ('covert') discrimination under what is now Art. 12(1) EC. The Commission agreed that there was discrimination but pointed to Art. 7(2) of Regulation 1612/68.[1129] AG Darmon noted that the formally equal application of a rule to all EU nationals 'does not totally rule out the possible existence of indirect or covert discrimination' (*Biehl*, point 3 of the AG's opinion). The Court found *prima facie* covert discrimination on grounds of nationality under Art. 7 of Regulation 1612/68; it explicitly referred to *Sotgiu*[1130] (*Biehl*, para. 14).

> Specifically, Mr Biehl's Luxembourg employer withheld sums from Mr Biehl's salary as income tax. When Mr Biehl moved back to Germany, the sum withheld exceeded the entire tax due to be paid for the entire year. Faced with the denial of a refund for the excess amount withheld based on the fact that he had left Luxembourg during the relevant tax year, Mr Biehl relied on the Treaty's general non-discrimination provision (now Art. 12(1) EC). He argued that even though the Luxembourg rule did not discriminate directly between taxpayers on grounds of nationality, it nevertheless constituted a covert form of discrimination since in fact it applied mainly to foreign nationals. The Court agreed. It pointed out that Art. 7 of Regulation 1612/68 prescribes equal treatment with respect to tax advantages because the principle of equal treatment of workers with regard to remuneration would be rendered ineffective if it could be undermined by discriminatory national provisions on income tax. Referring to *Sotgiu*, the Court then recalled that the rules regarding equality of treatment prohibit not only overt discrimination by reason of nationality but also all covert forms of discrimination which, by the application of other criteria of differentiation, lead to the same result. Regarding the residence criterion at issue, the Court held that '[e]ven though the criterion of permanent residence in the national territory [...] applies irrespective of the nationality of the taxpayer concerned, there is a risk that it will work in particular against taxpayers who are nationals of other Member States. It is often such persons who will in the course of the year leave the country or take up residence there.'

iii. Comments

The message of *Biehl* is clear: the prohibition against indirect discrimination is also applicable in the context of direct taxation. Further, the differentiation ground of habitual residence may lead to indirect discrimination on grounds of nationality. Notably, this is not a liberal or extensive interpretation of the term 'nationals' in the sense that it would include residents, as the term is used by Van Raad.[1131] Because

---

[1129]   Regulation 1612/68/EEC, *OJ* English Special Edition 1968 L 257/2, p. 475 (as amended).
[1130]   Case 152/73, [1974] *ECR* 153.
[1131]   Van Raad 1995, p. 194. Already in the context of the *Avoir fiscal* case, Van Raad 1986, p. 40, had asked 'whether the expression 'nationality', as employed in Article 7, also includes *residents*'.

nationality remains the decisive criterion, it would be more accurate to state that the term 'on grounds of' (nationality) is interpreted in an extensive way, in the sense that it includes not only formally discriminatory based on nationality but also measures in fact leading to such discrimination. Whether indirect discrimination exists in a particular case is not a matter of defining the term 'nationality' but rather depends on the specific circumstances of the case.[1132] With regard to the Court's findings in *Biehl*, Hein[1133] argues that for persons not familiar with EC case law it takes quite a bit of legal creativity ('bedarf es schon einiger jurisitischer Phantasie') to comprehend the Court's conclusion. In Hein's view, the decision confirms the Court's tendency to ensure the uniform application of EC law by limiting the Member States' competences. However, it should be remembered that by the time when *Biehl* was decided, the indirect discrimination approach was well established in EC case law and, as such, should not have caused surprise. Indeed, on the whole *Biehl* caused little uproar. Without further discussion, commentators often simply state that *Biehl* concerned indirect discrimination without discussing that concept any further (e.g. Farmer & Lyal,[1134] Hellebrekers,[1135] Müller,[1136] Terra & Wattel,[1137] Wouters).[1138] Easson[1139] is an exception; he emphasises the importance of finding indirect discrimination in the context of residence (though without making a distinction between habitual residence and tax residence). Finally, the generally slow development of EC tax law with respect to non-discrimination meant that, as in transport law,[1140] the concept of *indirect* discrimination emerged only a short time before that of restrictions in a wider sense.[1141]

iv. Fiscal or tax residence in *Commerzbank*: the case

The far more delicate criterion of fiscal or tax residence was at the centre of the later case *Commerzbank*[1142] which concerned British legislation granting a repayment

---

[1132]   The possibility of equating nationality with residence is also excluded by the possibility, recognised by the Court, that residents and non-residents are not comparable for tax law purposes; see later in this part, A.IV.4.c.
[1133]   Hein 1990, pp. 346-347.
[1134]   Farmer & Lyal 1994, p. 313.
[1135]   Hellebrekers 1991, p. 797.
[1136]   Müller 1992, p. 163.
[1137]   Terra & Wattel 2001, p. 48 subs.
[1138]   Wouters 1994, p. 200.
[1139]   Easson 1993, p. 82.
[1140]   See earlier in this part, A.I.4.k.
[1141]   Concerning this concept, see above Part 1, B.IV. For the area of taxation, see e.g. *Bachmann* (Case C-204/90, [1992] *ECR* I-249, para. 31-33). In this case, which was decided only two years after *Biehl*, the Court applied a restriction-based approach when answering questions related to the free movement of *services* (though not in the context of free movement of workers; see later in this part, A.II.4.b.i). Concerning the emergence of the restriction-based approach in the context of direct taxation, see also Lehner 2000, pp. 9 subs.
[1142]   Case C-330/91, [1993] *ECR* I-4017.

supplement on overpaid tax only to companies resident for tax purposes in Great Britain. The case concerned the refusal of the payment of interest on refunds to Commerzbank's UK branch, a permanent establishment engaged in granting loans to U.S. companies. AG Darmon explained that the criteria of residence and nationality overlap to a large extent and concluded that reliance on the differentiation criterion of tax residence amounted to indirect discrimination on grounds of nationality (*Commerzbank*, point. 46 subs. of the AG's opinion). The Court agreed and proceeded as it had in *Biehl* (*Commerzbank*, para. 14 and 15).

> The Court recalled that 'the rules regarding equality of treatment forbid not only overt discrimination by reason of nationality or, in the case of a company, its seat, but all covert forms of discrimination which, by the application of other criteria of differentiation, lead in fact to the same result'. It then continued: 'Although it applies independently of a company's seat, the use of the criterion of fiscal residence within national territory for the purposes of granting repayment supplement on overpaid tax is liable to work more particularly to the disadvantage of companies having their seat in other Member States. Indeed, it is most often those companies which are resident for tax purposes outside the territory of the Member State in question.'[1143]

v. Comments

The Court's reference in this case to indirect discrimination in the context of fiscal or tax residence was perceived as a far greater step than in *Biehl* (Wouters:[1144] 'then came the leap forward'; see also Keeling & Shipwright,[1145] Martín Jiménez).[1146] According to Wouters, the main contribution of the *Commerzbank* ruling 'undoubtedly lies in the fact that the Court confirms for the first time in the area of direct taxation that the use of the criterion of fiscal residence can amount to a covert form of discrimination', though some commentators did not agree at the time with this interpretation (e.g. Van Horzen,[1147] Thömmes & Kiblböck,[1148] Terra & Wattel).[1149] In hindsight,

---

[1143] An additional and interesting element of the case arises out of the fact that under the applicable double taxation Treaty, a company resident for tax purposes in the UK would not have qualified for a repayment of the tax at all. The UK government therefore considered that, rather than discrimination, the case actually involved preferential treatment of the Commerzbank company. Terra & Wattel 2001, p. 85.

[1144] Wouters 1994, p. 209.

[1145] Keeling & Shipwright 1995, p. 583.

[1146] Martín Jiménez 1999, p. 229.

[1147] Van Horzen 1993, p. 1880. According to this author, *Commerzbank* involved direct discrimination.

[1148] Thömmes & Kiblböck 1993. According to these authors, the question of whether the distinction between resident and non-resident tax payers could be maintained in the Common Market was still open after *Commerzbank*.

[1149] Terra & Wattel 2001, p. 86. These authors do not consider *Commerzbank* properly a tax case at all, but rather a case involving the payment of interest on government debts, similar to *Svensson and Gustavsson* (Case C-484/93, [1995] *ECR* I-3955) which was decided in the framework of free movement of capital and of services (see earlier in this part, A.I.4.m.ii).

clearly Wouters' analysis was correct. The importance assigned to the Court's ruling concerns the place of tax residence as a ground of differentiation in the context of international taxation, particularly in Europe. Unlike the USA, Mexico and the Philippines which each base their tax claims on the nationality of tax payers, European States rely on tax residence (Williams)[1150] and consider this 'a cornerstone of international taxation' (Wattel).[1151] As Vanistendael[1152] puts it: 'To anyone who is somewhat familiar with tax law, it is clear that the concept of *de facto* non-discrimination could very easily result in the disintegration of national tax systems.'[1153] Hatzopoulos[1154] goes so far as to speak about *an impossible cohabitation of national treatment and the criterion of fiscal residence*. The problem is aggravated by the fact that the OECD Model Tax Treaty,[1155] which supplies the model for most double taxation Treaties in Europe,[1156] only prohibits direct discrimination based on nationality. Vanistendael[1157] suggests that this situation may explain why the Court was willing later to mitigate the consequences of the prohibition against indirect discrimination on grounds of nationality in the area of direct taxation through a more generous approach to objective justification. This development will be discussed later.[1158] The Court's finding in *Schumacker*[1159] provided an additional way to reconcile the Treaty freedoms with international tax law,[1160] holding that residents and non-residents are not, as a rule, comparable (also to be discussed later).[1161] Obviously, where no comparability is available, a finding of indirect discrimination caused through different treatment of two persons or groups is excluded (see Wattel).[1162] In the area of free movement of capital this principle has been codified in Art. 58(1)(a) EC. Hatzopoulos[1163] speaks about 'a large loophole' but also points out that a combined use of the provisions on services together with those on capital (as in *Svensson and Gustavsson*)[1164] deprives the provision of any effect. As

---

[1150]   Williams 1994, p. 314.
[1151]   Wattel 1996, p. 223, and Wattel 1997, p. 424. See also AG Darmon, points 37 and 38 of his conclusions on the *Commerzbank* case (Case C-330/91, [1993] *ECR* I-4017) and AG Léger, points 35 subs. in his opinion on the *Schumacker* case (Case C-279/93, [1995] *ECR* I-225).
[1152]   Vanistendael 1994, pp. 310/311.
[1153]   On equality in European national tax laws, see Meussen 1999.
[1154]   Hatzopoulos 1995, p. 127.
[1155]   The text of the OECD Model Tax Convention on Income and Capital is available online at http://www.oecd.org/pdf/M00005000/M00005346.pdf.
[1156]   An example of a Treaty that does not follow that model (namely because it is too old) is the Double taxation Treaty concluded by Switzerland and the Netherlands (published in Switzerland in SR 0.672.963.61).
[1157]   Vanistendael 1994, p. 311.
[1158]   See below Part 3, A.II.2.b.ii.
[1159]   Case C-279/93, [1995] *ECR* I-225.
[1160]   See Wattel 1996.
[1161]   See later in this part, A.IV.4.b.i.
[1162]   Wattel 1996, pp. 229 subs.
[1163]   Hatzopoulos 1996, p. 579.
[1164]   Case C-484/93, [1995] *ECR* I-3955.

a result, the concept of indirect discrimination, slow to arrive in the area of direct taxation in the first place, is now rather limited in its actual application.

c. An interim conclusion (VIII)

In the specific areas of public procurement and direct taxation, there can be no doubts about the relevance of the legal concept of indirect discrimination. The Court's language is clear (covert discrimination, indirect discrimination), the definition given is that drawn from *Sotgiu*[1165] and, in at least the tax law cases, there are explicit references to this important precedent. However, it is *the specific context of its application* that is noteworthy, rather than the approach as such. In the case of public procurement, the Court applies the Treaty's general free movement rules where the concept of indirect discrimination is necessarily based on case law, rather than on secondary liberalising legislation which, in view of its wording, would not even require that label. In the case of direct taxation, the application of the indirect discrimination approach raises particular difficulties because of the central place of the criterion of fiscal residence in international taxation: if fiscal residence is the cornerstone of international taxation, the concept of indirect discrimination could jeopardize the national tax systems in relation to international taxation. However, later the Court itself substantially limited the consequences of the indirect discrimination approach in this context through judgments which stress comparability and justification and, thus, attempt to reconcile the Treaty freedoms with international tax law. Some have argued that from an EC point of view, it would be best to treat resident and non-resident taxpayers entirely equally by taxing them solely on the basis of an allocation of employment income and costs. Such treatment would require a change in the internationally accepted rule that taxation is based on residence, which in turn would require harmonization – an option that is not considered realistic at this point in time as far as the EU is concerned.[1166]

6.   SUMMARY AND CONCLUSION

These analyses of the Court's case law have thus far focused on the *first part* of the indirect discrimination formula. They have traced the recognition by the Court of the fact that *discrimination can be caused in an indirect way* in the sense of reliance on apparently neutral differentiation grounds which have disparate effects in terms of a prohibited ground. The development of the Court's case law in that regard can be summarised as follows:

[1165]   Case 152/73, [1974] *ECR* 153.
[1166]   Compare Peters & Snellaers 2001, p. 16.

Three early cases introduced the idea that discrimination can be of an indirect nature. In the first of these, *Ugliola*[1167] (decided in 1969, concerning free movement of workers and discrimination on grounds of nationality), the Court spoke of 'indirectly introducing discrimination'. However, the Court's approach appears not to have been surprising because of the obvious nature of the distinction in this particular case between nationals and foreigners in that the effect of the differentiation ground regarding the place of performance of military service was in fact the same as in the case of direct reliance on nationality. Whilst it did not acquire the importance of a landmark ruling, *Ugliola* remains important as the starting point of the development of the concept of indirect discrimination in EC law. In 1972, the Court used the same approach – though without referring to *Ugliola* – when it found sex discrimination in the staff case *Sabbatini*[1168] in relation to a differentiation based on a person's designation as head of a household as defined under EC Staff law in a sex-specific manner. Though the terminology used by the Court is less explicit than in *Ugliola*, the fact pattern of the *Sabbatini* case is more typical of indirect discrimination cases in that the persons benefiting from the differentiation were predominantly though not exclusively men and that those suffering from it predominantly though not exclusively women. The third of the foundational cases, *Sotgiu*[1169] (decided in 1974 in the context of free movement of workers), added the first *general definition* of the phenomenon of indirect discrimination (though only with regard to the formula's first part). The Court spoke about 'covert forms of discrimination' and described this notion as relating to 'all covert forms of discrimination which, by the application of other criteria of differentiation, lead in fact to the same result'. In addition, the case illustrates that the result need not in fact be precisely the same in that a merely *sufficiently disparate effect* is required. *Sotgiu* is the first case where a residence criterion was found to lead to *(prima facie)* indirect discrimination on grounds of nationality. Residence has remained the standard example in that context. Importantly, the Court in *Sotgiu* also explained that the reason for the new approach is the concern for the effectiveness of EC equality law. Not surprisingly, *Sotgiu* became the landmark case on indirect discrimination on grounds of nationality.

After *Sotgiu*, the Court went on to recognise the relevance of the concept of indirect discrimination to an ever broader range of fields and contexts. However, this development was preceded by *the confusing Defrenne II*[1170] *ruling* where the Court used the term 'indirect discrimination' in the context of the direct effect of the principle of equal pay for men and women. This use of terminology – direct effect only in the case of 'direct and overt discrimination', to the exclusion of 'indirect and disguised

---

[1167] Case 15/69, [1969] *ECR* 363.
[1168] Case 20/71, [1972] *ECR* 345.
[1169] Case 152/73, [1974] *ECR* 153.
[1170] Case 43/75, [1976] *ECR* 455.

discrimination' – was later abandoned. In addition, *Defrenne II* contains certain rather fleeting references to indirect discrimination in a substantive sense (which, however, tend to be overlooked in academic writing). In areas other than sex equality law, the first relevant case after *Sotgiu* concerned the *internal taxation of goods* (then Art. 95(1) of the EEC Treaty, now Art. 90 EC, prohibiting discrimination on grounds of the products' origin). In *Steinike & Weinlig*[1171] in 1977, the Court mentioned direct and indirect discrimination, though without explaining the concepts in detail. Actual instances of application are more difficult to find, particularly because the Court quite often did not identify the precise nature of the measure under consideration as either discriminatory (Art. 90(1) EC) or protective (Art. 90(2) EC). Arguably, *Marsala*[1172] serves as an example of indirect discrimination under Art. 90(1) EC. A similar picture emerges in relation to *freedom of establishment* (Art. 43 EC subs., prohibiting discrimination on grounds of nationality). A general remark on indirect discrimination can be found in *Thieffry*[1173] in 1977 but an actual application of the approach in a concrete case followed only much later, in *Data-processing contracts*.[1174]

1978 brought a particularly clear confirmation and application of the Court's case law concerning indirect discrimination in the field of *agriculture* (specifically, fisheries, based on Art. 2(1) of Regulation 101/76,[1175] prohibiting discrimination between vessels flying the flag of a Member State and registered in the Community territory, used in conjunction with what is now Art. 12(1) EC). In *Sea Fisheries*,[1176] the Court repeated the *Sotgiu* formula, this time expressly citing that decision as a precedent for the field of fisheries. The case, which concerned differentiation criteria concerning the length of fishing boats and the strength of their engines, also raised a question of the relationship between the concepts of indirect discrimination and discrimination in substance.

In *social security law,* the concept of indirect discrimination can be found both in the context of discrimination on grounds of sex and discrimination on grounds of nationality. The latter is relevant as a negative integration element in the framework of the Community's coordinating law which applies in the broader context of free movement of persons. A general reference to indirect discrimination in that particular context can be found as early as 1978, in *Kenny*.[1177] One year later, it was followed by a case illustrating its actual application, *Palermo-Toia*,[1178] which concerned the differentiation criterion of the nationality of a worker's children and illustrated its actual

---

[1171]   Case 78/76, [1977] *ECR* 595.
[1172]   Case 277/83, [1985] *ECR* 2049.
[1173]   Case 71/76, [1977] *ECR* 765.
[1174]   Case C-3/88, [1989] *ECR* 4035.
[1175]   Regulation 101/76/EEC, *OJ* 1976 L 20/19 (no longer in force).
[1176]   Case 61/77, [1978] *ECR* 417.
[1177]   Case 1/78, [1978] *ECR* 1489.
[1178]   Case 237/78, [1979] *ECR* 2645.

application. With regard to sex discrimination, the prohibition of indirect discrimination is explicitly stated in secondary social security law.

Kenny and *Sea Fisheries*, mentioned above, also concerned the *Treaty's general provision on discrimination on grounds of nationality* (originally Art. 7 of the EEC Treaty, then Art. 6 of the EC Treaty and now Art. 12 EC). In *Boussac*,[1179] a civil procedure case decided in 1980, the Court confirmed the indirect discrimination approach in the context of this provision alone. Given the wide reach of Art. 12(1) EC, *Boussac* opened a large field of application of the prohibition against indirect discrimination.

The first *sex discrimination* case where the concept of indirect discrimination was applied outside of Community Staff law was *Jenkins*,[1180] in 1981. It involved a differentiation ground, namely working time (worse treatment of part-time workers than full-time workers), that subsequently has acquired a similar importance in the context of sex discrimination as residence has in the context of discrimination on grounds of nationality. *Jenkins*, an equal pay case, was decided at a time when secondary law on other employment issues had already explicitly prohibited indirect sex discrimination. In this situation, the concept was not a surprising one, though its precise meaning was still open. In that regard, *Jenkins* caused confusion mainly for two reasons: 1) questions lingered with regard to the relationship of the indirect discrimination approach as applied in *Jenkins*, on the one hand, and the *Defrenne II*[1181] distinction between 'direct and overt discrimination' and 'indirect and disguised discrimination', on the other hand, 2) the Court's description of the modalities of the indirect discrimination approach notably referred to the employer's intent. Intent was no longer mentioned in *Bilka*[1182] which, by establishing the so-called Bilka test on indirect sex discrimination, became the general landmark case for the area of sex equality.

The Court's ruling in the *Seco* case[1183] in 1981 confirmed the relevance of the concept of indirect discrimination both in the context of *free movement of services* (Art. 49 EC subs.) and in that of discrimination on grounds of nationality. However, *Seco* itself was atypical since it concerned a situation of double regulation (an obligation of the employer to make social security payments in two countries for the persons providing services). In such cases, the problematic situation is not simply caused by the rules applicable in the host Member State but rather by their interplay with rules applicable in the State of origin as well. Subsequently, that type of case would be assessed in the light of the broader concept of restrictions in a wider sense rather than that of indirect discrimination. Indeed, in *Seco* the Court seems to have been able to find indirect discrimination only by relying on a slightly different definition than that

---

[1179] Case 22/80, [1980] *ECR* 3427.
[1180] Case 96/80, [1981] *ECR* 911.
[1181] Case 43/75, [1976] *ECR* 455.
[1182] Case 170/84, [1986] *ECR* 1607.
[1183] Joined Cases 62/81 and 63/81, [1982] *ECR* 223.

used previously. Examples of cases involving more typical factual situations followed
(e.g. *Data-processing contracts*).[1184] With regard to *transport services,* the general free
movement rules on services are not applicable, and the special Treaty rules (Arts. 70-80
EC) do not contain a general and directly applicable equality provision. Since
secondary law was particularly slow to develop, cases decided in an indirect discrimination framework appeared very late (and almost simultaneously with the concept of
restrictions in a wider sense). The first such case, *Corsica Ferries Italia*[1185] in 1994, concerned a differentiation based on the entitlement to *cabotage*. In this case, the identification of the discrimination found by the Court required a two-step approach ('doubly
indirect discrimination') because the discrimination was even more indirect and less
obvious than in ordinary cases. However, this factor made no difference in terms of
the unacceptability of the discrimination under EC law.

The concept of indirect discrimination was *also slow to emerge in the area of direct
taxation,* an area subject to particularly delicate national sensitivities where little
specific secondary EC law exists. Indirect discrimination appeared first in *Biehl*[1186] in
1990 and involved the criterion of habitual residence. However, the later *Commerzbank*[1187] decision attracted more attention due to the importance of the criterion of
tax residence which is a central pillar of international taxation in Europe. The Court
later substantially limited the consequences of its indirect discrimination case law, in
particular with regard to the issues of comparability and justification. As a consequence, the concept of indirect discrimination, slow to emerge in this area in the first
place, has proved to be of rather qualified importance in the field of direct taxation.
As in the case of direct taxation, statements concerning indirect discrimination in the
context of *public procurement* rest on the Treaty's general free movement provisions.
However, in such cases this is due not to the absence of specific secondary legislation
but rather to the Court's specific choice not to rely on explicitly worded secondary
law which would have rendered the label of indirect discrimination unnecessary
(Beentjes,[1188] *Data-processing contracts).*[1189]

Finally, the present writer was unable to find any indirect discrimination decisions
in the field of *free movement of capital,* even though discrimination was explicitly
mentioned in the original Treaty regime (Art. 67(1) of the EEC Treaty, concerning
nationality, the place of residence of the parties and the place where capital is invested)
and is claimed to be relevant as well to later law which no longer mentioned
discrimination (Directive 88/361,[1190] Art. 56(1) EC). In fact, for a long time the Court

---

[1184]   Case C-3/88, [1989] *ECR* 4035.
[1185]   Case C-18/93, [1994] *ECR* I-1783.
[1186]   Case C-175/88, [1990] *ECR* I-1779.
[1187]   Case C-330/91, [1993] *ECR* I-4017.
[1188]   Case 31/87, [1988] *ECR* 4635.
[1189]   Case C-3/88, [1989] *ECR* 4035.
[1190]   Directive 88/361/EEC, *OJ* 1988 L 178/5.

assessed free movement of capital cases in terms of restrictions, rather than in terms of discrimination, even under the original regime. Explicit findings of discrimination are rare and only quite recent; so far, they concern only blatant direct discrimination on grounds of nationality (*Konle*,[1191] *Albore*).[1192] It remains to be seen whether this new approach will eventually lead as well to explicit findings of indirect discrimination. Thus far, the concept appears only on the level of general references.

Thus, one may conclude that the first part of the indirect discrimination formula was *well established in most areas of EC law by the early 1980s*; direct taxation law and transport law are latecomers. Though the terminology varies, the basic idea behind the recognition of the concept of indirect discrimination is the same in each area of law and across the range of factual contexts discussed, namely that substance prevails over form. Discrimination not only can be caused through obvious and explicit reliance on prohibited discriminatory grounds but also through reliance on apparently neutral criteria with factually disparate effects in terms of prohibited discriminatory grounds. As the Court explained in *Sotgiu*, the concern underlying that approach is the effectiveness of the Community's equality law.

II. OBJECTIVE JUSTIFICATION

1. INTRODUCTORY REMARKS

Having examined the development through the Court's case law of the first part of the definition of indirect discrimination concerning the discrimination's indirect nature, the discussion now turns to the second part, *objective justification*, and how this element developed as part of the legal concept of indirect discrimination. In this context, the difference between objective justification and textual justification grounds must be recalled:[1193] whilst EC law in the context of particular prohibitions against discrimination may expressly provide for certain grounds for justification applicable even in cases of direct discrimination, the concept of indirect discrimination as it exists today *in itself* includes the much wider element of objective justification.[1194] The following search explores the Court's case law for specific statements which indicate an acceptance of that element. The most important findings will be as follows:

[1191]   Case C-302/97, [1999] *ECR* I-3099.
[1192]   Case C-423/98, [2000] *ECR* I-5965.
[1193]   On the question of the extent of this difference, see below Part 3, A.II.2.
[1194]   On the question of whether objective justification is truly a matter of justification in the proper sense of the word or rather of causation, as argued by an increasing number of academic writers, see later in this part, A.IV.3.e.

- The element of objective justification in a proper sense was not originally part of the legal concept of indirect discrimination (*Ugliola*,[1195] *Sabbatini*,[1196] *Sotgiu*).[1197]
- Over time, the Court began to use the term 'justification' in the context of objective differences (i.e. lack of comparability).
- Objective justification, proper, was first developed in the context of indirect sex discrimination (*Jenkins*,[1198] *Bilka*,[1199] *Rinner-Kühn*).[1200]
- Over time, this concept also appeared in the context of indirect discrimination on grounds of nationality, though first only in substance and then only much later as an explicit part of the indirect discrimination formula (*O'Flynn*).[1201]

2. EARLY DEVELOPMENTS

a. Ugliola and Sabbatini: a strict approach

i. Ugliola

No reference whatsoever to objective justification is found in *Ugliola*,[1202] the very first indirect discrimination case in EEC law (More).[1203] In fact, the Court mentioned 'indirectly introduced discrimination' only in the context of *express* grounds of derogation. Having observed that Art. 48 of the EEC Treaty (now Art. 39 EC) 'is subject to no reservations other than the restriction set out in paragraph (3) concerning public policy, public security and public health', the Court went on to state that apart from these restrictions 'Article 48 of the Treaty does not allow Member States to make any *exceptions to the equality of treatment* and protection required by the Treaty for all workers within the Community *by indirectly introducing discrimination* in favour of their own nationals alone based upon obligations for military service' (*Ugliola*, para. 3 and 6; emphasis added). In doing so, the Court seems to have treated indirect discrimination as a derogation from the principle of free movement. However, 'derogation' in this context must obviously be read as a 'breach of Art. 48', rather than as an additional form of justification similar in function to those of the provision's section 3. It is also noteworthy that although the German Government tried to justify the disregard of military service performed in another Member State for the purposes of

---

[1195] Case 15/69, [1969] *ECR* 363.
[1196] Case 20/71, [1972] *ECR* 345.
[1197] Case 152/73, [1974] *ECR* 153.
[1198] Case 96/80, [1981] *ECR* 911.
[1199] Case 170/84, [1986] *ECR* 1607.
[1200] Case 171/88, [1989] *ECR* 2743.
[1201] Case C-237/94, [1996] *ECR* I-2617.
[1202] Case 15/69, [1969] *ECR* 363, see earlier in this part, A.I.2.a.
[1203] More 1999, p. 526, footnote 57.

calculating a worker's seniority, it did not rely on extra-textual grounds but solely on the *express* ground of public security.[1204] In the face of such obvious discrimination, where only Germans were able to benefit from the contested rule, perhaps the very idea that some form of justification apart from that indicated in the Treaty could be argued did not even occur to anyone.

ii. *Sabbatini*

A somewhat broader discussion of the issue of justification can be found in *Sabbatini*.[1205] Although AG Roemer admitted that a system which relied on a sex-specifically defined status as head of household for the purposes of granting or withdrawing an expatriation allowance was not ideal, he considered it justified by reason of the pre-eminence granted to the husband at the time by the family law of most Member States, as well as justified by other economic, sociological and psychological considerations (*Sabbatini*, point 2, at p. 358 of the AG's opinion). However, the Court did not address this issue but rather applied the term justification in an entirely different context. The Court explained that '[t]he withdrawal of the allowance following the marriage of the recipient might be justified in cases in which this change in the family situation is such as to bring to an end the state of 'expatriation' which is the justification of the benefit in question' (*Sabbatini*, para. 11). This particular use of the term justification relates to the *very basis of the benefit* in question, namely the status of expatriation as the underlying reason for the expatriation allowance.[1206] Ultimately, the basis of a right concerns the comparability of the situations (here, of those who are expatriates to those who are not). In the framework of an Aristotelian understanding of equality, this is a precondition for equal treatment and thus must be distinguished from a situation where a person is, in principle, entitled to a benefit but may nonetheless be denied it on the basis of grounds which are held to be more important than the individual's entitlement. In all, the Court's approach to justification in *Sabbatini* contains no indication of an element of objective justification as it is understood today as part of the indirect discrimination formula.

[1204] AG Gand argued that even the express grounds could not be relied on because Art. 48(3) of the EEC Treaty referred to the right to enter a country and to take up employment only, but not to working conditions once employment had been taken up in an authorized manner. Much later, Martin still advocated such an interpretation, though he admits that the Court's case law goes further than that; Martin 1994, p. 48; Martin 1998, p. 599.

[1205] Case 20/71, [1972] *ECR* 345, see earlier in this part, A.I.2.b.

[1206] Compare Ms Sabbatini's argument that a difference in treatment is legally admissible only where there is a well-founded relationship between the criterion adopted and the difference between the rules; *Sabbatini*, p. 348.

b. Objective differences: Sotgiu (and later case law)

In the context of indirect discrimination on grounds of nationality, in the landmark case of *Sotgiu*[1207] the term 'objective justification' appears explicitly for the first time, invoked by both the Commission and AG Mayras. The Court, however, spoke only about objective *differences* that might prevent a finding of indirect discrimination when examining differences in the levels of separation allowances for workers employed away from home (*Sotgiu*, para. 12).

> Specifically, the Commission argued that, for purposes of determining the level of the allowance, reliance on a worker's place of residence at the time when he or she was recruited leads to concealed discrimination unless objectively justified. It explained that such justification might exist 'in a case in which, unlike workers recruited within the country, workers recruited abroad receive a separation allowance without having to find a home in the country of employment or to remove, and in which they receive the allowance at the lower rate for a practically unlimited period throughout the whole of their period of employment' (*Sotgiu*, p. 161). AG Mayras, too, mentioned the possibility that 'the difference in treatment is objectively justified by considerations of a non-discriminatory nature' (*Sotgiu*, opinion of the AG, p. 174). The Court stated that there would be no covert discrimination in the case of 'a separation allowance the conditions of allotment and rules for the payment of which took account of objective *differences* which the situation of workers may involve according to whether their residence, at the time [of] their taking up a given post, is within the territory of the State in question or abroad' (*Sotgiu*, para. 12; emphasis added). Regarding the case at hand, the Court acknowledged that there might be a difference in situation which 'may be a valid reason for differentiating between the amounts paid' (*Sotgiu*, para. 12).

Whilst according to AG Jacobs, it 'is clear from the *Sotgiu* judgment that covert discrimination is not prohibited by Article 38(2) if the difference in treatment is objectively justified' (*Scholz*,[1208] point 25 of the AG's opinion; in the same sense also Plötscher),[1209] others emphasise that the Court's reference in that case was to objective *differences* and, thus, to an issue of comparability, rather than of justification (Martin,[1210] see also Mattera).[1211] In the words of Weatherill & Beaumont,[1212] *Sotgiu* means that a host Member State may be required 'to apply its rules in a manner that reflects the migrant's objectively distinct situation'. As was noted before, comparability also played a role in earlier indirect discrimination cases (*Sabbatini*,[1213] regarding the

---

[1207]   Case 152/73, [1974] *ECR* 153, see earlier in this part, A.I.2.c.
[1208]   Case C-419/92, [1994] *ECR* I-505.
[1209]   Plötscher 2003, p. 56.
[1210]   Martin 1998, pp. 272, 292 and 600 subs. Consequently, Martin sees *Sotgiu* as one of the rare examples where the Court, in interpreting a specific non-discrimination provision, adhered to the definition of the general equality principle where comparability is the central notion.
[1211]   Mattera 1993, p. 67.
[1212]   Weatherill & Beaumont 1999, p. 632.
[1213]   Case 20/71, [1972] *ECR* 345; see earlier in this part, A.I.2.b.

basis of the expatriation benefit; *Ugliola*,[1214] regarding the consequences of military service for different groups of workers). What is new about *Sotgiu* is the explicit and very prominent place given to comparability in the context of indirect discrimination where it presents itself as *a second element* defining the concept – in other words, where comparability occupies a position that later would be held by the conceptually different element of objective justification.

Although the Court in *Sotgiu*[1215] did not yet use the term 'justification' in relation to objective differences, later it did not shy away from doing so. In *Palermo-Toia*,[1216] the social insurance fund argued that only by requiring the claimant's children to be French nationals could a duplication of social benefits to their mothers be avoided. It also pointed out that the allowance was intended as an incentive to bear and raise children and thereby increase the French national community. This latter argument can be read as related to justification proper (Wyatt).[1217] However, the Court[1218] did not address this argument. Rather, referring to *Sotgiu*, the Court preferred only to state generally that the condition concerning the nationality of the children must be regarded as indirectly discriminatory 'unless *justified* by objective differences' (emphasis added). The Court agreed with AG Warner, according to whom women of child-bearing age would unlikely be motivated to have many children in the hope of being entitled to a bonus at the age of 65 should they then be of insufficient means. The Court concluded that conditions of the type at issue are not acceptable under the law on free movement of workers (*Palermo-Toia*, para. 15-17). Except for the *term justification*, which is new, the Court's statement regarding objective differences corresponds to the relevant passage in *Sotgiu*. Unfortunately, the use of such confusing language is not limited to early case law but persists even today (e.g. the indirect discrimination cases *Mund & Fester*[1219] and *Pastoors*).[1220]

c.   The special approach in Boussac: avoiding the disadvantage

A rather unusual approach to justification in the context of indirect discrimination is reflected by *Boussac*,[1221] a case concerning a particularly simple and expeditious summary procedure under German civil procedural law that was not available where

---

[1214]   Case 15/69, [1969] *ECR* 363; see earlier in this part, A.I.2.a.
[1215]   Case 152/73, [1974] *ECR* 153.
[1216]   Case 237/78, [1979] *ECR* 2645 ; see earlier in this part, A.I.4.e.iii.
[1217]   Wyatt 1981, p. 45.
[1218]   It is obvious that the argument is not able to serve as justification in the framework of a prohibition of discrimination on grounds of nationality. After all, its underlying rationale is that it is preferable that the population in France is French rather than originating from other Member States. This is precisely the kind of approach that the EC provisions on free movement aim at eliminating.
[1219]   Case C-398/92, [1994] *ECR* I-467.
[1220]   Case C-29/95, [1997] *ECR* I-285. Concerning these cases, see e.g. Schwander 1994, Duintjer Tebbens 1996, Schlosser 1995, Verschuur 1995 and Mahler 1997.
[1221]   Case 22/80, [1980] *ECR* 3427, see earlier in this part, A.I.4.f.ii.

---

the debt was expressed in foreign currency. Faced with the claim that this infringed
Art. 7 of the EEC Treaty (now Art. 12 EC), Germany argued that the electronic
processing simplifying the *Mahnverfahren* could not be used in the case of debts
expressed in foreign currency because such claims then had to be dealt with manually.
The Court found this argument unconvincing[1222] but immediately added that this 'is
not such as to resolve the problem completely. A distinction based on the currency
in which debts are expressed, which applies only to the simplified procedure for
recovery of debts, does not amount, even indirectly, to discrimination on grounds of
nationality if the parties to the contract are free to select the currency in which the debt
is expressed and if ordinary proceedings remain available to creditors established on
the territory of the other Member States, whatever the currency in which the claim
is expressed' (*Boussac*, para. 12 and 13).

Academic commentators have expressed doubts as to how to interpret the Court's
approach. Grabitz & Hilf[1223] speak of a *de minimis* rule which may be connected with
the argument, brought forward by the German Government, that there were too few
discriminatory instances to be relevant in the present context. In a similar vein, AG
Mayras thought that the effect of the measure was negligible. The Court, however, did
not deal with this argument (see also Plötscher).[1224] Kon[1225] suggests that perhaps the
Court meant to accept 'legitimate occasional discrimination'.[1226] He criticizes the Court
for disregarding the possible economic advantages and disadvantages involved in
choosing a given currency and argues that the denial of the more effective remedy to
the majority of foreign creditors might constitute a serious erosion of the full and

---

[1222] The Court observed that the *Mahnverfahren* was available for foreign currency debts of debtors
established in the territory of other Brussels Convention States, even though in such a case the claims
had to be dealt with manually. The Court concluded that 'the need to provide for the electronic
processing of all claims subject to that procedure cannot be relied upon in relation to the recovery
of debts expressed in foreign currency from debtors established on national territory' (*Boussac*, para.
12). Thus, the Court did not deny the existence of differences in situation. It simply found it
unacceptable to rely on them in view of the fact that the *Mahnverfahren* was in fact used with regard
to certain claims expressed in foreign currency. In other words, the difference could not be deemed
relevant for the present purposes.

[1223] Grabitz & Hilf Commentary (as of 1989), n. 9 ad Art. 6 of the EC Treaty.

[1224] Plötscher 2003, p. 110, with further references.

[1225] Kon 1981, pp. 367/368.

[1226] In the context of his argument relating to 'legitimate occasional discrimination', Kon relies on
Schindler 1957, pp. 146/147, and Sundberg-Weitman 1977, p. 111. According to the former, there
is no prohibited discrimination if a measure *by accident* has a disparate effect. Schindler raises the
example where the fees payable by stock brokers are increased in a situation where most stock brokers
are foreigners. In his view, there is no discrimination in such a case as long as the amount of the
increase is reasonable, even if it accidentally affects only a certain group of persons. Discrimination
would exist only if the increase were too high ('übermässig'). In making this distinction, Schindler
seems to rely on the aim of the measure in question. Sundberg-Weitman argues that the distinction
between unlawful 'indirect discrimination' and legitimate 'occasional discrimination' should be made
on the basis of arbitrariness and that, therefore, the problem of separating the two concepts is in
reality the same as the question of whether or not there is comparability.

uniform application of the non-discrimination principle of Art. 7 of the EEC Treaty. In the present writer's analysis, the Court's statement means in fact that it accepted a notion of justification but one different not only from objective differences but also different from what is usually accepted in the framework of objective justification. The real reason for the Court's refusal to find discrimination in the *Boussac* case was simply that *it could be avoided.* This rationale does not constitute a 'cross-cutting reason' that would render the disadvantage *acceptable* in spite of the existence, in principle, of an entitlement of the person concerned. Rather, it is linked to the potential for the discrimination victim to exercise his or her own choice of behaviour. In accepting such 'justification', the Court's argument seems to be that the necessary *causal link* is missing between the disadvantage suffered by the victim of the alleged discrimination and the contested measure itself. The Court insinuates that the disadvantage was caused by the victim's own decision to get into the situation where the measure applied (in this case by expressing the debt in foreign currency). It is submitted that such a reasoning threatens to undermine non-discrimination law as a whole. After all, it could then be argued that a migrant worker suffering discrimination on grounds of nationality does not do so as a consequence of the host Member State's rules but rather of his or her decision to work in that state in the first place. By not going there, the disadvantage could have been avoided. However, the underlying rationale for the rules governing free movement of workers is, precisely, to encourage people to work in other Member States (or at least to make it possible for them without undue disadvantages flowing from the fact of their foreign nationality). This rationale is expressly stated in cases such as *Singh*[1227] and *De Groot.*[1228] It is further submitted that, *mutatis mutandis,* the same must apply in the many fields covered by Art. 12(1) EC. Fortunately, the *Boussac* approach to justification appears to be an aberration. For example, in the much more recent case *O'Flynn,*[1229] the Court did not accept the UK Government's argument that, in assessing the discriminatory nature of a given measure, it must be asked whether the failure to satisfy the contested condition results from the free choice of the person concerned. The Court emphasised that the reasons why a migrant worker chooses to make use of his or her freedom of movement within the Community are not to be taken into account in assessing whether a national provision is discriminatory. The Court added that the possibility of exercising such a fundamental freedom as the freedom of movement of persons 'cannot be limited by such considerations, which are purely subjective' (*O'Flynn,* para. 21).[1230]

[1227] Case C-370/90, [1992] *ECR* I-4265.
[1228] Case C-385/00, [2002] *ECR* I-11819.
[1229] Case C-237/94, [1996] *ECR* I-2617.
[1230] An *avoidance argument* is also made by Rating 1994, p. 106, in the context of sex discrimination. Rating suggests that discrimination resulting not from sex itself but from peoples' behaviour based on their own decisions (for instance in the context of traditional sex roles) should be irrelevant because it can be avoided. However, in that particular context the alleged freedom of choice of the

3. OBJECTIVE JUSTIFICATION IN SEX EQUALITY LAW

First indications regarding objective justification in the sense of justification proper can be found in the Court's case law on indirect *sex* discrimination in the 1980s. Three cases are of particular importance in this context. The first of these, *Jenkins*,[1231] marked a new approach but left a number of important questions unanswered. It was somewhat clarified though *Bilka*[1232] and further supplemented by *Rinner-Kühn*[1233] with regard to cases where discrimination is caused through Member State legislation. As the first of these relevant cases, *Jenkins* merits a particularly careful analysis.

a. A new approach in Jenkins

i. The case

In *Jenkins*,[1234] justification was extensively debated before the Court of Justice. Accused of sex discrimination, the employer tried to justify differences in pay between full-time and part-time workers by citing an alleged 'material difference other than the difference of sex' between the two groups of workers, a difference – it explained – not based either on the characteristics of the workers or on the quality of the work but rather merely intended to discourage absenteeism, to ensure a fuller use of machinery and to encourage greater productivity (*Jenkins*, p. 913 and 914). Ms Jenkins pointed to the U.S. Supreme Court decision *Griggs v. Duke Power Co.*,[1235] arguing that *prima facie* discrimination requires 'some special justification from the employer' (*Jenkins*, p. 936, see also p. 916). In her view, a measure with a disparate impact is to be regarded as discriminatory unless it is shown to be 'manifestly related to the services in question'. She did not contest that in certain situations a difference in pay might be objectively justified by factors unconnected with discrimination on grounds of sex, for example, such as superior skills and longer service. However, she added that such justification must be strictly confined to real and relevant factors that are personal to the workers concerned. Similarly, the Commission acknowledged that a difference between two workers occupying the same post may be explained by the operation of factors unconnected with any discrimination on grounds of sex but did not explain what it

---

persons concerned may rest largely on a fiction. In academic writing, it is also pointed out that such an approach would be difficult to put into practice (compare Wisskirchen 1994, p. 237). Further, giving that the traditional sex roles are at the basis of much of the existing sex discrimination (in particular, structural sex discrimination; see above Part 1, B.III.4.c), to accept them as they are would run counter to the entire project of striving for sex equality.

[1231] Case 96/80, [1981] *ECR* 911.
[1232] Case 170/84, [1986] *ECR* 1607.
[1233] Case 171/88, [1989] *ECR* 2743.
[1234] Case 96/80, [1981] *ECR* 911.
[1235] *Griggs v. Duke Power Co.*, 401 U.S. 424 (1971), see above Part 1, C.II.1.b.

meant by that notion (*Jenkins*, p. 921). AG Warner considered 'the *Griggs* approach' as suggested by Ms Jenkins appropriate because '[i]t is the only approach that reconciles the need to prevent discrimination against women disguised as differentiation between full-time and part-time workers with the need to prevent injustice to an employer who differentiates between full-time and part-time workers for sound reasons unconnected with their sex'. Arguing that earlier case law from other areas contained such an element, the AG suggested the following answer to be given to the national court (*Jenkins*, p. 936 subs.): 'Where there is a difference in time rates of pay related to the total number of hours worked each week, the provisions of Article 119 of the Treaty require the employer to show that the difference is justified on objective grounds unconnected with any discrimination on the basis of sex.'

The Court accepted the possibility of an objective justification (*Jenkins*, para. 11-14). It held that in the case of apparently sex-neutral rules, 'the fact that work paid at time rates is remunerated at an hourly rate which varies according to the number of hours worked per week does not offend against the principle of equal pay laid down in Article 119 of the Treaty in so far as the difference in pay between part-time work and full-time work is attributable to factors which are objectively justified and are in no way related to any discrimination based on sex'. It explained that '[s]uch may be the case, in particular, when by giving hourly rates of pay which are lower for part-time work than those for full-time work the employer is endeavouring, on economic grounds which may be objectively justified, to encourage full-time work irrespective of the sex of the worker.' The Court summed up its findings in the following statement: 'Where the hourly rate of pay differs according to whether the work is part-time or full-time it is for the national courts to decide in each individual case whether, regard being had to the facts of the case, its history and the employer's intention, a pay policy such as that which is at issue in the main proceedings although represented as a difference based on weekly working hours is or is not in reality discrimination based on the sex of the worker.'

ii. Comments

The arguments for justification made before the Court present a curious mixture. Some of them seem to be concerned with objective differences, as is perhaps most obvious in the case of Ms Jenkins' reference to superior skills and longer service which she regarded as 'differences personal to the workers concerned'. In contrast, the arguments brought forward by the employer, though alleged to relate to 'fundamental differences', in fact related to something different, namely a need on the part of the company – presumably particularly urgent in the context of part-time work – to discourage absenteeism, to encourage fuller use of machinery and to ensure greater productivity. Such concerns, relating to business necessity, are not related to objective differences but rather fall into the category of justification proper in the sense of 'cross-cutting reasons',[1236] as raised by the AG's remarks on the need to reconcile conflicting interests. But the Court accepted the idea of justification in the sense of 'factors which are objectively justified and in no way related to any discrimination based on sex'. At the time, commentators disagreed on what the Court intended and wondered whether the approach in *Jenkins* was consistent with the existing case law on indirect discrimination on grounds of nationality. Under Plender's[1237] analysis, the Court referred to two distinct tests. Under the first test, the use of the apparently neutral criterion must not be designed to camouflage the employer's object of treating men more favourably than women ('in no way related to any discrimination based on sex'). Under the second, there may be objective economic justification for the action of the employer.[1238] According to Martin,[1239] the Court in *Jenkins* 'seems to apply to the letter' the equality principle in its classical form (i.e. including the objective justification element as referring to objective differences) and therefore is consistent with the case law of that time on discrimination on grounds of nationality (see also Imbrechts,[1240] Snaith).[1241] In contrast, Szyszczak[1242] considered the case law on discrimination on grounds of nationality more favourable than that on sex discrimination. In her view, *Jenkins* reflects a deliberately evasive policy choice and pays mere lip service to the concern of seeking to identify and control indirect discrimination against women in the labour market. In particular, Szyszczak regretted that the Court did not adopt the solution (which she seems to interpret as relating to objective differences) suggested by AG Warner, whom she lauds for advocating a consistent approach. Similarly, Barrett[1243] considered the AG's approach more in line with the aims of Art. 119 than that eventually adopted by the Court. But Barrett goes even further and raises the question of whether an employer should ever be allowed to justify paying part-time workers at a lower rate on grounds of economic business benefits. She argues that 'such benefit, even if it were shown to exist, gained by means of the exploitation of part-time workers would be contrary to both aims of Article 119 and the social policy of the Community'.

The present writer agrees with those who found *a clear difference in approach*. The Court in *Jenkins* explicitly acknowledged that economic reasons may be acceptable in justifying indirect sex discrimination. In contrast, in the context of discrimination on grounds of nationality the Court had thus far only accepted express grounds for derogation (*Ugliola*)[1244] and objective differences (*Sotgiu*)[1245] as legitimate reasons for

---

[1236] See above Part 1, B.III.6.a.
[1237] Plender 1995, p. 78, also Plender 1982, pp. 634 and 649.
[1238] See also later in this part, A.IV.3.c.
[1239] Martin 1998, pp. 307 subs. and 615.
[1240] Imbrechts 1986, p. 240, footnote 41.
[1241] Snaith 1981, p. 197.
[1242] Szyszczak 1981, pp. 678 subs.; see also Prechal 1985, p. 172.
[1243] Barrett 1981, p. 189.
[1244] Case 15/69, [1969] *ECR* 363; see earlier in this part, A.II.2.a.i.
[1245] Case 152/73, [1974] *ECR* 153; see earlier in this part, A.II.2.b.

blocking a finding of indirect discrimination.[1246] *Jenkins* meant that in the area of sex discrimination it was then easier to find a redeeming element that would save a contested measure from being prohibited as indirect discrimination. But if that were so, why did the Court opt for a new approach in the specific context of sex equality law? The Court did not give any explanation on this point. Notably, it did not refer to the U.S. Supreme Court decision in *Griggs v. Duke Power Co.*,[1247] cited by both Ms Jenkins and AG Warner. It is, nevertheless, conceivable and perhaps even likely that the Court was influenced by the practicality of the business necessity approach set out in *Griggs*. In any case, this interpretation is reflected in comments on the later landmark case *Bilka*[1248] (discussed in the following section) concerning the same issue. However, notably whilst in *Griggs* business necessity was defined as related to job *performance*, the Court of Justice's test did not mention such a limitation. Finally, the acknowledgment of a need for objective justification was particularly meaningful in a legal context such as that of equal pay for men and women where there are no express derogations.[1249]

Possibly, the acceptance of objective justification was perceived by the Court as *filling a lacuna*, at least in the case of *indirect* discrimination which is often seen as a 'lesser' form of discrimination – that is, a form of discrimination which is perceived usually as having a less far reaching overall effect than direct discrimination.[1250] It has also been argued that the possibility of invoking objective justifications has to be seen as a *quid pro quo* for the enlargement of the notion of discrimination (and, thereby, of the field of application of provisions dealing with discrimination) which resulted from the Court's recognition that discrimination may be of an indirect nature (thus the GTE Commentary).[1251]

In *Jenkins*, not only did the Court not explain its reason for developing a new approach, but it also failed to clarify its *actual meaning and application*. According to Hervey,[1252] *Jenkins* left open a host of questions which go to the heart of the issue of objective justification, among them: What is the appropriate range of economic factors to consider? Are only 'job-related' justifications lawful or may broader justifications be allowed? What types of economic justifications are appropriate for an employer to consider – both present savings accruing to the existing discriminatory situation as well as the future costs involved in adopting a non-discriminatory policy? Should the fact that, absent a discriminatory policy, an employer might not be able to employ

---

[1246] In addition, in free movement law (purely) economic justification is excluded as a matter of principle; see later in this part, A.IV.3.c.
[1247] *Griggs v. Duke Power Co.*, 401 U.S. 424 (1971).
[1248] Case 170/84, [1986] *ECR* 1607.
[1249] Compare Part 1, B.III.6.c.
[1250] See further below Part 3, A.II.2.
[1251] GTE Commentary 1997, n. 25 ad Art. 119 of the EC Treaty.
[1252] Hervey 1991, pp. 808/809.

any (or as many) part-time workers be considered? Hervey is rightfully most concerned with the difficult question as to how to balance economic interests against the actual harmful impact of discriminatory policies on both individual women and men as well as on groups of victims collectively.

b. From Bilka to Rinner-Kühn

Rather than *Jenkins*, *Bilka*[1253] became the landmark case on objective justification for indirect sex discrimination. In *Bilka* (para. 29-31 and 36), the Court explained: 'If [...] it should be found that a much lower proportion of women than of men work full time, the exclusion of part-time workers from the occupational pension scheme would be contrary to Article 119 of the Treaty where, taking into account the difficulties encountered by women workers in working full-time, that measure could not be explained by factors which exclude any discrimination on grounds of sex. However, if the undertaking is able to show that its pay practice may be explained by objectively justified factors unrelated to any discrimination on grounds of sex there is no breach of Article 119. The answer to the first question referred by the national court must therefore be that Article 119 of the EEC Treaty is infringed by a department store company which excludes part-time employees from its occupational pension scheme, where that exclusion affects a far greater number of women than men, unless the undertaking shows that the exclusion is based on objectively justified factors unrelated to any discrimination on grounds of sex. [...] If the national Court finds that the measures chosen by Bilka correspond to a real need on the part of the undertaking, are appropriate with a view to achieving the objective pursued and are necessary to that end, the fact that the measures affect a far greater number of women than men is not sufficient to show that they constitute an infringement of Article 119.'

Anderman[1254] describes this test as containing 'within it the age-old labour law principle of deference to management discretion to pursue business objectives' (see also von Prondzynsky & Richards[1255] and, in particular regarding economic justification grounds, Shrubshall,[1256] Blom).[1257] According to Steiner,[1258] the main relevance of *Bilka* lies in the fact that the Court formulated a *stricter justification test than in Jenkins*.[1259] The so-called 'Bilka test for objective justification' contains *three elements* which would characterize objective justification for indirect discrimination in general, namely: 1) there must be an objective factor unrelated to the prohibited discriminatory

---

[1253]   Case 170/84, [1986] *ECR* 1607.
[1254]   Anderman 1996, p. 104.
[1255]   Von Prondzynsky & Richards 1995, p. 122.
[1256]   Shrubshall 1987, p. 53.
[1257]   Blom 1992, pp. 17 and 42.
[1258]   Steiner 1999, p. 141.
[1259]   Case 96/80, [1981] *ECR* 911.

ground, 2) there must be a genuine need on the part of the employer and 3) the measure must be suitable and necessary for attaining the aim pursued (proportionality). Whilst the first two elements relate to the aim or purpose of the measure, the third one concerns the means used for achieving that aim (Hervey).[1260] The importance of the element of proportionality did not come as a surprise, since it had long been held relevant in the context of justification in other areas of EC law (e.g. *De Peijper*[1261] and *Christmas Turkeys*,[1262] both concerning what was then Art. 36 of the EEC Treaty, now Art. 30 EC, concerning free movement of goods; e.g. see Usher,[1263] Tridimas).[1264] As one of the recognized general principles of EC law, proportionality has to be observed in all areas of EC law, as expressly confirmed in *Johnston*[1265] (para. 38).

Later, the Court developed a *slightly different test* for cases where the alleged indirect discrimination is caused by *Member State legislation*. First indications of this test are found in *Teuling*[1266] (*Ellis*,[1267] Luckhaus)[1268] but *Rinner-Kühn*[1269] is a much more explicit example. *Teuling* concerned a social security system under which the amount of the benefit was determined in part by family status. The Court pointed out that the system was indirectly discriminatory unless justified by factors which did not involve any discrimination on grounds of sex. In such a context, the purpose of the benefit must be considered. The Court, having found that the aim of providing a minimum subsistence benefit to persons with no income from work was an integral part of the relevant Member States' social policy, concluded that the system at issue was justified (*Teuling*, para. 13, 16 and 17). *Rinner-Kühn* concerned an exclusion from the payment of wages of part-time workers in the event of illness under national law. The Court explained that 'if the Member State can show that the means chosen meet a necessary aim of its social policy and they are suitable and requisite for attaining that aim, the mere fact that the provision affects a much greater number of female workers than male workers cannot be regarded as constituting an infringement of Article 119' (*Rinner-Kühn*, para. 14; emphasis added).

> In *Rinner-Kühn* the Court *did not follow AG Darmon* according to whom the presumption that national law is incompatible with the Treaty solely because it affects far more women

---

[1260] Hervey 1991, pp. 813 subs.
[1261] Case 104/75, [1976] *ECR* 613.
[1262] Case 40/82, [1984] *ECR* 283.
[1263] Usher 1998, pp. 49 subs.
[1264] Tridimas 1999, pp. 125 subs.
[1265] Case 222/84, [1986] *ECR* 1651. The Court stated generally that the principle of proportionality 'requires that derogations remain within the limits of what is appropriate and necessary for achieving the aim in view and requires the principle of equal treatment to be reconciled as far as possible with the requirements of public safety'.
[1266] Case 30/85, [1987] *ECR* 2497.
[1267] Ellis 1998, p. 297.
[1268] Luckhaus 1988, pp. 56 subs.
[1269] Case 171/88, [1989] *ECR* 2743.

than men is wholly justified only when the practice of an undertaking or an agreement between employers is involved. The AG argued that this situation concerns rules of law of modest status in the hierarchy of legal rules and above all of limited scope. The AG found it undesirable to establish the same presumption with regard to a legislative provision which is responsible for the common weal and must take into account a large number of social, economic and political circumstances amongst which the respective numbers of men and women are just one factor. Accordingly, he proposed the following answer to the national court (*Rinner-Kühn*, point 36 of the AG's opinion): 'A legislative provision which excludes part-time workers from the continued payment of their wages in the event of illness thereby affecting a much greater number of women than men is compatible with Article 119 of the EEC Treaty unless it is proved before the national court that the provision was based on objectives related to discrimination on grounds of sex.'

According to Szyszczak,[1270] the test in *Rinner-Kühn* is the same as in *Bilka*;[1271] only the contexts differ (see also Shaw).[1272] This difference lies in what is meant by the words 'based on objectives unrelated to discrimination on grounds of sex': in the case of an ordinary employer, the means chosen must correspond to a *real need on the part of the undertaking* whilst in the case of State legislation, the means chosen must meet *a necessary aim of the State's social policy* (though the latter test was later modified).[1273]

4. TOWARDS OBJECTIVE JUSTIFICATION IN OTHER AREAS

In contexts *other than sex discrimination*, objective justification as part of the indirect discrimination formula developed not only later but also with considerably less clarity and speed. An express formula comparable to that just discussed in the context of sex equality did not appear until the Court's decision in the *O'Flynn*[1274] case in 1996. The possibility of objective justification is, however, already suggested in earlier cases. The following sections trace that development.

a. Indirect discrimination on grounds of nationality: first indications

i. *Seco*

First indications of the inclusion of objective justification in the indirect discrimination formula outside sex equality law can be found in *Seco*,[1275] a case decided shortly after

---

[1270] Szyszczak 1990, p. 116.
[1271] Case 170/84, [1986] *ECR* 1607.
[1272] Shaw 1989, p. 433.
[1273] See later in this part, A.III.1.a.ii.
[1274] Case C-237/94, [1996] *ECR* I-2617.
[1275] Joined Cases 62/81 and 63/81, [1982] *ECR* 223; see earlier in this part, A.I.4.j.ii.

Jenkins,[1276] concerning the free movement of services. In *Seco*, the defendant offered a number of arguments in an attempt to justify the obligation imposed on employers to pay a share of social security contributions for foreign workers only temporarily resident in Luxembourg despite the fact that this practice did not result in an insurance entitlement for those workers and even though they were already insured in another Member State. None of these arguments related to justification proper,[1277] and each of them was rejected. The Court explained notably that 'legislation which requires employers to pay in respect of their workers social security contributions not related to any social security benefit for those workers, who are moreover exempt from insurance in the Member State in which the service is provided and remain compulsorily affiliated, for the duration of the work carried out, to the social security scheme of the Member State in which their employer is established, may not reasonably be considered justified on account of the general interest in providing workers with social security' (*Seco*, para. 10).

This statement has been interpreted as implying that the creation of a social security benefit for the workers through the employer's obligation to pay contributions might have been able to justify this obligation. Thus, Greenwood[1278] observed that '[t]he principle that workers should receive the best social security cover appears to override the prohibition of discrimination' (see also Druesne).[1279] Certain authors speak of justification in the general interest (Wyatt & Dashwood,[1280] Martin,[1281] Plötscher).[1282] As this justification does not relate to one of the three express justification grounds available in the context of free movement of services (public policy, public security, public health; Arts. 55 *juncto* Art. 46(1) EC), it must be understood as relating to *a*

[1276] Case 96/80, [1981] *ECR* 911.
[1277] For instance, the argument that the aim of the system was to avoid the temptation for employers to use foreign labour in order to alleviate their social security burdens as well as to prevent disadvantages for employers who could not escape the national minimum wages can be read in the context of objective differences. Employers established abroad may be able to reduce their wage related costs by avoiding the host State's minimum wage legislation and social security costs. For example, employers established in Luxembourg incurred higher costs because the enforcement of the legislation was much easier with regard to them. The defendant also maintained that since the Member States were free to refuse third country nationals employment as immigrating workers, they were also free to impose restrictions on their admittance. This argument concerns the free movement right at issue and not the possibility of limiting that right. Whilst EVI made its point in relation to free movement of workers, the case concerned the freedom to provide services of the companies employing the workers; see Gormley 1982, p. 209. Timmermans 1983, p. 318, points out that the employer's freedom to provide services affects the position of their employees but that this does not necessarily mean that the persons concerned qualify as workers within the meaning of Art. 48 of the Treaty (now Art. 39 EC).
[1278] Greenwood 1984, p. 53.
[1279] Druesne 1982, p. 80.
[1280] Wyatt & Dashwood 2000, p. 489.
[1281] Martin 1998, pp. 579/580.
[1282] Plötscher 2003, p. 150.

possibility of extra-textual justification. Under the present writer's analysis, *Seco* should be interpreted as providing a first, though not very explicit, indication of an element of objective justification in the context of indirect discrimination on grounds of nationality.

ii. *Data-processing contracts*

Another early example of the implicit acceptance of objective justification is *Data-processing contracts*,[1283] concerning a requirement of public ownership of a company to secure the award of public contracts. The Court rejected the Italian Government's arguments that the case concerned the exercise of official authority and, therefore, fell outside the scope of EC law altogether (Art. 45 EC, then Art. 55 of the Treaty), and that the express derogation of public policy (Art. 46(1) EC, then Art. 56 of the Treaty) applied. Italy further argued that it was necessary for the public authorities to control the performance of the contracts in question in order to adapt the work to meet developments that were unforeseeable at the time when the contracts were signed and that, for certain types of activities which the companies had to carry out, particularly in strategic sectors involving confidential data, the State must be able to employ an undertaking in which it can have complete confidence. In academic literature, this argument has been discussed in the context of express derogation provisions (Sanfilippo).[1284] However, both AG Mischo and the Court referred to general interest justifications (*Data-processing contracts*, point 35 of the AG's opinion and para. 11 of the judgment). The Court held that 'the Italian Government had sufficient legal powers at its disposal to be able to adapt the performance of contracts to meet future and unforeseeable circumstances and to ensure compliance with the general interest, and that in order to protect the confidential nature of the data in question the Government could have adopted measures less restrictive of freedom of establishment and freedom to provide services than those in issue, in particular by imposing a duty of secrecy on the staff of the companies concerned, breach of which might give rise to criminal proceedings. There is nothing in the documents before the Court to suggest that the staff of companies none of whose share capital is in Italian public ownership could not comply just as effectively with such a duty.' It seems clear, therefore, that the Court examined Italy's third argument in the context of objective justification, indicating thereby the relevance of that element in the context of indirect discrimination on grounds of nationality as well.

[1283]   Case C-3/88, [1989] *ECR* 4035; see earlier in this part, A.I.4.b.ii.
[1284]   Sanfilippo 1990, p. 423.

b. Steps on the way according to the Court

Eventually in general statements on the possibility of objective justification for indirect discrimination on grounds of nationality in *O'Flynn*,[1285] the Court mentioned three prior judgments as indirect precedents ('see, to that effect'; *O'Flynn*, para. 19), namely *Bachmann*,[1286] *Commission v Luxemburg*[1287] and *Allué II*.[1288] These cases are examined below.

i. Bachmann

Bachmann[1289] concerned Belgian tax legislation which made the deductibility of certain insurance contributions conditional upon their being paid in Belgium. The Court examined the case in the context of free movement not only of workers, where it found *prima facie* indirect discrimination[1290] on grounds of nationality (*Bachmann*, para. 8 subs.), but also services, where it found a restriction (*Bachmann*, para. 31-33). The Court's reference in *O'Flynn*[1291] related to the former. In *Bachmann*, the Belgian, Dutch and Danish Governments emphasised the need to ensure the cohesion of the tax system in relation to pensions and life assurance, an argument accepted by the Court in the context of indirect discrimination (*Bachmann*, para. 27). As in *Seco*[1292] and *Data-processing contracts*,[1293] the Court's acceptance is not accompanied by any general remarks on the possibilities of justification in the case of indirect discrimination.

> The Court noted that under the Belgian rules a connection existed between the deductibility of contributions on the one hand and the liability for tax payable by the insurers under pension and life assurance contracts on the other hand. It found that the cohesion of that type of system presupposed that, in the event of a State being obliged to allow the deduction of life assurance contributions paid in another Member State, it should be able to tax sums payable by insurers. The Court also stated that a mere undertaking by the insurer to pay the tax did not constitute an adequate safeguard measure. It concluded that a solution could be provided only by bilateral conventions between the Member States or by the adoption of Community harmonising measures (which did not exist at the time). Against that background, the Court held (*Bachmann*, para. 27 and 28): 'It follows that, as Community law

---

[1285] Case C-237/94, [1996] *ECR* I-2617.
[1286] Case C-204/90, [1992] *ECR* I-249.
[1287] Case C-111/91, [1993] *ECR* I-817.
[1288] Joined Cases C-259/91, C-331/91 and C-332/91, [1993] *ECR* I-4309.
[1289] Case C-204/90, [1992] *ECR* I-249.
[1290] As opposed to both the Commission and AG Mischo, the Court did not use express language. Nonetheless, the meaning of its finding is clear; see Roth 1993 (Bachmann), p. 391, and Vanistendael 1994, pp. 310 and 314.
[1291] Case C-237/94, [1996] *ECR* I-2617.
[1292] Joined Cases 62/81 and 63/81, [1982] *ECR* 223; see earlier in this part, A.II.4.a.i.
[1293] Case C-3/88, [1989] *ECR* 4035; see earlier in this part, A.II.4.a.ii.

stands at present, it is not possible to ensure the cohesion of such a tax system by means
of measures which are less restrictive than those at issue in the main proceedings, and that
the consequences of any other measure ensuring the recovery by the State concerned of
the tax due under its legislation on sums payable by insurers pursuant to the contracts concluded with them would ultimately be similar to those resulting from the non-deductibility
of contributions. In the light of the foregoing, it must be recognized that, in the field of
pensions and life assurance, provisions such as those contained in the Belgian legislation
at issue are justified by the need to ensure the cohesion of the tax system of which they form
part, and that such provisions are not, therefore, contrary to Article 48 of the Treaty.'

According to Boekhorst,[1294] the Court in *Bachmann* 'held that there could be public
policy reasons for the Belgian Government to infringe the fundamental freedoms of
the EEC Treaty'. However, in that the judgment contains no reference to Art. 48(3)
of the Treaty (now Art. 39(3) EC), the Court's statements must be understood as
relating to an *extra-textual* form of justification. Accordingly, the Court's reference
in *O'Flynn* to *Bachmann* as a precedent regarding objective justification makes perfect
sense.[1295]

ii. *Commission v Luxembourg*

The state of the law is less clear regarding the second decision referred to by the Court
in *O'Flynn*,[1296] namely *Commission v Luxemburg*,[1297] concerning a Luxembourg rule
making the payment of childbirth allowances conditional upon a requirement of prior
residence by the mother on the Luxembourg territory. The Court found that such a
measure constitutes *prima facie* indirect discrimination on grounds of nationality,
prohibited under Art. 7(2) of Reg. 1612/68[1298] (*Commission v Luxembourg*, para. 9 and
10). By way of a defence, the Luxembourg Government referred to public health
reasons, arguing that the contested measure intended to reduce infant mortality and
post-natal damages. These arguments were not accepted by the Court which stated
(*Commission v Luxembourg*, para. 12-14): 'In the circumstances of the present case,
a requirement of prior residence in the Grand Duchy is neither necessary nor
appropriate to attain the public health objective that is being sought. Whilst the
obligation to undergo certain medical examinations in the Grand Duchy is indeed
appropriate in the light of that objective, it is disproportionate not to take account of

---

[1294] Boekhorst 1992, p. 285.
[1295] Notably, most commentators seem to analyse the case in terms of public interest objectives or a rule
of reason as relevant in the context of the *wider concept of restrictions;* compare Fosselard 1993, pp.
482 subs.; Burgers 1995, p. 417; Farmer 1995, p. 315; Nowak & Schnitzler 2000, p. 629, and Martin
1998, pp. 603 and 608.
[1296] Case C-237/94, [1996] *ECR* I-2617.
[1297] Case C-111/91, [1993] *ECR* I-817.
[1298] Regulation 1612/68/EEC, *OJ* English Special Edition 1968 L 257/2, p. 475 (as amended).

medical examinations that may have been carried out in other Member States. Moreover, the argument of the Luxembourg Government is irrelevant as regards the second instalment of the childbirth allowance because, in the first place, the residence requirement for that instalment can also be met by the child's father and, in the second place, the compulsory postnatal examination of the mother has no connection with the requirement of residence prior to the birth. The Luxembourg Government's argument regarding the need to ensure that all the medical examinations take place under the supervision of a single doctor, cannot be accepted. It is enough to point out here that the Luxembourg legislation does not in any way require that the compulsory medical examinations should all take place under the supervision of the same doctor.'

In *O'Flynn*, the Court refers to the first part of these statements (para. 12) which concerns the express derogation ground of public health. This justification ground is available in the context of both direct and indirect discrimination. It is, therefore, difficult to see how the Court's statements could be understood as relating to objective justification as typically appropriate for indirect discrimination.[1299]

iii. *Allué II*

The third case to which the Court referred in *O'Flynn*,[1300] *Allué II*,[1301] is one of a series of cases concerning foreign language assistants which eventually led to an infringement procedure against Italy.[1302] Under Italian legislation, the contracts of foreign language assistants were concluded for only one year at a time but could later be extended for five more years. In principle, no such limit was applied to other types of lecturers. The dismissal of the applicants in the two *Allué* cases after six years of teaching raised questions in the context of the free movement of workers (then Art. 48 of the EEC Treaty, now Art. 39 EC).[1303] The Italian Government tried to justify these time limits by pointing out that no competitive recruitment procedure existed for the jobs in question making it necessary to have some means of getting rid of incompetent personnel. Italy also cited changing staff requirements and a need to ensure that the teachers had an up-to-date knowledge of their native language. In *Allué I*,[1304] the Court

---

[1299] Unfortunately, not much literature exists on this decision. According to the Court's list of case notes, there are only two case notes on this judgment of which only one is available to the present writer, namely Keunen 1994. It is not very helpful in the present context because, with regard to the issue of indirect discrimination, it is merely descriptive. The main focus of the note is on the field of application of Regulation 1408/71.

[1300] Case C-237/94, [1996] *ECR* I-2617.

[1301] Joined Cases C-259/91, C-331/91 and C-332/91, [1993] *ECR* I-4309.

[1302] Case C-212/99, [2001] *ECR* I-4923.

[1303] Since the employer also refused to pay social security contributions for the language assistants, further questions arose which related to the EC's social security law, but these are not discussed here.

[1304] Case 33/88, [1989] *ECR* 1591.

refused all these arguments (see Watson).[1305] Subsequently, the case has been called a prime example of the application of the indirect discrimination test (Johnson & O'Keeffe).[1306]

Allué II was prompted by a request for clarification of the *Allué I* decision which had been interpreted in various ways by Italian courts. In this case, the Italian Government claimed that the number of foreign-language assistants engaged by the universities depended on teaching requirements and resources available to the universities to pay such assistants and further that universities could ensure proper management only by using one-year contracts. To these arguments, the Court replied by stating that 'the provisions of the Treaty do not preclude the adoption by the Member States of measures which are applicable without distinction, which are intended to ensure the proper management of their universities and which could affect, in particular, the nationals of other Member States. However, such measures must respect the principle of proportionality, that is to say that they must be necessary and appropriate to attain the objective pursued.' (*Allué II*, para. 15). This response shows that the Court, in the context of *prima facie* indirect discrimination on grounds of nationality, expressly accepted the possibility of justification based upon needs relating to the proper management of universities (a possibility which the Court had previously only hinted at in *Allué I*; compare Martin).[1307] Again, this type of justification is not covered by the express derogation grounds provided for by the Treaty in the context of free movement of workers. *Allué II*, therefore, confirms that in the specific case of indirect discrimination on grounds of nationality extra-textual possibilities for justification do exist.[1308] Accordingly, the case could well serve as a precedent for *O'Flynn*.

c. Discrimination on grounds of nationality: the general statement in O'Flynn

None of the cases analysed thus far contains a *general* statement on objective justification as part of the indirect discrimination formula as applied in the context of discrimination on grounds of nationality. That development followed in *O'Flynn*[1309]

[1305] Watson 1989 (Free movement), p. 422.

[1306] Johnson & O'Keeffe 1994, p. 1328.

[1307] According to Martin, *Allué I* was in fact the first case in which the Court accepted objective justification; Martin 1993, p. 578, and Martin 1994, pp. 48/49.

[1308] Again, there are commentators who appear to put the Court's statements in the context of restrictions in a wider sense, rather than discrimination (e.g. Steindorff 1994, p. 96; Harms 2000, pp. 69/70). However, the indirect discrimination approach is confirmed by later cases on foreign language assistants, such as *Spotti* (Case C-272/92, [1993] *ECR* I-5185; for critical comments see Loewisch 1994), *Commission v Italy* (Case C-212/99, [2001] *ECR* I-4923) and *Pokrzeptowicz-Meyer* (Case C-162/00, [2002] *ECR* I-1049; concerning the Europe Agreement concluded by the EC and Poland; see Wolff 2002).

[1309] Case C-237/94, [1996] *ECR* I-2617.

which merely summarised and formalised the indirect discrimination test as applied in the earlier case law (Keunen).[1310]

i. The case

O'Flynn concerned UK legislation regarding funeral payments which provided a means-tested social benefit to defer the costs of funerals of qualifying family members. Mr O'Flynn, an Irish national living in the UK, was refused funeral payments for the burial of his son in Ireland on the basis of the place of the burial. Mr O'Flynn argued that a territoriality condition requiring the burial to take place within the UK is 'by its nature indirectly discriminatory against migrant workers' (*O'Flynn*, para. 8). The Court agreed and found *prima facie* indirect discrimination on grounds of nationality.[1311] In terms of *justification*, the UK argued that the purpose of the contested condition was to ensure, in the interest of public health, that at a minimum a simple funeral might take place in the UK in the event of death. To extend the payments to other cases would result in an unacceptable increase in costs as well as in practical difficulties. AG Lenz thought that the grounds relied on by the UK could not be 'justified by compelling reasons in the general interest', which would be the only way to save the contested measure (*O'Flynn*, point 32 of the AG's opinion). To grant Mr O'Flynn the same level of benefits as for a burial inside the UK would not have increased the costs. The Court agreed (*O'Flynn*, para. 36-29). On a general level, it explained that *prima facie* indirectly discriminatory measures are acceptable only if they are 'justified by objective considerations independent of the nationality of the workers concerned, and if they are proportionate to the legitimate aim pursued by the national law' (*O'Flynn*, para. 19). In that context, the Court mentioned the three precedents discussed earlier.

ii. Comments

As has already been indicated, the importance of *O'Flynn* with regard to objective justification lies in *the Court's explicit statements* on this issue. Here, for the first time the Court described the objective justification test in a general way as applicable in the case of indirect discrimination on grounds of nationality – though a test which, in fact, the Court had applied before. In that sense, *O'Flynn* is undoubtedly a landmark case (see the Schwarze Commentary,[1312] Peers).[1313] Nonetheless, commentators point out that *O'Flynn* did not add anything in terms of substance to the Court's approach

---

[1310] Keunen 2001, p. 329.
[1311] See later in this part, A.III.1.a.i.
[1312] Schwarze Commentary 2000, n. 37 ad Art. 39 EC.
[1313] Peers 1997, p. 160.

in earlier cases. One author,[1314] very appropriately, quotes Sartre: 'Donc recommençons. Cela n'amuse personne ... Mais il faut enfoncer le clou.' (So, let's begin once more. This will amuse no one, but it must sink in.) The present writer would agree that the added value of *O'Flynn* does not lie in the substance, that is, in the Court's description of the phenomenon of indirect discrimination on grounds of nationality as including the element of objective justification. Rather, the added value is the explicit formulation of indirect discrimination on grounds of nationality presented by the Court. In particular, *O'Flynn* and its precedents confirm that *objective justification is not just another term for objective differences.*[1315] As in sex equality law,[1316] objective justification according to the *O'Flynn* formula now included cross-cutting reasons and, as such, embraces the concept of justification proper.

5. FINDINGS AND CONCLUSION

These analyses can be summarised as follows. First, it is important to recall that the element of objective justification was not present in the Court's early case law on indirect discrimination. According to *Ugliola*,[1317] the only possible justifications available in a case involving free movement of workers were those explicitly granted through the law. In *Sabbatini*,[1318] justification was necessarily linked to the basis of, or the very reason for, the particular right in question. In *Sotgiu*,[1319] which contains the first general indirect discrimination formula, the second part of this formula was linked to objective differences and, as such, raised the issue of comparability. In *Palermo-Toia*,[1320] the Court confirmed this approach but then, confusingly, used the term 'justification'. A particular and problematic approach to justification is reflected in *Boussac*[1321] where the Court found a difference in treatment acceptable simply because it could be have been avoided by the potential victim, though that approach has not found its way into the Court's later case law.

Objective justification as part of the indirect discrimination formula first appeared in the context of *indirect sex discrimination*. The first relevant case, *Jenkins*,[1322]

[1314] X 1997, p. 542.
[1315] The present writer would, therefore, not agree with Scott 2002, p. 283, according to whom it may be argued that objective justification plays a rather different role in the context of free movement as opposed to, for example, sex discrimination, because in the former case 'objective justification plays a role in determining whether the products or services, for example, represent *like* products or services, and hence whether differential treatment amounts to discrimination' (emphasis added).
[1316] See earlier in this part, A.II.3.
[1317] Case 15/69, [1969] *ECR* 363.
[1318] Case 20/71, [1972] *ECR* 345.
[1319] Case 152/73, [1974] *ECR* 153.
[1320] Case 237/78, [1979] *ECR* 2645.
[1321] Case 22/80, [1980] *ECR* 3427.
[1322] Case 96/80, [1981] *ECR* 911.

concerned justification for indirect discrimination committed by an employer. This case left a number of questions open but commentators nevertheless noted the novelty of the Court's approach as compared to the case law on discrimination on grounds of nationality. *Jenkins* was later clarified in the landmark case of *Bilka*[1323] and subsequently somewhat modified in *Rinner-Kühn*[1324] in relation to discrimination resulting from Member State legislation. In cases involving actions by an employer, objective justification exists if the measure in question corresponds to a real need on the part of the undertaking, is appropriate with a view to achieving the objective pursued and is necessary to that end. In the case of Member State legislation, objective justification requires that the measure in question meets a necessary aim of the Member State's social policy and is suitable and requisite for attaining that aim. (Once more, this latter test was later modified).

With regard to *discrimination on grounds of nationality,* statements of a comparable general nature did not appear until long after the possibility of objective justification was recognised. First indications may be perceived in *Seco*[1325] and *Data-processing contracts.*[1326] When the Court eventually made explicit statements of a general nature in *O'Flynn,*[1327] it cited three relatively recent cases as indirect precedents. However, only two of these cases appear to be relevant in the present context (*Bachmann,*[1328] *Allué II*).[1329] According to the formula coined by the Court in *O'Flynn,* objective justification for indirect discrimination on grounds of nationality must be based on objective considerations independent of the nationality of the workers concerned and proportionate to a legitimate aim pursued by the measure in question.

III. SOME BASIC OVERALL FINDINGS

At this point some basic findings concerning the development of the legal concept of indirect discrimination through the Court's case law shall be summarised. The remarks below concentrate on discrimination on grounds of nationality and sex; in other contexts, the Court's case law does not seem to reflect a development of a similar explicit and general indirect discrimination formula. In addition, the following sections will draw attention to the answers to the questions first raised at the very beginning of this study: why the legal concept of indirect discrimination was needed in the first

---

[1323] Case 170/84, [1986] *ECR* 1607.
[1324] Case 171/88, [1989] *ECR* 2743.
[1325] Joined Cases 62/81 and 63/81, [1982] *ECR* 223.
[1326] Case C-3/88, [1989] *ECR* 4035.
[1327] Case C-237/94, [1996] *ECR* I-2617.
[1328] Case C-204/90, [1992] *ECR* I-249.
[1329] Joined Cases C-259/91, C-331/91 and C-332/91, [1993] *ECR* I-4309.

place, what it meant then and what it means today.[1330] The findings summarised below
form the basis for the subsequent discussion of a number of issues that are debated
in academic writing in relation to indirect discrimination.

1. WHAT DOES INDIRECT DISCRIMINATION MEAN?

a. Recalling the indirect discrimination formulae

i. Discrimination on grounds of nationality

In the early landmark case of *Sotgiu*,[1331] the Court recognised the possibility that
discrimination on grounds of nationality can have an indirect nature by referring to
'covert forms of discrimination which, by the application of other criteria of differentiation, lead in fact to the same result'. That often repeated formula was explicitly
recalled in *O'Flynn*[1332] where the Court, after more extensive general statements on
the meaning of indirect discrimination, gave the following definition: 'It follows from
all the foregoing case-law that, unless objectively justified and proportionate to its aim,
a provision of national law must be regarded as indirectly discriminatory if it is
intrinsically liable to affect migrant workers more than national workers and if there
is a consequent risk that it will place the former at a particular disadvantage.'

> The more extensive statements preceding this formula were as follows (*O'Flynn*, para. 17-
> 19): 'The Court has consistently held that the equal treatment rule laid down in Article 48
> of the Treaty and in Article 7 of Regulation No 1612/68 prohibits not only overt discrimina-
> tion by reason of nationality but also all covert forms of discrimination which, by the
> application of other distinguishing criteria, lead in fact to the same result (see inter alia Case
> 152/73 Sotgiu v Deutsche Bundespost [1974] ECR 153, paragraph 11; Case C-27/91 URSSAF
> v Le Manoir [1991] ECR I-5531, paragraph 10; Case C-111/91 Commission v Luxembourg
> [1993] ECR I-817, paragraph 9; and Case C-419/92 Scholz v Opera Universitaria di Cagliari
> [1994] ECR I-505, paragraph 7). Accordingly, conditions imposed by national law must
> be regarded as indirectly discriminatory where, although applicable irrespective of natio-
> nality, they affect essentially migrant workers (see Case 41/84 Pinna v Caisse d' Allocations
> Familiales de la Savoie [1986] ECR 1, paragraph 24; Case 33/88 Allué and Another v
> Università degli Studi di Venezia [1989] ECR 1591, paragraph 12; and Le Manoir, paragraph
> 11) or the great majority of those affected are migrant workers (see Case C-279/89
> Commission v United Kingdom [1992] ECR I-5785, paragraph 42, and Case C-272/92
> Spotti v Freistaat Bayern [1993] ECR I-5185, paragraph 18), where they are indistinctly

---

[1330]   The third question, namely whether a need still exists for the legal concept of indirect discrimination
         in today's EC law, will be the main focus point of the study's third part.
[1331]   Case 152/73, [1974] *ECR* 153.
[1332]   Case C-237/94, [1996] *ECR* I-2617.

applicable but can more easily be satisfied by national workers than by migrant workers (see Commission v Luxembourg, paragraph 10, and Case C-349/87 Paraschi v Landesversicherungsanstalt Wuerttemberg [1991] ECR I-4501, paragraph 23) or where there is a risk that they may operate to the particular detriment of migrant workers (see Case C-175/88 Biehl v Administration des Contributions [1990] ECR I-1779, paragraph 14, and Case C-204/90 Bachmann v Belgium [1992] ECR I-249, paragraph 9). It is otherwise only if those provisions are justified by objective considerations independent of the nationality of the workers concerned, and if they are proportionate to the legitimate aim pursued by the national law (see, to that effect, Bachmann, paragraph 27; Commission v Luxembourg, paragraph 12; and Joined Cases C-259/91, C-331/91 and C-332/91 Allué and Others v Università degli Studi di Venezia [1993] ECR I-4309, paragraph 15).'

In contrast to *Sotgiu*, this new formula presented the element of objective justification in the proper sense of the word (that is, as an element concerned with cross-cutting reasons rather than merely objective differences). Under the new formula, disparate effects need not be proven as existing in fact. Rather, it is sufficient that a measure be 'intrinsically liable to affect migrant workers more than national workers' and that 'there is a consequent risk that it will place the former at a particular disadvantage'. Thus, the mere *possibility* of a disparate effect is sufficient (so-called 'liability approach'). However, as Epiney[1333] observes, such an element was not entirely new in that a less strict approach regarding proof had begun to develop even before *O'Flynn*. In subsequent case law, the *O'Flynn* formula usually takes the place that *Sotgiu* once occupied (e.g. *Meints*,[1334] para. 45; *Österreichischer Gewerkschaftsbund, Gewerkschaft öffentlicher Dienst*[1335] para. 39 and 40, *Borawitz*,[1336] para. 25; *Collins*,[1337] para. 65; *Merida*,[1338] para. 21). However, this is by no means a consistent practice of the Court. Rather, the Court sometimes refers to *Sotgiu* (e.g. *Zurstrassen*,[1339] para. 18; *Commission v France*,[1340] par. 37; *Ferlini*,[1341] para. 57; *Bidar*,[1342] para. 51), or to precedents involving the same area of law (e.g. *Köbler*,[1343] para. 73; *Brenner Maut*,[1344] para. 52; *Germany v*

[1333] Epiney 1995, pp. 55 subs.
[1334] Case C-57/96, [1997] *ECR* I-6689.
[1335] Case C-195/98, [2000] *ECR* I-10497.
[1336] Case C-124/99, [2000] *ECR* I-7293.
[1337] Case C-138/02, judgment of 23 March 2004, n.y.r.
[1338] Case C-400/02, judgment of 16 September 2004, n.y.r.
[1339] Case C-87/99, [2000] *ECR* I-3337.
[1340] Case C-35/97, [1998] *ECR* I-5325.
[1341] Case C-411/98, [2000] *ECR* I-8081.
[1342] Case C-209/03, judgment of 15 March 2005, n.y.r.
[1343] Case C-224/01, judgment of 30 September 2003, n.y.r., a case concerning free movement of workers where reference is made to *Commission v Greece* (Case C-187/96, [1998] *ECR* I-1095).
[1344] Case C-205/98, [2000] *ECR* I-7367, a transport case where reference is made to *Corsica Ferries Italia* (Case C-18/93, [1994] *ECR* I-1783).

Commission,[1345] para. 83; *Öztürk*,[1346] para. 54) or simply to more recent judgments, regardless of the area of law involved (e.g. *Ciola*,[1347] para. 14). Though more recent and complete than prior decisions, thus far *O'Flynn* has failed to acquire a status comparable to that of the original landmark case *Sotgiu*, at least not in the early years after its appearance. Possibly, this is because *Sotgiu* clearly heralded a novel approach, whilst *O'Flynn* merely summarised and formalised an interpretation already in existence.

ii. Discrimination on grounds of sex

In the area of sex equality, *Bilka*,[1348] an undisputed landmark case providing for the full indirect discrimination formula, appeared early on. However, its formula is geared towards the specific facts of the case rather than framed in more general terms. After the somewhat unclear *Jenkins* decision,[1349] the Court stated in *Bilka* (para. 29-30 and 36) in relation to indirect sex discrimination *caused by an employer*:

'If [...] it should be found that a much lower proportion of women than of men work full time, the exclusion of part-time workers from the occupational pension scheme would be contrary to Article 119 of the Treaty where, taking into account the difficulties encountered by women workers in working full-time, that measure could not be explained by factors which exclude any discrimination on grounds of sex. However, if the undertaking is able to show that its pay practice may be explained by objectively justified factors unrelated to any discrimination on grounds of sex there is no breach of Article 119. [...] If the national Court finds that the measures chosen by Bilka correspond to a real need on the part of the undertaking, are appropriate with a view to achieving the objective pursued and are necessary to that end, the fact that the measures affect a far greater number of women than men is not sufficient to show that they constitute an infringement of Article 119.'

Bilka quickly became an often quoted landmark case (e.g. *Helmig*,[1350] para. 24: *Kording*,[1351] para. 20; *Hill and Stapleton*,[1352] para. 34).[1353] In more recent case law, the

---

[1345]   Case C-156/98, [2000] *ECR* I-6857, a taxation case where reference is made to *Commerzbank* (Case C-330/91, [1993] *ECR* I-4017).
[1346]   Case C-373/02, judgment of 28 April 2004, n.y.r., a social security case involving Turkish workers where reference is made to *Kocak and Örs* (Joined Cases C-102/98 and C-211/98, [2000] *ECR* I-1287).
[1347]   Case C-224/97, [1999] *ECR* I-2517, a case involving free movement of services where reference is made to a precedent from the area of free movement of workers, namely *Clean Car* (Case C-350/96, [1998] *ECR* I-2521).
[1348]   Case 170/84, [1986] *ECR* 1607.
[1349]   Case 96/80, [1981] *ECR* 911.
[1350]   Joined Cases C-399/92, C-409/92, C-425/92, C-34/93, C-50/93 & C-78/93, [1994] *ECR* I-5727.
[1351]   Case C-100/95, [1997] *ECR* I-5289.
[1352]   Case C-243/95, [1998] *ECR* I-3739.
[1353]   The Court may also refer to recent decisions from the specific area at hand, e.g. *Lewen* (Case C-333/97, [1999] *ECR* I-7243), para. 76, where the Court referred to *Boyle* (Case C-411/96, [1998] *ECR* I-6401).

Bilka test has sometimes been restated in general terms. Most notably, the Court in *Seymour-Smith*[1354] (para. 25) explained that the principle of equal pay 'excludes not only the application of provisions leading to direct sex discrimination, but also the application of provisions which maintain different treatment between men and women at work as a result of the application of criteria not based on sex where those differences of treatment are not attributable to objective factors unrelated to sex discrimination'.

With regard to objective justification, the Court in *Rinner-Kühn*[1355] (para. 14) reformulated the *Bilka* test for instances of indirect discrimination arising out of the application of *Member State legislation*. In order to be objectively justified, such national legislation must serve 'a necessary aim of the State's social policy' and be 'suitable and requisite for attaining that aim'. Later case law considerably softened this standard by referring merely to 'a legitimate aim' (first in *Commission v Belgium*,[1356] but later examples are *Molenbroek*, para. 13,[1357] and *Roks*,[1358] para. 34). Further, in the context of *social security law*, the Court in *Nolte*[1359] (para. 34) accepted as objective justification that in exercising its competence the national legislator was 'reasonably entitled to consider that the legislation in question was necessary in order to achieve [its] aim'. Similarly, the Court held in *Seymour-Smith* (para. 77) that if a *prima facie* indirect discrimination case exists, 'it is for the Member State, as the author of the allegedly discriminatory rule, to show that the said rule reflects a legitimate aim of its social policy, that that aim is unrelated to any discrimination based on sex, and that it could reasonably consider that the means chosen were suitable for attaining that aim'.

> Specifically, the Court explained (para. 68 subs.): 'It is settled case-law that if a Member State is able to show that the measures chosen reflect a necessary aim of its social policy and are suitable and necessary for achieving that aim, the mere fact that the legislative provision affects far more women than men at work cannot be regarded as a breach of Article 119 of the Treaty [...]. [...] It must also be ascertained, in the light of all the relevant factors and taking into account the possibility of achieving the social policy aim in question by other means, whether such an aim appears to be unrelated to any discrimination based on sex and whether the disputed rule, as a means to its achievement, is capable of advancing that aim. In that connection, the United Kingdom Government maintains that a Member State should merely have to show that it was reasonably entitled to consider that the measure

---

[1354] Case C-167/97, [1999] *ECR* I-623.
[1355] Case 171/88, [1989] *ECR* 2743.
[1356] Case C-229/89, [1991] *ECR* I-2205. Here, the Court actually used both terms (see para. 19 and 26).
[1357] Case C-226/91, [1992] *ECR* I-5943.
[1358] Case C-343/92, [1994] *ECR* I-571. According to Bieback 1997, p. 400, here the Court for the first time provided a standard formula regarding the concept of indirect discrimination in social security law.
[1359] Case C-317/93, [1995] *ECR* I-4625. See also *Megner and Scheffel* (Case C-444/93, [1995] *ECR* I-4741), para. 30.

would advance a social policy aim. It relies to that end on Case C-317/93 Nolte [1995] ECR
I-4625. It is true that in paragraph 33 of the Nolte case the Court observed that, in choosing
the measures capable of achieving the aims of their social and employment policy, the
Member States have a broad margin of discretion. However, although social policy is essentially a matter for the Member States under Community law as it stands, the fact remains
that the broad margin of discretion available to the Member States in that connection
cannot have the effect of frustrating the implementation of a fundamental principle of Community law such as that of equal pay for men and women. Mere generalisations concerning
the capacity of a specific measure to encourage recruitment are not enough to show that
the aim of the disputed rule is unrelated to any discrimination based on sex nor to provide
evidence on the basis of which it could reasonably be considered that the means chosen
were suitable for achieving that aim. Accordingly, the answer to the fifth question must be
that if a considerably smaller percentage of women than men is capable of fulfilling the
requirement of two years' employment imposed by the disputed rule, it is for the Member
State, as the author of the allegedly discriminatory rule, to show that the said rule reflects
a legitimate aim of its social policy, that that aim is unrelated to any discrimination based
on sex, and that it could reasonably consider that the means chosen were suitable for
attaining that aim.'

Barnard & Hepple[1360] note that such an application dilutes the test in that the element
of strict necessity is missing (also Hervey)[1361] and further that at least three tests for
objective justification now exist in the context of indirect sex discrimination: 'the strict
Bilka test for indirectly discriminatory conduct by employers [...], the weaker
Seymour-Smith test for indirectly discriminatory employment legislation, and the very
diluted test for social security legislation in *Nolte/Megner*' (see also O'Leary).[1362]
However, the present writer sees little or no qualitative difference between the two
latter tests (compare also Fredman).[1363]

iii. The formula's elements according to case law

In spite of the differences between these formulae in the context of indirect discrimination on grounds of both nationality and of sex, they share the *same basic structure*. The
two main elements of each version of the formula relate to 1) the discrimination's
indirect nature and 2) objective justification.[1364] Based on the Court's decisions, each

---

[1360] Barnard & Hepple 1999, p. 409, and Barnard & Hepple 2000, pp. 574 subs.
[1361] Hervey 2002, p. 122.
[1362] O'Leary 2002, p. 165.
[1363] Fredman 2002, p. 113.
[1364] As a more general element underlying equality and discrimination law, comparability – sometimes
mentioned by academic authors as part of the discrimination test (e.g. Burri 2000, p. 117) – is not
an explicit part of the indirect discrimination formula.

of these two elements may be further parsed (e.g. Rust,[1365] Bieback,[1366] also Drijber & Prechal).[1367] The first element, concerning the discrimination's indirect nature, is dependent upon two issues, namely a) reliance on a differentiatory ground that is formally neutral and b) a resulting disparate impact in terms of a separate but prohibited discriminatory ground. Objective justification can be similarly subdivided into issues involving a) a reliance on a legitimate aim which is independent of a prohibited discriminatory ground and b) the requirement that the measures employed for these purposes be proportionate – that is, they must be suitable and requisite (necessary). Thus, the overall structure of the indirect discrimination formula may be outlined as follows:

1) Indirect nature of the discrimination, meaning:
   a)   The existence of a formally neutral measure (that is, a measure or practice that does not directly and obviously rely on a forbidden discriminatory ground);
   b)   A disparate impact resulting from of the measure in the sense of an expressly prohibited ground (that is, the measure is only apparently neutral since, in practice, it causes a disadvantage for a group that is protected by a particular non-discrimination provision);
2) Absence of objective justification, including:
   a)   Reliance on a legitimate aim which is independent of the prohibited criterion (that is, the measure must have a legitimate, non-discriminatory aim);
   b)   Proportionality of the measure in that context, that is:
       aa) The measure is suitable in the context of the legitimate aim;
       bb) The measure is requisite (necessary) in that context.

Although, in this general form, the elements are the same for indirect discrimination on grounds of nationality and on grounds of sex, this study will demonstrate that there are important differences as far as their application is concerned[1368] and that, further, the formula as presented above may not in fact be complete, in particular with regard to proportionality.[1369]

b.   *Are there links between the development in the areas of discrimination on grounds of nationality and sex discrimination?*

According to some, certain *links must exist* between the development of the indirect discrimination formula in relation to discrimination on grounds of nationality, on

---

[1365]   Rust 1996, p. 443.
[1366]   Bieback 1997, p. 52.
[1367]   Drijber & Prechal 1997, pp. 137 subs.
[1368]   See later in this part, A.IV.2.d.
[1369]   See later in this part, A.IV.3.a.iv.

the one hand, and discrimination on grounds of sex, on the other hand (e.g.
Blomeyer,[1370] Rating).[1371] However, case law demonstrates that although the concept of
indirect discrimination developed in a parallel fashion in these two areas of law, that
development did not explicitly take place in an interdependent manner. When in
Sabbatini[1372] the Court recognized the potentially indirect nature of sex discrimination,
it did so without referring to Ugliola,[1373] which it decided three years earlier, as a precedent. Not in even in Jenkins,[1374] where AG Warner explicitly pointed to Sotgiu,[1375] did
the Court make such a reference. Similarly, when the Court dealt with objective justification in the context of discrimination on grounds of nationality in O'Flynn,[1376] it did
not refer to any of the prior relevant sex equality cases (Jenkins,[1377] Bilka,[1378] Rinner-
Kühn).[1379] In other words, although an implicit link seems to be likely, the decisions
through which the Court introduced and consolidated the legal concept of indirect
discrimination in the two areas are not explicitly built on precedents from one another.

c. The terminology used by the Court

The terminology used by the Court in the context of indirect discrimination *is not nor
has ever been uniform*. As previously mentioned, the term 'indirect discrimination'
as it first appeared in Geitling,[1380] was used in relation to an issue that differs from how
it is used today. In the first truly identifiable indirect discrimination cases, the Court
used a variety of expressions, 'indirectly introducing discrimination' (Ugliola),[1381] 'in
fact creating a difference' (Sabbatini),[1382] and 'covert discrimination' (Sotgiu).[1383] The
last term, covert discrimination, became a standard label, used over many decades.
However, 'indirect discrimination', sometimes together with 'disguised discrimination', was also used fairly early, at least in the context of cases involving discrimination
on grounds of nationality (Steinike & Weinlig,[1384] Palermo-Toia,[1385] Beentjes).[1386] More
recently, the terms most commonly used by the Court seem to be 'covert discrimina-

---

[1370] Blomeyer 1994, pp. 60/61.
[1371] Rating 1994, p. 94.
[1372] Case 20/71, [1972] *ECR* 345.
[1373] Case 15/69, [1969] *ECR* 363.
[1374] Case 96/80, [1981] *ECR* 911.
[1375] Case 152/73, [1974] *ECR* 153.
[1376] Case C-237/94, [1996] *ECR* I-2617.
[1377] Case 96/80, [1981] *ECR* 911.
[1378] Case 170/84, [1986] *ECR* 1607.
[1379] Case 171/88, [1989] *ECR* 2743.
[1380] Case 2/56, [1957/1958] *ECR* 3; see above Part 1, C.IV.
[1381] Case 15/69, [1969] *ECR* 363.
[1382] Case 20/71, [1972] *ECR* 345.
[1383] Case 152/73, [1974] *ECR* 153.
[1384] Case 78/76, [1977] *ECR* 595.
[1385] Case 237/78, [1979] *ECR* 2645.
[1386] Case 31/87, [1988] *ECR* 4635.

tion' (e.g. *ARGE Gewässerschutz*,[1387] para. 33 subs.; *Ferlini*,[1388] para. 59, *Bidar*,[1389] para. 51) and 'indirect discrimination' (e.g. *Italy v Commission*).[1390] The Court's simultaneous use of both terms in the landmark case *O'Flynn*[1391] confirms that they ought to be understood as synonymous (Drijber & Prechal).[1392]

In *sex discrimination* cases, the Court used the term 'indirect discrimination' for the first time in the Staff law case *De Angelis*[1393] (para. 18). Outside Staff law, at first the Court avoided such explicit language, possibly due to the confusion caused by its use of the term 'indirect discrimination' in the context of direct effect in *Defrenne II*.[1394] Instead, the Court spoke about a difference that is 'in reality discrimination based on the sex of the worker' (*Jenkins*)[1395] and about 'an indirect way of reducing the pay of part-time workers' (*Bilka*).[1396] Subsequently, 'indirect discrimination' has become a standard expression throughout sex equality law in general (e.g. *Teuling*,[1397] *Schnorbus*,[1398] *Seymour-Smith*),[1399] most likely because express prohibitions in secondary law (and also, more recently, because legal definitions)[1400] are framed in these terms. Nevertheless, the Court chooses at times to use such other terms as 'indirect disadvantage' (*Kachelmann*,[1401] para. 28), or more general descriptions, such as a provision which 'results as a matter of fact in discrimination against female workers by comparison with male workers' (*Steinicke*,[1402] para. 57).

2. WHY WAS THE LEGAL CONCEPT OF INDIRECT DISCRIMINATION 'INVENTED'?

In *Sotgiu*,[1403] the Court explained that a broad and comprehensive interpretation of the prohibition against discrimination on grounds of nationality covering both overt and covert discrimination 'is necessary to ensure the effective working of one of the fundamental principles of the Community which requires that equality of treatment

---

[1387] Case C-94/99, [2000] *ECR* I-11037.
[1388] Case C-411/98, [2000] *ECR* I-8081.
[1389] Case C-209/03, judgment of 15 March 2005, n.y.r.
[1390] Case C-361/98, [2001] *ECR* I-385.
[1391] Case C-237/94, [1996] *ECR* I-2617.
[1392] Drijber & Prechal 1997, p. 124, footnote 11.
[1393] Case 246/83, [1985] *ECR* 1253.
[1394] Case 43/75, [1976] *ECR* 455.
[1395] Case C-226/98, [2000] *ECR* I-2447.
[1396] Case 170/84, [1986] *ECR* 1607.
[1397] Case 30/85, [1987] *ECR* 2497.
[1398] Case C-79/99, [2000] *ECR* I-10997.
[1399] Case C-167/97, [1999] *ECR* I-623.
[1400] See later in this part, B.
[1401] Case C-322/98, [2000] *ECR* I-7505.
[1402] Case C-77/02, judgment of 11 September 2003, n.y.r.
[1403] Case 152/73, [1974] *ECR* 153.

of workers shall be ensured 'in fact and in law''. Yet, only one of the three foundational
cases explicitly addresses this *raison d'être* for the then new concept of indirect
discrimination. Such a broad and comprehensive interpretation was clearly intended
to identify circumventions of prohibitions against discrimination by *looking beyond
the mere form* of a contested measure. Accordingly, the maxim that 'substance prevails
over form' expresses the essence of the concept of indirect discrimination as developed
through the Court's case law. This comprehensive interpretation may particularly
impact certain areas, such as social law where the disparate effects of apparently neutral
measures are often due to underlying structural discrimination. For example, in
Jenkins[1404] the Court expressly acknowledged the difficulties of (some) female workers
to engage in full-time work and, against this background, some academic writers argue
that the concept of indirect sex discrimination law should be seen as a means to actively
combat the underlying structural discrimination itself.[1405]

IV. ISSUES FOR DEBATE ARISING FROM THE CASE LAW DEFINITION

1. INTRODUCTORY REMARKS

The case law discussed thus far raises a number of *questions relating to the meaning
and the aim of the legal concept of indirect discrimination.* The issues examined below
are divided into three categories. The first concerns the discrimination's indirect
nature; the second, objective justification; and the third, the aim behind the legal concept of indirect discrimination. In some cases, the issues call for a case law analysis
that goes into the ever increasing number of cases applying the concept in varying
concrete contexts, that is, far beyond the general definition of the legal concept of
indirect discrimination. As was stated earlier,[1406] this present study does not attempt
to provide a systematic and all encompassing analysis on that level. Others have
performed detailed and valuable work in that regard.[1407] Although their findings have
often been relied on in this study, it should be recalled that the primary focus here is

---

[1404]   Case 96/80, [1981] *ECR* 911.
[1405]   Ellis 1994 (Definition of Discrimination), p. 572, and Ellis 1998, pp. 122 and 186.
[1406]   See above Part 1, A.II.1.
[1407]   Among them notably Wisskirchen 1994, Steiner 1999 (both regarding indirect sex discrimination
in the context of employment law), Bieback 1997 (on sex discrimination in social security law), Burri
2000 (on sex discrimination in the specific context of part-time work), Drijber & Prechal 1997 (on
equal treatment of men and women as compared to other non-discrimination areas), Stampe 2001
(on sex discrimination in general), Sommer 1998, pp. 129 subs. (on discrimination specifically in
relation to pay), Gerards 2002 (on the application of the equality principle by the courts, in various
areas of EC law).

on *the Court's case law definition* (which remains relevant in important areas of EC non-discrimination law; the implications of the more recent legal definitions will be discussed later).[1408]

2. ISSUES RELATING TO THE FIRST PART OF THE INDIRECT DISCRIMINATION FORMULA

The following discussions relate to the *first part of the indirect discrimination formula* (the discrimination's indirect nature) and focus on the following issues: What is meant by 'indirect' discrimination? What is the nature of the link between indirect discrimination and the Aristotelian formula? How relevant is the legal concept of indirect discrimination in the context of openly formulated non-discrimination provisions? What is the applicable test in the context of the requisite disparate effect? What is the role of intent with regard to the first part of the indirect discrimination formula? And, what are the characteristics of the unique context of indirect sex discrimination as it applies to cases involving work of equal value?

a. What does 'indirect' mean?

Although illegal discrimination may be indirectly introduced in various ways, 'indirect' in the sense that the word operates as part of the legal term 'indirect discrimination' has a particular meaning. The case law discussed thus far confirms that the crucial element for present purposes is the discrimination ground. In other words, the 'indirectness' of the discrimination lies in the fact that discrimination *on grounds of the prohibited criterion* (such as nationality or sex) is caused indirectly, namely through reliance on a separate and apparently neutral criterion (for example, residence or working time). Indirect discrimination in this sense needs to be clearly distinguished from other ways of indirectly introducing discrimination, that is, from cases where elements other than the grounds for discrimination[1409] are concerned in an indirect manner (compare Jarass).[1410] Thus, it was seen that the indirect nature of an infrin-

---

[1408]   See later in this part, B.

[1409]   In the study's introductory part, a number of elements were proposed for the purposes of analysing discrimination provisions and cases, namely 1) the *type* of the provision (equality or non-discrimination provision), 2) the *object* of equality or discrimination (the persons, objects or actions to which the prescribed equality/forbidden discrimination refers), 3) the *ground* for equal treatment or non-discrimination, 4) the persons *protected* by the provision and 5) the persons *obliged* by the provisions; see above Part 1, B.V.2.

[1410]   Jarass 2000 (Unified Approach), p. 149.

gement can also relate to the category of the *protected*, as in the ECSC case *Geitling*.[1411] Further, the indirect nature of the infringement in a given case may relate to the *object* of the treatment, as in Art. 90(1) EC which mentions the direct and indirect imposition of taxation on goods as the object of its prohibition of discrimination (e.g. *Marsala*).[1412] It is suggested that in order to avoid confusion between these different situations it might be best to use the expression 'indirectly introducing discrimination' as a general and overarching term, including situations such as that of the ECSC case *Geitling* and the indirect imposition of tax under Art. 90(1) EC, and to reserve the term 'indirect discrimination' solely to discrimination caused through indirect reliance on a prohibited discrimination ground.

What, then, does it mean to indirectly rely on a prohibited discriminatory ground? In *O'Flynn*,[1413] the Court referred to 'distinguishing criteria' as well as to 'conditions'. According to Drijber & Prechal,[1414] the former terms concern the use of an apparently neutral criterion, such as residence or working time, whilst in the case of the latter term, no apparent distinguishing criteria are used but rather a discriminatory effect simply flows from requirements that can be met more easily by one group of persons than another. However, it would be a mistake to read too much into the fact that two separate terms are used. As Fuchsloch[1415] rightly notes, indirect discrimination always requires a differentiation, and regulatory systems that do not differentiate are as a practical matter inconceivable. It is submitted that, in fact, these two categories do not differ in terms of their effect in that there is always a differentiation in the sense that criteria and conditions both distinguish between two groups of persons or situations. Cases such as *Sotgiu*[1416] and *Biehl*,[1417] mentioned in *O'Flynn*, illustrate that what is called distinguishing criteria by the Court can also be said to involve a condition, and *vice versa*.

[1411] Case 2/56, [1957/1958] *ECR* 3; see above Part 1, C.IV. See also *Bond van Adverteerders* (Case 352/85, [1988] *ECR* 2085); Donner 1988, p. 93; see later Part 3. B.III.2.b.i. For the same phenomenon in the context of restrictions in a wider sense, see *Safir* (Case C-118/96, [1998] I-1897) and *Kohll* (Case C-158/96, [1998] *ECR* I-1931), also discussed later Part 3, B.IV.4.

[1412] Case 277/83, [1985] *ECR* 2049; see earlier in this part, A.I.4.a.iii. – For the same phenomenon in the context of restrictions in a wider sense, see *Choquet* (Case 16/78, [1978] *ECR* 2293), discussed below Part 3, B.II.2.a.iii. In that case, the requirement of a national driving licence – which is an issue of transport law – was examined in the context of rules concerning the free movement of persons and services because national rules on driving licences 'can exert an influence, both direct and indirect, on the exercise of rights guaranteed by the provisions of the Treaty relating to freedom of movement for workers, to establishment and, subject to the reference contained in Article 61(1) of the Treaty, to the provisions of services in general' (*Choquet*, para. 4).

[1413] Case C-237/94, [1996] *ECR* I-2617.

[1414] Drijber & Prechal 1997, pp. 124 and 138.

[1415] Fuchsloch 1995, pp. 122 and 131.

[1416] Case 152/73, [1974] *ECR* 153, see earlier in this part, A.I.2.c.

[1417] Case C-175/88, [1990] *ECR* I-1779; see earlier in this part, A.I.5.b.ii.

In *Sotgiu*, mentioned in *O'Flynn* as an example of the category of distinguishing criteria, the distinction made for the purposes of granting different allowances levels was that between two categories of workers employed away from their place of residence in Germany, namely those who lived in Germany at the time of their initial employment and those whose resided abroad. This situation can also be characterised as involving a condition: that is, in order to be granted the higher allowance, a person had to meet the condition that he or she be a resident in Germany at the time of the initial employment. In a parallel manner, underlying every condition is a distinction between those who are or who are not able to fulfil the condition. *Biehl*, also referred to in *O'Flynn* in the context of 'indistinctly applicable conditions', involved Luxembourg rules which allowed a refund of an over-deduction of tax only if the person concerned had been resident in Luxembourg during the whole of the relevant year. This rule can be seen as imposing a uniformly applicable condition in the sense that everyone seeking a refund had to fulfil the residence requirement. The underlying distinction is that between persons who can obtain the refund (namely those who had spent the full tax year in residence) and those who cannot obtain the refund (namely those who did not spend the full tax year in residence).

All cases discussed thus far in fact involve *a distinction or different treatment* (Fuchsloch),[1418] with the exception only of the special case of *Seco*[1419] which involved a situation that later would not even be examined in terms of indirect discrimination. The logical conclusion is that cases which do not result in different treatment of two groups envisaged by the discriminatory ground cannot qualify as indirect discrimination. Thus, the following conclusions may be drawn: a) indirect discrimination concerns treatment that differentiates between two groups (or situations); b) the differentiation ground that results in this distinction is not, formally speaking, one prohibited by the provision at issue, and c) but this ground is only formally neutral since in fact it has an effect similar to the explicitly prohibited one.

b. Indirect discrimination and the Aristotelian equality formula

In the previous section it was argued that indirect discrimination concerns *different treatment,* which implies that the groups or situations in question are comparable. However, in academic writing it is sometimes argued that indirect discrimination can also be seen as same treatment of non-comparable situations. This raises the question of the concept's place in the framework of the Aristotelian equality formula: is indirect discrimination caused through different treatment of likes (first part of the equality formula) or same treatment of unalikes (second part of the formula)?[1420]

[1418] Fuchsloch 1995, p. 39, footnote 231.
[1419] Joined Cases 62/81 and 63/81, [1982] *ECR* 223.
[1420] Regarding the Aristotelian formula, see above Part 1, B.II.1.b.

i. Indirect discrimination caused through different treatment

In the analysis of concrete cases undertaken thus far, the argument that a link exists between indirect discrimination and the same treatment of unalikes (or discrimination in substance) was found in the context of the cases *Sea Fisheries*,[1421] *Palermo-Toia*[1422] and *Seco*[1423] (Timmermans).[1424] Certain authors assert that in indirect discrimination cases *different situations are treated in the same way* but have significant disparate impacts on protected groups (as opposed to cases of direct discrimination, which involve unequal treatment of comparable situations; see in particular Barnard & Hepple;[1425] also Fredman,[1426] Govers,[1427] Wentholt,[1428] Hepple, Choussey & Choudhury,[1429] Hendriks,[1430] Waddington & Hendriks).[1431] De Schutter[1432] even argues that the prohibition against indirect discrimination obliges the potential discriminator to take account of particular factual differences which merit different treatment.

In contrast, Veldman[1433] insists that indirect discrimination is *a hidden kind of different treatment of comparable cases.* The present writer would agree with Veldman, at least as far as the case law thus far discussed is concerned. First, whilst there is indeed a factual difference between part-time workers and full-time workers or between persons resident or non-resident for tax purposes, the decisive question is whether this difference is relevant in the context of discrimination that focuses on a *different* issue (sex, nationality). Second, to claim that indirect discrimination cases involve same treatment is to disregard the fact that, in the types of cases that usually come before the Court, the focus is clearly on difference in treatment. This was the case even in the earliest indirect discrimination cases. Thus, the instance of indirect discrimination found in *Ugliola*[1434] resulted from a distinction made between persons called up for military service in Germany and persons called up in other countries. Under the rule in question, the former had their military service taken into account for the purposes of calculating their period of employment, but the latter did not. Because other legal rules tied the obligation to perform military service to the country of origin, the rule in question resulted in different treatment according to nationality. Similarly,

---

[1421] Case 61/77, [1978] *ECR* 417; see earlier in this part, A.I.4.d.ii.
[1422] Case 237/78, [1979] *ECR* 2645; see earlier in this part, A.I.4.e.iii.
[1423] Joined Cases 62/81 and 63/81, [1982] *ECR* 223; see earlier in this part, A.I.4.j.ii.
[1424] See in particular Timmermans 1978 and Timmermans 1982.
[1425] Barnard & Hepple 2000, p. 570.
[1426] Fredman 1999, p. 206.
[1427] Govers 1981, p. 27.
[1428] Wentholt 1990, p. 50.
[1429] Hepple, Choussey & Choudhury 2000, p. 30.
[1430] Hendriks 2000, p. 102.
[1431] Waddington & Hendriks 2002, p. 408.
[1432] De Schutter 1999, pp. 25 subs.
[1433] Veldman 1995, pp. 162 and 163.
[1434] Case 15/69, [1969] *ECR* 363.

in *Sabbatini*[1435] the instance of sex discrimination found by the Court resulted from a difference in treatment between officials who upon marriage became heads of households and those who did not. Under the rule in question, only the former retained their expatriation allowance. Thus, because of separate legal rules concerning the status of head of household, the rule in question resulted in different treatment of men and women. Such a difference in treatment was also at the centre of the landmark case *Sotgiu*[1436] where workers employed away from their place of residence were entitled to a higher allowance if they lived in Germany at the time of their initial employment. In this case, the Court explicitly referred to 'criteria of differentiation' and found that the differentiation made on the basis of residence resulted in a differentiation according to nationality. The same pattern can be found in later cases, again with the sole exception of *Seco.*[1437] More recently, the Court in *Schönheit and Becker*[1438] (para. 67) generally described indirect sex discrimination as 'the application of provisions which maintain *different treatment* between men and women at work as a result of the application of criteria not based on sex' (emphasis added). Similarly (and even more clearly), AG Jacobs explained in *Elsner-Lakeberg*[1439] (point 9 of the opinion): 'It is settled case-law that the principle of equal pay extends not only to direct sex discrimination but also to different treatment of men and women at work resulting from the application of criteria not based on sex, unless that different treatment is justified by objective factors unrelated to sex'. Accordingly, the conclusion to be drawn must be that the legal concept of indirect discrimination as reflected in the case law discussed thus far is linked to the first part of the Aristotelian equality formula.

ii. Indirect discrimination caused through same treatment?

However, this conclusion does not mean that indirect discrimination cannot also relate to the second part of the Aristotelian equality formula, as is sometimes argued (e.g. Fuchsloch).[1440] Lenaerts[1441] emphasises that the notions of formal discrimination and discrimination in substance, on the one hand, have to be distinguished from direct and indirect discrimination, on the other hand. Substantive discrimination may take the form of either direct or indirect discrimination. More specifically, there may be indirect discrimination in an instance where non-comparable cases are only apparently treated differently. Thus, under this view, there might be an indirect form of discrimination under the second part of the Aristotelian formula (see also Lenaerts & van

---

[1435] Case 152/73, [1974] *ECR* 153.
[1436] Case 20/71, [1972] *ECR* 345.
[1437] Joined Cases 62/81 and 63/81, [1982] *ECR* 223.
[1438] Joined Cases C-4/02 and 5/02, judgment of 23 October 2003, n.y.r.
[1439] Case C-285/02, judgment of 27 May 2004, n.y.r.
[1440] Fuchsloch 1995, p. 131.
[1441] Lenaerts 1991, p. 11, footnote 31.

Nuffel,[1442] Burri,[1443] the latter with further references). The present writer would agree
that, from a theoretical perspective, there is no logical reason why discrimination
should not be able to take an indirect form in the cases of non-comparable situations.

Whilst there is no explicit case law by the Court on indirect discrimination through
same treatment, the recent decision in the case *Merida*[1444] can be interpreted as implying such a finding. The case concerned the calculation under German social security
law of a temporary supplementary allowance paid to a former civilian employee of
the allied forces in Germany. In determining the basis for calculation, the German
authorities deducted what would have been the applicable German tax on wages. Mr
Merida, a Frenchman living in France and subject to French income taxation at a lower
rate than would have been the case in Germany, considered such a basis for calculation
contrary to Community law. In her opinion on the case, AG Stix-Hackl specifically
stated that '[i]ndirect discrimination arises through the application of different rules
to comparable situations or the application of the same rule to different situations and
where the measure concerned cannot be justified by an objective difference or as a
measure proportionate to its aim' (*Merida*, point 20 of the AG's opinion). In the AG's
view, the case indeed involved indirect discrimination on grounds of nationality (if
only *prima facie*), because the deduction of the amount of the German tax in all cases
tended to work to the detriment of foreign workers. The Court found (unspecified)
discrimination on grounds of nationality in a situation where Germany failed to apply
different rules to workers based on their tax residence. In effect, therefore, the Court
held that Germany was obliged to apply 'different methods of assessment depending
on the place of residence of the person concerned' (compare *Merida*, para. 29), in a
situation in which there was formally equal treatment but with a different effect
depending on the workers' (tax) residence (compare *Merida*, para. 24). This finding
implies that the positions of the two groups of workers were not comparable (namely
because of the different tax burden under the different national laws). Whilst the Court
did not explicitly say that persons with foreign residence tend to be foreigners, this
view is, clearly, implied. Accordingly, the Court's finding can be read as implying
indirect discrimination caused through same treatment of non-comparable situations.

> The Court began by recalling the prohibition of both overt and covert discrimination and
> then added generally that the principle of non-discrimination 'requires not only that
> comparable situations must not be treated differently but also that different situations must
> not be treated in the same way'. This is followed by a general definition of indirect discrimi-
> nation, in the sense that '[u]nless objectively justified and proportionate to its aim, a provi-
> sion of national law must be regarded as indirectly discriminatory it is intrinsically liable
> to affect migrant workers more than national workers and if there is a consequent risk that

---

[1442] Lenaerts & Van Nuffel 1995, pp. 120/121.
[1443] Burri 2000, p. 118.
[1444] Case C-400/02, judgment of 16 September 2004, n.y.r.

it will place the former at a particular disadvantage' (*Merida*, para. 21-23, referring to *O'Flynn*).[1445] As for the specific circumstances of the case at hand, the Court focused on the fact that the intent of the German rules was to ensure that the amount received by the former worker would correspond to 100% of the difference between the basis of assessment and the amount of unemployment benefit received by the worker. The Court found that in the case of workers residing in Germany this could indeed be achieved under the contested system. However, in a case like that of Mr Merida the system should have required the deduction of the actual French income tax, rather than the (higher) German tax to achieve the proper result. Consequently, taking account of the German wage tax had an unfavourable effect on frontier workers such as Mr. Merida. The Court refused Germany's attempt to defend its use of a single system for the calculation of benefit based on a claim of justifiable expediency.

c. Indirect discrimination in the context of openly worded non-discrimination provisions

As was stated earlier,[1446] the legal concept of indirect discrimination is particularly useful in the context of non-discrimination provisions that *list a limited number of discriminatory grounds* since here the concept may make it possible to bring cases involving different grounds within the scope of such a law. The situation differs in cases of non-discrimination provisions which do not mention any prohibited differentiation grounds at all or which provide for a non-exhaustive list of such criteria. These two situations are discussed below.

i. In the case of general non-discrimination or equality provisions (comparability)

In the case where an equality or non-discrimination rule *mentions no grounds at all*, the identification of a prohibited non-discriminatory ground is, strictly speaking, not even necessary. Instead, the only relevant question is whether a contested distinction concerns comparable or non-comparable situations (Bayefsky).[1447] In the framework of the law of the European Communities, where the general equality principle embodies such a rule, the so-called JET cases illustrate this point. These cases concerned the employment conditions applicable to the staff of a Euratom project which drew from research organisations established in various Member States. At issue was a distinction made on the basis of the provenance of the staff members in terms of the organisation sending them. The applicants complained of indirect discrimination on

---

[1445]   Case C-237/94, [1996] *ECR* I-2617.
[1446]   See above Part 1, B.III.4.a.
[1447]   Bayefsky 1990, p. 5.

grounds of nationality, based on Art. 96 of the EAEC Treaty.[1448] However, the Court
of Justice *(Ainsworth)*[1449] and later also the Court of First Instance *(Altmann)*[1450]
examined the case in the framework of the Community's general equality principle.
In that framework, both Courts simply focused on the question of whether the
situations of the different groups of staff were comparable, without examining whether
there was different treatment in terms of nationality (or any other specific discriminatory ground).

> Specifically, the JET cases concerned the employment rules and practices of the organisation
> Joint European Torus (JET) which was part of a research programme of the European
> Atomic Energy Community in the field of nuclear fusion and plasma physics. The
> organisation was hosted by the UK Atomic Energy Authority (UKAEA) which was a JET
> member. The other members were 12 research organizations located in other European
> States. The staff composing JET's project team were drawn from the various members.
> According to JET's Statutes, staff coming from the UKAEA were to remain in the employ-
> ment of that organisation whilst staff coming from other organisations were to be employed
> by the Commission as temporary workers. According to a practice by JET, British persons
> who wished to be hired as JET staff members had to apply through the UKAEA, which hired
> only British persons. There was an appreciable pay difference between the two categories
> of employment. The Commission staff were paid much better than the UKAEA staff even
> though both worked as members of the same project team. The JET cases arose because
> certain British staff members coming from UKAEA wished instead to be employed by the
> Commission but were refused.
>
> In *Ainsworth*, the applicants argued that the rules and practices in question operated solely
> to the disadvantage of British nationals and, therefore, constituted disguised discrimination
> on grounds of nationality under Art. 96 of the EAEC Treaty, similar to that condemned
> by the Court in *Sea Fisheries*.[1451] Though both Advocates General who wrote opinions on
> this case[1452] found an infringement of Euratom law, neither mentioned indirect discrimina-
> tion. The Court of Justice found that the practice to force British candidates to apply
> through the UKAEA violated the general equality principle but it refused to accept that a
> difference in payment based on the member organization which made the employee in
> question available to JET amounted to discrimination in that the situations of the different
> staff members were not comparable (*Ainsworth*, para. 25 subs.). The old edition of Kapteyn
> & VerLoren van Themaat[1453] interpreted this ruling as meaning that whilst the JET clearly

---

[1448]   Art. 96(1) EA reads: 'The Member States shall abolish all restrictions based on nationality affecting
the right of nationals of any Member State to take skilled employment in the field of nuclear energy,
subject to the limitations resulting from the basic requirements of public policy, public security or
public health.'

[1449]   Joined Cases 271/83 and 15, 36, 113, 158, 203/84 and 13/85, [1987] *ECR* 167.

[1450]   Joined Cases T-177/94 and T-377/94, [1996] *ECR* II-2041.

[1451]   Case 61/77, [1978] *ECR* 417.

[1452]   A second opinion was written after the case had been referred to the full Court and after there had
been a second hearing.

[1453]   Kapteyn & VerLoren van Themaat 1995, p. 729.

is a Community project, this does not mean that the working conditions fall fully under the Community rules (literally: 'have Community character'). In the present writer's analysis, the issue is rather one of comparability.

More than ten years later, the applicants in the follow-up case *Altmann* relied both on the principle of equal treatment and on the prohibition of discrimination on grounds of nationality, though, apparently, without referring specifically to indirect discrimination. Again, the decision was based on the general equality principle and the Court of First Instance focused on the comparability of the staff member's situations. The Court held that all members of the Project Staff were in a comparable situation, irrespective of the member organisation which made them available to JET, and that, consequently, there was a prohibited difference in treatment. The difference was found to be particularly pronounced in that it concerned not only employment but also included the security of employment as well as the prospect of recruitment as Community officials (*Altmann*, para. 81 subs.). In addition, the Court also found that circumstances had changed in such a way that all the factual circumstances referred to by the Court of Justice in support of its prior conclusion that there was objective justification for the difference in treatment established by the JET Statutes had lapsed (*Altmann*, para. 117 and 118). As a result, the Commission decision not to employ the British staff members as temporary Community servants had to be annulled.[1454] Tridimas[1455] lauds the Court for handing down a well-argued judgment on a delicate and complex issue, succeeding in undoing injustice whilst carefully distinguishing precedent.

The Court's choices regarding the appropriate legal framework for the analyses of the JET cases were decisive. Had the Court examined the contested differentiation in the framework of Art. 96 of the EAEC Treaty, as suggested by the applicants, its finding would in all likelihood have been one of *indirect* discrimination on grounds of nationality. As it was, both *Ainsworth* and *Altmann* were decided on the basis of the general equality principle, which is not framed in terms of specific discriminatory grounds. Accordingly, the Court did not have to identify a specific discriminatory ground and, consequently, there was no need to rely on the concept of indirect discrimination.

ii. In the case of a non-exhaustive list of discriminatory grounds

Strictly speaking, the legal concept of indirect discrimination is also not necessary in situations where the law mentions a non-exhaustive list of discriminatory grounds without specifying different appropriate levels of scrutiny. At least in theory, in such a framework it is always possible to find direct discrimination based on a ground not mentioned in the provision. (Though, in practice, the courts may nevertheless tend

---

[1454] At the same time, the Court of First Instance did not find the Commission's fault sufficiently serious in order to lead to liability for the damage caused; *Altmann*, para. 146 and 156.
[1455] Tridimas 1999, p. 68.

to analyse concrete cases in the framework of an explicitly mentioned ground.) In such
circumstances, there is no need to broaden the scope of the provision by looking
beyond the mere form of differentiation grounds relied on in a given case and, to that
extent, the distinction between direct and indirect discrimination is irrelevant. Given
that fact, the present author would disagree with Martin[1456] according to whom it is
precisely the non-exhaustive character of openly formulated provisions that allows
the further inclusion of disguised forms of discrimination into the general prohibition
against discrimination.[1457]

In contrast, the concept of indirect discrimination has important relevance where
a legal order applies various levels of scrutiny in the context of different discriminatory
grounds, as does the Council of Europe's Human Rights Convention. In such
framework, the concept may be particularly useful from the victim's perspective for
bringing a case into the field of application of a prohibition against discrimination with
a corresponding strict level of scrutiny (e.g. Gerards).[1458] As for EC law, an approach
based on various levels of scrutiny depending on the particular discriminatory ground
is sometimes raised in academic writing (e.g. Kischel,[1459] Alkema & Rop,[1460] Holtmaat),[1461] but the Court thus far has never based its case law on a *principled* approach
of that nature. Whilst it might be argued that the Court's generous approach to objective justification in the areas of agricultural law and social security law has the effect
of applying a comparatively low level of scrutiny, this is, rather, a matter of acknowledging wide competences (namely of the Commission in the case of agriculture[1462]
and of the Member States in the case of social security law)[1463] rather than of applying
a lower level of scrutiny. The Court's statement in *Orfanopoulos*[1464] (para. 65) is
perhaps more noteworthy in that the status of EU citizenship requires a particularly
strict interpretation of derogations with regard to the provisions on free movement
of workers because EU citizenship embodies the fundamental status of the nationals
of the EU Member States. It remains to be seen whether and how this will be reflected
in the practice of the Court's case law on free movement of workers (and of persons,
more generally).

[1456] Martin 1998, p. 266, also 263.
[1457] In addition, indirect discrimination does not provide a separate and additional discriminatory ground
to those already listed as prohibited in a given provision. Rather, indirect discrimination reflects the
recognition that explicitly prohibited discrimination can arise through reliance on a ground that is
not listed.
[1458] Gerards 2002, pp. 113 subs.
[1459] Kischel 1997, pp. 5 subs.
[1460] Alkema & Rop 2002.
[1461] Holtmaat 2003 (Stop de uitholling).
[1462] See earlier in this part, A.I.4.d.
[1463] See later in this part, A.IV.3.b.ii.
[1464] Joined Cases C-482/01 and C-493/01, judgment of 29 April 2004, n.y.r.

d. The assessment of the discriminatory effect

A closer analysis of the Court's case law on indirect discrimination reveals that the test to be applied for examining whether a given measure has a discriminatory effect or disparate impact differs depending upon whether the case of indirect discrimination is brought on grounds of nationality or on grounds of sex. The fact that, contrary to the wording of *Sotgiu*,[1465] the effect of relying on an indirectly discriminatory criterion is not (necessarily)[1466] the same as that of relying on a directly discriminatory criterion raises the question of how strong that link must be in order to amount to an actionable case of indirect discrimination. The following discussion will show that the Court's case law is not clear on that point in either of the two contexts discussed.

i. Indirect discrimination on grounds of nationality

In the foundational case of *Ugliola*[1467] the Court made no general remark with regard to the required extent of disparate impact. However, that is not surprising given that the effect of the contested rule in this case was the same as that of direct discrimination on grounds of nationality. In *Sotgiu*,[1468] the formula was that of the use of apparently neutral criteria which 'lead in fact to the same result' as the explicitly prohibited criterion. This *Sotgiu* formula was later repeated in *O'Flynn*[1469] but supplemented by additional statements. *O'Flynn* raised a question regarding the meaning of this formula. Whilst the UK Government pointed to the test applicable in situations of indirect *sex* discrimination, Mr O'Flynn argued that this test was not applicable in the different context of a claim of discrimination on grounds of nationality. The Court followed the suggestions of AG Lenz who agreed on the point that the approach for sex discrimination could not be transposed to discrimination on grounds of nationality (*O'Flynn*, points 19 subs. of the AG's opinion).[1470] The Court did not elaborate on the relationship between the case law on sex discrimination and on discrimination on grounds of nationality. Having recalled its earlier case law on discrimination on grounds of nationality, the Court simply summarised the test in the following way (*O'Flynn*, para. 20 and 21): 'It follows from all the foregoing case-law that, unless

---

[1465] Case 152/73, [1974] *ECR* 153.
[1466] See later Part 3, A.II.2.
[1467] Case 15/69, [1969] *ECR* 363; see earlier in this part, A.I.2.a.
[1468] Case 152/73, [1974] *ECR* 153.
[1469] Case C-237/94, [1996] *ECR* I-2617.
[1470] AG Lenz noted that the Court sometimes uses language that leads to the conclusion that there is discrimination by reason of nationality only if the relevant provision of a Member State *in fact* affects substantially more nationals of other Member States than its own nationals. The AG contrasted this situation with other decisions where the establishment of indirect discrimination is not made dependent on such a condition. He concluded that it is sufficient that the contested measure be *liable* to produce discriminatory effects for nationals of other Member States.

objectively justified and proportionate to its aim, a provision of national law must be regarded as indirectly discriminatory if it is intrinsically liable to affect migrant workers more than national workers and if there is a consequent risk that it will place the former at a particular disadvantage. It is not necessary in this respect to find that the provision in question does in practice affect a substantially higher proportion of migrant workers. It is sufficient that it is liable to have such an effect.' To this, the Court added explicitly that it 'is not necessary in this respect to find that the provision in question does in practice affect a substantially higher proportion of migrant workers. It is sufficient that it is liable to have such an effect'.

The Court's answer involves two distinct but intertwined issues, namely the question of the extent of impact of the rule or measure at issue (the number of persons negatively affected in order to constitute a *prima facie* case of indirect discrimination) as well as the requisite proof regarding that impact (the evidence required to establish the requisite level of negative impact). Regarding the *extent of the impact,* the Court stated that the measure must 'affect migrant workers more than national workers' and that it must 'place the former at a particular disadvantage'. Peers[1471] speaks about a *de minimis* rule; though in the present context this expression should not be understood in its classic sense since it does not concern the intensity of the disadvantage suffered by those discriminated against but rather the legal requirements regarding *the number of persons affected* by that disadvantage (see also Voogsgeerd).[1472] In fact, there is no *de minimis* rule in free movement law (though the Grabitz & Hilf Commentary[1473] appears to assert the opposite).

> The classic *de minimis* rule, based on the Roman legal saying '*de minimis non curat praetor*' (the judge does not deal with trifles), relates to an overall assessment, typically independent of the legal merits, of the circumstances of a given case from which it is concluded that the case is not worth dealing with. In its case law on discrimination the Court of Justice has made it clear that it does not recognize such a *de minimis* rule in relation to the intensity of the disadvantage. Thus, in *Corsica Ferries France I*[1474] (para. 8) the Court definitively stated that 'the articles of the EEC Treaty concerning the free movement of goods, persons, services

---

[1471] Peers 1997, p. 160.

[1472] Voogsgeerd 2000, p. 81. This author states specifically that the Court's formula for indirect discrimination on grounds of nationality as reflected in this decision is not based on a *de minimis* rule, based on the use of the word 'affect' in *O'Flynn*, rather than that of 'effect'. According to Voogsgeerd, the word 'effect' suggests a more quantitative approach to discrimination. In that case, a minor instance of discrimination would probably not constitute discrimination at all. Sufficient effects must then be established and that is only possible through statistical evidence. In contrast, under the *O'Flynn* formula, it is not the quantitative effect but rather the qualitative nature of the measure that determines whether there is a *prima facie* case of indirect discrimination.

[1473] Grabitz & Hilf Commentary (as of 1989), n. 9 ad Art. 6 of the EC Treaty. As was noted earlier in this part (see A.II.2.c), in the present writer's view, *Boussac* (Case 22/80, [1980] *ECR* 3427), relied on in this context by the Grabitz and Hilf Commentary, does not address the issue of a *de minimis* rule.

[1474] Case C-49/89, [1989] *ECR* I-4441.

and capital are fundamental Community provisions' and that 'any restriction, even minor, of that freedom is prohibited'. Similarly, in the *French Merchant Seamen*[1475] case (para. 46) the Court held that 'discrimination is prohibited even if it constitutes only an obstacle of secondary importance as regards the equality of access to employment and other conditions of work and employment'.[1476] Finally, the Court held in *Marsala*[1477] (para. 17) that 'even on the assumption that the reduction of the tax confers only a very limited advantage on producers of marsala, it must be pointed out that the purpose of the first paragraph of Article 95, which is to eliminate all forms of direct or indirect discrimination, could not be achieved if the advantages granted in respect of domestic products could escape the prohibition laid down by Article 95 by reason of their purportedly limited effect. Accordingly, even a tax relief the discriminatory effect of which is slight falls within the prohibition in Article 95.'

What remains unclear is what the Court might require in terms of *to what extent* foreigners, as opposed to nationals, as a group are negatively impacted by a rule. This question may be described as asking: To what degree must a particular rule be shown to work to the disadvantage of nationals from other Member States as opposed to a particular host State's own citizens? The terminology used by the Court varies, and there seems to be a subtle but important difference between 'a substantially higher proportion of migrant workers' and 'they affect essentially migrant workers' ('the impressionistic or eyeball approach')[1478] on the one hand, and formulae such as 'affecting migrant workers more than national workers', 'a particular disadvantage' and 'more easily be satisfied by national workers than by migrant workers' on the other hand. The second category simply seems to require a stronger negative effect on foreign nationals as a group than on the host Member State's own nationals. That is, of course, logically an absolute minimum. If the effect were the same for both groups of persons, there would be no difference in treatment and therefore, by definition, no discrimination at all.[1479]

In the present writer's view, it may simply be impossible to establish a specific threshold which acts as a means to convincingly rule out other approaches. In practice, such a precise definition of the requisite level of the disparity becomes largely irrelevant

---

[1475] Case 167/73, [1974] *ECR* 359.

[1476] This is even clearer in the German version: 'dass jegliche Diskriminierung untersagt ist, auch wenn wie in bezug auf Arbeitsplatzzugang und Arbeitsbedingungen die Gleichheit kaum nennenswert beeinträchtigt'.

[1477] Case 277/83, [1985] *ECR* 2049.

[1478] Barnard & Hepple 1999, p. 406.

[1479] In contrast, if the negative effect were greater for the Member State's own nationals, the case would involve reverse discrimination rather than discrimination on grounds of the nationality of other Member States as prohibited by EC free movement law. On reverse discrimination, see in particular Epiney 1995.

in view of the *low standards of proof* applicable[1480] in the case of indirect discrimination on grounds of nationality.[1481] As O'Hare[1482] explains, the '*O'Flynn* 'liability test' [...] alleviates the onerous burden on litigants to carefully select a pool of appropriate comparators and to present complex statistical evidence to establish a *prima facie* case of indirect discrimination' (see also Bell).[1483] Authors such as De Schutter[1484] and Vick[1485] point out that this approach has both advantages and disadvantages. One rather obvious advantage is the simple procedure for establishing a *prima facie* case of indirect discrimination. According to Barnard & Hepple,[1486] this approach allows a court to take account of social facts and to use its general knowledge, and Wyatt & Dashwood[1487] speak about a mere common sense assessment. As for potential disadvantages, the Court's formula only covers a limited range of situations, namely those where the potentially disparate effect is apparent from the criterion specified in the measure. Although in *O'Flynn*[1488] disparate effect was clearly evident because the differentiation ground relied on was based on geographic elements and as such was clearly linked to nationality (Hepple, Choussey & Choudhury;[1489] 'intrinsically liable to disadvantage migrants'), the disparate effect may not be so apparent when examining other types of criteria. Vick[1490] mentions another disadvantage, the potential danger that reliance on common sense as a legal standard may encourage tribunals to engage in speculation to an undesirable degree or to overly rely on anecdotal evidence.

ii.   A different test for indirect sex discrimination

Under the Court's case law definition, the disparate impact test differs somewhat in the context of indirect sex discrimination. Once again, the Court has not been very precise in defining the requisite extent of the disparate impact (Ellis).[1491] The contested measure must benefit 'a much lower proportion of women than of men' (*Jenkins*)[1492]

[1480]   According to Martin 1998, p. 310, the burden of proof plays no role whatsoever in the context of discrimination on grounds of nationality because a potential discriminatory effect of the measure is sufficient. However, showing that there is an inherent risk of discrimination still involves a kind of proof.

[1481]   Brown 2003, p. 206, argues that approach reflected in *O'Flynn* is the exception to the rule. However, it will be seen later that under the more recent legal definitions of indirect discrimination the liability approach provides the common standard; see later in this part, B.

[1482]   O'Hare 2001, p. 147.

[1483]   Bell 2002, p. 34.

[1484]   De Schutter 1999, pp. 115 subs.

[1485]   Vick 2001, p. 9.

[1486]   Barnard & Hepple 1999, p. 406.

[1487]   Wyatt & Dashwood 2000, p. 403.

[1488]   Case C-237/94, [1996] *ECR* I-2617.

[1489]   Hepple, Choussey & Choudhury 2000, p. 31.

[1490]   Vick 2001, p. 9.

[1491]   Ellis 1998, p. 118.

[1492]   Case 96/80, [1981] *ECR* 911.

or 'a considerably smaller percentage of women than of men' (*Bilka*,[1493] *Seymour-Smith*)[1494] or, conversely, it must disadvantage 'far more women than men' (*Lewen*),[1495] 'considerably more women than men' (*Helmig*)[1496] or 'a much higher percentage of women than men' (*Rinke*).[1497] However, according to Epiney,[1498] such descriptions are simply useless. Drijber & Prechal[1499] note that in specific cases the Court accepts with relative ease that the requisite level of disparate impact exists, but the Court does not provide the sort of guidance that might help employers, national authorities and courts trying to come to terms with the precise requirements of EC law.

Seymour-Smith[1500] is particularly telling in this context because, although the question of the indirect discrimination test was expressly raised, the Court's response failed to bring clarity to the situation. The case concerned a rule according to which a complaint of unfair dismissal could be registered with a court only if the prospective plaintiff had been employed for more than two years. In its reference for a preliminary ruling, the House of Lords wished to know '[w]hat is the legal test for establishing whether a measure adopted by a Member State has such a degree of disparate effect as between men and women as to amount to indirect discrimination for the purposes of Article 119 of the EC Treaty unless shown to be based upon objectively justified factors other than sex' (*Seymour-Smith*, para. 19). The Court answered as follows (*Seymour-Smith*, para. 58-62):

> 'As regards the establishment of indirect discrimination, the first question is whether a measure such as the rule at issue has a more unfavourable impact on women than on men. Next, as the United Kingdom Government was right to point out, the best approach to the comparison of statistics is to consider, on the one hand, the respective proportions of men in the workforce able to satisfy the requirement of two years' employment under the disputed rule and of those unable to do so, and, on the other, to compare those proportions as regards women in the workforce. It is not sufficient to consider the number of persons affected, since that depends on the number of working people in the Member State as a whole as well as the percentages of men and women employed in that State. As the Court has stated on several occasions, it must be ascertained whether the statistics available indicate that a considerably smaller percentage of women than men is able to satisfy the condition of two years' employment required by the disputed rule. That situation would be evidence of apparent sex discrimination unless the disputed rule were justified by objective factors unrelated to any discrimination based on sex. That could also be the case if the statistical evidence revealed a lesser but persistent and relatively constant disparity over a

---

[1493] Case 170/84, [1986] *ECR* 1607.
[1494] Case C-167/97, [1999] *ECR* I-623.
[1495] Case C-333/97, [1999] *ECR* I-7243.
[1496] Joined Cases C-399/92, C-409/92, C-425/92, C-34/93, C-50/93 & C-78/93, [1994] *ECR* I-5727.
[1497] Case C-25/02, judgment of 9 September 2003, n.y.r.
[1498] Epiney 1995, p. 61.
[1499] Drijber & Prechal 1997, p. 139.
[1500] Case C-167/97, [1999] *ECR* I-623.

long period between men and women who satisfy the requirement of two years' employment. It would, however, be for the national court to determine the conclusions to be drawn from such statistics. It is also for the national court to assess whether the statistics concerning the situation of the workforce are valid and can be taken into account, that is to say, whether they cover enough individuals, whether they illustrate purely fortuitous or short-term phenomena, and whether, in general, they appear to be significant (see Case C-127/92 Enderby [1993] ECR I-5535, paragraph 17). It is, in particular, for the national court to establish whether, given the answer to the fourth question, the 1985 statistics concerning the respective percentages of men and women fulfilling the requirement of two years' employment under the disputed rule are relevant and sufficient for the purposes of resolving the case before it.'

As Barnard & Hepple[1501] point out, this ruling did little to clarify the perplexing concept of indirect discrimination. In their view, the answers which the House of Lords received to its detailed questions, 'nearly two years later and eight years after the employees were dismissed, were not enlightening and did not merit the expense and time involved in making an Article 177[1502] reference'. These same authors[1503] also point out that the Court, in fact, provided not one, but two distinct tests. One test asked whether 'a considerably smaller percentage of women than men is able to satisfy the condition of two years' employment required by the disputed rule' (*Seymour-Smith*, para. 60), while the other asked whether 'a lesser but persistent and relatively constant disparity over a long period between men and women' existed (*Seymour-Smith*, para. 61). Authors such as Epiney & Freiermuth Abt[1504] agree with this double approach. However, in practical terms, both tests lack clarity. Not surprisingly, in this situation where two different tests exist, any attempt to establish a standard threshold for the determination of the requisite extent of disparate effects that must be met is even more difficult than it is in the context of discrimination on grounds of nationality, discussed in the previous section.[1505]

[1501] Barnard & Hepple 1999, pp. 399 and 403 subs. The authors also remark that AG Cosmas was of no help to the Court because he entirely misunderstood the nature of the alleged discrimination and misinterpreted the British legislation on the qualifying period in cases of sex discrimination (p. 405). See also Vick 2001, pp. 12 subs. and 17 subs.

[1502] After the Amsterdam revision Art. 234 EC.

[1503] Barnard & Hepple 2000, p. 572.

[1504] Epiney & Freiermuth Abt 2003, p. 78.

[1505] Nonetheless some academics have tackled this challenge in relation to the first test. Plötscher 2003, p. 239, footnote 103, suggests a ratio of at least 80% to 30% (apparently meaning of 'non-qualifiers' and 'qualifiers'). Barnard & Hepple 1999, p. 406, refer to the U.S. Employment Opportunity Commission Uniform Guidelines on Employee Selection Procedures in the context of race, sex or ethnic origin, according to which a selection rate of less than 80% of the group with the highest rate will generally be regarded as evidence of adverse impact. See also Goldman 1996, para. 342, who adds that the U.S. Supreme Court has rejected the use of any one sort of approach to demonstrating that a particular selection method has a disparate impact.

The perception of vagueness regarding the requisite extent of disparate impact is aggravated by the fact that the *requirements regarding the proof* of disparate impact are stricter under the Court's case law regarding indirect discrimination on grounds of sex than for discrimination on grounds of nationality (Prechal,[1506] Brown).[1507] Here, it is not sufficient that a given criterion is intrinsically liable to affect more persons of one sex than of the other. Rather, a factually disparate impact must be shown to exist. The problems experienced in practice in this context relate mainly to establishing proof through the means of statistics which appears to be necessary under the Court's case law in many, though not all, cases (e.g. *Kachelmann*,[1508] para. 24; *Schnorbus*,[1509] para. 38).

> No further proof is required where the Court is prepared to rely on common knowledge. Thus, the Court in *Kachelmann* simply held that '[i]t is common ground that in Germany part-time workers are far more likely to be women than men'. An example of a different kind is provided by *Schnorbus*, where the Court held that in a case where national provisions relied on a criterion that excludes all women, but nevertheless does not lead to direct discrimination, the provisions themselves are evidence of indirect discrimination, regardless of statistical evidence. In such a case, the requirement that 'a considerably smaller percentage of women than men' is affected by the criterion at issue is obviously fulfilled.[1510]

As AG Léger noted in his opinion on the *Nolte* case[1511] (point 53), the requirement *of statistical proof* is a tricky issue that can lead to a veritable battle with numbers. Apart from the relevant threshold, the questions most commonly discussed in this context concern the pool be examined in order to review the effect of the measure and the groups between whom the comparison needs to be made. The difficulties inherent in establishing statistical proof and its pitfalls have been described by numerous

---

[1506] Prechal 1993, p. 87.
[1507] Brown 2003, pp. 205 subs.
[1508] Case C-322/98, [2000] *ECR* I-7505.
[1509] Case C-79/99, [2000] *ECR* I-10997; see below Part 3, A.II.2.c.
[1510] See further below Part 3, A.II.2.c. According to De Schutter 2001, p. 84, statistical proof may also be relevant in the context of *direct* discrimination. As an example, he mentions the use of informal procedures (such as an interview) in the context of the hiring of personnel by an employer. In De Schutter's view, in such a case it is only statistics that can adequately support an allegation of discrimination (e.g. in the context of race discrimination, if after the interview all or a disproportionate number of persons with a certain ethnic background are excluded from the further hiring procedure: 'cela n'est-il pas attribuable, en effet, à al discrimination directe dont se rend coupable le recruteur?'. However, later in his study (p. 94), in the context of such informal procedures, De Schutter speaks about the merging of the concepts of direct and indirect discrimination in the sense that in such situations it may no longer make sense to distinguish between them. This is because one approach looks behind informal procedures for a direct, but masked discrimination, and the other attempts to find indirect discrimination based on the differential impact of informal procedures.
[1511] Case C-317/93, [1995] *ECR* I-4625.

authors (e.g. Pfarr & Bertelsmann,[1512] Prechal,[1513] Wisskirchen,[1514] Bieback,[1515] Winter,[1516] Steiner,[1517] Burri,[1518] De Schutter,[1519] Stampe,[1520] Fuchsloch,[1521] Browne).[1522] One particularly important principle seems to emerge from the Court's case law, namely that the comparison to be undertaken be *a relative, rather than an absolute one.* Under such an approach, the percentage of women (or, less often, men) in the disadvantaged group as compared with their percentage in the group that benefits from the contested measure is relevant with regard to proving disparate impact. Authors such as Burri[1523] and Barnard & Hepple[1524] observe that the validity of a relative approach to the issue of statistical proof is confirmed by *Seymour-Smith*. The latter authors suggest that, ideally, two comparisons should be made: one between 'the qualifiers', that is, those able to satisfy the requirement at issue (how many are men, and how many are women?) and one between 'the non-qualifiers', that is, those who do not satisfy the requirement (how many are women, and how many are men?). Because these tests may produce very different statistical results from one another, only by conducting both sorts of comparisons can their statistical results ensure that actual instances of disparate impact are recognized.

> To illustrate the possible differences which may result from the two sorts of comparisons, Barnard & Hepple cite an example given by a British judge, Lord Nicholls, where a workforce of a thousand persons comprises an equal number of men and women. In this example, under a comparison of qualifiers, 10% of the workforce worked part-time and 90% of these were women. In these circumstances, a scheme that favours full-time workers means that 98% of the men (490 out of a total of 500) and 82% of the women (410 out of a total of 500) can comply with the requirement (comparison of the qualifiers). In contrast, under a comparison of non-qualifiers, a mere 2% of the men (10 out of 500) compared with 18% of the women (90 out of 500) are disadvantaged. In other words, of those who are non-qualifiers, 10% are men and 90% are women.

[1512] Pfarr & Bertelsmann 1989, pp. 117 subs.
[1513] Prechal 1993, pp. 84 subs.
[1514] Wisskirchen 1994, p. 83.
[1515] Bieback 1997, pp. 76 subs.
[1516] Winter 1998, pp. 129 subs.
[1517] Steiner 1999, pp. 243 subs.
[1518] Burri 2000, pp. 306 subs.
[1519] De Schutter 2001, pp. 97 subs.
[1520] Stampe 2001, pp. 137 subs. Note that the relevant part of Stampe's study is not limited to EC law.
[1521] Fuchsloch 1995, pp. 167 subs. This author, relying on analytical logic, has even developed a formula that describes the required disparate impact in mathematical terms.
[1522] Browne 1999, in the context of U.S. discrimination law.
[1523] Burri 2000, pp. 315 subs.
[1524] Barnard & Hepple 2000, pp. 571 subs.; see also Fuchsloch 1995, pp. 169/170.

According to Fuchsloch,[1525] the relative approach illustrates why it is impossible to find an ultimately valid general description of the requisite extent of disparate impact to establish a violation in the context of indirect sex discrimination. According to Blomeyer,[1526] the practical problems arising in the context of proof could be avoided if the requirement were simply that the measure or rule at issue disadvantages more women than men and favours more men than women. However, it should be noted that, in practice, the Court does not often apply the relative approach. Thus, when assessing the circumstances involved in *Seymour-Smith*, in which the Court confirmed the relevance of the relative approach, in fact the Court considered only the pool of those able to benefit.[1527] It may therefore be concluded that in practice the test does not necessarily have to be a relative one. In any event, Blomeyer's suggestion would not do away with all the other problems linked to statistical proof which are bound to persist as long as that sort of proof is deemed relevant by the courts. Sjerps,[1528] whilst calling statistics an acceptable tool in principle, thinks that it has so many flaws that one ought to question the wisdom of using it at all. Similarly, Lundström[1529] argues that if the prohibition against sex discrimination is to have real effect, the Court should cease to require extensive statistical evidence in cases of indirect discrimination. In fact, for some (though not all) areas of sex equality law, the later introduction of a legal definition of indirect sex discrimination has brought about changes in approach which will be discussed later in the study.[1530]

iii. Are there good reasons for the difference in approach?

This section examines whether the Court should change the way it treats questions of whether an actionable level of disparate effect exists. The previous sections demonstrated that the Court uses various approaches depending on the discriminatory grounds under which the case is brought. AG Lenz in *O'Flynn*[1531] (points 19 subs. of the opinion) argued that sometimes a case of indirect sex discrimination can only be established through proof provided by a statistical investigation. According to the AG, one might conceive of many situations where, absent statistics, it is entirely unclear whether a particular measure impacts negatively more on women than on men. Similarly, Steiner[1532] argues that statistical evidence may be necessary in order to prove the causal relationship between the measures in question and the disadvantage

---

[1525]   Fuchsloch 1995, p. 179.
[1526]   Blomeyer 1994, p. 127.
[1527]   In *Seymour-Smith* (para. 63), the Court referred to statistics according to which 77,4% of the men and 68,9% of the women concerned fulfilled the condition for the beneficial treatment.
[1528]   Sjerps 1999, pp. 245 subs.
[1529]   Lundström 2001, p. 159.
[1530]   See later in this part, B.
[1531]   Case C-237/94, [1996] *ECR* I-2617.
[1532]   Steiner 1999, p. 244.

impacting upon one particular sex. Prechal,[1533] who acknowledges that, in principle, various areas of discrimination law may be used as appropriate sources of inspiration for one another, seems to accept the existing differences regarding how to prove disparate effect.

In contrast, the present writer argues that with regard to the appropriate threshold to be met in order to establish a legally sufficient disparate impact, the tests ought to be identical for discrimination on grounds of sex and on grounds of nationality, in the sense that it should be sufficient: first, that a measure be 'intrinsically liable to affect persons of one sex more than persons of the other sex' to be actionable; and, second, that statistical evidence should not be excluded as a legitimate way to establish proof of disparate impact should the need arise in a particular case. As De Schutter[1534] notes, statistical proof may be inconvenient and cumbersome but, nevertheless, has the advantage of a wide field of potential application because it is not limited to criteria that are suspect by their very nature, such as residence in the context of discrimination on grounds of nationality. Again, the discussion of the legal definitions of indirect discrimination which now exist for some areas of sex equality will show that certain steps in the direction of such a combined approach have subsequently been taken by the Community legislator.[1535]

e. The relevance of intent for the recognition of the potentially indirect nature of discrimination

Inevitable questions arise with regard to the role of intent in cases involving alleged instances of indirect discrimination. Though they are few, some authors argue that intent ought be made a requisite element of indirect discrimination, particularly in the context of economic law. Recalling that here discrimination was originally a subjective notion where intent was relevant, Bernard[1536] laments what he calls its 'objectivization' as 'une dénaturation de la notion'. In the same vein, Thümmel[1537] argues that there can be indirect discrimination under Art. 12(1) EC only if the contested rule intended from the outset to make a distinction based on nationality. In contrast, other commentators point out that, due to the very nature of indirect discrimination, frequently inadvertence on the part of the discriminator leads to discriminatory situations (e.g. Blom,[1538] Ellis).[1539]

[1533] Prechal 1993, p. 87.
[1534] De Schutter 2001, pp. 99/100, also 115.
[1535] See later in this part, B.
[1536] Bernard 1998, p. 15.
[1537] Thümmel 1994, p. 244: 'wenn die in Rede stehende Regelung von vornherein beabsichtigte, im Ergebnis eine Differenzierung nach der Staatsangehörigkeit herbeizuführen'.
[1538] Blom 1992, p. 104.
[1539] Ellis 1998, p. 113.

As was noted earlier,[1540] in EC law the discussion on this issue goes back to the Court's rather confusing reference to the discriminator's intent in the sex equality case *Jenkins*.[1541] It has been noted that the lack of any reference to intent in the landmark decision *Bilka*[1542] was taken to confirm that intent is irrelevant. In fact, in its original proposal for a Burden of Proof Directive,[1543] the Commission proposed to include an explicit statement to that effect in the legal definition of indirect discrimination. However, such a statement was omitted from the final text. Now it is generally accepted that intent is not a prerequisite for a finding of indirect sex discrimination and that the absence of proof of intent does not prevent such a finding.[1544] The same is true for discrimination on grounds other than of sex (e.g. the Grabitz & Hilf[1545] and the Calliess & Ruffert[1546] Commentaries, Epiney,[1547] De Schutter).[1548] According to Blom,[1549] the fact that the success of an indirect discrimination claim is no longer dependent on the proof of discriminatory intent is arguably one of the greatest advantages of the concept. As for the rationale underlying that approach, Barbera[1550] points out that the concept of indirect discrimination is based on the victim's perspective, rather than on the perspective of the perpetrator. The Grabitz & Hilf Commentary[1551] explains that the principle of the utmost effectiveness of equality law explains the irrelevance attributed to the alleged discriminator's motives (see also Ellis,[1552] Steiner).[1553]

f. The special case of 'work of equal value'

A final point to be discussed regarding the discrimination's indirect nature concerns indirect sex discrimination in the specific context of equal pay and, even more specifically, claims of such discrimination made in the context of work of (allegedly)

[1540] See earlier in this part, A.I.4.h.

[1541] Case 96/80, [1981] *ECR* 911.

[1542] Case 170/84, [1986] *ECR* 1607.

[1543] Proposal for a Council Directive on the burden of proof in the area of equal pay and equal treatment of men and women, *OJ* 1988 C 176/5. Art. 5(2) of the draft text read: 'Member States shall insure that the intentions of the respondent are not taken into account in determining whether the principle of equality has been infringed in any individual case.'

[1544] Neither is it necessary for a finding of *direct* discrimination; see above Part 1, B.III.5.b.i; also *Dekker* (Case C-177/88, [1990] I-3941), para. 24, in the context of the question of liability for sex discrimination; Ellis 1998, p. 115.

[1545] Grabitz & Hilf Commentary (as of 1989), n. 16 ad Art. 6 of the EC Treaty.

[1546] Calliess & Ruffert Commentary 2002, n. 6 ad Art. 12(1) EC.

[1547] Epiney 1995, pp. 100 subs.

[1548] De Schutter 2001, p. 93.

[1549] Blom 1992, p. 47.

[1550] Barbera 1994, p. 55.

[1551] Grabitz & Hilf Commentary (as of 1989), n. 16 ad Art. 6 of the EC Treaty.

[1552] Ellis 1998, p. 113.

[1553] Steiner 1999, p. 226.

equal value.[1554] With the exception of the landmark cases discussed earlier, the Court's
case law in this area draws attention to specific matters which have important consequences for the application of the concept of indirect discrimination (Sommer).[1555]

i.   Meaning and function of the concept of 'work of equal value'

In equal pay cases, the claim of indirect sex discrimination sometimes depends upon
the assessment of work as having equal value. In such a context, the nature of the
criteria used to determine the value of particular work are critical. In EC law, it is
important to note that the concept of 'work of equal value' is interpreted narrowly
in the sense that it relates only to the nature of the work, rather than also to the level
of its performance by individual workers (*Rummler*,[1556] para. 13 and 23; *Brunnhofer*,[1557]
para. 43; *Jämställdhetsombudsmannen*,[1558] para. 48; this approach is also reflected in
a Commission Memorandum on equal pay for work of equal value of 1994).[1559] As
Winter[1560] notes, these issues are often confused.[1561] For present purposes, the focus
on functions rather than on the people holding them means that the disadvantage
resulting from a (directly or indirectly) discriminatory evaluation does not directly
relate to the treatment of the workers themselves. Rather, the differences in the

---

[1554]   Both 'equal work' and 'work of equal value' are to be distinguished from the case, not mentioned
in Art. 141 EC, where the lower paid work is of higher value than work for which more is paid; see
Murphy (Case 157/86, [1988] *ECR* 673), para. 9; Winter 1998, p. 113.

[1555]   Sommer 1998, pp. 111 subs.

[1556]   Case 237/85, [1986] *ECR* 2101.

[1557]   Case C-381/99, [2001] *ECR* I-4961. However, the cases referred to by the Court in this context only
addressed the notion of 'same work' (rather than also that of 'work of equal value'), namely *Royal
Copenhagen* (Case C-400/93, [1995] *ECR* I/1275) and *Wiener Gebietskrankenkasse* (Case C-309/97,
[1999] *ECR* I-2865).

[1558]   Case C-236/98, [2000] *ECR* I-2189. The reference in this decision to training requirements should
be seen in the context of the Court's statement in *Wiener Gebietskrankenkasse* (C-309/97, [1999] *ECR*
I-2865, para. 18 and 19) that fundamentally different training may change the nature of the tasks
(or the purposes of the tasks) that can be assigned to different workers, thereby qualifying the work
as different. The Court in this context explicitly referred to AG Cosmas' opinion on this case (para.
32 subs.) where the AG distinguished between differences in training that affect that nature of the
work performed as such (fundamentally different training) and other differences in training (different
levels of the same training) that do not change the nature or purposes of the tasks.

[1559]   Memorandum on equal pay for work of equal value, COM(94) 6 fin., in particular at 5 and 22 subs.

[1560]   Winter 1998, pp. 109, 117 and 120.

[1561]   Burrows points out that the EC law approach may cause difficulties in practice since modern pay
systems are usually based on a mixture of job-related and performance-related criteria. In her view,
the existing equal pay legislation fails to capture these developments. She explains: 'My argument
is that human resources practices have outstripped the legislation with which we are working. What
is needed is therefore a re-appraisal of the legal structures, to modernise them and to have them reflect
current practice.' Prof. Noreen Burrows made these points in a presentation entitled 'Equal Pay for
Equal Work: The Impact of European Law' and given by her in the framework of the Conference
'Gender Equality and Europe's Future?', organised by the European Commission and held in Brussels
on 4 March 2003.

treatment of the types of work is primarily at issue. That treatment, in turn, results in different treatment of the workers themselves. Further, it should be recalled[1562] that the classification of work as either of equal or unequal value ultimately concerns *an issue of comparability*. Accordingly, allegations of indirect discrimination in that context concern a different conceptual level from such traditional indirect discrimination cases as *Jenkins*[1563] or *Bilka*.[1564]

ii. Consequences in the context of indirect sex discrimination

The stress placed on equal value has important consequences with regard to the acceptability of criteria for the classification of work which have a disparate effect in terms of sex. This point is illustrated by the Court's judgment in the *Rummler*[1565] case, concerning a national pay scale providing for seven wage groups according to the type of work carried out. The level of pay was determined on the basis of evaluations of the degree of knowledge, concentration, muscular demand, and responsibility required. According to her employer, Ms Rummler's work required merely slight or moderate muscular exertion but Ms Rummler herself claimed that her job should have been classified in a higher category in view of the fact that she packed parcels of more than 20 kg weight which, for her, represented heavy physical work. The Court held that if a given type of work requires a certain degree of physical strength, it is acceptable to rely on the specified criterion for determining the value of the work (*Rummler*, para. 14). In essence, the Court's finding accepted the principle that essential job requirements – in other words, the elements characterising and distinguishing the sort of work – may be taken into account. It further results from *Rummler* that such criteria are the only acceptable sorts of reasons for differentiations in pay. The practical issue in *Rummler* was that certain types of physical work require more effort from women on average than from men. The Court acknowledged that although reliance on the criterion of muscular demand may place women workers at a disadvantage, the difference in treatment may 'be objectively justified by the nature of the job when such a difference is necessary in order to ensure a level of pay appropriate to the effort required by the work and thus corresponds to a real need on the part of the undertaking' (*Rummler*, para. 24; see Ellis).[1566] The Court's reference to *Bilka*[1567] in this context has clear implications in the context of indirect discrimination. Accordingly, the

---

[1562] See above Part 1, B.II.1.c.
[1563] Case 96/80, [1981] *ECR* 911.
[1564] Case 170/84, [1986] *ECR* 1607.
[1565] Case 237/85, [1986] *ECR* 2101.
[1566] Ellis 1998, p. 157. To remunerate women more highly than men would have the unfortunate consequence that women would become more expensive to employ than men. This result would be counterproductive. Ellis applauds the Court for having avoided that trap.
[1567] Case 170/84, [1986] *ECR* 1607.

conclusion must be that in the case of *prima facie* indirect sex discrimination which is caused in the framework of the evaluation of work, the only possible excuse on which the employer might rely is a lack of comparability of the work. Logically, no other justification is available.

A second lesson to be learnt from *Rummler* is that in examining cases involving evaluation systems alleged to be indirectly discriminatory, the focus of the analysis must *not be merely on one criterion*. The Court emphasised that the classification system as whole must be assessed (*Rummler*, para. 15): 'Even where a particular criterion, such as that of demand on the muscles, may in fact tend to favour male workers, since it may be assumed that in general they are physically stronger than women workers, it must, in order to determine whether or not it is discriminatory, be considered in the context of the whole job classification system, having regard to other criteria influencing rates of pay. A system is not necessarily discriminatory simply because one of its criteria makes reference to attributes more characteristic of men. In order for a job classification system as whole to be non-discriminatory and thus to comply with the principles of the Directive, it must, however, be established in such a manner that it includes, if the nature of the tasks in question so permits, jobs to which equal value is attributed and for which regard is had to other criteria in relation to which women workers may have a particular aptitude.' (See De Bruijn, Bajema & Timmerman,[1568] Schiek;[1569] also Arnull).[1570]

Both issues show that in cases of alleged indirect discrimination in relation to the valuation of work of supposedly equal value the concept of indirect discrimination is *not applied in the usual way*. Such cases require a two step analysis. First, it must be established whether the individual criteria relied on are relevant in the context of the type of work at issue. Although reliance on a particular criterion might suggest indirect discrimination because of its disparate impact, a finding of discrimination will not in fact be made if, and insofar as, the criteria correspond to a legitimate job requirement – but no other sort of 'justification' is acceptable. Second, where an individual criterion is part of a job classification system, that system will have to be analysed as whole rather than only with regard to its individual components. However, the system will be found to be discriminatory if it is not balanced in the sense that it takes unequal account of criteria with a disparate effect upon the sexes. Ellis[1571] applauds the fact that after *Rummler* it is possible to allege that a classification system falls short of the requirements of EC law. Nonetheless, Ellis still believes that it is far from clear exactly when a job classification system is discriminatory as a whole, not least because there

---

[1568] De Bruijn, Bajema & Timmerman 1992, pp. 22 subs.
[1569] Schiek 1997, p. 173.
[1570] Arnull 1987, pp. 62-63.
[1571] Ellis 1998, p. 160.

will always be room for argument regarding how to evaluate the specific demands of any particular job.

3. ISSUES RELATING TO THE SECOND PART OF THE INDIRECT DISCRIMINATION FORMULA

The following sections will examine a number of issues related to the second part of the indirect discrimination formula, namely the objective justification test itself and its application. Particular focus will be given to issues regarding the validity of economic justification grounds, the procedural implications of objective justification and, finally, the question of whether objective justification is a matter of causation rather than of justification.

a. Objective justification: a vague test

i. The test as formulated by the Court

As Prechal[1572] points out, the standards applicable with regard to objective justification are vital to the effectiveness of the concept of indirect discrimination as a whole. Accordingly, objective justification is said to be the chief issue and the biggest challenge in indirect discrimination law (Sjerps,[1573] Morris).[1574] Unfortunately, the Court's case law is not very specific with regard to the elements and the modalities of the justification test. In the context of indirect discrimination on grounds of *nationality*, objective justification simply requires that the contested measure is based on 'objective considerations independent of the nationality of the workers concerned' and that it is 'proportionate to the legitimate aim pursued by the national law' (*O'Flynn*,[1575] para. 19). In relation to indirect *sex* discrimination, the Court generally mentioned 'objectively justified factors unrelated to any discrimination on grounds of sex' which are 'appropriate with a view to achieving the objective pursued and [...] necessary to that end'. In the case of actions by employers, the measure must correspond 'to a real need on the part of the undertaking' (*Bilka*,[1576] para. 30). As far as Member State legislation is concerned, where the Court was specifically asked about the issue in *Seymour-Smith*,[1577] the Court explained that the Member State must show that the contested rule reflects a legitimate aim of its social policy, that the particular aim is unrelated

---

[1572] Prechal 1993, pp. 86 subs.
[1573] Sjerps 1994, p. 96.
[1574] Morris 1995, p. 217.
[1575] Case C-237/94, [1996] *ECR* I-2617; see earlier in this part, A.II.4.c.
[1576] Case 170/84, [1986] *ECR* 1607; see earlier in this part, A.II.3.b.
[1577] Case C-167/97, [1999] *ECR* I-623.

to any discrimination based on sex, and that it could reasonably consider that the
means chosen were suitable for attaining that aim (para. 77).

ii. Acceptable justification grounds

The preceding description of the elements of the objective justification test has led to
a number of critical comments. One important point concerns the *legitimacy of the
measure's aim*, in particular in the context of the dilution of the test in the area of sex
discrimination caused through national social legislation (as previously mentioned).[1578]
With a view to how to improve the test, Wentholt[1579] insists that the contested
measure's aim must be sufficiently important to outweigh the prohibition against
discrimination and that it must actually serve its given purpose (see also Dierx &
Siegers).[1580] The latter means, *inter alia*, that under no circumstances must it be linked
to a prohibited criterion. For example, the aim to reduce part-time work would be
unacceptable precisely because predominantly women perform (or would like to
perform) part-time work. Similarly, Blom[1581] suggests that the acceptability of the aim
in question should not be tested merely on a theoretical level but also by balancing
the concrete interests in a particular case. In her view, a court dealing with objective
justification 'should, ideally, ask the following questions in this order: 1: Is the goal
which the measure intends to serve a legitimate one, i.e. could it, theoretically, justify
a measure which disadvantages members of one sex? Of course, if the goal put forward
is linked to the sex of the person concerned, it will definitely fall at this first hurdle.
2: Can the measure in fact achieve the objective? 3: Is there no viable, less harmful
alternative to the measure in question? 4: Lastly, does not the achievement of the goal,
although legitimate, disproportionately harm the interests of the people affected?' The
first and the last of these questions involve a balancing exercise. They differ in that the
first 'is more or less in the abstract' (meaning that some interests will simply never
justify disparate impact) whereas the last question balances the interests of the
individual actors in each particular case.

A further problem in the context of evaluating the legitimacy of a given justification
ground concerns the role of *intent*. Drijber & Prechal,[1582] noting that the debate on
the relevance of intent on the part of the alleged discriminator as a requisite element
for a *prima facie* finding of indirect discrimination is a discussion from the distant
past,[1583] further observe that intent may still play some role in the context of objective
justification, particularly with regard to the wide discretion left to the Member States

---

[1578] See earlier in this part, A.III.1.a.ii.
[1579] Wentholt 1990, p. 88.
[1580] Dierx & Siegers 1990, p. 559.
[1581] Blom 1992, p. 59.
[1582] Drijber & Prechal 1997, p. 142.
[1583] See earlier in this part, A.I.4.h.

in the determination of the legitimacy of a given aim in the context of social policy. Thus, the problems linked to intent may return through the back door. Similarly, O'Leary[1584] suspects that, although the Court may have discounted intent as a relevant criterion, it may simply have replaced intent with an emphasis on the purpose of the particular employment policy or piece of legislation. Recalling AG Darmon's suggestion in *Rinner-Kühn*[1585] that national legislation should only be regarded as incompatible with EC law if it was intended to discriminate, O'Leary even goes so far as to suggest that 'it is arguable that, over time and overall, specifically in the context of Member State social security legislation, Darmon's level of scrutiny has won through'.

iii. Over- and underinclusiveness

Gerards[1586] advocates that a further element should be examined after the legitimacy of the aim served by an allegedly justifiable measure but before its proportionality. Gerards calls for a test of *over- or underinclusiveness*, a test drawn from U.S. law. At present, no such a test exists in EC case law in the contexts of either direct or indirect discrimination. The Court does not examine whether a given measure too narrowly defines the group to whom benefits are granted or upon whom disadvantages are imposed with regard to the aim of the contested measure (underinclusiveness) or too broadly for that purpose (overinclusiveness). According to Gerards, the inclusion of such a test element would make the Court's discrimination test more sophisticated. It would also clarify the court's reasoning.

iv. Proportionality

In academic writing it is sometimes argued that the Court's objective justification test requires clarification in relation to the element of proportionality. According to the indirect discrimination formula given by the Court, proportionality means that the measure in question must be suitable and requisite. According to some, it should be explicitly added that there are *no other and less restrictive means* to achieve the goal in question (e.g. Wisskirchen,[1587] with further references; see also Plötscher).[1588] According to others, this element, though not explicitly mentioned on the level of the indirect discrimination formula, is already inherent in the Court's case law (e.g. Bieback,[1589]

[1584]   O'Leary 2002, p. 149.
[1585]   Case 171/88, [1989] *ECR* 2743; see earlier in this part, A.II.3.b.
[1586]   Gerards 2002, pp. 46 subs. and 304, as well as Gerards 2003, pp. 93 subs.
[1587]   Wisskirchen 1994, pp. 112 subs.
[1588]   Plötscher 2003, pp. 125 subs.
[1589]   Bieback 1997, pp. 103 subs.

based on the concrete test applied in *Teuling*,[1590] para. 18). In the present writer's view, the requirement that a measure must be requisite in itself implies that there are no other and less restrictive means. Further, in *Collins*[1591] (para. 72) the Court explicitly stated that for a measure to be proportionate it cannot go beyond what is necessary in order to attain the objective in question. This characterization is also found in the Court's general case law on the principle of proportionality, as is particularly exemplified by *Fedesa*.[1592] In *Fedesa* (para. 13), the Court explained that by virtue of the principle of proportionality, the lawfulness of the prohibition of an economic activity is subject to the condition that prohibitory measures are appropriate and necessary in order to achieve the objectives legitimately pursued by the legislation in question; when there are several apparently appropriate means available, the least onerous must be chosen, and the disadvantages caused must not be disproportionate to the aims pursued. Such a definition includes an element that is often seen as the third aspect of proportionality (particularly in the German tradition, see Emiliou,[1593] Jarass,[1594] Epiney & Freiermuth Abt),[1595] namely *proportionality stricto sensu* which requires that the seriousness of the intervention and the gravity of the reasons for justifying it are in adequate proportion to each other. Again, this element, though not explicitly part of the justification formula, appears to be implied in some of the Court's earlier decisions (e.g. Gerards,[1596] concerning *Schnorbus*,[1597] para. 28; see also Blom,[1598] Burri,[1599] Drijber & Prechal).[1600]

v. Can this vague test be improved on the conceptual level?

Given the characteristics of the objective justification test just described, More[1601] speaks about 'yet another abstract legal notion', and Piso[1602] points to the lack of predictability of the case law flowing from it.[1603] Although many critics complain about the present state of the objective justification test, it may be impossible to formulate

---

[1590]   Case 30/85, [1987] *ECR* 2497.
[1591]   Case C-138/02, judgment of 23 March 2004, n.y.r.
[1592]   Case C-331/88, [1990] *ECR* I-4023.
[1593]   Emiliou 1996, pp. 25 subs. However, the same author also noted that the use of terminology and the number of the elements in Germany lack consistency.
[1594]   Jarass 2000 (Unified Approach), p. 160.
[1595]   Epiney & Freiermuth Abt 2003, p. 101.
[1596]   Gerards 2002, pp. 288, also 46 subs.
[1597]   Case C-79/99, [2000] *ECR* I-10997.
[1598]   Blom 1992, p. 48.
[1599]   Burri 2000, pp. 323 and 469, notes that this element is also present in the test applied by the Dutch Equal Treatment Commission in the framework of Dutch non-discrimination law, some of which implements EC equality law; Burri 2000.
[1600]   Drijber & Prechal 1997, p. 142.
[1601]   More 1993, p. 70.
[1602]   Piso 1998, pp. 301, 306 and 319.
[1603]   More generally on this issue, see Gerards 2002, pp. 2 subs.

an adequately broad test on the conceptual level. Burri[1604] suggests that the Court impose an explicit duty on potential discriminators to evaluate the possibility of implementing non-discriminative or, at least, less damaging measures. However, given that much indirect discrimination is unintentional, it is doubtful that such a requirement could have much impact in practice. Piso[1605] points to the varying and developing social contexts of discrimination and concludes that a 'complete' formula is neither feasible nor desirable (see also Ebsen,[1606] Wisskirchen,[1607] Bieback).[1608] At most, one might attempt to further refine the elements of the objective justification test. In the absence of clearer legislation, Piso suggests that the Court of Justice adhere in a strict manner to its own definition of objective justification, that it apply it consistently and that it give clearer and stricter guidance to the national courts with regard to the elements of the test.

b. Applying the objective justification test

i. Who should determine the legitimacy of a claim of objective justification?

Regarding the application of the objective justification test to concrete cases, a first question must be asked: Who should actually determine the legitimacy of such claims? In giving preliminary rulings,[1609] the Court of Justice's function is limited to providing authoritative interpretation of Community law provisions. The application of such interpretations to concrete cases is, strictly speaking, a matter for the national court (*Da Costa*,[1610] p. 38). However, it is well established that the Court often gives the national courts such specific 'guidance' regarding how to apply EC law, that it appears to perform that task of application of the law for itself. Prechal[1611] and Watson[1612] found that the Court hesitates less to scrutinize and assess justifications brought forward in the context of indirect discrimination on grounds of nationality than on sex. In fact, the case law analyses in this present study demonstrate that the Court simply examined the concrete justification grounds brought forward in the context of indirect discrimination on grounds of nationality without making any general statements on the nature of objective justification.[1613] In contrast, at least in the early sex discrimina-

---

[1604] Burri 2000, p. 345.
[1605] Piso 1998, p. 326.
[1606] Ebsen 1993, p. 13.
[1607] Wisskirchen 1994, p. 120.
[1608] Bieback 1997, p. 97.
[1609] The preliminary ruling procedure forms the procedural background to the majority of the indirect discrimination cases coming before the Court.
[1610] Joined Cases 28, 29 and 30/62, [1963] *ECR* 31.
[1611] Prechal 1993, p. 90.
[1612] Watson 1995, pp. 43 subs.
[1613] See earlier in this part, A.II.4.

tion cases, the Court only remarked on the general meaning of objective justification but left the determination of the legitimacy of specific claims to the national court (e.g. *Jenkins*,[1614] para. 14; *Bilka*, para. 36).[1615] More recently, the Court itself sometimes determines the legitimacy of such claims regarding justification grounds and also rules on issues of proportionality (e.g. *Seymour-Smith*,[1616] para. 67 subs.). In all, there seems to be no consistency in, nor clear criteria for the Court's choices in these matters (e.g. Hervey,[1617] Darmon & Huglo,[1618] Prechal,[1619] Asscher-Vonk & Wentholt,[1620] Drijber & Prechal,[1621] Piso,[1622] Tobler,[1623] Burri).[1624]

Who should determine the legitimacy of claims in a given case may also depend on the nature of the questions put forward by the national courts in their requests for preliminary rulings. Bieback[1625] notes that in this procedure the Court of Justice has no choice but to focus on the questions referred to it. The range of particular questions referred by national courts may limit the Court's ability to reach all issues which might otherwise be relevant in the context of a specific case. Still, the Court sometimes provides guidance to the national court on certain issues without even having been asked to do so (e.g. *Bowden*).[1626] Not to be outdone, even after having obtained from the Court of Justice a preliminary ruling, some national courts tend to search for possible objective justifications other than those mentioned in their references. Prechal[1627] therefore suggests the use of encompassing and 'interrogative references', as were employed in the *Molenbroek* case.[1628] Piso[1629] emphasises that the national courts in their references specifically ask about *every* justification ground raised before them.

As for the Court of Justice's approach to the questions put to it, academic writers sometimes caution that certain issues should not be left to the national courts because to do so jeopardizes the uniform application of Community law (Burri,[1630] Barnard

---

[1614]   Case 96/80, [1981] *ECR* 911.
[1615]   Case 170/84, [1986] *ECR* 1607.
[1616]   Case C-167/97, [1999] *ECR* I-623.
[1617]   Hervey 1991, pp. 816 subs.
[1618]   Darmon & Huglo 1992, p. 12.
[1619]   Prechal 1993, pp. 86 subs.
[1620]   Asscher-Vonk & Wentholt 1994, p. 76.
[1621]   Drijber & Prechal 1997, pp. 144 subs.
[1622]   Piso 1998, p. 55.
[1623]   Tobler 1999, p. 397.
[1624]   Burri 2000, pp. 343 subs.
[1625]   Bieback 1997, pp. 95 subs.
[1626]   Case C-133/00, [2001] *ECR* I-7031. This example concerns indirect discrimination, though not the issue of objective justification.
[1627]   Prechal 1993, pp. 86 subs. and 92.
[1628]   Case C-226/91, [1992] *ECR* I-5943.
[1629]   Piso 1998, p 327.
[1630]   Idem.

& Hepple).[1631] According to Drijber & Prechal,[1632] the legitimacy of a general class of aims should always be assessed by the Court of Justice. But, insofar as this is possible, the Court should also deal with the legitimacy of such grounds in the framework of the specific case. Such a two-tiered examination should certainly be possible where legal measures are at issue. Other cases may depend on their particular circumstances. As an example of what should be left to the national court, Drijber & Prechal mention disputes concerning alleged sex discrimination in the context of pay classification systems. In the present writer's view, the Court could also consider enumerating a list of aims that are, in principle, acceptable in the form of an open catalogue, similar to the Court's case law on mandatory requirements in the area of free movement of goods.[1633]

ii. The test: strict in principle, lenient in practice?

Academic research has found that when the Court chooses to assess for itself a specific argument relating to objective justification, the strictness of its approach may vary according to the area of law under consideration. In 1990 Currall[1634] found that the Court thus far had never once accepted a claim of objective justification in the context of indirect discrimination on grounds of *nationality*. Since then, cases such as *Bachmann*[1635] demonstrate that objective justification may indeed be accepted, though apparently only rarely. In contrast, such acceptance is common in the context of indirect *sex* discrimination, where some commentators have even noted the increased use of standardised excuses (e.g. the GTE Commentary).[1636] Particularly in *social security law,* objective justification appears to be accepted relatively easily. It is generally thought that here the Court applies the proportionality test loosely, requiring only reasonable or rational justification of discriminatory practices. The Court's stance on objective justification is seen to have gone from robust to downright confused and indeed far too permissive of practices and rules which disadvantage one sex over another (O'Leary).[1637] Accordingly, it is said that the Court does not properly apply its own demanding test (Bieback)[1638] which in turn raises questions about its commitment to equality in more than a purely formal sense (Sohrab;[1639] see further e.g.

[1631]   Barnard & Hepple 1999, p. 411.
[1632]   Drijber & Prechal 1997, p. 144.
[1633]   See the Court's approach in *Cassis de Dijon* (Case 120/78, [1979] ECR 649), para. 8.
[1634]   Currall 1990, p. 19.
[1635]   Case C-204/90, [1992] *ECR* I-249, see earlier in this part, A.II.4.b.i.
[1636]   GTE Commentary 1997, n. 61 ad Art. 119 of the EC Treaty.
[1637]   O'Leary 2002, p. 182.
[1638]   Bieback 1997, p. 400.
[1639]   Sohrab 1994, p. 109.

Sjerps,[1640] Manolkidis,[1641] Ellis,[1642] Drijber & Prechal,[1643] Burri,[1644] Hervey;[1645] also Piso).[1646]

Regarding the reasons for the Court's particular restraint in the area of social security law, Manolkidis[1647] mentions the obvious (and rather mundane) point of the costs involved. Shaw[1648] speaks of a 'key policy decision' made by the Court to leave a relatively wide discretion to the Member States as they modernize their welfare systems, both in view of the sex equality principle and because of the increasing demographic pressures which they are experiencing. Bieback[1649] refers to the division of competences according to which social policy is, first and foremost, for the Member States to regulate (though it should be noted that subsequently the Amsterdam revision has provided for a more explicit role for the Community in this field).[1650] However, Blom[1651] rightly points out that it is perfectly possible to allow a wide margin of discretion and then to test proportionality in a rather strict way. Also, in recent years the Court has emphasised that 'the broad margin of discretion which the Member States enjoy in matters of social policy may not have the effect of frustrating the implementation of a fundamental principle of Community law such as that of equal treatment of men and women' (*Steinicke*,[1652] para. 63, with further references). Obviously, this should have consequences for the application of the objective justification test.

[1640]   Sjerps 1994, p. 95.

[1641]   Manolkidis 1997, pp. 101 subs.

[1642]   Ellis 1997, p. 175; Ellis 1994 (Definition of Discrimination), p. 576.

[1643]   Drijber & Prechal 1997, pp. 141 subs. and 164.

[1644]   Burri 2000, p. 345.

[1645]   Hervey 2002, pp. 121 subs.

[1646]   Piso 1998, p. 314.

[1647]   Manolkidis 1997, p. 102.

[1648]   Shaw 2001, p. 108.

[1649]   Bieback 1997, p. 400.

[1650]   Before the Amsterdam revision, there was no provision specifically granting the Community a competence in the area of social law. Directives adopted in this field were based on general competence provisions (Arts. 100 and 235 of the Treaty, now Arts. 94 and 308 EC). The fact that the Member States in this situation accepted a Community competence of an implicit nature is evidenced by the fact that the Court was never asked to annul the sex equality Directives adopted on the basis of such general provisions. (This differs from measures adopted on the basis of specific social policy provisions, see the action for annulment in *UEAPME*; Case T-135/96, [1998] *ECR* II-2335). Since the Amsterdam revision, the Community enjoys various explicit competences in the field of social policy, though the Community's role remains limited to supporting and complementing the activities of the Member States in that field (Art. 137 EC); see Tobler 2000 (Sex Equality Law), pp. 145 subs.

[1651]   Blom 1992, p. 106.

[1652]   Case C-77/02, judgment of 11 September 2003, n.y.r.

c. Specifically: justification based on economic considerations

A further issue for debate is the type of justification grounds that are acceptable under Community law and, more specifically, the question of whether *economic grounds* can be relied on. In that regard, there appear to be fundamentally different starting points for social law as opposed to free movement law. As will be seen below, in free movement law (purely) economic grounds of justification are not accepted as a matter of principle in relation to all types of infringements. In contrast, in social (e.g. sex equality) law the starting point is that economic grounds may be acceptable in the context of indirect discrimination.

i. Economic justification in free movement law

In the area of free movement, a *general prohibition of economic justification* applies (Drijber & Prechal).[1653] With regard to the free movement of persons and services, the principle is explicitly written into law in Art. 2 of Directive 64/221[1654] and has often been recognized in the Court's case law (e.g. *Bond van Adverteerders*,[1655] para. 34; *Ciola*,[1656] para. 16). In the context of free movement of goods, the Court held in *Commission v Italy*[1657] (p. 329) that what was then Art. 36 of the EEC Treaty (now Art. 30 EC) 'is directed against eventualities of a non-economic kind' (see also *Campus Oil*,[1658] para. 35, and, *Commission v Greece*,[1659] para. 30). More recently, the Court affirmed generally in the *Golden Shares* cases that 'economic grounds can never serve as justification' for obstacles to free movement (e.g. *Commission v Portugal*,[1660] para. 52). However, in terms of its application, this principle seems to have been somewhat mitigated. As was mentioned earlier, at least in the context of direct taxation, the Court in principle (though hardly ever in practice) accepts that the cohesion of a tax system may serve as a possible ground for justification.[1661] AG Lenz argued that such a concern is in fact economic in nature and can, therefore, never serve as a legitimate justification (*Safir*,[1662] point 36 of the AG's opinion, in relation to the objectives of national fiscal cohesion and effective fiscal supervision). But the Court apparently did not regard this

---

[1653] Drijber & Prechal 1997, p. 140.
[1654] Directive 64/221/EEC, *OJ* English Special Edition 1964, No. 850/64, p. 117.
[1655] Case 352/85, [1988] *ECR* 208.
[1656] Case C-224/97, [1999] *ECR* I-2517. Compare however Plötscher 2003, p. 123f., who, when discussing the possibility of justification in this case, does not mention the exclusion of economic justification at all.
[1657] Case 7/61, [1961] *ECR* 317.
[1658] Case 72/83, [1984] *ECR* 2727.
[1659] Case C-398/98, [2001] *ECR* I-7915.
[1660] Case C-367/98, [2002] *ECR* I-473, concerning the free movement of capital, an area where the only economic derogation ground provided for by the Treaty concerns third countries (Art. 59 EC).
[1661] See later Part 3, A.II.2.b.ii.
[1662] Case C-118/96, [1998] I-1897.

as an obstacle. Further, there are cases of an economic nature where the financial balance of systems regarding social security, health and the like are relied on in the context of objective justification for restrictions to free movement. In *Kohll*[1663] (para. 41), the Court explained that 'aims of a *purely* economic nature cannot justify a barrier to the fundamental principle of freedom to provide services' but continued to say that 'it cannot be excluded that the risk of seriously undermining the financial balance of the social security system may constitute an overriding reason in the general interest capable of justifying a barrier' (emphasis added). This means that purely economic considerations are excluded but broader considerations with a financial aspect to them may be acceptable.[1664]

ii. Specifically: economic justification in the context of indirect sex discrimination

Whilst in free movement law the starting point is that economic justifications are excluded, such justification has expressly been accepted by the Court in relation to *indirect sex discrimination*. In *Jenkins*[1665] (para. 12), the Court spoke about 'economic grounds which may be objectively justified' when employers try to justify measures with a disparate effect in terms of sex. Similarly, the Court in *Bilka*[1666] (para. 36) mentioned the possibility of relying on 'a real need on the part of the undertaking'. It is, therefore, clear that in this context market forces or business necessity may be relied on as legitimate economic grounds for the purposes of objective justification (e.g. Gerards,[1667] O'Leary).[1668] In academic writing, various cases are cited as examples (though it is debatable whether and to what extent they actually concern economic justifications). Kenner[1669] cites *Kachelmann*[1670] as a case where the economic needs of an employer (so-called 'operational needs') were allowed to counterbalance the social rights of employees (regarding the right to non-discrimination in relation to dismissal). This case is particularly clear because the Court itself speaks of economic reasons for the dismissal in question (*Kachelmann*, para. 35, see also para. 9). Foubert[1671] draws attention to *Enderby*,[1672] where the Court accepted a claim which involved the state

---

[1663]   Case C-158/96, [1998] *ECR* I-1931; see further below Part 3, B.IV.4.b.
[1664]   In the context of EEA law, compare the so-called single practice rule cases *Brändle* (Case E-4/00, [2000-2001] *EFTA Court Reports* 123), para. 34 and 35; *Mangold* (Case E-5/00, [2000-2001] *EFTA Court Reports* 163), para. 29, and *Tschannett* (Case E-6/00, [2000-2001] *EFTA Court Reports* 203), para. 32.
[1665]   Case 96/80, [1981] *ECR* 911.
[1666]   Case 170/84, [1986] *ECR* 1607.
[1667]   Gerards 2002, pp. 237 and 274 subs.
[1668]   O'Leary 2002, p. 145.
[1669]   Kenner 2003, p. 464.
[1670]   Case C-322/98, [2000] *ECR* I-7505.
[1671]   Foubert 2002, p. 43, with further references.
[1672]   Case C-127/92, [1993] *ECR* I-5535.

of the employment market as a legitimate justification for an employer increasing the pay of a particular job category in order to attract candidates. The same example is mentioned by O'Leary[1673] who further cites *Nolte*[1674] where the Court accepted Germany's argument that it had a legitimate interest in fostering the existence and supply of so-called minor employment in order to respond to a 'social and presumably economic demand'. O'Leary also notes more generally that, under *Teuling*[1675] in the context of social security law, the fundamental principle of equality 'may simply be trumped' by a Member State pointing to the laudable social policy objectives behind the legislation in the face of presumably, strained, budgetary circumstances.

As far as *budgetary considerations* are concerned, the Court has held repeatedly that they cannot justify sex discrimination (e.g. *Roks*,[1676] para. 35 subs.; *Jørgensen*,[1677] para. 39 subs.; *Steinicke*,[1678] para. 66 subs.; *Schönheit and Becker*,[1679] para. 85). The Court explained that though such considerations may underlie a Member State's choice of social policy and influence the nature or scope of the social protection measures which it wishes to adopt, such considerations do not in themselves constitute an aim pursued by a Member State's social policy. The Court added that 'to concede that budgetary considerations may justify a difference in treatment between men and women which would otherwise constitute indirect discrimination on grounds of sex would mean that the application and scope of a rule of Community law as fundamental as that of equal treatment between men and women might vary in time and place according to the state of the public finances of Member States'. At the same time, the Court found that reasons relating to the need to ensure sound management of public expenditure on specialised medical care and also to guarantee people's access to such care may justify measures of social policy. According to Epiney & Freiermuth Abt,[1680] the decisive criterion in determining the acceptability of particular financial considerations is whether the aim is to maintain a specified and limited social policy scheme (e.g. social insurance system). According to Kenner,[1681] the Court simply used the language of social aims to justify policies that are ultimately driven by economic considerations.

The conclusion is that although purely budgetary concerns cannot serve as legitimate justification for indirect sex discrimination, they may nevertheless play an important part in the context of broader aims of social policy of a Member State trying to justify national legislation with a disparate impact in terms of sex. To that extent, a parallel can be drawn with the Court's approach in free movement law. With regard

---

[1673] O'Leary 2002, pp. 156, 169 and 174.
[1674] Case C-317/93, [1995] *ECR* I-4625.
[1675] Case 30/85, [1987] *ECR* 2497.
[1676] Case C-343/92, [1994] *ECR* I-571.
[1677] Case C-226/98, [2000] *ECR* I-2447.
[1678] Case C-77/02, judgment of 11 September 2003, n.y.r.
[1679] Joined Cases C-4/02 and 5/02, judgment of 23 October 2003, n.y.r.
[1680] Epiney & Freiermuth Abt 2003, p. 96.
[1681] Kenner 2003, p. 462.

to indirect sex discrimination, although employers cannot rely on purely budgetary reasons, nevertheless, they may still be able to rely on economic grounds in a broader sense, namely in the framework of business necessity. Again, it is noteworthy that the Court in this context explicitly used the term of 'economic grounds'.

iii. Who should bear the costs of non-discrimination?

Fredman[1682] observes that little attention has been paid to the question of why economic needs should be allowed to trump equality considerations. One plausible rationale might be that of the freedom of both employers and Member States to pursue their own legitimate interests. This idea is linked to the assumption, mentioned by Foubert,[1683] that, in today's society, employers usually discriminate out of economic self-interest rather than because of irrational prejudices. Along the same lines, it might be argued more generally that the primary motivation of most private employers for being in business at all is of an economic nature and that the ramifications of their actions are, necessarily, of an economic nature.

Ultimately, the issue of economic justification is linked to the question *of who should bear the cost* of non-discrimination legislation. As De Schutter[1684] explains, non-discrimination legislation may lead to a partial transfer of the cost of achieving equality from the collectivity (meaning the society as a whole as represented by the State) to individual economic agents. In systems that accept economic justifications, the employer is not encouraged to contribute to the elimination of discrimination if it would impact negatively on the economic health of the enterprise. Such a system is based on two ideas, namely 1) that the alleged requirements of the market do not significantly reinforce stereotypes and prejudices that may lead to discrimination and, thus, are neutral and 2) that the fight against discrimination is a task belonging solely to the State. In contrast, the cost to the employer is higher under a system that does not allow economic justification. Such a system is based on the ideas 1) that businesses can be required to contribute individually to the collective task of progressively eliminating discrimination because such a goal is in the interest of society as a whole and 2) that the alleged requirements of the market do not form a neutral context for the employer's actions, but on the contrary serve to reinforce stereotypes and prejudices that may lead to discrimination.[1685] In comparison, the latter approach is more long-term oriented.

[1682]   Fredman 2002, p. 25.
[1683]   Foubert 2002, pp. 59 subs.
[1684]   De Schutter 2001, pp. 111 subs. and 137 subs.
[1685]   Though De Schutter rightly remarks that shifting some of the responsibility for fighting discrimination risks being regarded as a substitute for a more structural approach to further equality of opportunities.

Not surprisingly, commentators' reactions to the Court's acceptance of economic justification grounds vary widely. On the one hand, Arnull[1686] argues that the balance struck by the Court between equal treatment and the operation of the market is not unreasonable since it is limited to conduct which is not intended to disadvantage women and produces such negative results simply through circumstances beyond the control of the employer.[1687] Clearly, such reasoning is based on the view that employers should not be required to contribute individually to the collective task of eliminating sex discrimination. On the other hand, Foubert[1688] argues that the Court's willingness to accept economic justification 'may indicate that, once judges lose touch with the raw instances of overt discrimination, they easily – and maybe unknowingly -, revert to traditional societal concepts, inclusive of their inherent sex discriminatory aspects'. Similarly, Shaw[1689] reproaches the Court for importing too many market-based criteria into the concept of objective justification, and Fredman[1690] argues that '[i]f market forces may be used to justify indirect discrimination, there is a distinct danger that discriminatory practices which are functional to the market will simply be perpetuated'. Such critics suggest that, if a legal system that allows employers to enact discriminatory measures when such measures are merely economically useful, a courts' finding of justification amount to no more than an acceptance of discrimination against women whenever it can be shown to correspond roughly to the needs of men. Accordingly, Hervey[1691] argues that an approach based on excluding, or at least questioning, market justifications might significantly improve the definition of unlawful discrimination. Market justification would then no longer be presumptively neutral, but would require a showing of actual neutrality.

In the present writer's view, the basic principle should be that employers should not be allowed to derive benefits from behaviour with a discriminatory effect. However, given that EC equality law necessarily functions within a market order,[1692] it is questionable whether a *total* exclusion of economic justification is feasible, particularly in view of the potential backlash. To that extent, a fixed stance against discrimination supported by a rigid system might not necessarily be the most effective one. However, it could be argued that the same is true for discrimination on grounds of nationality where economic justification has long been outlawed on the level of principle. The present writer is unable to find any convincing reasons for applying a different starting position with regard to the principle of sex discrimination. In the

---

[1686] Arnull 1999, p. 488.
[1687] Similarly, Novak 1997, p. 1592, argues in relation to free movement law that economic justification should be accepted in principle.
[1688] Foubert 2002, p. 47.
[1689] Shaw 2001, p. 125.
[1690] Piso 1998, pp. 130 subs.
[1691] Hervey 1996, p. 406.
[1692] On the economic function of equality and non-discrimination law, see above Part 1, B.II.4.

interest of consistency, such a difference ought to be abandoned. Accordingly, it is
submitted that at least the principle that purely economic reasons are unacceptable
should be a general one that also applies in relation to sex discrimination. Of course,
it may not be easy in each case to draw a line between economic and social aims
(Drijber & Prechal).[1693] However, Burri[1694] is certainly right in arguing that the Court's
statements in *Schröder*[1695] (para. 57) on the prevalence of the social over the economic
aim of Art. 141 EC must have consequences in the present context. Accordingly, the
social aims of the prohibition of indirect discrimination (rather those of economic
justification) must be accorded particular importance in the process of weighing
interests.

d. Procedural implications of the objective justification element

In the Court's indirect discrimination formula, the element of objective justification
has important procedural implications in that it reverses the usual distribution of the
burden of proof. Already under the case law definition of indirect discrimination,
coined long before the adoption of the Burden of Proof Directive[1696] with its explicit
rules, the burden of proof for the existence of objective justification was placed on the
defendant (*Bilka*,[1697] para. 30: 'if the undertaking is able to show that its pay practice
may be explained by objectively justified factors unrelated to any discrimination on
grounds of sex', and para. 31: 'unless the undertaking shows that the exclusion is based
on objectively justified factors unrelated to any discrimination on grounds of sex').
According to O'Leary,[1698] this is clearly one of the essential aspects of the Court's
attitude towards indirect (sex) discrimination.

Whilst these procedural implications are generally recognised as an important
aspect of the legal concept of indirect discrimination, there have also been voices taking
the issue considerably further. Barrett[1699] is an early example. Pondering the meaning
of the Court's statements in *Jenkins*[1700] regarding intent and objective justification,
Barrett thought at the time that possibly the Court viewed the difference between part-
time and full-time work as capable of constituting a material difference, provided that
the employer had a genuine business-related *motive,* not simply the desire to
discriminate against women, for making the distinction. Barrett thought that if this
were the correct interpretation, the purpose of establishing the adverse impact of the

---

[1693] Drijber & Prechal 1997, p. 140.
[1694] Burri 2000, p. 391.
[1695] Case C-50/96, [2000] *ECR* I-743.
[1696] Directive 97/80/EC, *OJ* 1998 L 14/6 (as amended).
[1697] Case 170/84, [1986] *ECR* 1607.
[1698] O'Leary 2002, p. 151.
[1699] Barrett 1981, pp. 177 and 184/185.
[1700] Case 96/80, [1981] *ECR* 911.

differential treatment of women was then only to shift the full burden of proof on the employer. This tentative interpretation was rendered irrelevant through later case law that clarified that the employer's intent was irrelevant to a *prima facie* case of indirect sex discrimination.[1701]

Much later, a similar thought was considered by Blomeyer[1702] who argued that the procedural aspects of the legal concept of indirect sex discrimination represent the concept's very essence. Under this view, the concept is intended to overcome so-called *non liquet* situations, that is, situations where neither the existence nor the inexistence of elements necessary for the application of a given rule can be proven. Writing before the adoption of the Burden of Proof Directive (and with no expectation that it might ever be adopted), Blomeyer argued that, in the context of the equal pay principle, the burden of proof rule can be derived from an interpretation of Art. 119 of the Treaty itself. Relying notably on the Court's findings in the cases *Jenkins*,[1703] *Bilka*[1704] and *Danfoss*,[1705] Blomeyer explained that the Court starts from a legal presumption (namely that there is indirect discrimination on grounds of sex if it is predominantly women who are disadvantaged by the measure or act at issue) and that those legal presumptions constitute burden of proof rules: if the plaintiff succeeds in showing the disparate impact, the presumed fact – namely the existence of discrimination on grounds of sex – is accepted through a fiction without any further proof. The responsibility to provide counter-proof then falls to the defendant. The result of this construction is that it is the defendant who has to bear the risk of a *non liquet* situation. Though logical within its own framework, the disadvantage of Blomeyer's approach lies in the fact that it explicitly denies that the concept of indirect sex discrimination has any social policy function. Given that a substantive and a procedural function need not be mutually exclusive (see Bieback's[1706] discussion of both aspects; also Ebsen),[1707] it is not surprising that Blomeyer's view has not been adopted into mainstream academic writing.

e. The place of objective justification in the discrimination analysis

Academic writers take opposing positions with regard to what constitutes the *proper function* of the element of objective justification in the discrimination analysis. The traditional view sees objective justification simply as a specific form of justification (in the proper sense). In contrast, a more recent view links objective justification to causation in cases of alleged discrimination.

[1701] See earlier in this part, A.I.4.h.
[1702] Blomeyer 1994, pp. 44, 88 and 119 subs.
[1703] Case 96/80, [1981] *ECR* 911.
[1704] Case 170/84, [1986] *ECR* 1607.
[1705] Case 109/88, [1989] *ECR* 3199.
[1706] Bieback 1997, pp. 35 and 38.
[1707] Ebsen 1993, p. 12.

i. Objective justification as an issue of justification (proper)

According to the traditionally held view, the decisive difference between direct and indirect discrimination with regard to justification lies in the fact that direct discrimination can be justified only on the basis of grounds expressly mentioned in the Treaty (a so-called closed system), whilst in the case of indirect discrimination there exists an additional possibility of objective justification embodied in the last part of the formula indirect discrimination (an open system; e.g. Craig & de Búrca,[1708] see also Burri,[1709] Blom,[1710] Barnard).[1711] Justification is thus understood in the strict sense of the word – that is, in the sense of an element involving cross cutting-reasons.[1712] Under such an approach, a finding of objective justification means that, although in fact indirect discrimination is present in terms of the measure's effect, this discrimination is not prohibited by the law because there are other rationales that are deemed more important than the concern for equality ('There is discrimination, but it is justified.'). Bamforth[1713] describes this as the situation where all the elements of discrimination are present, but there is a saving factor or a defence.

ii. Objective justification as an issue of causation

In contrast, according to an increasing number of academic writers, in the context of indirect discrimination objective justification does not concern justification but rather is an element defining discrimination – meaning that if there is legitimate 'justification', then discrimination simply does not exist. Bamforth[1714] describes this as the situation where there is an element preventing a finding of discrimination in the first place. Blomeyer[1715] provides an example. According to Blomeyer, understanding the concept of indirect discrimination as containing a *burden of proof rule*, as described in the previous section, means that if objective justification exists, then the existence of discrimination on grounds of sex has not been proven. In other words, it has not been shown that sex was the cause for the disadvantage suffered.

The view that objective justification relates to the definition itself of the term indirect discrimination is shared by a number of authors, though in a different context.

[1708] Craig & de Búrca 2003, p. 720. Literally: 'The possible grounds for justifying indirect discrimination are broad, and not confined to the exceptions set out in the Treaty or in secondary legislation.'
[1709] Burri 2000, pp. 119 and 211.
[1710] Blom 1992, p. 55.
[1711] Barnard 2004, in various contexts, e.g. p. 258.
[1712] See above Part 1, B.III.6.a.
[1713] Bamforth 1996, p. 50.
[1714] Idem.
[1715] Blomeyer 1994, p. 127.

The argument has perhaps been made most forcefully by Ellis[1716] in the context of sex discrimination. In this view, discrimination is a civil wrong ('the tort of discrimination') which as such logically must have two ingredients: harm and causation (the harm must result from the application of a prohibited classification). Regarding indirect sex discrimination,[1717] Ellis explains the meaning of the causation approach as follows: '[I]f the adverse consequences to one sex can be shown to be attributable to an acceptable and gender-neutral factor, then there is no discrimination. The *cause* of the adverse impact is something other than sex discrimination.'[1718] And: 'Where an employer 'justifies' apparent indirect discrimination, there is proof that the disadvantage is attributable to some other cause than sex, such as the efficient running of a business.'[1719] At least theoretically, such causation is usually fairly easy to demonstrate in cases of direct discrimination but not in that of indirect discrimination where, in a formal manner, other, neutral criteria are at play. Consequently, the legislator grants the benefit of the doubt to the putative victim in indirect discrimination cases by assuming the existence of indirect discrimination once proof of adverse impact is established unless causation can be disproved. Proof of objective justification discharges this burden of proof.

Ellis' view is shared by a growing number of academic writers (e.g. Kentridge,[1720] Watson,[1721] Barnard,[1722] Szyszczak,[1723] Bieback),[1724] though not always for the same

---

[1716] See Ellis 1994 (Enderby), p. 391; Ellis 1994 (Definition of Discrimination), p. 572; Ellis 1996, pp. 18 subs.; Ellis 1997, p. 174; Ellis 1998, pp. 124 and 136.

[1717] According to Ellis, the issue of causation in the case of indirect discrimination is a logical parallel to that of direct discrimination. Regarding *direct* sex discrimination, see Ellis 1998, in particular pp. 109/110, 124 and 136, as well as Ellis 1994 (Enderby), p. 389 (the latter in the context of AG Lenz's use of the term justification in the context of an issue of causation in *Enderby* (Case C-127/92, [1993] *ECR* I-5535), point 24 subs. of the AG's opinion. In essence, Ellis points out that only discrimination *based on sex* is prohibited under the equal pay principle, which means that differences which are not attributable to sex remain possible. Thus, the way is open for the employer to plead that some factor other than sex is the cause of the pay discrepancy. In terms of its practical relevance, Ellis relies on this approach in order to warn against accepting extra-textual justification in the case of direct pay discrimination. She argues that acceptance of such justification would confuse the issues of causation and of harm.

[1718] Ellis 1998, p. 136.

[1719] Ellis 1994 (Enderby), p. 391.

[1720] Referring to an earlier edition of Ellis' textbook; Kentridge 1994, p. 202.

[1721] Watson 1995, pp. 42 and 45.

[1722] Barnard 1996 (Commercial Discrimination), p. 70.

[1723] Szyszczak 1996, p. 58.

[1724] Bieback 1997, p. 102.

reasons (e.g. Somek,[1725] Martin,[1726] Meyer,[1727] Plötscher).[1728] In fact, certain Advocates General have taken the same approach (e.g. AG Jacobs in his opinion on the *Schnorbus*[1729] case, point 35; AG Cosmas in his opinion on *Italy v Commission*,[1730] point 32).

AG Cosmas' statements in *Italy v Commission*, a transport case, are particularly illustrative. The AG first observed generally that 'in the case of direct discrimination, proof of its existence is by definition self-evident: both the existence of different treatment of similar situations and the similar treatment of different situations (de facto discrimination) and the unlawful nature of that treatment (de jure discrimination) may be directly inferred from reference in the measures at issue of a prohibited criterion. Conversely, a finding of indirect discrimination presupposes a complex reasoning based, in the first instance, on a thorough analysis of the concrete factual situation governed by the measure at issue, and on an examination of whether, in light of that situation, the apparent neutrality of the criterion applied leads in the end to unfair discrimination in practice. The second stage is the finding that that discrimination is unlawful, that is to say that it is indirectly but closely connected to a prohibited criterion. In other words, under the above reasoning it is appropriate to determine initially whether the emergence in practice of discrimination is, in general terms, the unavoidable consequence of the criterion applied or whether it is rather a random consequence not attributable to the provision at issue. It is not always easy to reach that determination immediately, nor may it, in any event, prejudge the existence of de jure discrimination, whether reliance is placed on the precepts of common experience or on statistical data. For that reason, what is henceforth required is an inquiry from the opposite starting point into whether the provision adopted is objective in nature. That inquiry should logically be conducted on the basis of a reasoning process which examines whether the provision at issue is proportionate, that is to say necessary, appropriate and not unduly burdensome, in relation to its purpose. That purpose must be connected with an overriding general-interest requirement, as interpreted in each given case. That purpose may indeed be defined generally by a legal provision, which is the case in regard to Article 8(1) of Regulation No 2408/92[1731] which provides that the objective of the measures at issue must concern distribution of traffic between the airports within an airport system.' The following

---

[1725] Somek 2001, p. 193, footnote 89, though the author seems to make the same statement in an even more general context.

[1726] Martin 1998, p. 312. In arguing that 'objective justification' is not an issue of justification, Martin relies on the Court's general definition of the equality principle. Martin at the time thought that the Court had never recognised true justification. However, subsequently *Schnorbus* (Case C-79/99, [2000] *ECR* I-10997) appeared; see further below Part 3, A.II.2.c.

[1727] Meyer 2002, p. 37.

[1728] Plötscher 2003, p. 61.

[1729] Case C-79/99, [2000] *ECR* I-10997.

[1730] Case C-361/98, [2001] *ECR* I-385.

[1731] AG Cosmas is referring to Regulation 2408/92/EEC, *OJ* 1992 L 240/8 (as amended). Art. 8(1) of this Regulation reads: 'This Regulation shall not affect a Member State's right to regulate without discrimination on grounds of nationality or identity of the air carrier, the distribution of traffic between the airports within an airport system.'

remarks made by AG Cosmas reflect the causation approach: 'If the provision at issue is proportionate to its objective, it must be regarded as lawful even if it results in de facto discrimination because then plainly that discrimination cannot be attributed to the provision at issue but either occurs randomly or is attributable to the legitimate objectives of the law of which the provision at issue constitutes the culmination. It is, then, to be inferred from the foregoing that, whenever it is a question of determining indirect discrimination the proportionality of the provision at issue has to be reviewed in relation to the legitimate purpose for which that provision was adopted. That review should not be seen exclusively as an element of the possible justification for the indirect discrimination but should be deemed to constitute an element of the reasoning leading to a finding of discrimination, a fact that distinguishes the logic of indirect discrimination from that of direct discrimination.'

Under the present writer's analysis, the causation approach as advocated by Ellis and others can be compared to the role of the mandatory requirements in the *Cassis de Dijon* case law under Art. 28 EC (concerning free movement of goods) and, more generally, to the role of objectives of general interest in the context of restrictions in a wider sense.[1732] In *Cassis de Dijon*[1733] (para. 8), the Court stated that, in the absence of harmonisation, goods lawfully produced in one Member State must be admitted for import into other Member States unless the importing Member State can rely on mandatory requirements. According to the predominant view, this must be understood as meaning that national measures hindering or limiting the import of such goods in the interest of mandatory requirements do not fall within the *scope* of Art. 28 EC in the first place, rather than constituting restrictions that are *justified* in the interest of mandatory requirements.[1734] In other words, they are not measures having an equivalent effect to a quantitative restrictions to imports to begin with (e.g. the von der Groeben & Schwarze Commentary;[1735] see also Epiney,[1736] Jarass).[1737] The reason usually given for this interpretation relates to the fact that the justification grounds available under Art. 30 EC form a closed list which, in addition, must be interpreted restrictively (*Irish Souvenirs*,[1738] para. 7). Within such a system, it is not possible to expand the scope of Art. 30 EC and add other grounds of justification through mere judicial interpretation. The formula of the mandatory requirements as relating to the scope of Art. 28 EC made it possible to avoid that problem – though, in effect, the Court's case law did in fact introduce new possibilities of escape for the Member

---

[1732] See above Part 1, B.IV.
[1733] Case 120/78, [1979] *ECR* 649.
[1734] The Court's case law has not always been clear on this issue; see Martin 1998, pp. 294 subs.
[1735] Von der Groeben & Schwarze Commentary 2004, n. 190 ad Art. 28 EC.
[1736] Epiney 1995, p. 42.
[1737] Jarass 2000 (Elemente), p. 719.
[1738] Case 113/80, [1981] *ECR* 1625.

States.[1739] Similarly, the acceptance by the Court of objective justification for indirect discrimination is an example of how the Court sometimes acts to allow certain categories of interests to be classified as legitimate exceptions without having to amend the Treaty. In that sense, the causation approach fits into the logic of the system.

However, in the present writer's view, the causation approach is not convincing for the following reasons. First, it is submitted that the objective justification test's proportionality requirement with its element of balancing interests indicates that objective justification is concerned with justification proper (compare Jarass).[1740] Second, it can be argued that the causation approach deprives the concept of indirect discrimination of its fundamental *raison d'être* (to ensure the effectiveness of EC equality law)[1741] even at an initial stage of the analysis. Under the causation approach, the particular disadvantage suffered by the group disparately affected by the contested measure would not even be recognised. As Hervey[1742] explains, this aspect is relevant from an emotional point of view, since 'it is one thing to be told that under the law you have been discriminated against, but it is justified for an over-riding reason, and quite another thing to be told that the law does not regard the activity as discrimination at all'. In the present writer's view, causation should be viewed as a factor relevant solely to the *first* part of the indirect discrimination formula where the decisive point is that the disadvantage suffered is due to, for example, sex. The requisite causal link is established by the factually disparate effect of an apparently neutral criterion. Since such disadvantage continues unabated where objective justification is accepted, it is submitted that it is more honest to view objective justification as a form of justification in the proper sense.

iii. The relevance of the distinction between the two approaches

From a *practical point of view* the distinction between the two approaches may not be so very relevant. Bamforth[1743] calls the distinction legalistic and Steiner[1744] considers that it has no practical relevance as long as two points are clear, namely that the objective justification test involves a weighing of the interests (those of the alleged discriminator and those of the victim of the alleged discrimination) and that it is the alleged discriminator who has to establish justification.[1745] The present writer would

---

[1739] Accordingly, Martin 1998, p. 291, speaks about '*une creation prétorienne*'. Oliver 1999, p. 804, declares that he would find a construction based on justification more convincing.

[1740] Jarass 2000 (Unified Approach), pp. 155 and 157, in the context of textual derogations and general good justification for indistinctly applicable measures, respectively.

[1741] See later in this part, A.IV. 4.

[1742] Hervey 2002, p. 105, footnote 31.

[1743] Bamforth 1996, p. 50.

[1744] Steiner 1999, p. 273.

[1745] This latter point seems to be doubted by Hervey 2002, p. 105, footnote 31.

agree. As Kentridge[1746] puts it in the context of indirect sex discrimination, objective justification seen as an issue of causation 'does not make [the practice] fair to the women who are disadvantaged by it. The point at which such a policy is found to be justifiable is the point at which the law compromises between equality and commercial rationality.' In that sense and with the exception of the emotional aspect, mentioned above, the effect of objective justification, however understood, is the same as of that of cross-cutting reasons or justification proper (compare also Bär).[1747] As an advantage of the traditional approach, Blom[1748] points out that it may lead to the application of stricter requirements for the justifications put forward because they are conceived of as exceptions. The causation approach tends to give the comfortable feeling that equality need not give way to economic interests but in reality does not resolve the question of which interests are sufficiently important to justify disparate impact. For that reason, the traditional approach appears preferable and ultimately more effective in attaining a state of equality.

Finally, it should be added that thus far most of the discussion over the merits of the traditional and causation approaches has taken place on the academic level. There are no clear indications in the Court's case law as to which is the more preferable view. Regarding discrimination on grounds of nationality, the Court's language in the landmark case O'Flynn[1749] does not forcefully point in the direction of the causation approach (compare, however, Martin).[1750] Whereas, in the context of sex discrimination, there are admittedly some expressions that might be interpreted as referring to causation (Jenkins,[1751] para. 11; Bilka,[1752] para. 29). However, as far as the present writer can see, the Court thus far has not explicitly pronounced a view on the issue. In particular, there are no such statements in the cases Schnorbus[1753] and Italy v Commission[1754] in whose contexts the causation approach was expressly advocated by Advocates General Jacobs and Cosmas.

[1746] Kentridge 1994, p. 203.
[1747] Baer 2004, p. 176.
[1748] Blom 1992, p. 56.
[1749] Case C-237/94, [1996] ECR I-2617.
[1750] Martin 1998, pp. 607 subs. Without referring to causation, this author perceives in O'Flynn a change in the case law since in Bachmann (Case C-204/90, [1992] ECR I-249), the Court began by stating that there is indirect discrimination and only afterwards turned to the issue of objective justification. In contrast, in O'Flynn the Court held that there is indirect discrimination only in the absence of objective justification which, according to Martin, illustrates a different kind of approach. According to Martin, this does not correspond to what the Court really wanted to do (and was actually doing), namely to continue with the Bachmann case law.
[1751] Case 96/80, [1999] ECR I-623 (para. 25).
[1752] Case 170/84, [1986] ECR 1607.
[1753] Case C-79/99, [2000] ECR I-10997.
[1754] Case C-361/98, [2001] ECR I-385.

It might perhaps be argued that in some cases *implicit* indications can be found, but in the present writer's view they are too uncertain to settle the matter. For instance, the Court held in *Bond van Adverteerders*[1755] (para. 32) that 'national rules which are not applicable to services without distinction as regards their origin and which are therefore discriminatory are compatible with Community law only if they can be brought within the scope of an express derogation'. This statement was made against the background of a case that concerned *direct* discrimination,[1756] but the Court repeated this statement also in the context of cases that seem to involve *indirect* discrimination, such as *Distribuidores Cinematográficos*[1757] and *Ciola*.[1758] If the limitation of the justification possibilities to express grounds also applies in the case of indirect discrimination, this could be interpreted in favour of the causation approach: given the undeniable existence of the objective justification element, the Court's statement makes sense only if that element is not seen as relating to justification proper. However, as case law stands at present, the Court's rulings regarding the reach and the meaning of the *Bond van Adverteerders* statement does not seem sufficiently clear to settle the question. Clarification will have to come from future case law.

4. ISSUES RELATING TO THE AIM OF THE LEGAL CONCEPT OF INDIRECT DISCRIMINATION

Issues for debate also arise in the context of the underlying rationale of the legal concept of indirect discrimination, which is to ensure the effectiveness of the Community's equality law. The following sections will first put this aim in a broader context and then consider factors that may limit the degree to which effectiveness can be achieved in practice.

a. Effectiveness in a broader context

Although the Court did not rely on Art. 5 of the EEC Treaty (now Art. 10 EC) when, in *Sotgiu*,[1759] it declared that the concern for the effectiveness of EC equality law was the underlying rationale of the legal concept of indirect discrimination. Sundberg-Weitman[1760] argues that 'there can be no doubt that, under Article 5 of the Treaty, Member States are generally prohibited from taking such arbitrary measures 'as could jeopardize the attainment of the objectives of this Treaty'. A different treatment which, although not directly linked with nationality, has the same or essentially the same effect

---

[1755] Case 352/85, [1988] *ECR* 2085.
[1756] At least in the present writer's analysis, the Court itself did not qualify the nature of the discrimination.
[1757] Case C-17/92, [1993] *ECR* I-2239, see para. 15 and 16.
[1758] Case C-224/97, [1999] *ECR* I-2517, see para. 14 and 16.
[1759] Case 152/73, [1974] *ECR* 153.
[1760] Sundberg-Weitman 1977, p. 110.

as discrimination on grounds of nationality would therefore, in any case, violate Article 5.' The Calliess & Ruffert Commentary[1761] links the concept of indirect discrimination to the well known general principle of *effet utile* (or useful effect) of Community law[1762] in whose context Art. 10 EC often plays an important role (compare e.g. Temple-Lang,[1763] Mortelmans,[1764] Hinton).[1765] In fact, apart from being aimed at the effectiveness of discrimination law itself, the concept of indirect discrimination also takes its place in the context of a broader concern for effectiveness of Community law in general. A particularly illustrative example is the system set up by the Treaty concerning fiscal barriers to the free movement of goods. It consists of a carefully constructed safety net consisting of a combination of provisions of various natures including the prohibition against financial charges (Art. 25 EC), the prohibition against discriminatory (including indirectly discriminatory) taxation (Art. 90(1) EC) and the prohibition against protective taxation (Art. 90(2) EC). In this context, the legal concept of indirect discrimination is but one element in a sophisticated larger system.

The concept of charges having an equivalent effect in Art. 25 EC (formerly Arts. 12 and 13 of the EEC Treaty) is based on the approach that substance prevails over form, as reflected in the Court's definition of such charges as 'a duty imposed unilaterally either at the time of importation or subsequently [...] which, if imposed specifically upon a product imported from a Member State to the exclusion of a similar domestic product, has, by altering its price, *the same effect* upon the free movement of products as a customs duty' (*Gingerbread*,[1766] page 432; emphasis added). Further, the Court stressed that this concept, 'far from being an exception to the general rule prohibiting customs duties, is on the contrary necessarily complementary to it and enables that prohibition to be made effective. This expression, invariably linked to that of 'customs duties', is evidence of a general intention to prohibit not only measures which obviously take the form of the classic customs duty but also all those which, presented under other names or introduced by the indirect means of other procedures, would lead to the same discriminatory of protective results as customs duties.'

[1761] Some examples are *Leonesio* (Case 93/71, *ECR* 287), para. 21 (regarding the possibility of direct effect of provisions of a Regulation); *Marleasing* (Case C-106/89, [1990] *ECR* I-41359, para. 8 (regarding *interprétation conforme*), and *Francovich* (Joined Cases C-6/90 and C-9/90, [1991] *ECR* I-5357), para. 36 (regarding the duty of the Member States to make good damages caused through their breaches of Community law).

[1762] Important features of EC law such as primacy and direct effect have been developed by the Court using this reasoning, e.g. *Van Gend en Loos* (Case 26/62, [1963] *ECR* 1), p. 13; *Van Duyn* (Case 41/74, [1974] *ECR* 1337), para. 12; *Costa* (Case 6/64, [1964] *ECR* 585), pp. 593 subs.; *Grad* (Case 9/70, [1970] *ECR* 825), para. 5. On effectiveness in a more general context, see Snyder 1993 (Effectiveness), pp. 40 subs.

[1763] For an academic analysis, see in particular Temple-Lang 1990.

[1764] Mortelmans 1998.

[1765] Hinton 1999.

[1766] Joined Cases 2 and 3/62, [1962] *ECR* 425.

The Court also explained that the importance of what were then Arts. 12 and 13 (now, after amendment, Art. 25 EC) of the Treaty 'is such that, in order to prevent their evasion by different customs or fiscal practices, the Treaty sought to forestall any possible breakdown in the application' and that Art. 95 of the EEC Treaty (now Art. 90 EC) must be seen in this context: 'Article 95, which is to be found in that part of the Treaty dealing with the 'policy of the Community' and in the chapter relating to 'tax provisions', seeks to fill in any loophole which certain taxation procedures might find in the prescribed prohibitions.'[1767] The Court further emphasised that this concern is taken so far as to forbid two forms of infringement under Art. 90 EC. As was noted earlier,[1768] it is in the framework of the prohibition against discrimination under the first section of this provision that the concept of indirect discrimination has its place. Art. 90(2) EC then is the last link in the chain.

b. Limits to effectiveness inherent in the indirect discrimination formula

The fact that effectiveness is the historical aim of the indirect discrimination approach begs the question as to the extent to which the concept is able to achieve it. Obviously, some limits are inherent in the indirect discrimination formula itself. The degree of its effectiveness in practice is dependent upon the meaning assigned to each of the concept's elements. Thus, the easier it is to meet the requirements regarding the *level of the negative effect* and also those regarding the level of proof, the more likely that a case will fall within the prohibition. With regard to the case law-based definition of indirect discrimination,[1769] the prohibition of indirect discrimination is, from the outset, more effective in the context of discrimination on grounds of nationality than in that of sex, due to more stringent requirements regarding proof in the latter case.

Similar considerations apply regarding *objective justification*: the higher the threshold for establishing an acceptable objective justification, the higher the degree of effectiveness that can be reached (though at some point, a danger of a backlash might be reached). In that context, it is important to remember that the Court's statement on effectiveness in *Sotgiu*[1770] was made at a time when objective justification had not yet been recognized as an integral part of the concept of indirect discrimination. Obviously, the effectiveness of the concept depends upon the possibility of such justification, a fact that is particularly problematic in the context of indirect sex discrimination where economic justifications are recognized.[1771] More[1772] even argues that 'the admission of objective justification for measures having a discriminatory impact surely destroys the meaning of a disparate impact analysis'. However, that problem arises regardless of the kind of justification, be it in the context of direct or

---

[1767]   See also *Diamantarbeiders* (Joined Cases 2/69 and 3/69, [1969] *ECR* 211), para. 7/10.
[1768]   See earlier in this part, A.I.4.a.i.
[1769]   Regarding legal definitions, see later in this part, B.
[1770]   Case 152/73, [1974] *ECR* 153.
[1771]   See earlier in this part, A.IV.3.c.
[1772]   More 1993, p. 70.

indirect discrimination. As Leader[1773] aptly notes, 'discrimination law presents a deceptive face. It is not aiming totally to eliminate the practice [...]. Instead, the appearance of cross-cutting justifications for unequal treatment places the reduction of discrimination alongside other objectives, working towards the simultaneous satisfaction of all of them. But simultaneous satisfaction is partial satisfaction, and an invitation to frustration for those who take seriously the promise behind the law.' However, Loenen[1774] disagrees, based on a very pragmatic view that focuses on the workability of the concept in practice. In her view, the possibility of objective justification should not be seen as a weak point in the concept of indirect discrimination, but as part of its strength. The combination of having to demonstrate disparate impact in order to establish a *prima facie* case of discrimination coupled with the opportunity to refute such a claim makes the concept so workable in practice. Loenen therefore argues that the combination 'directs attention to all kinds of treatment with a adverse effect on vulnerable groups as problems of equality, without rigidly prohibiting all such treatment. Thus it is able to challenge dominant standards with a detrimental effect on vulnerable groups. If applied carefully, the objective justification test can be a very useful tool in eradicating quite a lot of less obvious forms of discrimination without ignoring other important goals and interest which may be at stake.'[1775]

Whilst both views have their merits, the fact remains that the shortcomings of the concept of indirect discrimination in terms of effectiveness seem particularly problematic in the context of *social law* where it is often hoped that the concept may serve as a means to combat the structural discrimination[1776] that is often underlying situations of indirect discrimination. Pfarr[1777] lauds the concept for recognising existing factual differences between men and women but at the same time notes that it does not, as such, alter the traditional sex roles. For example, the principle that part-time workers should receive the same pay as full-time workers lest there be indirect sex discrimination, may make part-time work somewhat more attractive (or somewhat less unattractive, as others would see it),[1778] but it has generally not led many men to seek and take up part-time work in order to be able to accept their share of care work. Accordingly, Fuchsloch[1779] speaks of a concept aiming only at 'factual neutrality', and Ellis[1780] calls it a 'static notion'. Arguably, Stampe's[1781] argument that the only function

---

[1773] Leader 1996, p. 120; see also Apollis 2002, p. 40.
[1774] Loenen 1999, p. 202.
[1775] For a similar view, see O'Leary 2002, p. 149, who at the same time points to the weaknesses of the indirect discrimination test in terms of ensuring effective, substantive equality.
[1776] See above Part 1, B.III.5.c.
[1777] Pfarr 1988, pp. 38 and 43.
[1778] Compare Junter-Loiseau & Tobler 1999, p. 358, who speak of part-time work as 'la forme d'emploi la plus sexuée qui soit'.
[1779] Fuchsloch 1995, p. 131.
[1780] Ellis 1997, p. 173.
[1781] Stampe 2001, p. 132.

of the concept of (indirect) discrimination is the prevention of social differences from
having effects on employment relationships, seems to be in accord with Ellis and
Stampe.

These points of criticism are reflected in the evaluation by academic writers of the
concept of indirect discrimination in light of various understandings of equality.[1782]
On the one hand, the concept's concern with the actual effect of a measure rather than
only with its outward appearance (substance prevails over form) makes it possible
to link it to the notion of substantive equality (in the context of sex equality see,
for instance, Blom,[1783] Senden,[1784] Peters,[1785] Holtmaat,[1786] Wentholt,[1787] Burri,[1788]
Prechal,[1789] many of them with further references; in a more general context, Hepple,
Choussey & Choudhury).[1790] On the other hand, the concept's inherent limits lead
some writers to place it between formal equality and substantive equality (e.g.
Loenen,[1791] Veldman,[1792] Fuchsloch,[1793] Steiner,[1794] Burri).[1795] Yet others link it to equality of opportunity (Hepple:[1796] 'an interesting and important half-way idea between
'equality of opportunity' and the narrower usage of 'discrimination''; also Wisskirchen,[1797] Lacey,[1798] Stampe,[1799] Fredman).[1800]

c. Limits of a more general nature

Besides the limits that are inherent in the concept's definition, there are also limits *of
a more general nature* to effectiveness. Below, the issues of comparability and different
treatment are discussed. A third element, the single source of that treatment, is
examined afterwards under a separate heading.

[1782]   It should be noted that the *Court* has never linked the concept of indirect discrimination to a specific
notion of equality.
[1783]   Blom 1992, pp. 3 and 104.
[1784]   Senden 1996, p. 159.
[1785]   Peters 1996, p. 188, and Peters 1999, p. 253.
[1786]   Holtmaat 1996 (Deeltijdwerk), p. 9.
[1787]   Wentholt 2000, p. 62.
[1788]   Burri 2000, p. 116.
[1789]   Prechal 2004, p. 537.
[1790]   Hepple, Choussey & Choudhury 2000, p. 27.
[1791]   Loenen 1992, p. 254, also 24.
[1792]   Veldman 1995, pp. 184 and 186.
[1793]   Fuchsloch 1995, p. 108.
[1794]   Steiner 1999, p. 318.
[1795]   Burri 2000, p. 117.
[1796]   Hepple 1990, p. 413.
[1797]   Wisskirchen 1994, p. 44.
[1798]   Lacey 1992, p. 101.
[1799]   Stampe 2001, p. 124.
[1800]   Fredman 2002, p. 115.

i. Comparability

As was noted in the introduction,[1801] Drijber & Prechal[1802] have found that a questionable use of the element of *comparability* as a means to determine the outcome of alleged indirect discrimination cases seems to be on the rise in EC law, arguably because it allows the Court to avoid delicate issues. *Schumacker*,[1803] a direct taxation case arising under Art. 39 EC, provides an illustrative example.[1804] Here, the Court observed that residents and non-residents are not, as a rule, comparable for taxation purposes, since it is usually only part of the total income of a non-resident that is taxed by the host country.[1805] As a consequence, 'the fact that a Member State does not grant to a non-resident certain tax benefits which it grants to a resident is not, as a rule, discriminatory since those two taxpayers are not in a comparable situation' (*Schumacker*, para. 34).

Among the numerous comments which the judgment received, few focus on comparability,[1806] though Wattel[1807] is an interesting exception. He argues that the Court's approach is wrong in principle but that it might be explained by the particular problems arising when trying to apply the concept of indirect discrimination to the area of direct taxation. In Wattel's opinion, the Court should not have made a distinction between residents and non-residents in that these are comparable for the purposes of Community law. The Court, therefore, should have found *prima facie* indirect discrimination but should have then accepted in principle (though not in the case at hand) a potential justification on grounds of the coherence between unlimited tax liability and the taking into account of personal circumstances. As it stands, the Court's approach can be seen as one of avoiding the issue of indirect discrimination by focusing instead on comparability, without solving the more fundamental problems of applying the concept of indirect discrimination in the field of income taxation. Wattel observes that such approach pre-empts the issue of indirect discrimination, and thereby limits the effectiveness of the concept of indirect discrimination.

[1801] See above Part 1, B.III.3.b.

[1802] Drijber & Prechal, p. 163.

[1803] Case C-279/93, [1995] *ECR* I-225. Mr Schumacker was a Belgian living in Belgium but working in Germany. As a non-resident, his income earned in Germany was subject to limited taxation. In that context, his personal and family circumstances (Mr Schumacker was married) were not taken into account. As a consequence, certain benefits available to resident persons subject to unlimited taxation were withheld. Mr Schumacker thought that the application of the more favourable splitting tariff for married persons should be applied to him and therefore asked for a refund.

[1804] In sex equality law, see for instance *Gruber* (Case C-249/97, [1999] ECR I-5295) and *Österreichischer Gewerkschaftsbund, Gewerkschaft der Privatangestellten* (Case C-220/02, judgment of 8 June 2004, n.y.r.).

[1805] According to the Court, the situation is different where the major part of a worker's income is concentrated in the state of his or her residence.

[1806] E.g. Burgers 1995, De Weerth 1995, Farmer 1995, Kiblböck 1995, Knobbe-Keuk 1995.

[1807] Wattel 1995.

Wattel[1808] explains: 'In its *Schumacker* decision, the Court of Justice of the European Communities tried to reconcile the European non-discrimination principle with the common differential treatment of resident and non-resident taxpayers in international tax law. As was to be expected, these two proved to be irreconcilable. The Court therefore made a compromise: non-residents may fiscally be discriminated against, unless they earn the income entirely or almost entirely in the work state and do not earn enough income in their home state to be able to benefit from the home state personal allowances.' According to Wattel, this compromise falls short of satisfying principles and in addition is not even practical. As for the Court's reasoning, he finds it surprising and at odds with former case law such as *Biehl*,[1809] *Bachmann*[1810] and *Commerzbank*.[1811] Wattel criticises the fact that a finding of non-comparability pre-empts the entire discrimination issue which means that the free movement of persons is deprived of meaning in the context of tax law. At the same time, he acknowledges that there were good reasons for the Court's caution in the specific context of the taxation law. Wattel suspects that the Court 'did not want to run long settled and delicately balanced international tax law and practice into incalculable uncertainty and maybe chaos. It moulded its settled non-discrimination case law to more or less fit settled international tax law, in particular the principles of division of tax jurisdiction between residence state and source state contained in the OECD Model Tax Treaty. The Court probably considered the limits reached of negative integration (integration through interdictions). Reconciling international tax law with Community law is a matter for positive European integration (integration through decisions by the Council). The Court could not go any further than it did without risking to damage rather than remedy. I think that was a wise decision, but I do not understand why the Court did not simply say so, instead of unnecessarily construing residents and non-residents as different cases, which they are not, at least for Community law purposes.'

ii. Different treatment

A finding of indirect discrimination may also be avoided at the level of the assessment of the question of *whether there is different treatment*. *Helmig*,[1812] a sex discrimination case, is a prime example for a problematic approach in that regard (compare Prechal[1813] who calls it a good example of a 'comparison trap'). In this case, the Court in essence found that there is no difference in treatment if both full-time and part-time workers alike are only entitled to overtime payment[1814] if they work more than the regular weekly working time allotted to the status of full-time work. The Court focused on the fact that the overall pay of part-time and full-time workers per hour was the same.

[1808] Wattel 1995, p. 347.
[1809] Case C-175/88, [1990] *ECR* I-1779.
[1810] Case C-204/90, [1992] *ECR* I-249.
[1811] Case C-330/91, [1993] *ECR* I-4017.
[1812] Joined Cases C-399/92, C-409/92, C-425/92, C-34/93, C-50/93 & C-78/93, [1994] *ECR* I-5727.
[1813] Prechal 2004, p. 544.
[1814] On this issue, see already Peter 1988.

Accordingly, it found that the contested overtime pay practice did not constitute indirect sex discrimination against the part-time workers.

In *Helmig* a number of female part-time workers claimed that they were entitled to overtime supplements for hours worked in addition to their own regular working time at the same rate as that applicable for overtime worked by full-time employees in addition to their normal working time. However, under the applicable collective agreement, part-time workers were entitled to overtime supplements only where the weekly working time fixed for full-time workers was exceeded. The national court, turning to the Court of Justice for a preliminary ruling, asked specifically whether such a case involved indirect sex discrimination. AG Darmon explained that the provision at issue was not discriminatory *per se*, given the fact that it applied to all employees in the same way. In the AG's analysis, both full-time and part-time workers were subject to the same demands in the case of overtime work beyond the normal working hours, namely a greater physical effort and a reduction of leisure-time, which are compensated for by the overtime supplement on identical terms, regardless of the working hours provided for in the individual contracts. In the AG's view, to base the right to overtime payment on the individually contracted working time 'would in fact give rise to a real inequality because, *for the same number of hours worked*, some workers would be paid the supplement, and others not' (*Helmig*, points 20 subs., specifically 29, of the AG's opinion). The Court followed this reasoning in its entirety and found that there was no difference in the overall pay of full-time and of part-time workers (*Helmig*, para. 28-30): 'A part-time employee whose contractual working hours are 18 receives, if he works 19 hours, the same overall pay as a full-time employee who works 19 hours. Part-time employees also receive the same overall pay as full-time employees if they work more than the normal working hours fixed by the collective agreements because on doing so they become entitled to overtime supplements. Consequently, the provisions at issue do not give rise to different treatment as between part-time and full-time employees and there is therefore no discrimination [...].'

The Court's finding in *Helmig* has been heavily criticised, most prominently by Holtmaat,[1815] as reflecting a one-sided view of the facts and a formalistic approach to sex discrimination (see further Steyger,[1816] Fenwick,[1817] Veldman,[1818] Hervey,[1819]

[1815]   Holtmaat 1995, Holtmaat 1996 (Deeltijdwerk), Holtmaat 1999 (Overtime Payments). – The article published in *Nemesis* led to a lively academic debate in this journal in which Holtmaat's views were criticised; see Veldman 1996 and Loenen 1996 (Holtmaat en Helmig). For Holtmaat's reaction, see Holtmaat 1996 (Alle dingen).
[1816]   Steyger 1995, pp. 9 and 10.
[1817]   Fenwick 1995, p. 335.
[1818]   Veldman 1996, pp. 35/36.
[1819]   Hervey 1996, p. 405.

Szyszczak,[1820] Drijber & Prechal,[1821] Hervey & Shaw,[1822] Tobler,[1823] Barnard & Hepple,[1824] Freivogel & Steiner).[1825] The problem lies in the fact that the Court failed to see what many see as an obvious difference in treatment at issue: this is, in order to be entitled to overtime payments, full-time workers merely had to work more than their regular working time. In contrast, part-time workers had to work more than their individually contracted working time (namely their regular weekly working time) plus the additional number of hours necessary to meet the number of hours regularly constituting full-time work (the particular number depended on the number of hours specified in their individual contracts for part-time work). In other words, the difference in the situations of the workers was that only full-time workers were entitled to overtime payments when working more than their regular working time. Holtmaat emphasises that the problem with the Court's approach in *Helmig* is of a fundamental nature in that the Court's decision disregards both the reasons why women often work part-time and also how overtime-work impacts upon their specific situations. The background against which a case like *Helmig* should be seen is a *conflict of time*, that is, a conflict regarding the questions of how time is valued and of how people use it. Holtmaat finds that the time concept underlying the approach shared by the Advocate General and the Court is limited and inadequate. It distinguishes only between working time and leisure time and disregards the time used for care which is particularly relevant in the case of part-time workers, given that they are typically women who have taken family responsibilities upon themselves. In fact, the demand to perform over-time work encroaches on time set aside by the part-time workers to use for other purposes as much as, if not even more than, it does in the case of full-time workers. In addition, Holtmaat argues that both the Court and the Advocate General failed to recognise the special character of care time which is more cyclical than linear in nature (compare Huften & Kravaritou).[1826] Against that background, *Helmig* not only shows that the Court's appraisal of the facts will determine the outcome of the indirect discrimination test but, more fundamentally, that the Court may miss – or even wish to avoid – the whole point of a case.

That the mistake in *Helmig* could have been avoided is illustrated by a decision of the Dutch Equal Treatment Commission (*Commissie Gelijke Behandeling*)[1827] in a comparable situation where the Commission found *different treatment* and indirect

---

[1820] Szyszczak 1997, p. 47.
[1821] Drijber & Prechal 1997, p. 137.
[1822] Hervey & Shaw 1998, p. 54.
[1823] Tobler 1999, p. 397.
[1824] Barnard & Hepple 2000, p. 570.
[1825] Freivogel & Steiner 2001, p. 998.
[1826] Hufton & Kravaritou 1999.
[1827] Judgment 1-90-10 CGB, mentioned by Loenen 1996 (Holtmaat en Helmig), p. 123. On the Dutch Equal Treatment Commission, see Blom 1995.

sex discrimination.[1828] The decisive point in the Commission's approach was that, as opposed to the Court of Justice, it took account of the time spent by women on care. Indeed, in the recent decision *Elsner-Lakeberg*,[1829] the Court of Justice recognized the fact that the same rule for overtime payment for all workers implies *a different burden* in relation to the individual working time and, therefore, leads to different treatment between full-time and part-time workers (*Elsner-Lakeberg*, para. 17 and 18). In the present writer's analysis, this judgment implies a correction of the Court's earlier approach in *Helmig* (though according to AG Jacobs the finding of a difference in treatment in *Elsner-Lakeberg* could in fact be reached even on the basis of that earlier decision; *Elsner-Lakeberg*, points 20 and 21 of the AG's opinion).

In *Elsner-Lakeberg*, a part-time teacher complained about a rule according to which overtime pay was granted only for extra work consisting of more than three teaching hours. The rule applied equally to both full-time workers (teaching 98 hours per month) and part-time workers (Ms Elsner-Lakeberg herself taught 60 hours per month.) in spite of their different ordinary working time. Perhaps understandably against the background of the Court's decision in *Helmig*, the defendants saw nothing problematic in the contested rule. They claimed that equality of remuneration was ensured for both regular working hours and additional hours, arguing that 'part-time teachers are treated in exactly the same manner as full-time teachers' and that 'the additional hours are remunerated in exactly the same manner' (*Elsner-Lakeberg*, para. 11). In contrast, AG Jacobs thought that the situation was different from that in *Helmig*. He pointed out that the Court in that earlier case found same treatment because part-time workers received the same overall pay as full-time workers for the same number of hours worked. Whereas in the present case, the effect of the contested national legislation was that 'a part-time employee who is contracted to work for 15 hours, who works an additional 2.5 hours and who thus works 17.5 hours in total would be paid for only 15 hours work and would therefore not receive the same overall pay as a full-time employee receives for 17.5 hours worked'. AG Jacobs concluded that, on the basis of the Court's case-law, there was different treatment of part-time and full-time workers. The Court, however, focused on the additional burden imposed on the different categories of workers, rather than on the amount of pay that they receive. According to the Court, there was different treatment due to the fact that the requirement of at least three additional working hours meant roughly 3% of additional work for the full-time workers but 5% for a part-time worker in the situation of Ms Elsner-Lakeberg. If it affects considerably more women than men, such treatment constitutes *prima facie* indirect discrimination on grounds of sex.

[1828] On the indirect discrimination test employed by the Commission, see Gerards 2003.
[1829] Case C-285/02, judgment of 27 May 2004, n.y.r.

d. Awareness and avoidance

Despite the fact that the effectiveness of non-discrimination law is limited in practice
for the various reasons mentioned in the previous sections, the concept may still have
the merit of increasing the awareness of authorities, courts and the public in relation
to the existence of discrimination. At the very least, it can help in making potential
discriminators and victims aware of the fact that discrimination can take forms that
may not be immediately obvious and that it is therefore always necessary to consider
not only the form of a measure but also its effect in practice. As insignificant as it may
appear to be in view of the larger aim of effectiveness, such awareness is in itself an
important achievement that should not be underestimated. At the same time, recent
developments illustrate that awareness concerning the problem of indirect discrimination does not necessarily lead to the desired result, namely that such discrimination
ceases to exist. Instead, some employers try to actively avoid a finding of indirect
discrimination in a way that will thwart the effectiveness of Community law.
Allonby,[1830] a case concerning a part-time college lecturer who was formally dismissed
but then technically rehired through a third organisation, provides an example. The
college found that part-time teachers had become more expensive given that under
recently adopted national sex equality legislation they became entitled to pay at the
same rate as full-time teachers (in other words, because the law now addressed the
issue of indirect discrimination against women based on part-time work). Hiring part-
time lecturers through a third party, the Education Lecturing Services (ELS), allowed
the college to keep low the costs since ELS paid at a rate below that paid by the college
to full-time college lecturers. A further consequence of the new arrangement was that
the teachers could no longer participate in the college's occupational pension scheme
since, under other national legislation, such schemes were open only to persons
employed directly. In court, Ms Allonby argued that she had a right to equal pay
against ELS based on a comparison of her pay and that of her former full-time colleagues who continued to be employed directly by the college. AG Geelhoed and the
Court disagreed, based on the doctrine of the single source of discriminatory behaviour. According to the AG, the dismissal rather than the difference in pay can be
challenged under EC sex equality law in a situation like that of Ms Allonby. (The
Commission had taken the same view.). In that regard, the Court simply observed that
the question was no longer relevant since an amicable agreement had been reached
between Ms Allonby and the college with regard to the dismissal. As for access to the
pension scheme, both the AG and the Court thought it possible that the rules on the
access to the occupational pension scheme in question might indirectly discriminate
against women (*Allonby*, points 51 und 79 of the AG's opinion, and para. 44 subs.,
56 and 75 of the judgment).

[1830] Case C-256/01, judgment of 13 January 2004, n.y.r.

Referring to the Court's finding in *Lawrence*[1831] that in order to amount to discrimination, a difference in treatment must be attributable to a single source, Ms Allonby argued that in her case the single source was the College's decision to use ELS as an intermediary. AG Geelhoed and the Court disagreed. The Court found that in a case like that of Ms Allonby the different treatment complained of stemmed from different sources. According to the Court, the fact that the level of pay received by Ms Allonby was influenced by the amount which the college paid ELS was not a sufficient basis for concluding that the college and ELS constituted a single source to which the differences in pay can be attributed. The Court also agreed with its AG on the fact that the rules of the national pension scheme might amount to indirect sex discrimination. Such a finding presupposes that persons in the same situation as that of Ms Allonby are workers within the meaning of Art. 141 EC. Importantly, the Court held that it is not the formal status of a person like Ms Allonby as a service provider that is decisive because self-employment may be of a merely fictitious nature (compare Evtimov).[1832] Regarding the possibility of bringing an action against the college for discriminatory dismissal, the Court's statements seem to recognise it implicitly: 'As regards her [Ms Allonby's] relationship with the College, it must be held that, following the amicable settlement reached between Ms Allonby and the College while the case was pending before the Court, the question whether Ms Allonby suffered indirect discrimination on grounds of sex as a result of her dismissal and the question whether, if appropriate, she may still claim elements of remuneration from the College on the basis of Article 141(1) EC no longer arise.'

As Ms Allonby rightly pointed out before the Court of Justice, the facts of her case are representative of a more general trend in employment relationships that has major importance with regard to the effectiveness of the equal pay principle, in particular with regard to the practice of *contracting work out* in order to reduce the costs of activities which are performed predominantly by women. It is clear from the facts of the case that the college circumvented the prohibition against indirect discrimination towards women by outsourcing part-time personnel. AG Geelhoed explicitly raised the question 'whether the courts must turn a blind eye to the fact that in the circumstances of the main proceedings a legal device has been used precisely, it should been noted, in order to evade the consequences of the principle of equal treatment laid down in Article 141 EC' (*Allonby*, point 43 of the AG's opinion). The Commission

---

[1831] Case C-320/00, [2002] *ECR* I-7325; see also Plötscher 2003, p. 48. – The *Lawrence* case itself is less of a case of avoidance of non-discrimination law by the employer since here the outsourcing of cleaning personnel was the result of the process of compulsory competitive tendering imposed by a law. In such a case, the problem might lie on the level of the law and its criteria for the award of contracts; compare earlier in this part, A.I.5.a (public procurement). *Lawrence* concerned cleaning personnel formerly employed by the North Yorkshire County Council which, following an equal pay action, was obliged to raise the pay of its part-time staff. Following the tendering process, the cleaning was outsourced to private undertakings which re-employed a number of female staff originally employed by the Council at lower pay rates. The Court's finding in *Lawrence* has been called highly unfortunate by Prechal 2004, p. 547.

[1832] Evtimov 2004, p. 215.

spoke about a misuse of law (*Allonby*, point 49 of the AG's opinion). It initially thought
that in order to counter that misuse the college should continue to be regarded as the
employer for purposes of ensuring equal pay. It then said that such misuse could
undermine the operation of the principle of equality laid down in Art. 141 EC. Accordingly, in cases such as Ms Allonby's the decisive factor should not be the legal
relationships between the original employer and his part-time employees, but the
factual relationships which nonetheless remain unaltered. Later, the Commission
changed its view and distanced itself from what the AG calls 'this idea based on a legal
fiction', due to practical problems posed by such a solution (*Allonby*, point 49 of the
AG's opinion). The Commission finally concluded that Ms Allonby's dismissal by the
college, rather than ELS' pay policy, was open to challenge.

> AG Geelhoed described the Commission's change of mind and the reasons for it in the
> following manner (*Allonby*, point 49 of the AG's opinion): 'First, there is no common
> source, within the meaning of the *Lawrence* judgment, which could be held responsible for
> the difference in treatment and could correct that difference. For the termination of
> employment is a fact; there is therefore no longer any link from the point of view of employ-
> ment law between the College and Ms Allonby which could serve as the basis for restoring
> equality in terms of pay conditions. The question then arises as to how long the legal fiction
> could be used in order to hold the original employer responsible for differences in pay. For
> by the simple effluxion of time variations in conditions of pay may increase further. Initially
> the Commission sought to attribute liability to the body which in its view could be held
> responsible from the outset for the difference occurring, namely the College when it decided
> to restructure its organisation. The problem in that connection is that the College cannot
> be held entirely responsible for the difference occurring between Ms Allonby and her
> comparator. For the fee which Ms Allonby receives for the services provided by her is agreed
> between her and ELS. The College cannot be held liable for that even if it endeavours in
> its relations with ELS to ensure that equivalence is maintained as between the remuneration
> paid to its employees and the subcontractors engaged by ELS. Moreover, it goes without
> saying that over time maintenance of parity in pay conditions becomes more difficult. This
> may be accounted for again by the lack of a single source which could be held liable for
> preserving and restoring parity.'

The Court did not expressly address the issue of circumvention or misuse of the law
but simply pointed to the legal possibilities other than an equal pay action that a person
in the situation of Ms Allonby might have. Though perhaps conceptually sound, the
outcome of this case is particularly unfortunate for Ms Allonby in particular who,
when agreeing to the settlement with the college on the issue of her dismissal, did not
yet know whether she might succeed in her equal pay claim against ELS.

5. FINDINGS AND CONCLUSION

a. Garrone's definition revisited

Having examined the development of the legal concept of indirect discrimination through the Court's case law, the main elements found in the course of this analysis are summarised below by revisiting the definition of indirect discrimination by Garrone[1833] which was the starting point in this present study's introduction. Again, according to this definition: '[t]he use of apparently neutral criteria may [...] lead to discrimination which is then termed indirect discrimination. Such discrimination is presumed to exist if a measure predominantly disadvantages persons who are members of a group that is protected against the use of a criterion prohibited as regards other persons – in this case there is an indirect distinction; this indirect distinction is discriminatory unless the contrary is proven. Such proof may be brought in two ways: a) the measure at issue does not lead to inequality because similar situations are treated similarly or different situations are treated differently, without taking into account in any way the prohibited criterion; b) the measure does not lead to discrimination in the strict sense, because it aims at a legitimate objective and is proportionate in that regard. Obviously, an objective may be legitimate only if it has nothing to do with the prohibited criterion.'

A first point to be noted is the fact that Garrone distinguishes between 'indirect *distinction*' and 'indirect *discrimination*'. The former notion appears to correspond to that of *prima facie* indirect discrimination in the sense of a presumption of the existence of discrimination. According to Garrone, this requires that a measure disadvantages predominantly persons of a group that is protected against reliance on a certain differentiation criterion. The Court's landmark decisions on indirect discrimination are based on the same approach, though it must be added that in the cases decided by the Court the effect of an indirectly discriminatory measure can go further and practically be the same as that of direct discrimination (*Ugliola*).[1834]

Garrone's definition was formulated in the framework of the author's search for a *general theory on indirect discrimination*. Indeed, Garrone suggests that the concept displays the same features in all areas of EC law. In a broader context, this corresponds to the view that equality is 'un principe unique aux apparences multiples', 'un principe général de droit communautaire dont le contenu est unique à travers toutes ses applications, malgré des apparences multiples dues aux fonctions diverses assumées par ce principe' (Lenaerts).[1835] According to More,[1836] 'the same concept and the same

---

[1833] Garrone 1994, p. 448.
[1834] Case 15/69, [1969] *ECR* 363.
[1835] Lenaerts 1991, p. 3.
[1836] More 1999, p. 517.

test apply whether it be taxation, maternity rights, or production quotas for ferrous scrap'. Though this may be true in terms of the basic idea underlying the concept, the case law analysis undertaken in this study showed that the development of the legal notion of indirect discrimination was not the same in the various areas and that there are important differences in the test to be applied under the Court's case law. In particular, there are different standards for discrimination on grounds of nationality and grounds of sex as far as the required level of disparity of impact and proof of that impact are concerned. Whilst descriptions such as 'a substantially higher proportion of persons of one group' are used in both contexts, alternatively a lower standard can also be sufficient for sex discrimination. In that latter context, proof must be brought for the actual disparity in effect which in many cases requires complicated assessments involving statistical evidence. In contrast, in the context of indirect discrimination on grounds of nationality the mere possibility of the prohibited discriminatory effect is sufficient ('liability test'). It was suggested that there is no valid legal reason why there should be such a difference and that rather the liability test should apply in both cases (without, however, excluding the possibility statistical proof).

According to Garrone's definition, an indirect distinction amounts to indirect discrimination *unless the contrary is proven*. Justification through reliance on express derogation grounds is not mentioned in the definition, but it is obvious that the possibility of claiming such justification will always exist. Garrone mentions two possibilities as counterproof. One of them is to show that there is no legally prohibited inequality because similar situations are treated similarly or different situations are treated differently. This is clearly a reference to the Aristotelian equality formula which underlies EC equality law in general. With regard to similar treatment of similar situations, here the defence is that there is, in fact, no difference in treatment. The discussion of the *Helmig*[1837] case showed that whilst such an approach is acceptable within its own (Aristotelian) framework, there may be cases where the nature of the treatment is assessed in a problematic manner. If so, it wrongly limits the reach of the legal concept of indirect discrimination. As for different treatment of different situations, the defence mentioned by Garrone is the lack of comparability (the 'objective differences' approach, as formulated in *Sotgiu*).[1838] Again, a problematic assessment of comparability may result in wrongly avoiding a finding of indirect discrimination, as discussed in the context of *Schumacker*.[1839] Logically, comparability should be dealt with at the very beginning of the non-discrimination analysis. In contrast, Garrone's way of referring to it corresponds to a problematic approach that can also be observed in the Court's case law, namely that of conceiving of objective differences as a type of 'objective justification'.

[1837]   Joined Cases C-399/92, C-409/92, C-425/92, C-34/93, C-50/93 and C-78/93, [1994] *ECR* I-5727.
[1838]   Case 152/73, [1974] *ECR* 153.
[1839]   Case C-279/93, [1995] *ECR* I-225.

As a second possibility of counter-proof, Garrone mentions a legitimate objective and proportionality. This roughly corresponds the element of objective justification as recognised by the Court of Justice as part of the indirect discrimination formula in the landmark cases *Bilka*[1840] and *O'Flynn*.[1841] These case law analyses showed that a number of problems have arisen concerning the meaning and the application of this test and that they are especially noticeable in certain fields (in particular social security law in the context of sex discrimination). For some of these problems there may be practical solutions, such as interrogative references for preliminary rulings and a more proactive and consistent approach by the Court in applying its own test. However, the underlying problem is that the notion of objective justification is vague. Whilst it is not possible to fix its meaning once and for all in a general description, it was nevertheless suggested that a somewhat clearer and more concrete definition should be feasible. In particular, the Court should clarify the number and precise nature of the elements relevant in the context of proportionality.

Under Garrone's definition, a finding of objective justification means that there is no indirect discrimination. Such a definition does not fully explain the *nature or function of objective justification* in that context. It was noted that according to an academic argument the element of objective justification relates to the causation of discrimination, rather than to its justification in the proper sense of the word. Whilst such an approach may seem logical, it was also argued that case law provides no clear indication that the Court would follow the causation approach. Indeed, it was suggested that there are good reasons for upholding the traditional view which regards objective justification as a special form of justification in the sense of cross-cutting reasons which require a balancing of interests.

Garrone's use of the term 'indirect distinction' further raises the question of how the concept of indirect discrimination is *linked to the Aristotelian equality formula*. In that regard, it was noted that, with the exception of the atypical case of *Seco*,[1842] all the cases discussed when tracing the development of the concept of indirect discrimination through the Court's case law concerned discrimination through different treatment. As such, they are linked to the first part of the Aristotelian equality formula ('treating likes alike'). Whilst some have argued that this linkage correctly reflects the role of the concept, the present author takes a different view: that there is no reason why, in the case of non-comparability, discrimination should not be able to take an indirect form as well. The Court's recent case *Merida*[1843] appears to be such a case, though the Court itself does not explicitly say so.

[1840]   Case 170/84, [1986] *ECR* 1607.
[1841]   Case C-237/94, [1996] *ECR* I-2617.
[1842]   Joined Cases 62/81 and 63/81, [1982] *ECR* 223.
[1843]   Case C-400/02, judgment of 16 September 2004, n.y.r.

An aspect not mentioned by Garrone (understandably, since it is not part of a definition), is the *aim of the legal concept of indirect discrimination*. In that regard, it was noted that the Court's historical concern was the effectiveness or *effet utile* of equality law. The concept of indirect discrimination is intended to catch disguised forms of discrimination and thereby to prevent the circumvention of the prohibition following the principle that substance prevails over form. The degree of effectiveness that can be achieved in practice is linked to the elements and requirements of the concept of indirect discrimination, particularly concerning the level of disparity of impact and objective justification. It was noted that the Court's statements about effectiveness as the *raison d'être* of the concept of indirect discrimination were made before objective justification was recognised as one of its components. It was further seen that a lack of effectiveness is often bemoaned in social law, and particularly in social security law. It is also said that the concept of indirect discrimination is static in the sense that it does not aim at changing the societal structures underlying its very existence (such as traditional sex roles in the context of sex discrimination). In view of these limits, academic writers do not think that the concept of discrimination is based on an idea of fully substantive equality or equality of opportunity. On a very modest level, it might be said that its main strength is its potential to raise awareness in relation to the existence of discrimination.

b. Consistency, precision and effectiveness

Overall, the discussion undertaken so far illustrates that the legal concept of indirect discrimination should be assessed in the light of the keywords: consistency, precision and effectiveness. But, then one must ask: Are the definitions of the legal concept of indirect discrimination as developed by the Court in the different areas of EC law consistent with each other? Are they sufficiently precise, and are they capable of achieving the concept's aim? In the event of a negative answer, is a better definition feasible? The following brief remarks on these issues concern only the *case law* definition of indirect discrimination. They will be revisited in the context of the legal definitions[1844] as they presently exist in EC law.

As far as *consistency* is concerned, it was found that the case law definitions of indirect sex discrimination on the one hand and of indirect discrimination on grounds of nationality on the other hand differ in relation to the requirements for both disparate impact and proof. It was argued that there is no conceivable reason why that should be the case and that the same definition should be applicable in all areas of law. Another point of inconsistency is the possibility of economic justification in the context of indirect sex discrimination, as opposed to discrimination on grounds of

---

[1844] See later in this part, B.

nationality (at least on the level of the starting points). Again, it was argued that there is no reason why that should be the case.

Concerning the *precision* of the definition, it was found that the indirect discrimination formula as developed by Court's case law is vague in various respects. First, it does not indicate the precise level of requisite disparate impact, and there are other uncertainties regarding the precise comparison to be made in that context. Second, it gives no clear indication as to which aims and goals are legitimate for the purposes of objective justification. Third, it lacks clarity regarding the elements making up the proportionality test and their meaning. In the future, at least some of these problems could be remedied by a further degree of clarity on the level of either the general definition or through case law. Concerning the determination of precisely which goals and aims are legitimate in the context of objective justification, it was suggested that the Court should explain, against the background of specific cases, what constitutes 'a legitimate aim'. The Court might also consider enumerating several acceptable aims in the form of an open catalogue.

Finally, it was seen that the concept of indirect discrimination is rather limited in terms of its *effectiveness*, in part because of its own limitations (such as lack of precision) but also due to some issues of a more general nature, such as the limited scope of non-discrimination law and the tricky issue of comparability. Accordingly, increasing the concept's effectiveness is only partially a matter of definition on the conceptual level.

B. THE DEVELOPMENT OF THE
LEGAL DEFINITIONS

I. INTRODUCTORY REMARKS

As Ellis[1843] has argued, the original lack of a legal definition of indirect discrimination allowed the Court to proceed purposively with an eye focused on the objectives to be served by the law rather than being trapped by over-technical aspects of a legal definition. However, over time the creation of such a definition has been suggested, in particular in the context of sex discrimination, by both the Commission (see Burri)[1844] and also by academic writers. These suggestions were made in response to such developments as the manner in which the British courts addressed questions of objective justification (von Prondzynsky & Richards;[1845] further Prechal).[1846] Legal definitions can be found in an increasing number of legal instruments. The first appeared in the Burden of Proof Directive of 1997[1847] and was followed by later versions in the Race Directive[1848] and the General Framework Directive,[1849] both adopted in 2000, further in the revised Second Equal Treatment Directive of 2002,[1850] in the Goods and Services Directive of 2004[1851] and in the proposed Recasting Directive.[1852] In contrast, some other recent Community measures do not contain such definitions (e.g. EC Staff law,[1853] the EU Charter of Fundamental Rights,[1854] the new Directive on free movement and residence of EU citizens[1855] and the new Social

---

[1843] Ellis 1994 (Definition of Discrimination), p. 572.

[1844] Burri 2000, p. 298.

[1845] Von Prondzynsky & Richards 1995, p. 131.

[1846] Prechal 1993, p. 97.

[1847] Directive 97/80/EC, *OJ* 1998 L 14/6 (as amended).

[1848] Directive 2000/43/EC, *OJ* 2000 L 180/22.

[1849] Directive 2000/78/EC, *OJ* 2000 L 303/16.

[1850] Directive 2002/73/EC, *OJ* 2002 L 269/15.

[1851] Directive 2004/113/EC, *OJ* 2004 L 373/37.

[1852] Proposal for a Directive on the implementation of the principle of equal opportunities and equal treatment of men and women in matters of employment and occupation, COM(2004) 279 fin.

[1853] See Art. 1d of Regulation 259/68/EEC, Euratom, ECSC, *OJ* 1968 L 56/1 (as amended). For a consolidated text, see http://www.europa.eu.int/comm/dgs/personnel_administration/statut/tocen100.pdf).

[1854] Charter of fundamental rights of the European Union, *OJ* 2000 C 364/1; inserted into the Treating establishing a Constitution for Europe, *OJ* 2004 C 310.

[1855] Directive 2004/38/EC, *OJ* 2004 L 158/77.

Security Regulation).[1856] In fact, some of them simply provide a right to equal
treatment, without even mentioning the term 'discrimination'. Below, the development of some of the early legal definitions is discussed.

II. CODIFICATION: THE BURDEN OF PROOF
DIRECTIVE (SEX DISCRIMINATION)

The first legal definition of indirect discrimination in EC law concerned sex equality
law. The definition contained in the Burden of Proof Directive[1857] can be called *a first
generation* because it largely reflects the case law definition in its area of application.
As the very first version of such a legal definition in EC law, its development shall be
traced in some detail.

1. THE DEVELOPMENT OF THE DEFINITION

The adoption of the Burden of Proof Directive was preceded by some years of legal
and political debate leading to a number of draft texts with differing legal bases and
differing content (Lanquetin,[1858] Ellis).[1859] The Commission's original proposal of
1988[1860] suggested the following definition of indirect discrimination (Art. 5(1) of the
draft text): 'For the purposes of the principle of equality referred to in Article 1 (2),
indirect discrimination exists where an apparently neutral provision, criterion or
practice disproportionately disadvantages the members of one sex, by reference in
particular to marital and family status, and is not objectively justified by any necessary
reason or condition unrelated to the sex of the person concerned.' In its Explanatory
Memorandum[1861] the Commission, referring to *Jenkins*,[1862] explained that this
definition was intended to reflect the Court's case law on indirect sex discrimination.
The European Parliament[1863] found nothing to criticise but the Economic and Social

---

[1856] Regulation 883/2004/EC, *OJ* 2004 L 166/1.
[1857] Directive 97/80/EC, *OJ* 1998 L 14/6 (as amended).
[1858] Lanquetin 1998, p. 688.
[1859] Ellis 1998, p. 9.
[1860] Proposal for a Council Directive on the burden of proof in the area of equal pay and equal treatment
of men and women, *OJ* 1988 C 176/5.
[1861] COM(88) 269 fin.
[1862] Case 96/80, [1981] *ECR* 911.
[1863] The only amendment suggested by Parliament with regard to Art. 5(1) did not concern the definition
of indirect discrimination as such but rather the expression 'principle of equality'. Parliament
suggested 'principle of equal treatment' instead; *OJ* 1989 C 12/180.

Committee (ECOSOC)[1864] argued that indirect discrimination cannot be directly ascribed to identifiable circumstances and, therefore, advocated that the term 'disproportionately' should be deleted. The proposal also met with criticism outside the Community institutions. For instance, the Dutch *Emancipatieraad* (Emancipation Council) feared that a legal definition would block the further development of the concept by the Court. It also noted that the proposal's terminology did not conform to that of the Court's case law (Burri).[1865] In academic writing, Blomeyer[1866] considered it a positive step that the Commission used the strict formula of 'necessary reason or condition' in the context of objective justification but criticised the fact that this point was not further defined. Blom[1867] thought that the concept of 'justified indirect discrimination' constituted a contradiction in terms. The proposal never made its way into law. Having discussed it on several occasions during the following years, the Council was unable to reach the unanimity required for its adoption due to UK opposition, which lead to the proposal's withdrawal.[1868]

Eventually, the Social Agreement[1869] offered the possibility of adopting social legislation with a qualified majority of eleven of the (then) twelve Member States, though this legislation would have no legal effect in the UK (see Tobler).[1870] On this basis, in 1996 the Commission presented a new proposal.[1871] In this version, the proposed legal definition of indirect sex discrimination read as follows (Art. 2(2) of the draft text): 'For the purposes of the principle of equal treatment referred to paragraph 1, indirect discrimination exists where an apparently neutral provision, criterion or practice disproportionately disadvantages the members of one sex, by reference in particular to marital or family status, unless the aim pursued by the application of the provision, criterion or practice is objectively justified and the means of achieving it are appropriate and necessary.' Again, according to the Commission[1872] this definition set out the concept of indirect discrimination as defined by the Court in the area of sex equality law. This time, ECOSOC agreed[1873] but criticism was voiced from other sides. Bieback[1874] considered the new version's wording unfortunate, even though its reach was wider than that of the original proposal and more precise with

---

[1864]   Opinion on the proposal for a Council Directive on the burden of proof in the area of equal pay and
         equal treatment for women and men, *OJ* 1988 C 337/58.
[1865]   Burri 2000, p. 303, footnote 360.
[1866]   Blomeyer 1994, pp. 110 subs.
[1867]   Blom 1992, p. 55.
[1868]   See *OJ* 1998 C 40/4.
[1869]   *OJ* 1992 C 191/90 (attached to the Social Protocol).
[1870]   Tobler 2000 (Sex Equality Law), p. 138.
[1871]   Proposal for a Council Directive on the burden of proof in cases of discrimination based on sex, *OJ*
         1996 C 332/11.
[1872]   COM (96)340 fin.
[1873]   Opinion of the Economic and Social Committee on the 'Proposal for a Council Directive on the
         burden of proof in cases of discrimination based on sex', *OJ* 1997 C 133/34.
[1874]   Bieback 1997, p. 26.

regard to objective justification. The report of the European Parliament's Committee on Women's Rights (Ghilardotti Report)[1875] welcomed the new definition as more closely reflecting the Court's wording in *Bilka*[1876] but at the same time argued for even stronger wording to more closely follow the Court's strictest case law. It wished to avoid the danger – perceived in the light of some of the more recent cases – of shortening the reach of the concept of indirect discrimination and of broadening the definition of objectively justified factors. In the latter context, the importance of the words 'appropriate' and 'necessary' were emphasised, because otherwise 'we risk slipping from the case law already gained'. The report further stated that it 'would not want to see a development of double standards on discrimination, whereby discrimination on the basis of nationality remains watertight and absolutely unacceptable, whereas discrimination on the basis of sex has a more flexible definition'. The Committee therefore proposed the following definition: 'For the purposes of the principle of equal treatment referred to in paragraph 1, indirect discrimination exists where an apparently neutral provision, criterion or practice disproportionately disadvantages the members of one sex, by reference inter alia to marital or family status, unless the aim pursued corresponds to a real need of the undertaking or meets a necessary aim of the social policy of a Member State, in itself is completely unrelated to gender and as such is objectively justified, and unless the means of achieving this aim are appropriate and necessary.' This was approved by the European Parliament.[1877] As a consequence, in 1997 the Commission presented an amended proposal[1878] that corresponded to the version suggested by the European Parliament.[1879] The Council, however, opted in favour of yet another different version. The final text[1880] of Art. 2(2) of the Directive reads: 'For purposes of the principle of equal treatment referred to in paragraph 1, indirect discrimination shall exist where an apparently neutral provision, criterion or practice disadvantages a substantially higher proportion of the members of one sex unless that provision, criterion or practice is appropriate and necessary and can be justified by objective factors unrelated to sex.'

[1875] Report on the proposal for a Council Directive on the burden of proof in cases of discrimination based on sex, A4/0115/97, PE 220.959 fin., at pp. 14 subs. The report is named after the *rapporteur* of the European Parliament's Committee on Women's Rights, Ms Ghilardotti.

[1876] Case 170/84, [1986] *ECR* 1607.

[1877] *OJ* 1997 C 132/215.

[1878] Amended proposal for a Council Directive on the burden of proof in cases of discrimination based on sex, *OJ* 1997 C 185/21.

[1879] See the Commission's Explanatory Memorandum, COM(97) 202 fin.

[1880] Directive 97/80/EC, *OJ* 1998 L 14/6 (as amended).

2. THE DEFINITION AS ADOPTED

When adopting this definition, the Council explained that it departed from the Commission's amended proposal only in that it did not fully adopt the terms used by the Court and that all essential aspects appearing in the Commission's proposal had been included.[1881] Academic opinions dispute this issue. According to authors like Rust[1882] and O'Leary,[1883] the definition confirms the Court's test, whilst Lanquetin[1884] sees the definition as merely 'inspired' by the Court's case law. Similarly, AG Jacobs in his opinion on the *Schnorbus* case (point 32)[1885] observes that the Directive's definition 'encapsulates much of the development in case-law since the distinction was first drawn by the Court', which implies that it is not identical. Barnard & Hepple[1886] note that the formulation in the Burden of Proof Directive is stricter than that in *Seymour-Smith*[1887] since there the element of necessity is missing (compare also Burri).[1888] Some commentators fear that the differences may cause confusion because, due to the Directive's limited scope,[1889] the Court's case law definition continues to remain valid in certain areas. In the present writer's analysis, the definition in the Directive is stricter than the Commission's proposals as far as *the level of the disparate impact* is concerned. Whilst the proposal merely required a disproportionate disadvantage, the text adopted by the Council refers to a disadvantage on a substantially higher level. This is in line in line with the Court's case law definition of indirect sex discrimination. At the same time, Fredman[1890] argues that there might be a change in the comparison to be made, in that under the new formulation there is no longer any need to show that the difference is between those who can comply and those who cannot.[1891] Concerning the *proof* of disparate impact, the Directive follows the approach of previous sex discrimination case law which requires proof of an actual disparity. With regard to the element of *objective justification*, the text closest to the Court's previous case law appears to be that proposed by the European Parliament

---

[1881] Common Position No 37/97 adopted by the Council with a view to the adoption of Council Directive 97/.../EC on the burden of proof in cases of discrimination based on sex, *OJ* 1997 C 307/6.
[1882] Rust 1997, p. 152.
[1883] O'Leary 2002, p. 137.
[1884] Lanquetin 1998, p. 690.
[1885] Case C-79/99, [2000] *ECR* I-10997.
[1886] Barnard & Hepple 2000, p. 575.
[1887] Case C-167/97, [1999] *ECR* I-623, para. 77. According to *Seymour-Smith* (para. 77), the aim must be unrelated to any discrimination based on sex, and the Member State must reasonably consider that the means chosen are suitable for attaining that aim.
[1888] Burri 2000, p. 304.
[1889] See later in this part, B.IV.2.
[1890] Fredman 2002, p. 111.
[1891] On the requirement of a relative comparison, see earlier in this part, A.IV.2.d.ii.

which relies on, and combines, the *Bilka*[1892] and *Rinner-Kühn*[1893] tests (a real need of
the undertaking and a necessary and legitimate aim of the State's social policy, respectively). The text eventually adopted is much less explicit. According to Koukoulis-
Spiliotopoulos,[1894] it falls short of the case law definition. In addition, the new definition reverses the logical order of the elements that are relevant in the context of
objective justification: it begins with the proportionality test and only then mentions
the aim or goal of the measure. These elements are mentioned side by side, as if
independent of each other whilst according to the case law definition proportionality
is a function of the legitimate aim (the measure must be suitable and requisite in view
of goal which it aims to achieve). Finally, the new definition refers to apparently
neutral *'provisions, criteria and practices'*. According to Fredman,[1895] the inclusion of
the latter term is the most important advance, in that it is not necessary to prove an
absolute bar and in that a looser practice or provision will suffice.

III. A NEW GENERATION

After the Burden of Proof Directive,[1896] legal definitions of indirect discrimination
appeared in an increasing number of legislative measures. Of these, the first three are
discussed below; later definitions essentially follow the same pattern. The Directives
discussed include two groundbreaking[1897] Directives adopted in the framework of the
anti-discrimination package of 2000[1898] on the basis of Art. 13 EC in 'record-breaking
speed for social Europe' (EUROPE),[1899] namely the Race Directive[1900] and the so-called
General Framework Directive.[1901] Also discussed is the Revised Second Equal

---

[1892] Case 170/84, [1986] *ECR* 1607.
[1893] Case 171/88, [1989] *ECR* 2743.
[1894] Koukoulis-Spiliotopoulos 2001, p. 42.
[1895] Fredman 2002, pp. 107 subs.
[1896] Directive 97/80/EC, *OJ* 1998 L 14/6 (as amended).
[1897] See: the Commission in its Green Paper on Equality and Non-discrimination in an enlarged European
Union, COM(2004) 379 fin.
[1898] Besides these Directives, the package includes an Action Programme (Council Decision establishing
a Community Action Programme to combat discrimination (2001-2006), *OJ* 2000 L 303/23).
Regarding race discrimination, see also the Joint Action adopted by the Council on the basis of Article
K.3. EU (Joint Action adopted by the Council on the basis of Article K.3 of the Treaty on European
Union, concerning action to combat racism and xenophobia, *OJ* 1996 L 185/5). For the pre-
Amsterdam State of Law, see Guild 1997.
[1899] EUROPE No 7732 of 7 June 2000, p. 7, 'Council comes to political agreement on directive banning
discrimination on grounds of race or ethnic origin – other session results'. On the genesis of this
package, see Kenner 2003, pp. 395 subs.
[1900] Directive 2000/78/EC, *OJ* 2000 L 180/22.
[1901] Directive 2000/78/EC, *OJ* 2000 L 303/16.

Treatment Directive[1902] (the new Goods and Services Directive[1903] as well as the proposed Recasting Directive[1904] follow the same approach). Due to certain important differences from the Burden of Proof Directive, these Directives represent a *second generation* of legal definitions of indirect discrimination.

1. THE RACE DIRECTIVE

a. The development of the definition

With regard to the Race Directive, Art. 2(2)(b) of the Commission's original proposal[1905] for a legal definition of indirect discrimination provided that 'indirect discrimination shall be taken to occur where an apparently neutral provision, criterion or practice is liable to affect adversely a person or group of persons of a particular racial or ethnic origin, unless that provision, criterion or practice is objectively justified by a legitimate aim which is unrelated to the racial or ethnic origin of a person or group of persons and the means of achieving that aim are appropriate and necessary'. In the amended version of the proposal,[1906] the text was slightly altered. It stated that 'indirect discrimination shall be taken to occur where an apparently neutral provision, criterion or practice is intrinsically liable to affect adversely a person or group of persons of a particular racial or ethnic origin and if there is a consequent risk that it will place those persons at a particular disadvantage, unless that provision, criterion or practice is objectively justified by a legitimate aim which is unrelated to the racial or ethnic origin of a person or group of persons and the means of achieving that aim are appropriate and necessary'. In its Explanatory Memorandum relating to the original draft, the Commission claimed that its definition was consistent with the case law of the Court of Justice on indirect discrimination in the fields of equal treatment for women and men and of free movement of workers. However, that is in fact not possible given the differences found earlier in this study with regard to the case law regarding the two fields, notably in relation to the element of the disparate impact.[1907] Instead, the draft definitions appear to be based on the case law definition of indirect discrimination on grounds of nationality (O'Hare),[1908] though they are not entirely consistent with

---

1902 Directive 2002/73, *OJ* 2002 L 269/15.
1903 Directive 2004/113/EC implementing the principle of equal treatment between men and women in the access to and supply of goods and services, OJ 2004 L 373/37.
1904 Proposal for a Directive on the implementation of the principle of equal opportunities and equal treatment of men and women in matters of employment and occupation, COM(2004) 279 fin.
1905 Proposal for a Council Directive implementing the principle of equal treatment between persons irrespective of racial or ethnic origin, COM(99) 566 fin.
1906 Amended proposal for a Council Directive implementing the principle of equal treatment between persons irrespective of racial or ethnic origin, *OJ* 2000 C 311 E/169, COM(2000) 328 fin.
1907 See earlier in this part, A.IV.2.d.
1908 O'Hare 2001, p. 146.

that definition either. As Hepple, Choussey & Choudhury[1909] point out, both the
O'Flynn[1910] definition and that of the Burden of Proof Directive[1911] concern adverse
impact on members of a group, whilst the proposed definition also mentioned an individualised approach. For that reason, these authors called it 'fundamentally flawed'.
The text eventually adopted,[1912] though worded slightly differently, is essentially based
on the same approach. Art. 2(2)(b) of the Directive provides that 'indirect discrimination shall be taken to occur where an apparently neutral provision, criterion or practice
would put persons of a racial or ethnic origin at a particular disadvantage compared
with other persons, unless that provision, criterion or practice is objectively justified
by a legitimate aim and the means of achieving that aim are appropriate and necessary'.

b. The definition as adopted

A first point to be made regarding the definition finally opted for in the Race Directive
is that, in keeping with the Burden of Proof Directive,[1913] it refers to provisions, criteria
and practices, rather than only to criteria or conditions as was the case with the earlier
case law definitions. As was noted earlier,[1914] this may or may not indicate a difference
in approach. Further, in the new definition the *level of the disparate impact* is described
as a 'particular disadvantage'. Notably, this wording differs from that in the Burden
of Proof Directive in that it does not refer to proportions of those who are disadvantaged but more generally to a particular disadvantage of one group as compared to
other persons. The significance of this difference remains unclear. As far as the *proof*
of disparate impact is concerned, it is generally stated that the definition is based on
a liability test, as is the definition developed by the Court in its case law concerning
indirect discrimination on grounds of nationality (e.g. Sewandono,[1915] Holtmaat,[1916]
De Schutter,[1917] Brown,[1918] Kenner).[1919] This test is, arguably, easier than that applicable
in the Burden of Proof Directive[1920] (Bell,[1921] Waddington & Hendriks).[1922] In fact, this
seems to have been the Commission's intention (Waddington & Bell,[1923] quoting Odile

---

[1909] Hepple, Choussey & Choudhury 2000, p. 31.
[1910] Case C-237/94, [1996] *ECR* I-2617.
[1911] Directive 97/80/EC, *OJ* 1998 L 14/6 (as amended).
[1912] Directive 2000/43/EC, *OJ* 2000 L180/22.
[1913] Directive 97/80/EC, *OJ* 1998 L 14/6 (as amended).
[1914] See earlier in this part, B.II.
[1915] Sewandono 2001, p. 221.
[1916] Holtmaat 2001 (Uit de keuken), p. 114.
[1917] De Schutter 2001, p. 96.
[1918] Brown 2003, p. 206.
[1919] Kenner 2003, p. 407.
[1920] Directive 97/80/EC, *OJ* 1998 L 14/6 (as amended).
[1921] Bell 2001, p. 593.
[1922] Waddington & Hendriks 2002, p. 7, at 423.
[1923] Waddington & Bell 2001, p. 594.

Quintin, Director-General for Employment and Social Affairs at the Commission). At the same time, the Directive's preamble[1924] states that the appreciation of the facts from which it may be inferred that there has been direct or indirect discrimination is a matter for national bodies in accordance with national law, and that national law 'may provide in particular for indirect discrimination to be established by any means including on the basis of statistical evidence' (recital 15; see also Recital 16 of the General Non-Discrimination Directive). Accordingly, statistical evidence may still be relevant (though Fredman[1925] points out that statistics on race may be particularly difficult to collect).

Barnard & Hepple[1926] draw the attention to the fact that Art. 2(2)(b) requires a comparison between the treatment of 'persons of a racial or ethnic origin' and that of 'other persons'. Pointing to the individualised approach of the original proposal, these authors argue that the final wording does not make clear that the disadvantage must be suffered by a group of persons of a particular racial or ethnic group to which an individual belongs. They explain that '[l]iterally interpreted, there will be discrimination if two or more individuals 'of a racial or ethnic origin' (presumably the same origin) suffer a particular disadvantage, even without evidence that the racial or ethnic group as such suffers from that disadvantage'. In the authors' view, this 'loses the crucial objective of equality of results in favour of the notion of formal equality between individuals', and results in an assimilation of the concepts of direct and indirect discrimination. From this, they conclude that the Directive shows 'a remarkable lack of understanding of indirect discrimination as a concept which is concerned with the effects of apparently neutral provisions on the group to which an individual belongs' and they hope that the Court will opt for a purposive interpretation in line with the approach reflected in *O'Flynn*.

With regard to the element of *objective justification* in this definition, according to Sewandono[1927] it follows the pattern of case law on indirect sex discrimination (also Barnard).[1928] However, it should be noted that this definition is similar only with regard to its more generally formulated part ('objectively justified factors unrelated to any discrimination on grounds of sex'); otherwise it is more specific. In particular, in a more detailed manner the case law definition sets out the requirements for objective

---

[1924] Concerning the relevance of preambles, Bell argues that even though preambles are not binding on the Court, depending on the issue the Court is unlikely to disregard them. Bell in this context refers to AG Tizzano's opinion in the *BECTU* case (Case 173/99, [2001] *ECR* I-4881, point 41 of the AG's opinion); Bell 2002, p. 116. A clear example of the Court's taking into account statements made in the preamble that are not reflected in the provisions of the Directive can be found in *Grzelczyk* (Case C-184/99, [2001] *ECR* I-6193), see Iliopoulou & Toner 2002, p. 611, footnote 8, and p. 613, footnote 12.
[1925] Fredman 2001, p. 162.
[1926] Barnard & Hepple 2000, pp. 568 and 583.
[1927] Sewandono 2001, p. 221.
[1928] Barnard 2000, p. 291.

justification in the two specific cases of indirect sex discrimination – those resulting
from acts of an employer and those resulting from State action through legislation.
Barnard & Hepple[1929] point out that the Race Directive requires a single standard for
objective justification according to which measures 'must be 'appropriate and necessary' to achieve a legitimate aim, and not simply one of a number of 'reasonable'
courses of action'.

Finally, it should be noted that the Race Directive provides only for *minimum
protection* (Art. 6(1)). According to Whittle,[1930] this means that Member States are
generally 'allowed, and should be actively encouraged, to extend the principle of equal
treatment that is embodied in the [...] Directive to areas of activity beyond employment (a horizontal expansion), as well as improve on the level and quality of the
protection that it affords (a vertical expansion)'. The concept of indirect discrimination
is concerned with this latter aspect. It can therefore be argued that the Member States
are not tied to the letter of the Directive's definition but instead may provide for a
different test to the extent that such a test provides a higher level of protection to
people suffering from the relevant type of discrimination. More favourable rules under
national law may deal with every aspect of the indirect discrimination test, including
the level of requisite disparate impact and its corresponding acceptable levels and
forms of proof and objective justification. De Schutter[1931] raises the possibility of
prescribing an approach based on statistics, arguing that in some cases it is easier to
establish proof through statistics than to satisfy the liability test. Again, future case law
that will have to show what the precise meaning of the definition of indirect discrimination in the Race Directive is and whether and to what extent it differs from that
derived through previous case law.

2. THE SO-CALLED GENERAL FRAMEWORK DIRECTIVE

a. *The development of the definition*

A legal definition can also be found in the second Directive adopted on the basis of
Art. 13 EC,[1932] which is the so-called General Framework Directive[1933] (concerning

---

[1929] Barnard & Hepple 2000, p. 575.
[1930] Whittle 2002, p. 305.
[1931] De Schutter, p. 96.
[1932] Whittle & Bell 2002, pp. 681 subs., argue that Art. 137(2) EC would have been a more appropriate
legal basis for this Directive.
[1933] Directive 2000/78/EC, OJ 2000 L 303/16. The usual name by which this Directive is called merits some
comment. Obviously, the 'Framework Directive' is derived from the Directive's official title. However,
this name is somewhat misleading because the term 'framework' is usually applied to Directives of
a general nature which are then fleshed out by a number of more specific Directives (so-called

discrimination on the grounds of religion or belief, disability, age and sexual orientation). The Commission originally proposed[1934] a definition according to which 'indirect discrimination shall be taken to occur where an apparently neutral provision, criterion or practice is liable to affect adversely a person or persons to whom any of the grounds referred to in Article 1 applies, unless that provision, criterion or practice is objectively justified by a legitimate aim and the means of achieving it are appropriate and necessary.' (Art. 2(2)(b) of the original proposal, which is identical in the amended proposal).[1935] In its Explanatory Memorandum, the Commission stated:

'Unlike direct discrimination, which can be described as a difference of treatment on the grounds of a specific characteristic, indirect discrimination is much more difficult to discern. In the field of sex discrimination, the European Court of Justice has required statistical evidence to prove indirect discrimination. However, adequate statistics are not always available. For example, there may be too few persons in a firm who are affected by the provision in question or where the provision, criterion or practice has just been introduced, statistics may not yet be available. The definition of indirect discrimination in paragraph 2(b) is inspired by the case-law of the European Court of Justice in cases involving the free movement of workers. According to this definition, an apparently neutral provision, criterion or practice will be regarded as indirectly discriminatory if it is intrinsically liable to adversely affect a person or persons on the grounds referred in Article 1. The 'liability test' may be proven on the basis of statistical evidence or by any other means that demonstrate that a provision would be intrinsically disadvantageous for the person or persons concerned. The emphasis on an objective justification in cases of indirect discrimination is put on two elements. Firstly, the aim of the provision, criterion or practice which establishes a difference of treatment must deserve protection and must be sufficiently substantial to justify it taking precedence over the principle of equal treatment. Secondly, the means employed to achieve that aim must be appropriate and necessary. The definition of indirect discrimination should be construed in conjunction with the general rules on the burden of proof set out in Article 9. The principle of equal treatment under Article 2 as applied in the context of disability entails an identification and removal of barriers in the way of persons with disabilities who, with reasonable accommodation, are able to perform the essential functions of a job. The concept has become central to the construction

---

'individual Directives'). The Directive on safety and health of workers at work (Directive 89/391/EEC, OJ 1989 L 183/1, as amended) may serve as an example, and the Maternity Directive (Directive 92/85/EEC, OJ 1992, L 348/1) is one of the individual Directives fleshing it out. In contrast, Directive 2000/78 is not a Framework Directive in the traditional sense (see House of Lords 2000 (EU proposals), para. 45). For that reason, the present writer prefers the term 'Horizontal Directive' used by authors such as Hepple, Choussey & Choudhury 2000, p. 27, and De Schutter 2001, p. 63. However, because insisting on this title risks confusion, in this present study the present author will use the term 'General Framework Directive' with regard to Directive 2000/78/EC.

[1934] Proposal for a Council Directive establishing a general framework for equal treatment in employment and occupation, COM(99) 565 fin.

[1935] Amended proposal for a Council Directive establishing a general framework for equal treatment in employment and occupation, OJ 2001 C 62 E/152, COM(2000) 652 fin.

of modern legislation combating disability-based discrimination and is also expressly
recognised at an international level.'

Criticism of this proposed definition was broadly similar to that concerning the Race
Directive.[1936] For example, the Select Committee on the European Union of the UK
House of Lords[1937] noted that the definition differed significantly from that found in
the Burden of Proof Directive[1938] and that, although it drew heavily on that developed
by the Court of Justice in its case law on free movement (*O'Flynn*),[1939] it was not fully
consistent with that definition. Accordingly, the new definition would likely create
confusion and increase the problems facing the courts and potential litigants. In the
Committee's view, there was no need to diverge from the definition found in the
Burden of Proof Directive whose inherent limits (with regard to such matters as the
requirements regarding proof) could be avoided by a purposive interpretation. The
European Scrutiny Committee of the UK House of Commons[1940] noted the inconsistency with that of the proposed Action Programme to combat discrimination.[1941]

Subsequently, the draft text underwent a number of changes.[1942] The definition
of indirect discrimination contained in the Directive's final text[1943] is worded as follows
(Art. 2(2)(b) of the Directive): 'For the purposes of paragraph 1: [...] indirect
discrimination shall be taken to occur where an apparently neutral provision, criterion
or practice would put persons having a particular religion or belief, a particular
disability, a particular age, or a particular sexual orientation at a particular disadvantage compared with other persons unless: (i) that provision, criterion or practice is
objectively justified by a legitimate aim and the means of achieving that aim are
appropriate and necessary, or (ii) as regards persons with a particular disability, the
employer or any person or organisation to whom this Directive applies, is obliged,
under national legislation, to take appropriate measures in line with the principles
contained in Article 5 in order to eliminate disadvantages entailed by such provision,
criterion or practice.' (Art. 5 of the General Framework Directive obliges employers
to make reasonable accommodations for persons with disabilities.)

[1936] Directive 2000/43/EC, *OJ* 2000 L 180/22.
[1937] House of Lords 2000 (EU proposals), para. 78 subs.
[1938] Directive 97/80/EC, *OJ* 1998 L 14/6 (as amended).
[1939] Case C-237/94, [1996] *ECR* I-2617.
[1940] House of Commons 2000, para. 4.32, point v.
[1941] Council Decision establishing a Community Action Programme to combat discrimination (2001-
2006), OJ 2000 L 303/23.
[1942] In the end, it was only after six hours of extremely difficult negotiations that political agreement was
reached; Europe No 7824 of 19 October 2000, p. 6, 'Approving a general directive, Council bans all
forms of employment and work discrimination within Union'; Neue Zürcher Zeitung of 19 October
2000, 'EU-Arbeitsminister für Gleichbehandlung'.
[1943] Directive 2000/78/EC, *OJ* 2000 L 303/16.

b. The definition as adopted

Concerning the requirement of *disparate impact,* the definition in the General Framework Directive is characterised by the same elements that were previously included in the Race Directive[1944] but cannot be found in the Court's case law definitions:[1945] the General Framework Directive refers to *'provisions, criteria and practices'* (rather than only to criteria and conditions such as in the previous case law definitions), it provides for an individualised approach,[1946] it describes the level of the requisite impact as a *particular disadvantage* and, with regard to proof of that impact, it is based on a liability test[1947] whilst allowing for the possibility of prescribing proof by statistics under national law.[1948] Like the Race Directive, the Framework Directive is based on a *minimum approach* (Art. 8(1) of the Directive). Academic writers point to the difficulties that may arise in the context of statistical proof in relation to certain discriminatory grounds because of their specific characteristics (e.g. Bell,[1949] Whittle,[1950] De Schutter,[1951] Bell & Waddington,[1952] Meenan).[1953]

> Bell points out that obtaining reliable statistical data on *sexual orientation* would be very difficult indeed, given that individuals can and do conceal their sexuality, especially in employment contexts. Also, conflicts with the privacy rights of individual employees may arise. In the context of *disability,* Whittle emphasises that reliance on the use of statistical data to establish an adverse impact is inappropriate. As opposed to the discriminatory grounds of sex, race and religion which can (relatively)[1954] easily be classified into clearly defined groups, the same is not possible with disabilities because people with disabilities do not form a homogeneous group. As a consequence, statistical data on disabilities is unlikely to be accurate or even available (see also Hendriks).[1955] In the context of *age,* Meenan points to the fact that, more so than with regard to other grounds, peoples' ages are subject to constant change. More generally, De Schutter observes that statistical proof requires that

---

[1944] Directive 2000/78/EC, *OJ* 2000 L 180/22.
[1945] See earlier in this part, B.II.
[1946] Waddington & Hendriks 2002, p. 425, seem to welcome this approach.
[1947] De Schutter 2001, p. 95; Waddington & Bell 2001, p. 593.
[1948] The House of Lords 2000 (Framework Directive), para. 35 subs., though finding the final definition more workable than that originally proposed, considered that it followed neither the terms of the Court's judgment in *O'Flynn* (Case C-237/94, [1996] *ECR* I-2617) nor those of the Burden of Proof Directive.
[1949] Bell 2001, p. 660.
[1950] Whittle 2002, p. 309.
[1951] De Schutter 2001, p. 105.
[1952] Bell & Waddington 2003, p. 363.
[1953] Meenan 2003, p. 13.
[1954] In view of the phenomenon of intersexuals or persons with ambiguous genitalia, it would be more appropriate to say 'relatively easily'. See the information provided by the Intersex Society of North America at http://www.isna.org/faq.htm#anchor637790.
[1955] Hendriks 2000, pp. 29 subs.

the groups be accurately identified which is particularly difficult when the differences
between the groups is simply a matter of degree (e.g. handicap, age, and to some extent even
race and ethnic origin) or when the comparison requires knowing the details of persons'
private lives (sexual orientation or, sometimes, their religions).

The definition of indirect discrimination in the General Framework Directive also
differs from the case law definitions with regard to *objective justification* in that it
provides for two possibilities. First, Art. 2(2)(b)(i) provides the usual possibility of
objective justification as known from the Court's case law in the same manner as the
Race Directive ('unless that provision, criterion or practice is objectively justified by
a legitimate aim and the means of achieving that aim are appropriate and necessary').
Second, Art. 2(2)(b)(ii) provides for a new and particular type of justification concerning persons with a particular disability. According to this subsection, there is no
indirect discrimination if 'the employer or any person or organisation to whom this
Directive applies, is obliged, under national legislation, to take appropriate measures
in line with the principles contained in Articles 5 in order to eliminate disadvantages
entailed by such provision, criterion or practice'.

In academic writing, interpretations of Art. 2(2)(b)(ii) differ. According to Hepple,
Choussey & Choudhury,[1956] the provision entails a reconciliation of the duty to make
reasonable adjustments with the prohibition against indirect discrimination, which
the authors declare necessary if the concept of indirect discrimination is to be applied
at all to disability discrimination. Waddington & Bell[1957] think that subsection (ii)
provides for another type of justification in addition to the standard objective justification. Whittle[1958] argues that if a rule or practice is deemed to be indirectly discriminatory because of its disparate impact it can nevertheless be retained as long as the
employer is under a duty to provide reasonable accommodation independent of
whether or not such measures have already been actually taken. Yet another interpretation is suggested by the UK Government[1959] based on the provision's legislative
history. In this view, the intent of Art. 2(2)(b)(ii) is to give the Member States a choice
between a combination of direct discrimination with reasonable adjustments following
the UK model, on the one hand, and a combination of direct and indirect discrimination with reasonable adjustments, on the other hand.

[1956] Hepple, Choussey & Choudhury 2000, p. 31.
[1957] Waddington & Bell 2001, p. 594. The authors refer to 'Art. 2(b)', but it appeared upon inquiry that
what they mean is indeed Art. 2(2)(b)(ii); see also Waddington & Hendriks 2002, p. 415.
[1958] Whittle 2002, p. 305.
[1959] See the statements by the UK Minister in charge, The Rt. Hon. Tessa Jowell, in House of Lords 2000
(Framework Directive), p. 6 of the Minutes of the Evidence taken Wednesday, 15 November 2000.
See further UK Department of Trade and Industry 2002, at para. 14.10, and House of Commons,
p. xxii.

The background to the UK view is as follows. The fact that the Commission's original proposal for the Directive did not include the second 'unless clause' was perceived as problematic by the UK Government. The UK Disability Discrimination Act (DDA) did not incorporate the concept of indirect discrimination. Rather, discrimination was defined as either less favourable treatment or a failure to comply with a duty to make reasonable adjustments (see House of Commons).[1960] The UK Government feared that under the proposed EC definition employers would have to bring forward a form of double justification incorporating objective justification and reasonable accommodation. The UK therefore suggested an amendment that simply omitted any reference to handicap in the definition. This, however, proved unacceptable to the Commission and other Member States, notably Sweden and Ireland. Given that the adoption of the Directive required unanimity, a compromise had to be reached. According to UK Government, this compromise consisted in letting the Member States choose between the UK approach (combination of direct discrimination with reasonable adjustments), on the one hand, and the Swedish/Irish option (combination of direct and indirect discrimination with reasonable adjustments), on the other hand. It should be noted that this interpretation was questioned by the House of Lords.[1961]

From the point of view of persons with a handicap, these varied interpretations are hardly satisfactory. In the present writer's analysis, there may be a more favourable interpretation (though, admittedly, it is not readily apparent from the provision's wording). Accordingly, subsection (ii) should be read as concerning only a particular sort of case, in the sense that if national legislation requires, as the Directive puts is, 'appropriate measures in line with the principles contained in Article 5 in order to eliminate disadvantages entailed by such provision, criterion or practice', such measures directed at persons with a particular handicap in themselves ought not be considered as constituting indirect discrimination. In other words, the 'extras' that handicapped persons get by way of reasonable accommodation cannot be contested as being indirectly discriminatory by those who do not get them.[1962] But then, it could be argued on a more fundamental level that Art. 2(2)(b)(ii) is superfluous in view of the existence of the Directive's Art. 5 which obliges (not merely 'allows') the Member States to provide reasonable accommodation. Another more favourable reading is mentioned by Hepple, Choussey & Choudhury[1963] who recommend the approach taken by the Ontario Human Rights Code, section 11(2). They explain: 'A provision, criterion or practice should not be regarded as appropriate and necessary in the case of indirect discrimination which disadvantages disabled persons [...], unless the needs

---

[1960] House of Commons, para. 4.28.
[1961] House of Lords 2000 (Framework Directive), para. 40 and 41.
[1962] Regarding the relationship in terms of substance between indirect discrimination and accommodation, see Jolls 2001, who argues in the context of US law that in specified instances of disparate impact (in European terms: indirect discrimination) anti-discrimination and accommodation are identical. The author discusses examples such as the no-beard and English-only requirements as well as height and weight as job selection criteria; see pp. 653 subs.
[1963] Hepple, Choussey & Choudhury 2000, pp. 31 subs.

of that group cannot be reasonably accommodated without causing undue hardship
on the person responsible for accommodating those needs, having regard to factors
such as financial and other costs and health and safety requirements.' In other words,
in the case of indirect discrimination on grounds of handicap, there should be
justification only if reasonable accommodation is not possible. Or to put it differently
still: as long as reasonable accommodation is possible, there can be no justification
for indirect discrimination in the case of disability. Again, case law will have to identify
the precise meaning of the definition of indirect discrimination in the General
Framework Directive, in particular with regard to whether and to what extent it differs
from the traditional case law definitions.

3. THE REVISED SECOND EQUAL TREATMENT
DIRECTIVE (SEX DISCRIMINATION)

a. The development of the definition

In the field of sex equality law, the Commission repeatedly expressed its view that the
original Second Equal Treatment Directive[1964] (concerning sex discrimination in
relation to access to employment, vocational training and promotion, and working
conditions) should be amended.[1965] A first proposal[1966] was made in reaction to the
Court's ruling in the *Kalanke* case[1967] and concerned only positive action. This proposal
was rejected by the European Parliament[1968] which called for a new proposal based
on the provisions of the Amsterdam Treaty. In 2000, the Commission presented a
proposed text[1969] adding the following subparagraph to Art. 2(1) of the Directive:
'Indirect discrimination, for the purposes of the first subparagraph, shall exist where
an apparently neutral provision, criterion or practice disadvantages a substantially
higher proportion of the members of one sex unless that provision, criterion or
practice is appropriate and necessary and can be justified by objective factors unrelated
to sex.' In its comments, the Commission explained that this article gives 'a definition
of the notion of indirect discrimination coherent with Directive 97/80/EC [the Burden

---

[1964] Directive 76/207/EEC, *OJ* 1976, L 39/40.
[1965] Regarding the process of amendment of this Directive, see Tobler 2003, pp. 76 subs.
[1966] Proposal for a Council Directive amending Directive 76/207/EEC on the implementation of the
principle of equal treatment for men and women as regards access to employment, vocational training
and promotion, and working conditions, *OJ* 1996 C 179/8.
[1967] Case C-450/93, [1995] *ECR* I-3051.
[1968] See *OJ* 1999, C 175/67.
[1969] Proposal for a Directive of the European Parliament and of the Council amending Council Directive
76/207/EEC on the implementation of the principle of equal treatment for men and women as regards
access to employment, vocational training and promotion, and working conditions, COM(2000)
334 fin., *OJ* 2000 C 337 E/204.

of Proof Directive] and that of the (proposed) legislation, based on Article 13 of the Treaty, to combat discrimination on grounds other than sex in matters of employment'. Although the parallel with the Burden of Proof Directive[1970] is obvious (O'Hare),[1971] the alleged parallel with the definitions in the Race[1972] and the General Framework[1973] Directives is by no means apparent. Holtmaat[1974] observed that the proposed definition did *not* follow their approach, and the UK House of Lords[1975] warned that these differences may create an unsatisfactory state of affairs and a danger of confusion, particularly in cases involving instances of multiple discrimination. It was also pointed out that these pieces of legislation would provide various levels of protection and different definitions of the same key-concepts (Waddington & Bell,[1976] Holtmaat).[1977] It is therefore not astonishing that ECOSOC[1978] in principle welcomed a legal definition, but felt that the definition should be reworded to make it consistent with that in the Art. 13 Directives. Subsequently, the Conciliation Committee reached agreement on the final text of the revised Directive.[1979] Art. 2(2) of the Revised Second Equal Treatment Directive[1980] states: 'For the purposes of this Directive, the following definitions shall apply: […] indirect discrimination: where an apparently neutral provision, criterion or practice would put persons of one sex at a particular disadvantage compared with persons of the other sex, unless that provision, criterion or practice is objectively justified by a legitimate aim, and the means of achieving that aim are appropriate and necessary […].'

b. The definition in comparison

According to former Commissioner Anna Diamantopoulou,[1981] the final version of the definition is line with that in the Race Directive[1982] and the General Framework

---

[1970] Directive 97/80/EC, *OJ* 1998 L 14/6 (as amended).
[1971] O'Hare 2001, p. 147.
[1972] Directive 2000/43/EC, *OJ* 2000 L 180/22.
[1973] Directive 2000/78/EC, *OJ* 2000 L 303/16.
[1974] Holtmaat 2001 (Uit de keuken), pp. 114 and 117; see also Bell 2001, pp. 659 subs.
[1975] House of Lords 2000 (Framework Directive), para. 36.
[1976] Waddington & Bell 2001, p. 588.
[1977] Holtmaat 2001 (Uit de keuken), p. 114.
[1978] Opinion of the Economic and Social Committee on the 'Proposal for a Directive of the European Parliament and of the Council amending Council Directive 76/207/EEC on the implementation of the principle of equal treatment for men and women as regards access to employment, vocational training and promotion, and working conditions', *OJ* 2001 C 123/81.
[1979] Joint text approved by the Conciliation Committee provided for in Article 251(4) of the EC Treaty, 2000/0142 (COD); see also Neue Zürcher Zeitung of 19 April 2002, 'Gegen sexuelle Belästigung am Arbeitsplatz. Die EU verstärkt die Gleichbehandlungs-Richtlinie'.
[1980] Directive 2002/73, *OJ* 2002 L 269/15.
[1981] 'Anna Diamantopoulou welcomes new tough new EU rules against sexual harassment at work', see http://europa.eu.int/comm/employment_social/news/2002/apr/092_en.html, last accessed 14 July 2003.
[1982] Directive 2000/43/EC, *OJ* 2000 L 180/22.

Directive[1983] (an aim mentioned in consideration 6 of the Directive's preamble).
Indeed, all of them refer to indirectly discriminatory 'provisions, criteria or practices'
as well as to 'a particular disadvantage', all of them reflect the liability approach whilst
not excluding statistical proof in principle, and all of them provide only for minimum
protection (Art. 8e of the Revised Second Equal Treatment Directive). However, the
definition differs from that in the Burden of Proof Directive.[1984] Consequently, there
are now two different legal definitions applicable in the area of sex equality – plus a
case law definition that differs from those two on some points (e.g. Epiney &
Freiermuth Abt).[1985]

IV. COMPARISON AND FINDINGS

Against the background of the development of the legal definitions as just described,
the following section tries to make an overall comparison and to draw certain
conclusions. It begins by recalling the various legal definitions and then turns to the
differences between the Directives' fields of application. Finally, the new definitions
are compared to the case law definitions in terms of their consistency, precision and
effectiveness.

1. RECALLING THE LEGAL DEFINITIONS

It was seen that the development discussed above led to two generations of legal
definitions for indirect discrimination. The first generation codified the Court's case
law in the area of sex discrimination. According to Art. 2(2) of the Burden of Proof
Directive:[1986]

> 'indirect discrimination shall exist where an apparently neutral provision, criterion or
> practice disadvantages a substantially higher proportion of the members of one sex unless
> that provision, criterion or practice is appropriate and necessary and can be justified by
> objective factors unrelated to sex'.

The second generation of legal definitions added a new dimension. Art. 2(2)(b) of the
Race Directive[1987] provides that:

[1983]   Directive 2000/78/EC, OJ 2000 L 303/16.
[1984]   Directive 97/80/EC on the burden of proof in cases of discrimination based on sex, OJ 1998 L 14/6
        (as amended). On the respective fields of application of these Directives, see immediately below.
[1985]   Epiney & Freiermuth Abt 2003, p. 164.
[1986]   Directive 97/80/EC, OJ 1998 L 14/6 (as amended).
[1987]   Directive 2000/43/EC, OJ 2000 L 180/22.

'indirect discrimination shall be taken to occur where an apparently neutral provision, criterion or practice would put persons of a racial or ethnic origin at a particular disadvantage compared with other persons, unless that provision, criterion or practice is objectively justified by a legitimate aim and the means of achieving that aim are appropriate and necessary'.

Largely the same definition can be found in the General Framework Directive[1988] (concerning discrimination on the grounds of religion or belief, disability, age and sexual orientation) where Art. 2(2)(b) states:

'indirect discrimination shall be taken to occur where an apparently neutral provision, criterion or practice would put persons having a particular religion or belief, a particular disability, a particular age, or a particular sexual orientation at a particular disadvantage compared with other persons unless: (i) that provision, criterion or practice is objectively justified by a legitimate aim and the means of achieving that aim are appropriate and necessary, or (ii) as regards persons with a particular disability, the employer or any person or organisation to whom this Directive applies, is obliged, under national legislation, to take appropriate measures in line with the principles contained in Articles 5 in order to eliminate disadvantages entailed by such provision, criterion or practice'.

Finally, Art. 2(2) of the Revised Second Equal Treatment Directive[1989] provides that there is indirect discrimination:

'where an apparently neutral provision, criterion or practice would put persons of one sex at a particular disadvantage compared with persons of the other sex, unless that provision, criterion or practice is objectively justified by a legitimate aim, and the means of achieving that aim are appropriate and necessary'.

2. DIFFERENT FIELDS OF APPLICATION

Obviously, these definitions apply only in the fields covered by the respective Directives. These *differ so considerably* that Fredman[1990] speaks of 'a hierarchy of directives, with race and ethnic origin given the widest reach, followed by gender discrimination [...] and trailed by the discrimination on grounds of age, religion, sexual orientation and disability'. The widest field of application of the existing legal definitions is that of the *Race Directive*.[1991] According to Art. 3(1), it includes conditions for access to employment, to self-employment and to occupation, further access to vocational

---

[1988] Directive 2000/78/EC, *OJ* 2000 L 303/16.
[1989] Directive 2002/73/EC, *OJ* 2002 L 269/15.
[1990] Fredman 2001, p. 151.
[1991] Directive 2000/43/EC, *OJ* 2000 L 180/22.

guidance, vocational training and advanced vocational training and retraining, employment and working conditions, membership of and involvement in organisations of workers or employers or any organisation whose members carry on a particular profession, social protection, social advantages,[1992] education as well as access to, and supply of, goods and services that are available to the public. According to Kenner,[1993] this extends the reach of the Directive to areas that are on the very fringe of the Community's competence. Even so, Community law in this area clearly falls short of the approach suggested by Schiek[1994] which calls for the adoption of a prohibition against personal discrimination[1995] as a general principle of European contract law. On the other hand, Sjerps[1996] argues that there are, and should be, limits to the reach of non-discrimination law. For example, differentiation between the sexes may be prohibited in the realm of paid work, but it is 'a highly relevant and acceptable criterion in the realm of love'. Sjerps concludes that '[t]he prohibition of all forms of unequal treatment based on sex is as impossible as it is undesirable'.

In contrast, the field of application of the *General Framework Directive*[1997] is much narrower. According to Art. 3(1), it includes access to employment, self-employment, occupation, vocational guidance, vocational training and advanced vocational training, further employment and working conditions as well as membership of and involvement in organisations of workers or employers or any organisation whose members carry on a particular profession. Notably, social security is not part of the packet, and neither is the access to goods and services.

The situation is most complicated in the area of sex equality since here two different legal definitions exist. First, according to Art. 3, the *Burden of Proof Directive*[1998] concerns situations covered by the principle of equal pay (today Art. 141(1) and (2) EC and the Equal Pay Directive),[1999] by the Second Equal Treatment Directive[2000] (which, at the time when the Directive was adopted, did not yet contain its own legal definition of indirect discrimination), by the Maternity Directive[2001] (insofar as discrimination based on sex is concerned) and by the Parental Leave Directive.[2002] In each these areas, the Directive does not apply to criminal procedures, unless otherwise provided for by the Member States. In addition, since there is now a legal definition

---

[1992] On this term, see e.g. Ellis 2003.
[1993] Kenner 2003, p. 401.
[1994] Schiek 2000, p. 26.
[1995] Schiek describes personal discrimination as 'discrimination against natural persons on grounds of personal characteristics ascribed to them as being permanent and servicing as starting points for social exclusion' and as 'discrimination on grounds of ascribed otherness'.
[1996] Sjerps 1999, p. 238.
[1997] Directive 2000/78/EC, *OJ* 2000 L 303/16.
[1998] Directive 97/80/EC, *OJ* 1998 L 14/6 (as amended).
[1999] Directive 75/117/EEC, *OJ* 1975 L 45/19.
[2000] Directive 76/207/EEC, *OJ* 1976 L 39/40.
[2001] Directive 92/85/EEC, *OJ* 1992, L 348/1.
[2002] Directive 96/34/EC, *OJ* 1996 L 145/4 (as amended).

for indirect sex discrimination in the Revised Second Equal Treatment Directive,[2003] it would seem to follow that the definition provided by the Burden of Proof Directive will no longer be relevant in that particular context. With regard to the definition in *the Revised Second Equal Treatment Directive,* it applies to access to employment, vocational training, promotion and working conditions other than pay (Art. 1 of the Directive). This leaves certain areas of sex discrimination law where there is as yet no applicable legal definition, notably social security law,[2004] the matters dealt with by the Fifth Equal Treatment Directive[2005] and those criminal procedures excluded from the field of application of the Burden of Proof Directive. In these areas, the definition of indirect sex discrimination must still be based on the Court's case law. Consequently, *three different definitions of indirect sex discrimination* exist side by side, one derived from case law and two from legislation. Contrary to what is argued by Waddington & Hendriks,[2006] to that extent the Revised Second Equal Treatment Directive does not resolve the disparity between the definitions found in the Burden of Proof Directive, on the one hand, and in the Race Directive and the General Framework Directive, on the other hand.

However, this situation may change in view of the fact that the Commission identified the Directives on equal treatment between men and women as an area in need of recasting for modernisation.[2007] In April 2004, the Commission proposed a Recasting Directive on the implementation of the principle of equal opportunities and equal treatment of men and women in matters of employment and occupation.[2008] The Directive is intended to simplify the existing acquis in the field of sex equality law by recasting the content of a number of Directives and related case law in one single instrument. As the Commission states in the Explanatory Memorandum, one aim of the proposal is to extend the application of the definitions contained in the Revised Second Equal Treatment Directive[2009] to all areas covered by the proposal. This includes in particular a single definition of direct and indirect discrimination (recital 5 of the preamble, Art. 2 of the proposed Directive). Under the proposed Directive, this definition would apply in relation to a) access to employment, including promotion, and to vocational training, b) working conditions, including pay, and c) occupational security schemes (Art. 1 of the proposed text). Accordingly, the new Directive

---

[2003] Directive 2002/73/EC, *OJ* 2002 L 269/15.

[2004] Directive 79/7/EEC, *OJ* 1979 L 6/24 (Third Equal Treatment Directive) and Directive 86/378/EEC, *OJ* 1986 L 225/40 (Fourth Equal Treatment Directive; as amended).

[2005] Directive 86/613/EEC, *OJ* 1986 L 359/56.

[2006] Waddington & Hendriks 2002, p. 423.

[2007] Annex 2 of the Commission's Communication on Updating and simplifying the Community acquis, COM(2003) 71, which in turn is based on the Commission's Better Regulation Initiative of the year 2002, COM(2002) 278.

[2008] Proposal for a Directive on the implementation of the principle of equal opportunities and equal treatment of men and women in matters of employment and occupation, COM(2004) 279 fin.

[2009] Directive 76/207/EEC, *OJ* 1976 L 39/40, as amended by Directive 2002/73/EC, OJ 2002 L 269/15.

would repeal the Equal Pay or First Equal Treatment Directive,[2010] the Second Equal
Treatment Directive (as amended),[2011] the Fifth Equal Treatment Directive,[2012] the
amendment to the Fourth Equal Treatment Directive (that is, the provisions concerning occupational pensions, which are considered pay)[2013] and the Burden of Proof
Directive (including its extension to the UK).[2014] For present purposes, the latter in
particular is important since it means that the legal definition of indirect sex discrimination as now contained in the Burden of Proof Directive will be abolished. At the
same time, there will still be two definitions, since for matters falling under the
Third[2015] and the Fourth[2016] Equal Treatment Directives (sex equality in social security)
the old case law definition will continue to apply.

Finally, it should be recalled that of all prohibitions against discrimination in EC
law the prohibition of *discrimination on grounds of nationality* has the widest reach,
due to Art. 12(1) EC which applies to all areas of the Treaty, and due to the Court's
case law on Art. 18 EC (travel and residence rights of EU citizens) which in turn has
broadened the field of application of Art. 12 EC.[2017] However, Art. 3(2) of the Race
Directive[2018] specifically states that the Directive does not cover difference of treatment
based on nationality.[2019] As there is no legal definition of discrimination on grounds
of nationality,[2020] the relevant definition in this area – and, presumably, in other areas
concerning other types of discrimination for which there is no legal definition – is still
the *case law definition* of O'Flynn.[2021]

[2010] Directive 75/117/EEC, *OJ* 1975 L 45/19.
[2011] Directive 76/207/EEC, *OJ* 1976 L 39/40, as amended by Directive 2002/73/EC, OJ 2002 L 269/15.
[2012] Directive 86/378/EEC, *OJ* 1986 L 225/40.
[2013] Directive 96/97/EC, *OJ* 1997 L 46/20.
[2014] Directive 97/80/EC, *OJ* 1998 L 14/6, and Directive 98/52/EC, *OJ* 1998 L 205/66.
[2015] Directive 79/7/EEC, *OJ* 1979 L 6/24.
[2016] Directive 86/378/EEC, *OJ* 1986 L 225/40.
[2017] See above Part 2, A.I.4.f.
[2018] Directive 2000/43/EC, *OJ* 2000 L 180/22.
[2019] The same provision excludes the right to entry into and residence by *third country nationals*.
According to Bell 2002, pp. 36 subs., the lack of any prohibition of discrimination against third
country nationals in EC free movement law shows the market integration approach in this area of
law (rather than a social citizenship model); Bell 2002, pp. 36 subs.
[2020] Such a definition was not contained in the Proposal for a European Parliament and Council
Regulation amending Council Regulation (EEC) No 1612/68 on freedom of movement for workers
within the Community, *OJ* 1998 C 344/9, Art. 1a of which provided: 'Within the scope of this
Regulation, all discrimination on grounds of sex, racial or ethnic origin, religion, belief, disability,
age or sexual orientation shall be prohibited.' The proposal has subsequently been withdrawn
(COM(2004) 542 (01)).
[2021] Case C-237/94, [1996] *ECR* I-2617.

3. PRECISION, EFFECTIVENESS AND CONSISTENCY OF THE NEW DEFINITIONS

The final issue addressed in the present context is whether the legal definitions, if compared to those of the Court's case law, represent an improvement in terms of precision, effectiveness and consistency.

a. Precision

An examination of the new legal definitions in terms of their precision leads to the conclusion that they are, in fact, equally vague as the case law definitions. First, as far as the required *disparate impact* is concerned, expressions such as 'disadvantages a substantially higher proportion' (Burden of Proof Directive)[2022] and 'put at a particular disadvantage' (Race Directive,[2023] General Framework Directive,[2024] Revised Equal Treatment Directive)[2025] are in no way clearer. Neither do the definitions indicate the precise framework of the comparison to be made in that context. For instance, does the wording of the definition in the Burden of Proof Directive mean that a comparison between the proportions of the 'qualifiers' is no longer necessary, as is argued by Fredman?[2026] Second, it was noted that the *objective justification* test as worded in the Burden of Proof Directive is rather strange in that it turns around the usual order of the elements. The test formulated in the other three Directives appears to have been better structured. The elements constituting the proportionality test are the same as under the old case law definition, namely only two ('appropriate and necessary', which corresponds to the earlier version of 'suitable and requisite'). What the formula lacks is an explicit reference to proportionality *stricto sensu* (that is, the requirement that the seriousness of the intervention and the gravity of the reasons for justifying it are in adequate proportion to each other). Since this point nevertheless appears to still be relevant, it should have been specifically addressed in the definition.

Again, it must be admitted that it is simply not possible to solve all the existing problems on the level of a general definition of indirect discrimination. When Prechal[2027] suggested a legal definition, she stated that it should simply mention the separate elements of the indirect discrimination test and leave the rest to case law. The author argued that flexibility is the strength, as opposed to the weakness, of the concept and that an evolution on a case by case basis is a valuable asset. Indeed, it is impossible to fully codify the concept, since striking the correct balance in each case is a matter

---

[2022] Directive 97/80/EC, *OJ* 1998 L 14/6 (as amended).
[2023] Directive 2000/43/EC, *OJ* 2000 L 180/22.
[2024] Directive 2000/78/EC, *OJ* 2000 L 303/16.
[2025] Directive 2002/73/EC, *OJ* 2002 L 269/15.
[2026] Fredman 2002, p. 111.
[2027] Prechal 1993, p. 97.

of opinion. Today's legal definitions appear to be a reflection of this reality. Thus,
further explanatory case law aiming to clarify problematic issues is a valued aspect of
EC law. Nonetheless, Prechal has suggested that the legislative definition include an
unrestricted list of possible 'suspect criteria' (that is, criteria which often have caused
indirect discrimination) in order to alert the addressees of the Directives to certain
types of indirect discrimination. Such a list is absent from the Burden of Proof
Directive as well as the Race and the General Framework Directives, though in a very
limited form such as list is included in Art. 2(1) of the Revised Second Equal Treatment
Directive ('no discrimination whatsoever on grounds of sex either directly or indirectly
by reference in particular to marital or family status'). However, it will be recalled that
whether reliance on an apparently neutral criterion amounts to indirect discrimination
still depends on the context and the factual circumstances of each given case.[2028]

b. Effectiveness

Whether the new definitions will make the concept of indirect discrimination more
effective than under the prior case law definition alone will largely depend on the
precise meaning given their elements as clarified through future case law. As stated
earlier, much depends on the strictness of the test. In that regard, the extension of the
relevance of the liability test to indirect sex discrimination (namely under the Revised
Second Equal Treatment Directive)[2029] as well as the possibly simpler requirements
regarding the comparisons to be made in order to assess disparate impact appear to
be improvements. At the same time, as discussed in the context of the case law
definition,[2030] other factors (which do not spring directly from the definition as set out
either in the case law or in legislation) limit the effectiveness of the concept of indirect
discrimination and will persist until confronted directly.

c. Consistency

Whilst it is certainly possible to have definitions of indirect discrimination in the
various areas of EC law that are consistent with each other, the analysis of the new legal
definitions showed that such consistency has been achieved only to some degree. The
definitions in the Race Directive,[2031] the General Framework Directive[2032] and the
Revised Sex Equality Directive[2033] are all based on the idea of minimum protection

---

[2028]   On the qualification of discrimination on grounds of marital or family status as indirect sex
discrimination, see further below Part 3, A.III.2.b.ii.
[2029]   Directive 2002/73/EC, OJ 2002 L 269/15.
[2030]   See earlier in this part, A.IV.4.
[2031]   Directive 2000/43/EC, OJ 2000 L 180/22.
[2032]   Directive 2000/78/EC, OJ 2000 L 303/16.
[2033]   Directive 2002/73/EC, OJ 2002 L 269/15.

and on the liability approach. Whilst the latter also appears in the case law definition on indirect discrimination on grounds of nationality, neither the Burden of Proof Directive[2034] nor the case law definition for indirect sex discrimination is based on that approach. There also seems to be differences regarding the comparison to be undertaken in the framework of the assessment of disparate impact. As a special feature, the General Framework Directive provides possibly for a specific sort of justification in the context of handicap (Art. 2(2)(b)(ii)). As a further difference, (purely) economic justification for indirect discrimination is not acceptable in the context of free movement law but is explicitly accepted in the context of indirect sex discrimination caused by individual employers.

Obviously, the simplest approach to take care of these inconsistencies would be to adopt one single non-discrimination Directive, at least within the field of application of Art. 13 EC,[2035] which would include discrimination on all grounds mentioned in that provision (thus, including sex).[2036] However, given the recent adoption of three different Directives based on Art. 13 EC,[2037] this is clearly not the approach contemplated by the Community at present. Obviously, this is due at least in part to the various fields of application to which the various existing measures apply.[2038] There may also be doubts about whether such a common Directive is desirable for other reasons. In particular, it could be argued that a 'one size fits all' approach is not appropriate given the specific characteristics of the various types of discrimination. At the same time, Hepple, Choussey & Choudhury[2039] are right in arguing that although a general concept of equality and non-discrimination is not necessarily a unified one, the same concept could be applied to each ground of discrimination within its specific context. According to these authors, a single measure would have the advantage of recognising the indivisibility of the concept of equality.[2040] In the present writer's view,

---

[2034] Directive 97/80/EC, OJ 1998 L 14/6 (as amended).

[2035] Arts. 13(1) and 141(3) EC cannot be relied on simultaneously because they provide for different legislative procedures (Art. 13(1) EC: consultation procedure; Art. 141(3) EC: co-decision procedure); see Case C-338/01, judgment of 29 April 2004, n.y.r., para. 57. The proposed Recasting Directive (Proposal for a Directive on the implementation of the principle of equal opportunities and equal treatment of men and women in matters of employment and occupation, COM(2004) 279 fin.) is based on Art. 141(3) EC.

[2036] See earlier in this part, A.I.5.a.

[2037] Namely the Race Directive (Directive 2000/43/EC, OJ 2000 L 180/22), the General Framework Directive (Directive 2000/78/EC, OJ 2000 L 303/16), and the Goods and Services Directive (Directive 2004/113/EC, OJ 2004 L 373/37).

[2038] See earlier in this part, B.IV.2.

[2039] Hepple, Choussey & Choudhury 2000, pp. 21 subs.

[2040] The authors made this argument in their study on UK anti-discrimination law which consists of a large number of legal instruments covering various kinds of discrimination. For the UK national law as it existed in 2000, they mention thirty Acts, thirty-eight statutory instruments and eleven codes of practice. The authors criticise that not only is there 'too much law' but also that this law is written in a language and style that renders it largely inaccessible to those whose actions it is intended to influence. Finding the UK law inconsistent and inherently unsatisfactory, the authors recommend the creation of a single Equality Act.

it would be both possible and desirable to have only one Directive, at least under Art.
13 EC, even if a unified field of application were not feasible for political reasons and
even if certain types of discrimination call for specific justification grounds. Yet a
further step would be a general definition of indirect discrimination that is applicable
in the context of indirect discrimination on grounds of nationality as well as of any
other type of discrimination relevant under Community law. Such a definition, if
agreed upon, would best be inserted into the EC Treaty itself, in a general provision
on equality and non-discrimination. Finally, it needs to be remembered that total
uniformity of the law as applicable in the Member States is excluded anyway, due to
the minimum character[2041] of the Race Directive,[2042] the General Framework Directive[2043] and the Revised Sex Equality Directive.[2044] Depending upon how the Directives
are variously implemented in the Member States, there may be a lack of consistency
even with regard to any one type of discrimination. However, given that the flexibility
left to the Member States is to be used in the interest of potential victims of indirect
discrimination, this inconsistency seems far less problematic than that presently found
on the level of Community law between the various types of discrimination.

[2041] On minimum harmonization and its effects on the uniformity of the laws of the Member States, see
for instance Temmink 1995, Rott 2003.
[2042] Directive 2000/43/EC, *OJ* 2000 L 180/22.
[2043] Directive 2000/78/EC, *OJ* 2000 L 303/16.
[2044] Directive 2002/73/EC, *OJ* 2002 L 269/15.

PART THREE:
DEMARCATIONS

Examining the legal concept of indirect discrimination naturally leads to the question of its relationship to other related concepts. This is the focus of the third part of this present study, which examines the differences under EC law between indirect discrimination and direct discrimination, on the one hand (below A.), and indirect discrimination and restrictions in a wider sense, as relevant in the context of free movement, on the other hand (below B.). As a preliminary remark, it should be noted that the cases discussed in this context are meant to be *mere – though representative – examples*. The aim is not (and naturally cannot be) to present a case study that is all-encompassing.

A. DIRECT AND INDIRECT DISCRIMINATION

I. PRELIMINARY REMARKS

The perceived difference between direct and indirect discrimination is particularly important from a practical point of view: from the perspective of the victim of the alleged discrimination, a finding of direct discrimination will always be preferable because of the difficulties involved in proving disparate impact and because of the (usually) more limited justification possibilities in the case of direct discrimination. For the same reasons, the alleged discriminator will prefer an analysis based on the concept of indirect discrimination. The following sections begin by discussing the differences between the two concepts on a conceptual level (below II.) and thereafter turn to problems that may arise in the framework of the analysis of concrete cases (below III.).

II. DEMARCATION ON THE CONCEPTUAL LEVEL

1. INTRODUCTION

On the conceptual level, two issues must be discussed, namely whether and to what extent a significant difference exists between direct and indirect discrimination in terms of 1) the effect of the discriminatory measures and 2) the justification for taking such measures. Since the definitions of the concepts found in legislation do not give detailed guidance on these issues, indications must be found in the Court's decisions in concrete cases. The main findings of these analyses are as follows:

- Under the Court's case law, the effect of directly and indirectly discriminatory measures can be the same or nearly the same. The precise criterion for the dividing line remains unclear.
- The traditionally assumed dividing line between direct and indirect discrimination in terms of justification is not a strict one (though thus far it is only in the context of direct taxation and agricultural law that the Court has been willing to openly accept non-textual grounds of derogation for direct discrimination).
- Under certain more recent non-discrimination law, objective justification is now also relevant in the context of direct discrimination.

2. THE EFFECT OF DIRECTLY AND INDIRECTLY DISCRIMINATORY MEASURES

a. The issue

In *Sotgiu*[2045] (para. 11), the Court held that not only overt discrimination is prohibited 'but also all covert forms of discrimination which, by the application of other criteria of differentiation, lead in fact *to the same result*' (emphasis added). However, as was noted earlier,[2046] that holding is not to be taken literally. Rather, it is decisive that the contested measure has (or, in the context of discrimination on grounds of nationality and under the second generation legal definitions, tends to have), a *disproportionate* adverse effect, meaning that it disproportionately disadvantages members of one group and/or disproportionately benefits members of another group. Accordingly, Sjerps[2047] emphasises that it is incorrect to say that indirect discrimination is differentiation having the same result as direct discrimination. Nevertheless, there are instances in the Court's case law where the effect of an *apparently neutral* measure is the same, or largely the same, as in the case of direct reliance on the prohibited differentiation criterion. This raises the question of whether such cases should indeed be examined in the framework of indirect discrimination or rather in the framework of direct discrimination. The examples discussed below concern differentiations related to military service in two different legal contexts, namely discrimination on grounds of nationality and discrimination on grounds of sex.

b. Discrimination on grounds of nationality: Ugliola, De Vos *and* Mora Romero

As far as discrimination on grounds of nationality is concerned, the first relevant case is one of the foundational cases on indirect discrimination, namely *Ugliola*.[2048] It will be recalled that the case concerned the rule that the period of basic military service or reserve training was to be taken into account in calculating the duration of a worker's employment only if such service was performed in Germany and that the Court found that tying the benefit in question to the performance of service in the host Member State amounts to discrimination prohibited under the law on free movement of workers. As was noted earlier, the basis for this finding appears to have been the particularly far-reaching effect of the contested rule, which made the discrimination quite obvious ('discrimination in favour of their own nationals alone'). In fact, it can well be argued that cases with such a far reaching effect should be analysed in terms

---

[2045]   Case 152/73, [1974] *ECR* 153.
[2046]   See above Part 2, A.I.2.c.
[2047]   Sjerps 1999, p. 328, footnote 2.
[2048]   Case 15/69, [1969] *ECR* 363, see above, Part. 2, A. I.2.a. as well as II.2.a.i.

of *direct* discrimination and that the concept of indirect discrimination should be reserved to those cases where the effect of relying on an apparently neutral criterion is not the same as in the case of direct discrimination. At the same time, it was seen that the perceived difference between direct and indirect discrimination was less important at the time when *Ugliola* was decided because objective justification was not yet part of the latter concept.

However, that situation had long since changed when *De Vos*[2049] reached the Court. Like *Ugliola*, this case concerned the place of performance of military service as a differentiation ground and the allegation of discrimination on grounds of nationality in the context of the free movement of workers. Mr De Vos, a Belgian national working in Germany, complained because his employer discontinued the usual payments towards supplementary old-age and survivors' insurance during his absence from work due to military service performed in Belgium. Under German law, an employer was obliged to continue the payments only if the service was performed in Germany. Asked whether this concerns a social advantage within the meaning of Art. 7 of Regulation 1612/68,[2050] the Court held this was not the case because the benefit in question was essentially linked to the performance of military service, rather than being granted because of a person's objective status as a worker or by virtue of the mere fact of his or her residence on the national territory (*De Vos*, para. 22). Given this finding, the Court did not address the substantive issues raised by the case, including the nature of the alleged discrimination. Denys[2051] comments that the decision is a rare example where the Court did not dynamically interpret the concept of social advantages. That author further considers *De Vos* a paramount example of *direct* discrimination on grounds of nationality. Whilst the present writer would agree with this finding for the reasons given in the previous sections, the Court's approach in *Ugliola* as well as in the later social security case *Mora Romero*[2052] make it more likely that the Court would have analysed the *De Vos* in the same framework, which was that of *indirect* discrimination on grounds of nationality, based on a merely formal examination of the differentiation criterion in question as apparently neutral.

Mora Romero concerned the son of a Spanish worker who had died in Germany as the result of an accident at work. Mr Mora Romero received an orphan's benefit under the German social security system, which was suspended during his period of military service performed in Spain and paid again thereafter. When Mr Mora Romero reached the age of 25 years, the social insurance authorities refused to continue the payment for a period equivalent to the military service, arguing that such continuation was available only in cases of service performed in Germany. Mr Mora Romero

---

[2049] Case C-315/94, [1996] *ECR* I-1417.
[2050] Regulation 1612/68/EEC, *OJ* English Special Edition 1968 L 257/2, p. 475 (as amended).
[2051] Denys 1996 (Stille vormgeving), p. 128.
[2052] Case C-131/96, [1997] I-3659.

complained about discrimination on grounds of nationality because, 'under German law, only German nationals can perform military service in that Member State' (*Mora Romero*, point 19 of the AG's opinion). AG Ruiz-Jarabo Colomer agreed, pointing out that '[i]n practice [...], orphans of German nationality who continue their education or training beyond the age of 25 will be the only ones who can claim the deferred payment of the benefit which they have not received while performing military service' (*Mora Romero*, point 36 of the AG's opinion). Neither the applicant nor the AG in this context spoke of *indirect* discrimination but the Court did, albeit only implicitly. Answering the questions put to it by the national court in the framework of social security law,[2053] the Court recalled the prohibition of both 'overt and covert' discrimination on grounds of nationality and continued: 'The refusal to assimilate military service in another Member State to military service completed in the State concerned is liable to result in nationals of other Member States being unable to benefit from the right to extension of the orphan's benefit beyond the age of 25 for a period equal to that of their military service where the beneficiary's training is interrupted by reason of such service.' (*Mora Romero*, para. 35). The Court's finding, therefore, was clearly based on *indirect* discrimination on grounds of nationality (compare Plötscher).[2054] Overall, *Mora Romero* reinforces the impression that the Court will judge the existence of direct or indirect discrimination based on *formal* considerations (that is, based on the question whether or not the criterion relied on is formally direct), rather than giving consideration to the far reaching effect of some apparently neutral differentiation criteria (which would be a more substantive approach).

c.   Discrimination on grounds of sex: Schnorbus

The next case to be examined, *Schnorbus*,[2055] is particularly interesting because the question of whether a criterion with an automatic exclusionary effect leads to direct or rather to indirect sex discrimination was explicitly raised before the Court. It therefore deserves particular attention.

i.   The case

In order to become fully qualified lawyers under German law, students have first to pass the so-called First State Examination, then complete a period of practical training (the so-called *Referendariat*) and finally pass the so-called Second State Examination. The *Referendariat* is a prerequisite for taking the second required examination. Ms

---

[2053]   The rules on free movement of workers were not applicable because Mr Mora Romero's father had died at a time when Spain was not yet a member of the European Communities; see *Mora Romero*, para. 17.

[2054]   Plötscher 2003, p. 114.

[2055]   Case C-79/99, [2000] *ECR* I-10997.

Schnorbus applied to be admitted for the *Referendariat* in the Land Hessen but there were more applications than places available for the relevant period. The law provided that in such cases admission could be postponed up to one year, with certain derogations. Art. 24(2) of the Hessen Law on Legal Training (*Juristenausbildungsgesetz*, JAG) stated that the postponement rule shall 'not apply if the deferment would result in particular hardship'. Art. 14a of the Legal Training Regulations (*Juristenausbildungsordnung*, JAO) defined this latter term as including, among other issues, 'service pursuant to Article 12(a)(1) or (2) of the Grundgesetz', which meant compulsory military or civil service. When admission was postponed in her case, Ms Schnorbus argued that reliance on that criterion for the purposes of granting exemptions discriminated against women because it is only men who perform (meaning both: have to perform and can perform) compulsory service. The national court turned to Court of Justice to learn whether such a rule involves direct or indirect sex discrimination. In doing so, it referred to statistics showing that the percentage of female applicants admitted as hardship cases to practical training commencing in March 1998 was considerably lower than that of male applicants, even though women accounted for approximately 60% of the total number of applications.

Before the Court, the Land Hessen contended that there was neither direct nor indirect sex discrimination because the category of persons favoured were determined in view of disadvantages arising from a deferment that may be suffered by men and women alike. The Commission agreed that there was no direct discrimination but believed that the statistics relied on by the national court revealed indirect discrimination. AG Jacobs dealt with the issue on a general level. He explained (*Schnorbus*, points 33 and 38-41 of the AG's opinion): 'To state matters simply, it may be said that discrimination on grounds of sex arises where members of one sex are treated more favourably than the other. The discrimination is direct where the difference in treatment is based on a criterion, which is either explicitly that of sex or necessarily linked to a characteristic indissociable from sex. It is indirect where some other criterion is applied but a substantially higher proportion of one sex than of the other is in fact affected. [...] It is true that under German law as it stands women cannot be accorded priority under the rule in issue whereas the overwhelming majority of men can, as a direct result of the fact that the criterion used – completion of compulsory national service – relates to an obligation imposed by law on all men and on men alone. This might be compared to the situation as regards pregnancy. The Court has held, in a series of cases starting with *Dekker*, that since only women can be refused employment on grounds of pregnancy, such a refusal constitutes direct discrimination on grounds of sex. However, there is a distinction to be drawn between a criterion based on an obligation imposed by law on one sex alone and a criterion based on a physical characteristic inherent in one sex alone. No amount of legislation can render men capable of bearing children, whereas legislation might readily remove any discrimination between men and women in relation to compulsory service. In the present case, therefore, there is no direct discrimination because the rule in issue differentiates between those who have and those who have not completed compulsory national service as a result of a statutory obligation, and not between men and women as such.'

In contrast, the judgment is much less explicit and extremely short (*Schnorbus*, para. 32 subs.). The Court pointed out that the contested rule 'provides for a number of circumstances which may be taken into account for priority access to practical legal training. They include the completion of compulsory military or civilian service. In such a case, the benefit of the priority envisaged by the abovementioned provisions cannot be regarded as being directly based on the sex of the persons concerned. According to the criteria established by the case-law of the Court, only provisions which apply differently according to the sex of the persons concerned can be regarded as constituting discrimination directly based on sex […].' After having excluded direct sex discrimination, the Court did, however, find indirect sex discrimination, based on the nature of the rule alone (that is, independently of statistical proof of its effect). According to the Court, 'it is not necessary in this case to analyse the specific consequences of the application of the JAO. It is sufficient to not that, by giving priority to applicants who have completed compulsory military or civilian service, the provisions at issue themselves are evidence of indirect discrimination since, under the relevant national legislation, women are not required to do military or civilian service and therefore cannot benefit from the priority accorded by the abovementioned provisions of the JAO to applications in circumstances regarded as cases of hardship. The answer to the third question must therefore be that national provisions such as those at issue in the main proceedings constitute indirect discrimination on grounds of sex.'

ii. Comments

In the context of the German law relevant in *Schnorbus*, the criterion of compulsory military or civil services was such that the persons favoured by the contested rule were exclusively men; no woman could ever benefit from that particular hardship clause. Indeed, as AG Jacobs noted, '100% of those who meet it [meaning: the criterion] are necessarily men, 0% are women'. As had the Advocate General, the Court took account of this far-reaching effect only in the context of the *indirect* discrimination analysis, more specifically in that of the first part of the indirect discrimination test (disparate impact), where it led to doing away with the necessity of statistical proof. Only few academic writers seem to agree with such an approach (e.g. Puissochet).[2056] In contrast, Hanau & Preis[2057] had argued long before *Schnorbus* that a condition relating to

---

[2056] Puissochet 2002, p. 21: '[...] the court had no difficulty in recognising that the law of Land Hessen was favourable to men and thus constituted indirect discrimination based on sex.' Puissochet was Judge Rapporteur at the Court of Justice in this very case.

[2057] Hanau & Preis 1988, p. 171.

military service should *not* be seen as a case of indirect but instead of 'pretended' (*vorgeschobene*) sex discrimination, a concept strictly to be distinguished from indirect discrimination. They explained that an employer by the very use of such a criterion shows that only men are aimed at. Similarly, Bieback[2058] considers that if a criterion is exclusively linked factually or legally to one sex, the application of the rules on direct sex discrimination is justified; he explicitly mentions military service (see also Steiner,[2059] Tobler).[2060] The Court's *reasons* for refusing to find direct sex discrimination are not clear. Veldman[2061] argues that it is due to the Court's having taken the category of hardship cases as a whole as a basis for its analysis (rather than only compulsory military or civil service), but in the present writer's view that was not in fact the Court's focus.

> Veldman refers to para. 32 of the judgment, arguing that in the framework of such a 'package analysis', a finding of *direct* discrimination is not possible because the hardship package does not as a whole distinguish between men and women. However, the Court's reference to the *Grant* case[2062] (which clearly concerned a single differentiation ground) does not seem to support that view. If the package approach were indeed the point the Court wished to make, it would have been more logical to refer to a precedent like *Rummler*[2063] (where the Court based its analysis on a group of elements for a job classification system rather than on the one specific element contested by the plaintiff).[2064] But more importantly, when the Court in *Schnorbus* considered *indirect* discrimination, it did not assess the effect of the hardship package as a whole but very clearly only the aspect of the specific case of military service (as did AG Jacobs when elaborating on 'a characteristic indissociable from sex'). It would have been inconsistent to examine an individual criterion in the context of indirect discrimination after first having rejected direct discrimination on the basis of a package approach.[2065] The present writer would therefore conclude that the Court's analysis of the *Schnorbus* case is based on the *individual* differentiation ground of compulsory military or civil service.[2066]

[2058] Bieback 1997, p. 76.

[2059] Steiner 1999, p. 88.

[2060] Tobler 2001 (Schnorbus), p. 239.

[2061] Veldman 2001, p. 119.

[2062] Case C-249/96, [1998] *ECR* I-621.

[2063] Case 237/85, [1986] *ECR* 2101.

[2064] In that particular context, this approach is dictated by Art. 1 of the Equal Pay Directive (Directive 75/117/EEC, *OJ* 1975 L 45/19); see above Part 2, A.IV.2.f.

[2065] See also the later case *Griesmar* (Case C-366/99, [2001] *ECR* I-9383), which concerned the possibility of receiving benefits in the framework of a French pension system and where AG Alber made some statements concerning the system as a whole which he compared with that at issue in *Schnorbus* (*Griesmar*, point 65 of the AG's opinion).

[2066] It should be added that this assessment concerns simply the Court's approach as it appears from the judgment. Obviously, where an entire system is at issue, that system also has to be assessed as a whole in order to determine whether it is discriminatory. Such an evaluation would have to check whether factors that are specifically female (such as maternity) are taken into account as well.

It seems more likely (or at least possible) that the Court, in determining whether the approach for direct rather than for indirect sex discrimination was proper, opted for the approach suggested by the Advocate General. With his reference to *characteristics indissociable from sex* in the context of direct sex discrimination, it appears that AG Jacobs took the same view as had Govers.[2067] The AG limited his consideration of 'characteristics indissociable from sex' to cases involving *physical* characteristics based on nature and inherent in one sex alone, to the exclusion of criteria imposed by the law, which could be easily be changed.[2068] However, in the present writer's view the argument that the negative effect of a criterion imposed by the law can be removed by changing the law is unconvincing: if it is easy to do away with such discrimination, it is also easy to bring it about. Also, the fact alone that a change of law is possible in theory does not help as long as the relevant Member State is not obliged to change the law (and actually changes it). Instead, it is submitted that a measure's effect should be decisive. The present writer would therefore agree with the approach advocated by Hanau & Preis and Bieback according to which there is direct discrimination if a criterion is exclusively linked factually *or* legally to one group.

> It might be added that in the specific case of *Schnorbus* the problem of determining whether direct or indirect discrimination is present could have been avoided if the Court had clearly based its final finding (that there is no discrimination) on the lack of comparability, as was appropriate in this case. As it stands, the Court's statement that a rule of the type at issue 'takes account of the delay experienced in the progress of their education by applicants who have been required to do military service or civilian service, is objective in nature and prompted solely by the desire to counterbalance to some extent the effects of that delay' (*Schnorbus*, para. 44) remains unclear. It is a matter of objective justification as relied on by AG Jacobs or of positive action as expressly inquired after by the national court or perhaps even of unspecified objective differences? In the present writer's view, a solution on the basis of comparability is the most convincing.[2069] Given that, from a conceptual point of view, comparability needs to be dealt with before addressing the nature of the alleged discrimination, there would have been no need to go into the subtle and perhaps theoretical dividing line between direct and indirect discrimination and the Court's problematic and unclear statements on this issue could have been avoided.

[2067] Govers 1981, p. 27.

[2068] In a different context, AG Cosmas argued that direct discrimination can also arise due to social circumstances; *Wiener Gebietskrankenkasse* (Case C-309/97, [1999] *ECR* I-2865), point 63 of the AG's opinion. The AG interprets the Court's finding in *Jenkins* (Case 96/80, [1981] *ECR* 911) as being based on a fact known from general experience, namely the difficulties of women to engage in full-time work. The AG explains that discrimination relating to such a fact may, formally, appear to be indirect discrimination, but in fact is rather a form of direct discrimination because membership of the occupational group in question is determined at the outset on the basis of sex. Note that the German version of the judgment refers to *social* determination ('da die betreffende Berufsgruppe sozial durch das Geschlecht festgelegt ist').

[2069] The temporary setbacks that only women can suffer are connected to childbearing, an aspect that was not at issue in the *Schnorbus* case.

d. An interim conclusion (I)

The previous sections discussed the differences between the concepts of direct and indirect discrimination on the conceptual level in terms of the measures' effects. It was seen that under the Court's case law the effect of direct and indirectly discrimination can be similar or even the same. Perhaps this should not be surprising given that previously the General Programmes on free movement in the areas of establishment[2070] and services[2071] had referred to 'requirements that are applicable irrespective of nationality but have the effect of *exclusively* or principally excluding foreigners' (emphasis added). Similarly, Lenaerts & Nuffel[2072] define indirect discrimination as arising 'where, although not making use of an unlawful distinguishing criterion, a provision has effects *coinciding with* or approaching those of such distinguishing criterion as a result of its use of other distinguishing criteria which are not as such prohibited' (emphasis added). However, if the effect of indirect discrimination can be precisely the same as that of direct discrimination, then it is not clear why there should be differences on the level of justification.[2073] It is therefore preferable to draw a dividing line between the two concepts on the level of their effect, based on the principle that substance prevails over form. Veldman[2074] proposes the following: First, if the ground formally relied on is prohibited in itself, then the case involves direct discrimination, independently of the intentions of the discriminator (who in fact may wish to discriminate on a different ground than the one apparently relied on, like in the *Dan Air* case mentioned by Harrison).[2075] Secondly, if the ground relied on is not prohibited as such, it needs to be checked whether the case involves the exceptional situation where it is not possible to distinguish between this ground and that of sex, such as in the case of pregnancy. If that is the case, the conclusion should still be that there is direct discrimination. Thirdly, if that is not the case but there is a disparate impact concerning a prohibited criterion, this means that there is *prima facie* indirect discrimination. In the present writer's view, that approach is useful as a starting point, with the addition that the second element of this test should be modified so that once

---

[2070] General Programme for the abolition of restrictions on freedom of establishment, *OJ* English Special Edition, Second Series, IX, p. 7.

[2071] General Programme for the abolition of restrictions on freedom to provide services; *OJ* English Special Edition, Second Series, IX, p. 3.

[2072] Lenaerts & Van Nuffel 1999, p. 118.

[2073] Assuming that indeed there is such a difference; see further immediately below.

[2074] Veldman 1998, pp. 2 subs.

[2075] Harrison 1996, p. 271. In this Danish case, the air carrier *Dan Air* limited the recruitment of cabin personnel to women, arguing that male applicants tended to be homosexual and that this could lead to a health risk in the case of an air accident. Harrison does not further explain the nature of the alleged health risk (possibly HIV infection?). In the case at issue medical evidence was produced showing that there was no such risk. Harrison notes that such a situation involves direct discrimination on grounds of sex and, possibly (that is, depending on the factual composition of the group of male applicants), also indirect discrimination on grounds of sexual orientation.

a criterion, though formally neutral, has in fact the effect of favouring *all* persons of one group and/or of disadvantaging *all* persons of the other group, it must be understood as leading to *direct* discrimination.

3. JUSTIFICATION

a. Introductory remarks

Having examined the differences between the legal concepts of direct and indirect discrimination in terms of the effect of the prohibited measures, the next point to be discussed is justification. The traditional assumption (and, in the words of O'Leary & Fernández Martín,[2076] 'the theory imbibed by students of EC law since the latter part of the 1980s') is that in the case of direct discrimination only justification grounds expressly mentioned in the law can be relied on, whilst in the case of indirect discrimination there is the additional and open category of objective justification (e.g. Blom,[2077] Craig & de Búrca,[2078] Barnard,[2079] Hervey,[2080] Burri,[2081] Borchardt;[2082] compare also Jarass).[2083] As far as direct discrimination is concerned, this view is reflected in the Court's ruling in *Bond van Adverteerders* (para. 32)[2084] where it is stated that 'national rules which are not applicable to services without distinction as regards their origin and which are therefore discriminatory are compatible with Community law only if they can be brought within the scope of an express derogation'. In this context, the system with relation to justification is therefore a *closed* one. In contrast, objective justification in the context of indirect discrimination operates in an *open* system. The range of possible justification grounds for justification is by definition wider than the specific justification grounds expressly mentioned in Community non-discrimination law and, therefore, can be seen as a form of extra-textual justification.[2085] The following sections examine the question of to what extent the traditionally perceived dividing line is a strict one. Two specific issues emerge in this context. First, is the system indeed a closed one as far as direct discrimination is concerned? Second, is the concept of objective justification, as typically understood in the context of indirect discrimination,

---

[2076] O'Leary & Fernández Martín 2002, p. 164.
[2077] Blom 1992, p. 55.
[2078] Craig & de Búrca 2003, p. 720.
[2079] Barnard 2000, pp. 127 and 213; also Barnard 2004, in particular p. 235.
[2080] Hervey 2002, p. 105.
[2081] Burri 2000, pp. 119 and 211.
[2082] Borchardt 2002, p. 301, n. 683.
[2083] Jarass 2000 (Unified Approach), pp. 154 subs.
[2084] Case 352/85, [1988] *ECR* 2085.
[2085] That is, if its function is understood to relate to justification rather than to causation; on this issue, see above Part 2, A.IV.3.e.

indeed limited to that situation (or may it also apply to cases of direct discrimination)?[2086]

b. Is there extra-textual justification for direct discrimination?

Obviously, the question whether extra-textual justification is possible is particularly urgent in cases where a non-discrimination provision does not mention justification at all, in other words where a particular provision is absolutely worded.[2087] The examples discussed below are Arts. 34(2), 90(1) and 12(1) EC. In the context of provisions that do mention justification grounds (relatively worded provisions) only direct taxation and sex discrimination outside equal pay will be examined. The principle of equal pay for men and women is discussed separately due to the fact that the question of whether it should be seen as absolutely or as relatively worded is debated.

i.   Absolutely worded provisions: Arts. 34(2), 90(1) and 12 EC as examples

As far as absolutely worded provisions are concerned, there is only one area where case law clearly accepts the possibility of justification, namely *Art. 34(2) EC* (agricultural law; Usher,[2088] Gerards).[2089] In *Denkavit*[2090] (para. 17), the Court ruled that a difference in treatment in the field of agriculture does not amount to prohibited discrimination if it 'corresponds to the needs of the market in question and the requirements of the common market organization'. In *Sermide*[2091] (para. 28), the Court explained more generally that non-discrimination in agricultural law means that comparable situations must not be treated differently and different situations must not be treated in the same way 'unless such treatment is objectively justified'. In practice, this means that there is discrimination within the meaning of Art. 34(2) EC only if the difference in treatment is manifestly unjustified or arbitrary (Plender;[2092] see also Martin).[2093] According to Barents,[2094] justification in this context is so closely linked to proportionality that the latter is really the only test to be applied. In the context of Art. 34(2) EC, therefore, the Court accepts the possibility of justification in spite of the fact that the

---

[2086]   Meaning within the discrimination framework; on objective justification and restrictions in a wider sense, see below B.
[2087]   See above Part 1, B.III.6.c.
[2088]   Usher 2001, p. 42.
[2089]   Gerards 2002, pp. 239 subs.
[2090]   Case 35/80, [1981] *ECR* 45.
[2091]   Case 106/83, [1984] *ECR* 4209.
[2092]   Plender 1995, p. 76.
[2093]   Martin 1998, pp. 268/269.
[2094]   Barents 1994 (Agricultural Law), pp. 224 and 336, also 537.

provision itself does not mention it (see Tridimas,[2095] Schwarze,[2096] Gerards,[2097] the von der Groeben & Schwarze Commentary).[2098] Technically, the Court achieved this by modelling its interpretation of Art. 34(2) EC after the Community's general equality principle where an element of justification is part of the principle's very definition.[2099] It is said that the Court's choice for this approach can most likely be explained by the special characteristics of agriculture as an area of wide discretion particularly with regard to the Commission. This feature is often emphasised by academic writers. Blumann[2100] points to the increasing diversity and disparity of situations in this particular field, and Barents[2101] points to the interventionist nature of EC agricultural policy. Gencarelli[2102] even speaks about a specific and typical meaning of equality in the context of agricultural law ('quasiment un principe d'égalité typique du droit agricole communautaire'), which allows for different treatment leading to negative repercussions if in the interest of legal certainty and the effectiveness of the regulation at issue.

There is *no case law of comparable clarity with regard to other absolutely worded provisions.* Accordingly, various interpretations of the Court's case law in other areas abound. For example, the Grabitz & Hilf Commentary[2103] considers that economic, social or environmental aims provide possible justification grounds for different treatment in the context of *Art. 90(1) EC* concerning the internal taxation of goods.[2104] In contrast, Craig & de Búrca[2105] and Barnard[2106] insist that justification is possible only in the case of indirect but not in that of direct discrimination (the latter citing *Commission v France,*[2107] para. 33, where the Court refused to accept arguments related to public health, pointing out that Art. 30 EC cannot be relied on in the context of Art. 90(1) EC). However, other academic commentators seem to ignore the issue altogether (e.g. the von der Groeben & Schwarze Commentary)[2108] or mention only very specific case law dealing with acceptable measures outside the context of justification in the

---

[2095] Tridimas 1999, pp. 53 subs.
[2096] Schwarze Commentary 2000, n. 71 ad Art. 34 EC.
[2097] Gerards 2002, pp. 239 subs.
[2098] Von der Groeben & Schwarze Commentary 2004, n. 54 ad Art. 34 EC.
[2099] See above Part 1, B.II.1.c.
[2100] Blumann 1996, p. 123.
[2101] Barents 1994 (The Significance), p. 537, and Barents 1994 (Agricultural Law), pp. 224 and 336.
[2102] Gencarelli 2001, p. 671.
[2103] Grabitz & Hilf Commentary (as of 1989), n. 33-35 ad Art. 90 EC.
[2104] The Schwarze Commentary mentions such issues in the context of comparability; n. 11 ad Art. 90 EC.
[2105] Craig & de Búrca 2003, pp. 596 subs.
[2106] Barnard 2004, p. 52.
[2107] Case C-302/00, [2002] I-2055.
[2108] Von der Groeben & Schwarze Commentary 2004, ad Art. 90 EC.

proper sense (e.g. Kapteyn & VerLoren van Themaat,[2109] for example in relation to 'parafiscal' charges).[2110]

The picture is similarly unclear as far as the Treaty's general provision on discrimination on grounds of nationality, *Art. 12(1) EC* (originally Art. 7(1), later Art. 6(1) of the Treaty), is concerned. Tridimas[2111] argues that if no exceptions were permitted, it would follow that the residual content of Art. 12 would be wider than the specific provisions of the Treaty prohibiting discrimination on grounds of nationality. Such an interpretation he considers unjustified, adding that the very notion of discrimination suggests difference in treatment without good justification[2112] (see also e.g. the von der Groeben & Schwarze Commentary,[2113] Epiney,[2114] Kapteyn & VerLoren van Themaat,[2115] Kischel).[2116] Others insist that there is no possibility of justification under Art. 12(1) EC (e.g. the Grabitz & Hilf Commentary,[2117] Feige,[2118] the Mégret Commentary,[2119] Blomeyer,[2120] Dony,[2121] the Schwarze Commentary;[2122] for an overview on the pros and cons see Rossi).[2123] According to Plötscher,[2124] the problem with this debate lies in the fact that most writers are not sufficiently clear about the meaning of the legal concept of discrimination on which they rely. In particular, a provision that does not explicitly mention justification grounds may nevertheless contain that element if discrimination as such is defined as 'unjustified different treatment' (as advocated by him). This point leads back to the debate on the function of objective justification (justification or causation). As was noted in that context,[2125] in the present writer's view objective justification should not be seen as a matter of

---

[2109] Kapteyn & VerLoren van Themaat 2003, pp. 517 subs.

[2110] See further the Lenz & Borchardt Commentary 2003, n. 26 subs. ad Art. 90 EC; and Demaret 2000, pp. 175 and 181 subs.

[2111] Tridimas 1999, p. 79.

[2112] Gerards 2002, pp. 226, 264 subs. and 305, also speaks of the possibility of justification in the context of Art. 12(1) EC but by that means the possibilities of relying on objective differences. In the present writer's analysis, the example mentioned by this author, *Hayes and Hayes* (Case C-323/95, [1997] *ECR* I-1711) concerns the comparability of the cases.

[2113] Von der Groeben & Schwarze Commentary 2004, n. 3 ad Art. 12 EC.

[2114] Epiney 1995, pp. 94 subs.

[2115] Kapteyn & VerLoren van Themaat 2003, pp. 134 subs.

[2116] Kischel 1997, p. 5.

[2117] Grabitz & Hilf Commentary (as of 1989), n. 7 and 22 ad Art. 6 of the EC Treaty.

[2118] Feige 1973, pp. 44 subs.

[2119] Mégret Commentary (as of 1972), p. 49, n. 71.

[2120] Blomeyer 1994, p. 95.

[2121] Dony 1999, pp. 53/54.

[2122] Schwarze Commentary 2000, n. 52 subs. ad Art. 12(1) EC. The Commentary refers to *Saldanha* (Case C-122/96, [1997] *ECR* I-5325). Here, the Court, when faced with the defendant's justification arguments, simply stated that the rule at issue did discriminate on grounds of nationality (*Saldanha*, para. 29).

[2123] Rossi 2000, p. 212.

[2124] Plötscher 2003, pp. 68 and 130 subs.

[2125] See above Part. 2, A.IV.3.e.ii.

causation but rather of justification proper. In that framework, the above debate remains valid and there appear to be no easy answers.

ii. Relatively worded provisions: the example of direct taxation

The question of justification poses itself differently in the context of provisions that explicitly provide for derogation possibilities. As a general principle, these have to be interpreted restrictively; in particular, the list of grounds cannot be extended (e.g. *van Duyn*,[2126] para. 18 and *Orfanopoulos*,[2127] para. 65, both regarding free movement of workers where the requirements are particularly strict; *Kapper*,[2128] para. 72, in relation to provisions of Directives; in a very general sense *Changzhou Hailong Electronics*,[2129] para. 39; see also Schilling).[2130] Whilst in practice the principle of narrow interpretation is not always applied in a consistent manner (e.g. *Van Duyn, Hofmann*,[2131] *Sirdar*),[2132] as far as the present writer is able to see there is only one specific context where the Court was willing to openly[2133] deviate from the closed system and to accept extra-textual justification, namely that of direct taxation (Hatzopoloulos).[2134] The first relevant statement can be found in *Avoir fiscal*[2135] (para. 19), where the Court remarked in a general sense that 'the possibility cannot altogether be excluded that a distinction based on the location of the registered office of a company or the place of residence of a natural person may, under certain conditions, be justified in an area such as tax law'. That is not surprising in the context of natural persons because here it relates to indirect discrimination on grounds of nationality with its open element of objective justification. However, in the case of companies such a possibility constitutes direct discrimination and must be read as relating to extra-textual justification (Wouters,[2136]

[2126] Case 41/74, [1974] *ECR* 1337.

[2127] Joined Cases C-482/01 and C-493/01, judgment of 29 April 2004, n.y.r. In this case, the Court emphasised that the status of EU citizen requires a particularly strict interpretation of the derogations to free movement of workers.

[2128] Case C-476/01, judgment of 29 April 2004, n.y.r.

[2129] Case T-255/01, judgment of 23 October 2003, n.y.r. In this case, the Court of First Instance stated very generally that 'any derogation from or exception to a general rule must be interpreted strictly'.

[2130] Schilling 1996.

[2131] Case 184/83, [1984] *ECR* 3047.

[2132] Case C-273/97, [1999] *ECR* I-7403.

[2133] Some authors think that the Court sometimes implicitly deviates from the principle, namely when it considers in substance excuses that are not mentioned in the law in the context of direct discrimination, even if only to reject them (e.g. Wouters 1999, p. 104, concerning *Bosman* (Case C-415/93, [1995] *ECR* I-4921). In the present writer's view, such an approach is not by itself sufficient indication for a deviation from the principle; compare Tobler 2001 (Rechtvaardiging), p. 124.

[2134] Hatzopoulos 1996, p. 584, writes that with regard to the closed justification system, 'there has been admitted one single exception in relation to tax measures'.

[2135] Case 270/83, [1986] *ECR* 273.

[2136] Wouters 1999, p. 104.

see also Thömmes).[2137] In later taxation cases, the Court held that the need to safeguard the cohesion of a tax system might justify rules that are liable to restrict fundamental freedoms. This was first stated in the context of *indirect* tax discrimination (*Bachmann*),[2138] but later confirmed more generally (*Metallgesellschaft*, para. 67).[2139] Though in practice the Court rarely accepts the cohesion of the tax system as justification against the background of particular cases, on the level of principle it still has life.

It has been noted that the concept of the cohesion of the tax system is complex (Thömmes:[2140] 'einen der schillerndsten Begriffe, die das europäische Steuerrecht bislang hervorgebracht hat'). In fact, it is rarely accepted by the Court in concrete circumstances. Other than in *Bachmann* and in *Commission v Belgium*,[2141] the Court always found that the necessary direct link of the contested measure with the cohesion of the tax system was missing.[2142] Terra & Wattel[2143] speak about 'downsizing of the fiscal cohesion justification' (see also Wattel,[2144] Van de Wetering,[2145] Binon,[2146] Wernsmann).[2147] The exception seems to stand in spite some uncertainty as to whether it was overruled by *Svensson and Gustavsson*.[2148] In para. 15 of that decision, the Court stated that the discrimination found could only be justified on the basis of express derogations, which do not include economic justification. This has been interpreted as indicating a clear departure from the *Bachmann* case law by Hatzopoulos.[2149] At the same time, he concludes from the fact that the Court continued by specifically distinguishing the *Bachmann* type of case from the factual situation under examination that it did not mean to completely overrule *Bachmann* (see also Thömmes).[2150]

Against this background, AG Léger explained that national discriminatory rules 'may, despite such discrimination, be justified for overriding reasons of public interest. The exceptions to the principle of non-discrimination laid down by that article [Art. 39 EC] are not merely those referred to in paragraphs 3 and 4 thereof. The Court thus

---

[2137] Thömmes 1997, pp. 802, 805 subs. and 818 subs.
[2138] Case C-204/90, [1992] *ECR* I-249, see above Part 2, A.II.4.b.i.
[2139] Joined Cases C-397/98 and C-410/98, [2001] *ECR* I-1727.
[2140] Thömmes 1997, p. 826.
[2141] Case C-300/90, [1992] *ECR* I-305.
[2142] In all other cases, the Court found that the required direct link did not exist; see *Weidert & Paulus* (Case C-242/03, judgment of 15 July 2004, n.y.r.), para. 20 subs.
[2143] Terra & Wattel 2001, p. 71.
[2144] Wattel 1996, pp. 241 subs., and Wattel 1997, pp. 425 and 427 subs.
[2145] Van de Wetering 1996.
[2146] Binon 1996.
[2147] Wernsmann 1999, pp. 763 subs. According to this author, the cohesion of the national tax systems should in fact not be able to serve as a justification ground because the necessary link will always be missing.
[2148] Case C-484/93, [1995] *ECR* I-3955.
[2149] Hatzopoulos 1996, p. 585.
[2150] See also Thömmes 1997, p. 828.

applies the 'rule of reason' to discriminatory tax rules intended to temper the effects of bringing within the scope of Articles 48 and 52 national rules which apply without distinction and prevent or hamper the free movement of workers' (*Schumacker*,[2151] points 44 subs. of the AG's opinion). The conclusion must be that, in the specific context of direct taxation, there is a possibility of extra-textual justification. At the same time, the Court's reference to 'an area such as tax law' indicates that the special approach in this area is due to its specific features, notably the importance of the criterion of residence in international taxation, as mentioned earlier.[2152]

iii. Relatively worded provisions: the example of sex discrimination in areas other than pay

In the context of other relatively worded provisions, there is no equally explicit case law as that concerning direct taxation. Accordingly, the matter is much debated, in particular in the context of sex discrimination where the Equal Treatment Directives on issues other than pay[2153] provide for certain possibilities of different treatment.[2154] In his opinion on the *Birds Eye Walls*[2155] case (points 12 subs.), AG van Gerven famously suggested that there should be possibilities of extra-textual justification for direct sex discrimination.[2156] The Court, however, found that the situations at issue in *Birds Eye Walls* were not comparable[2157] and therefore did not address the issue. According to Veldman,[2158] the Court's *avoidance strategy* in this case as well as in *Helmig*[2159] comes down to accepting justification for direct sex discrimination. In contrast, Ellis[2160] thinks that the approach in *Helmig* shows the Court's 'real dislike of the argument that direct discrimination can be justified'.

[2151] Case C-279/93, [1995] *ECR* I-225.

[2152] See above Part 3, A.I.5.b.

[2153] Directive 76/207/EEC, *OJ* 1976, L 39/40 (Second Equal Treatment Directive, as revised by Directive 2002/73/EC, *OJ* 2002 L 269/15); Directive 79/7/EEC, *OJ* 1979 L 6/24 (Third Equal Treatment Directive); Directive 86/378/EEC, *OJ* 1986 L 225/40 (Fourth Equal Treatment Directive, subsequently revised by Directive 96/97/EC, *OJ* 1997 L 46/20) and Directive 86/613/EEC, *OJ* 1986 L 359/56 (Fifth Equal Treatment Directive). – Pay equality will be discussed in the following section.

[2154] On the nature of such possibilities, see above Part 1, B.III.6.b.

[2155] Case C-132/92, [1993] *ECR* I-5579.

[2156] See also the same AG's remarks in *Smith* (Case C-408/92, [1994] *ECR* I-4435), points 17 and 18. According to Hepple 1994, p. 48, the AG repeated this argument also in his opinion on the *Neath* case (Case C-152/91, [1993] *ECR* I-6935). However, in the present writer's view, the AG's statements in that context relate to objective differences rather than to objective justification; see Tobler 2001 (Rechtvaardiging), p. 125, footnote 37.

[2157] See above Part 1, B.I.2.b.ii.

[2158] Veldman 1996, p. 36.

[2159] Joined Cases C-399/92, C-409/92, C-425/92, C-34/93, C-50/93 & C-78/93, [1994] *ECR* I-5727; see above Part 2, A.IV.4.c.ii.

[2160] Ellis 1994 (Definition of Discrimination), p. at 569.

In the particular context of pregnancy and discrimination,[2161] the academic debate essentially centers around two cases, *Habermann-Beltermann*[2162] and *Webb*[2163] (in fact, AG van Gerven referred to the circumstances of this latter case, then pending, when in his opinion on the *Birds Eye Walls* case he suggested that there should be a possibility of justification for direct sex discrimination). In *Habermann-Beltermann* (para. 25) the Court held that 'termination of a contract for an indefinite period on grounds of the woman' s pregnancy, whether by annulment or avoidance, cannot be justified by the fact that she is temporarily prevented, by a statutory prohibition imposed because of pregnancy, from performing night-time work'. In *Webb* (para. 27), the Court held that '[i]n circumstances such as those of Mrs Webb, termination of a contract for an indefinite period on grounds of the woman' s pregnancy cannot be justified by the fact that she is prevented, on a purely temporary basis, from performing the work for which she has been engaged'. The weight given by the Court to the limited duration of the worker's unavailability was read by many as leaving open the possibility of justification based on the unavailability of the worker concerned, at least for temporary employment contracts (e.g. Veldman,[2164] Fenwick & Hervey,[2165] Drijber & Prechal,[2166] Ellis,[2167] Arnull,[2168] Vegter).[2169] However, since then the Court's decision in *Tele Danmark*[2170] has made clear that this is not the case (*Tele Danmark*, para. 28, referring to *Dekker*[2171] and *Mahlburg*).[2172] According to AG Ruiz-Jarabo Colomer, the erroneous interpretation by some authors of the Court's case law on pregnancy discrimination before *Tele Danmark* is due to their being 'overly-faithful to the exact words used by the Court' (*Tele Danmark*, point 27 of the AG's opinion).[2173] Whether the Court's denial of extra-textual justification is limited to the specific issue at hand in *Tele Danmark* (namely the unavailability of workers because of *pregnancy*) or whether it reflects a general attitude by the Court concerning extra-textual justification for direct sex discrimination, remains to be seen.

[2161]   Regarding the qualification of discrimination on grounds of pregnancy as direct sex discrimination, see earlier in this part, A.III.3.a.

[2162]   Case C-421/92, [1994] *ECR* I-1657.

[2163]   Case C-32/93, [1994] *ECR* I-3567.

[2164]   Veldman 1995, pp. 181 subs.

[2165]   Fenwick & Hervey 1995, p. 452.

[2166]   Drijber & Prechal 1997, p. 133.

[2167]   Ellis 1998, pp. 135 subs.

[2168]   Arnull 1999, p. 497.

[2169]   Vegter 2000, p. 119.

[2170]   Case C-109/00, [2001] *ECR* I-6993.

[2171]   Case C-177/88, [1990] *ECR* I-3941.

[2172]   Case C-207/98, [2000] *ECR* I-549.

[2173]   This confirms the opinion expressed earlier by the present author; Tobler 2001 (Rechtvaardiging), p. 124.

iv. A special case: equal pay for work of equal value

As was noted earlier,[2174] it is debated whether the principle of equal pay for men and women in its present form under Art. 141 EC is to be regarded as absolutely or as relatively worded. After the Treaty revision of Amsterdam, which introduced Art. 141(4) EC on positive action, this issue depends on whether that latter section is seen as a derogation or rather as an equality provision in itself. In any case, positive action aside, neither Art. 141(1) nor (2) EC mention any justification grounds. At least to that extent they are worded in an absolute manner. However, even in that narrower framework the question of whether justification for direct sex discrimination should nevertheless be possible is hotly debated. According to some academic writers, it is open in so far as there is no explicit decision by the Court of Justice on the matter (see Burri,[2175] Meyer).[2176] Some are in favour of justification (e.g. Steiner,[2177] Rating,[2178] the Calliess & Ruffert Commentary,[2179] Kischel,[2180] Meyer,[2181] Epiney & Freiermuth Abt).[2182] In contrast, Ellis[2183] is vehemently opposed, both for practical and conceptual reasons, and Hepple[2184] even speaks about 'a dangerous heresy'.

In the present writer's view, case law such as *Abdoulaye*[2185] (para. 16), *Mouflin*[2186] (para. 28) and *Evrenopoulos*[2187] (para. 26 subs.) appear to indicate that the Court is *not* willing to accept extra-textual justification: if the Court accepts different treatment in this area, it is because of a lack of comparability rather than because of justification in the proper sense.[2188] In *Evrenopoulos* (para. 26-28), which concerned widower's pensions, the Court held explicitly that 'Article 119 prohibits any discrimination in matters of pay as between men and women, whatever the system which gives rise to such inequality [...]. It is clear from the documents before the court in the main proceedings that the provision at issue directly discriminates against men in that the award to a widower of a pension falling within the meaning of 'pay' as used in Article 119 is subject to specific conditions, which are not applied to widows. Clearly, there

---

[2174] See above Part 1, B.III.6.c.
[2175] Burri 2000, p. 297, footnote 344.
[2176] Meyer 2002, p. 95.
[2177] Steiner 1983, p. 413, see also p. 421.
[2178] Rating 1994, p. 97.
[2179] Calliess & Ruffert Commentary 2002, n. 61 and 64 ad Art. 141 EC.
[2180] Kischel 1997, p. 4.
[2181] Meyer 2002, p. 97.
[2182] Epiney & Freiermuth Abt 2003, pp. 86 subs.; also Epiney & Freiermuth Abt 2004, p. 63.
[2183] Ellis 1998, p. 136.
[2184] Hepple 1994, p. 48, see also Hepple 1997, p. 145.
[2185] Case C-218/98, [1999] *ECR* I-5723.
[2186] Case C-206/00, [2001] *ECR* I-10201.
[2187] Case C-147/95, [1997] *ECR* I-2057.
[2188] The present writer would therefore not agree with Gerards 2002, p. 250, according to whom the Court in the context of sex equality law almost never relies on the element of comparability.

is no rule of Community law under which the maintenance in force of such a discriminatory provision could be justified.'

Admittedly, certain statements by the Court are difficult to place in this framework. For example, in *Brunnhofer*[2189] the Court seems to mention objective justification in the context of direct pay discrimination. However, in the present writer's analysis this must be read as relating to objective differences rather than to objective justification in its proper sense.[2190] In *Brunnhofer*, the Court stated that the principle of equal treatment for men and women 'prohibits comparable situations from being treated differently unless the difference is objectively justified' and that 'the fundamental principle laid down in Article 119 of the Treaty [...] precludes unequal pay as between men and women for the same job or work of equal value, whatever the mechanism which produces such inequality [...], unless the difference in pay is justified by objective factors unrelated to any discrimination linked to the difference in sex' (*Brunnhofer*, para. 28 and 30). In this context, the Court referred to both comparability and objective justification. Regarding the former, the Court explained (*Brunnhofer*, para. 60): 'If the plaintiff in the main proceedings adduced evidence to show that the criteria for establishing the existence of a difference in pay between a woman and a man and for identifying comparable work are satisfied in this case, *a prima facie case of discrimination* would exist and it would then be for the employer to prove that there was no breach of the principle of equal pay.' (Emphasis added.) The Court mentioned two ways through which the employer might establish that no such breach occurred: first, by a simple counter-proof (*Brunnhofer*, para. 61) and, second, by showing the existence of 'objective factors unrelated to any discrimination based on sex, by proving that there was a *difference*, unrelated to sex, to explain the payment of a higher monthly supplement to the chosen comparator' (*Brunnhofer*, para. 62, emphasis added). In the context of objective justification, the Court again stated that pay differences can be justified 'by objective factors unrelated to any discrimination based on sex' (*Brunnhofer*, para. 65 subs.). The Court here referred to precedents concerning *indirect* discrimination, which may seem confusing. In the present writer's view, this may be explained by the fact that certain 'objective factors' that are often dealt with by the Court in the context of objective justification for indirect discrimination (such as professional training) in reality reflect objective differences (as expressly recognised by the Court in *Wiener Gebietskrankenkasse*,[2191] para. 19). Read in this way, it is not

---

[2189] Case C-381/99, [2001] *ECR* I-4961; compare also the AG's remarks in *Lawrence* (Case C-320/00, [2002] *ECR* I-7325), point 56 of the AG's opinion.

[2190] On the confusion in terminology in the Court's case law regarding these two issues, see above Part 2, II.2.b.

[2191] Case C-309/97, [1999] *ECR* I-2865. In this case, which concerned indirect discrimination, the Court recalled that 'discrimination involves the application of different rules to comparable situations or the application of the same rule to different situations' and then referred to a number of factors relevant in this context, such as the nature of the work, the training requirements and the working conditions (*Wiener Gebietskrankenkasse*, para. 15 and 17). This is noteworthy because, in indirect discrimination cases, such elements traditionally appear in the context of objective justification, while here they are placed in the context of comparability. In para. 19, the Court remarked: 'As Advocate General Cosmas stated at point 32(c) of his Opinion, professional training is not merely one of the factors that may be an objective justification for giving different pay for doing the same work [...];

surprising that these same factors can also be relevant in the context of direct discrimination and consequently their presence does not indicate an availability of extra-textual justification proper.

c. A new legislative approach

More recently, the question of the extent to which broad justification possibilities exist also for direct discrimination arises on the level of the written law since in certain non-discrimination legislation objective justification is explicitly mentioned as a justification ground. Below, three examples are discussed, the Fixed-Term Work Directive,[2192] the Part-Time Work Directive[2193] and the provisions on age discrimination in the General Framework Directive,[2194] all of which are linked to issues of sex discrimination.[2195]

i. The example of the Part-Time Work Directive

In the Part-Time Work Directive,[2196] Clause 4(1) of the Framework Agreement attached to the Directive provides that '[i]n respect of employment conditions, part-time workers shall not be treated in a less favourable manner than comparable full-time workers solely because they work part time unless different treatment is justified

---

it is also one of the possible criteria for determining whether or not the same work is being performed.' See also point 33 of the AG's opinion (though note that in the English version the last sentence contains a translation mistake; as other language versions show, the Advocate General here means to refer to employees of the different groups which perform duties of the *same* (rather than of a different) nature or purpose).

[2192] Directive 1999/70/EC, *OJ* 1999 L 175/43.

[2193] Directive 97/81/EC, *OJ* 1998, L 14/9 (as amended).

[2194] Directive 2000/78/EC, *OJ* 2000 L 303/16.

[2195] A general reference to justification based on objective reasons can also be found in Art. 5(1) of the Commission's Proposal for a Directive on working conditions for temporary workers (COM(2002) 149 fin.) where Art. 5(1) provides: 'Temporary workers during their posting, shall receive at least as favourable treatment, in terms of basic working and employment conditions, including seniority in the job, as a comparable worker in the user enterprise, unless the difference in treatment is justified by objective reasons. Where appropriate, the *pro rata temporis* principle applies.' In this context, the link with indirect sex discrimination is somewhat less obvious. As the Commission explains in its Explanatory Memorandum, '[t]he situation with regard to equality for men and women varies greatly depending on the Member State. In some countries, mainly those where temporary work is most common in industry, construction and public works, such as Austria (87%), Germany (80%), France (74%), Luxembourg (77%), Spain (62%) and Belgium (60%), the sector is dominated by men. In other countries, such as the Netherlands, Portugal and the United Kingdom, there is a fair balance between the sexes. In Finland and in Sweden, however, women are very much in the majority, accounting for some 80% of all temporary workers' (point 2.3., see also point 2 of the impact assessment form).

[2196] Directive 97/81/EC, *OJ* 1998, L 14/9 (as amended).

on objective grounds'.[2197] In that context, it needs to be remembered that prior to the existence of the Directive discrimination on grounds of working time was already prohibited under Community if it amounted to *indirect sex discrimination*.[2198] Through the adoption of a Directive with a specific prohibition against discrimination against part-time workers, reliance on the differentiation ground of working time became a discriminatory ground in its own right, thereby leading to direct discrimination (if only in an asymmetrical way, namely regarding only part-time workers).[2199] Accordingly, the broad justification possibilities provided for by Clause 4(1) must be seen in that context. This seems to be the result of the Directive's particularly difficult legislative history during which the Commission had presented several unsuccessful drafts which 'were *all* more precise, *all* were wider in scope (all included social security); and *all* either admitted no exceptions at all, or allowed for only one, minor exception to the general rules to be established' (Jeffrey).[2200] Eventually, Art. 4(2) of the Social Agreement[2201] made the adoption of the Directive possible through Community implementation of agreements concluded by the European Social Partners (see now Art. 139 EC). The actual content of the Directive was formulated by the Social Partners rather than by the Commission (though the Commission had to examine it in the framework of Community implementation, see *UEAPME*).[2202] According to Delarue,[2203] the Social Partners deliberated carefully on the Agreement's every word – resulting in a Directive that is less strict than previously proposed by the Commission. In the absence of relevant case law by the Court of Justice, it is open as to the meaning of the reference to 'objective reasons' in Clause 4(1). As Burri[2204] notes, the Directive is silent on the relationship of that term to the concept of objective justification as developed by the Court in the framework of indirect sex discrimination. Schmidt[2205] observes that the Directive's wording seems to reflect the Court's approach in that latter context. Indeed, given the history of the discriminatory ground of part-time work in EC law, it would not be surprising if this were what the Social Partners had in mind. In other words, they might simply have wished to codify the Court's case law. If so, this would mean that there are very broad justification possibilities, which are subject only to the requirement of proportionality. Arguably, this deprives the

---

[2197] See also Art. 2(2) of an older Fixed-Term Work Directive which addresses specifically health and safety matters, Directive 91/383, *OJ* 1991 L 206/19.

[2198] See above Part 2, A.I.4.h.

[2199] See above Part 1, B.III.5.b.ii.

[2200] Jeffrey 1998, p. 201. Compare for instance Art. 2 of the Proposal for a Council Directive on voluntary part-time work, *OJ* 1982 C 62/7.

[2201] *OJ* 1992 C 191/90.

[2202] Case T-135/96, [1998] *ECR* II-2335.

[2203] Delarue 1998, p. 182.

[2204] Burri 2000, p. 377.

[2205] Schmidt 1998, p. 577.

prohibition of discrimination on grounds of part-time work in the Directive of much of its meaning as a form of *direct* discrimination.

ii. The example of the Fixed-Term Work Directive

As Caracciolo di Torella & Masselot[2206] note, some of the issues concerning temporary employment contracts mentioned above in the context of pregnancy discrimination, can now be dealt with under the Fixed-Term Work Directive.[2207] The fact that this Directive provides for an open system of justification (Clause 4(1) of the Directive's Annex),[2208] raises the question of whether this means that discrimination on grounds of pregnancy could be justified in that framework. It is submitted that it follows from *Tele Danmark*[2209] that this is not the case: that judgment emphasises that pregnancy discrimination is sex discrimination and that for such cases there is *specific applicable* EC legislation (namely the Maternity Directive[2210] and the Second Equal Treatment Directive)[2211] which also applies in the context of fixed-term contracts. In the present writer's analysis, this conclusion follows from the Court's statements that the two Directives do not make any distinction, with regard to the scope of the principle of equal treatment for men and women, according to the duration of the employment relationship in question. On the contrary, if the legislator had wished to exclude the applicability of these Directives to cases of sex discrimination arising in the context of fixed-term work, it would have had to say so explicitly when adopting the Fixed-Term Work Directive.

iii. The example of age discrimination

Objective reasons are also mentioned as a justification ground in the General Framework Directive[2212] in Art. 6(1) in the specific context of direct age discrimination. In the Directive, the general reference to objective justification is followed by a list mentioning specific examples. As Fredman[2213] notes, age discrimination is in many ways different from other types of discrimination, and age has traditionally been considered a legitimate factor for differentiation between groups of employees (see also Kenner,[2214]

[2206]   Carracciolo di Torella & Masselot 2001, p. 257.
[2207]   Directive 1999/70/EC, *OJ* 1999 L 175/43.
[2208]   See also Art. 2(2) of an older Fixed-Term Work Directive which addresses specifically health and safety matters, Directive 91/383, *OJ* 1991 L 206/19.
[2209]   Case C-109/00, [2001] *ECR* I-6993. In that case, the Directive was not applicable.
[2210]   Directive 92/85/EEC, *OJ* 1992 L 348/1.
[2211]   Directive 76/207/EEC, *OJ* 1976 L 39/40 (as amended).
[2212]   Directive 2000/78/EC, *OJ* 2000 L 303/16. This Directive provides for an impressive arsenal of justification grounds (see Arts. 2(5), 4, 5 and 6).
[2213]   Fredman 2002, pp. 59 subs.
[2214]   Kenner 2003, p. 417.

Meenan).[2215] Art. 6(1) results from a debate during the legislative process on the question of whether or not a closed justification system is appropriate in this particular context (Holtmaat).[2216] In view of the result, Waddington & Bell[2217] speak about an 'open-ended possibility for Member States to justify direct age discrimination' and a parallel with the approach adopted by the European Court of Human Rights in the context of Art. 14 ECHR where, in principle, justification is available for any type of discrimination provided that the measure in question pursues a legitimate aim and is proportionate in that regard. Clearly, this approach is less beneficial to the victims of alleged discrimination than is the traditional Community approach. According to Fredman,[2218] it possibly presents the biggest challenge under the new Directive as far as age discrimination is concerned. Similarly, O'Hare[2219] criticises the fact that the scope of the exception could open the way for Member States to effectively curtail the application of the equal treatment principle in the light of their own labour market conditions. According to this author, Art. 6(1) in fact raises questions about the EU's commitment to age discrimination. Meenan[2220] explicitly addresses the blurring of boundaries between direct and indirect discrimination: 'Setting a maximum age for recruitment could arguably be similar in operation and in effect to an indirectly discriminatory provision, criterion or practice with which a person cannot comply or which places a person at a particular disadvantage because they are a certain age. If indirect discrimination is taken to mean discrimination which affects, or is more likely to affect a group then Article 6 is unusual. Article 6 concerns justification for direct age discrimination but appears to allow the Member States to treat people of a certain age as a group.'

iv. Not a universal approach

The three examples mentioned above show that in some cases there are now extra-textual possibilities of justification for *direct* discrimination based on express legislation, rather than only for indirect discrimination based on the Court's case law and on the legislation codifying it. However, it should be noted that not all recent non-discrimination legislation provides for such wide possibilities of justification. For example, in the Revised Second Equal Treatment Directive[2221] there is no reference to objective justification outside the definition of indirect discrimination. Further, it

---

[2215] Meenan 2003, pp. 12 subs.
[2216] Holtmaat emphasises that a closed system is still possible in view of the fact that it offers more protection; Holtmaat 2001, p. 112.
[2217] Waddington & Bell 2001, p. 599.
[2218] Fredman 2002, p. 65.
[2219] O'Hare 2001, p. 153.
[2220] Meenan 2003, p. 20.
[2221] Directive 2002/73/EC, *OJ* 2002 L 269/15.

is submitted that Art. 52(1) of the Charter of Fundamental Rights[2222] as adopted in 2000 and the corresponding provision in the Constitutional Treaty,[2223] Art. II-112, do not indicate a general change in approach towards broad objective justification. According to Art. 52(1) of the Charter, '[a]ny limitation on the exercise of the rights and freedoms recognised by this Charter must be provided for by law and respect the essence of those rights and freedoms. Subject to the principle of proportionality, limitations may be made only if they are necessary and genuinely meet objectives of general interest recognised by the Union or the need to protect the rights and freedoms of others.' The reference to 'objectives of general interest' would seem to point in the direction of an open system of justification. However, the Member States are bound by the Charter 'only when implementing Union law' (Art. 51(1) of the Charter and Art. II-111 of the Constitutional Treaty, respectively). In that framework, Member States obviously remain bound by the individual provisions of that law. It is therefore submitted that Arts 52(1) and Art. II-112(1) express a general principle on derogations rather than being substantive provisions in themselves that generally allow wide justification possibilities in the general interest for all areas of the Treaty.

d. An interim conclusion (II)

The starting point for the above discussion was the traditional assumption that there is a difference between direct and indirect discrimination in terms of justification: in the case of direct discrimination, justification is possible only on grounds of derogations expressly mentioned in the law; in the case of indirect discrimination, there is the additional possibility of objective justification. The discussion showed that this dividing line is not as strict as it might at first appear, though at least in one case the Court expressly put an end to widespread speculations regarding the possibility of justification for direct sex discrimination (discrimination on grounds of pregnancy, *Tele Danmark*).[2224] In the specific contexts of direct taxation and agricultural law, the Court was willing to openly deviate from the text of the written law and to accept extra-textual justification for direct discrimination. There are other areas where the Court's case law is unclear. Further, it was seen that the concept of objective justification, historically relevant in the context of indirect discrimination, appears on the level of *direct* discrimination in certain recent non-discrimination Directives. Depending on the Court's interpretation of that concept, this might further blur the dividing line between direct and indirect discrimination.

[2222] Charter of Fundamental Rights of the European Union, *OJ* 2000 C 364/1.
[2223] Treaty establishing a Constitution for Europe, *OJ* 2004 C 310.
[2224] Case C-109/00, [2001] *ECR* I-6993.

This leaves the question of whether, from a theoretical point of view, justification should[2225] differ *as a matter of principle* for direct and indirect discrimination. Again, this question is debated in academic writing. Some authors argue that the rules should be the same, though they may do so for different reasons. Nowak & Schnitzler,[2226] for instance, point to the system of the Treaty. However, given the fact that the Treaty does not even mention indirect discrimination, it is not clear (at least to the present writer) to what extent the system of the Treaty could be of any relevance. Others make the point that for the victims of discrimination there is no difference between the effects of direct or indirect discrimination and that, therefore, there should also be no difference in terms of justification (e.g. Kirsten,[2227] Wisskirchen,[2228] Kingreen,[2229] Novak,[2230] Rossi).[2231] However, this is true only in some cases. On the level of the general effect of a measure reliance on an indirectly discriminatory criterion does not negatively affect the entire group or category that is protected, but rather only a certain part of it. Epiney[2232] provides yet another example, arguing that the application of the same (strict) rules is the logical consequence of the *raison d'être* of the concept of indirect discrimination, namely the useful effect of the prohibition against discrimination. However, it was noted earlier[2233] that this kind of argument could be used against any type of justification and that there is a further possibility of a backlash effect against an approach which is perceived as 'too strict'. In a more general context, Kingreen[2234] suggests that justification in the general interest should be integrated into the textual derogation ground of public policy, which in turn should be interpreted as a safety net in view of the other textual derogations. As a result, restrictions of whatever nature could be justified only on the basis of express derogation grounds. However, it should

---

[2225] According to some, this is not a matter open to debate but an established fact. However, such voices are exceptions (at least those who do not base their view on the causation approach; see above Part 2, A.IV.3.e). Weiss 1999, p. 496, is an example. (In the present writer's view, the further references given by this author are not to the point.). According to Weiss, both direct and indirect discrimination can only be justified on the basis of express derogation grounds. Such views appear to be rooted in a failure to view objective justification in the broader context of the EC legal system with regard to indirect discrimination. Thus, Weiss concludes from *O'Flynn* (Case C-237/94, [1996] *ECR* I-2617) that there is no difference on the level of justification between distinctly and indistinctly applicable measures.

[2226] Nowak & Schnitzler 2000, p. 628.

[2227] Kirsten 1990, p. 285.

[2228] Wisskirchen 1994, p. 43.

[2229] Kingreen 1999, pp. 72, 121 and 151.

[2230] Novak 1999, p. 85. This author's critique is particularly harsh. He writes: 'Zu kritisieren bleibt der vom Gerichtshof verwendete Ansatz der indirekten Diskriminierung, der durch seine ständige Wiederholung auch nicht richtig wird. [...] Mittlerweile ist der Befund zulässig, dass der EuGH selbst nicht mehr weiss, was eine Diskriminierung ist.'

[2231] Rossi 2000, p. 213.

[2232] Epiney 1995, p. 98.

[2233] See above Part 2, A.IV.4.b.

[2234] Kingreen 1999, pp. 157 subs.

be noted that this argument is made in the limited context of free movement of goods, persons and services, where public policy always appears as a textual derogation ground. It is difficult to see how it could be helpful in other areas where that is not the case, such as sex equality law or the internal taxation of goods (Art. 90 EC). Wattel[2235] observes that most people would be glad to see the differences in justifiability disappear, 'as it would rid us of having to consider mind boggling species of discrimination (direct/indirect, overt/covert, inverse, substantive/formal, generaliza-tion [treating alike what is different] etc.)'. He suggests that any restrictive measure, whether or not discriminatory, should be tested under the justifications put forward for it and under the appropriateness and proportionality tests. He admits that distinctly applicable measures are more suspect but adds that 'it escapes me why it would be inconceivable that they can well be justified and proportionate on the basis of justif-ication grounds not included in the text of the EC Treaty'. Bieback[2236] suggests a less far-reaching and more pragmatic approach. He argues that in the case of rather obvious indirectly discriminatory criteria, such as body size or physical strength in the context of sex discrimination, it is difficult to justify a different justification test than that applicable in the context of direct discrimination. He therefore believes that a sharp theoretical dividing line between direct and indirect discrimination does not make sense. Instead, every single criterion should be assessed on a case-to-case basis in terms of the intensity of its link with the prohibited ground. To some extent, Holtmaat's[2237] suggestion, mentioned earlier, to distinguish between discrimination in a neutral and in a strict sense supports a case-by-case assessment as well. In this author's view, justification for discrimination in a strict sense (such as discrimination on grounds of sex and race) must be closely scrutinized. Here, a closed system is appropriate, certainly in the context of direct discrimination. Similarly, Hervey[2238] argues that the recognition of sex equality as a fundamental right in EC law has impli-cations for its justification. Whilst acknowledging that fundamental rights are not absolute, this author insists that they are not to be easily justified but, rather, 'one would expect them to be subject to what other legal systems term a 'strict scrutiny' test which probably translates into a strong version of the proportionality principle in EC law'.

At present EC law does not reflect such approaches (though compare now *Orfanopoulos*).[2239] It is submitted that within the existing system a useful answer to

---

[2235] Wattel 2004, p. 84.
[2236] Bieback 1997, p. 76.
[2237] Holtmaat 2002, p. at 170; see above Part 1, B.III.2.
[2238] Hervey 2002, p. 104.
[2239] Again, possibly a first indication in the direction of the development of a system with different levels of scrutiny can be found in *Orfanopoulos* (Joined Cases C-482/01 and C-493/01, judgment of 29 April 2004, n.y.r.), para. 65. where the Court stated that the status of EU citizenship requires a particularly strict interpretation of derogations from the provisions on free movement of workers; see above Part 2, A.IV.2.c.ii.

the above questions presupposes the clarification of a number of issues discussed earlier. First, there should be a clearer demarcation between objective differences and justification.[2240] Second, it should be clarified whether objective justification is a matter of causation or rather of justification proper.[2241] Third, the range of express justification grounds should be reconsidered. The written derogation provisions in the EC Treaty law on free movement have been in existence since the origins of the Community. As Mortelmans[2242] observes, they are now outdated in view of social problems (such as the pollution of the environment), of technical developments (such as in internet technology) and of the Court's case law on the rule of reason as applicable in the area of free movement in the case of restrictions in a wider sense. The provisions should therefore be reconsidered and amended. It is submitted that, in the interest of the effectiveness of non-discrimination law, such a revised list of derogations grounds would ideally maintain the traditional EC approach by being specific and limited in nature (though it must be acknowledged that it will be impossible to codify all possible derogation grounds in an exhaustive list – social, technical and other developments would soon raise new problems and call for a further development of the law). It is probable that in such a clarified framework a distinction between direct and indirect discrimination in terms of justification would be less important, simply because more justification grounds would be available.

III. APPLYING THE CONCEPTS IN CONCRETE CASES

1. INTRODUCTORY REMARKS

In the following part, the discussion on the demarcation line between direct and indirect discrimination turns to the *assessment of concrete cases*. Determining whether a concrete case concerns direct or rather indirect discrimination requires a number of preliminary steps. First, the *case* must be analysed from a factual perspective in order to identify both the differentiation criterion at its centre and the persons to whom that criterion applies. Second, the potentially applicable *law* must be analysed in order to identify the differentiation criteria expressly prohibited by it and, thus, to determine which criteria give rise to direct discrimination. Thirdly, the reach of the directly discriminatory criteria must be determined. Below, a number of examples are discussed in order to illustrate some of the problems that may arise in the course of these steps. The main points made in that context are:

[2240] See above Part 2, A.II.2.b.
[2241] See above Part 2, A.IV.3.e.
[2242] Mortelmans 1997, p. 190.

- A correct analysis of the facts of a case is a prerequisite for the correct identification of the applicable legal framework.
- Not every expressly mentioned discriminatory ground relates to direct discrimination. The law may also list indirectly discriminatory grounds.
- In concrete cases, much depends on the reach of directly discriminatory criteria. The examples of discrimination on grounds of pregnancy and discrimination against sexual minorities show that the Court's case law on that issue is sometimes rather unpredictable.
- In spite of arguments to the contrary, certain provisions of Community law may not even require an analysis in terms of direct or indirect discrimination, due, for example, to their explicit wording or an individual approach by the Court in particular factual contexts.

2. ANALYSING THE CASE AND THE LAW

a. Analysing the case

i. Which ground forms the basis for the distinction?

Examining an allegation of discrimination in a concrete case requires first of all a careful analysis of the facts. Whether discrimination is direct or indirect depends on the *ground on which the contested differentiation relies*. But, determining the true nature of the applicable grounds can be a more difficult task than at first it might appear. As the following examples demonstrate, this is particularly true for situations where a *combination of grounds seems to be at issue*, whilst in fact only one of them is relevant.

A first example is provided by *Marsman*.[2243] This case concerned the obligation falling to an employer to obtain prior official consent when seeking to dismiss a seriously disabled employee. In the case of foreign nationals, this obligation arose only if certain additional conditions were met, including that the employee be a resident of Germany or of what was then West-Berlin. The Court found an (unspecified) infringement of the right to free movement of workers (*Marsman*, para. 4). Later, AG Mayras interpreted this finding as showing 'that a condition requiring residence within the territory of the host country may be a factor of discrimination' (*Sotgiu*,[2244] p. 173 of the AG's opinion). However, in *Marsman* the residence requirement was imposed only on foreign nationals. Thus, residence served merely as an *additional* criterion for a clear differentiation between nationals and foreigners. In such a situation, nationality, rather than residence, is the decisive differentiation ground. It follows that the Court's

---

[2243] Case 44/72, [1972] *ECR* 1243.
[2244] Case 152/73, [1974] *ECR* 153.

finding ought to be understood as one involving direct discrimination on grounds of nationality (see Wyatt & Dashwood),[2245] and, consequently, the Advocate General's focus on residence was misplaced.

The *Hoeckx*[2246] case provides another example and involved a similar situation. According to Belgian law, foreign nationals were entitled to a minimum subsistence allowance (the so-called 'minimex') only if they had resided in Belgium for at least five years immediately preceding the date on which the allowance was to be awarded. The Court explained that in such a case 'the residence requirement is an additional condition imposed on workers who are nationals of a Member State but not national workers' and that this 'constitutes a clear case of discrimination on the basis of the nationality of workers' (*Hoeckx*, para. 24). The Commission and the AG, discussing a hypothetical situation, pointed out that to impose an identical residence requirement of five years on both Belgians and foreigners would not be sufficient to avoid discrimination since such a requirement would, 'by its very nature, [be] more difficult for a migrant worker to fulfil than for a national worker' (*Hoeckx*, p. 980 of the AG's opinion). In such a hypothetical case, the distinction would shift from nationality to residence and, thereby, from direct to indirect discrimination on grounds of nationality.

Further examples for cases apparently involving a combination of differentiation grounds are *Beune*[2247] and *Vroege*.[2248] The former concerned rules under which the amount of a pension was calculated differently for married male former civil servants and for married female former civil servants to the disadvantage of the men. The Court found direct discrimination on grounds of sex, adding specifically that the fact that only married men rather than single men were placed at a disadvantage could not alter this conclusion (*Beune*, para. 51, see also point 46 of the AG Jacobs' opinion).[2249] *Vroege* involved rules that limited participation in a pension scheme to men and unmarried women employed for an indeterminate period of time and working at least 80% of the normal full working day. As AG van Gerven rightly noted, such a case involves both direct and indirect sex discrimination: the former results from the exclusion of married women from participation in the scheme and the latter from the exclusion of persons working less than 80% (*Vroege*, point 12 of the AG's opinion). The Court, however, only looked at the criterion of working time (*Vroege*, para. 41).

[2245] Wyatt & Dashwood 2000, p. 400.
[2246] Case 249/83, [1985] *ECR* 973.
[2247] Case C-7/93, [1994] *ECR* I-4471.
[2248] Case C-57/93, [1994] *ECR* I-4541.
[2249] In that sense, the present writer would disagree with Barnard's conclusion that the Court construes the concept of sex broadly by recognizing 'gender-plus' discrimination (sex and marital status) as sex discrimination (Barnard 2000, p. 221). This analysis was made in the context of *Liefting* (Case 23/83, [1984] *ECR* 3225).

Finally, it is also possible that the apparent combination of differentiation grounds in a given case implicates *different levels of the non-discrimination analysis*, such as the discriminatory ground and the object of discrimination.[2250] *Bickel and Franz*[2251] provides an example. Mr Bickel, a German national, and Mr Franz, an Austrian national, were refused the right to use the German language in criminal proceedings before a court in Bolzano, Italy, despite the fact that this right was granted to legal residents of the Bolzano province. In such a situation, language is the object rather than the ground on which the different treatment is based: residents and non-residents were treated differently with regard to the language that they could use in court. The Court explained that 'Italian nationals are at an advantage by comparison with nationals of other Member States. The majority of Italian nationals whose language is German are in a position to demand that German be used throughout the proceedings in the Province of Bolzano, *because they meet the residence requirement* laid down by the rules in issue; the majority of German-speaking nationals of other Member States, on the other hand, cannot avail themselves of that right because they do not satisfy that requirement. Consequently, rules such as those in issue in the main proceedings, which make the right, in a defined area, to have criminal proceedings conducted in the language of the person concerned conditional on that person being resident in that area, favour nationals of the host State by comparison with nationals of other Member States exercising their right to freedom of movement and therefore run counter to the principle of non-discrimination laid down in Article 6 of the Treaty.' (*Bickel and Franz*, para. 24-26; emphasis added). This finding has appropriately been described as one of indirect discrimination on grounds of nationality (Novak,[2252] Luijendijk,[2253] Rossi,[2254] Desolre).[2255]

ii. Whose treatment is at issue?

The second important question to be asked in the framework of the analysis of the facts of a given case is *to whom the differentiation ground relates* or, more simply, whose treatment is at issue. Again, this point may determine the nature, direct or indirect, of the alleged discrimination. For example, in *Palermo-Toia*,[2256] reliance on the nationality of the worker's children in order to refuse their mother an old-age benefit was found to lead to indirect discrimination against her on grounds of nationality.

[2250] Compare the structural elements for the analysis of discrimination provisions and cases as set out above Part 1, B.V.2.

[2251] Case C-274/96, [1998] *ECR* I-7637.

[2252] Novak 1999, p. 85.

[2253] Luijendijk 1999, p. 349.

[2254] Rossi 2000, p. 213.

[2255] Desolre 2000, p. 317. – Other commentators do not discuss the nature of the discrimination at all; e.g. Bulterman 1999 and Safferling 2000.

[2256] Case 237/78, [1979] *ECR* 2645; see above Part 2, A.I.4.e.iii.

Had the mother's own nationality been the key issue, the case would have involved direct discrimination (see *Palermo-Toia*, para. 10).

There may also be cases where it is *possible to analyse the facts in several ways* and where the Court's own choice of focus then determines the direct or indirect nature of the discrimination. This is illustrated by the *Schmid*[2257] case, which was brought by a father with regard to his handicapped daughter. Ms Schmid was refused disability benefits in Belgium because of her German nationality (which was also her father's nationality). In his opinion on this case, AG Lenz focused on the handicapped daughter. He found that Ms Schmid was the victim of *direct* discrimination on grounds of nationality, though he added that it would also be possible to focus on the applicant himself as the person of reference in which case 'the nationality requirement would at least constitute indirect discrimination' (*Schmid*, points 68 and 69 of the AG's opinion). Indeed, the Court did focus on the father in his capacity as a worker and explained that any provision making entitlement to a social advantage conditional upon nationality is incompatible with Art. 7 of Regulation 1612/68[2258] because the nationality of the country of residence is more easily fulfilled by the offspring of national workers than by the offspring of migrant workers (*Schmid*, para. 24 subs.). In other words, the Court found *indirect* discrimination on grounds of nationality.

Lindman[2259] provides another example of how one set of discriminatory circumstances may be viewed in a variety of ways. Ms Lindman complained of discrimination because her winnings from a lottery held in Sweden were included in her taxable income in Finland whilst winnings from lotteries licensed and operated in Finland were exempt from tax. Her argument would seem to be one of *indirect* discrimination on grounds of nationality, based on the fact that the contested differentiation criterion was the country where the service was lawfully offered, rather than the taxable person's nationality. It is clear that Ms Lindman focused on the treatment of herself as a recipient of a service, and so did AG Stix-Hackl.[2260] The Court, however, chose to focus on the treatment of the lottery as the service provider (*Lindman*, para. 21-23). It found that 'foreign lotteries are treated differently for tax purposes from, and are in a disadvantageous position compared to, Finnish lotteries' and spoke about manifest discrimination[2261] (by which the Court appears to mean *direct* discrimination on grounds of nationality).

[2257] Case C-310/91, [1993] *ECR* I-3011.
[2258] Regulation 1612/68/EEC, *OJ* English Special Edition 1968 L 257/2, p. 475 (as amended).
[2259] Case C-42/02, judgment of 13 November 2003, n.y.r.
[2260] Though the AG did not speak about discrimination but rather about a restriction which made foreign lotteries less attractive; *Lindman*, points 53 and 59 of the AG's opinion.
[2261] The Court added that the fact that gaming providers established in Finland are subject to tax as organisers of gambling does not rid the Finnish legislation of its manifestly discriminatory character, since that tax is not analogous to the income tax charged on winnings from taxpayers' participation in lotteries held in other Member States.

The possibility of such a choice of focus, independent of who actually brought the case, obviously raises questions concerning what constitutes justification which, as was noted earlier,[2262] is traditionally thought to differ in the cases of direct and indirect discrimination. In *Schmid*, this issue is not touched upon. In *Lindman*, the Court addressed the Finnish Government's attempt to rely on overriding reasons in the public interest merely by observing that the national court had disclosed no evidence enabling conclusions as to the gravity of the risks connected to playing games of chance or to the existence of a particular causal relationship between such risks and participation by nationals of one Member State concerning lotteries organised in another Member State. In contrast, there are no remarks of a principled nature on the question of whether justification grounds other than those expressly mentioned in the Treaty can be relied on in the case of 'manifest discrimination' (*Lindman*, para. 26). The present writer would submit that, ideally, the choice of focus in cases such as *Schmid* and *Lindman* should be made in the interest of the plaintiffs.

b.   Analysing the law

The analysis of the case in terms of its facts must be followed by *the analysis of the potentially relevant law*. The proper determination of whether a case involves indirect as opposed to direct discrimination depends on the ability to correctly identify the criteria at issue in a particular anti-discrimination provision of law. This requires first of all the *identification* of the criteria leading to direct discrimination. Examples of cases involving residence as well as marital and family status demonstrate that such analyses can be more difficult than might be anticipated.

i.   The example of residence in the context of free movement

Residence is often seen as the quintessential example of an indirectly discriminatory differentiation ground in the context of discrimination on grounds of nationality. As AG Jacobs in his opinion on *Pusa*[2263] (point 17) has pointed out, 'discrimination on the basis of residence has been a recurrent theme in the Court's case-law as a form of indirect discrimination on grounds of nationality'. However, whether such discrimination has indeed to be seen as indirect *depends on its legislative framework*. Depending on the area, the differentiation ground of residence can give rise to either direct or to indirect discrimination. The Treaty rules on free movement provide an illustrative example. Thus, the relevance of a differentiation based on residence was obvious under the original rules on free movement of *capital* which prohibited 'any discrimination based on the nationality or on the place of residence of the parties or on the place

---

where such capital is invested'.[2264] In that context, reliance on a residence criterion clearly gave rise to direct discrimination. The situation is also clear with regard to free movement of *workers*, since under Art. 39 EC the only ground leading to direct discrimination is nationality. Accordingly, reliance on a worker's residence can lead to no more than a finding of indirect discrimination (e.g. *Sotgiu*).[2265] In the present writer's analysis, the same applies in the case of free movement of *services* (though as was noted earlier,[2266] this issue is debated in academic writing). In contrast, the issue is somewhat more complex in the context of freedom of *establishment* where discrimination on grounds of nationality is prohibited in relation to both natural and legal persons (Art. 43 EC). As was stated earlier,[2267] for companies the place of residence is the legal equivalent of nationality, which means that use of such a criterion leads to a finding of direct discrimination on grounds of nationality (e.g. the von der Groeben & Schwarze Commentary).[2268] Nonetheless, it has been noted that there is considerable uncertainty as to what constitutes direct discrimination in the context of the secondary establishment of companies. Edwards[2269] therefore suggests that, as a rule, different treatment of companies based on their seat should be seen as leading to indirect rather than to direct discrimination (see also Scott,[2270] Gundel).[2271] With regard to natural persons, reliance on a residence criterion in the context of establishment can be regarded only as indirect discrimination.

ii. The example of marital and family status

Similar problems arise in relation to the differentiation ground of marital and family status. Clear examples are the former Arts. 12(1), second subparagraph, and 27(2), introduced in 1998 through a revision of the Staff Regulations.[2272] They provided that temporary staff and officials, respectively, 'shall be selected without distinction as to race, political, philosophical or religious beliefs, sex or sexual orientation and without reference to their marital status or family situation.'[2273] It is obvious that here marital

---

[2264] Though only to the extent necessary to ensure the proper functioning of the common market, Art. 67 of the EEC Treaty.
[2265] Case 152/73, [1974] *ECR* 153; see above Part 2, A.II.2.c.
[2266] See above Part 2, A.II.4.j.
[2267] See above Part 2, A.II.4.b.
[2268] Von der Groeben & Schwarze Commentary 2004, n. 71 ad Art. 43 EC.
[2269] Edwards 2000, pp. 245 subs. and 257.
[2270] Scott 2002, p. 281.
[2271] Gundel 2001, pp. 81 and 85.
[2272] Regulation 781/98/EC, ECSC, Euratom, *OJ* 1998 L 113/4.
[2273] It should be noted that, as far as marital status was concerned, this did not go beyond the issue of selection for purposes of employment as a staff member. Further, the general equal treatment provision of the Staff Regulations, Art. 1a(1), also inserted in 1998, was without prejudice to provisions requiring a specific marital status. In this regard, compare also the General Framework Directive (Directive 2000/78/EC, *OJ* 2000 L 303/16) whose preamble (point 22) provides that '[t]his Directive

status and family situation were mentioned in the framework of a list of criteria for *direct* discrimination (the most recent version of the Staff Regulations is framed differently).[2274]

In contrast, according to some commentators the situation is less clear with regard to sex equality law where it is stated that there shall be no discrimination whatsoever on ground of sex 'either directly or indirectly by reference in particular to marital or family status' (Art. 2(1) of the Second Equal Treatment Directive,[2275] Art. 4(1) of the Third Equal Treatment Directive,[2276] Art. 5(1) of the Fourth Equal Treatment Directive,[2277] Art. 3 of the Fifth Equal Treatment Directive).[2278] In the original draft text of the Second Directive,[2279] equal treatment was defined as 'the elimination of all discrimination based on sex or on marital or family status' without making any distinction between direct and indirect discrimination (Burri).[2280] This would have meant that discrimination on grounds of marital or family status would have constituted direct sex discrimination. Today, some authors still wonder 'whether discriminations on the grounds of marital and family status are prohibited *per se*, or whether they are only prohibited where they also constitute some form of sex discrimination' (Ellis;[2281] see also Harrison,[2282] Blomeyer).[2283] In Langenfeld's[2284] view, the former is the case. In contrast, Steiner[2285] considers it obvious that the criterion must be related to sex (see also Kyriazis,[2286] Bieback,[2287] Lutjens).[2288] When answering a parliamentary question concerning the Second Equal Treatment Directive,[2289] the Commission explained that

---

is without prejudice to national law on marital status and the benefits dependent thereon'.

[2274] In today's version of the Staff Regulations, Art. 1d(1) provides that for the purposes of these Staff Regulations, non-marital relationships shall be treated as marriage provided that certain conditions are fulfilled; see the consolidated text of the Staff Regulations, available at http://www.europa.eu.int/comm/dgs/personnel_administration/statut/tocen100.pdf).

[2275] Directive 76/207/EEC, *OJ* 1976 L 39/40 (as amended).

[2276] Directive 79/7/EEC, *OJ* 1979 L 6/24.

[2277] Directive 86/378/EEC, *OJ* 1986 L 225/40 (as amended).

[2278] Directive 86/613/EEC, *OJ* 1986 L 359/56.

[2279] COM(75)36 fin.

[2280] Burri 2000, p. 284, footnote 301. – Marital and family status were mentioned in a comparable way in the definition of indirect discrimination in the Commission's 1988 proposal for a burden of proof Directive; Proposal for a Council Directive on the burden of proof in the area of equal pay and equal treatment of men and women, *OJ* 1988 C 176/5; see Blomeyer 1994, pp. 110/111. There is, however, no such reference in the final text of Directive 97/80/EC, *OJ* 1998 L 14/6 (as amended).

[2281] Ellis 1998, p. 198.

[2282] Harrison 1996, p. 276.

[2283] Blomeyer 1994, p. 111.

[2284] Langenfeld 1990, p. 233.

[2285] Steiner 1999, p. 99.

[2286] Kyriazis 1990, p. 100.

[2287] Bieback 1997, p. 111.

[2288] Lutjens 1990, p. 141.

[2289] Written Question No 2295/80 by Mrs Lizin to the Commission: the notion of 'indirect discrimination' in the directives on equal treatment, *OJ* 1981 C 129/22.

the reference to marital or family status related to *indirect* discrimination. The Court in *Teuling*[2290] later confirmed this, in the context of social security law. This example shows that differentiation grounds that are explicitly mentioned in the law need not necessary relate to direct discrimination. As the Bigler-Eggenberger & Kaufmann Commentary[2291] explains, explicit mention of a criterion potentially giving rise to indirect discrimination is useful in view of the burden of proof: indirect discrimination is automatically presumed if based on such a criterion, without any need for proof of a disparate impact (though such a presumption is open to counter-proof by the alleged discriminator).

c. An interim conclusion (III)

Regarding the demarcation line between situations involving direct as opposed to indirect discrimination, the previous sections emphasised the importance of performing a *careful analysis of the facts and the law* involved in each concrete case of alleged discrimination. The examples discussed demonstrated that this is often a difficult challenge. On the level of the analysis of the facts, both the correct ground upon which the contested distinction is made and also precisely whose treatment is at issue must be identified. It was seen that in some cases there may be more than one possible approach, and it was argued then that the choice should be made in the interest of the plaintiffs. On the level of legislation, it was seen that the proper context of a differentiation criterion that is explicitly mentioned in such law must be identified based on its framework. Accordingly, the same criterion can be related to either direct or indirect discrimination. For example, residence, often seen as the quintessential example of a ground leading to *(prima facie)* indirect discrimination on grounds of nationality in the context of free movement law, may lead either to direct discrimination (e.g. in relation to companies and freedom of establishment) or to *(prima facie)*

[2290] Case 30/85, [1987] *ECR* 2497. The main importance of this case is the fact that for the first time the question was raised as to whether a social security system can lead to indirect discrimination on grounds of sex. The Court's positive answer to that aspect of the question received generally positive comments, e.g. Luckhaus 1988. Using the traditional description of indirect discrimination, the Court explained that 'it should be pointed out that a system of benefits in which, as in this case, supplements are provided for which are not directly based on the sex of the beneficiaries but take account of their marital status or family situation and in respect of which it emerges that a considerably smaller proportion of women than of men are entitled to such supplements is contrary to Article 4 (1) of the directive if that system of benefits cannot be justified by reasons which exclude discrimination on grounds of sex' (*Teuling*, para. 13). The Court noted that in the Netherlands a significantly greater number of married men than of married women received a supplement linked to family responsibility. This resulted from the fact that at the time there were considerably more married men than married women who carried on occupational activities and therefore considerably fewer women who had a dependant spouse. However, the Court agreed with the AG that in the circumstances of the case there was objective justification.

[2291] Bigler-Eggenberger & Kaufmann Commentary (on the Swiss Sex Equality Act), n. 30 ad Art. 3 GlG (writing in the context of Swiss law).

indirect discrimination (e.g. in relation to workers). Similarly, reliance on the differentiation criterion of marital and family status may lead either to direct discrimination or to indirect discrimination, depending on the legal context.

3. THE REACH OF DIRECTLY DISCRIMINATORY GROUNDS

In practical terms, problems in drawing the dividing line between direct and indirect discrimination when assessing concrete cases also arise notably because the *reach* of a directly discriminatory ground is not clear. Below, this point is illustrated by the Court of Justice's interpretation of non-discrimination law in two specific contexts, namely discrimination on grounds of pregnancy and, briefly, (certain instances of) discrimination against sexual minorities. In both contexts, direct and indirect discrimination play a role, and in both contexts the Court's approach to these issues was unpredictable.

a. The example of discrimination on grounds of pregnancy

Pregnancy has long been seen as one of the most important issues of sex equality (MacKinnon:[2292] 'a nerve center of gender relations'). Against this background, it is obvious that the legal classification of discrimination based on grounds of pregnancy and biological motherhood or maternity[2293] is particularly important. At the time when there were no specific relevant EC law provisions nor case law bearing directly on these matters, academic writers debated whether pregnancy discrimination should be seen as either direct or indirect sex discrimination in the broader framework of EC sex equality law. For example, Kyriazis[2294] argued that in a situation where a pregnant woman is refused employment because of her pregnancy that ground must be viewed as a sex-neutral criterion with a disproportionate negative effect on women. In Kyriazis' view, such treatment would only constitute direct discrimination if pregnancy were, in fact, a continuous state relating to a large majority of women. Similar views were expressed by Hanau & Preis[2295] who thought, however, that the issue concerned a borderline case since only women can be pregnant. The case law discussed below shows that Court of Justice took a qualified approach.

[2292] MacKinnon 2001, pp. 386/387.
[2293] Maternity in the biological sense relates to aspects specific to women, such as a woman's recovery from giving birth and breastfeeding. This is opposed to social parenthood which is not by nature sex-specific, but can (and should) concern both men and women.
[2294] Kyriazis 1990, p. 109. This was apparently written before the *Dekker* case (Case C-177/88, [1990] *ECR* I-3941) was decided.
[2295] Hanau & Preis 1988, p. 200.

i. Direct sex discrimination: *Dekker*

The very first case involving an allegation of pregnancy discrimination that reached the Court, *Dekker*,[2296] arose because it was unclear under the applicable Dutch law at the time whether such discrimination should be seen as direct or indirect sex discrimination (see Asscher-Vonk,[2297] Wentholt).[2298] *Dekker* concerned the refusal to hire a pregnant woman because of insurance problems. Having applied for a job, Ms Dekker was found to be the most suitable candidate. However, when it became known that she was pregnant, she was refused employment. Under the applicable rules, the insurer was allowed to refuse reimbursement to the employer for all or part of the daily benefits in the event that the employee became unable to perform his or her duties within six months of commencement of the insurance if, at the time when the insurance took effect, it was to be anticipated from the state of health of the employee that such incapacity would supervene this period. Under circumstances involving a pre-existing pregnancy, the potential employer, VJV, would not have been able to get payments for the time of Ms Dekker's pregnancy leave. VJV found the hiring of a replacement for Ms Dekker unaffordable, and, consequently, also the hiring of Ms Dekker herself.

This situation led to various arguments regarding the nature of the alleged discrimination under the Second Equal Treatment Directive (in its original version).[2299] The Commission focused on the insurance problem. Pointing out that since only women can become pregnant, the six-month rule is liable to affect women more than men, the Commission concluded that '[r]egardless of whether direct discrimination is involved here, the legislation at any rate has the effect of indirect discrimination' (*Dekker*, p. I-3951). In contrast, others focused on VJV's refusal to employ a pregnant woman and argued in favour of a finding of direct sex discrimination. Ms Dekker in particular pointed out that the ground cited by her employer as precluding her appointment can never apply to a man. For the same reason, the Dutch Government considered it 'legitimate to speak of direct distinction in treatment' (*Dekker*, p. I-3949). AG Darmon agreed, arguing that taking account of motherhood in order to justify a refusal of employment is '*ipso facto* direct sex discrimination' (*Dekker*, point 23 of the AG's opinion).

> The AG famously observed: 'Defining the question sometimes supplies the answer to it. Is there any event more closely connected to the specific nature of womanhood? Is it conceivable to treat female workers on an equal footing with their male counterparts without taking account of motherhood? [...] Consequently, it appears that, in Ms Dekker's case,

---

[2296] Case C-177/88, [1990] *ECR* I-3941.
[2297] Asscher-Vonk 1993, p. 387.
[2298] Wentholt 1990, p. 78.
[2299] Directive 76/207/EEC, *OJ* 1976, L 39/40.

refusal of employment on account of forthcoming motherhood, by taking account of an event, which affects only female workers, is direct discrimination. Thus, I do not think it is possible to apply to this case the judgments of the Court in the Jenkins, Bilka and Rinner-Kühn cases on indirect discrimination, which have never been applicable except in the presence of factors capable in theory of affecting either sex – part-time work, for example – but found in actual fact to be associated with the circumstances of a woman more commonly than with those of a man. At the expense of stating the obvious, motherhood can only ever affect women; taking account of it in order to justify a refusal of employment is therefore *ipso facto* direct discrimination on grounds of sex.'

The Court agreed. It began by observing that the answer to the question whether the refusal of employment is indirectly or directly discriminatory 'depends on whether the fundamental reason for the refusal of employment is one which applies without distinction to workers of either sex, or conversely, whether it applies exclusively to one sex' (*Dekker*, para. 10). The Court continued (*Dekker*, para. 12 and 17): '[I]t should be observed that only women can be refused employment on grounds of pregnancy and such a refusal therefore constitutes direct discrimination. [...] It should be stressed that the reply to the question whether the refusal to employ a woman constitutes direct or indirect discrimination depends on the reason for that refusal. If that reason is to be found in the fact that the person concerned is pregnant, then the decision is directly linked to the sex of the candidate.' The Court added that direct discrimination could not be justified on grounds relating to the financial loss, which the employer would suffer over the course of her maternity leave.

The Court's findings in *Dekker* should be examined on two levels. The first of these concerns the Court's general statement on the nature of discrimination on grounds of pregnancy and the second concerns the specific circumstances of the particular case. On the *general level*, most commentators agree with the Court's finding that disadvantageous treatment on grounds of pregnancy is direct sex discrimination,[2300] though others voice other views. Wintemute,[2301] whilst acknowledging that pregnancy discrimination can be viewed as direct sex discrimination in some cases, argues that it is in

---

[2300] It should be added that, obviously, a finding of direct discrimination is possible only if the treatment in question is indeed related to the pregnancy in the sense that pregnancy is the *cause* for the treatment. This can be illustrated by the Court's decision in *Speybrouck* (Case T-45/90, [1992] *ECR* II-33), a case concerning the dismissal of an employee of the European Parliament during her pregnancy. The Court of First Instance confirmed that dismissal on grounds of pregnancy is direct discrimination. However, it added that 'only an employee dismissed on account of pregnancy may invoke the protection deriving from that fundamental right'. Ms Speybrouck had been dismissed for 'serious political reasons'. The Court found that the required link with pregnancy had not been proven (*Speybrouck*, para. 49-52). In fact, Ms Speybrouck had not claimed that her dismissal was attributable to the fact that she was pregnant. Rather, she argued rather that under Staff law there is a fundamental and general right whereby pregnant women are protected against any dismissal.

[2301] Wintemute 1998, pp. 28 subs. According to Wintemute, the outcome of the Court's later case law on pregnancy discrimination is easier to reconcile from this point of view.

any case better viewed as *prima facie* indirect sex discrimination. According to Julén,[2302] indirect discrimination might be more appropriate in that direct sex discrimination (in her view) relates to unchangeable biological laws, whilst pregnancy discrimination often involves the social division of sex roles, which gives women the task of being primary care takers. In a similar vein, Foubert[2303] argues that on an individual level the result of *Dekker* was certainly positive, but that defining pregnancy discrimination as direct sex discrimination makes it impossible to dig for the underlying causes of such discrimination. In the present writer's[2304] analysis, the Court's finding of direct discrimination simply reflects the sheer obviousness of a situation that overshadows every other approach, rendering them 'unrealistic'. As Prechal[2305] noted (at a time, when there was not yet a legal definition of indirect sex discrimination based on the liability approach), an indirect discrimination approach would have led to absurd results since in that case a possible plaintiff would first have had to prove that it is considerably more women who get pregnant than men (see also Fuchsloch,[2306] Ellis,[2307] McGlynn).[2308]

The conclusion from *Dekker* must be that a differentiation ground that is by definition linked to the explicitly prohibited ground in the way pregnancy is linked to sex must be read as 'sex' itself. Veldman[2309] speaks of pregnancy discrimination as conceptually situated between direct and indirect sex discrimination, but, in the Court's case law, it simply appears as a particular variety of direct sex discrimination. In such a case, a finding of direct discrimination does not require that the two groups whose treatment is compared consist exclusively of men and exclusively of women. Rather, in the case of pregnancy discrimination only the disadvantaged group consists exclusively of one sex (women), whilst the group of advantaged contains all persons that are not pregnant, including non-pregnant women.[2310]

However, it is debated whether the above reasoning can be applied to *specific situations of the kind at issue in Dekker*. After all, the primary reason for the refusal of employment in that case was not the pregnancy itself but rather its financial implications, an aspect that was taken into account by the Court only in the context of the issue of justification. Flynn[2311] observes that the Court in fact assimilated both the fact

---

[2302] Julén 2001, p. 180.
[2303] Foubert 2002, p. 149.
[2304] Tobler 1998, p. 68.
[2305] Prechal 1991, p. 666.
[2306] Fuchsloch 1995, p. 124. Literally: 'eine Frage der Offenkundigkeit'. The author in this context speaks about 'definitorische Diskriminierung'.
[2307] Ellis 1994 (Definition of Discrimination), p. 568.
[2308] McGlynn 2001, pp. 208 subs.
[2309] Veldman 1998, p. 3.
[2310] It will be recalled that this was precisely the starting point for the problematic assessment made by the U.S. and Canadian Supreme Courts in *Geduldig v. Aiello*, 417 U.S. 484 (1974) and *Bliss v. Attorney General of Canada* [1979] 1 S.C.R. 183, respectively; see above Part 1, B.III.3.c.
[2311] Flynn 2000, p. 266, footnote 39.

of pregnancy as well as the financial costs associated with it into one issue. Rodière[2312] states that a focus on the financial implications on the earlier level of causation would have led to a finding of indirect sex discrimination, as reflected in the Commission's submissions.[2313] Nielsen,[2314] whilst lauding the Court for offering stronger protection to pregnant women 'by choosing to call discrimination on grounds of adverse financial effects of pregnancy direct, as opposed to indirect, discrimination', considers the *Dekker* decision to be incorrect, or at least unconvincing, when examined against the background of the various national laws regarding who has to bear the financial burden arising out of pregnancy and childbirth. Nielsen points out that under Danish law it is possible that the father's employer accepts that burden which in her analysis means that discrimination on grounds of pregnancy in the circumstances of *Dekker* can constitute nothing more than indirect sex discrimination. Nielsen therefore suggests that *Dekker* should be read as meaning 'that in countries where pregnancy costs are put solely on women and women's employers, discrimination on grounds of pregnancy costs is direct discrimination while in countries at another stage of development where costs related to procreation are put both on the male and the female workforce, and their respective employers, this form of discrimination is (if at all gender-related) indirect sex discrimination'. As it stands, the Court did not address such issues and simply spoke about direct sex discrimination. This can perhaps be interpreted as showing that the Court was determined to avoid the pitfalls of an indirect discrimination approach and its element of objective justification.

Subsequently, the Court notably opted for a *different approach* in *Habermann-Beltermann*,[2315] which concerned an allegation of sex discrimination under the Second Equal Treatment Directive (in its original version)[2316] with regard to the dismissal of a night-nurse. Here, the Court expressly noted that 'the unequal treatment in a case such as this, unlike the *Dekker* case referred to by the national court, is not based directly on the woman' s pregnancy but is the result of [a] statutory prohibition on night-time work during pregnancy', which in turn was based on Art. 2(3) of the Second Equal Treatment Directive (*Habermann-Beltermann*, para. 16 and 18). As Fenwick & Hervey[2317] note, the Court's focus on the statutory prohibition excluded a finding of direct sex discrimination in this case, thereby leaving open the possibility of objective justification.[2318] Possibly, the reason for the difference in approach between *Dekker*

[2312]   Rodière 1991, p. 574.
[2313]   To that extent, therefore, *Dekker* can be seen as an example of the difficulties that may arise when trying to determine the ground that is relevant for the legal analysis; see earlier in this part, A.III.2.a.i and 3.
[2314]   Nielsen 1992, p. 166.
[2315]   Case C-421/92, [1994] *ECR* I-1657.
[2316]   Directive 76/207/EEC, *OJ* 1976, L 39/40.
[2317]   Fenwick & Hervey 1995, p. 452.
[2318]   Other writers seem to think that the Court found direct discrimination; e.g. Jaqmain 1994, p. 355; Ellis 1998, p. 204.

and *Habermann-Beltermann* was the fact that the latter case involved Community law itself which specifically allowed a prohibition of night-work for pregnant women without also obliging employers to allocate day-work or to grant leave to such women.[2319] In contrast, the insurance problems arising in *Dekker* were not related to Community law but arose only because national law permitted it. The Court may have felt that to decide otherwise in *Dekker* would in effect allow the Member States to circumvent the prohibition of discrimination.

ii. At the most indirect sex discrimination: *Hertz*

In *Hertz*,[2320] the Court set limits to the direct discrimination approach just discussed. Based upon the fact that *Hertz* and *Dekker*[2321] were decided on the same day and also in that both cases were decided by an identical formation of the Court, Arnull[2322] concludes that *Hertz* was intended to qualify *Dekker*. *Hertz* concerned a woman dismissed on account of a pregnancy-related illness, which occurred after the expiration of a statutory pregnancy/maternity leave. AG Darmon 'confessed' that he was tempted to propose a direct sex discrimination approach ('a solution whereby medical conditions which were directly, definitely and preponderantly due to pregnancy or confinement would enjoy a sort of immunity in the sense that the principle of equality of treatment would restrain the employer from dismissing the employee for a reasonable period after the event in question'). However, he thought that in the final analysis Community law as it stood at the time did not require such an approach. Moreover, such an approach might create a backlash against women. The AG therefore suggested the solution that was eventually adopted by the Court (*Dekker*, point 43 subs. of the AG's joint opinion on *Dekker* and *Hertz*). The Court explained that in the case of an illness manifesting itself after the expiration of the statutory pregnancy/maternity leave, there is no reason to distinguish an illness attributable to pregnancy or confinement from any other illness. According to the Court, '[m]ale and female workers are equally exposed to illness. Although certain disorders are, it is true, specific to one or other sex, the only question is whether a woman is dismissed on account of absence due to illness in the same circumstances as a man; if that is the case, then there is no direct discrimination on grounds of sex.' (*Hertz*, para. 16 and 17).

The above discussion shows that under EC law not all disadvantageous treatment, which in fact is on grounds of pregnancy or biological motherhood, is seen as direct sex discrimination. Rather, only during the pregnancy and the statutory pregnancy or maternity leave is it granted legal recognition as discrimination on grounds of

---

[2319] This obligation was later introduced through the Maternity Directive (Art. 7 of Directive 92/85/EEC, *OJ* 1992, L 348/1).

[2320] Case C-179/88, [1990] *ECR* I-3979.

[2321] Case C-177/88, [1990] *ECR* I-3941.

[2322] Arnull 1999, p. 496.

pregnancy (and thereby directly on sex).[2323] Thereafter, it is considered to be on grounds of illness (and as such could amount to no more than indirect sex discrimination if it can be shown that considerably more women than men suffer from such long-term 'illnesses'). Shaw[2324] in this context speaks about a remoteness element (a notion well known in EC free movement law).[2325] It may be supposed that the Court's reasons for this qualified approach to pregnancy discrimination were similar to those mentioned by AG Darmon in *Hertz*, namely essentially of a practical nature. Most likely, the Court considered that some dividing line had to be drawn because otherwise there might be no legal escape from a situation where a female worker is unable to work and cannot be dismissed, possibly for many years, which might result in a backlash effect. Understandable as this may seem from a practical point of view, the fact nevertheless remains that *Hertz* does not sit easily with *Dekker* and even less so with the Court's later statement in *Webb*[2326] concerning the non-comparability of pregnancy with illness. In that sense, *Hertz* can be seen as drawing an artificial border line between what is legally held to fall under the terms 'pregnancy' on the one hand and what is held to be an illness like any other (e.g. Traversa,[2327] Shaw,[2328] Fredman,[2329] Tobler,[2330] Caracciolo de Torella & Masselot).[2331]

An additional problem results from the fact that the *length of pregnancy leave differs greatly* among the various Member States. At the time of *Hertz*, Member States were not even obliged to grant any such leave (but rather simply *entitled* to do so under Art.

[2323]   After *Hertz*, the Court elaborated on the temporal aspects of the distinction between the *Dekker* and the *Hertz* type of situations. In *Brown* (Case C-394/96, [1998] *ECR* I-4185), it held that taking account of absences from work of a pregnant woman during the entire pregnancy and during the statutory pregnancy leave for the purposes of calculating the total length of absence which then leads to dismissal – whether during the period mentioned or only after the expiry of the pregnancy leave – constitutes direct discrimination. For a critical analysis of the equality approach underlying this ruling, see Ellis 1999. With this decision the Court overruled its earlier decision *Larsson* (Case C-400/95, [1997] *ECR* I-2757) based on which it had been possible to take account of absences before the beginning of the pregnancy leave.

[2324]   Shaw 1991, p. 320.

[2325]   In free movement law, this concerns situations where a potentially limiting effect in terms of free movement is considered to be too remote in order to be attributable to the specific measure at issue. For an example from the area of the free movement of services, see *Grogan* (Case C-159/90, [1991] *ECR* I-4685), para. 24. See also the Torfaen Borough Council's argument in *Torfaen Borough Council* (Case C-145/88, [1989] *ECR* 3851, point 9 of the AG's opinion); this is one of the so-called Sunday Trading cases that can be seen as precursor to the Court's decision in *Keck* (Joined Cases C-267/91 and C-268/91, [1993] *ECR* I-6097).

[2326]   Case C-32/93, [1994] *ECR* I-3567.

[2327]   Traversa 1991, p. 436.

[2328]   Shaw 1991, p. 230.

[2329]   Fredman 1992, p. 122.

[2330]   Tobler 1996, pp. 139 subs.

[2331]   Carracciolo di Torella & Masselot 2001, p. 245.

2(2) of the Second Equal Treatment Directive; *Hertz*, para. 15).[2332] Subsequently, Art. 8 of the Maternity Directive[2333] prescribed a leave of at least 14 weeks duration. As mere minimum harmonization, this leaves a certain discretion to the Member States, which has led to considerable differences in the length of the various pregnancy leaves under national law. In combination with the Court's decision in *Hertz*, this in turn leads to various borderlines between direct and indirect discrimination depending upon the particular rules of the Member State where a given case arises. Whilst differences in regulation are inherent in a minimum harmonization approach, the fact remains that in the present context they have particularly disturbing consequences.

iii. Specific legislation: doing away with the need to distinguish between direct and indirect discrimination?

Noting that pregnancy cases provide perhaps the best example of the old adage that 'hard cases make bad law', Ellis[2334] called for a separate corpus of rules governing pregnancy outside traditional sex discrimination law (see also Hepple, Choussey & Choudhury).[2335] Subsequently, some of the problems discussed above have been solved through the adoption of the Maternity Directive[2336] through which disadvantageous treatment on grounds of pregnancy became a legislative category of its own (Ellis).[2337] With this Directive, the demarcation line between direct and indirect discrimination in the context of pregnancy and maternity has to some extent (that is, within the Directive's field of the application) lost its practical importance, since these provisions are not framed in terms of discrimination (Mancini & O'Leary[2338] speak of a 'special protection approach').[2339] In particular, Art. 10 of the Directive expressly states that it is unlawful to dismiss a pregnant worker from the beginning of pregnancy until the end of the statutory maternity leave. Nonetheless, this provision does not do away with the problems arising from the different lengths of maternity leave under the various

---

[2332] Compare, however, Fredman 1991, p. 122, according to whom *Hertz* had the effect of making a period of maternity leave obligatory.

[2333] Directive 92/85/EEC, *OJ* 1992, L 348/1.

[2334] Ellis 1997, p. 182.

[2335] Hepple, Choussey & Choudhury 2000, p. 227, suggest that subjecting a woman to any disadvantage or detriment for a reason related to pregnancy or childbirth should be a substantive wrong, not tied to discrimination.

[2336] Directive 92/85/EEC, *OJ* 1992 L 348/1. Based on the former Art. 118a of the EEC Treaty, in a formal sense the Maternity Directive is not a sex equality Directive though its preamble recognises a link with that issue.

[2337] Ellis 1999, p. 631.

[2338] Mancini & O'Leary 1999, p. 340. The authors note that the Maternity Directive takes 'some pressure off the Court and relieves it of the need to wrestle with the equal treatment/non-discrimination tools which are at its disposal in an area where comparisons of male and female are often if not always untenable'.

[2339] Compare, however, Honeyball 2000, pp. 50 subs., according to whom the non-discrimination approach is maintained.

national legislations, as mentioned. Beyond the limited reach of the Directive, the non-discrimination approach with all its inherent difficulties remains relevant, including the problem of distinguishing when to find direct as opposed to indirect sex discrimination. As *Boyle*[2340] illustrates, it is even possible that both sets of rules, and thereby also both approaches (discrimination and special protection) apply in one and the same case. That, of course, is not a satisfactory state of affairs.

b. The example of discrimination against sexual minorities

In the Court's case law, the reach of the directly discriminatory ground of sex has also been decisive when determining whether disadvantageous treatment of *sexual minorities*, such as homosexuals and transsexuals, gives rise to discrimination under EC law. In a situation where there was no specific EC law on the issue, primarily arguments claiming direct sex discrimination were made, though the discussion below will show that indirect discrimination has also been argued, in the context first of sex discrimination but later also of discrimination on grounds of nationality.

i. Direct or indirect sex discrimination?

The first case involving sexual minorities that came before the Court concerned the dismissal of a transsexual worker because of his/her change of physical sex (so-called gender reassignment). In *P. v S.*[2341] (para. 20 and 21),[2342] the Court held that such a case involves discrimination on grounds of sex because the contested treatment was based 'essentially, if not exclusively, on the sex of the person concerned'. In the present writer's analysis,[2343] the judgment means that discrimination on grounds of sex includes not only the situation where a person *is* of a given sex and for that reason is treated in a disadvantageous way but also the different situation where a person *develops* from one sex in the direction of the other and consequently suffers disadvantageous treatment. This result is due to the fact that the Court in interpreting the term 'sex' did not limit itself to a textual or historical interpretation. Though the Court did

---

[2340]   Case C-411/96, [1998] *ECR* I-6401. According to this decision, the rights granted under the Maternity Directive concern only the leave as stipulated by the Maternity Directive (at least 14 weeks) and by the relevant Member State (the actual choice made by the Member State within the framework of the Directive). The employment rights granted by the Maternity Directive do not relate to a leave granted by the employer which is longer than that required by the law. Rather, the treatment of women workers with regard to that part of the leave must be examined under the Second Equal Treatment Directive.

[2341]   Case C-13/94, [1996] *ECR* I-2143. See also *Grant* (Case C-249/96, [1998] *ECR* I-621), para. 41 and 42.

[2342]   Heerma van Vos 1997, p. 286, rightly notes that the Court's finding of sex discrimination in this case is limited to the *specific issue of gender reassignment* and does not extend to transsexuality in a more general sense.

[2343]   Tobler 2001 (Same-Sex Couples), pp. 275 subs.

not specify whether the *P. v S.* involved direct as opposed to indirect discrimination, it is usually assumed that it meant *direct* sex discrimination (e.g. Flynn,[2344] Wintemute,[2345] Carolan;[2346] compare, however, the Léger Commentary).[2347] Indeed, the Court's statement that the discrimination is based 'essentially, if not exclusively, on the sex of the person concerned' points in this direction and is in line with the argument made earlier by Pannick[2348] that the dismissal of a male to female transsexual because of her sex change constitutes sex discrimination ('Since the employer would have [...] kept her in the job had she remained male, the less favourable treatment is arguably on the ground of her sex.'). Indeed, if it is recognised (as it should be), that gender reassignment necessarily results in a sex change (rather than in some sort of a 'third sex'; Hauser),[2349] then the finding that P. would not have been dismissed if she had remained a man is inevitable and the contrast between the treatment of a man and a woman is obvious.[2350] The Court's approach in *P. v S.* appears to be similar to that in the case of discrimination on grounds of sex in the context of pregnancy,[2351] namely in reaction to the sheer obviousness of the discrimination and independent from conceptual considerations.

Encouraged by the Court's approach in *P. v S.*, the lesbian applicant in the *Grant*[2352] case also relied on the prohibition of (direct) sex discrimination when faced with discrimination on grounds of her homosexual orientation. However, the Court held that the refusal to provide travel concessions to homosexual couples whilst they were granted to heterosexual couples, whether or not formally married, did not amount to sex discrimination in relation to pay (Art. 141(1) and (2) EC). Notably, the Court pointed out that the condition that the worker must live in a stable relationship with a person of the opposite sex in order to benefit from the travel concessions applied regardless of the sex of the worker concerned. Under the rules in question, travel concessions were refused to a male worker if he was living with a person of the same sex, just as they were refused to a female worker if she was living with a person of the same

---

[2344] Flynn 1997, p. 386. Flynn even suggests that the need for a leave to undergo and recuperate from surgery or complications arising from the surgery might be protected by the prohibition against direct sex discrimination, subject to limits similar to those expressed in *Hertz* (Case C-179/88, [1990] *ECR* I-3979).

[2345] Wintemute 1997, p. 339.

[2346] Carolan 1999, p. 45.

[2347] Léger Commentary 2000, n. 20 ad Art. 141 EC.

[2348] Pannick 1985, p. 221 (as quoted by Wintemute 1997, p. 342, footnote 30).

[2349] Hauser 1996, p. 579. Hauser observes that it would be paradoxical to refuse protection through the non-discrimination principle to a transsexual person undergoing gender reassignment, under the pretext that he or she does not belong to either sex and, therefore, is *a priori* not 'discriminable'.

[2350] That, however, does not answer questions that have been raised in the context of the *comparison* lying at the basis of the Court's finding in *P. v S.* In academic comments, this is a hotly debated issue, particularly in comparison with the Court's approach in *Grant* (discussed immediately below).

[2351] See earlier in this part, A.III.3.a.

[2352] Case C-249/96, [1998] *ECR* I-621.

sex. The Court concluded that '[s]ince the condition imposed by the undertaking's regulations applies in the same way to female and male workers, it cannot be regarded as constituting discrimination directly based on sex' (*Grant*, para. 28).

Few of the many commentators who struggled to reconcile *Grant* with *P. v S.* discuss the *nature* of the alleged discrimination at issue in *Grant*,[2353] Veldman[2354] being a notable exception. In her analysis, *Grant* is primarily an example of indirect discrimination on grounds of homosexuality in that the measure in question in fact disadvantaged homosexual persons. However, such an argument could be relevant only in the context of the laws of Member States that already recognized an explicit prohibition against discrimination on grounds of homosexuality, such as the Netherlands (Velman's origin).[2355] With regard to sex discrimination, Veldman agrees that there is no direct discrimination but suggests that the case might be understood as involving *prima facie* indirect discrimination (though likely open to objective justification), in that persons of the same sex as their partner were automatically negatively affected.[2356] However, such an approach works only where the explicitly prohibited criterion of sex refers not only to the sex of the worker herself (or himself) but also to the sex of the worker's partner. This view was indeed raised by AG Elmer in *Grant* (point 16 of the opinion;[2357] and in a broader context also in academic writing before *Grant* was

---

[2353] Most commentators focus on the much debated question whether the Court based its findings on the correct comparison and whether *Grant* is consistent with *P. v S.*; e.g. Tobler 2001 (Same-Sex Couples), pp. 272 subs. (with further references); since then in particular Carey 2001, pp. 99 subs., Bell 2002, pp. 107 subs., and Kaddous 2004, pp. 604/605.

[2354] Veldman 1998, pp. 2 subs.

[2355] In a case comparable to *Grant*, the Dutch Equal Treatment Commission found that the exclusion of non-married persons from travel benefits leads, among other things, to indirect discrimination on grounds of sexual orientation (Commissie Gelijke Behandeling, judgment 96/52 of 20 June 1996, RN 1997/713); see Hendriks 1998, p. 846.

[2356] Before *Grant*, an argument of indirect sex discrimination of a different kind was made by Harrison 1996, pp. 272 subs. The author argued that the proportion of the male gay population is considerably higher than the proportion of the female lesbian population (though the author notes that such an argument depends on statistical evidence regarding the unequal distribution of homosexuality among the population which is difficult to obtain).

[2357] This would seem to correspond to the concept of discrimination by association, as known in UK law (e.g. *Weathersfield Ltd (t/a Van & Truck Rentals) v Sargent* [1999] I.C.R. 425, *Showboat Entertainment Centre v Owens* [1984] I.C.R. 65). In the context of U.S. law, compare Sulds & Israel 1999. It would seem that under EC law, a similar result as that of discrimination by association can be reached only through a generous interpretation of the Community legislation's *scope*, as illustrated by the Court's decision in *Drake* (Case 150/85, [1986] *ECR* 1995). In this case, the Court held that a woman caring for her disabled mother and therefore temporary unable to take up paid work is part of the working population covered by the Third Equal Treatment Directive (Directive 79/7/EEC, OJ 1979 L 6/24) even though the risk at issue (namely chronic illness) did not concern her own heath but rather that of the person she cared for. The Court explained this approach by stating that under a different interpretation 'it would be possible, by making formal changes to existing benefits covered by the Directive, to remove them from its scope' (*Drake*, para. 25); see also Ellis 1998, pp. 277 subs.

decided, e.g. Heinze,[2358] Wintemute,[2359] Harrison).[2360] According to the Court of Justice, that is precisely not the case under EC law where the focus is on the sex of the worker. Instead, the Court pointed to the recently expanded competence of the Community which under Art. 13 EC after the Amsterdam revision[2361] explicitly authorized legislation on discrimination on grounds of sexual orientation.

ii. Indirect discrimination on grounds of nationality?

The approach reflected in *Grant* was essentially confirmed in the Staff law cases *D v Council*[2362] and *D and Sweden v Council*.[2363] They are mentioned in the present context because they added a new element to the debate on direct and indirect discrimination in the context of homosexuality. Mr D., a Swedish national living in a homosexual partnership registered in Sweden, complained about a Council decision which refused him a family benefit. Having lost his case before the Court of First Instance, Mr D. turned to the Court of Justice where he included a new argument in his plea that is relevant for the present purposes, namely that the refusal to recognise his partnership as equivalent to a marriage constitutes discrimination on grounds of nationality. Obviously, this must be understood as relating to *indirect* discrimination, based on the idea that reliance on a traditional notion of marriage by EC law[2364] is liable to disadvantage predominantly nationals of specific Member States (namely those that

---

[2358] Heinze 1994, pp. 217 subs.

[2359] Wintemute 1995, p. 335.

[2360] Harrison 1996, pp. 272 subs. – Such authors tend to argue that the term 'sex' should not be reduced to differences between men and women but rather include any kind of discrimination arising from sexuality, sexual behaviour, or sexual norms. Academic writers in that context often refer to the links between the social phenomena of discrimination on grounds of sex and on grounds of sexual orientation; compare Helfer 1999, p. 202; Bell 1999, p. 80 (speaking about multiple discriminations), and the Bigler-Eggenberger & Kaufmann Commentary (on the Swiss Sex Equality Act), n. 27 ad Art. 3.

[2361] It is interesting to compare the Court's insistence on an explicit Community competence with the approach taken by the Canadian Supreme Court in *Vriend v. Alberta* [1998] 1 S.C.R. 493 and *M. v. H.* [1999] 2 S.C.R. 3. In these cases, the Supreme Court found that the Canadian Charter of Rights and Freedoms grants protection against discrimination on grounds of sexual orientation even though attempts to explicitly include this discriminatory ground in section 15(1) of the Charter had failed. Hovius 2000, p. 23, comments that 'the Supreme Court of Canada, in effect, amended legislation over the express objection of the legislature'. However, from a legal point of view this finding was not revolutionary: section 15(1) is formulated in an open way and thus by definition leaves room for the recognition of discriminatory grounds not explicitly mentioned in the provision. This differs from EC law where discrimination on grounds of sex was the only available ground in the context of the employment law binding the Member States.

[2362] Case T-264/97, [1999] *ECR*-SC I-A-1 and II-1.

[2363] Joined Cases C-122/99 P and C-125/99 P, [2001] *ECR* I-4319. Generally on Staff law and discrimination on grounds of homosexuality, see Snyder 1993 (The Community), pp. 247 subs. (though this work refers to an earlier stage in the development of the EU Staff law).

[2364] In EC law, the concept of marriage is in principle interpreted in a traditional, heterosexual sense, see *Reed* (Case 59/85, [1986] *ECR* 1283); compare Tobler 2001 (Begriff der Ehe).

have legal regimes which regard same-sex couples in a manner equivalent or similar to marriage; this includes countries where marriage itself is defined in a neutral way in terms of sexual orientation).[2365] AG Mischo did not find Mr D's approach convincing. He argued that since it is not necessary in Sweden for registered partners to be of Swedish nationality, there is no issue of different treatment with regard to nationality (*D and Sweden v Council*, points 101 subs. of the AG's opinion). However, the AG's counterargument disregards the point at the centre of an indirect discrimination approach that the majority of Community staff members in registered partnerships tend to be nationals of the country of registration. In that sense, it is submitted that the argument of indirect discrimination on grounds of nationality is not necessarily without merit. The Court found the argument inadmissible because it was brought up too late in the proceedings (*D and Sweden v Council*, para. 54).

iii. Specific legislation: doing away with the need to distinguish between direct and indirect discrimination?

Subsequently, new provisions of EC law (in particular the General Framework Directive[2366] and the revised Staff law) explicitly addressed discrimination on grounds of sexual orientation. In principle, the inclusion of such provisions makes possible not only findings of direct but also of indirect discrimination on that ground. However, there are limits, for instance where the law makes an express reservation with regard to sexual orientation discrimination caused through reliance on a person's marital status, as was the case with Art. 1a(1) as inserted into the Staff Regulations in 1998.[2367] In fact, the request by Sweden for registered partnership to be treated as being equivalent to marriage under the revised regime was explicitly rejected. Instead, the Community legislature chose to instruct the Commission to study the consequences (especially those of a financial nature) of such a measure and to submit proposals, if appropriate. In the meantime, the existing regime with regard to provisions requiring a particular civil status would be allowed to continue to operate as before. Thus, in practice, the amendments to the 1998 Staff Regulations did not provide a remedy for the problems arising in cases such as that of Mr D in *D v Council*[2368] and *D and Sweden*

[2365] Same-sex marriage is currently possible in the Netherlands and in Belgium. Spain is expected to follow. In certain other Member States, registration is possible; compare the special issue *Registrierte Partnerschaft. Partenariat enregistré*, AJP 3/2001, Berthou & Masselot 2002.
[2366] Directive 2000/78/EC, *OJ* 2000 L 303/16.
[2367] Regulation 781/98/EC, ECSC, Euratom, *OJ* 1998 L 113/4. A similar reservation can also be found in consideration 22 of the preamble to the General Framework Directive (Directive 2000/78/EC, *OJ* 2000 L 303/16).
[2368] Case T-264/97, [1999] *ECR*-SC I-A-1 and II-1.

v Council.[2369] This situation has rightly been criticised in that it maintained an indirect form of discrimination on grounds of homosexuality (Waaldijk,[2370] see also Carolan).[2371] Under the present Staff Regulations,[2372] Art. 1d(1) provides that 'non-marital partnerships shall be treated as marriage provided that all the conditions listed in Article 1(2)(c) of Annex VII are fulfilled'. These conditions are: '(i) the couple produces a legal document recognised as such by a Member State, or any competent authority of a Member State, acknowledging their status as non-marital partners, (ii) neither partner is in a marital relationship or in another non-marital partnership, (iii) the partners are not related in any of the following ways: parent, child, grandparent, grandchild, brother, sister, aunt, uncle, nephew, niece, son-in-law, daughter-in-law; (iv) the couple has no access to legal marriage in a Member State; a couple shall be considered to have access to legal marriage for the purposes of this point only where the members of the couple meet all the conditions laid down by the legislation of a Member State permitting marriage of such a couple.

c. An interim conclusion (IV)

These analyses illustrate the fact that the reach of criteria, the reliance on which constitutes direct discrimination, is particularly important since it may determine whether a given case has to be examined in the framework of direct or indirect discrimination. The examples of pregnancy discrimination and of discrimination against sexual minorities demonstrated that this may be a difficult issue and that the Court's case law on such matters is not always predictable. This is particularly true in the context of discrimination against sexual minorities, where the Court has found that discrimination on grounds of gender-reassignment of a transsexual person is (direct) discrimination on grounds of sex (*P. v S.*),[2373] whilst discrimination on grounds of homosexuality is not (*Grant*).[2374] As for disadvantageous treatment that in fact is related to pregnancy or maternity, the case law analyses showed that both direct and indirect sex discrimination may be relevant, depending on the circumstances of the particular case in terms of the duration of a specified benefit period at issue. Nonetheless, the Court in *Dekker*[2375] was willing to find direct sex discrimination in

---

[2369]   Joined Cases C-122/99 P and C-125/99 P, [2001] *ECR* I-4319. Generally on Staff law and discrimination on grounds of homosexuality, see Snyder 1993 (The Community), pp. 247 subs. (though that work refers to an earlier stage in the development of the EU Staff law).

[2370]   Waaldijk 1997, pp. 118/119.

[2371]   Carolan 1999, pp. 45 and 47.

[2372]   Regulation 259/68/EEC, Euratom, ECSC, OJ 1968 L 56/1 (as amended). For a consolidated text, see http://www.europa.eu.int/comm/dgs/personnel_administration/statut/tocen100.pdf).

[2373]   Case C-13/94, [1996] *ECR* I-2143.

[2374]   Case C-249/96, [1998] *ECR* I-621.

[2375]   Case C-177/88, [1990] *ECR* I-3941.

the context of pregnancy even though the disadvantage at issue in that case was in fact attributable to financial considerations (which, in turn, were related to pregnancy). This illustrates that the Court's case law on pregnancy discrimination is not easy to comprehend, a fact that prompted Mancini & O'Leary[2376] to observe that '[t]hose confused by what could be regarded as the Court's 'multi-speed' approach to pregnant workers are to be forgiven'.[2377] Further, it was seen that the adoption of specific legislation clarifies the situation only to a certain degree. In some situations, the concepts of direct and indirect discrimination are no longer relevant due to specific legislation, but outside the fields of application of such legislation these concepts remain important. In still other situations, a particularly confusing challenge emerges when both the legislative and the conceptual approaches apply in a given case.

4. EXPLICIT PROVISIONS: NO NEED FOR DISTINGUISHING BETWEEN DIRECT AND INDIRECT DISCRIMINATION

Although the demarcation line between direct and indirect discrimination is extremely important in many cases, it needs nevertheless to be added that there are situations in which indirect discrimination in particular is argued before the Court and in academic writing but where the Court does not find it necessary to rely on the concept or even to engage in conceptual considerations of different forms of discrimination. The examples discussed in this section concern situations where the Court simply based its decisions on the relevant provisions' explicit wordings. The case law examined in this context relates to the issues of residence and language, both of them often said to involve indirect discrimination on grounds of nationality.

[2376] Mancini & O'Leary 1999, p. 339.

[2377] On a more general note, it can be argued that the Court's case law on the nature of pregnancy discrimination is one piece in a larger legal system that does not yet fully reflect the following view, expressed by Chief Justice Dickson of the Canadian Supreme Court, in *Brooks v. Canada Safeway Ltd.* [1989] 1 S.C.R. 1219, note 34, p. 1243/1244: 'Combining paid work with motherhood and accommodating the childbearing needs of working women are ever-increasing imperatives. That those who bear children and benefit society as a whole thereby should not be economically or socially disadvantaged seems to bespeak the obvious. It is only women who bear children; no man can become pregnant. As I argued earlier, it is unfair to impose all the costs of pregnancy upon one half of the population. It is difficult to conceive that distinctions or discriminations based upon pregnancy could ever be regarded as other than discrimination based on sex, or that restrictive statutory conditions applicable only to pregnant women did not discriminate against them as women.' – For more general criticism of the Court's case law on the post-birth period see in particular Kilpatrick 1996, p. 96, and Carracciolo di Torella & Masselot 2001, p. 258.

a. Residence in Arts. 73, 77(2) and 78(2) of Regulation 1408/71

Indirect discrimination on grounds of nationality has been argued in relation to a number of the provisions of Regulation 1408/71[2378] in which residence appears. A first example is Art. 73, providing that 'an employed or self-employed person subject to the legislation of a Member State shall be entitled, in respect of the members of his family who are residing in another Member State, to the family benefits provided for by the legislation of the former State, as if they were residing in that State, subject to the provisions of Annex VI'. Art. 73 was at issue in *Bronzino*,[2379] a case that involved an Italian national working in Germany who was refused a family benefit for his three children residing in Italy and registered there as persons seeking employment. Under the applicable German law, entitlement to the allowance required that the children had to be at the disposal of an employment office situated within the German territory and covered by the German legislation, which was in fact only possible in the case of persons residing in Germany. Indirect discrimination (on grounds of nationality) was argued by the Portuguese Government (which in that context referred to *Pinna I*)[2380] and by AG Jacobs (though in his case only as a second line of argument; point 22 of the AG's joint opinion on the *Bronzino* and *Gatto* cases). The Court explained that '[t]he purpose of Article 73 is to prevent a Member State from being able to refuse to grant family benefits on account of the fact that a member of the worker' s family resides in a Member State other than that providing the benefits. Such a refusal could deter Community workers from exercising their right to freedom of movement and would therefore constitute an obstacle to that freedom.' From this, the Court concluded that 'a condition of entitlement to certain family benefits whereby a worker's child must be registered with the employment office of the Member State providing the benefits, a condition which can be fulfilled only if the child resides within the territory of that State, comes within the scope of Article 73 and must therefore be considered to be fulfilled where the child is registered with the employment office of the Member State in which he resides' (*Bronzino*, para. 12).

[2378] Regulation 1408/71/EEC, *OJ* English Special Edition 1971(II) L 149/2, p. 416 (as amended; later replaced by Regulation 883/2004/EC, *OJ* 2004 L 166/1). Besides the provisions discussed in this section, indirect discrimination has also been argued in the context of Art. 10 of the Regulation, see Fuchsloch 1995, p. 51. According to Fuchsloch, Art. 10 constitutes an explicit prohibition of indirect discrimination on grounds of nationality. Art. 10 provides that '[s]ave as otherwise provided in this Regulation invalidity, old-age or survivors' cash benefits, pensions for accidents at work or occupational diseases and death grants acquired under the legislation of one or more Member States shall not be subject to any reduction, modification, suspension, withdrawal or confiscation by reason of the fact that the recipient resides in the territory of a Member State other than that in which the institution responsible for payment is situated'. In the present writer's analysis, it is clear that this provision determines the level of the prescribed treatment (*no* reduction, modification, and so forth) and for that reason is *not* a discrimination provision in the strict sense; see above Part 1, B.V.1.b.

[2379] Case C-228/88, [1990] I-531, see also the parallel case *Gatto* (Case C-12/89, [1990] *ECR* I-557).

[2380] Case 41/84, [1986] *ECR* 1, to be discussed later in this part, A.III.4.c).

Commenting on this judgment, AG La Pergola spoke about indirect discrimination on grounds of nationality (*Stöber and Piosa Pereira*,[2381] point 44 of the AG's opinion), Kokott[2382] spoke about a '*de facto* impediment', Wyatt[2383] spoke about choice of law rules and the GTE Commentary[2384] spoke about a legal fiction regarding the residence of the relevant family members. The language chosen by the Court ('must therefore be considered to be fulfilled'), appears to confirm the GTE Commentary and is in line with AG Jacobs' argument of 'notional residence', according to which Member States are obliged to regard other conditions of eligibility for benefits as satisfied if they are satisfied in the country where the members of the migrant worker's family reside. Importantly for present purposes, the Court did not mention discrimination but simply relied on the wording of Art. 73 Regulation 1408/71.

The same phenomenon can be observed in *Athanasopoulos*,[2385] a case concerning Arts. 77(2) and 78(2) of the same Regulation[2386] where indirect discrimination on grounds of nationality was argued by AG van Gerven (*Athanasopoulos*, points 8 and 22 of the AG's opinion). Here, the Court held that persons residing abroad 'have to be treated *as if* residing' in the Member State responsible for the payment of the benefit in question (*Athanasopoulos*, para. 20 and 47; emphasis added). In both cases, the Court was able to answer the questions put to it based on the mere wording of the relevant provisions, without having to rely on labels such as direct or indirect discrimination, indeed, without mentioning discrimination at all. This is interesting because it might be argued that the duty to treat non-residents as if they were in fact residents corresponds to a prohibition against treating non-residents different from residents, in other words, to a prohibition of discrimination *directly on grounds of residence*. In contrast, these indirect discrimination arguments related to discrimination on grounds of nationality, as generally relevant under the Regulation as well as its broader framework, which is free movement of persons. By focusing on the concept of fictional

---

[2381] Joined Cases C-4/95 and C-5/95, [1997] *ECR* I-511.
[2382] Kokott 1990, p. 928.
[2383] Wyatt 1986, p. 711.
[2384] GTE Commentary 1991, n. 108 ad Art. 51 of the EC Treaty.
[2385] Case C-251/89, [1991] *ECR* I-2797. This case involved the rights of persons residing in a Member State other than Germany to family benefits and to supplements making up for the difference between the German child allowance and the allowance the persons already drew in the other Member State. Deductions applied in the context of such supplements were calculated on the basis of the net annual income of the recipient and his or her family members. It was claimed that the tax assessment necessary in this context was made only with regard to persons residing within Germany while in other cases a reduction was systematically made to the level of the basic amount (without calculating the deduction applicable in the specific case on the basis of the actual net income).
[2386] The former provision states that benefits for dependent children of pensioners 'shall be granted in accordance with the following rules, irrespective of the Member State in whose territory the pensioner or the children are residing'; the latter stipulates that orphans' benefits 'shall be granted in accordance with the following rules, irrespective of the Member State in whose territory the orphan or the natural or legal person actually maintaining him is resident'.

residence instead, the Court was able to avoid the difficulties that might otherwise arise in such a situation.

b. Language requirements under Art. 3(1) of Regulation 1612/68

Mutatis mutandis, a similar phenomenon can be observed in the context of language requirements. According to some authors, imposing such requirements is generally an obvious form of indirect discrimination on grounds of nationality (e.g. Craig & de Búrca,[2387] see also the von der Groeben & Schwarze Commentary,[2388] Malmstedt).[2389] Again, the case law shows that such a label is necessary only where the wording of the law is not sufficiently explicit to answer the question posed in a given case. The final sentence of Art. 3(1) of Regulation 1612/68[2390] is an example.[2391] Art. 3(1) prohibits (i) measures that 'limit the application for and offers of employment, or the right of foreign nationals to take up and pursue employment or subject these to conditions not applicable with respect to their own nationals' and (ii) provisions applicable irrespective of nationality but whose aim or effect is to deter nationals of other Member States from accepting employment. According to the final sentence, the provision 'shall not apply to conditions relating to linguistic knowledge required by reason of the nature of the post to be filled'. According to the Court, this is an exception to sub-section ii (*Groener,*[2392] para. 12) which, in academic writing, is often linked to indirect

---

[2387] Craig & de Búrca 2003, p. 716.

[2388] Von der Groeben & Schwarze Commentary 2004, n. 84 subs. Ad Art. 43 EC.

[2389] Malmstedt 2001, p. 97.

[2390] Regulation No 1612/68/EEC, *OJ* English Special Edition 1968 L 257/2 (as amended). Regarding the issue of language, see already Regulation 3/58/EEC, *OJ* 1958 No 30, p. 561, which was the former version of Regulation 1408/71, and 48(1) of Regulation 574/72/EEC, *OJ* 1972 L 74/1.

[2391] There are other cases where indirect discrimination has been argued in the context of language. However, in those cases the Court did not address the substance of the law in question. Examples are the *French Tourist Guides* case (Case C-154/89, [1991] *ECR* I-659), where AG Lenz raised the question of whether the requirement to take the examination in a language other than that of the State of establishment constitutes indirect discrimination; he left the question open. Another example is the Commission's reference to *Maris* (Case 55/77, [1977] *ECR* 2327) in *Palermo-Toia* (Case 237/78, [1979] *ECR* 2645, p. 2650) as authority for the prohibition of indirect discrimination in the context of language requirements under Art. 84(4) of Regulation 1408/71. In this case, the Court only addressed questions of personal scope. As a third example, consider the applicant in *Kik* (Case T-120/99, [2001] *ECR* II-2235) who argued that the language regime set up by Art. 115 of the Trade Mark Regulation (Regulation 40/94, *OJ* 1994 L 11/1, as amended) infringes Art. 12 EC which, in her opinion, allowed her to employ any of the official languages of the European Community in trade mark proceedings. In the appeals case (Case C-361/01 P, judgment of 9 September 2003, n.y.r., para. 39 of the AG's opinion), the appellants submitted that the language regime set up by Art. 115 'is contrary to Art. 12 EC because it favours certain official languages and hence certain citizens of the Union'. These arguments imply indirect discrimination on grounds of nationality. The Court did not address them as such.

[2392] Case C-379/87, [1989] *ECR* 3967.

discrimination on grounds of nationality. De Witte[2393] explains that 'when a Member State requires that access to employment be conditioned upon linguistic proficiency, there is a presumption of an indirect discrimination against foreign workers, unless it can be shown that such proficiency is needed for that particular job' (compare also McMahon,[2394] Albers).[2395] Accordingly, the *Groener* case is often discussed as a case involving *prima facie* indirect discrimination on grounds of nationality for which there was objective justification[2396] (e.g. Craig & de Búrca,[2397] Bell,[2398] Plötscher,[2399] Barnard).[2400]

Groener arose because a Dutch national was refused appointment to a permanent full-time post[2401] of art teacher in Ireland due to the fact that she had failed a test intended to assess her knowledge of the Gaelic language. In court,[2402] Ms Groener argued that the language requirement was unlawful under the Community rules on free movement of workers, especially in view of the fact that the teaching in question was carried out in English. Whilst acknowledging that the Irish language was not necessary for the work of an art teacher teaching in English, the Court recognised the legitimacy of a national policy for the promotion of a language that is both the national language and the first official language, though it emphasised that such a policy must not encroach upon the fundamental freedoms and that it must not be disproportionate in relation to the aim pursued. In that latter context, the Court pointed to the important role played by teachers in the daily life of the school as well as the privileged relationship that they have with their pupils, and from that concluded that it was not unreasonable to require them to have some knowledge of a country's first language (*Groener*, para. 19 subs.).[2403] In its judgment, the Court did not elaborate on the type

---

[2393]   De Witte 1992, p. 293.

[2394]   McMahon 1990, p. 131.

[2395]   Albers 1999, p. 334.

[2396]   There are also commentators who speak about a rule of reason approach as relevant in the context of the (broader) notion of restrictions in a wider sense: Albers 1990, p. 307, cites *Groener* as an example of the application of the rule of reason in cases involving cultural matters (in making this statement, Albers refers to AG van Gerven's statements in his conclusion on the case *Fedicine* (Case C-17/92, [1993] *ECR* I-2239)).

[2397]   Craig & de Búrca 2003, pp. 716 subs.

[2398]   Bell 2002, p. 35.

[2399]   Plötscher 2003, p. 117.

[2400]   Barnard 2004, p. 236.

[2401]   As Candela Sobriano 2002, p. 33, notes, curiously Ms Groener was not required to be able to speak Gaelic when she was working on a part-time basis but only afterwards when she applied to be appointed full-time, for the same type of work.

[2402]   Before going to Court, Ms Groener complained to the European Parliament. The Commission then initiated an enforcement procedure which, however, did not go to the Court; see Mortelmans 1990, p. 309.

[2403]   It would seem that the Court's benevolent interpretation of the final sentence of Art. 3(1) in *Groener* was at least partially due to the easiness of the language test at issue. At the time at least, Ms Groener appeared to have been the only foreign-national to ever have failed the test (see McMahon 1990, pp. 137 and 138). The judgment may also have been influenced by the fact that *Groener* was the first case

of the infringement and according to McMahon[2404] even actively avoided any examination in terms of indirect discrimination. It is submitted that discussing the final sentence of Art. 3(1) of Regulation 1612/68 in terms of a derogation of a prohibition of indirect discrimination was simply not necessary given the provision's explicit wording.

c. An interim conclusion (V)

The examples just discussed are intended to illustrate that the concept of indirect discrimination, and thus also the demarcation line between direct and indirect discrimination, may be less relevant than is sometimes argued due to specific characteristics of particular provisions or situations. Thus, it was found that Arts. 73, 77(2) and 78(2) of Regulation 1408/71[2405] as well as the final sentence of Art. 3(1) of Regulation 1612/68[2406] are worded in such an explicit way that their references to residence and language, respectively, require no analysis in terms of either direct or indirect discrimination on grounds of nationality. Indeed, it was seen that the Court in case law concerning these provisions does not use such terminology but simply relies on the wording of the provisions which, by itself, is sufficient for dealing with concrete cases.

This finding is confirmed by illustrative counterexamples. In the context of residence, the former Art. 73(2) of Regulation 1408/71 stipulated a reservation in favour of France to the principle of equal treatment with regard to family benefits for family members residing in another Member States, as provided for by section 1 of the same provision.[2407] In other words, section 2 maintained the precise residence criterion declared to be irrelevant in section 1.[2408] The discrepancy between the two sections

---

in which the court had to weigh cultural interests against other interests of the common market; Candela Sobriano 2002, p. 32.

[2404] McMahon 1990, pp. 137 and 138, at 137, speaking about 'de facto discrimination'.

[2405] Regulation 1408/71/EEC, OJ English Special Edition 1971(II) L 149/2, p. 416 (as amended; later replaced by Regulation 883/2004/EC, OJ 2004 L 166/1).

[2406] Regulation No 1612/68/EEC, OJ English Special Edition 1968 L 257/2, as amended.

[2407] Art. 73(2) provided that a worker subject to French legislation 'shall be entitled, in respect of members of his family residing in the territory of a Member State other than France, to the family allowances provided for by the legislation of the Member State in whose territory those members of the family reside; the worker must satisfy the conditions regarding employment on which French legislation bases entitlement to such benefits'.

[2408] The distinction between foreign workers employed in France on the one hand and foreign workers employed elsewhere on the other hand had not existed in the original version of the relevant legislation, which was Regulation 3/58, OJ 1958 No 30, p. 561. Under the rules of that Regulation, a worker was entitled to family allowances according to the provisions of the legislation of the worker's host Member State up to the amount of the allowances granted under the legislation of the state of residence of the family members. Regulation 1408/71 abolished the latter element; see *Pinna I* (Case 41/84, [1986] ECR 1), para. 17.

should have been remedied by the end of 1972[2409] but proposals made by the Commission to this effect were not adopted. Eventually, the validity of Art. 73(2) was challenged in *Pinna I*[2410] where the Court found indirect (covert) discrimination on grounds of nationality (*Pinna I*, para. 23 subs.; see also *Pinna II*,[2411] para. 11 and 12). As a consequence of this ruling, Art. 73(2) EC was abolished.[2412] As opposed to the provision at issue in *Bronzino* (where the Portuguese Government argued indirect discrimination by relying, precisely, on *Pinna I*), the wording of Art. 73(2) alone was not able to provide the answer to the question put to the Court. Instead, the validity of the provision had to be assessed based on an examination of its effect in the light of the requirements of Arts. 48 and 51 of the Treaty (now Arts. 39 and 42 EC). In this framework, with its focus on discrimination on grounds of *nationality*, the concept of indirect discrimination was needed. It is therefore not surprising that Van Raepenbusch[2413] observes that *Pinna I* fits in perfectly with the Court's earlier case law on indirect discrimination on grounds of nationality (see also Wyatt,[2414] Rodière;[2415] further Watson).[2416] Much more recently, the distinction between provisions depending on their wording was confirmed by *Commission v Belgium*[2417] where the Court found a residence requirement in relation to a career interruption benefit to amount to indirect discrimination on grounds of nationality in the context of Art. 39 EC and of Art. 7 of Regulation 1612/68[2418] but merely spoke about a disregard for the terms

---

[2409] Art. 98 of Reg. 1408/71 provided: 'Before 1 January 1973 the Council shall, on a proposal from the Commission, re-examine the whole problem of payment of family benefits to members of families who are not residing in the territory.'

[2410] Case 41/84, [1986] *ECR* 1.

[2411] Case 359/87, [1989] *ECR* 585.

[2412] Mavridis 1997, pp. 204 subs., notes that after *Pinna* the Court no longer invalidated provisions of coordinating secondary social security law found to be (indirectly) discriminatory. Instead, it now 'neutralises' them by pointing to the directly effective prohibition of discrimination under the Treaty.

[2413] Van Raepenbusch 1986, p. 511.

[2414] Wyatt 1986, p. 711. According to Wyatt, the Court's reasoning with regard to the concept of indirect discrimination was strong, though in his opinion the argument that different rules should apply to migrants according their Member State of employment is clearly untenable as such; that in itself would have been a sufficient basis for a finding of an infringement,

[2415] Rodière 1989, p. 310. This author criticises the Court's recourse to the concept of indirect discrimination though not because he considers the discrimination approach inappropriate but only because in his view the case concerned non-comparable situations.

[2416] Watson 1989 (Equal treatment), p. 349. Watson interprets the ruling as stating that not only must the letter of the law be examined but also its practical application: a measure stating clearly that both non-nationals and nationals must be treated equally may still offend the principle of equal treatment if, in its application, a non-national may be disadvantaged to a greater extent than his national counterpart. It is submitted that this reflects a misplaced focus in the present context, namely on the French social security rules. Even though the Court referred to these rules, the case was not concerned with them but rather with the difference regarding residence in sections 1 and 2 of Art. 73 of the Regulation as created by the Community legislator.

[2417] Case C-469/02, judgment of 7 September 2004, n.y.r.

[2418] Regulation 1612/68/EEC, *OJ* English Special Edition 1968 L 257/2, p. 475 (as amended).

of the law in the context of Art. 73 of Regulation 1408/71 (*Commission v Belgium*, para. 15 and 16).

In the context of language, counterexamples are provided by the Court's case law on the place where linguistic abilities were acquired. In *Groener* (para. 19 and 23; see also point 33 of the AG's opinion), the Court explained that '[t]he EEC Treaty does not prohibit the adoption of a policy for the protection and promotion of a language of a Member State which is both the national language and the first official language. However, the implementation of such a policy must not encroach upon a fundamental freedom such as that of the free movement of workers. Therefore, the requirements deriving from measures intended to implement such a policy must not in any circumstances be disproportionate in relation to the aim pursued and the manner in which they are applied must not bring about discrimination against nationals of other Member States. [...]. Moreover, the principle of non-discrimination precludes the imposition of any requirement that the linguistic knowledge in question must have been acquired within the national territory.' This was confirmed in *Angonese*[2419] (para. 45) where the Court held that a requirement to provide evidence of linguistic knowledge exclusively by means of a diploma issued in one particular province of a Member State leads to discrimination on grounds of nationality contrary to Article 48 of the EC Treaty. In these cases, the discrimination[2420] mentioned by the Court related to the national origin of the required linguistic knowledge, rather than to the language requirement as such[2421] (von Toggenburg,[2422] Palermo).[2423] In the framework of the prohibition of discrimination on grounds of nationality, this can only be indirect

---

[2419] Case C-281/98, [2000] *ECR* I-4139. It may be added that the language issue is not the central aspect of this case which instead is famous because of the Court's finding that Art. 39 EC has horizontal direct effect not only with regard to rule-making associations or organisations not covered by public law, as held in *Walrave and Koch* (Case 36/74, [1974] *ECR* 1405) and *Bosman* (Case C-415/93, [1995] *ECR* I-4921), but also with regard to private persons. In that regard, the Court explained that the reasoning adopted in *Defrenne II* (Case 43/75, [1976] *ECR* 455) with regard to what was then Art. 119 of the Treaty (now, after amendment, Art. 141(1) and (2) EC) applied *a fortiori* to Art. 39 EC (*Angonese*, para. 30 subs.).

[2420] Though, some authors speak more generally about an 'obstacle to mobility', rather than about discrimination; e.g. Streinz & Leible 2000, p. 463.

[2421] Indeed, that requirement was not contested by Mr Angonese (see *Angonese*, para. 12; also AG Fennelly in point 42 of his opinion). – Compare also *Haim II* (Case C-424/97, [2000] *ECR* I-5123), para. 58. In this case, the Court held that linguistic requirements can justify restrictions of fundamental freedoms guaranteed by the Treaty. The case concerned an Italian dentist holding a Turkish diploma and wishing to work in Germany as a practitioner under a social security scheme. The Directive on mutual recognition of dentists' diplomas, which in Art. 18(3) explicitly mentions language requirements, did not apply because Ms Haim's diploma did not originate in a Member State (Directive 78/686/EEC, *OJ* 1978 L 233/1, as amended). The case was therefore decided based on the Treaty rules on freedom of establishment.

[2422] Von Toggenburg 2000, p. 246.

[2423] Palermo 2001, p. 315.

discrimination (see Körber,[2424] Lenaerts & Foubert)[2425] – a label that is necessary in this context because there is no EC law provision explicitly dealing with geographic requirements regarding language abilities. Similarly, given the fact that the Race Directive[2426] does not contain specific provisions on language, language requirements having a disadvantageous effect in terms of race or ethnic origin, or being liable to do so, may amount to indirect discrimination on those grounds.

5. USING EU CITIZENSHIP AS A SHORTCUT?

Finally, there are also certain recent cases involving EU citizenship where the Court does not seem to find the distinction between direct and indirect discrimination relevant or necessary. In this case, this is not due to the wording of the relevant provisions (Arts. 17 subs. and 12 EC) but rather to the Court's unique approach to certain situations. Below, two cases serve as examples, namely *Pusa*[2427] and *Gaumain-Cerri*.[2428]

a. Pusa

Mr Pusa, a Finnish national living in Spain, received a disability pension in Finland from which a certain sum was withheld for the purposes of repaying a creditor. Under Finnish law, a certain amount was protected from such an action. In calculating the protected amount, the taxes paid by beneficiaries of pensions *in Finland* were taken in to account but no account was taken of taxes paid in other Member States. In his opinion on this case, AG Jacobs observed that if the case were to be assessed in terms of discrimination (which, however, he did not think necessary), the issue could be presented in terms of discrimination on the basis of residence, and that 'discrimination on the basis of residence has been a recurrent theme in the Court's case-law as a form of indirect discrimination on grounds of nationality' (*Pusa*, point 17 of the AG's opinion). The Court found a difference in treatment in terms of nationality but did not mention indirect discrimination. It explained (*Pusa*, para. 18 subs.): 'In that a citizen of the Union must be granted in all Member States the same treatment in law as that accorded to the nationals of those Member States who find themselves in the same situation, it would be incompatible with the right of freedom of movement were a citizen, in the Member State of which he is a national, to receive treatment less favourable than he would enjoy if he had not availed himself of the opportunities

---

[2424]   Körber 2000, p. 933, speaking of discrimination in substance, but clearly meaning indirect discrimination.
[2425]   Lenaerts & Foubert 2001, p. 292.
[2426]   Directive 2000/43/EC, *OJ* 2000 L 180/22.
[2427]   Case C-224/02, judgment of 29 April 2004, n.y.r.
[2428]   Joined Cases C-502/01 and C-31/02, judgment of 8 July 2004, n.y.r.

offered by the Treaty in relation to freedom of movement [...]. Those opportunities could not be fully effective if a national of a Member State could be deterred from availing himself of them by obstacles raised to his residence in the host Member State by legislation of his State of origin penalising the fact that he has used them [...]. National legislation which places at a disadvantage certain of its nationals simply because they have exercised their freedom to move and to reside in another Member State would give rise to inequality of treatment, contrary to the principles which underpin the status of citizen of the Union, that is, the guarantee of the same treatment in law in the exercise of the citizen's freedom to move [...]. Such legislation could be justified only if it were based on objective considerations independent of the nationality of the persons concerned and proportionate to the legitimate aim of the national provisions [...].'

As a starting point, it should be noted that the Court based its findings on equality or non-discrimination in terms of *nationality*. At the same time, the definition of inequality of treatment given by the Court does not focus on nationality, nor does the Court analyse the effect of the contested regulation in terms of nationality. Here, in terms of the nationality of the persons whose income is at issue, the effect results from making a distinction based on the country where taxes are paid. But the Court's focus is simply on whether or not a person has exercised his or her freedom of movement and residence. This focus appears to be due to the specific circumstances of the case where an individual living in another Member State complains about legislation in his or her Member State of origin. It is clear that in such a case the complaint cannot be about discrimination on grounds of the migrant person's foreign nationality. Indeed, in cases decided in the framework of free movement of persons the issue presents itself either as concerning a specific right[2429] enjoyed by migrant persons, such as the right to residence (e.g. *Singh*),[2430] or as concerning the broad concept of a restriction in a wider sense[2431] (e.g. *Schilling and Fleck-Schilling*).[2432] *Pusa*, however, is not based on the concept of restrictions in a wider sense but clearly on discrimination on grounds of nationality. In his opinion on the case, AG Jacobs (*Pusa*, point 16 subs. of the AG's opinion) argued that it is not necessary to establish discrimination on

---

[2429] Compare above Part 1, B.V.1.

[2430] Case C-370/90, [1992] *ECR* I-4265.

[2431] See Part 1, B.IV.

[2432] Case C-209/01, judgment of 13 November 2003, n.y.r. In this case, the Court stated that '[a]ny Community national who, irrespective of his place of residence and his nationality, has exercised the right to free movement for workers and who has been employed in a Member State other than that of residence falls within the scope of Article 48 of the Treaty' (para. 23). It further recalled that 'provisions which prevent or deter a national of a Member State from leaving his State of origin to exercise his right to freedom of movement constitute an obstacle to that freedom even if they apply without regard to the nationality of the workers concerned' (para. 25). Accordingly, the Court found that the refusal of a tax deduction with regard to the costs for a household assistant because that assistant is employed in a different country and because he or she is not subject to the national statutory pension scheme constitutes a barrier to free movement (para. 37). See also Pernice 2003, p. 185.

grounds of nationality in order for Art. 18 EC to apply since this provision prohibits any unjustified burden imposed on EU citizens seeking to exercise the right to freedom of movement or residence, independent of whether the burden affects nationals of other Member States more significantly than those of the Member State imposing it. The AG in this context specifically mentioned the concept of 'non-discriminatory restrictions' as prohibited in free movement law as a result of the Court's case law. However, the Court did not explicitly address this issue but simply reiterated its earlier statements on equal treatment irrespective of nationality. In that context, the Court's silence on indirect discrimination in the context of a formally neutral measure is noteworthy.

b. Gaumain-Cerri

A further element appears to have been added though the Court's judgment in *Gaumain-Cerri*.[2433] This case involved the refusal of the payment of social security benefits to care providers because they resided in a country different from that where they performed their work. Having found that such benefits fall within the ambit of Regulation 1408/71,[2434] the Court had to address the question whether such a refusal is acceptable under EC law. AG Tizzano expressly argued that such a case involves *indirect* discrimination on grounds of nationality prohibited under Art. 7(2) of Regulation 1612/68[2435] (*Gaumain-Cerri*, point 137 subs. of the AG's opinion). The Court merely spoke about discrimination in a general sense. It explained (*Gaumain-Cerri*, para. 31 subs.): 'It thus remains to be examined, in a situation in which the law of the competent State applies, whether the competent institution may refuse to grant a particular care insurance benefit, namely the payment of the old age insurance contributions on behalf of the third party assisting the reliant person, on the ground that that third party is not resident within the competent Member State. In cases such as those in the main proceedings, the reply must in any event be in the negative, without it being necessary to take a position, as did a number of interveners which submitted observations to the Court, on the issue of whether the third parties concerned are to be regarded as workers within the meaning of Article 39 EC or of Regulation No 1408/71. It is not disputed that, in the main proceedings, those third parties possess Union citizenship conferred by Article 17 EC. The status of Union citizenship enables nationals of the Member States who find themselves in the same situation to enjoy within the scope of the Treaty the same treatment in law, subject to such exceptions as are expressly provided for [...]. However, in cases such as those constituting the

---

[2433] Joined Cases C-502/01 and C-31/02, judgment of 8 July 2004, n.y.r.

[2434] Regulation 1408/71/EEC, *OJ* English Special Edition 1971(II) L 149/2, p. 416 (as amended; later replaced by Regulation 883/2004/EC, *OJ* 2004 L 166/1).

[2435] Regulation 1612/68/EEC, *OJ* English Special Edition 1968 L 257/2, p. 475 (as amended).

subject-matter of the main proceedings, refusal to pay the old age insurance contributions on behalf of a third party assisting a reliant person on the ground that he is not resident in the competent State, the legislation of which is applicable, leads to different treatment of persons finding themselves in the same situation, that is to say of providing assistance on a non-professional basis, within the meaning of the legislation of the competent State, to persons covered by the care insurance provided for under that same legislation. In that context, in view of the purpose of the activity carried on by third parties assisting reliant persons, the condition as to residency of such third parties appears to afford different treatment to comparable situations, rather than to constitute a factor objectively establishing a difference in their situations and thus justifying such different treatment, and therefore constitutes discrimination prohibited by Community law.'

Possibly, the concept of indirect discrimination was not relevant in *Gaumain-Cerri* because the Court relied on the general principle of equality rather than on a specific prohibition of discrimination on grounds of nationality, as suggested by AG Tizzano. Such an interpretation may follow from the fact that the Court, after having stated that citizens who find themselves in the same situation have a right to equal treatment, focused entirely on comparability without ever addressing nationality as a relevant differentiation criterion. Nationality appears to be relevant only as the necessary link to EU citizenship (in other words, because it determines the persons who may derive rights from Art. 18 EC). Should this interpretation be correct, it would mean that the Court's approach is noteworthy because in earlier case law on EU citizenship and the right to equal treatment the Court always explicitly referred to equal treatment *as regards nationality* (guaranteed by Art. 12 EC; e.g. *Grzelczyk*,[2436] para. 31; *D'Hoop*,[2437] para. 28; *Garcia Avello*[2438] para. 23; *Pusa*,[2439] para. 16; see e.g. Timmermans;[2440] Jessurun d'Oliveira,[2441] the von der Groeben & Schwarze Commentary).[2442] The same approach can also be found in later cases (*Trojani*,[2443] para. 39 subs.). In *Gaumain-Cerri*, the Court still speaks about equal treatment and discrimination but no longer specifically about equal treatment with regard to *nationality*. Should the Court's focus indeed be on the general equality principle, this would explain why the concept of indirect discrimination was not relied on by the Court: as was seen earlier,[2444] it is not necessary

---

[2436]   Case C-184/99, [2001] *ECR* I-6193.
[2437]   Case C-224/98, [2002] *ECR* I-6191.
[2438]   Case C-148/02, judgment of 2 October 2003, n.y.r. – According to Barnard 2004, p. 419, both *D'Hoop* and *Garcia Avello* demonstrate 'the fluidity of concepts' in this area and 'mixing models based on discrimination on grounds of nationality with those based on obstacles to market access'.
[2439]   Case C-224/02, judgment of 29 April 2004, n.y.r.
[2440]   Timmermans 2003, pp. 197 subs.
[2441]   Jessurun d'Oliveira 2003, pp. 2239 subs.
[2442]   Von der Groeben & Schwarze Commentary 2004, n. 8 ad Art. 18 EC.
[2443]   Case C-456/02, judgment of 7 September 2004, n.y.r.
[2444]   See above Part 2, A.IV.2.c.

in that context because the principle is not framed in terms of specific discriminatory grounds.

c. An interim conclusion (VI)

The EU citizenship cases, just discussed, seem to indicate that in this particular context indirect discrimination (and, thus, also the demarcation between direct and indirect discrimination) could be less relevant than is sometimes argued due to the Court's approach to certain specific situations. In *Pusa*,[2445] the Court had to interpret provisions on citizenship in view of a situation where a citizen had migrated to another Member State and from there complained about the legislation of his state of origin. In other words, the complaint was not in fact one of discrimination because of the plaintiff's foreign nationality. It was seen that outside EU citizenship such cases are dealt with in the framework of the broad concept of restrictions in a wider sense but that the Court in *Pusa* was, apparently, not willing to recognise the relevance of that concept in the framework of EU citizenship. The Court appears to have addressed the difficulty presented by this situation with a shift in focus to the citizen's having made use of his or her right to free movement. In doing so, the Court side stepped any issue involving the distinction between direct and indirect discrimination. In fact, it was a shift away from nationality. Against this background, *Gaumain-Cerri*[2446] appears to present an alternative and possibly more elegant solution: here, the Court's reasoning appears to have shifted away from discrimination on grounds of nationality altogether and settled rather on the general equality principle. As this principle is not framed in terms of specific discriminatory grounds, the only issue is the comparability of situation – direct and indirect discrimination are no longer relevant concepts in such a context.

IV. OVERALL CONCLUSION: A RATHER UNCLEAR DIVIDING LINE

The following conclusions emerge. On the level of principle, the distinction between direct and indirect discrimination seems easy enough. Based on the Court's statements in *Dekker*,[2447] the decisive point is whether the fundamental reason for the contested treatment is one that applies without distinction to persons of different groups (potential indirect discrimination) or, conversely, whether it applies exclusively to persons of a group protected by a non-discrimination provision (direct discrimina-

---

[2445] Case C-224/02, judgment of 29 April 2004, n.y.r.
[2446] Joined Cases C-502/01 and C-31/02, judgment of 8 July 2004, n.y.r.
[2447] Case C-177/88, [1990] *ECR* I-3941.

tion). However, case law analyses demonstrate that in practice matters are less clear cut both on the conceptual level and on that of the examination of concrete cases. On the *conceptual level,* there appears to be no clear dividing line in terms of the effect of the prohibited measures nor in terms of the possibilities of justification. Cases like *Ugliola*[2448] and *Schnorbus*[2449] show that the Court may find indirect discrimination even where the effect of an apparently neutral differentiation ground is the same or largely the same as that of expressly relying on a prohibited criterion. It was argued that this rather formal approach is unsatisfactory and that it may also have problematic consequences on the level of justification, at least if the traditionally assumed difference between direct and indirect discrimination in terms of justification possibilities is to be maintained. However, it was seen in some areas (direct taxation and agriculture) that the Court explicitly accepted extra-textual justification even for direct discrimination. In addition, certain recent non-discrimination legislation provides for openly formulated justification possibilities for direct discrimination which might well prove to be identical to those available in the context of indirect discrimination (e.g. the Part-Time Work Directive,[2450] further the General Framework Directive[2451] in relation to age discrimination). On the conceptual level, therefore, the dividing line between the concepts of direct and indirect discrimination is not a very clear one.

As far as the *assessment of concrete cases* is concerned, issues concerning the demarcation between direct and indirect discrimination may arise on various levels. First, the facts of the case must be analysed carefully to determine the differentiation ground accurately as well as the person whose treatment is at issue because these issues will be decisive in determining the applicable legal and conceptual framework. Second, the potentially relevant law must be examined in terms of the differentiation grounds that lead to direct discrimination and their reach in order to ascertain which grounds might have to be examined in the framework of indirect discrimination. The examples of the grounds of pregnancy, gender reassignment and homosexuality showed that in practice this may pose difficult questions and that sometimes the Court's case law appears unpredictable. In some cases, the problem may be solved or somewhat mitigated through the adoption of specific secondary legislation. Nonetheless, such legislation may leave certain problems involving demarcation unresolved due primarily to the inherent limits to the reach of legislation. Finally, it was seen that in some cases the concept of indirect discrimination and its distinction from direct discrimination is less relevant than is often argued before the Court and in academic writing. Thus, the law relevant in a given case of alleged discrimination may in fact contain explicit wording which by itself enables the Court to answer the questions before it. Through

---

[2448]   Case 15/69, [1969] *ECR* 363.
[2449]   Case C-79/99, [2000] *ECR* I-10997.
[2450]   Directive 97/81/EC, *OJ* 1998, L 14/9 (as amended).
[2451]   Directive 2000/78/EC, *OJ* 2000 L 303/16.

another example, it was seen that subtle shifts by the Court in interpreting Art. 18 EC on EU citizenship in the particular situation where a citizen complains about the law of his or her own Member State appear to do away with the need to qualify discrimination as either direct or indirect. More generally, De Schutter[2452] argues that there may be specific instances where it does not make sense to try to distinguish between direct and indirect discrimination to begin with, such as in the case of what the author calls 'masked discrimination', a form of direct discrimination that is practiced in such a discrete manner that proof becomes a decisive issue.[2453] According to De Schutter, in such cases there is an intersection between the notions of direct and indirect discrimination in that certain situations can be analysed in either framework depending on what is seen as the intention of the alleged discriminator. In the end the concepts may be merging so that it is useless to try to keep them apart other than through the mode of proof. However, as far as the present writer can see, the Court so far has never been faced with a case precisely of that type.[2454]

[2452] De Schutter 2001, pp. 82 subs.

[2453] Presumably, this refers to cases such as *Yick Wo v. Hopkins* and *Wo Lee v. Hopkins*, 118 U.S. 356 (1886); see above Part 1, B.II.1.a.

[2454] In addition, a case like *Danfoss* (Case 109/88, [1989] *ECR* 3199) shows that the issue of proof may arise even before the nature of the discrimination can be determined. *Danfoss* concerned a pay system lacking so totally in transparency that it was impossible to identify the criteria at the basis of the contested pay differences. The Court held that in such a case 'it is for the employer to prove that his practice in the matter of wages is not discriminatory, if a female worker establishes, in relation to a relatively large number of employees, that the average pay for women is less than that for men' (*Danfoss*, para. 16).

B. INDIRECT DISCRIMINATION AND RESTRICTIONS IN A WIDER SENSE

I. INTRODUCTORY REMARKS: APPROACHING A VAGUE DIVIDING LINE

If the dividing line between direct and indirect discrimination has been found to be rather unclear, some academic writers have argued that it is positively vague in the case of indirect discrimination and restrictions in a wider sense.[2455] On the conceptual level, the distinction between them is obviously made difficult in that both concern formally indistinctly applicable measures and both offer open justification possibilities. On the level of application, it is said that the Court cases do not apply clear cut rules as to which concept is to be applied to a particular situation; instead, it often appears to be a question of where to place the emphasis in a particular case. It is even questioned whether the Court in free movement law nowadays considers it at all necessary to distinguish between different kinds of infringements (e.g. Druesne,[2456] Moitinho de Almeida,[2457] de Búrca,[2458] Drijber,[2459] the Schwarze Commentary,[2460] Somek,[2461] Novak & Schnitzler,[2462] the Calliess & Ruffert Commentary,[2463] Martin).[2464] Against this background, the following sections begin by examining why the Court developed the concept of restrictions in a wider sense rather than simply relying on indirect discrimination (below II.). Further questions that will be examined are whether a distinction can be made between the two concepts in view of the nature of effect of the infringement (below III.) and whether a distinction can be perceived on the level of the application of the two concepts to concrete cases and in specific contexts in the Court's case law (IV.).

[2455]   As was explained earlier, this concept is relevant in the areas of free movement law; see above Part 1, B.IV.
[2456]   Druesne 1982, p. 77.
[2457]   Moitinho de Almeida 1994, p. 256.
[2458]   De Búrca 1997, pp. 20 subs.
[2459]   Drijber & Prechal 1997, pp. 124/125.
[2460]   Schwarze Commentary 2000, n. 75 ad Art. 49 EC.
[2461]   Somek 2001, pp. 188 subs.
[2462]   Nowak & Schnitzler 2000, p. 631.
[2463]   Calliess & Ruffert Commentary 2002, n. 56 ad Art. 50 EC.
[2464]   Martin 1998, pp. 583 subs.

II. WHY A NEW APPROACH?

1. INTRODUCTORY REMARKS

Usually a new legal concept is developed in order to address particular sorts of situations that are not covered by existing concepts. Below, this study examines the function which the concept of restrictions in a wider sense is supposed to fulfil, specifically as compared to the role which the older concept of indirect discrimination has played. The discussion focuses on three specific areas, namely prudential supervision, mutual recognition of diplomas and mutual recognition of driving licences. It begins with three early cases, namely *Van Binsbergen*[2465] (decided in 1974), *Thieffry*[2466] (1977) and *Choquet*[2467] (1978) but then also examines a number of more recent and particularly important cases, namely *Kraus*,[2468] *Gebhard*[2469] and *Vlassopoulou*.[2470] The main findings will be as follows:

– The legal concept of restrictions in a wider sense was developed against the background of national law intended to serve concerns of general interest that were not covered by the narrowly construed textual derogations to the free movement rules.
– At the time, the concept of indirect discrimination would not have been able to adequately address such concerns because it lacked the element of objective justification (though later, once that element was included, the Court still did not change its approach).
– Also, the Court seems to have been reluctant to apply a discrimination approach in areas where secondary law was needed in order to reconcile the conflicting interests of the general interest and individuals' rights to free movement.
– Unlike indirect discrimination, the concept of restrictions in a wider sense makes the imposition of positive duties possible.

2. THREE EARLY CASES

a. The cases

i. Prudential supervision: *Van Binsbergen*

The historical starting point for the development of a restriction-based approach is found in the area of prudential supervision, that is, of national rules governing the

---

[2465] Case 33/74, [1974] *ECR* 1299.
[2466] Case 71/76, [1977] *ECR* 1199.
[2467] Case 16/78, [1978] *ECR* 2293.
[2468] Case C-19/92, [1993] *ECR* I-1663.
[2469] Case C-55/94, [1995] *ECR* I-4165.
[2470] Case C-340/89, [1991] *ECR* I-2357.

professions (and relating to issues other than diplomas). The first relevant case, *Van Binsbergen*,[2471] concerned the question of whether it is acceptable under Community law for a Member State to require that attorneys-at-law acting before its courts be permanently based on its territory. The case arose in the Netherlands and involved Mr van Binsbergen's legal representative who, in the course of legal proceedings, moved to Belgium, thereby ceasing to fulfil the Dutch residence requirement. Indirect discrimination on grounds of nationality was argued by AG Mayras who, however, considered that the Dutch rule might be justified in the interest of the proper functioning of the administration of justice (*Van Binsbergen*, p. 1318 subs.). In contrast, the Court did not refer to indirect discrimination but only spoke about restrictions. It stated that the requirement of habitual residence may have the result of depriving the rules on free movement of services of their useful effect, but then added that in the case of services of a particular nature, specific requirements imposed on the person providing the service cannot be considered incompatible with the Treaty where they have as their purpose the application of professional rules justified by the general good (*Van Binsbergen*, para. 10-15).

> The Court began by pointing out that 'the restrictions to be abolished pursuant to Articles 59 and 50 include all requirements imposed on the person providing the service by reason in particular of his nationality or of the fact that he does not habitually reside in the state where the service is provided, which do not apply to persons established within the national territory or which may prevent or otherwise obstruct the activities of the person providing the service'. The Court continued: '[...] a requirement that the person providing the service must be habitually resident within the territory of the state where the service is to be provided may, according to the circumstances, have the result of depriving Article 59 of all useful effect, in view of the fact that the precise object of that Article is to abolish restrictions on freedom to provide services imposed on persons who are not established in the State where the service is to be provided. However, taking into account the particular nature of the services to be provided, specific requirements imposed on the person providing the service cannot be considered incompatible with the Treaty where they have as their purpose the application of professional rules justified by the general good – in particular rules relating to organization, qualifications, professional ethics, supervision and liability – which are binding upon any person established in the State in which the service is provided, where the person providing the person providing the service would escape from the ambit of those rules being established in another Member State. [...] In accordance with these principles, the requirement that persons whose functions are to assist the administration of justice must be permanently established for professional purposes within the jurisdiction of certain courts or tribunals cannot be considered incompatible with the provisions of Articles 59 and 60, where such requirement is objectively justified by the need to ensure observance of professional rules of conduct connected, in particular, with the administration of justice and with respect for professional ethics.' To this the Court added that the above only applies

---

[2471]   Case 33/74, [1974] *ECR* 1299.

in situations where the provision of services is subject to some sort of qualification or regulation and when the requirement of residence is fixed by reference to the territory of the state in question. The Court concluded (*van Binsbergen*, para. 17): 'It must therefore be stated in reply to the question put to the Court that the first paragraph of Article 59 and the third paragraph of Article 60 of the EEC Treaty must be interpreted as meaning that the national law of a Member State cannot, by imposing a requirement as to habitual residence within that state, deny persons established in another Member State the right to provide services, where the provision of services is not subject to any special condition under the national law applicable.'[2472]

ii. Recognition of foreign diplomas: *Thieffry*

Thieffry[2473] concerned a Belgian lawyer who, after having established himself in Paris, obtained there the recognition of his doctorate in Belgian law as a qualification equivalent to a licentiate's degree in French law. Mr Thieffry also earned the French certificate for the profession of *avocat* (bar exam). His application to be admitted to the Paris bar was nevertheless rejected on the grounds that he did not hold a *French* licentiate or doctor's degree. Mr Thieffry maintained that this constituted 'discrimination based on the nationality of his diploma', arguing that discrimination based on nationality must be rejected, whether it was applied to the person holding the diploma or to the diploma itself. Recalling that Community law on freedom of establishment prohibits not only overt but also disguised or covert discriminations, the Commission and AG Mayras considered that the rules of the type at issue fall under that prohibition (*Thieffry*, p. 773 and 782 subs.).

> The Commission, referring to the General Programme on establishment[2474] and to (unspecified) case law, pointed out that 'discriminations on the basis of nationality are not only overt discriminations, but can also be disguised discriminations' and that 'the conditions to which the right to take up or pursue activities as a self-employed person is made subject by any law, regulation or administrative action and which, although applicable irrespective of nationality, mainly or exclusively impede foreigners in the taking up and pursuing of such activities, constitute restrictions within the meaning of Article 52 of the Treaty. The requirement of a French diploma is in fact a condition which impedes almost exclusively, and at all events mainly, nationals of the other Member States.' AG Mayras agreed. Referring to *Sotgiu*,[2475] he explained: 'Let me point out, indeed, that discrimination in connexion with the right of establishment does not only consist of direct and overt restrictions imposed

---

[2472] The same approach is reflected in other early prudential supervision cases, such as *Van Wesemael* (Joined Cases 110/78 and 111/78, [1979] *ECR* 35) and *A.J. Webb* (Case 279/80, [1981] *ECR* 3305) which confirmed the Court's approach in *Van Binsbergen*; see Morse 1979, p. 376; X 1981.

[2473] Case 71/76, [1977] *ECR* 1199.

[2474] General Programme for the abolition of restrictions on freedom of establishment, *OJ* English Special Edition, Second Series, IX, p. 7.

[2475] Case 152/73, [1974] *ECR* 153.

by reason of nationality of the persons seeking to avail themselves thereof, but can also consist of disguised discrimination based for example on residence [...]'. In the AG's view, 'in the circumstances of the case before the Court today, the demand of the Paris Bar Council that the person concerned should possess the *French* diploma of licentiate in law constitutes, with regard to the principle of freedom of establishment, a disguised restriction on, or at least an obstacle to, the exercise by Community nationals of their right of establishment in the profession of advocate in France'. In the AG's analysis, the relevant legal provisions were 'not discriminatory in theory, but can result in discrimination in practice, because it will in general be easier for a national than for a foreigner to satisfy the requirements imposed'. Therefore, the French requirement 'in fact constitutes an indirect and disguised but quite definite restriction with regard to nationals of other Member States desirous of entering the profession of advocate in France'.

The Court, though mentioning the prohibition of both direct and indirect discrimination on grounds of nationality, did not find such discrimination. Instead, it spoke simply about 'an unjustified restriction' to the freedom of establishment and in that context pointed to the need for specific secondary legislation regarding the mutual recognition of diplomas which was necessary in order to reconcile the freedom of establishment with the application of national professional rules justified by the general good (*Thieffry*, para. 12 and 19).

The Court first recalled the Treaty system regarding free movement of persons and, more specifically, freedom of establishment. It mentioned Art. 57 of the Treaty (now Art. 47 EC) which assigns the Council the duty to issue Directives about the mutual recognition of diplomas and about the coordination of national provisions concerning the taking up and the pursuit of activities as self-employed persons. The Court noted that this provision is 'directed towards reconciling freedom of establishment with the application of national professional rules justified by the general good, in particular rules relating to organization, qualification, professional ethics, supervision and liability, provided that such application is effected without discrimination' (*Thieffry*, para. 12). The Court affirmed that the General Programme provides useful guidance for the implementation of the Treaty provisions and addresses both overt and disguised discrimination. Against the background of the case at hand, the Court then explained that freedom of establishment is subject to observance of professional rules justified by the general good and that and that it is to be attained by measures enacted by the Member States. It found that there was 'an unjustified restriction on that freedom where, in a Member State, admission to a particular profession is refused to a person covered by the Treaty who holds a diploma which has been recognized as equivalent qualification by the competent authority of the country of establishment and who furthermore has fulfilled the specific conditions regarding professional training in force in that country, solely by reason of the fact that the person concerned does not possess the national diploma corresponding to the diploma which he holds and which has been recognized as an equivalent qualification' (*Thieffry*, para. 19).

iii. Recognition of foreign driving licences: *Choquet*

The third case to be mentioned in the present context, *Choquet*,[2476] concerned a Frenchman residing in Germany and holding a driving licence issued in France. He suffered criminal prosecution for driving a motor vehicle without possessing a licence considered valid under German law. As a driver residing in Germany, German law obliged him to hold a German licence. Mr Choquet argued that this infringed the national treatment principle under Community law. Similarly, the national court in its reference for a preliminary ruling pointed out 'that the acquisition of a fresh driving licence may [...] create language difficulties and involve the person concerned in expenses which are so disproportionate that they may amount to discrimination against nationals of the other Member States in contravention of Article 7 of the Treaty and may impede the exercise of the right to freedom of movement which is guaranteed by Article 48' (*Choquet*, para. 2). In contrast, the Court of Justice did not refer to discrimination but spoke more generally about 'an obstacle to freedom of movement' (*Choquet*, para. 7). It found that whilst the requirement to obtain a national driving licence was not in principle incompatible with Community law, such a requirement may be regarded as prejudicing in an indirect way the exercise of free movement rights 'if it appears that the conditions imposed by national rules on the holder of a driving licence issued by another Member State are not in due proportion to the requirements of road safety' (*Choquet*, para. 9).

> Specifically, the Court stated that 'national rules relating to the issue and mutual recognition of driving licences by the Member States can exert an influence, both direct and indirect, on the exercise of rights guaranteed by the provisions of the Treaty relating to freedom of movement for workers, to establishment and, subject to the reference contained in Article 61(1) of the Treaty, to the provisions of services in general' (*Choquet*, para. 4). The Court recognised that such rules fell primarily within the scope of the responsibility of the Member States concerning traffic safety. It noted that the national rules differed 'to such an extent that the mere recognition of driving licences for the benefit of persons who elect to reside permanently within the territory of a Member State other than the State which issued them with a driving licence cannot be contemplated unless the requirements for the issue of those driving licences are harmonized to a sufficient extent'. From this the Court concluded: 'In these circumstances the requirements imposed by a Member State on persons established within its territory, in so far as the recognition of driving licences issued by other Member States is concerned, cannot be regarded as amounting by themselves to an obstacle to freedom of movement for workers, to freedom of establishment or to the liberalization of the provision of services.' (*Choquet*, para. 7). However, the Court added that whilst the requirement to obtain a national driving licence was not in principle incompatible with Community law, such a requirement 'may be regarded as indirectly prejudicing the exercise

---

[2476]   Case 16/78, [1978] *ECR* 2293.

of the right of freedom of movement, the right of freedom of establishment or the freedom to provide services guaranteed by Articles 48, 52 and 59 of the Treaty respectively, and consequently as being incompatible with the Treaty, if it appears that the conditions imposed by national rules on the holder of a driving licence issued by another Member State are not in due proportion to the requirements of road safety' (*Choquet*, para. 9). As examples, the Court mentioned the insistence by the host Member State on a driving test which clearly duplicates a test taken in another Member State for the classes of vehicle which the person concerned wishes to drive, linguistic difficulties arising out of the procedure laid down for the conduct of any checks and the imposition of exorbitant charges for completing the requisite formalities.

b. Indirect discrimination or restriction?

It appears that in all three cases (indirect) discrimination on grounds of nationality was argued before the Court. Commenting on the decisions, some academic writers thought that the Court's finding was indeed (or could have been) one of (a broadly understood type of) indirect discrimination (regarding *Van Binsbergen*,[2477] see Martin,[2478] O'Leary & Fernández Martín,[2479] the Lenz & Borchardt Commentary;[2480] regarding *Thieffry*, X,[2481] Dauwe,[2482] Colin & Sinkondo,[2483] the von der Groeben & Schwarze Commentary,[2484] Eberhartinger,[2485] Borchardt,[2486] more generally also the Léger Commentary;[2487] regarding *Choquet*, the Lenz & Borchardt Commentary,[2488] the former GTE commentary,[2489] Plender;[2490] also Martin).[2491] Others thought that the

---

[2477] In the area of prudential supervision, the argument of indirect discrimination is often found in relation to the later case *A.J. Webb* (Case 279/80, [1981] *ECR* 3305). According to Martin 1998, p. 567, this case clearly was examined in the framework of discrimination; see further Druesne 1982, p. 77; O'Leary 1999, p. 400; Streinz & Leible 2000, p. 462, footnote 462; also AG Jacobs in *Säger* (Case C-76/90, [1991] *ECR* I-4221), point 21 of the AG's opinion; AG Mancini in *Bond van Adverteerders* (Case 352/85, [1988] *ECR* 2085), point 10 of the AG's opinion, and AG van Gerven in *Rush Portuguesa* (Case C-113/89, [1990] *ECR* I-1417), point 8 of the AG's opinion.

[2478] Martin 1998, p. 564.

[2479] O'Leary & Fernández Martín 2002, p. 168.

[2480] Lenz & Borchardt Commentary 2003, n. 20 ad Arts. 49/50 EC.

[2481] X 1978 (Thieffry), pp. 959 subs.

[2482] Dauwe 1978, p. 229.

[2483] Colin & Sinkondo 1993, p. 43.

[2484] Von der Groeben & Schwarze Commentary 2004, n. 82 ad Art. 43 EC.

[2485] Eberhartinger 1997, p. 47.

[2486] Borchardt 2002, p. 328, n. 740.

[2487] Léger Commentary 2000, n. 75 ad Arts. 49-50 EC.

[2488] Lenz & Borchardt Commentary 2003, n. 5 ad Art. 43 EC.

[2489] GTE Commentary 1997, n. 41 und 43 ad Art. 52 of the EC Treaty.

[2490] Plender 1982, p. 634, footnote 20.

[2491] Martin 1994, p. 47. Martin speaks about 'objective discrimination', a term that refers to situations 'dans lesquelles le simple fait que de n'être pas ressortissant national peut justifier, dans le chef de l'intéressé, l'exigence d'une condition qui n'est pas imposée aux nationaux, telles la détention d'un permis de conduire national'.

Court applied a concept of *restrictions* that may be justified in the interest of the general good (regarding *Van Binsbergen*, e.g. Morse,[2492] Kok;[2493] regarding *Thieffry* and *Choquet*, e.g. Mattera).[2494] In hindsight, it is clear that the latter interpretation is correct. Nevertheless, from a merely conceptual point of view, an analysis of the three cases in terms of indirect discrimination on grounds of nationality would certainly appear to have been possible: after all, all of them involved a difference in treatment (in *Van Binsbergen*, between attorneys-at-law permanently established in the Netherlands and those permanently established outside the Netherlands in that only the former could act before Dutch courts; in *Thieffry* between attorneys-at-law holding national and foreign diplomas in that only the former were admitted to the bar; and in *Choquet* between persons holding national and foreign driving licences in that only the former were allowed to drive a car, which in turn affected foreigners' possibilities to engage in economic activities) and in all three cases the differentiation ground relied on was formally neutral as far as nationality is concerned but in fact predominantly disadvantaged foreigners (permanent residence in *Van Binsbergen*, possession of a national diploma in *Thieffry* and of a national driving licence in *Choquet*).

If an analysis in the framework of indirect discrimination would have been possible in terms of the nature of the infringements at issue in the three cases, why did the Court opt for a different approach? In the present writer's analysis, the main factor might have been the specific subject matters of the cases and the ensuing *need for specific secondary legislation* in order to reconcile matters of general interest with free movement. As Kraus[2495] points out in the context of diplomas, 'the right to take up employment or to establish oneself in another Member State or to provide cross-border services would be quite meaningless if those who wish to exercise these fundamental freedoms could not make use of their diplomas and professional qualifications abroad. On the other hand, the protection of the consumer or, more generally, the public interest calls for mechanisms to ensure that certain professions or activities cannot be exercised unless the person concerned possesses the appropriate specialised qualifications.' As far as prudential supervision and diplomas are concerned, the Treaty recognised their relevance as possible obstacles to free movement by expressly envisaging the adoption of specific secondary legislation (Art. 57(1) and (2) of the EEC Treaty, now Art. 47(1) and (2) EC, made applicable in the area of free movement of services by virtue of Art. 55 EC; Wägenbaur).[2496] In this area, therefore, the Community

---

[2492]   Morse 1975, p. 69.
[2493]   Kok 1976, p. 259. According to Kok, *Van Binsbergen* is situated on the dividing line between the principle of free movement and the legitimate concern for prudential supervision.
[2494]   Mattera 1991, pp. 192 subs. This author interpreted *Thieffry* as containing the 'fecund seed' for a general theory on restrictions in the field of free movement of persons and of services.
[2495]   Kraus 2003, p. 248.
[2496]   Wägenbaur 1977, p. 261.

had been given both the competence and the task to legislate on these issues in order to address the difficulties that might arise in the context of free movement.[2497]

At the time of *Van Binsbergen* and *Thieffry*, the fact that specific legislation did not yet exist explains why the Court had to base its decisions on the Treaty rules. This was possible because the Court had held earlier that the absence of secondary legislation envisaged by the Treaty in the area of freedom of establishment did not prevent Art. 52 of the EEC Treaty (now Art. 43 EC) from having direct effect (*Reyners*,[2498] para 26 and 30). In other words, the Treaty provisions could be applied even in the absence of specific secondary legislation. However, Nicolaysen[2499] points out that the Court 'of course' could not simply do away with the need for secondary legislation expressly envisaged by the Treaty but had to find a way in which to take care of *interests related to the general good*.[2500] Under the approaches in existence at the time, the need to reconcile the legitimate requirements regarding prudential supervision and rules on diplomas with the right of free movement would have caused difficulties. First, it would have been impossible to rely on the express derogation grounds of public policy, public security and public health (Art. 46 EC, made applicable in the area of free movement of services by virtue of Art. 55 EC) since these derogations have to be construed narrowly.[2501] Second, the definition of indirect discrimination as it existed at the time did not yet include the element of objective justification in the sense of cross-cutting reasons[2502] but allowed for 'justification' only in terms of objective *differences*

[2497] To some extent, this can be compared to the situation involving medical and allied and pharmaceutical professions under Art. 47(3) EC, though that provision is more explicit in that it specifies that in its field of application the progressive abolition of restrictions of free movement 'shall be dependent upon coordination of the conditions for their exercise in the various Member States'. Thus, here the Treaty itself regulates the relationship between the approximation of law in a given area and the abolition of discrimination; see Steindorff 1965, p. 42.

[2498] Case 2/74, [1974] *ECR* 631. In the *Reyners* case itself the situation at issue differed from those in the above three cases in that it did not concern hindrances to free movement caused in the context of formally neutral rules concerning diplomas or prudential supervision, but a rather straightforward example of direct discrimination on grounds of nationality. Mr Reyners, a Dutch national, wished to work as an attorney-at-law in Belgium. He held the necessary Belgian diplomas but did not fulfil the requirement of Belgian nationality. The argument was made that Art. 52 could be directly effective only once the secondary legislation envisaged by the Treaty was adopted. In para. 30, the Court specifically held that the Directives had become superfluous at the end of the transitional period with regarding to implementing the rule on nationality.

[2499] Nicolaysen 1978, p. 228.

[2500] This is also reflected in the Commission's remarks in the later case of *Heylens* (Case 222/86, [1987] *ECR* 4097) where a reference to indirect discrimination is immediately followed by the remark that problems arising in this context are to be solved through secondary law. The Court examined the case in the framework of the concept of restrictions in a wider sense; see X 1988, p. 517; Mattera 1991, pp. 194/195, and Timmermans 1989, p. 291.

[2501] See above Part 2, A.IV.3.e.ii.

[2502] It will be recalled that first indications in that regard can be found 1982 in *Seco* (Joined Cases 62/81 and 63/81, [1982] *ECR* 223); see above Part 2, A.II.4. The element was not recognized in the context of sex discrimination until 1981, in *Jenkins* (Case 96/80, [1981] *ECR* 911); see above Part 2, A.II.3.

(comparability).[2503] Although AG Mayras in *Van Binsbergen* suggested the inclusion of the element of objective justification (as he had done earlier in the context of *Sotgiu*),[2504] the Court was obviously not willing to follow him. In that situation, if the Court meant to acknowledge the legitimacy of national professional rules of conduct in the context of the administration of justice or of certain national requirements regarding diplomas, it had to do so under a new and different approach. It therefore developed the concept of restrictions in a wider sense with its element of justification in the interest of the general good, which was thus able to accommodate these concerns. As Snell[2505] notes in the context of *Van Binsbergen*, the idea behind the Court's approach was to ensure that legitimate national measures could be saved even if Art. 46 EC was unavailable. In addition, Dauwe[2506] notes that a finding of indirect discrimination would not have solved the problem with regard to diplomas since the Court was looking for more than a mere negative obligation, that is, for the positive duty to assess foreign diplomas. In the framework of a legal order such as EC free movement law, the concept of discrimination is quite limited in that positive obligations are not part of the prohibition of discrimination itself but rather constitute additional and separate duties, such as the Member States' duty under Art. 10 EC to actively ensure compliance with the fundamental freedoms on their territory (compare the *Strawberries* case;[2507] Jarass)[2508] and the employer's duty to actively provide reasonable accommodation for employees with a handicap under Art. 5 of the General Framework Directive.[2509] Also, it is submitted that the principle that difficulties arising in the context of differences between the legal orders of different Member States cannot be considered as leading to discrimination may also play a role in the present context; this will be discussed later.[2510]

The case of driving licences is somewhat different since here there is no Treaty provision explicitly recognizing a need for action in this area of law. Nevertheless, similar considerations may apply. The relevance of national rules on driving licences in the context of free movement outside the area of transport itself[2511] was recognised by the Court when it pointed out that such rules can exert an influence on the exercise

---

[2503] See above Part 2, A.II.2.b.

[2504] Case 152/73, [1974] *ECR* 153.

[2505] Snell 2002, p. 183.

[2506] Dauwe 1978, p. 229.

[2507] Case C-265/95, [1997] *ECR* I-6959. Although the case specifically concerned the free movement of goods, the principle emerging from it is of general importance.

[2508] Jarass 2000 (Unified Approach), p. 150.

[2509] Directive 2000/78/EC, *OJ* 2000 L 303/16. Compare, however, the argument that a failure to fulfil this duty amounts to a form of discrimination; see above Part 1, B.III.5.b.iii.

[2510] See later in this part, B.IV.2.a.

[2511] The Treaty only very generally states that free movement of services in the area of transport is to be achieved through special rules (Arts. 61(1) EC). There, the reference is generally to road transport but not to the specific issue of driving licences and its relationship to issues of free movement (Arts. 79 subs. EC).

of free movement rights, both directly an indirectly. For present purposes, it is important to note that the term 'indirect' as used in this context concerns the *indirect relevance* of rules on driving licences in the context of free movement outside transport law ('indirectly prejudicing the exercise of the right of freedom of movement'),[2512] rather than the nature of the infringement at issue in this particular case. As was already noted, the Court's approach in that latter context was clearly restriction-based. As in the case of diplomas, it includes an element of positive obligation: the fact that national requirements regarding driving licences must not duplicate a test taken in another Member State implies that foreign tests must be taken into account, examined and recognised in so far as refusal would lead to an unnecessary duplication. Finally, the need for secondary legislation in order to reconcile the requirements of traffic safety with free movement was eventually acknowledged in legislation itself (e.g. the preamble of the Second Directive on driving licences).[2513]

3. CONFIRMATION IN A CHANGED LEGAL CONTEXT

The restriction-based approach as reflected in the three early cases just discussed was confirmed in later case law even after the legal concept of indirect discrimination allowed for objective justification going beyond mere objective differences. Below, three important examples are discussed.

a. Kraus

The first example, *Kraus*,[2514] came to the Court of Justice after a number of important prudential supervision cases had already been decided in the framework of a restriction-based approach, among them notably *Insurance and Co-insurance*,[2515] the *Tourist Guides* cases[2516] and *Säger*.[2517] Whilst the concept of indirect discrimination was not important to any of them, it once again played a prominent role in *Kraus* in an argument made by AG van Gerven. *Kraus* concerned a lawyer faced with German legislation requiring an official authentication of his LL.M. degree from the University of Edinburgh, at a cost of 130 DM, whilst no such procedure was necessary with regard to German degrees. Noting that this system was not directly aimed at foreigners but

---

[2512] Compare above Part 2, A.IV.2.a.
[2513] Directive 91/439/EEC, *OJ* 1991 L 237/1 (as amended).
[2514] Case C-19/92, [1993] *ECR* I-1663.
[2515] Case 205/84, [1986] *ECR* 3755.
[2516] Case C-154/89, [1991] *ECR* I-659; Case C-180/89, [1991] *ECR* I-709; Case C-198/89, [1991] *ECR* I-727, and Case C-375/92, [1994] *ECR* I-923.
[2517] Case C-76/90, [1991] *ECR* I-4221. On this landmark case, see, for example, Roth 1993 (Kraus), pp. 151/152, Van Empel 1993, p. 669, and Speyer 1991, p. 588.

rather at foreign diplomas, AG van Gerven suggested an indirect discrimination approach based on the *Sotgiu*[2518] line of authority (*Kraus*, point 7 of the AG's opinion). The Court, however, after having stated that a situation of the type at issue in *Kraus* falls within the ambit of Community law,[2519] applied a restriction-based approach (*Kraus*, para. 32).

Academic commentators differ on the question of whether a case like *Kraus* should be seen in the framework of the concept of restrictions in a wider sense or rather of indirect, or even direct, discrimination on grounds of nationality (e.g. Roth,[2520] Denys,[2521] Johnson & O'Keeffe,[2522] O'Leary,[2523] Martin,[2524] Adobati,[2525] Kaldellis,[2526] Barnard).[2527] Again, given the formally neutral nature of the national rule and its quite obvious disparate effect in terms of nationality, indirect discrimination on grounds of nationality would appear to be a possibility. Given that the element of objective justification had already been included in the Court's definition of that concept, it would also have allowed for taking concerns of general interest into account. In addition, in the context of prudential supervision there is normally no issue of positive duties. Against this background, the suggestion of AG van Gerven's made perfect sense. However, it would seem that by then the restriction-based approach was so firmly established that the Court did not find it necessary or advisable to go back to an analysis in the framework of indirect discrimination with its inherent difficulties concerning comparability, proof and the limits with regard to positive duties.

b. Gebhard

Kraus was later confirmed in *Gebhard*,[2528] which has been called the culmination point in the evolution from a discrimination-based to a restriction-based approach (e.g.

[2518] Case 152/73, [1974] *ECR* 153.

[2519] *Kraus*, para. 14 subs., regarding the issue of reverse discrimination; see also Smith 1994, pp. 72 subs., and Denys 1994.

[2520] Roth 1993 (Kraus), p. 1254.

[2521] Denys 1994, pp. 650/651.

[2522] Johnson & O'Keeffe 1994, p. 1333.

[2523] O'Leary 1999, p. 401.

[2524] Martin 1994, p. 50, and Martin 1998, p. 587.

[2525] Adobati 1995, p. 112.

[2526] Kaldellis 2001, p. 38. This author argues that *Kraus* has to be seen as a ruling on 'indirect, or even direct, discrimination', though in the present writer's analysis his arguments really relate to indirect discrimination. Kaldellis refers to Craig & de Búrca 1998, p. 747, according to whom 'it can be argued that the restriction in *Kraus* was in fact indirectly discriminatory'. Kaldellis at the time referred to the 2nd edition of the text book; in the 3rd edition, the language used is slightly different: 'could' instead of 'can' (see p. 786). It is therefore unclear to the present writer how the argument made by Kaldellis could relate to direct discrimination.

[2527] Barnard 2004, p. 258.

[2528] Case C-55/94, [1995] *ECR* I-4165.

Ysewijn).[2529] Mr Gebhard, a German attorney-at-law, worked for a number of years for an Italian law firm. Eventually, he set up his own chambers in Milan and worked from there using the Italian professional title of *avvocato*. This led to problems, first because under Italian law foreign lawyers were entitled only to carry on temporary activities[2530] and, second, because the Milan Bar Council prohibited Mr Gebhard from using the title *avvocato*. The Court, referring to the need for secondary Community legislation as indicated by Art. 47 EC, explained that the taking-up and pursuit of certain self-employed activities may be conditioned on complying with provisions justified by the general good, such as rules relating to organization, qualifications, professional ethics, supervision and liability, including rules concerning use of professional titles. However, it added that 'national measures liable to hinder or make less attractive the exercise of fundamental freedoms guaranteed by the Treaty must fulfil four conditions: they must be applied in a non-discriminatory manner, they must be justified by imperative requirements in the general interest; they must be suitable for securing the attainment of the objective which they pursue; and they must not go beyond what is necessary in order to attain it' (*Gebhard*, para. 37).

The restriction-based framework of the Court's decision in *Gebhard* is acknowledged by numerous authors (e.g. Huglo,[2531] Denys,[2532] Kaldellis,[2533] O'Leary,[2534] Craig & de Búrca).[2535] Lombay[2536] almost enthusiastically exclaimed: 'Gone is a case law which indicated that national treatment alone was sufficient, with no review of purpose or proportionality. It is open season on indistinctly applicable national measures [...].' Nevertheless, some commentators still argue in favour of indirect discrimination on grounds of nationality (Martin).[2537]

[2529]   Ysewijn 1997, p. 29.

[2530]   This was based on the Italian law implementing the Lawyers' Services Directive (Directive 77/249/EEC, *OJ* 1977 L 78/17, as amended). The national court's question was whether the Italian law was in line with this Directive. However, working in Italy on a permanent basis, Mr Gebhard was in fact not a service provider. Instead, the Court found his situation to fall under the rules on freedom of establishment (*Gebhard*, para. 20 subs.). It nevertheless indicated that even if Mr Gebhard had indeed been a service provider, he would have been entitled to equip himself with the infrastructure necessary for providing his services.

[2531]   Huglo 1996, p. 745.

[2532]   Denys 1996, p. 36.

[2533]   Kaldellis 2001, p. 39.

[2534]   O'Leary 1999, p. 401.

[2535]   Craig & de Búrca 2003, pp. 784 subs.

[2536]   Lombay 1996, p. 1982. This author sees *Gebhard* as an example of a case involving a truly indistinctly applicable measure.

[2537]   Martin 1998, p. 594. Besides a restriction, the case also concerned an instance of direct discrimination on grounds of nationality, namely the prohibition against foreigners to set up offices in Italy.

c. Vlassopoulou

As far as foreign diplomas are concerned, the restriction-based approach reflected in *Thieffry*[2538] was confirmed in *Vlassopoulou*,[2539] which sums up the development of the Court's case law on this issue.[2540] The case concerned a Greek lawyer who, holding Greek legal diplomas and a German Ph.D., was not admitted to the German bar because she did not hold a lower law degree from a German university (first or second state examination). AG van Gerven once more emphasised the importance of the prohibition of indirect discrimination on grounds of nationality but then nevertheless pointed to the concept of restrictions in a wider sense (*Vlassopoulou*, para. 6 and 10). The Court found that Community nationals can be placed at a disadvantage through the non-recognition of a diploma[2541] and stated that the Member States have a duty to examine foreign diplomas and to accept them in so far as they are equivalent to the relevant national diplomas. The Court in this context also mentioned Art. 5 of the EC Treaty (now Art. 10 EC; *Vlassopoulou*, para. 15 subs.).

Again, there are commentators who argue that the requirement of a national diploma leads to indirect discrimination on grounds of nationality (e.g. Stein,[2542] Kingreen,[2543] the von der Groeben & Schwarze Commentary,[2544] Nachbaur,[2545] Martin).[2546] However, it is quite clear that the approach applied by the Court is that of restrictions in a wider sense (e.g. Fierstra,[2547] Johnson & O'Keeffe).[2548] It was now the established approach as far as requirements of a national diploma were concerned. Comparing the Court's approach in *Vlassopoulou* to that in *Schöning-Kougebetopoulou*,[2549] where the Court in effect found indirect discrimination on

---

[2538]   Case 71/76, [1977] *ECR* 765.
[2539]   Case C-340/89, [1991] *ECR* I-2357. The case came to the Court of Justice at a time when the first general Directive on the mutual recognition of diplomas (Directive 89/48/EEC, *OJ* 1989 L 19/16; as later amended) was already in existence, but not yet applicable to the case; see Poma 1992, p. 672.
[2540]   See generally Görlitz 2002.
[2541]   *Vlassopoulou* (para. 16): 'It must be stated in this regard that, even if applied without any discrimination on the basis of nationality, national requirements concerning qualifications may have the effect of hindering nationals of the other Member States in the exercise of their right of establishment guaranteed to them by Article 52 of the EEC Treaty. That could be the case if the national rules in question took no account of the knowledge and qualifications already acquired by the person concerned in another Member State.'
[2542]   Stein 1992, p. 635.
[2543]   Kingreen 1999, p. 66.
[2544]   Von der Groeben & Schwarze Commentary 2004, n. 83 ad Art. 43 EC.
[2545]   Nachbaur 1991, p. 471.
[2546]   Martin 1994, p. 51, and 1998, p. 586. This author in particular points to the Court's reference to Art. 5 of the Treaty (now Art. 10 EC) which, in his opinion, indicates that the Court simply wished to rely on a wide notion of discrimination.
[2547]   Fierstra 1992, p. 441.
[2548]   Johnson & O'Keeffe 1994, p. 1332.
[2549]   Case C-15/96, [1998] *ECR* I-47.

384

grounds of nationality, Novak[2550] criticises that the Court does not know any longer what is and what is not discrimination (see also O'Leary).[2551] It is submitted that this kind of comment disregards the difference between cases involving the mutual recognition of *formal* qualifications such as were at issue in *Vlassopoulou* (including related work experience; *Hocsman*,[2552] para. 40), on the one hand, and mere professional experience as a form of *informal* qualification, on the other hand. In the latter context the Court consistently applies an indirect discrimination approach (e.g. *Roviello*,[2553] concerning practical experience as a tiler; *Scholz*[2554] and *Schöning-Kougebetopoulou*,[2555] both concerning work experience in another Member State). Similarly, an indirect discrimination approach can be detected in the context of qualification-related requirements other than diplomas (e.g. *Commission v Belgium*).[2556]

[2550] Novak 1999, p. 85.

[2551] O'Leary 1999, p. 407.

[2552] Case C-238/98, [2000] *ECR* I-6623.

[2553] Case 20/85, [1988] *ECR* 2805. Mr Roviello applied for a disability pension in Germany. In the course of the evaluation of his situation, he was found to be able to perform unskilled work. According to German legislation, a disability pension could be refused if the applicant could be assigned to work in the category immediately below his or her own, based on the categories of highly skilled, skilled, semi-skilled and unskilled work. Mr Roviello argued that, having worked in Italy as a tiler, his former work was on the level of a skilled worker. However, the German authorities insisted on basing his status on solely his former occupation in Germany, which was on the lower level of a semi-skilled worker. As a result, Mr Roviello was refused a pension. This approach by the German legislation was based on point 15 of Annex VI, Part C, of Regulation 1408/71/EEC, *OJ* English Special Edition 1971(II) L 149/2, p. 416 (as amended and later replaced by Regulation 883/2004/EC, *OJ* 2004 L 166/1). The Court found that Point 15, though formally neutral in terms of nationality, affected essentially migrant workers and therefore did not guarantee equal treatment (*Roviello*, para. 14 subs.).

[2554] Case C-419/92, [1994] *ECR* I-505. Ms Scholz, a former German citizen but later an Italian by marriage, participated in an open competition organised by the University of Cagliari, Italy, for the recruitment of canteen staff. In the framework of the procedure, previous professional experience in the public service was a relevant element. Ms Scholz complained about the fact that the university refused to take into account her work experience in the German post office. In his opinion, AG Jacobs spoke about unjustified 'covert or disguised discrimination' (*Scholz*, point 17 of the opinion). The Court agreed and expressly held that such a case involves 'unjustified indirect discrimination' on grounds of nationality (*Scholz*, para. 7-10). – The fact that Ms Scholz herself was an Italian meant that the case also involved the question of reverse discrimination; see White 1994, pp. 310 subs.

[2555] Case C-15/96, [1998] ECR I-47. *Schöning-Kougebetopoulou* concerned the calculation of seniority for the purposes of promotion in the civil service in Germany. As in *Scholz*, periods of employment in another Member State were not taken into account. Dr. Schöning-Kougebetopoulou complained of indirect discrimination on grounds of nationality. Again, AG Jacobs suggested that such a case involves indirect discrimination (*Schöning-Kougebetopoulou*, points 11 subs. of the AG's opinion) and, again, the Court agreed, explaining that the contested rules manifestly worked to the detriment of migrant workers (*Schöning-Kougebetopoulou*, para. 23). Like the AG, the Court referred to *O'Flynn* (Case C-237/94, [1996] *ECR* I-2617).

[2556] Case C-65/03, judgment of 1 July 2004, n.y.r. In this case, the Commission accused Belgium of infringing Arts. 12, 149 and 150 EC by maintaining certain rules on the recognition of foreign diplomas and certificates of study. The Commission claimed that under Belgian law holders of foreign secondary education diplomas who wish to get access to higher education must pass an aptitude test where they are not able to prove 'that they qualify for admission in their own country of origin to a university with no entry examination or other condition of access' (*Commission v Belgium*, para.

It is submitted that the Court's approach is not surprising given that such issues are not mentioned in the Treaty as needing further attention through secondary legislation.

4.   NO NEED FOR THE DEMARCATION UNDER SPECIFIC SECONDARY LAW

As Handoll[2557] notes, the importance of the Court's restriction-based case law has declined as more areas have become subject to specific Community legislation. This is also true for the examples discussed above. After the early cases on diplomas, Crisham[2558] expressed the hope that the Council 'will not wait for further 'backdoor' actions by the Court' but would speedily adopt the necessary Directives. There is now a host of specific Directives[2559] and two general Directives on the mutual recognition of diplomas.[2560] The Commission plans to consolidate this regulatory framework.[2561] Similarly, secondary legislation that includes elements of prudential supervision exists in a variety of contexts, such as the provision of services,[2562] freedom of establishment[2563] and the mutual recognition of diplomas.[2564] Rather than being framed in terms of negative integration,[2565] such legislation is of a specific nature which means that *the demarcation between indirect discrimination and restrictions in a wider sense is no longer relevant* as far the equivalence of diplomas is concerned (compare Everling).[2566]

---

13). This was the consequence of national legislation according to which equivalence granted to foreign diplomas 'shall under no circumstances have the effect [...] of giving the recipient access to studies to which he does not have access in the country in which the diploma or certificate was awarded'. The Court found indirect discrimination on grounds of nationality prohibited by Art. 12 EC (*Commission v Belgium,* para. 28 and 29).

[2557]   Handoll 1995, para. 6.13. The author adds that the Court's case law continues to act as a spur to legislation in areas where secondary legislation has yet to be developed and that the case law forms the basis for the exercise of rights of free movement where specific Directives do not apply.

[2558]   Crisham 1978, p. 370.

[2559]   The first of these specific (sectoral) Directives was adopted in 1977, concerning nurses responsible for general care; Directive 77/452/EEC, *OJ* 1977 L 176/1.

[2560]   Directive 89/48/EEC, *OJ* 1989 L 19/16 (as amended), and Directive 92/51/EEC, *OJ* 1992 L 209/25 (as amended). These general Directives and the more specific ones were amended through Directive 2001/19/EC, *OJ* 2001 L 206/1 (the so-called SLIM Directive).

[2561]   See the Commission's Proposal for a Directive of the European Parliament and of the Council on the recognition of professional qualifications, COM(2002) 119 fin., and Amended proposal for a Directive of the European Parliament and of the Council on the recognition of professional qualification, COM(2004) 317(1).

[2562]   E.g. Art. 4(2) of Directive 77/249/EEC, *OJ* 1977 L 78/17 (as amended).

[2563]   E.g. Art. 3(1) of the Directive 98/5, *OJ* 1998 L 77/36 (as amended); see also Art. 6 and 7.

[2564]   E.g. Art. 17(1) of Directive 93/16, *OJ* 1993 L 165/1, as amended.

[2565]   See above Part 2, A.I.4.e.i.

[2566]   Everling 1997, p. 624.

With regard to driving licences, the picture is somewhat more complex. A first Directive, adopted in 1980,[2567] introduced a limited system for the mutual recognition of licences based on a Community model driving licence. Under that system a licence issued by a Member State would remain valid for up to a maximum of a year following the taking up of residence by its holder in another Member State. At the request of the holder within that period, the host Member State was in principle obliged to issue him or her with a Community model driving licence. This meant that the problem arising in cases such as *Choquet*[2568] was taken care of insofar as the first year of residence in the host Member State was concerned, as illustrated by the *Skanavi*[2569] case (see Huglo).[2570] However, this was true only with regard to the recognition of the licence as such, but not with regard to *sanctions* imposed by national law in the context of requirements to exchange the licence. The reason for this is that the Directive did not cover sanctions. If disproportionate to the gravity of the infringement, sanctions may amount to an obstacle to the free movement of persons (*Skanavi*, para. 27 subs.; *Awoyemi*,[2571] para. 24 subs.).[2572] In that context, the concepts of indirect discrimination and restrictions in wider sense as well as their demarcation remain relevant. The remaining obstacles with regard to the mutual recognition of driving licences were eventually removed under the Second Directive on driving licences[2573] which did away with the duty to exchange the licence by providing for full mutual recognition. Again, in the framework of such explicit provisions there is no longer a need to determine

---

[2567] Directive 80/1263/EEC, *OJ* 1980 L 375/1 (no longer in force).
[2568] Case 16/78, [1978] *ECR* 2293.
[2569] Case C-193/94, [1996] *ECR* I-929. Ms Skanavi, a Greek national, took up residence in Germany on 15 October 1992 without exchanging her Greek driving licence in the course of one year as required under German law. On 28 October 1993 (that is, just a little over a year after she had come to Germany), she was stopped by the police while driving a car and found to possess only a Greek driving licence. Though the Court's decision in *Skanavi* is clearly based on a restriction-based approach, again there are commentators who put the case in the context of indirect discrimination (e.g. the GTE Commentary 1997, n. 41 and 42 ad Art. 52 of the EC Treaty; see also Denys 1996 (Stille vormgeving), p. 128, who speaks about 'discrimination in substance' (materiële discriminatie) but at the same time notes that the rule at issue predominantly disadvantages foreigners.
[2570] Huglo 1996, p. 746.
[2571] Case C-230/97, [1998] *ECR* I-6781.
[2572] Third country nationals can rely on the provisions of the Directive but are not able to rely on the prohibition of obstacles caused through sanctions because the Community rules on free movement of persons are applicable to Community nationals only; *Awoyemi*, para. 27. Mr Awoyemi, a Nigerian national, was the holder of a Community model driving licence issued in the UK that he had obtained when established there. When later living in Belgium, he was stopped and prosecuted for not being in possession of a Belgian licence. Under Belgian law, he should have exchanged his foreign licence for a Belgian one within one year after having established himself in Belgium. The Court explained that the right to have one's licence recognised is not dependent on the licence holder's nationality but rather on the Community origin of the licence itself. The Court added, however, that the licence must be an original Community licence and not one obtained in the first Member State in exchange for a licence issued by a third country (*Awoyemi*, para. 22 and 44).
[2573] Directive 91/439/EEC, *OJ* 1991 L 237/1 (as amended).

the nature of the infringement of the free movement rules resulting from the refusal by a Member State to recognise a foreign licence.[2574]

5. AN INTERIM CONCLUSION (I)

The starting point for these analyses has been the question of *why the Court of Justice developed the new concept* of restrictions in a wider sense rather than simply relying on the pre-existing concept of indirect discrimination. The analysis of early restriction-based case law showed that the subject matters at issue (prudential supervision, the recognition of foreign diplomas and of foreign driving licences) share certain characteristics: all of them involve important concerns of general interest, and all of them in effect *call for specific legislation* on their relationship with the requirements of free movement. Against this background, it was argued that the Court may have been reluctant to examine such cases in an indirect discrimination framework, in particular because that concept, due to the lack of the element of objective justification at the time, did not allow for the taking into account of issues of general interest. Since such concerns could not be dealt with under the narrowly construed textual exceptions to the Treaty's free movement rules, their recognition called for a new legal concept. Thus, at the time the concept of restrictions in a wider sense was *subtler* than that of indirect discrimination. Later, when the concept of indirect discrimination was expanded to include an element of objective justification, the Court appears to have seen no reason for returning to an analysis in the framework of this more burdensome and limited concept. Further, it was noted that the concept of restrictions in a wider sense made it possible to impose certain *positive obligations* (such as for the active examination of foreign diplomas and driving licences) which would not have been possible under the Community's non-discrimination law. Specific legislation will often do away with the need to analyse an infringement in terms of its nature (indirect discrimination or restriction in a wider sense). However, this may be limited to certain specific issues, such as formal professional qualifications (as opposed to mere professional experience) and the mutual recognition of driving licences (as opposed to national sanctions imposed in the context of exchange requirements).

[2574] In a different context, Szyszczak 1992, p. 127, argues that rules of the kind at issue are potentially indirectly discriminatory on grounds of race, since they might be used to exclude applicants who do not possess European qualifications.

III. ON THE CONCEPTUAL LEVEL: IS THERE A DIFFERENCE IN EFFECT?

1. INTRODUCTORY REMARKS

Having discussed the genesis of the restriction-based approach, the analysis now turns to the question of whether the Court's case law reveals differences on the conceptual level between indirect discrimination and restrictions in a wider sense. It was already noted[2575] that at an early stage of the development there was indeed a difference as far as *justification* was concerned, namely as long as the concept of indirect discrimination did not contain an element of objective justification in the sense of cross-cutting reasons. Once that had changed, both concepts in principle allowed for an unlimited range of justification grounds (e.g. the Schwarze Commentary).[2576] Some academic writers go so far as to treat the terms 'objective justification' and 'general interest justification' as interchangeable (e.g. AG Fennelly in his opinion on the *Clean Car*[2577] case, point 28; Martin;[2578] Hilson;[2579] see also Scott).[2580] Indeed, the only difference that might be perceived in the context of justification concerns the acceptability of economic justification. As was stated earlier, economic justification may be acceptable in the context of indirect sex discrimination but not in that of free movement.[2581] Further, these concepts may vary from one another to a greater or lesser degree depending upon how one views the functions of objective justification (in the case of indirect discrimination) and of general interest justification (in the case of restrictions in a wider sense), namely as either justification proper or as a matter of causation.[2582]

As for the *effect of the contested measure*, the discussion of the early restriction cases showed that it was not decisive for the development of the new approach. In particular, the measures at issue in these cases were not truly indistinctly applicable in the sense that they had precisely the same effect in the relevant Member State on its own nationals and on foreigners. In other words, they were not neutral in terms of their effect (Arnull).[2583] It is, therefore, not surprising that indirect discrimination was

---

[2575] See above Part 2, II.2.
[2576] Schwarze Commentary 2000, n. 37 ad Art. 39 EC.
[2577] Case C-350/96, [1998] *ECR* I-2521.
[2578] Martin 1998, notably p. 631.
[2579] Hilson 1999, p. 461, in respect of free movement of goods. According to Hilson, the mandatory requirements aspect of the *Cassis de Dijon* case law is the equivalent of a non-Treaty-based justification in the context of indirect discrimination.
[2580] Scott 2002, p. 279.
[2581] See above Part 2, IV.3.c.
[2582] See above Part 2, A.IV.3.e. Note also Jarass' view according to which reliance on the general interest should be seen in the context of justification rather than of the scope of the relevant provisions even in its original field of application (free movement of goods); Jarass 2000 (Elemente), p. 719.
[2583] Arnull 1999, pp. 347 subs.

argued in each case. Kaldellis'[2584] label of such cases as 'inflated models of indirect discrimination' appears understandable. This raises the question of whether in the Court's case law there are examples of truly indistinctly applicable measures which could not have been examined in an indirect discrimination framework and which, therefore, had to be examined in that of restrictions in a wider sense. The main findings in that regard will be as follows:

- The concept of restrictions in a wider sense appears to be able to cover measures with a wide range of effects, though in most cases the types of effect are similar to that of indirect discrimination.

- Restriction-based cases involving truly indistinctly applicable measures are extremely rare.

- In such cases, the Court's finding of a restriction is not based on a comparison of the treatment suffered by domestic and foreign actors.

- Whilst not all restriction cases can also be analysed in the framework of indirect discrimination, the opposite is possible.

2. IN SEARCH OF TRULY INDISTINCTLY APPLICABLE MEASURES: THE EXAMPLE OF CROSS-BORDER TELEVISION

In search of truly indistinctly applicable measures, academic writers have pointed to various cases that, under their analyses, fall into this category.[2585] In fact, such cases are very rare. As Kingreen[2586] notes, a careful analysis of the facts will almost always reveal some additional obstacles for foreigners.[2587] In search of an example of truly indistinctly applicable measures, the discussion below deals with cross-border television, particularly interesting for present purposes because of the Court's different

---

[2584] Kaldellis 2001, p. 32.

[2585] E.g. O'Leary 1999, p. 405, regarding *Kraus* (Case C-19/92, [1993] *ECR* I-1663; compare however the analysis earlier in this part, B.II.3.a. Kingreen 1999, pp. 132 subs., mentions the transfer rules in *Bosmann* (Case C-415/93, [1995] *ECR* I-4921). Yet another example, Martin 1998, p. 577, concerning *De Agostini* (Joined Cases C-34/95, C-35/95 and C-36/95, [1997] *ECR* I-3843). In contrast, according to Novak 1997, p. 1591, *De Agostini* involved a discriminatory measure. In fact, the Court left it to the national court to decide whether a national rule prohibiting television advertising directed at children had the same effect for domestic and foreign producers (para. 42 subs., in the context of what is now Art. 28 EC). In the context of free movement of services, the Court simply found a restriction (para. 50).

[2586] Kingreen, p. 122.

[2587] This, however, does not necessarily mean that such a measure amounts to indirect discrimination as that concept requires a disparate effect of a certain intensity; see above Part 2, A.IV.2.d.

approaches in two cases involving similar factual situations, namely *Debauve*[2588] and *Collectieve Antennevoorziening*.[2589]

a. Debauve

i. The case

Debauve concerned Belgian television legislation under which national broadcasting was performed by two organizations holding legal monopolies and subject to a prohibition against broadcasting commercial advertisements. Cable diffusion of broadcasts produced outside Belgium was subject to the same prohibition. This legislation led to practical problems: since programmes carried into Belgium were carried into other countries as well, the Belgian prohibition in practice prevented the broadcast of programmes containing advertising from reaching several other countries regardless of whether their own legislation allowed such advertising. The Belgian legislation raised questions with regard to the freedom to provide services under the EC Treaty. Particularly difficult was the question of whether 'Articles 59 and 60 of the Treaty of Rome [must] be interpreted as having direct effect against all national rules insofar as such rules do not create any formal discrimination against the person providing the services on the ground of his nationality or of his place of residence (in the present instance, the prohibition on retransmitting advertisements)' (*Debauve*, para. 7).[2590] Before the Court, arguments concerning both indirect discrimination on grounds of nationality and restrictions in a wider sense were made (*Debauve*, p. 845 subs.). The Commission and AG Warner proposed a restriction based approach (*Debauve*, p. 859 and 870 subs.). In contrast, the respondents (three officers of companies allegedly infringing the Belgian rules on commercial advertising) pointed to the Court's case law on indirect discrimination (*Debauve*, p. 851). The Court did not elaborate on the difference between these two approaches but simply stated that '[i]n the absence of any approximation of national laws and taking into account the considerations of general interest underlying the restrictive rules in this area, the application of the laws in question cannot be regarded as a restriction upon freedom to provide services as long as those laws treat all such services identically whatever their origin or the nationality of place of establishment of the persons providing them' (*Debauve*, para. 13). The Court added

---

[2588] Case 52/79, [1980] *ECR* 833.

[2589] Case C-288/89, [1991] *ECR* I-4007. For the parallel enforcement procedure, see *Commission v The Netherlands* (Case C-535/89, [1991] *ECR* I-4069).

[2590] Another question was whether such rules 'introduce discrimination based on the geographical locality of the foreign broadcasting station which would be able to transmit advertisements only within its natural receiving zone, as these zones may, because of the differences in density of population, be of very different interest from the advertising point of view' (*Debauve*, p. 837). The Court answered that difficulties arising from natural phenomena can, by definition, not be described as discrimination within the meaning of Community law (*Debauve*, para. 21).

that in such a framework Member States are allowed to have differing systems and to regulate, restrict or even totally prohibit television advertising on their territory. Restrictions or prohibitions could extend to television advertising originating in other Member States if they actually applied on the same terms to national television organizations. The Court concluded (*Debauve*, para. 16): 'The answer must therefore be that Articles 59 and 60 of the Treaty do not preclude national rules prohibiting the transmission of advertisements by cable television – as they prohibit the broadcasting of advertisements by television – if those rules are applied without distinction as regards the origin, whether national or foreign, of those advertisements, the nationality of the person providing the service, or the place where he is established.'

ii. Comments

There are differing academic opinions concerning the *legal framework of the Court's finding*. Following Timmermans,[2591] *Debauve* confirms that the Treaty not only prohibits formal discrimination but that same treatment may also be prohibited, namely if there is no objective justification (though at the same time, he speaks of a rule of reason approach similar to that developed by the Court with regard to Art. 28 EC). According to Martin,[2592] the ruling could not be clearer ('on ne peut pas être plus claire') on the point that the Court interpreted Art. 59 in the light of discrimination only, to the exclusion of the wider notion of restrictions (similarly Barnard).[2593] But whatever the correct interpretation might be, for present purposes it is more interesting to ask *why the Court refused to find an infringement*. Again, various explanations have been offered. Jones[2594] thought that the case did not involve trans-frontier broadcasting in the first place. According to March Hunnings,[2595] the Court simply did not consider the Belgian rules to have the requisite disparate impact for a finding of an infringement. The present writer would agree in the sense that the decisive aspect of *Debauve* appears to be that the disadvantage caused by the Belgian rules to foreign broadcasters did not concern the Belgian territory but rather the territory of other Member States. Within Belgium, there was no difference either in treatment or in effect. In such a situation, the explanation may lie in the Court's focus on the *Belgian* territory. It is submitted that this is logical within a legal system such as EC free movement law where the Member States rights and duties concern only their own territory (see AG Léger's opinion on *Hedley Lomas*,[2596] point 31-38, with further references). Nonetheless, the

---

[2591] Timmermans 1981, pp. 139 and 141.
[2592] Martin 1998, p. 566.
[2593] Barnard 2004, p. 349.
[2594] Jones 2000, p. 301.
[2595] March Hunnings 1980, p. 466. The author in this context refers to *discrimination* but his statement can also be seen in a wider context.
[2596] Case C-5/94, [1996] *ECR* I-2553.

necessary consequence of the approach in the *Debauve* case was the disregard of the disadvantages caused in fact by the Belgian rules to foreign broadcasters in relation to their activities outside Belgian. Interestingly, the Court would later take a different approach.

b. Collectieve Antennevoorziening

i. The case

Collectieve Antennevoorziening[2597] concerned Dutch broadcasting rules which, in an earlier version, provided for different treatment of foreign and domestic broadcasters (which in *Bond van Adverteerders*[2598] led the Court to a finding of what seems to be direct[2599] discrimination on grounds of nationality under the Treaty rules on the freedom to provide services; see Kohnstamm,[2600] Martin;[2601] also De Blois).[2602] After the revision of the Dutch rules, the *Mediawet* (Media Act) provided that programmes transmitted by cable from abroad and containing advertisements specifically intended for the Dutch public must be produced by a separate legal person and, further, that advertisements must be clearly identifiable as such, clearly separated from other programming, not broadcast on Sundays and not exceeding 5% of the total airtime. The same conditions applied to programmes broadcast within the Netherlands. The

---

[2597] Case C-288/89, [1991] *ECR* I-4007.
[2598] Case 352/85, [1988] *ECR* 2085.
[2599] Though AG Mancini had spoken about 'carefully concealed discrimination' and 'a paradigm of covert discrimination'; *Bond van Adverteerders*, point 10 of the AG's opinion. At the time, the Dutch *Kabelregeling* (Cable Regulation) prohibited the distribution by cable of radio and television programmes transmitted from other Member States if they contained advertising intended especially for the public in the Netherlands and if they used subtitles in Dutch. As far as domestic broadcasting was concerned, the *Omroepwet* (law on broadcasting) prohibited advertising altogether but otherwise gave the broadcasters the right to choose the form and content of their programmes. This did not, however, mean that there was no advertising on Dutch television. Rather, responsibility for advertising in the context of domestic broadcasting was conferred on a foundation, STER (*Stichting Etherreclame*) which sold air time to the advertisers. In other words, there was advertising on Dutch broadcasting stations but no advertisements intended for the Dutch public and using subtitles could be broadcasted from abroad.
[2600] Kohnstamm 1988, p. 1270.
[2601] Martin 1998, p. 581. – As Donner 1988, p. 93, notes, this (direct) discrimination had been brought about in an indirect way: the Court found different treatment of the domestic and foreign established broadcasters due to the regulations relating to STER rather than directly to the broadcasters themselves; compare also above Part 2, A.IV.2.a.
[2602] De Blois 1990. Most commentators do not elaborate on the nature of the discrimination at issue. Instead, they focus on the much debated question of whether the case involved a service within the meaning of the Treaty and whether there was justification; e.g. Van Empel 1989, pp. 427/428; Albers 1999, p. 101. Friden 1990, p. 236, notes that, thus far, the Court's case law regarding television services had only concerned the import of television services, but not the export of the services by cable operators to foreign broadcasters which were also mentioned by the Court in *Bond van Adverteerders*.

Collectieve Antennevoorziening[2603] case arose because ten cable network operators were fined for broadcasting foreign produced programmes containing advertising. Two of the main issues arising in this context were whether there was any difference at all in treatment and what would be the consequence of a negative finding on this point. The arguments made before the Court included discrimination in substance, indirect discrimination on grounds of nationality and restrictions in a wider sense. According to AG Tesauro, the advertising rules were 'applicable without distinction, both on the formal and (in principle) substantive levels' and as such non-discriminatory restrictions that could be justified in the interest of the general good (*Collectieve Antennevoorziening*, point 19 of the opinion). Faced with these various arguments, the Court began by observing that there are two possible hindrances to the freedom to provide services, namely discriminations and restrictions in a wider sense (*Collectieve Antennevoorziening*, para. 10 subs.). Applying this to rules of the type in question, the Court found that they were not discriminatory (a fact that had been explicitly pointed out by the national court) but nevertheless not acceptable since they constituted unjustified restrictions for foreign cable network operators and broadcasting companies (*Collectieve Antennevoorziening*, para. 17): 'It must be noted at the outset that conditions such as those imposed by the second sentence of Article 66(1)(b) of the Mediawet contain a two-fold restriction on freedom to provide services. First, they prevent operators of cable networks established in a Member State from transmitting radio or television programmes supplied by broadcasters established in other Member States which do not satisfy those conditions. Secondly, they restrict the opportunities afforded to those broadcasting bodies to include in their programmes for the benefit in particular of advertisers established in the State in which the programmes are received advertising intended specifically for the public in that State.' The Court found that the restrictions were not justified.

ii. Comments

In spite of its clear language, some commentators put the Court's finding in *Collectieve Antennevoorziening* in the context of indirect discrimination on grounds of nationality (e.g. Castillo de la Torre,[2604] Martin,[2605] Arnull,[2606] also Wyatt & Dashwood).[2607] In the present writer's view, O'Leary[2608] is right in interpreting the Court's decision as an

---

[2603]   Case C-288/89, *ECR* I-4007.
[2604]   Castillo de la Torre 1995, p. 142, footnote 142.
[2605]   Martin 1998, pp. 571/572 and 582 (though this author admits that the indirect discrimination approach may not be entirely satisfactory in the present context).
[2606]   Arnull 1999, p. 349.
[2607]   Wyatt & Dashwood 2000, p. 490.
[2608]   O'Leary 1999, p. 402.

explicit departure from the discrimination-based approach.[2609] The most noteworthy aspect of the case is that it concerns a similar situation as in the earlier case of *Debauve*.[2610] There, the Court had refused to find an infringement of the free movement rules because there was no different treatment in the territory of the host Member State concerned. The situation in *Collectieve Antennevoorziening* was the same: the Dutch rules certainly made it difficult to broadcast foreign programmes containing advertising but no more so than in the case of Dutch programmes. However, this time the Court found a prohibited restriction, independent of a comparison of the treatments of programmes broadcast from abroad with those broadcast within the Netherlands. The conclusion must be that now the Court was now willing to find a restriction (though not discrimination) caused through a truly indistinctly applicable measure. To that extent, *Collectieve Antennevoorziening* represents a new type of restriction case which is different not only from indirect discrimination cases but also from the restriction-based cases discussed thus far.

As far as the specific area of television broadcasting is concerned, the Community later adopted legislation which no longer requires the designation of an infringement as either discrimination or a restriction in a wider sense. Under the Television Without Frontiers Directive's[2611] home state control principle, the only relevant issue is whether or not a foreign established service provider falls under the relevant state's jurisdiction. As the Court held in *Commission v United Kingdom*[2612] (para. 74), 'under Article 2(1), all broadcasts transmitted by broadcasters under the jurisdiction of that Member State or over which it is required to exercise jurisdiction pursuant to the second indent of Article 2(1) must comply with the law applicable to broadcasts intended for the public in that Member State'.

3. AN INTERIM CONCLUSION (II)

The above discussion began by stating that there is no difference on a conceptual level between of the concepts of indirect discrimination and of restrictions in a wider sense as far as *justification* is concerned. As for the *effect of the measures* covered by the two concepts, AG Lenz observed that the dividing line is not always clear but that in any event, it can be inferred from the Court's case law that 'any provision which, *de jure* or *de facto*, impedes the freedom to provide services *may* constitute an infringement'

[2609]   Feenstra 1993, p. 427, seems to go even further. According to this author, the judgment confirms that the interpretation of the Treaty rules on the free movement of services has grown similar to that of the rules on free movement of goods under Art. 28 EC.

[2610]   Case 52/79, [1980] *ECR* 833; see earlier in this part, B.III.2.a.

[2611]   Directive 89/552/EEC, *OJ* 1989 L 298/23 (as amended).

[2612]   Case C-222/94, [1996] *ECR* I-4025.

(*TV10*,[2613] point 40 of the AG's opinion). The analysis of that case law showed that the concept of restrictions in a wider sense is capable of covering measures with a very wide range of effects, including measures with a disparate impact on the host Member State's territory (the 'inflated models of indirect discrimination', such as in *Vlassopoulou*[2614] and *Kraus*)[2615] as well as those which do not involve any differentiation either in treatment or in effect on the host Member State's territory (as in *Collectieve Antennevoorziening*).[2616] Given the Court's different approach in the context of free movement of goods based on *Keck*,[2617] this latter element is often criticised in academic writing. Kingreen,[2618] for example, has suggested that the prohibition of restrictions of free movement should be limited generally to what he terms a 'substantive concept of discrimination' *('materieller Diskriminierungsbegriff)*, that is, measures limiting market access as well as measures partitioning markets but to the exclusion of measures merely regulating a market if they do not have a discriminatory effect. For present purposes, the central finding is that the wide concept of restrictions as developed by the Court is perfectly capable of encompassing instances of indirect discrimination. To that extent, it is not possible to draw a clear dividing line between them. However, the case of truly indistinctly applicable measures highlighted the fact that the *analytical framework* is different in that the concept of restrictions in a wider sense is not comparison-based. This is, in fact, inherent in the Court's very definition of the concept in *Kraus* (para. 32) as it relates to measures that are 'liable to hamper or to render less attractive the exercise by Community nationals [...] of fundamental freedoms guaranteed by the Treaty'. As Voogsgeerd[2619] puts it, under a restriction-based approach 'all references to a 'comparability test' are gone. Every negative impact on the protected group is *prima facie* forbidden if the treatment falls within the scope of the specific right to free movement.' In contrast, the definition of the legal concept of indirect discrimination is clearly based on a comparison, as is apparent from the Court's statements in the landmark decision *O'Flynn*[2620] (para. 20: 'intrinsically liable to affect migrant workers more than national workers') and from provisions such as Art. 2(2) of the Revised Second Equal Treatment Directive[2621] ('a particular disadvantage compared with persons of the other sex'). This fundamental difference means that the application in practice of the concept of restrictions in a wider sense is much easier.

[2613] Case C-23/93, [1994] *ECR* I-4795.
[2614] Case C-340/89, [1991] *ECR* I-2357.
[2615] Case C-19/92, [1993] *ECR* I-1663.
[2616] Case C-288/89, [1991] *ECR* I-4007.
[2617] Joined Cases C-267/91 and C-268/91, [1993] *ECR* I-6097.
[2618] Kingreen 1999, pp. 120 subs. and 184 subs.
[2619] Voogsgeerd 2000, p. 71, see also p. 83; see further Hakenberg 2000, p. 99, and Denys 1996 (Vrije dienstverlening), p. 36.
[2620] Case C-237/94, [1996] *ECR* I-2617.
[2621] Directive 2002/73/EC, *OJ* 2002 L 269/15.

IV. ASSESSING CONCRETE CASES

1. INTRODUCTORY REMARKS

In the following, the discussion turns to the question of whether a distinction can be made between indirect discrimination and restrictions in a wider sense on the level of their *application to concrete cases and in specific contexts*. This discussion will show that on the level of application the distinction does not get easier but in fact becomes more uncertain. The main findings will be as follows:

- There seems to be only one clear category where the Court, after first having followed the indirect discrimination approach, turned to the concept of restrictions in a wider sense, namely double regulation cases.
- Sometimes, the Court does not clearly distinguish between the two concepts but oscillates between them.
- In certain cases, the Court even obviously and quite deliberately avoided putting the case before it into either of the two frameworks.

2. DIFFERENT RELEVANCE OF THE CONCEPTS FOR DIFFERENT CATEGORIES OF CASES?

The first question to be examined in the present context is whether there are certain categories of cases that are invariably analysed either in the framework of indirect discrimination or in that of restrictions in a wider sense, be it because of their particular characteristics or because of their subject matter. The discussion below begins with the Court's change of approach in cases concerning double regulation and then turns to the argument that indirect discrimination is less relevant in various core areas of free movement.

a. Taking double regulation cases out of indirect discrimination

An analysis of the Court's more recent case law gives the impression that there is one type of case which is consistently examined in the framework of the concept of restrictions in a wider sense, namely double regulation cases. This was, however, not always the case. The Court's change in approach can best be illustrated by comparing the judgments in the indirect discrimination case *Seco*[2622] and the restriction case *Vander Elst*,[2623] cases that are very similar in terms of their factual situations.

[2622]   Joined Cases 62/81 and 63/81, [1982] *ECR* 223; see already above Part 2, A.I.4.j.ii. and A.II.4.a.i.
[2623]   Case C-43/93, [1994] *ECR* I-3803.

i. Contrasting *Seco* and *Vander Elst*: the cases

In that *Seco* has already been discussed, it will suffice to recall that it concerned Luxembourg legislation under which employers using foreign staff only temporarily resident in Luxembourg were obliged to pay the employer's share of social security contributions even though this did not lead to any benefits for the employees. For foreign employers, this resulted in a double burden since they also had to pay social security contributions in their country of origin. The Court held that such circumstances involve indirect discrimination on grounds of nationality (*Seco*, para. 8 and 9). The facts of the *Vander Elst* case are largely comparable to those of *Seco*. Mr Vander Elst was a Belgian operator of a specialist demolition business in Brussels. When working in France, he employed third country nationals (Moroccans) who were legally resident in Belgium, held Belgian work permits, were covered by the Belgian Social security system and for whom Mr Vander Elst had obtained French visas. However, the French authorities further required French work permits for which an additional fee had to be paid. Both AG Tesauro and the Court recalled the prohibition of discrimination on grounds of nationality as well as of restrictions in a wider sense but then analysed the case in the framework only of the latter. According to AG Tesauro, the effect of the contested national legislation was to restrict the freedom to provide services within the Community. It constituted 'a wholly unjustified duplication of burdens and formalities liable to put the foreign service provider at a disadvantage in competing with national providers of services' (*Vander Elst*, point 17 of the AG's opinion). The Court agreed. As in *Seco*, it assessed the case from the perspective of the employer's rights as service providers rather than from the perspective of the workers.[2624] It found that the contested requirements went beyond what could be laid down as a precondition for the provision of services and that, therefore, they were contrary to the Treaty. In that context, the Court also made reference to *Seco* (*Vander Elst*, para. 14-22).

> The Court began by explaining that Art. 59 of the EEC Treaty (now Art. 49 EC) 'requires not only the elimination, against a person providing services who is established in another Member State, of all discrimination on the ground of his nationality but also the abolition of any restriction, even if it applies without distinction to national providers of services and to those of other Member States, when it is liable to prohibit or otherwise impede the activities of a provider of services established in another Member State where he lawfully provides similar services [...]. Similarly, the Court has already held that national legislation which makes the provision of certain services on national territory by an undertaking established in another Member State subject to the issue of an administrative licence constitutes a restriction on the freedom to provide services within the meaning of Article

---

[2624]   Obviously, the employees were also affected by the French rules, though only in an indirect way, namely through the treatment of their employers; see Peers 1995, pp. 303 and 309.

59 of the Treaty [...]. Furthermore, it is apparent from the judgment in Joined Cases 62/81 and 63/81 Seco and Desquenne & Giral v Etablissement d' Assurance contre la Vieillesse et l' Invalidité [1982] ECR 223 that legislation of a Member State which requires undertakings established in another Member State to pay fees in order to be able to employ in its own territory workers in respect of whom they are already liable for the same periods of employment to pay similar fees in the State in which they are established proves financially to be more onerous for those employers, who in fact have to bear a heavier burden than those established within the national territory. Finally, as one of the fundamental principles of the Treaty, freedom to provide services may be restricted only by rules which are justified by overriding reasons in the general interest and are applied to all persons and undertakings operating in the territory of the State where the service is provided, in so far as that interest is not safeguarded by the rules to which the provider of such a service is subject in the Member State where he is established [...]. In any event, as the Court has emphasized on several occasions, a Member State may not make the provision of services in its territory subject to compliance with all the conditions required for establishment and thereby deprive of all practical effectiveness the provisions whose object is to guarantee the freedom to provide services [...].'

Concerning the case at hand, the Court explained: 'In the circumstances, it is important to note, first, that the Moroccan workers employed by Mr Vander Elst were lawfully resident in Belgium, the State in which their employer was established and where they had been issued with work permits. Secondly, it is apparent from the documents and hearings before the Court that the short-stay visas held by the persons concerned, issued by the French Consulate at their request, constituted valid documents permitting them to remain in France for as long as was necessary to carry out the work. Consequently, the national legislation applicable in the host State concerning the immigration and residence of aliens had been complied with. Finally, as regards the work permits which are the focus of the main proceedings, they are required in order for a national of a non-member country to be employed by an undertaking established in France, whatever the nationality of the employer, because a short-stay visa is not equivalent to a permit. Such a system is intended to regulate access to the French labour market for workers from non-member countries. Workers employed by an undertaking established in one Member State who are temporarily sent to another Member State to provide services do not in any way seek access to the labour market in that second State, if they return to their country of origin or residence after completion of their work [...]. Those conditions were fulfilled in the present case. In those circumstances, the requirements at issue go beyond what may be laid down as a precondition for the provision of services. Accordingly, those requirements are contrary to Articles 59 and 60 of the Treaty.' The Court added that Community law does not preclude Member States from extending their legislation, or collective labour agreements relating to minimum wages to any person employed within their territory or from enforcing those rules by appropriate means. However, it pointed out that the application of the Belgian system excluded any substantial risk of workers being exploited or of competition between undertakings being distorted (*Vander Elst*, para. 22-26).

ii. Comments

The parallels between the situations in *Seco* and *Vander Elst* in terms of their facts is as striking as is the difference in the Court's approaches to them. Both cases concerned situations of double regulation where the host Member State's rules had a particularly burdensome effect on foreign employers due to the existence of similar rules in the State of origin. In *Seco*, the double burden thus arising concerned social security contributions which had to be paid in both countries, whereas in *Vander Elst* the double burden consisted of the requirement of work permits imposed by both countries. However, whilst *Seco* was examined in the framework of the concept of indirect discrimination on grounds of nationality, the Court's decision in *Vander Elst* is clearly restriction-based (see Castillo de la Torre,[2625] Khan).[2626] As was noted earlier,[2627] the Court's approach in *Seco* has to be seen against the background of a slightly different definition of indirect discrimination than that used in earlier cases. In contrast, in *Vander Elst* the Court did not even mention indirect discrimination, though it referred to *Seco*. Peers[2628] concludes from this that the Court believed the contested legislation in *Vander Elst* was (indirectly) discriminatory. At the same time, he considers that the Court's emphasis on the character of the rules as 'indistinctly applicable' suggests that any national legislation that impedes a Community company's right to use its third-country staff to provide services in another Member State will breach the Treaty rules on free movement of services. It therefore seems that in Peers' analysis *Vander Elst* contains a mixture of both elements, indirect discrimination and restriction. The present writer does not find this view convincing. *Seco* is often mentioned as a precedent in later decisions which are clearly not based on an indirect discrimination but rather a restriction approach. *Vander Elst* is simply an example of this tendency. It therefore seems more logical to interpret *Vander Elst* as indicating a change of approach in the context of double burden rules away from indirect discrimination and towards restrictions in a wider sense. This in line with Roth's[2629] observation that as of a certain moment in the Court's case law the notion of discrimination has to be understood as excluding cases of double regulation (see also Plötscher).[2630] In those circumstances, the reference to *Seco* may simply have been meant to stress that a duplication of rules in the host Member State can be prohibited or, even more generally, to acknowledge the factual parallel with the earlier *Seco* case.

Arguably, this shift by the Court has to be seen against the broader background of the meaning of discrimination under EC law. As the Court stated in a variety of

---

[2625] Castillo de la Torre 1995, p. 142.
[2626] Khan 1994, p. 603.
[2627] See above Part 2, A.I.4.j.iii.
[2628] Peers 1995, p. 306.
[2629] Roth 1993 (Säger), p. 151.
[2630] Plötscher 2003, p. 150.

contexts, difficulties arising in the context of differences between the legal orders of different Member States cannot be considered as leading to discrimination (e.g. *Walt Wilhelm*,[2631] para. 13; *Van Dam*,[2632] para. 10; more recently *Schröder*,[2633] para. 52, *Kristiansen*,[2634] para. 38; see also the von der Groeben & Schwarze Commentary).[2635] In the context of indirect discrimination, an example of the application of the *Walt Wilhelm* principle can be found in *Kocak and Örs*,[2636] where the Court held that the fact that legislation of a worker's host Member State does not (fully) take account of the difficulties arising from the legal situation in the worker's State of origin (here: an Association state) cannot be considered as leading to indirect discrimination on grounds of nationality (*Kocak and Örs*, para. 51).

The case involved German rules concerning the recognition of birth dates of Turkish workers for social security purposes in the event of changes in relation to the date of birth based on decisions taken in Turkey. At the time, German law accorded the same probative value to civil status documents originating from Germany with those from abroad. However, for rights dependent on a specific age, the German Code of Social Law (*Sozialgesetzbuch*) provided that the applicable date of birth was that which resulted from the first declaration made by the person entitled to those rights.[2637] Another date was recognised only in exceptional circumstances, including the existence of an even older document. Messrs. Kocak and Örs applied for retirement benefits, relying on changes regarding their date of birth as pronounced by a Turkish court (they were actually older than they previously declared). The recently substituted date was rejected on the grounds that it was not based on the workers' original declaration. The German social security institutions argued in particular that the circumstances and the evidence brought forward (namely medical opinions and statements of witnesses) did not have sufficient weight to cast doubt upon the probative value of the original entry in the register of civil status. They also stressed that if altering the dates of birth meant that the amount of social benefit paid out was affected, the cost incurred would be extremely high, unexpected and possibly even capable of upsetting the financial equilibrium of the system. Both the national court and the Commission mentioned indirect discrimination on grounds of nationality under the EEC-Turkish Association Agreement,[2638] but the Court of Justice explicitly excluded such a finding. In doing so, it emphasised that the migrant workers' difficulties resulted from *Turkish* law and its practice. The Court held: 'It is not permissible, on the basis of the principle of non-

---

[2631] Case 14/68, [1969] *ECR* 1.
[2632] Joined Cases 185/78 to 204/78, [1979] *ECR* 2345.
[2633] Case C-50/96, [2000] ECR I-743.
[2634] Case C-92/02, judgment of 4 December 2003, n.y.r.
[2635] Von der Groeben & Schwarze Commentary 2004, n. 6 ad Art. 12 EC.
[2636] Joined Cases C-102/98 and C-211/98, [2000] *ECR* I-1287.
[2637] Regarding an earlier version of the German law, see later in this part, B.IV.3.b.
[2638] Agreement establishing an Association between the European Economic Community and Turkey, confirmed on behalf of the Community by Council Decision 64/732, *OJ* 1977 L 361/29. The case also concerned an Additional Protocol belonging to the Association Agreement, approved and confirmed on behalf of the Community by Council Regulation 2760/72, *OJ* 1977 L 361/61.

discrimination on grounds of nationality [...], to require a Member State which lays down rules regarding the determination of dates of birth for the purpose of establishing a social security number and of awarding a retirement pension to take account of particular circumstances which derive from the Turkish legislation on civil status and of the detailed arrangements for its application.'

It can perhaps be argued that double regulation cases must be seen in this same context in that a finding of an infringement of free movement law on the part of the host Member State in effect imposes positive obligations on that State to take account of particular circumstances which derive from the situation in the country of origin, to use the language in *Kocak and Örs*, just quoted. Following the *Walt Wilhelm* principle, the legal concept of discrimination does not apply to that situation. Accordingly, the recognition of such a positive duty requires a different approach, which is that of restrictions in a wider sense. Not only may this analysis explain why the Court turned away from the indirect discrimination approach as reflected in *Seco*,[2639] but it also highlights once more the exceptional nature of this particular case.

b. Indirect discrimination: less relevant in core areas of Community law?

Searching for elements which might indicate the dividing line between the concepts of indirect discrimination and of restrictions in a wider sense, Voogsgeerd[2640] has argued that the more a case has to do with core areas of Community law (meaning free movement law), the less is there room for a discrimination approach. However, whilst it is certainly true that the broad interpretation of the concept of restrictions in a wider sense has limited the field of application of the concept of indirect discrimination in free movement law, the fact remains that the Court in this area continues to rely on the indirect discrimination approach quite frequently. This shows that O'Leary[2641] is correct in pointing out that, in spite of the Court's tendency to move towards a restriction-based approach, discrimination as a criterion is far from obsolete in free movement case law. Indeed, the Court regularly mentions both approaches as co-existing, and sometimes even explicitly raises direct discrimination, indirect discrimination and restrictions in a wider sense in the same case (e.g. *Graf*,[2642] para. 18).

[2639] Joined Cases 62/81 and 63/81, [1982] *ECR* 223.

[2640] Voogsgeerd 2000, at 83.

[2641] O'Leary 1999, pp. 406 subs.

[2642] Case C-190/98, [2000] *ECR* I-493. This case raised the question of whether Art. 39 EC precludes national legislation which denies entitlement to compensation on termination of employment in the case of a worker who terminates his contract of employment himself in order to take up employment with a new employer established in that Member State or in another Member State but grants such compensation in the case of a worker whose contract ends without the termination being at his own initiative or otherwise attributable to him. The Court answered in the negative. It noted that the contested rules applied irrespective of the nationality of the worker concerned (implying that such rules could not constitute direct discrimination). Further, they did not affect migrant

Some examples of recent free movement cases where the Court relied on the concept of indirect discrimination are 1) from the area of free movement of workers: *Kaba*,[2643] *Ferlini*,[2644] *Borawitz*,[2645] *Commission v Italy* (foreign language assistants),[2646] *Commission v Luxembourg*,[2647] *Köbler*,[2648] *Collins*[2649] and *Commission v Belgium*,[2650] 2) from the area of freedom of establishment: *Société Baxter*[2651] (taxation, also regarding free movement of workers) and *Germany v Commission*[2652] (taxation), and 3) from the area of free movement of services: *Ciola*[2653] and *Commission v France*.[2654] As was said earlier,[2655] there is as yet no case concerning free movement of capital where the Court has explicitly found indirect discrimination.

3. OSCILLATING BETWEEN INDIRECT DISCRIMINATION AND RESTRICTIONS

If double regulation cases provide an example of where the Court has made a clear decision in favour of one particular approach, there are also examples where the Court seems to oscillate between the two concepts of indirect discrimination and restrictions in a wider sense without clearly deciding in favour of one of them. The two examples discussed below are *Konstantinidis*[2656] and *Dafeki*.[2657]

a. Konstantinidis

i. The case

Mr Konstantinidis, a Greek national living and working in a self-employed capacity in Germany, encountered difficulties concerning the registration of his name when

---

workers to a greater extent than national workers; therefore, they did not disadvantage the former in particular (implying that they could not lead to indirect discrimination either). Consequently, they could only constitute a restriction. However, the Court found that there was no such restriction in the situation at issue because the potential effect of precluding or deterring a national of a Member State from leaving his or her country in order to exercise his or her right of free movement was too uncertain and indirect a possibility to be capable of being regarded as liable to hinder freedom of movement.

[2643] Case C-356/98, [2000] *ECR* I-2623.
[2644] Case C-411/98, [2000] *ECR* I-8081.
[2645] Case C-124/99, [2000] *ECR* I-7193.
[2646] Case C-212/99, [2001] *ECR* I-4923.
[2647] Case C-299/01, [2002] *ECR* I-5899.
[2648] Case C-224/01, judgment of 30 September 2003, n.y.r.
[2649] Case C-138/02, judgment of 23 March 2004, n.y.r.
[2650] Case C-469/02, judgment of 7 September 2004, n.y.r.
[2651] Case C-254/97, [1999] *ECR* I-4809.
[2652] Case C-156/98, [2000] *ECR* I-6857.
[2653] Case C-224/97, [1999] *ECR* I-2517.
[2654] Case C-225/98, [2000] *ECR* I-7445.
[2655] See above Part 2, A.I.4.m.
[2656] Case C-168/91, [1993] *ECR* I-1191.
[2657] Case C-336/94, [1997] *ECR* I-6761.

he wished to get married in his host country. Under German law, a person's name in the official registers must correspond to the name as stated on the birth certificate, and names written in non-Roman characters must be transliterated into Roman characters. In the case of Mr Konstantinidis, this was done by a qualified translator who, applying a system of transliteration developed by the International Organization for Standardization (ISO), came up with 'Hréstos Kónstantinidés'. This was, however, different from the English transliteration in Mr Konstantinidis' passport, which was 'Christos Konstantinidis'. Finding the ISO-spelling intensely distasteful, Mr Konstantinidis argued[2658] that it did not adequately reflect the way his name was pronounced in Greek. This led to court proceedings and to a reference for a preliminary ruling to the Court of Justice on the question whether rules of the type at issue infringe EC law. The Commission and AG Jacobs suggested a finding of *indirect discrimination* on grounds of nationality. Given that among the languages of all the Member States only the Greek language was written in non-Roman characters, they argued that the German rules on transliteration were more likely to affect Greek nationals than nationals of Germany or any other Member State. The AG explained that there is every justification for requiring the names of Greek migrant workers to be written in Roman characters in the Member States that do not use the Greek alphabet. However, he added that that does not mean that there is objective justification for writing Greek names in a manner that is unphonetic, illogical, arbitrary, inconsistent with long-established practice and offensive to the persons concerned (*Konstantinidis*, points 10 and 20 subs. of the AG's opinion).

The Court began by observing that Mr Konstantinidis worked as a self-employed person and therefore the national court's question concerned the freedom of establishment (*Konstantinidis*, para. 10 and 11). According to the Court, the question to be examined was whether the contested rules 'are capable of placing him [meaning: Mr Konstantinidis] at a disadvantage in law or in fact, in comparison with the way in which a national of that Member State would be treated in the same circumstances'. In its further statements, the Court spoke only very generally about an incompatibility with the rules on free movement (*Konstantinidis*, para. 14-17): 'There is nothing in the Treaty to preclude the transcription of a Greek name in Roman characters in the registers of civil status of a Member State which uses the Roman alphabet. It is therefore for the Member State in question to adopt legislative or administrative measures

---

[2658]   AG Jacobs praised Mr Konstantinidis for his way of presenting his arguments (point 12 of the AG's opinion: 'Mr Konstantinidis did not submit written observations, but he did give the Court a rare opportunity to hear a litigant in person when he represented himself at the hearing. His essential argument, presented with a simple eloquence and brevity which many professional advocates would do well to emulate, is that 'Hréstos Kónstantinidés' is an insulting, unpronounceable parody of his name, which is offensive to his religious sentiments. He also points out that, having been known to his clients as 'Christos Konstantinidis' for eight years, he must now suffer either the inconvenience of telling them that he has a new name or the confusion of using different names for different purposes.'

laying down the detailed rules for such transcription, in accordance with the prescriptions of any international conventions relating to civil status to which it is a party. Rules of that kind are to be regarded as incompatible with Article 52 of the Treaty only in so far as their application causes a Greek national such a degree of inconvenience as in fact to interfere with his freedom to exercise the right of establishment enshrined in that article. Such interference occurs if a Greek national is obliged by the legislation of the State in which he is established to use, in the pursuit of his occupation, a spelling of his name derived from the transliteration used in the registers of civil status if that spelling is such as to modify its pronunciation and if the resulting distortion exposes him to the risk that potential clients may confuse him with other persons. It should therefore be stated in reply to the national court that Article 52 of the Treaty must be interpreted as meaning that it is contrary to that provision for a Greek national to be obliged, under the applicable national legislation, to use, in the pursuit of his occupation, a spelling of his name whereby its pronunciation is modified and the resulting distortion exposes him to the risk that potential clients may confuse him with other persons.'

ii. Comments

Commenting on *Konstantinidis*, Lawson[2659] remarks that the Court avoided 'the question whether there was (indirect) discrimination'. Indeed, the Court's reasoning in *Konstantinidis* seems to oscillate between the concepts of indirect discrimination and of restrictions in a wider sense. Whilst the reference to comparatively equal treatment evokes the concept of discrimination, the concrete examination of the contested rules is not framed in those terms. Rather, the language used by the Court ('interfere with his freedom', 'risk that potential clients may confuse him with other persons') evokes the concept of restrictions in a wider sense. Unsurprisingly, the decision has been commented upon in both contexts (c.g. Schockweiler,[2660] Loiseau,[2661] Dony,[2662] Pintens,[2663] Plötscher;[2664] see also Gaurier,[2665] the Geiger Commentary).[2666] As AG Jacobs' suggestions show, a careful application of the concept of indirect discrimination would also have achieved the final result of the Court's decision. Alternatively, a restriction-based approach would also have served the purpose, as is evidenced by the academic comments on this issue. As it is, the Court left the matter open. In fact, the most convincing approach would have been to recognise *a difference in*

[2659] Lawson 1993, p. 402.
[2660] Schockweiler 1995, p. 501.
[2661] Loiseau 1995, pp. 509/510.
[2662] Dony 1999, p. 55.
[2663] Pintens 1995, p. 103.
[2664] Plötscher 2003, p. 121.
[2665] Gaurier 1995, 495; with interesting observations on the meaning of a personal name.
[2666] Geiger Commentary 2000, n. 14 ad Art. 43 EC.

situation between persons who, in a Member State other than Greece, wish to rely on documents written in Greek and persons holding comparable documents written in Roman letters. In such a situation, an Aristotelian equality approach[2667] requires adequate different treatment. This would mean that a requirement of transliteration is adequate in principle (treating unalikes *unalike*) but that the rules applied in that context must lead to a transliteration that corresponds as closely as possible to the actual pronunciation in the language concerned (treating unalikes unalike *according to the difference*). Lack of respect of this latter requirement would then constitute a form of discrimination. However, it was seen earlier[2668] that EC law normally focuses on equal treatment and that the Court in that framework relies on the non-comparability of situations only in order to explain why different treatment allegedly constituting discrimination is lawful, rather than in order to call for a specified different form of treatment.

b. Dafeki

i. The case

The second example of an oscillating approach on the part of the Court is even clearer. *Dafeki*[2669] concerned the recognition in a host Member State of foreign documents on the civil status of migrant persons. After having worked for many years in Germany, Ms Dafeki, a Greek, applied for an early retirement benefit based on her Greek birth certificate. A Greek court in accordance with the Greek procedure applicable in cases where archives and registers have disappeared had rectified this document in relation to Ms Dafeki's date of birth. Ms Dafeki was refused the requested benefit based on doubts concerning the accuracy of the Greek court's rectification. Under German law at the time, there was a legal presumption of accuracy of official documents only in relation to documents drawn up on the basis of official registers kept under German law. In all other cases, the documents had to be evaluated by the German courts in accordance with the rule of free assessment of evidence.[2670] Against this background, Ms Dafeki, supported by the Greek Government, complained of indirect discrimination on grounds of nationality prohibited under EC free movement law. The German Government and the Commission countered by pointing to significant differences between the Member States with regard to the maintenance and rectification of registers of civil status and, in particular, to the fact that it is not uncommon in Greece

---

[2667] See above Part 1, B.II.1.b.
[2668] See above Part 1, B.II.2.b.
[2669] Case C-336/94, [1997] *ECR* I-6761.
[2670] Later, the law recognized no difference regarding the probatory force of official documents depending on their origin. According to the new rules, determination of a worker's age for the purposes of retirement was to be based on the worker's own original declaration. The Court was confronted with these revised rules in *Kocak and Örs* (Joined Cases C-102/98 and C-211/98, *ECR* I-1287); see earlier in this part, B.IV.2.a.ii.

to alter the date of birth by judgment of a single judge simply upon evidence of two witnesses.

The Court began by stating that the situation of Ms Dafeki fell within the scope of Art. 39 EC (then Art. 48 of the Treaty) which prohibits discrimination on grounds of nationality and that the German rules, though applicable irrespective of the nationality of the worker, in practice operated to the detriment of workers who are nationals of other Member States. The Court acknowledged the existence of considerable differences between the national legal orders with regard to the rectification of dates of birth. It stated that, in the absence of a Community system of harmonization or mutual recognition, the Member States are not required to treat as equivalent subsequent rectifications of certificates of civil status made by the competent authorities of their own State and those made by the competent authorities of other Member States. To this, the Court added (*Dafeki*, para.19): 'Nevertheless, exercise of the rights arising from freedom of movement for workers is not possible without production of documents relating to personal status, which are generally issued by the worker's State of origin. It follows that the administrative and judicial authorities of a Member State must accept certificates and analogous documents relative to personal status issued by the competent authorities of the other Member States, unless their accuracy is seriously undermined by concrete evidence relating to the individual case in question.'

ii. Comments

The Court's reasoning in *Dafeki* is curious. It clearly begins with a *prima facie* recognition of indirect discrimination on grounds of nationality against foreign workers, caused through a difference in treatment with regard to the probatory force of documents according to their provenance. However, this is immediately qualified by the statement that, as a matter of principle, the Member States are *not* obliged to treat foreign documents in the same way as domestic documents (Droz,[2671] Van der Steen),[2672] which seems to imply that there is no room for a finding of discrimination. Further, the fact that the Court later recognised a positive duty upon the Member States to accept foreign documents unless their authority is seriously undermined by concrete evidence recalls the restriction-based approach in *Choquet*[2673] where the Court was faced with a similar situation. There might have been at least three alternatives to the Court's rather confusing approach in *Dafeki*. The first, and probably most realistic alternative would have been that suggested by AG La Pergola. He acknowledged that the German rules involved a difference in treatment but excluded a finding

---

[2671] Droz 1998, p. 336.
[2672] Van der Steen 2000, p. 33. This author notes that the Court's relatively lenient approach as reflected in the *Dafeki* case does not apply to all declarations originating in other Member States. Stricter rules may apply where the matter has been harmonised.
[2673] Case 16/78, [1978] *ECR* 2293; see earlier in this part, B.II.2.a.iii.

of discrimination based on the argument that documentation of matters concerning the status of persons is a matter for national law. He added, however, that the Member States are not totally free since they have to observe the principles of equivalence and effectiveness as minimum requirements regarding national procedural law. The latter in particular requires that the national rules must not make it impossible in practice to exercise a right conferred by Community law.[2674] In the AG's view, the rules at issue in *Dafeki* did not meet this requirement (*Dafeki*, points 4 and 5 of the AG's opinion). In other words, the AG approached the case from a *procedural* rather than from a substantive perspective which appears to be very appropriate in a case involving rules on the probatory force of foreign official documents. As a second possibility, the Court could have kept within the discrimination framework and focused on the question of *comparability*. It could have examined whether Greek nationals and German nationals relying on rectified birth certificates originating from their respective countries are in a different situation and whether this difference is such as to call for different treatment. The answer could have been that there is a relevant difference only if the authority of the foreign documents is seriously undermined by concrete evidence. Finally, it could be argued that since *Dafeki* concerned the *recognition of a foreign court decision*, this was not a matter for substantive Community law but rather of private international law.

4. THE 'AVOIDANCE CASES'

If the Court's approach in the cases just discussed was unclear, there are also examples where the Court quite obviously avoids a clear labelling of an infringement as either (indirect) discrimination or a restriction in a wider sense. The examples discussed

---

[2674] *Rewe (Saarland)* (Case 33/76, [1976] *ECR* 1989), para. 5; later e.g. *Van Schijndel* (Joined Cases C-430/93 and C-431/93, [1995] *ECR* I-4705), para. 17, and *Recheio* (Case C-30/02, judgment of 17 June 2004, n.y.r.), where the Court stated in para. 17 that 'it is for the domestic legal system of each Member State to designate the courts and tribunals having jurisdiction and to lay down the detailed procedural rules governing actions for safeguarding rights which individuals derive from Community law, provided, first, that such rules are not less favourable than those governing similar domestic actions (principle of equivalence) and, second, that they do not render virtually impossible or excessively difficult the exercise of rights conferred by Community law (principle of effectiveness)'. According to Tridimas 2000, p. 39, 'the requirement of equivalence prohibits not only direct but also indirect discrimination against claims based on Community law'. Tridimas explains: 'Where a procedural rule applies to certain categories of claims most of which are claims based on Community law, and a more favourable rule applies to other categories of claims most of which are claims based on national law, the first rule may run counter to the requirement of equivalence unless it is objectively justified.'

below are *Safir*[2675] (mentioned by the Lenz Commentary[2676] as the first 'avoidance case'), and *Kohll*.[2677]

a. Taxation of life insurance: Safir

i. The case

Safir[2678] concerned Swedish legislation on the taxation of capital life insurance which differed according to whether the insurance had been taken out with a company established in Sweden or abroad. In the former case, the tax system focused on the companies who must pay tax on the yield from capital insurance (the proceeds received by the insured from such policies were not subject to tax and the premiums were not tax-deductible). In the case of companies established abroad, a tax of 15%, subject to certain possibilities of tax exemptions or reductions, was levied on the premiums paid by the persons who had taken out insurance with such companies. The main aim of this system was to achieve competitive neutrality. Ms Safir, who had taken out a policy with a company established in the UK,[2679] complained that the Swedish tax system infringed EC law. A number of Member State Governments disagreed and further argued that the system was in any event justified by virtue of the aims of national fiscal cohesion and effective fiscal supervision. AG Tesauro thought it clear that the Swedish rules could well constitute an obstacle for insurance companies intending to conduct their business in Sweden without having a fixed place of business there. In his analysis, the restrictions were 'clearly, albeit indirectly, based upon the place of establishment of the provider of services and are consequently liable to restrict its cross-border activities: they are therefore in patent conflict with Article 59 of the Treaty' (*Safir*, point 23 of the AG's opinion). The AG urged the Court to determine the nature of the alleged breach as either 'formally discriminatory' or 'applicable without distinction'. Observing that discriminatory measures can be justified only if covered by one of the derogations expressly laid down in the Treaty, the AG insisted on the importance of this determination, though he acknowledged that it is sometimes difficult to make. According to AG Tesauro, *Safir* presented the Court with an opportunity to clarify the matter (*Safir*, point 23 subs. of the AG's opinion).

[2675] Case C-118/96, [1998] I-1897.
[2676] Lenz Commentary 1999, n. 20 ad Art. 49/50 EC.
[2677] Case C-158/96, [1998] *ECR* I-1931. Another important case in that context is *Decker* (Case C-120/95, [1998] *ECR* I-1831). This case will not be discussed because it concerns an area excluded from the reach of this present study, namely free movement of goods (Art. 28 EC); see above Part 1, B.V.1.b.ii.
[2678] Case C-118/96, [1998] *ECR* I-1897.
[2679] Interestingly enough, this company happened to be a wholly owned subsidiary of a Swedish company (*Safir*, point 6, footnote 3 of the AG's opinion).

When urging the Court to determine the precise *nature of the alleged infringement*, the AG emphasised that 'this question is not as banal as it may seem' because the classification of the measure is not always easy in relation to the free movement of services and it is difficult to arrive at a clear and unequivocal definition of discriminatory measures on the basis of the Court's case law. According to the AG, 'the Court considers as formally discriminatory only those national provisions which lay down a different regime for foreign nationals and/or providers of services 'originating' in another Member State. However, where the legislation in question is intended to apply to all persons exercising the activity concerned on the territory of a given Member State, even where it expressly lays down a residence or establishment condition (thereby making it impossible for providers established in another Member State to exercise the activity), it is classified as applicable without distinction.' The AG further pointed out that in a concrete case the determination of the category at issue may depend on where the emphasis is put. Concerning *justification*, the AG wrote: 'I would point out first of all that, according to the Court's case-law, a national provision which is discriminatory can be justified, and therefore be declared compatible with Community law, only if it is covered by one of the derogations expressly laid down in the Treaty. In *Bond van Adverteerders*, subsequently confirmed in other cases, the Court made clear that 'national rules which are not applicable to services without distinction as regards their origin and which are therefore discriminatory are compatible with Community law only if they can be brought within the scope of an express derogation'.' With regard to the grounds relied on by the Swedish Government in the case at hand, AG Tesauro pointed out that they are not covered by the express derogations provided for in the Treaty and that, in any event, they pursue an economic objective which, as such, can never serve as justification. The AG acknowledged that the objectives relied on are covered by the notion of the general interest, but he considered them not to be proportionate (*Safir*, 35 and 36 of the AG's opinion).

According to the Court, the question to be asked was whether legislation of the type at issue 'creates obstacles to the freedom to provide services and whether, should this be the case, such obstacles are justified on the grounds relied on by the Swedish Government' (*Safir*, para. 25). The Court generally observed that Art. 59 of the Treaty (now Art. 49 EC) precludes the application of any national legislation which, without objective justification, impedes a provider of services from actually exercising the freedom to provide services or has the effect of making the provision of services between Member States more difficult than the provision of services exclusively within one Member State. According to the Court, national legislation of the type at issue was liable to dissuade both foreign established insurance companies from operating in the relevant Member State and their potential clients from taking out an insurance with them. According to the Court, the contested rules could not be justified as other, more transparent and less restrictive systems were conceivable.

ii. Comments

It is submitted that the Court's judgment in *Safir* lacks clarity in more than one respect. First, though the national court's questions related to free movement of both services *and* capital, the Court did not elaborate on the distinction between them. Having found that such a tax system infringes the Treaty rules on the freedom to provide services, the Court simply stated that it was not necessary to determine whether such legislation was also incompatible with the other provisions mentioned by the national court in its questions (*Safir*, para. 35). In contrast, AG Tesauro had argued that it is always necessary to establish precisely whether a provision of national law, especially when related to the banking or insurance sectors, is to be defined as a (potential) restriction on freedom to provide services or on free movement of capital (*Safir*, point 17 subs. of the AG's opinion). In the same context, Cabral & Cunha[2680] point to the residual character of the Treaty provisions regarding services. For present purposes, the question is interesting because of the lack of practical relevance of the concept of indirect discrimination in the Court's case law on free movement of capital, as discussed earlier.[2681]

Second, it is clear that the Court did not make an effort to explicitly analyse the contested rules in the light of the two categories mentioned by AG Tesauro (e.g. Wattel,[2682] the Lenz Commentary,[2683] O'Leary & Fernández Martín).[2684] Wattel observes that the ruling leaves open whether the Swedish system led to direct discrimination, to indirect discrimination or to a restriction in the wider sense. According to Martin,[2685] it is direct discrimination, according to Wathelet[2686] and Notaro[2687] it is an obstacle to free movement in a wide sense and according to (De Jong)[2688] it is simply discrimination with regard to foreign insurance companies. In the present writer's view, Wattel is correct in arguing that direct discrimination must be excluded. As a starting point, it must be determined who is affected by the contested rules. In the case of the Swedish law, the taxation of the premiums concerned first of all the service *recipients*, that is, the insured persons. Obviously, rules which differentiate based on the establishment of the company cannot lead to direct discrimination on grounds of the nationality or their clients. In contrast, indirect discrimination can easily be argued based on the claim that foreigners are more likely to take out insurance policies

---

2680   Cabral & Cunha 1999, p. 401.
2681   See above Part 2, A.I.4.m.
2682   Wattel 1999, pp. 191 subs.
2683   Lenz Commentary 1999, n. 20 ad Art. 49/50 EC.
2684   O'Leary & Fernández Martín 2002, p. 172.
2685   Martin 1998, p. 583.
2686   Wathelet 2002, p. 15.
2687   Notaro 1998, p. 269.
2688   De Jong 1999, p. 113.

with foreign established firms.[2689] Given its broad scope, it would also have been possible to rely on the concept of a restriction in a wider sense. To that extent, a clear label appears to have been possible. However, the Court also found an obstacle to the freedom of insurers to *provide* their services. In that regard, the situation is more complex since here the issue is not one of different taxation to the disadvantage of the foreign companies (who in principle were not even subject to the Swedish taxation system) but rather one of discouraging potential clients from taking out insurance with them because of those persons' tax treatment. In other words, the issue here was not a difference in the treatment of the companies themselves but rather of the *effect* on these companies due to the different treatment of their clients. Should this be seen as a form of direct discrimination induced in an indirect manner (similar to the situation of *Geitling*),[2690] as indirect discrimination or as a restriction in a wider sense? It is submitted that this very question might explain the Court's refusal to determine the precise nature of the infringement in *Safir*: possibly, in the Court's view, the situation was simply too complicated to settle on any one specific label that would have been appropriate for all the aspects of the case.

Further, using clear labels in relation to the two aspects of infringement might also have led to difficulties with regard to *justification*, especially had the Court found both a formally discriminatory measure and an indistinctly applicable measure. What would then have been the appropriate framework for evaluating the potential justifications: the closed list of the Treaty or the open possibilities of objective justification or justification in the general interest?[2691] According to Cabral & Cunha,[2692] it is striking that the Court in *Safir* did not take a position with regard to the nature of the infringement and nevertheless proceeded to examine their possible justification in the general interest. In doing so, it missed the opportunity to bring some clarity to its case law on this matter with the obviously undesirable consequence of 'muddying the waters'. Similarly, Wattel[2693] comments that an explicit statement by the Court to the

---

[2689] As for *Safir*, it is not clear from the case whether Ms Safir herself was a Swedish or a foreign national.

[2690] Case 2/56, [1957/1958] *ECR* 3, where the element of indirectness related to the persons to be protected rather than to the differentiation criterion employed; see above Part 1, C.IV.

[2691] In such a case, the situation should be different from that, for instance, in *Köbler* (Case C-224/01, judgment of 30 September 2003, n.y.r., para. 72 subs.) where the Court found both indirect discrimination (namely in relation to foreign workers) and a restriction (namely in relation to workers established in Austria) and, therefore, was able to generally mention the possibility of justification by pressing reasons of public interest. *Köbler* concerned a regime making the eligibility for a length of service increment for professors dependent on the professor's having completed 15 years of service in that capacity in an Austrian university or institution of higher education. The Court found indirect discrimination in para. 73, since the regime 'operates to the detriment of migrant workers who are nationals of Member States other than the Republic of Austria' and a restriction in a wider sense in para. 74, since the regime deters workers established in Austria from leaving the country to exercise their right to free movement.

[2692] Cabral & Cunha 1999, p. 401.

[2693] Wattel 1999, p. 192.

effect that it does not matter for the purposes of justification which of these two types of infringement is at issue would be welcomed – should that indeed be what the Court thinks. He adds that such a statement should then also clarify whether it applies only in relation to fiscal obstacles or to other limited areas of free movement, or whether it is of a more general nature.[2694] However, as far as the *specific issue of direct taxation* is concerned, it could be argued that a generous approach regarding justification (should that indeed be what the Court intended) should not have come as a surprise. After all, it was long before *Safir* that the Court had recognised the possibility of justification in the interest of the cohesion of the national tax system even in the context of direct discrimination.[2695]

b. Insurance for medical services: Kohll

i. The case

The 'avoidance approach' described above in relation to *Safir*[2696] can also be found in *Kohll*,[2697] a case that concerned the reimbursement in Luxembourg for dental treatment in the context of the free movement of services. Under the relevant insurance scheme, patients were obliged to obtain prior authorization for medical services performed abroad. In defence of this system, the insurance institution, various Member State Governments and the Commission argued that the control of health expenditure and notably the danger of upsetting the financial balance of the insurance scheme must be taken into consideration. The Luxembourg Government also relied on the issue of the protection of public health and the need to ensure quality medical services for all. As in *Safir*, AG Tesauro stressed the importance of placing a measure in its proper category because of the consequences that this has on the level of justification (*Kohll*, points 45 subs. of the AG's opinion). As in *Safir*, the Court did not specify the nature of the infringement in the sense suggested by the AG. It simply stated that rules of the type at issue 'deter insured persons from approaching providers of medical services established in another Member State and constitute, for them and their patients, a

---

[2694] As for the specific circumstances of *Safir*, the Court's statement that less restrictive measures would have been possible was criticised by Wattel (p. 194) according to whom the alternatives mentioned by the Court only *seem* to be less restrictive. However, as AG Tesauro noted even before the judgment in the *Safir* case was handed down, Sweden did in fact revise its tax system by introducing an undifferentiated system for the taxation of insurance policy yields received by policyholders (which thus applied irrespective of the place of establishment of the insurance company). The AG commented (*Safir*, point 38 of the AG's opinion): 'This fact, which can be interpreted in only one way, is significant to say the least.' In other words, a less restrictive system was not only conceivable but also regarded as appropriate in Sweden.

[2695] See above Part 3, A.II.2.b.ii.

[2696] Case C-118/96, [1998] I-1897.

[2697] Case C-158/96, [1998] *ECR* I-1931.

barrier to freedom to provide services' (*Kohll*, para. 35). Addressing justification, the Court recalled that aims of a purely economic nature cannot justify a barrier to the fundamental principle of freedom to provide services, but then added that '[i]t cannot be excluded that the risk of seriously undermining the financial balance of the social security system may constitute an overriding reason in the general interest capable of justifying a barrier of that kind' (*Kohll*, para. 41). However, the Court found that the reimbursement of the costs of treatment in other Member States in accordance with the tariff of the State of insurance[2698] has no significant effect on the financing of the social security system.[2699]

ii. Comments

As in the case of *Safir*, academic commentators note that the Court in *Kohll* examined the possibility of a public interest justification without first having determined the precise nature of the infringement (e.g. Giesen,[2700] Temmink,[2701] du Pré,[2702] O'Leary & Fernández Martín).[2703] As in *Safir*, they discuss a range of possibilities (e.g. Van Raepenbusch,[2704] Van der Mei,[2705] Wyatt & Dashwood,[2706] Heselhaus,[2707] Nowak & Schnitzler,[2708] Dauck & Nowak,[2709] Keunen).[2710] Academic writers offer different explanations for the Court's approach. Berg[2711] points out that *Kohll* only concerned

---

[2698] This is what Mr Kohll had requested. One commentator notes that Mr Kohll was 'a constructive applicant'. Had he asked for reimbursement of the German tariffs, the outcome of the case would have been different ('dan was dit juridische feest niet doorgegaan'); Van der Burgh 1998, p. 1209.

[2699] The Court also addressed the argument of public health (which, however, is less interesting for the present purposes since explicit derogation grounds are available for all types of infringements). The Court observed that the objective of maintaining a balanced medical and hospital service open to all, although intrinsically linked to the method of financing the social security system in so far as it contributes to the attainment of a high level of health protection, may fall within that derogation. Referring to *Campus Oil* (Case 72/83, [1984] *ECR* 2727), the Court held that Art. 56 of the Treaty allows Member States to restrict the freedom to provide medical and hospital services in so far as the maintenance of a treatment facility or medical service on national territory is essential for the public health and even the survival of the population. However, the Court found in this case that the rules under consideration were not proved necessary to that end (*Kohll*, para. 50 subs.).

[2700] Giesen 1999, pp. 845/846.

[2701] Temmink 1998, p. 277.

[2702] Du Pré 1998, p. 368.

[2703] O'Leary & Fernández Martín 2002, p. 172.

[2704] Van Raepenbusch 1998, pp. 696/697.

[2705] Van der Mei 1998 (Decker), p. 191.

[2706] Wyatt & Dashwood 2000, p. 491.

[2707] Heselhaus 2001, p. 645, footnote 7.

[2708] Nowak & Schnitzler 2000, p. 629.

[2709] Dauck & Nowak 2001, p. 745, footnote 26.

[2710] Keunen 2001, p. 360, see also p. 158. – In the parallel case of *Decker* (Case C-120/95, [1998] *ECR* I-1831), direct discrimination was argued by Scott 2002, p. 272.

[2711] Berg 1999, p. 588 footnote 14.

reimbursement, rather than immediate access to treatment as such. Giesen[2712] thinks that the Court wished to rely on *flexible justification* regardless of the nature of the infringement. In the present writer's analysis, the reasons may have been the same as in *Safir*, namely the complexity of a situation that possibly constitutes of a combination of different types of infringements. Again, the contested treatment in the first place affected the service *recipients* whose different treatment according to whether the services were to be obtained at home or abroad leaves room for the argument of either indirect discrimination on grounds of nationality (namely based on the assumption that foreign nationals are more likely to wish for treatment abroad than Luxembourg nationals)[2713] or of a restriction in a wider sense. Again, the contested rules also indirectly affected the service *providers* and as such are difficult to classify. Again, the Court may simply have wished to avoid the problems posed by such a situation when faced with what it considered as legitimate interests of the national legislator in relation to national social security systems.[2714]

5. AN INTERIM CONCLUSION (III)

The previous sections examined the question of whether and to what extent the Court in analysing concrete cases distinguishes between the concepts of indirect discrimination and of restrictions in a wider sense. It was said that there is only one situation where the Court consistently applies one particular approach, namely double regulation cases (*Vander Elst*),[2715] though that is the result of a change in its approach which also had consequences on the meaning of the concept of indirect discrimination. By putting such cases in the framework of restrictions in a wider sense, the Court in effect stepped back from the unusually broad definition of indirect discrimination on which

---

[2712] Giesen 1999, pp. 845 subs. This would, arguably, mean that the Court's approach in *Kohll* could be compared to the Court's much criticised approach in the *Wallonian Waste* case (Case C-2/90 [1992] *ECR* I-4431; see e.g. Mortelmans 1997, p. 186; in contrast, Craig & de Búrca 2003, p. 634, do not think that this is a correct interpretation of the *Wallonian Waste* case; see also Barnard 2004, p. 118.

[2713] Though note that Mr Kohll himself was a Luxemburg national.

[2714] Though less obviously, because the Court in that case had not been urged to specify the nature of the infringement, an avoidance strategy also seems to be at the basis of *Geraerts-Smits* (Case C-157/99, [2001] *ECR* I-5473); see Pieter van der Mei 2002, pp. 198 subs. Again, there are commentators who consider that the case in fact concerned indirect discrimination on grounds of nationality; e.g. Dauck & Nowak 2001, pp. 744 subs. These authors comment that the Court's approach of accepting general interest justification made an adequate outcome possible in the case at hand. Similarly, Steyger 2002, p. 106, explains that the Court tried to maintain a fair balance between the free movement of services and the necessity to keep social security systems a workable concept for the Member States; see further Davies 2002. Van der Burgh 2001, p. 1167, emphasizes that the need to maintain medical services for all was already discussed in *Kohll*, but not accepted as legitimate justification under the specific circumstances of that case. – More recently, see in particular *Müller-Fauré* (Case C-385/99, [2003] *ECR* I-4509).

[2715] Case C-43/93, [1994] *ECR* I-3803.

it based its judgment in the early double regulation case of *Seco*.[2716] However, apart from cases involving double regulation, the Court's decisions do not reveal a clear dividing line between other situations that are examined in either of the two frameworks. In some cases, the Court's reasoning even seems to oscillate between the two concepts (*Konstantinidis*,[2717] *Dafeki*),[2718] and in others the Court pointedly avoids the labelling of an infringement in terms of its specific nature (*Safir*,[2719] *Kohll*).[2720] After *Kohll*, some academic writers generally concluded that the making of categories in terms of different types of infringement of free movement law is no longer necessary (see O'Leary,[2721] Nowak & Schnitzler,[2722] Hakenberg,[2723] Steen,[2724] Van der Mei,[2725] Novak,[2726] Streinz & Leible).[2727] However, it should be noted that not all cases discussed by them fall into that category. For example, Nowak & Schnitzler[2728] point to the Court's ruling in *Terhoeve*.[2729] In fact, the reason why the Court did not find indirect discrimination in that particular case (but rather applied a restriction-based approach) was simply that the facts did not support the argument that there was a (sufficiently) disparate impact. For that reason, the present writer would also disagree with Voogsgeerd's[2730] argument that the Court ignored the concept of discrimination because the case concerned 'the core area of free movement' which it wished to protect

---

[2716]   Joined Cases 62/81 and 63/81, [1982] *ECR* 223.
[2717]   Case C-168/91, [1993] *ECR* I-1191.
[2718]   Case C-336/94, [1997] *ECR* I-6761.
[2719]   Case C-118/96, [1998] I-1897.
[2720]   Case C-158/96, [1998] *ECR* I-1931.
[2721]   O'Leary 1999, p. 406.
[2722]   Nowak & Schnitzler 2000, p. 628.
[2723]   Hakenberg, p. 99.
[2724]   Steen 1998, p. 160.
[2725]   Van der Mei 1998 (Cross-Border Access), pp. 279 subs.
[2726]   Novak 1998, p. 368.
[2727]   Streinz & Leible 2000, p. 462.
[2728]   Nowak & Schnitzler 2000, p. 630.
[2729]   Case C-18/95, [1999] *ECR* I-345. The case concerned the question whether Community law on free movement of workers precludes a Member State (here, the Netherlands) from levying greater social security contributions than those payable by a worker who remained in that Member State on a worker who had transferred his residence in the course of a year from this Member State to another in order to take up employment. Mr Terhoeve maintained that such a system led to indirect discrimination on grounds of nationality. However, he was unable to contradict the counter-argument by the Dutch authorities that nearly half of the taxpayers (in the Netherlands, the general social security contributions are levied together with the taxes) in that country who were actually or notionally non-resident were Netherlands nationals (as Mr Terhoeve himself). The Court recalled that provisions which preclude or deter a national of a Member State from leaving his or her country of origin in order to exercise the right to freedom of movement constitute an obstacle to that freedom even if they apply without regard to the nationality of the workers concerned. It concluded (*Terhoeve*, para. 41): 'It follows that national legislation of the kind at issue in the main proceedings constitutes an obstacle to freedom of movement for workers, prohibited in principle by Article 48 of the Treaty. It is therefore unnecessary to consider whether there is indirect discrimination on grounds of nationality [...] or to consider the set of presumptions which might apply in that regard.'
[2730]   Voogsgeerd 2000, p. 72.

by easing the burden of proof for the worker concerned. Nonetheless, Keunen[2731] is right in observing that *Terhoeve*, the first social security case to be decided under a restriction-based approach, illustrates that the dividing line between indirect discrimination on grounds of nationality on the one hand and a prohibited restriction in a wider sense on the other hand can be razor-sharp.[2732] The example shows that whether or not the Court chooses in a given instance to find (indirect) discrimination or rather a restriction in a wider sense may depend on the particular facts of the individual case before it. Neither can it be concluded that the avoidance approach is now generally applied in cases involving a *requirement of prior authorization* which are, in fact, often seen as typical restriction cases (e.g. Szyszczak[2733] in the context of free movement of capital; e.g. *Analir*,[2734] in the context of Regulation 3577/92/EEC,[2735] concerning maritime transport). As a result, the distinction between the various concepts remains important on the conceptual level though it is sometimes difficult to see the differences in their actual application.

V. OVERALL CONCLUSION: A VERY VAGUE DIVIDING LINE

Overall, these analyses give the impression of a very vague dividing line between the concepts of indirect discrimination and of restrictions in a wider sense, and indeed there are numerous similarities between them. From a practical perspective, the most important of these similarities concerns the equally open[2736] possibilities of justification under the two concepts. As far as the effect of the measures is concerned, it appears

---

[2731] Keunen 2001, pp. 351 subs.

[2732] Keunen adds that the Court's finding might have been different if it had applied less strict rules regarding the proof of the alleged disparate impact, namely the liability approach as expressed in *O'Flynn* (Case C-237/94, [1996] *ECR* I-2617). However, the present writer suspects that in such a case the Dutch Government might still have been able to bring the same counter-proof.

[2733] Szyszczak 2002, p. 274.

[2734] Case C-205/99, [2001] *ECR* I-1271. This case concerned Spanish rules governing regular maritime cabotage liner and public-interest shipping which made the provision of island cabotage services subject to prior administrative authorization. The Court pointed out that '[i]t is settled case law that freedom to provide services requires not only the elimination of all discrimination on grounds of nationality against providers of services who are established in another Member State, but also the abolition of any restriction, even if it applies without distinction to national providers of services and to those of other Member States, which is liable to prohibit, impede or render less attractive the activities of a provider of services established in another Member State where he lawfully provides similar services'. In making this statement, the Court referred to a number of earlier restriction cases, among them *Säger* (Case C-76/90, [1991] *ECR* I-4221) and *Corsica Ferries France II* (Case C-266/96, [1998] *ECR* I-3949).

[2735] Regulation 3577/92/EEC, *OJ* 1992 L 364/7.

[2736] Regarding the possibilities of relying on economic justification which may differ according to the particular context, see above Part 2, A.IV.3.e.

possible to distinguish between the two concepts in so far as comparability is not a constitutive element of the concept of restrictions in a wider sense, which therefore – in contrast to indirect discrimination – is capable of covering even truly indistinctly applicable measures (e.g. *Collectieve Antennevoorziening*).[2737] However, it was seen that the Court's restriction-based decisions are by no means limited to that particular situation and that the concept was not even developed in that context. Instead, the foundational cases discussed concerned measures with some sort of a disparate impact in terms of nationality (*Van Binsbergen*,[2738] *Thieffry*,[2739] *Choquet*).[2740] In this type of case, an analysis of such cases in terms of indirect discrimination would also have been possible, at least where there were no positive duties at issue, and for that reason they have been described as 'inflated models of indirect discrimination on grounds of nationality'. In other cases, it was seen that the Court in its reasoning does not always carefully distinguish between indirect discrimination and restrictions in a wider sense with the result that it is not clear what its actually findings are in a given case (e.g. *Konstantinidis*,[2741] *Dafeki*).[2742] When urged to clearly distinguish between the two concepts against the background of concrete cases and to clarify the link between different types of infringement and different justification possibilities, the Court has even pointedly avoided the issue (e.g. *Safir*,[2743] *Kohll*).[2744]

As a result, the dividing line between indirect discrimination and restrictions in a wider sense is far from clear. Only in one particular situation does the Court seem to clearly and consistently apply one particular approach, namely double regulation which is now always examined in the framework of the concept of restrictions in a wider sense. It was said that for present purposes this is particularly interesting because it indicates a move away from the unusually broad definition of indirect discrimination underlying the early double regulation case *Seco*[2745] which appeared not to be linked to a comparative difference in treatment on grounds of nationality. To that extent, the development of the Court's case has confirmed the most fundamental difference between the two concepts: indirect discrimination remains necessarily comparison-based.

[2737] Case C-288/89, [1991] *ECR* I-4007.
[2738] Case 33/74, [1974] *ECR* 1299.
[2739] Case 71/76, [1977] *ECR* 765.
[2740] Case 16/78, [1978] *ECR* 2293.
[2741] Case C-168/91, [1993] *ECR* I-1191.
[2742] Case C-336/94, [1997] *ECR* I-6761.
[2743] Case C-118/96, [1998] I-1897.
[2744] Case C-158/96, [1998] *ECR* I-1931.
[2745] Joined Cases 62/81 and 63/81, [1982] *ECR* 223.

418

C. DO WE STILL NEED THE CONCEPT OF INDIRECT DISCRIMINATION?

I. RECALLING THE STARTING POINT AND THE MAIN FINDINGS

The final sections of this study bring together the most important findings of the work presented thus far and draw some conclusions. At the beginning it was stated that the study essentially asks why the concept of indirect discrimination was needed in EC law when it was first developed, what it meant then and over the course of its later development, and whether today it is still necessary. This was undertaken through two main research questions,[2746] one concerning the development of the concept itself (How and why did the legal concept of indirect discrimination develop in EC law?) and one concerning its place in today's EC law (How is it to be distinguished from other concepts and, ultimately, is it still necessary today?). The analyses carried out in order to answer the *first of these questions* showed that the Court considered the legal concept of indirect discrimination necessary in view of the effectiveness of EC equality law: it should not be possible to circumvent prohibitions of discrimination by relying on formally neutral differentiation grounds with a discriminatory effect. The arguments employed by the Court in this context were familiar to other areas of Community law and illustrate the maxim that substance must prevail over form. The case law analysis built a complex picture of how the definition of indirect discrimination with its two main elements (the discrimination's indirect nature and objective justification) developed in different areas of EC law and at different points in time through the Court's case law and, later, through the adoption of legal definitions. This led to the conclusion that the case law *lacks consistency* in that different definitions arise depending upon the context. In the context of sex equality law, several definitions exist even within one single area. A further conclusion was that the definitions, whether based on case law or on written legislation, *lack precision*: they do not determine the precise level of requisite disparate impact, and they are unclear regarding the comparison to be made. Further, they do not indicate which aims and goals are legitimate for the purposes of objective justification, and they are not sufficiently clear regarding both the number of elements making up the proportionality test or their

---

[2746] See above Part 1, A.I.4.

meanings. It was noted that all of this negatively impacts upon the *effectiveness* of the legal concept of indirect discrimination.

The *second research question* focused on the place of the concept of indirect discrimination in today's legal order of the European Community, in particular on how it is to be distinguished from other concepts. The study examined the dividing line in the Court's case law between, first, direct and indirect discrimination and, second, between indirect discrimination and restrictions in a wider sense. It found that the demarcation line between *direct and indirect discrimination* seems easy to establish only on the level of principle. Based on the Court's general statements, the decisive point is whether the fundamental reason for the contested treatment is one that applies exclusively to persons of a group protected by a non-discrimination provision (direct discrimination) or, conversely, without distinction to persons of different groups (indirect discrimination). It was seen that in applying this distinction the Court has adopted a formal approach rather than focusing on the effect of the contested treatment. Accordingly, the Court may find indirect discrimination even in cases where the effect of the reliance on an apparently neutral criterion is the same or almost the same as in the case of a directly prohibited criterion. It was further found that on the level of justification the traditionally assumed dividing line between direct and indirect discrimination is not a strict one in that there are areas where the Court accepts extra-textual justification even in the case of direct discrimination (direct taxation and agriculture). In addition, some comparatively recent non-discrimination legislation allows for open justification possibilities in the case of direct discrimination. Against this background, the conclusion was that the dividing line in the Court's case law between direct and indirect discrimination is rather unclear and in some respect problematic.

Regarding *indirect discrimination and restrictions in a wider sense,* the distinction proved to be even more difficult, first, because of their shared feature of open justification possibilities and, second, due to the wide reach of the concept of restrictions in a wider sense which has been applied to a broad range of measures. It was stated that the most important conceptual difference lies in the fact that the concept of restrictions is not necessarily comparison-based, which means that it can also include truly indistinctly applicable measures. At the same time, there are many restriction-based cases concerning formally neutral measures with a disparate effect many of which might just as well have been examined in the framework of indirect discrimination. Indeed, except for double regulation cases which are now consistently examined in the framework of a restriction-based approach, it is difficult to see a clear division based on the Court's case law.

As for the *importance of the legal concept of indirect discrimination* under the law as it stands, it was found that the concept *is in fact less important* than is sometimes argued in academic writing and in submissions made before the Court of Justice. Whilst there is a tendency to almost automatically mention indirect discrimination in the context of certain criteria that are seen as paramount examples in that context (such as residence and language requirements in relation to indirect discrimination on grounds of nationality), the Court in some specific contexts does not use such language but simply relies on a provision's explicit wording or on an alternative concept such as fictional residence. It was also noted that whether a given differentiation ground is indeed a suspect criterion in the context of indirect discrimination depends on the framework of the applicable law. The assessment of concrete cases therefore requires a careful analysis of the factual circumstances and of the legal context. Further, in certain areas the legal concept of indirect discrimination lost importance over time through developments in the law or of special approaches by the Court. At the same time, the relevance of the concept of indirect discrimination may *widen* through the new legal basis provisions which provide for new fields of application of the concept of discrimination as such, as is the case with Art. 13 EC and the secondary law adopted on its basis.

II. WHAT APPROACH FOR THE FUTURE?

1. INTRODUCTORY REMARKS

Though the concept of indirect discrimination on the whole may be less important than is sometimes argued, there are nevertheless large areas of EC law where it remains relevant and where solutions need to be found for the demarcation problems previously discussed, in particular in the area of free movement with its co-existing prohibitions of (direct and indirect) discrimination and of restrictions in a wider sense. Perhaps the situation as it exists today can be compared to a knitted garment that was made for a child when small and that was 'made to grow' with the child through various additions and alterations. Now that the child has grown, the garment still fits in terms of size but is a patchwork made up of various pieces, not all of which fit easily together. It is complicated and lacks elegance. The question that remains is how to deal with this situation in the future. In addressing the question of whether we still need the legal concept of indirect discrimination, the concept's function must be recalled, namely to ensure the effectiveness of EC equality law by making it possible to look beyond the mere form of a contested measure. Below, three possibilities for a future approach are discussed. The first is to simply maintain the *status quo* for reasons of convenience. In the metaphor of the knitted garment, this would mean continuing to use the garment as it is (below II.). A second possibility is to improve the definition of indirect discrimination and to clarify the dividing lines between the various concepts – that is, to first clearly separate and, thereafter, better link the various pieces of the garment (below III.). The third and most far reaching possibility is to give up the distinction between (some or all of) the different concepts – in other words, to unravel the garment and to reuse the wool for making something new that is no longer a patch-work but rather made out of one single piece that covers all types of infringement, including what is now indirect discrimination (below IV.).

2. KEEPING THE STATUS QUO: THE 'LABEL OF CONVENIENCE' APPROACH

a. A pragmatic approach ...

From a practical point of view, the most likely approach is that the Court will simply maintain the *status quo* either using a specific label (direct discrimination, indirect discrimination, restrictions in a wider sense) or keeping its terminology deliberately vague, depending upon what a given case requires in its view in order to arrive at a pragmatic and convincing solution. The Court's approach in the area of free movement of capital[2747] provides a particularly illustrative example for such a 'label of convenience approach'. For a long time, the Court spoke only about restrictions. However, even after the revised basic Treaty provision (Art. 56 EC) no longer even mentioned discrimination, the term still appeared in the Court's case law, namely in the context of measures that explicitly relied on the investors' nationality (*Konle*,[2748] *Albore*).[2749] Given the blatant nature of such infringements, the Court may have felt that the label 'discrimination' better encapsulated or more clearly described the unacceptable nature of the contested measures than did the label of a mere 'restriction'. However, the Court has so far never mentioned indirect discrimination in this context, arguably because it was not necessary from a practical point of view in order to arrive at the conclusion that there is an infringement in a given case. In contrast, indirect discrimination proved to be the most convenient label in the landmark case *O'Flynn*,[2750] due to the wording of the national court's questions and the clear-cut facts which, indeed, immediately evoked the concept of indirect discrimination on grounds of nationality. Though *O'Flynn* was decided at a time when the restriction-based approach was also well established in the area of free movement of workers (*Bosman*),[2751] there was no need to rely on that framework rather than that of indirect discrimination.

In such cases, clear labels have the particular advantage of being easily recognisable to the judgments' addressees. On the other hand, it was seen that in some situations the Court may be inclined to disregard consistency for the purposes of a particular

---

[2747]   See above Part 2, A.I.4.m.
[2748]   Case C-302/97, [1999] *ECR* I-3099.
[2749]   Case C-423/98, [2000] *ECR* I-5965.
[2750]   Case C-237/94, [1996] *ECR* I-2617.
[2751]   Case C-415/93, [1995] *ECR* I-4921.

case before it. Thus, the Court may wish to use less explicit language when a case is complex in terms of its factual situation or where it requires a particular approach to the issue of justification (*Safir*,[2752] *Kohll*).[2753] Though perhaps conceptually rather unconvincing, the 'label of convenience approach' has the advantage of allowing valuable flexibility in dealing with particular cases. To some extent, it may also be possible to interpret the Court's approach as a refusal to submit to the wide spread obsession with formulas of an almost mathematical nature on legal equality, non-discrimination and, in the context of free movement, restrictions in a wider sense. Whilst the desire for clear and easily applicable formulae is certainly understandable from the point of view of legal certainty, some cases do not easily fit into such formulae. Insisting that a given formula needs to be applied in precisely the same way in all circumstances may jeopardise the very aim and effectiveness of the law. Such an approach is, therefore, not always appropriate. As AG Lenz explained in the context of sex discrimination (*Enderby*,[2754] point 15 of the AG's opinion): 'The purpose of a conceptual scheme is to comprehend methods by which women are placed at a disadvantage in their working lives and not to create additional obstacles to claims being made before the courts in respect of sex-related pay discrimination. For this reason, a formalistic approach should not be adopted when categorizing actual instances where women are placed at a disadvantage at work. In accordance with the result-oriented line taken by the Court in the past, a pragmatic approach ought to be pursued.'

b. … and its meaning for the importance of the legal concept of indirect discrimination

Obviously, maintaining the 'label of convenience' approach in the future implies a choice in favour of recognizing the continued importance of the legal concept of indirect discrimination, however limited it might be due to the various factors discussed in this study. Viewed from this perspective, the answer to the second research question is clearly a positive one: yes, we do still need the legal concept of indirect discrimination as a tool to further the effectiveness of EC law. However, it needs to be added that the extent of this importance varies according to the legal context. Thus, in areas where the prohibited behaviour is defined only in terms of discrimination (as in EC social law or under Art. 90 EC), the concept of indirect discrimination will necessarily be more important than in EC free movement law where there is an alternative and, to a large extent, competing concept of restrictions in a wider sense. In addition, yet another dimension must be considered in the context of social law, where it is often hoped that the concept of indirect discrimination will serve as a tool

---

[2752] Case C-118/96, [1998] *ECR* I-1897.
[2753] Case C-158/96, [1998] *ECR* I-1931.
[2754] Case C-127/92, [1993] *ECR* I-5535.

for combating structural discrimination.[2755] In such a framework, the importance of the concept also depends on the existence of alternative avenues under EC law for tackling structural discrimination. Given, in fact, the very limited effect of the legal concept of indirect discrimination in this particular context,[2756] Ellis[2757] has argued that, in order to be truly effective, equality law needs to have a positive as well as a negative face. In recent years, elements of a positive duty to combat (structural) discrimination have been introduced into EC law, as mentioned in this present study's introductory part.[2758] It is clear that to the extent that such positive duties are able to tackle structural discrimination, the focus will shift away from the legal concept of indirect discrimination as a tool in that particular context. However, it should be remembered that the concept's main (and, comparatively speaking, much more successful) function in practice is that of guaranteeing that substance prevails over form. In that context indirect discrimination remains particularly important in an area such as social law.

3. IMPROVING THE *STATUS QUO* BY SHARPENING DEFINITIONS AND DISTINCTIONS

A second possibility for dealing with the present situation would be to maintain the distinction between the existing concepts (e.g. Barnard)[2759] whilst sharpening the definitions and distinctions between them. Below, some suggestions to that effect are presented. Obviously, an approach based on such suggestions implies a positive answer to the second research question: yes, we still need the legal concept of indirect discrimination as a tool to further the effectiveness of EC law. In fact, it will be seen that under this approach that concept would regain some ground since the concept of restrictions in a wider sense would be defined more narrowly than at present.

a. Improving the definition of indirect discrimination

The starting point for an improved definition of indirect discrimination should be the concern for more precision, consistency and effectiveness. However, as was noted earlier, this can be achieved only to a certain extent. In particular, the element of effectiveness depends only somewhat on the concept's definition. Nevertheless, more precision and a stricter objective justification test would also help. In that regard, it was said that some possibilities of justification appear necessary in view of legitimate needs to balance conflicting interests. As for precision, it was found that on the level

---

[2755]   See above Part 2, A.III.2.
[2756]   See above Part 2, A.IV.4.b.
[2757]   Ellis 2001, p. 62.
[2758]   See above Part 1, B.II.3.c.
[2759]   Barnard 2000, p. 220.

of a general definition it can be achieved only to a limited extent. The present writer agrees with Prechal[2760] that a proper definition of indirect discrimination should remain on a rather general level and simply mention the concept's constituent elements, leaving the details to clarifying case law. These *constituent elements* should in any case encapsulate the two main aspects of the definition of indirect discrimination, namely 1) the discrimination's indirect nature (that is, the apparently neutral nature of a measure in terms of an explicitly prohibited type of discrimination and its factually disparate effect) and 2) objective justification (legitimate aim, proportionality).

In describing these elements, a number of factors should be taken into account. First, a general definition that aspires to be applicable in all areas if EC law must not only refer to persons but must also include a wider term, such as 'situations'. As was noted in this study's introduction,[2761] the object of equality or discrimination is not necessarily a person. Second, it would be sufficient if the definition refers to 'measures', rather than to 'provisions, criteria, conditions and/or practices', all of which can be considered to be covered by that former notion. Further, disparate effect should be described in the sense of a particular disadvantage that exists, from a comparative perspective, for some persons or situations. In terms of the modalities of the comparison to be made, the definition should indicate a framework that is as straight forward as possible. In particular, it should not be based on a double relative test. Regarding proof of the required level of the disparate impact, the definition should provide for both possibilities, proof on the basis of the liability approach and proof by showing that a disparate effect actually exists. Also, proportionality should be defined on the basis of the three elements indicated in *Fedesa*,[2762] that is, the aim of the measure must be legitimate, the means for achieving that aim must be appropriate and necessary, and the seriousness of the intervention and the gravity of the reasons justifying must be in adequate proportion to each other (proportionality *stricto sensu*). Finally, the definition need not contain an indication of the reason for the existence of the concept of indirect discrimination (namely effectiveness of equality law) because that element does not describe the meaning of the concept but rather the broader context in which it has to be placed. (As such, it should certainly be emphasised in the Court's case law.) Further details should be left to the case law, including in particular the precise level of the required disparate impact and the modalities of the comparison to be made in that context as well as the legitimacy of aims relied on in the context of objective justification and the proportionality of the measures adopted in order to achieve such aims. The former can be defined more specifically on the level of general

---

[2760]   Prechal 1993, p. 97.
[2761]   See above Part 1, B.V.2.
[2762]   Case C-331/88, [1990] *ECR* I-4023.

case law in the form of an open list of examples whereas the latter must be assessed on a case-to-case basis.

Against this background, the following *three alternative forms of definitions* are suggested as better than the existing ones. *The first* of these leans heavily on the second generation legal definition as reflected in the Race Directive,[2763] the General Framework Directive[2764] and the Revised Second Equal Treatment Directive.[2765] It provides as follows:

> 'Indirect discrimination shall be taken to occur where an apparently neutral measure would, or in fact does, put persons or situations protected by a non-discrimination provision at a particular disadvantage compared with other persons or situations, unless the measure is justified by a legitimate aim, the means for achieving that aim are appropriate and necessary, and the seriousness of the intervention and the gravity of the reasons justifying it are in adequate proportion to each other.'

In the second suggestion, the definition is divided into two sentences in order to distinguish more clearly between the different steps that have to be taken in the discrimination analysis. In this definition, the term 'prohibited indirect discrimination' is used in the context of objective justification in order to indicate an understanding that 'there is indirect discrimination, but it is justified'. In other words, it embraces the justification rather than the causation approach.[2766] This definition reads:

> 'There shall be a presumption of indirect discrimination where an apparently neutral measure would, or in fact does, put persons or situations protected by a non-discrimination provision at a particular disadvantage compared with other persons or situations. This presumption can be rebutted by proof that the measure is justified by a legitimate aim, that the means for achieving that aim are appropriate and necessary, and that the seriousness of the intervention and the gravity of the reasons justifying it are in adequate proportion to each other. In such a case, there shall be no prohibited indirect discrimination.'

Finally, the *third suggestion* takes up Garrone's[2767] terminology by differentiating between indirect distinction and indirect discrimination:

> 'There shall be an indirect distinction where an apparently neutral measure would, or in fact does, put persons or situations protected by a non-discrimination provision at a particular disadvantage compared with other persons or situations. Such a distinction is prohibited as indirect discrimination unless the measure is justified by a legitimate aim,

---

[2763] Directive 2000/43/EC, *OJ* 2000 L 180/22.
[2764] Directive 2000/78/EC, *OJ* 2000 L 303/16.
[2765] Directive 2002/73/EC, *OJ* 2002 L 269/15.
[2766] See above Part 2, A.IV.3.e.
[2767] Garrone 1994, p. 448.

the means for achieving that aim are appropriate and necessary, and the seriousness of the intervention and the gravity of the reasons justifying it are in adequate proportion to each other.'

b. Demarcations: clarifying the dividing lines

i. Direct and indirect discrimination

The dividing line between direct and indirect discrimination could be clarified on two levels, namely that of the nature of the prohibited measure and that of justification. In terms of the measure's *nature*, it is suggested that the number of situations covered by the concept of *direct* discrimination should be greater than is now the case. To start with, the criterion of 'measures obviously relying on a prohibited ground' should be understood as including grounds that are intrinsically linked to the prohibited ground. In such cases, the link with the prohibited criterion is obvious, as recognised by the Court of Justice in the case of pregnancy and sex. The category of direct discrimination should also apply to formally neutral measures that have the same effect as obvious reliance on a prohibited ground and as well as to formally neutral measures disadvantaging or benefiting exclusively persons of one group (or one type of situation), since here the measure's discriminatory effect is still particularly far reaching. In other words, here the Court's approach should be less focused on form and more on substance. Consequently, the concept of *indirect* discrimination should be limited to formally neutral measures with a disparate impact of a lesser nature, namely where the group of persons (or the situation) benefiting from (or disadvantaged by) the measure does not consist exclusively of members of one group (or types of situations). Accordingly, the two concepts are characterised by the following elements:

Direct discrimination:
– Measures obviously relying on a prohibited ground, including grounds intrinsically linked to it;
– Formally neutral measures with the same effect as obvious reliance on a prohibited ground;
– Formally neutral measures which exclude only persons (situations) of one group or benefit only persons of one group (or one type of situation).

Indirect discrimination:
Formally neutral measures with a considerable disparate effect – except for cases where the effect of the measure is the same as that of direct discrimination and for cases where the measures disadvantages or benefits exclusively persons of one group.

In terms of *justification*, the clearest demarcation between direct and indirect discrimination would maintain and strictly apply the traditional system which distinguishes between a closed class of strictly applied textual justification grounds, on the one hand, and an open class of objective justification, on the other hand. Problems resulting from the narrow nature of some textual derogations should be solved by a formal revision of the relevant provisions. Issues concerning objective differences should not be framed in terms of derogations (but rather positively as requirements of equality understood in a substantive sense). Purely economic justification should be generally excluded. This would result in the following distinction between direct and indirect discrimination in terms of possibilities of justification:

Direct discrimination:
Only a closed class of strictly interpreted express (textual) justification is available, understood as cross-cutting reasons, to the exclusion of objective differences and to the exclusion of purely economic considerations.

Indirect discrimination:
–   The closed class of express justification grounds as also available in the context of direct discrimination;
–   In addition the open class of objective justification, again excluding considerations of a purely economic nature.

ii.   Indirect discrimination and restrictions in a wider sense

In the context of the concepts of indirect discrimination and restrictions a distinction such as just proposed cannot be made on the level of *justification* since both concepts provide for open justification possibilities.[2768] Such a distinction does, however, appear possible on the level of the *nature* of the prohibited measure. One, rather radical, possibility would be to suggest that the concept of *restrictions* in a wider sense be limited to cases of truly indistinctly applicable measures, that is, measures that do not make a distinction either in treatment or in effect between different groups of persons or situations. However, it was seen that such cases are extremely rare in practice and that, in addition, they raise the fundamental question of whether the prohibitions in EC free movement law should indeed extend so far. In relation to the free movement of goods, the Court has decided this issue with regard to certain types of selling arrangements (*Keck*);[2769] in other contexts, it continues to be debated.[2770] Whatever

---

[2768]   Here, again, purely economic considerations should generally be unable to serve as justification.
[2769]   Joined Cases C-267/91 and C-268/91, [1993] *ECR* I-6097.
[2770]   Compare AG Léger's remarks in his opinion on *Van Lent* (Case C-232/01, judgment of 2 October 2003, n.y.r., footnote 10 of the AG's opinion) to those by AG Ruiz-Jarabo Colomer in his opinion on the Spanish and UK *Golden Shares* cases (Case C-463/00, [2003] *ECR* I-4581, and Case C-98/01,

the correct approach, it is clear that the Court's case law in its present state does not reserve the concept of restrictions in a wider sense to cases involving truly indistinctly applicable measures. In this situation, it may be more realistic to suggest that the concept of restrictions in a wider sense should be understood as including all truly indistinctly applicable measures with a negative effect on free movement as well as formally neutral measures with a different effect on different groups (or situations) if that effect is an additional burden due to double regulation or if the issue requires a positive duty. The concept should also cover whatever hinders free movement but cannot be brought under the prohibitions of either direct or indirect discrimination. This would result in the following distinction between indirect discrimination and restrictions in a wider sense in terms of the measures' effect:

Indirect discrimination:
Formally neutral measures with a sufficiently serious disparate effect – except double regulation cases.

Restrictions in a wider sense:
–   Truly indistinctly applicable measures, that is, measures that do not make a distinction either in treatment nor in effect but still negatively affect free movement;
–   Indistinctly applicable measures in the sense of formally neutral measures that hinder free movement, without being covered by the concepts of either direct or indirect discrimination;
–   Formally neutral measures with a different effect in the sense of an additional burden caused through double regulation.

4.   ABOLISHING (CERTAIN) DISTINCTIONS

A much more radical approach to deal with the present situation of insufficiently clear distinctions would be to give up certain, or even all, conceptual distinctions. Below, this idea is discussed in two different contexts, first that of free movement law where there is the prohibition not only against discrimination but also against restrictions

---

[2003] *ECR* I-4641). According to AG Léger, the Court's case law in the area of free movement of persons implements the essential criterion identified by *Keck*. In the *Golden Shares* cases, AG Ruiz-Jarabo Colomer remarked that it would be desirable for the Court to temper the rigour with which it applied its principles on restrictions applicable without distinction as in *Keck* – which implies that the Court had not done that yet. The Court did not address the issue in terms of principle but simply pointed out that the contested measures did not have comparable effects to those which the judgment in *Keck* regarded as not falling within the scope of Art. 28 EC.

in a wider sense, and then in the context of other areas where there is only a prohibition against discrimination.

a. In free movement law

i. Abolishing the concept of *indirect* discrimination

In free movement law, the closeness of the concepts of indirect discrimination and of restrictions in a wider sense immediately suggests that it might not be useful to further distinguish between them. For example, Epiney[2771] argued that in the area free movement of persons the concept of indirect discrimination should be abolished altogether and that the only distinction should be that between distinctly and indistinctly applicable measures. The same view might be underlying AG Tesauro's distinction in the context of the cases *Safir*[2772] and *Kohll*[2773] between formally discriminatory and indistinctly applicable measures. Similarly, the Commission in its Communication on intra-EU investment[2774] mentions only two categories of infringements, namely discriminatory and non-discriminatory measures (the latter being described as 'applied to nationals and other EU investors alike'). Given that the concept of restrictions in a wider sense as presently interpreted by the Court is capable of covering measures with disparate effects, and given further that it provides for open justification possibilities, it would easily be possible to use that concept for all formally neutral measures, including those that are today found to constitute indirect discrimination. This would mean that we do not need the legal concept of indirect discrimination any longer in the area of free movement. In fact, such an approach would do away with a number of problems related to the concept of indirect discrimination, in particular concerning the comparison that must be undertaken and the level of proof that must be adhered to. There seem to be only two disadvantages to such an approach, namely the loss of indirect discrimination as a 'label of convenience' in particularly clear cases and, possibly, a perceived lack of consistency if the same situation amounts to a restriction in free movement law and to indirect discrimination in areas where there is no such concept as restrictions in a wider sense, as in social law.

ii. Abolishing the concept of discrimination altogether

On a conceptual level, these arguments can be taken an admittedly big step further by proposing the *abolition of the notion of discrimination altogether* for the area of free

---

[2771] Epiney 1995, pp. 60 subs.
[2772] Case C-118/96, [1998] *ECR* I-1897.
[2773] Case C-158/96, [1998] *ECR* I-1931. The opinion on this case can be found in Case C-120/95, [1998] *ECR* I-1831.
[2774] Communication on certain legal aspects concerning intra-EU investment, *OJ* 1997 C 220/15.

movement in favour of retaining only that of restrictions in a wider sense, though in a modified form. This is not at all a likely scenario but it shall nevertheless be briefly described. It is submitted that a single standard concept of restrictions could be defined as follows: 'There is a restriction of the right to free movement where a measure hinders or makes less attractive the exercise of free movement rights or is liable to do so, unless it is justified by imperative requirements in the general interest, if the means for achieving that aim are appropriate and necessary and if the seriousness of the intervention and the gravity of the reasons justifying it are in adequate proportion to each other. Purely economic concerns cannot serve as justification.' This definition is similar to that used by the Court in the context of its general statement in *Gerhard*[2775] (para. 37) except that it is expressly not limited to indistinctly applicable measures. It is further modified insofar as it expands upon the liability approach mentioned in *Gerhard* ('liable to hinder or make less attractive'), a reference to the proof of an actually existing obstacle. This latter element has been taken from the suggestions made earlier for an improved definition of indirect discrimination.

The advantages of such an approach are evident, at least as far as the *nature of the infringement* is concerned: apart from the simplicity of a single standard, it would do away with the problems linked to comparison and proof that characterise the concept of discrimination. At the same time, it is obvious that, given the traditional distinction in relation to *justification* between direct discrimination on the one hand and indirect discrimination and restrictions in a wider sense on the other hand, the most important impact and the most difficult challenges of a modified single standard concept of restrictions, as suggested, lie on that level. Under the proposed definition, restrictions can be justified by imperative requirements in the general interest, provided that the means for achieving that aim are appropriate and necessary and provided further that the seriousness of the intervention and the gravity of the reasons justifying it are in adequate proportion to each other. Again, this is similar to the Court's general statement in *Gebhard* (para. 37) which has been somewhat expanded in light of the suggestions made in the context of an improved definition of indirect discrimination by adding the element of proportionality in the narrow sense. Obviously, such an approach would upset the present system of the Treaty. Moving away from the closed system would mean that the determination of the legitimacy of a given justification ground is put back in the hands of the courts rather than being decided – at least on the level of principle – by the legislator. As the experiences from EC social law show, the drawback might be that such a system tempts the courts to accept all kinds of justification, though it is also conceivable that a corrective might be built in by following the approach suggested by Holtmaat,[2776] namely that a distinction should be made on the level of justification depending on whether discrimination is 'neutral' or

---

[2775] Case C-55/94, [1995] *ECR* I-4165.
[2776] Holtmaat 2002, p. 170; see above Part 1, B.III.2.

'pejorative' (discrimination in a neutral and in a strict sense). Holtmaat argues that justification grounds must weigh very heavily in the framework of the latter.[2777]

b. In areas where there is only a prohibition of discrimination

i. The *status quo*: indirect discrimination as an important concept

The suggestion for a single standard, discussed above in the context of EC free movement law, would be even more radical in areas that are framed solely in terms of discrimination and where there is no alternative form of concept such as restrictions in a wider sense.[2778] In EC law, this includes not only the whole of social law but also important provisions of economic law, such as Art. 90(1) EC on the internal taxation of goods, Art. 34(2) EC on the framing of the Community's agricultural policy, as well as Art. 12(1) EC (see Plötscher).[2779] As EC law stands, a single standard within the meaning just discussed is not conceivable. As was stated earlier, given that there is no alternative concept that could take its place, it is clear that here the legal concept of indirect discrimination is indispensable as an admittedly limited tool in the effort to further the effectiveness of EC law.

ii. Changing the equality paradigm: the example of the Canadian approach

This situation could, however, change if the legal framework around equality and non-discrimination were to be redefined in such a way that it would itself somehow resemble the concept of restrictions in a wider sense. An example in that context is Section 15(1)[2780] of the Canadian Charter of Rights and Freedoms of 1982 which is part of the Canadian Constitution.[2781] It was adopted specifically to reverse the restrictive interpretations then placed by the Canadian Supreme Court on the phrase

---

[2777] Compare also the Court's statement in *Orfanopoulos* (Joined Cases C-482/01 and C-493/01, judgment of 29 April 2004, n.y.r.), para. 65, that the status of EU citizenship requires a particularly strict interpretation of derogations from the provisions on free movement of workers because EU citizenship is the fundamental status of the nationals of the EU Member States; see above Part 2, A.IV.2.c.ii.

[2778] At least several authors have tried to draw parallels to the concept of restrictions in a wider sense. Martin argues that there is no room for that concept in the context of equal pay for men and women. Rather, there the concept of positive action comes into play. Positive action, like restrictions in a wider sense, requires more than the application of a strict prohibition of discrimination; Martin 1998, pp. 273 and 316 subs.; see also De Schutter 1999, pp. 26 subs. and 36 subs.

[2779] Plötscher 2003, p. 103, in relation to Art. 12 EC, with further references.

[2780] Section 15(1) provides: 'Every individual is equal before and under the law and has the right to the equal protection and equal benefit of the law without discrimination and, in particular, without discrimination based on race, national or ethnic origin, color, religion, sex, age or mental or physical disability.'

[2781] For the full text, see http://lois.justice.gc.ca/en/charter/.

'equality before the law' in the Canadian Bill of Rights (Mahoney,[2782] Vizkelety,[2783] Hovius).[2784] The new interpretation results from the landmark case of *Andrews*,[2785] decided by the Canadian Supreme Court in 1989, in the context of discrimination on grounds of nationality. Mr Andrews was a British national permanently resident in Canada who had applied to be admitted to the British Columbia Bar as a solicitor. Though he held British law degrees and fulfilled all the other requirements provided for by the Barristers and Solicitor's Act, he was refused because he was not a Canadian citizen. The Supreme Court found that this requirement constituted an infringement of a right guaranteed by the Charter. In its decision, it generally explained the meaning of discrimination as follows (*Andrews*, p. 3 subs.): 'Section 15(1) of the Charter provides for every individual a guarantee of equality before and under the law, as well as the equal protection and equal benefit of the law without discrimination. [..] The 'similarly situated should be similarly treated' approach will not necessarily result in equality nor will every distinction or differentiation in treatment necessarily result in inequality. […] Discrimination is a distinction which, whether intentional or not but based on grounds relating to personal characteristics of the individual or group, has an effect which imposes disadvantages not imposed upon others or which withholds or limits access to advantages available to other members of society. Distinctions based on personal characteristics attributed to an individual solely on the basis of association with a group will rarely escape the charge of discrimination, while those based on an individual's merits and capacities will rarely be so classed. […]'.

According to Mahoney,[2786] *Andrews* is a groundbreaking constitutional case with which the Canadian Supreme Court 'launched a promising new era for equality jurisprudence quite unique in the Western World', in particular by rejecting the traditional 'similarly situated approach' (that is, the requirement of comparability of situations). For that same reason, the case was also mentioned by the American scholar MacKinnon[2787] as an application of the non-Aristotelian approach to equality and discrimination developed by her against the background of U.S. sex equality law as of the late 1970s.[2788] Later, the Canadian Supreme Court in *Law*[2789] (para. 88) summarised the guidelines relating to the discrimination approach under the Charter. Writing for the Court, Justice Iacobucci emphasised that it is inappropriate to attempt to confine the analysis under s. 15(1) of the Charter to a fixed and limited formula. Instead, a purposive and contextual approach to discrimination analysis is to be

---

[2782] Mahoney 1992, pp. 765 subs.
[2783] Vizkelety 1999, p. 224.
[2784] Hovius 2000, p. 6.
[2785] *Andrews v. Law Society of British Columbia* [1989] 1 S.C.R. 143.
[2786] Mahoney 1992, pp. 760 and 775 subs.; see also more generally Mahoney 1994.
[2787] MacKinnon 1991, p. 1296.
[2788] Regarding MacKinnon's dominance approach, see above, Part 1, B.III.3.c.ii.
[2789] *Law v. Canada (Minister of Employment and Immigration)* [1999] 1 S.C.R. 497.

preferred, in order to permit the realization of the strong remedial purpose of the equality guarantee, and to avoid the pitfalls of a formalistic or mechanical approach. He described the approach adopted and regularly applied by his Court as focusing upon three central issues, namely: (1) whether a law imposes differential treatment between the claimant and others in purpose or effect; (2) whether one or more enumerated or analogous grounds of discrimination are the basis for the differential treatment; and (3) whether the law in question has a purpose or effect that is discriminatory within the meaning of the equality guarantee.

As for the *relevance of the legal concept of indirect discrimination* in such a framework, Loenen[2790] observes that under the Canadian approach the distinction between direct and indirect discrimination seems to collapse altogether, because disadvantage is determinative whatever the distinction or lack of distinction being made.[2791] In the present writer's opinion, this is convincing given the indirect discrimination concept's necessary link to comparability.[2792] As Justice McLachlin of the Canadian Supreme Court (now the Supreme Court's President) noted following *Andrews* in *Meiorin*[2793] (para. 47), all that is required is that the claimant establish that either the purpose or the effect of the measure infringes section 15 of the Charter. As a result, the distinction between direct and indirect (adverse impact) discrimination has little legal importance. Under the Charter, 'the employer cannot dictate the nature of what it must prove in justification simply by altering the method of discrimination' (*Meiorin*, para. 48). In *Meiorin* itself, in the context of the Canadian Human Rights Code, the Court rejected a distinction between direct and indirect discrimination and, in particular, the use of a different *justification test*, though apparently more for practical than for conceptual reasons.

The case is particularly interesting in the present context because it takes up many of the problems that exist in relation to indirect discrimination and discussed in the framework of this present study. Ms Meiorin, a fire fighter, challenged fitness standards for fire fighters established by the government which were found to have a disproportionately negative effect

---

[2790]   Loenen 1999, p. 203.

[2791]   Against this background, it may be interesting to note that in Loenen & Rodrigues' book Vizkelety's article on adverse effect discrimination in Canadian law is placed in the chapter on 'Adverse Impact' which deals with indirect discrimination. However, the paper does not seem to fit here in that it does not link the Canadian equality approach to the issue of indirect discrimination. Instead, the link made is that with substantive equality; see Vizkelety 1999.

[2792]   In contrast, Kingreen's suggestion of limiting prohibited restrictions of the fundamental freedoms to what he terms 'substantive discrimination' (Kingreen 1999, pp. 120 subs. and 184 subs.) remains firmly comparison-based. Thus, it is not comparable to innovative approaches such as those under Canadian constitutional law or under MacKinnon's discrimination theory.

[2793]   *British Columbia (Public Service Employee Relations Commission) v. BCGSEU* [1999] 3 S.C.R. 3 (Meiorin).

on women and which were not proven to be necessary for the job.[2794] Writing for the Court, Justice McLachlin pointed to the difficulties inherent in the conventional distinction between direct and indirect discrimination and developed a new approach instead (Meiorin, para. 19 subs.). She explained that the conventional analysis had been helpful in the interpretation of the early human rights statutes, and indeed had represented a significant step forward, but that it does not serve the purpose of contempory human rights legislation. Rather, the complexity and unnecessary artificiality of aspects of the conventional analysis attest to the desirability of simplifying the guidelines that structure the interpretation of human rights legislation in Canada. Justice McLachlin noted that there are a number of difficulties with the conventional approach which make a compelling case for revising the analysis, including in particular the artificiality of the distinction between direct and indirect discrimination as well as practical difficulties in determining adverse effect and in applying employers' defences. Regarding the first of these issues, she emphasised that the distinction is unrealistic, in that a modern employer with a discriminatory intention would rarely frame the rule in directly discriminatory terms when the same effect – or an even broader effect – could be easily realized by couching it in neutral terms. Accordingly, the bifurcated analysis gives employers with a discriminatory intention and the forethought to draft the rule in neutral language an undeserved cloak of legitimacy. The Justice also noted that the distinction under the conventional analysis ultimately serves to legitimise systemic discrimination, since it does not challenge the underlying standards, the imbalances of power or the discourse of dominance. She further called the belief that unintentional discrimination is less deserving of legal censure inconsistent with the goal of human rights legislation. Against this background, Justice McLachlin proposed *a unified approach* in the form of a three-step test for determining whether a prima facie discriminatory standard is a bona fide occupational requirement (in other words, whether it can be justified). Under the new and unified test, an employer 'may justify an impugned standard by establishing on the balance of probabilities: (1) that the employer adopted the standard for a purpose rationally connected to the performance of the job; (2) that the employer adopted the particular standard in an honest and good faith belief that it was necessary to the fulfilment of that legitimate work-related purpose; and (3) that the standard is reasonably necessary to the accomplishment of that legitimate work-related purpose. To show that the standard is reasonably necessary, it must be demonstrated that it is impossible to accommodate individual employees sharing the characteristics of the claimant without imposing undue hardship upon the employer.' (*Meiorin*, para. 54). The Court agreed unanimously.

For purposes of the present study, it might be argued that the Canadian approach with its focus on disadvantage comes close to the concept of restrictions in a wider sense, as relevant in EC free movement law, in particular because it is not based on the requirement of comparability of situation. Though discussed here in the context of social law, the facts of the *Andrews* case itself illustrate that such an approach need not

---

[2794] Whilst this case concerned employment, the Court held later that the new approach applied to all situations under the relevant human rights code; see *British Columbia (Superintendent of Motor Vehicles) v. British Columbia (Council of Human Rights)* [1999] 3 S.C.R. 868 (Grismer).

be limited to that particular area of law. Instead, it could generally underlie equality law so as to form a single and encompassing legal standard. However, it is clear that, given the still firm basis of EC non-discrimination law on a comparison-based Aristotelian understanding of equality, such a radical change of paradigm appears extremely unlikely in EC law at this point of time.

In conclusion, the above discussion was intended to demonstrate that an equality system where the legal concept of indirect discrimination is no longer necessary is conceivable, even outside the area of free movement law where the legal concept of restrictions in a wider sense offers a ready alternative. In that sense, we no longer need the concept. However, it was seen that there are difficulties and drawbacks which make it unlikely for the EC to fundamentally change its present approach. Against this background, it seems certain that the legal concept of indirect discrimination is here to stay, at least in areas of law where discrimination is the only prohibited type of action. Thus, there are still two viable options for dealing with the present situation: first, by trying to sharpen the definitions and demarcations and, second, by simply maintaining the *status quo,* for reasons of convenience. At least in the short term, the latter patchwork approach clearly appears to be the most likely scenario. Nonetheless, other more consistent and straightforward solutions may eventually make their way into the Court's case law.

TABLES

A. EC LEGISLATION

I. REGULATIONS

Regulation 38/64/EEC (Règlement relatif à la libre circulation des travailleurs à l'intérieur de la Communauté; text not available in English), OJ No. 62 of 17 April 1964, p. 965 (no longer in force).

Regulation 259/68/EEC, Euratom, ECSC laying down the Staff Regulations of Officials and the Conditions of Employment of Other Servants of the European Communities, OJ 1968 L 56/1 (as amended). For a consolidated text indicating the numerous amendments, see http://www.europa.eu.int/comm/dgs/personnel_administration/statut/tocen100.pdf.

Regulation 1612/68/EEC on freedom of movement for workers within the Community, OJ English Special Edition 1968 L 257/2, p. 475 (as amended).

Regulation 1408/71/EEC on the application of social security schemes to employed persons, to self-employed persons and to members of their families moving within the Community, OJ English Special Edition 1971(II) L 149/2, p. 416 (as amended; meanwhile replaced by Regulation 883/2004 on the coordination of social security systems, OJ 2004 L 166/1).

Regulation 574/72/EEC fixing the procedure for implementing Regulation (EEC) No 1408/71 on the application of social security schemes to employed persons and their families moving within the Community, OJ 1972 I 74/1.

Regulation 101/76/EEC laying down a common structural policy for the fishing industry, OJ 1976 L 20/19 (no longer in force).

Regulation 4055/86/EEC applying the principle of freedom to provide services to maritime transport between Member States and between Member States and third countries, OJ 1986, L 378/1 (as amended).

Regulation 2408/92/EEC on access for Community air carriers to intra-Community air routes, OJ 1992 L 240/8 (as amended).

Regulation 3577/92/EEC applying the principle of freedom to provide services to maritime transport within Member States (maritime cabotage), OJ 1992 L 364/7 (as amended).

Regulation 3118/93/EEC laying down the conditions under which non-resident carriers may operate national road haulage services within a Member State, OJ 1993 L 279/1 (Regulation on road cabotage (goods)).

Regulation 40/94/EC on the Community trade mark, OJ 1994 L 11/1 (as amended).

Regulation 1279/96/EC, Euratom concerning the provision of assistance to economic reform and recovery in the New Independent States and Mongolia, OJ 1996 L 165/1 (TACIS-Regulation, no longer in force).

Regulation 781/98/EC, ECSC, Euratom amending the Staff Regulations of Officials and Conditions of Employment of Other Servants of the European Communities in respect of equal treatment, OJ 1998 L 113/4.

Regulation 44/2001/EC on jurisdiction and the recognition and enforcement of judgments in civil and commercial matters, OJ 2001 L 12/1 (Brussels I Regulation, as amended).

Regulation 883/2004/EC on the coordination of social security systems, OJ 2004 L 166/1.

II. DIRECTIVES

First Directive for the implementation of Article 67 of the Treaty, OJ English Special Edition 1959-1962, p. 49 (no longer in force).

Directive 64/221/EEC on the co-ordination of special measures concerning the movement and residence of foreign nationals which are justified on grounds of public policy, public security and public health, OJ English Special Edition 1964, No. 850/64, p. 117.

Directive 70/32/EEC on the provision of goods to the State, to local authorities and other official bodies, OJ 1970 L 13/1.

Directive 71/304/EEC concerning the abolition of restrictions on freedom to provide services in respect of public works contracts and on the award of public works contracts to contractors acting through agencies or branches, OJ 1971 L 185/1.

Directive 71/305/EEC concerning the coordination of procedures for the award of public works contracts, OJ 1971 L 185/5 (no longer in force).

Directive 75/117/EEC on the approximation of the laws of the Member States relating to the application of the principle of equal pay for men and women, OJ 1975 L 45/19 (First Equal Treatment Directive or Equal Pay Directive).

Directive 76/207/EEC on the implementation of the principle of equal treatment for men and women as regards access to employment, vocational training and promotion, and working conditions, OJ 1976 L 39/40 (Second Equal Treatment Directive, as amended).

Directive 77/91/EEC of 13 December 1976 on coordination of safeguards which, for the protection of the interests of members and others, are required by Member States of companies within the meaning of the second paragraph of Article 58 of the Treaty, in respect of the formation of public limited liability companies and the maintenance and alteration of their capital, with a view to making such safeguards equivalent, OJ 1977 L 26/1 (Second Company Law Directive; as amended).

Directive 77/249/EEC to facilitate the effective exercise by lawyers of freedom to provide services, OJ 1977 L 78/17 (Lawyers' Services Directive; as amended).

Directive 78/686/EEC concerning the mutual recognition of diplomas, certificates and other evidence of the formal qualifications of practitioners of dentistry, including measures to facilitate the effective exercise of the right of establishment and freedom to provide services; OJ 1978 L 233/1 (as amended).

Directive 79/7/EEC on the progressive implementation of the principle of equal treatment for men and women in matters of social security, OJ 1979 L 6/24 (Third Equal Treatment Directive).

First Directive 80/1263/EEC on the introduction of a Community driving licence, OJ 1980 L 375/1 (First directive on driving licences; no longer in force).

Directive 86/378/EEC on the implementation of the principle of equal treatment for men and women in occupational social security schemes, OJ 1986 L 225/40 (Fourth Equal Treatment Directive, as amended).

Directive 86/613/EEC on the application of the principle of equal treatment between men and women engaged in an activity, including agriculture, in a self-employed capacity, and on the protection of self-employed women during pregnancy and motherhood, OJ 1986 L 359/56 (Fifth Equal Treatment Directive).

Directive 88/361/EEC for the implementation of Article 67 of the Treaty, OJ 1988 L 178/5.

Directive 89/48/EEC on a general system for the recognition of higher-education diplomas awarded on completion of professional education and training of at least three years' duration, OJ 1989 L 19/16 (as amended).

Directive 89/391/EEC of 12 June 1989 on the introduction of measures to encourage improvements in the safety and health of workers at work, OJ 1989 L 183/1 (General Framework Directive on health and safety at work; as amended).

Directive 89/552/EEC on the coordination of certain provisions laid down by Law, Regulation or Administrative Action in Member States concerning the pursuit of television broadcasting activities, OJ 1989 L 298/23 (Television Without Frontiers Directive; as amended).

Directive 90/434/EEC on the common system of taxation applicable to mergers, divisions, transfers of assets and exchanges of shares concerning companies of different Member States, OJ 1990 L 225/1 (Taxation Merger Directive; as amended).

Directive 90/435/EEC on the common system of taxation applicable in the case of parent companies and subsidiaries of different Member States, OJ 1990 L 225/6 (Parent-Subsidiary Directive; as amended).

Directive 91/383/EEC supplementing the measures to encourage improvements in the safety and health at work of workers with a fixed-duration employment relationship or a temporary employment relationship, OJ 1991 L 206/19 (Fixed-Term Work Directive).

Directive 91/439/EEC of 29 July 1991 on driving licences, OJ 1991L 237/1 (Second Directive on driving licences; as amended).

Directive 92/51/EEC on a second general system for the recognition of professional education and training to supplement Directive 89/48/EEC, OJ 1992 L 209/25 (as amended).

Directive 92/85/EEC on the introduction of measures to encourage improvements in the safety and health at work of pregnant workers and workers who have recently given birth or are breastfeeding (tenth individual Directive within the meaning of Article 16(1) of Directive 89/391/EEC), OJ 1992 L 348/1 (Maternity Directive).

Directive 93/16/EEC to facilitate the free movement of doctors and the mutual recognition of their diplomas, certificates and other evidence of formal qualifications, OJ 1993 L 165/1, as amended (Doctors' Directive).

Directive 93/89/EEC on the application by Member States of taxes on certain vehicles used for the carriage of goods by road and tolls and charges for the use of certain infrastructure, OJ 1993 L 279/32 (Directive on road taxes; no longer in force).

Directive 96/34/EC on the framework agreement on parental leave concluded by UNICE, CEEP and the ETUC, OJ 1996 L 145/4 (Parental Leave Directive; as amended).

Directive 96/97/EC amending Directive 86/378/EEC on the implementation of the principle of equal treatment for men and women in occupational social security schemes, OJ 1997 L 46/20.

Directive 97/80/EC on the burden of proof in cases of discrimination based on sex, OJ 1998 L 14/6 (Burden of Proof Directive; as amended).

Directive 97/81/EC concerning the Framework Agreement on part-time work concluded by UNICE, CEEP and the ETUC, OJ 1998, L 14/9 (Part-Time Work Directive; as amended).

Directive 98/5/EC to facilitate practice of the profession of lawyer on a permanent basis in a Member State other than that in which the qualification was obtained, OJ 1998 L 77/36 (Lawyers' Home Title Directive; as amended).

Directive 98/52/EC on the extension of Directive 97/80/EC on the burden of proof in cases of discrimination based on sex to the United Kingdom of Great Britain and Northern Ireland, OJ 1998, L 205/66.

Directive 1999/70/EC concerning the framework agreement on fixed-term work concluded by ETUC, UNICE and CEEP, OJ 1999 L 175/43 (Fixed-Term Work Directive).

Directive 2000/43/EC implementing the principle of equal treatment between persons irrespective of racial or ethnic origin, OJ 2000 L 180/22 (Race Directive).

Directive 2000/78/EC establishing a general framework for equal treatment in employment and occupation, OJ 2000 L 303/16 (General Framework Directive).

Directive 2001/19/EC amending Council Directives 89/48/EEC and 92/51/EEC on the general system for the recognition of professional qualifications and Council Directives 77/452/EEC, 77/453/EEC, 78/686/EEC, 78/687/EEC, 78/1026/EEC, 78/1027/EEC, 80/154/EEC, 80/155/EEC, 85/384/EEC, 85/432/EEC, 85/433/EEC and 93/16/EEC concerning the professions of nurse responsible for general care, dental practitioner, veterinary surgeon, midwife, architect, pharmacist and doctor, OJ 2001 L 206/1 (SLIM Directive).

Directive 2002/73/EC amending Council Directive 76/207/EEC on the implementation of the principle of equal treatment for men and women as regards access to employment, vocational training and promotion, and working conditions, OJ 2002 L 269/15 (Revised Second Equal Treatment Directive).

Directive 2003/48/EC on taxation of savings income in the form of interest payments, OJ 2003 L 157/38 (as amended).

Directive 2004/17/EC coordinating the procurement procedures of entities operating in the water, energy, transport and postal services sectors, OJ 2004 L 134/1.

Directive 2004/18/EC on the coordination of procedures for the award of public works contracts, public supply contracts and public service contracts, OJ 2004 L 134/114.

Directive 2004/38/EC on the right of citizens of the Union and their family members to move and reside freely within the territory of the Member States amending Regulation (EEC) No 1612/68 and repealing Directives 64/221/EEC, 68/360/EEC, 72/194/EEC, 73/148/EEC, 75/34/EEC, 75/35/EEC, 90/364/EEC, 90/365/EEC and 93/96/EEC, OJ 2004 L 158/77.

Directive 2004/113/EC implementing the principle of equal treatment between men and women in the access to and supply of goods and services, OJ 2004 L 373/37.

B. CASE LAW

I. COURT OF JUSTICE OF THE EUROPEAN COMMUNITIES

1. Court of Justice

2. Court of First Instance

II. EFTA COURT[2795]

III. PERMANENT COURT OF INTERNATIONAL JUSTICE[2796]

IV. EUROPEAN COURT OF HUMAN RIGHTS[2797]

V. CANADIAN SUPREME COURT[2798]

2795 See http://www.eftacourt.lu/decidedcases.asp.
2796 See http://www.worldcourts.com/pcij/eng/pcij-decisions.htm.
2797 See http://www.echr.coe.int/Eng/Judgments.htm.
2798 See http://www.scc-csc.gc.ca/judgments/index_e.asp.

VI. U.S. SUPREME COURT[2799]

C. LITERATURE QUOTED

Adobati 1995
Enrica Adobati, 'Laurea ed accesso alla libera professione nell'Unione Europea', *Diritto comunitario e degli scambi internazionali* 1995, 91-116.
Albers 1999
Hendrik S.J. Albers, *Europees Gemeenschapsrecht en cultuur: eenheid en verscheidenheid*, Deventer: Kluwer 1999.
Alkema & Rop 2002
E.A. Alkema & A.C. Rop, 'Gelijk zijn en gelijk krijgen – aspecten van gelijkheid in de rechtspraktijk', in: M. Kroes, J.P. Loof & H.-M.Th.D. ten Napel (eds), *Gelijkheid en rechtvaardigheid. Staatsrechtelijke vraagstukken rondom ,minderheden'*, Deventer: Kluwer 2002, 31-77.
Anderman 1996
Steve Anderman, 'Constitutional Law and Labour Law Dimensions of Art. 119: The Case of Justification for Indirect Discrimination', in: Janet Dine & Bob Watt (eds), *Discrimination Law. Concepts, Limitations, and Justifications*, London/New York: Longman 1996.
Apollis 1980
Gilbert Apollis, 'Le principe de l'égalité de traitement en droit économique communautaire', *Revue du marché commun* 1980, 72-84 (first part) and 140-159 (second part).

[2799] See http://www.findlaw.com/casecode/supreme.html.

Arioli 1992

Kathrin Simone Arioli, *Frauenförderungsmassnahmen im Erwerbsleben unter besonderer Berücksichtigung der Verfassungsmässigkeit von Quotenregelungen*, Zürich: Schulthess 1992.

Aristotle 1980

Aristotle, *The Nichomachean Ethics*, translated and edited by W. David Ross, edition revised by John Ackrill & James O. Urmson, Oxford: Oxford University Press 1980.

Aristotle 2000

Aristotle, *Nicomachean ethics*, translated and edited by Roger Crisp, Cambridge: Cambridge University Press 2000.

Arnull 1987

Anthony Arnull, (Case note on *Danfoss*), *EL Rev* 1987, 62-63.

Arnull 1999

Anthony Arnull, *The European Union and its Court of Justice*, Oxford: Oxford University Press 1999.

Arrowsmith 2004

Sue Arrowsmith, 'An assessment of the new legislative package on public procurement', *CML Rev* 2004, 1277-1325.

Asscher-Vonk 1993

I.P. Asscher-Vonk, 'Gevolgen van het Dekker-arrest voor sanctionering van gelijke-behandelingsregels', *Sociaal Maandblad Arbeid* 1993, 386-394.

Asscher-Vonk 1997

I.P. Asscher-Vonk, 'Artikel 6A EG-Verdrag, zoals voorgesteld bij het Verdrag van Amsterdam en discriminatie op grond van leeftijd', *NTER* 1997, 279-282.

Asscher-Vonk & Wentholt 1994

Irene Asscher-Vonk & Klaartje Wentholt, *Wet gelijke behandeling van mannen en vrouwen*, Deventer: Kluwer 1994.

Baer 2004

Susanne Baer, 'Europäische Richtlinien gegen Diskriminierung', in: Doris König, Joachim Lange, Ursula Rust & Hanna Beate Schöpp-Schilling (eds), *Gleiches Recht – gleiche Realität? Welche Instrumente bieten Völkerrecht, Europarecht und nationals Recht für die Gleichstellung von Frauen?*; Rehburg-Loccum: Evangelische Akademie Loccum 2004, 173-183.

Ballestero 1994

Maria Vittoria Ballestero, 'Le azioni positive fra egualianza e diritto diseguale', *Le nuove leggi civili commentate* 1994, 11-21.

Bamforth 1993

Nicholas Bamforth, 'The Changing Concept of Sex Discrimination', *The Modern Law Review* 1993, 872-880.

Bamforth 1996

Nicholas Bamforth, 'Setting the Limits of Anti-Discrimination Law: Some Legal and Social Concepts', in: Janet Dine & Bob Watt (eds), *Discrimination Law. Concepts, Limitations, and Justifications*, London/New York: Longman 1996, 49-62.

Banton 1996

Michael Banton, *International Action Against Racial Discrimination*, Oxford: Clarendon Press 1996.

Barbera 1994

Marzia Barbera, 'La nozione di discriminazione', *Le Nuove Leggi Civili Commentate* 1994, 46-73.

Barents 1977

René Barents, (Case note on *Steinike & Weinlig*), *SEW* 1977, 730-736.

Barents 1994 (Agricultural Law)

René Barents, *The Agricultural Law of the EC. An Inquiry into the Administrative Law of the European Community in the Field of Agriculture*, Kluwer Law and Taxation Publishers: Deventer/Boston 1994.

Barents 1994 (The Significance)

René Barents, 'The Significance of the Non-Discrimination Principle for the Common Agricultural Policy: Between Competition and Intervention', in: Deirdre Curtin & Ton Heukels (eds), *Institutional Dynamics of European Integration. Essays in Honour of Henry G. Schermers*, Volume II, Dordrecht/Boston/London: Martinus Nijhoff Publishers 1994, 527-548.

Barnard 1996 (Commercial Discrimination)

Catherine Barnard, 'Gender and Commercial Discrimination', in: Janet Dine & Bob Watt (eds.), *Discrimination Law. Concepts, Limitations, and Justifications*, London/New York: Longman 1996, 63-76.

Barnard 1996 (Economic objectives)

Catherine Barnard, 'The economic objectives of Article 119', in: Tamara K. Hervey & David O. O'Keeffee (eds), *Sex Equality Law in the European Union*, Chichester: Wiley 1996, 320-334.

Barnard 1998

Catherine Barnard, 'The Principle of Equality in the Community Context: *P, Grant, Kalanke and Marschall*: Four Uneasy Bedfellows?', *Cambridge Law Journal* 1998, 352-377.

Barnard 2000

Catherine Barnard, *EC Employment Law*, 2nd edition, Oxford: Oxford University Press 2000.

Barnard 2004

Catherine Barnard, *The Substantive Law of the EU. The Four Freedoms*, Oxford: Oxford University Press 2004.

Barnard & Hepple 1999

Catherine Barnard & Bob Hepple, 'Indirect Discrimination: Interpreting *Seymour-Smith*', *Cambridge Law Journal* 1999, 399-412.

Barnard & Hepple 2000

Catherine Barnard & Bob Hepple, 'Substantive Equality', *Cambridge Law Journal* 2000, 562-585.

Barrett 2004

Gavin Barrett, 'Re-examining the Concept and Principle of Equality in EC Law', in: P. Eeckhout & T. Tridimas (eds), *Yearbook of European Law 2003*, Oxford: Oxford University Press 2004, 117-153.

Barrett 1981

J.M. Barrett, 'Part-time workers and equal pay: the case of Jenkins v Kingsgate', Human Rights Review 1981, 174-193.

Bartlett & Harris 1998
    Katharine T Bartlett & Angela P. Harris, *Gender and Law. Theory, Doctrine, Commentary*, 2nd edition, New York: Aspen Law & Business 1998.
Bayer 2002
    Walter Bayer, 'Zulässige und unzulässige Einschränkungen der europäischen Grundfreiheiten im Gesellschaftsrecht', *Betriebs-Berater* 2002, 2289-2291.
Bayefsky 1990
    Anne F. Bayefski, 'The principle of equality or non-discrimination in international law', *Human Rights Journal* 1990, 1-34.
Beaumont 2002
    Paul, 'Human Rights: Some Recent Developments and Their Impact on Convergence an Divergence of Law in Europe', in: Paul Beaumont, Carol Lyons & Neill Walker (eds), *Convergence and Divergence in European Public Law*, Oxford: Hart Publishing 2002, 151-175.
Behrens 1992
    Peter Behrens, 'Die Konvergenz der wirtschaftlichen Freiheiten im europäischen Gemeinschaftsrecht', *EuR* 1992, 145-162.
Bell 1999
    Mark Bell, 'Shifting Conceptions of Sexual Discrimination at the Court of Justice: from *P v S* to *Grant v SWT*', *European Law Journal* 1999, 63-81.
Bell 2001
    Mark Bell, 'Sexual Orientation Discrimination in Employment: An Evolving Role for the European Union', in: Robert Wintemute & Mads Andenas (eds), *Legal Recognition of Same-Sex Partnerships. A Study of National, European and International Law*, Oxford/Portland: Hart 2001, 653-676.
Bell 2002
    Mark Bell, *Anti-Discrimination Law and the European Union*, Oxford: Oxford University Press 2002.
Bell & Waddington 2003
    Mark Bell & Lisa Waddington, 'Reflecting on inequalities in European equality law', *EL Rev* 2003, 349-369.
Berg 1999
    Werner Berg, 'Grenzüberschreitende Krankenversicherungsleistungen in der EU. Auswirkungen der Urteile EuGH, EuZW 1998, 345 – Kohll und EuGH, EuZW 1998, 343 – Decker auf das deutsche Gesundheitswesen', *EuZW* 1999, 587-591.
Bernard 1996
    Nicolas Bernard, 'What are the Purposes of EC Discrimination Law?', in: Janet Dine & Bob Watt (eds), *Discrimination Law. Concepts, Limitations, and Justifications*, London/New York: Longman 1996, 77-99.
Bernard 1998
    Nicolas Bernard, 'La libre circulation des marchandises, des personnes et des services dans le traité CE sous l'angle de la compétence', *CDE* 1998, 12-45.
Berthou & Masselot 2002
    Katell Berthou & Annick Masselot, 'Le mariage, les partenariats et la CJCE: ménage à trois', *CDE* 2002, 679-694.

Bieback 1997

Karl-Jürgen Bieback, *Die mittelbare Diskriminierung wegen des Geschlechts. Ihre Grundlage im Recht der EU und ihre Auswirkungen auf das Sozialrecht der Mitgliedstaaten*, Baden-Baden: Nomos 1997.

Bigler-Eggenberger 2003

Margrith Bigler-Eggenberger, *Justitias Waage – wagemutige Justitia? Die Rechtsprechung des Bundesgerichts zur Gleichstellung von Mann und Frau*, Basel: Helbing & Lichtenhahn 2003.

Bigler-Eggenberger & Kaufmann Commentary 1997

Margrith Bigler-Eggenberger & Claudia Kaufmann (eds), *Kommentar zum Gleichstellungs-gesetz*, Basel/Frankfurt: Helbing & Lichtenhahn 1997.

Binon 1996

Jean-Marc Binon, 'Avantages fiscaux en assurance de personnes et droit européen. Après les arrêts Schumacker, Wielockx et Svensson, quelle place reste-t-il pour la jurisprudence Bachmann?', *Revue du Marché Unique Européen* 1996 (2), 129-14.[2800]

Bleckmann 1976

Albert Bleckman, 'Considérations sur l'interprétation de l'article 7 du Traité C.E.E.', *RTDE* 1976, 469-481.

Blom 1992

J.A.H. Blom, *Indirect discrimination in EC law and its application in Member States*, LL.M. thesis EUI Florence, Florence: European University Institute 1992.

Blom 1995

J. Blom, 'Equal Treatment. The Dutch Equal Treatment Commission', *ILJ* 1995, 84-89.

Blomeyer 1994

Christian Blomeyer, *Das Verbot der mittelbaren Diskriminierung gemäss Art. 119 EGV. Seine Funktion im deutschen Arbeitsrecht*, Baden-Baden: Nomos 1994.

Blumann 1996

Claude Blumann, *Politique agricole commune. Droit communautaire agricole et agro-alimentaire*, Paris: Litec 1996.

Bobbio 1996

Norberto Bobbio, 'Égalité et inégalité, le clivage décisive', *Esprit* April 1996, 19-32.

Boch 1998

Christine Boch, 'Où s'arrête le principe d'égalité ou de l'importance d'être bien-portante', *CDE* 1998, 177-190.

Boekhorst 1992

Paul J. Boekhorst, 'Tax Discrimination Permitted for Reasons of Coherence of Tax System', *European Taxation* 1992, 284-286.

Börner 1973

Bodo Börner, 'Diskriminierungen und Subventionen', in Börner Bodo (ed), *Studien zum deutschen und europäischen Wirtschaftsrecht*, Köln/Berlin/Bonn/München: Carl Heymanns Verlag 1973, 49-79.

[2800] Note: as of 2000, the Journal is called *Revue du Droit de l'Union Européenne (ex Revue du Marché Unique Européen)*.

Borchardt 2002
Klaus-Dieter Borchardt, *Die rechtlichen Grundlagen der Europäischen Union*, 2nd edition, Heidelberg: C.F. Müller Verlag 2002.

Boutard Labard 1988
Marie-Chantal Boutard Labard, (Case note on *Clinical Biological Laboratories*), *Journal du droit international* 1988, 510-511.

Bovis 2002
Christopher Bovis, 'Recent case law relating to public procurement: a beacon for the integration of public markets', *CML Rev* 2002, 1025-1056.

Breitenmoser & Husheer 2002
Stephan Breitenmoser & André Husheer, *Europarecht*, volume II 'Binnenmarkt- und Aussenwirtschaftsrecht der EG, Europäischer Grundrechtsschutz (EU, Europarat, OSZE)', 2nd, revised and enlarged edition, Zurich: Schulthess 2002.

Breitenmoser 2003
Stephan Breitenmoser, 'Sectoral Agreements between the EC and Switzerland – Contents and Context', *CML Rev* 2003, 1137-1186.

Brian & McIntyre 1995
J. Arnold Brian/Michael J. McIntyre, *International Tax Primer*, Boston/The Hague/London: Kluwer 1995.

Brown 2003
Christopher Brown, 'The Race Directive: Towards Equality for *All* the Peoples of Europe?', in: P. Eeckhout & T. Tridimas (eds), *Yearbook of European Law 2001-2002*, Oxford: Oxford University Press 2003, 195-227.

Browne 1999
Kingsley R. Browne, 'The Use and Abuse of Statistical Evidence in Discrimination Cases', in: Titia Loenen & Peter R. Rodrigues (eds), *Non-Discrimination Law: Comparative Perspectives*, The Hague/London/Boston: Kluwer Law International 1999, 411-423.

Bulterman 1999
Mielle Bulterman, (Case note on *Bickel and Franz*), *CML Rev* 1999, 1325-1334.

Burgers 1995
I.J.J. Burgers, (Case note on *Schumacker*), SEW 1995, 416-423.

Burri 2000
Susanne Burri, *Tijd delen. Deeltijd, gelijkheid en gender in Europees- en nationaalrechtelijk perspectief*, Ph.D. thesis, Utrecht: Utrecht University 2000.

Burton 1981/82
Steven J. Burton, 'Comment on "Empty Ideas": Logical Positivist Analyses of Equality and Rules', *The Yale Law Journal* 91 (1981/82) 1136-1152.

Cabral & Cunha 1999
Pedro Cabral & Patrícia Cunha, 'The internal market and discriminatory taxation: just how (un)steady is the ground?', *EL Rev* 1999, 396-402.

Callender & Meenan 1994
Rosheen Callender & Francis Meenan (for the European Commission), *Equality in Law between Men and Women in the European Community: Ireland*, Dordrecht/Boston/London:

Martinus Nijhoff and Office for Official Publications of the European Communities: Luxembourg 1994.

Calliess & Ruffert Commentary 2002

Christian Calliess & Matthias Ruffert (eds), *Kommentar des Vertrages über die Europäische Union und des Vertrages zur Gründung der Europäischen Gemeinschaft (EUV/EGV)*, 2nd edition, Neuwied/Kriftel: Luchterhand 2002.

Candela Sobriano 2002

Mercedes Candela Sobriano, 'Les exigences linguistiques: une entrave légitime à la libre circulation?', *CDE* 2002, 9-44.

Carey 2002

Nelius Carey, 'From Obloquy to Equality: In the Shadow of Abnormal Situations', in: P. Eeckhout & T. Tridimas (eds), *Yearbook of European Law 2001*, Oxford: Oxford University Press 2002, 79-111.

Carolan 1999

Bruce Carolan, 'Hope fades for EU recognition of same-sex partnerships', *Gazette of the Incorporated Law Society of Ireland* 1999, 44-47.

Carracciolo di Torella & Masselot 2001

Eugenia Carracciolo & Annick Masselot, 'Pregnancy, maternity and the organisation of family life: an attempt to classify the case law of the Court of Justice', *EL Rev* 2001, 239-260.

Castillo de la Torre 1995

Fernando Castillo de la Torre, 'La libre circulation des services et les ressortissant des pays tiers: quelques réflexions au sujet de l'arrêt Vander Elst', *Revue du Marché Unique Européen* 1995 (2), 131-159.

Charro 2002

Pablo Charro, (Case note on *Concordia Bus*), *CML Rev* 2002, 179-191.

Chavret 1969

John Chavret, 'The Idea of Equality as a substantive principle of society', *Political Studies* 17 (1969) 1-13.

Chemerinksy 1983

Erwin Chemerinsky, 'In Defense of Equality: A Reply to Professor Westen', *Michigan Law Review* 81 (1983) 575-599.

Christensen 2001

Ann Christensen, 'Structural Aspects of Anti-Discrimination Legislation and Processes of Normative Change', in: Ann Numhauser-Henning (ed), *Legal Perspectives on Equal Treatment and Non-Discrimination*, The Hague: Kluwer Law International 2001, 31-60.

Clapham & Weiler 1993

Andrew Clapham & Joseph Weiler, 'Lesbians and Gay Men in the European Community Legal Order', in: Kees Waaldijk & Andrew Clapham (eds), *Homosexuality: A European Community Issue. Essays on Lesbian and Gay Rights in European Law and Policy*, Dordrecht: Martinus Nijhoff Publishers 1993, 6-69.

Colin & Sinkondo 1993

Jean-Pierre Colin & Marcel Sinkondo, 'Principe de non-discrimination et protection de la concurrence en droit international et en droit communautaire', *Revue du Marché commun et de l'Union européenne* 1993, 36-55.

Colneric 1996

Ninon Colneric, 'Making Equality Law More Effective: Lessons from the German Experience', *Cardozo Women's Law Journal* 1996, 229-250.

Cook 2003

Rebecca Cook, 'Obligations to Adopt Temporary Special Measures Under the Convention on the Elimination of All Forms of Discrimination Against Women' in: Ineke Boerefijn, Fons Coomans, Jenny Goldschmidt, Rikki Holtmaat & Ria Wolleswinkel (eds), *Temporary Special Measures. Accelerating de facto Equality of Women under Article 4(1) UN Convention of the Elimination of All Forms of Discrimination Against Women*, Anwerpen/Oxford/New York: Intersentia 2003, 119-141.

Cottier & Mavroidis 2000

Thomas Cottier & Petros C. Mavroidis. (eds; associate editor: Patrick Blatter), *Regulatory Barriers and the Principle of Non-Discrimination in World Trade Law*, Ann Arbor: The University of Michigan Press 2000.

Craig & de Búrca 1998

Paul Craig & de Búrca Gráinne, *EU Law, Texts, Cases, and Materials*, 2nd edition, Oxford: Oxford University Press 1998.

Craig & de Búrca 2003

Paul Craig/de Búrca Gráinne, *EU Law, Texts, Cases, and Materials*, 3rd edition, Oxford: Oxford University Press 2003.

Crisham 1977

Catherine A. Crisham, (Case note on *Defrenne II*), *CML Rev* 1977, 108-118.

Crisham 1978

C.A. Crisham, (Case note on *Thieffry*), *CML Rev* 1978, 359-370.

Crisham 1981

C.A. Crisham, 'The equal pay principle: some recent decisions of the European Court of Justice', *CML Rev* 1981, 601-612.

Crosby 1996

Faye Crosby, 'A Rose by Any Other Name', in: Kathrin Airoli (ed), *Quoten und Gleichstellung von Frau und Mann*, Basel/Frankfurt a.M.: Helbing & Lichtenhahn 1996, 151-167.

Currall 19990

Julian Currall, 'Unlawful Discrimination in Employment – An Outline of the European Community Rules and Case-Law', *Georgia Journal of International and Comparative Law* 1990, 13-27.

Curtin 1989

Deirdre Curtin, *Irish Employment Equality Law*, Dublin: Round Hall Press 1989.

Dahlgaard Dingel 1999

Dorthe Dahlgaard Dingel, *Public Procurement. A Harmonization of the National Judicial Review of the Application of European Community Law*, The Hague/London/Boston: Kluwer Law International 1999.

D'Amato 1983

Anthony D'Amato, 'Is Equality a totally Empty Idea?', *Michigan Law Review* 1983, 600-603.

Daniele 1997

Luigi Daniele, 'Non-Discriminatory Restrictions to the Free Movement of Persons', *ELRev* 1997, 191-200.

Darmon & Huglo 1992

Marco Darmon & Jean-Guy Huglo, 'L'égalité de traitement entre les hommes et les femmes dans la jurisprudence de la Court de justice des Communautés européennes: un univers en expansion', *RTDE* 1992, 1-25.

Dashwood 1977

Alan Dashwood, 'State aids. Preliminary rulings on the EEC State aids provisions', *EL Rev* 1977, 367-373.

Dauck & Nowak 2001

Kirsten Dauck & Carsten Nowak, 'Das Recht auf unionsweite, bestmögliche medizinische Versorgung', *Europarecht* 2001, 741-745.

Dauwe 1978

Brigitte Dauwe, (Case note on *Thieffry*), *SEW* 1978, 227-230.

Davies 2002

Gareth Davies, 'Welfare as a Service', *Legal Issues of Economic Integration* 2002, 27-40.

De Blois 1990

Matthijs de Blois, (Case note on *Bond van Adverteerders*), *CML Rev* 1990, 371-381.

De Bruijn, Bajema & Timmerman 1992

Jeanne de Bruijn, Cristien Bajema & Greetje Timmerman, 'Indirecte discriminatie in functiewaardering. Onderzoeksverslag naar deugdelijkheid van FW-systemen', *Nemesis* 1992 no. 5, 21-29.

de Búrca 1997

Gráinne de Búrca, 'The Role of Equality in European Community Law', in: Alan Dashwood & Síofra O'Leary (eds), *The Principle of Equal Treatment in EC Law*, London/Dublin/Hong Kong: Sweet & Maxwell 1997, 13-34.

de Búrca 2002

Gráinne de Búrca, 'Unpacking the Concept of Discrimination in EC and International Trade Law', in: Catherine Barnard & Joanne Scott Joanne (eds), *The Law of the Single European Market. Unpacking the Premises*, Oxford/Portland, Oregon: Hart Publishing 2002, 181-195.

Défalque 1987

Lucette Défalque, 'Le concept de discrimination en matière de libre circulation des marchandises', *CDE* 1987, 471-491.

De Jong 1999

M.G. de Jong, (Case note on *Safir*), *SEW* 1999, 112-115.

Delarue 1988

R. Delarue, 'De Europese kaderakkoorden over ouderschapsverlof en deeltijdse arbeid: voorbereiding, totstandkoming, omzetting en perspectieven', in: Liber Amicorum Blanpain, Brugge: Die keure 1998, 169-188, at 182.

Del Valle Galvez 2003

Alejandro del Valle Galvez, 'Extranjería, Ciudadanía, Fronteras y Tribunal de Luxemburgo', in: Ninon Colneric, David Edward, Jean-Pierre Puissochet & Dámaso Ruiz-Jarabo Colomer (eds), *Une communauté de droit. Festschrift für Gil Carlos Rodriguez Iglesias*, Berlin: BWV Berliner Wissenschafts-Verlag 2003, 207-218.

Demaret 2000

Paul Demaret, 'The Non-Discrimination Principle and the Removal of Fiscal Barriers to Intra-Community Trade', in: Thomas Cottier & Petros C. Mavroidis (eds), *Regulatory Barriers and the Principle of Non-Discrimination in World Trade Law*, Ann Arbor: The University of Michigan Press 2000, 171-189.

Denys 1994

Christine Denys, 'Les notions de discrimination et de discrimination à rebours suite à l'arrêt Kraus', *CDE* 1994, 643-662.

Denys 1996 (Stille vormgeving)

C Denys. 'De stille vormgeving van het burgerschap', *NTER* 1996, 127-131.

Denys 1996 (Vrije dienstverlening)

C. Denys, 'Vrije dienstverlening door advocaten: nieuw leven ingeblazen?', *NTER* 1996, 34-37.

De Schutter 1999

Olivier de Schutter, 'Le concept de discrimination dans la jurisprudence de la Cour de Justice des Communautés européennes (égalité de traitement et liberté de circulation)', in: Emmanuelle Brisbosia, Emmanuelle Dardenne, Paul Magnette & Anne Weyembergh (eds), *Union Européenne et nationalités. Le principe de non-discrimination et ses limites*, Brussels: Bruylant 1999, 11-44.

De Schutter 2001 .

Olivier de schutter, *Discriminations et marché du travail. Liberté et égalité dans les rapports d'emploi*, Brussels: P.I.E.-Peter Lang 2001.

Desolre 2000

Guy Desolre, 'Le principe de non-discrimination, la liberté de circulation et les facilités linguistiques en matière judiciaire', *CDE* 2000, 311-321.

De Weerth 1995

Jan de Weerth, 'Der gegenwärtige Stand des Gemeinschaftsrechts und das Steuerrecht. Zugleich eine Anmerkung zum EuGH-Urteil vom 14. 2. 1995 „Schumacker"', *Recht der internationalen Wirtschaft* 1995, 395-398.

De Witte 1992

Bruno de Witte, 'Surviving in Babel? Language Rights and European Integration', in: Yoram Dinstein & Mala Tabory (eds), *The Protection of Minorities and Human Rights*, Dordrecht/Boston/London: Martinus Nijhoff Publishers 1992, 277-300.

Dierx & Siegers 1990

Janny Dierx & Jacques Siegers, 'Indirecte discriminatie van deeltijdwerkers', *NJB* 1990, 554-560.

Donner 1988

J.P.H. Donner, 'een onduidelijke uitspraak?', *Informatierecht* 1988, 91-94.

Dony 1999

Marianne Dony, 'Les discriminations fondées sur la nationalité dans la jurisprudence de la Cour de Justice des Communautés européennes', in: Emmanuelle Brisbosia, Emmanuelle

Dardenne, Paul Magnette & Anne Weyembergh (eds), *Union Européenne et nationalités. Le principe de non-discrimination et ses limites*, Brussels: Bruylant 1999, 45-62.

Dourado 2002

Ana Paula Dourado, 'From the *Saint-Gobain* to the *Metallgesellschaft* case: scope of non-discrimination of permanent establishments in the EC Treaty and the most-favoured-nation clause in EC Member States tax treaties', *EC Tax Review* 2002, 147-156.

Driessen-Reilly & Driessen 2003

Miriam Driessen-Reilly & Bart Driessen, 'Don't shoot the messenger: a look at Community law relating to harassment in the workplace', *EL Rev* 2003, 493-506.

Drijber & Prechal 1997

Berend Jan Drijber & Sacha Prechal, 'Gelijke behandeling van mannen en vrouwen in horizontaal perspectief' (Preadvies van de Nederlandse Vereniging voor Europees Recht), *SEW* 1997, 112-167.

Drijber 2002

Berend Jan Drijber, 'Gouden aandelen van hun glans ontdaan', *NTER* 2002, 237-241.

Droz 1998

Georges A.L. Droz, (Case note on *Dafeki*), *Revue critique de droit international privé* 1998, 334-337.

Druesne 1982

Gérard Druesne, 'Liberté de prestation des services et travailleurs salariés', *RTDE* 1982, 75-81.

Duintjer Tebbens 1996

H. Duintjer Tebbens, (Case note on *Mund & Fester*), *SEW* 1996, 313-315.

Du Pré 1976

F.M. du Pré, (Case note on *Defrenne II*), *SEW* 1976, 578-586.

Du Pré 1998

F.M. Pré, 'Het EG-verdrag door een ziekenfondsbrilletje', *Sociaal maandblad arbeid* 1998, 364-376.

Dworking 2000

Ronald Dworkin, *Sovereign Virtue. The Theory and Practice of Equality*, Cambridge/London: Harvard University Press 2000.

E.K. 1991

E.K., (Case note on *Commission v Greece*), *Droit fiscal* 1991, 1750-1751 (numbers 2328 and 2329).

Easson 1993

A.J. Easson, *Taxation in the European Community*, London/Atlantic Highlands, NJ: The Athlone Press 1993.

Eberhartinger 1997

Michael Eberhartinger, 'Konvergenz und Neustrukturierung der Grundfreiheiten', *EWS* 1997, 43-52.

Ebke 2002

Werner F. Ebke, (Case note on the *Golden Shares* cases), *EWS* 2002, 335-338.

Ebsen 1993

Ingwer Ebsen, 'Zur Koordinierung der Rechtsdogmatik beim Gebot der Gleichberechtigung von Männern und Frauen zwischen Europäischem Gemeinschaftsrecht und innerstaatlichem Verfassungsrecht', *RdA* 1993.

Eckart 1988

Christel Eckart, 'Wie Teilzeitarbeit zur Frauenarbeit gemacht wurde', in: Ute Gerhard & Jutta Limbach (eds), *Rechtsalltag von Frauen*, Frankfurt: Suhrkamp 1988, 46-59.

Eeckhout 2000

Piet Eeckhout, 'After Keck and Mithouard: Free Movement of Goods in the EC, Market Access, and Non-Discrimination', in: Thomas Cottier & Petros C. Mavroidis (eds), *Regulatory Barriers and the Principle of Non-Discrimination in World Trade Law*, Ann Arbor: The University of Michigan Press 2000, 191-206.

Edwards & McKie 1996

Julia Edwards & Linda McKie, 'Women's Public Toilets. A Serious Issue for the Body Politic', *The European Journal of Women's Studies* 3 (1996) 215-230.

Edwards 2000

Vanessa Edwards, 'Secondary Establishment of Companies – the Case Law of the Court of Justice', in: P. Eeckhout & T. Tridimas (eds), *Yearbook of European Law 1998*, Oxford: Oxford University Press 2000, 221-257.

Ellis 1994 (Definition of Discrimination)

Evelyn Ellis, 'The Definition of Discrimination in European Community Sex Equality Law', *EL Rev* 1994, 563-580.

Ellis 1994 (Enderby)

Evelyn Ellis, (Case note on *Enderby*), *CML Rev* 1994, 387-394.

Ellis 1996

Evelyn Ellis, 'Gender Discrimination in the European Community', in: Janet Dine & Bob Watt (eds), *Discrimination Law. Concepts. Limitations and Justifications*, London/New York: Longman 1996, 14-30.

Ellis 1997

Evelyn Ellis, 'The Principle of Equality of Opportunity Irrespective of Sex: Some reflections on the present state of European Community Law and its future development', in: Alan Dashwood & Síofra O'Leary (eds), *The Principle of Equal Treatment in E.C. Law*, London/Dublin/Hong Kong: Sweet & Maxwell 1997, 172-188.

Ellis 1998

Evelyn Ellis, *EC Sex Equality Law*, 2nd edition, Oxford: Clarendon Press 1998.

Ellis 1999

Evelyn Ellis, (Case note on *Brown*), *CML Rev* 1999, 625-633.

Ellis 2001

Evelyn Ellis, 'The Importance of a Structural Analysis in the Field of Anti-Discrimination Law', in: Ann Numhauser-Henning Ann (ed), *Legal Perspectives on Equal Treatment and Non-Discrimination*, The Hague: Kluwer Law International 2001, 61-63.

Ellis 2003

Evelyn Ellis, 'Social Advantages: a new lease of life?', *CML Rev* 2003, 639-659.

Emiliou 1996

Nicholas Emiliou, *The Principle of Proportionality in European Law. A Comparative Study*, London/The Hague/Boston: Kluwer Law International 1996.

Epiney 1995

Astrid Epiney, *Umgekehrte Diskriminierungen. Zulässigkeit und Grenzen der discrimination à rebours nach europäischem Gemeinschaftsrecht und nationalem Verfassungsrecht*, Köln/Berlin/Bonn/München: Carl Heymanns 1995 (at the same time: Habilitation, Mainz University 1994).

Epiney & Freiermuth Abt 2003

Astrid Epiney & Marianne Freiermuth Abt, *Das Recht der Gleichstellung von Mann und Frau in der EU*, Baden-Baden: Nomos 2003.

Epiney & Freiermuth Abt 2004

Astrid Epine & Marianne Freiermuth Abt, ,Gleichstellungsrecht in der EU: Grundlagen, Meilensteine und neuere Entwicklungen', in: Astrid Epiney & Ira von Danckelmann (eds), *Gleichstellung von Frauen und Männern in der Schweiz und der EU/L'Egalité entre femmes et hommes en Suisse et dans l'UE*, Zurich/Basel/Geneva: Schulthess 2004, 53-87.

Ermacora 1971

Felix Ermacora, *Diskriminierungsschutz und Diskriminierungsverbot in der Arbeit der Vereinten Nationen*, Wien/Stuttgart: Wilhelm Braumüller, Universitäts-Verlagsbuchhandlung 1971.

Europäische Kommission 2000

Europäische Kommission, *CECA, EKSF, EGKS, EKAX, ECSC, EHTY, EKSG, 1952-2002: Fünfzig Jahre Europäische Gemeinschaft für Kohle und Stahl*, Luxembourg: Office des Publications officielles des Communautés européennes 2002.

Everling 1997

Ulrich Everling, 'Das Niederlassungsrecht in der EG als Beschränkungsverbot', in: Wolfgang Schön (ed), *Gedächtnisschrift für Brigitte Knobbe-Keuk*, Köln: Verlag Dr. Otto Schmidt 1997, 607-625.

Evtimov 2004

Erik Evtimov, 'Kein gleiches Entgelt bei Collegetätigkeit von Lehrkräften über Drittfirmen – Ausschluss selbstständiger Lehrer aus Betriebsrentensystem', *EuZW* 2004, 210-215.

Farmer 1995

Paul Lyal, 'Article 48 EC and the taxation of frontier workers', *EL Rev* 1995, 310-318.

Farmer & Lyal 1994

Paul Farmer & Richard Lyal, *EC Tax Law*, Oxford: Clarendon Press 1994.

Fauchald 1998

Ole Kristian Fauchald, *Environmental Taxes and Trade Discrimination*, London/The Hague/Boston: Kluwer Law International 1998.

Feenstra 1993

Jaap Feenstra, (Case note on *Collectieve Antennevoorziening* and *Commission v Netherlands*), *CML Rev* 1993, 424-432.

Feige 1973

Konrad Feige, *Der Gleichheitssatz im Recht der EWG*, Tübingen: Mohr 1973.

Fenwick 1995
    Helen Fenwick, 'Indirect Discrimination in Equal Pay Claims: Backward Steps in the
    European Court of Justice?', *European Public Law* 1995, 331-339.
Fenwick 1998
    Helen Fenwick, 'From Formal to Substantive Equality: the Place of Affirmative Action in
    European Union Sex Equality Law', *European Public Law* 1998, 507-516.
Fenwick & Hervey 1995
    Helen Fenwick & Tamara Hervey, 'Sex Equality in the Single Market: new directions from
    the European Court of Justice', *CML Rev* 1995, 443-470.
Fernández Martín 1996
    José Fernández Martín, *The EC Public Procurement Rules. A Critical Analysis*, Oxford:
    Clarendon Press 1996.
Fierstra 1990
    M.A. Fierstra (Case note on *Beentjes*), *SEW* 1990, 76-79.
Fierstra 1992
    M.A. Fierstra, (Case note on *Vlassopoulou*), *SEW* 1992, 441-443.
Fleischer 2003
    Holger Fleischer, (Case note on the *Golden Shares* cases), *CML Rev* 2003, 493-501.
Flynn 1997
    Leo Flynn, (Case note on *Grant*), *CML Rev* 1997, 367-387.
Flynn 2000
    Leo Flynn, 'Equality between Men and Women in the Court of Justice', in: P. Eeckhout &
    Takis Tridimas (eds), *Yearbook of European Law 1998*, Oxford: Oxford University Press
    2000, 260-287.
Fosselard 1993
    Denis Fosselard, 'L'obstacle fiscal à la réalisation du marché interieur', *CDE* 1993, 472-500.
Foubert 2002
    Petra Foubert, *The Legal Protection of the Pregnant Worker in the European Community. Sex
    Equality, Thoughts of Social and Economic Policy and Comparative Leaps to the United States
    of America*, The Hague/London/New York: Kluwer Law International 2002.
Fredman 1992
    Sandra Fredman, 'European Community Discrimination Law: A Critique', *ILJ* 1992, 119-
    134.
Fredman 1996
    Sandra Fredman, 'The Poverty of Equality: Pensions and the ECJ', *ILJ* 1996, 91-109.
Fredman 1999
    Sandra Fredman, 'After *Kalanke* and *Marschall*: Affirming Affirmative Action', in: Alan
    Dashwood & Angela Ward (eds), *The Cambridge Yearbook of European Legal Studies 1998*,
    Cambridge: Hart Publishing 1999, 199-215, at 206.
Fredman 2001
    Sandra Fredman, 'Equality: A New Generation?', *ILJ* 2001, 145-168.
Fredman 2002
    Sandra Fredman, *Discrimination Law*, Oxford: Oxford University Press 2002.

Freivogel & Steiner 2001

Elisabeth Freivogel & Oliver Steiner, 'Die Regelung der Ueberzeitzuschläge und das Verbot der Geschlechterdiskriminierung', *AJP* 2001, 993-1001.

Friden 1990

Georges Friden, 'The 'Bond van Adverteerders' Case and recent legal development in EEC 'Television Law'', *Leiden Journal of International Law* 1990, 231-238.

Fuchsloch 1995

Christine Fuchsloch, *Das Verbot der mittelbaren Geschlechtsdiskriminierung. Ableitung, Analyse und exemplarische Anwendung auf staatliche Berufsausbildungsförderung*, Baden-Baden: Nomos 1995.

Gardner 1989

John Gardner, 'Liberals and Unlawful Discrimination', *Oxford Journal of Legal Studies* Spring 1989, 1-22.

Gardner 1996

John Gardner, 'Discrimination as Injustice', *Oxford Journal of Legal Studies* 1996, 353-367.

Garrone 1994

Pierre Garrone, 'La discrimination indirecte en droit communautaire: vers une théorie générale', *RTDE* 1994, 425-449.

Gaspard, Servan-Schreiber & Le Gall 1992

Françoise Gaspard, Claude Servan-Schreiber & Ann Le Gall, *Au pouvoir, citoyennes! Liberté, égalité, parité*, Paris: du Seuil 1992.

Gaspard 2003

Françoise Gaspard, 'La Convention CEDAW et l'Union européenne', in: AFFJ & EWLA (ed), *L'Egalité entre femmes et homes et la vie professionnelle. Le point sur les dévelopments actuels en Europe*, Paris: Editions Dalloz 2003, 175-183.

Gaurier 1995

Dominique Gaurier, (Case note on *Konstantinidis*), *European Review of Private Law* 1995, 483-496.

Geiger Commentary 2000

Rudolf Geiger, *EUV/EGV. Kommenar*, 3rd and revised edition, München: Beck 2000.

Gencarelli 2001

F. Gencarelli, 'L'Evolution du droit agricole communautaire', *Revue du droit de l'Union européenne* 2001, 655-688.

Gerards 2002

J.H. Gerards, *Rechterlijke toetsing aan het gelijkheidsbeginsel*, Den Haag: Sdu Uitgevers 2002.

Gerards 2003

J.H. Gerards, 'Het toetsingsmodel van de CGB voor de beoordeling van indirect onderscheid', in: Commissie Gelijke Behandeling & D.J.B. Wolff (eds), *Gelijke behandeling: oordelen en commentaar 2002*, Deventer: Kluwer 2003, 77-95.

Gianformaggio 1996

Letizia Gianformaggio, 'Egualianza formale e sostanziale: il grande equivoco', *Il Foro Italiano* 1996, 1961-1976.

Giesen 1999
Richard Giesen, (Case note on *Decker* and *Kohll*), *CML Rev* 1999, 841-850.

Gimeno Verdejo & Rojes I Pujol 1999
Carlos Gimeno Verdejo & María Isabel Rojes I Pujol, 'Crónica de la Jurisprudencia del Tribunal de Justicia de las Comunidades Europeas', *Cuadernos Europeos de Deusto* 1999, 211-223.

Görlitz 2002
Niklas Görlitz, 'Immer noch unterschätzt: Die gemeinschaftsrechtlichen Vlassopoulou-Grundsätze', *Europäisches Wirtschafts- und Steuerrecht. Betriebs-Berater für Europarecht* 2002, 20-31.

Goldman 1996
Alvin L. Goldman, *Labor and Employment Law in the United States*, Boston/The Hague/London: Kluwer Law International 1996.

Gori 1985
Paolo Gori, 'Il principio della parità di trattamento dell'uomo e della donna nella giurisprudenza della corte di guistizia delle comunità europee', *Rivista di diritto europeo* 1985, 1-33.

Gormley 1982
Laurence Gormley, 'Services and double social security contributions' (Case note on *Seco*), *EL Rev* 1982, 207-209.

Gormley 1992
Laurence Gormley, 'Workers and services distinguished', *EL Rev* 1992, 63-67.

Gormley 1994
Laurence Gormley, 'Pay your money and take your chance?', *EL Rev* 1994, 644-653.

Govers 1981
A.W. Govers, 'Gelijkheid van vrouw en man in het Europees sociaal recht', in: A.W. Govers & A.E. Bosscher (eds)., *Gelijkheid van vrouw en man in het Europees sociaal recht. Preadviezen uitgebracht voor de gezamenlijke vergadering van de Vereniging voor Arbeidsrecht en de Vereniging voor Europees Recht op 27 november 1981 te 's-Gravenhage*, Alphen aan den Rijn: Samson 1981, 5-83.

Goyder 2003
D.G. Goyder, *EC Competition Law*, 4th edition, Oxford: Oxford University Press 2003.

Grabitz & Hilf Commentary (various dates, as of 1989)
Eberhard Grabitz & Meinrad Hilf (eds), *Das Recht der Europäischen Union*, München: Beck, various editions, as of 1989.

Greaves 2000
Rosa Greaves, *EC Transport Law*, Harlow etc.: Longman 2000.

Greenawalt 1983
Kent Greenawalt, 'How Empty is the Idea of Equality?', *Columbia Law Review* 83 (1983) 1167-1185.

Greenwood 1984
Christopher Greenwood, 'Freedom to Provide Services in EEC Law', *Business Law Review* 1984, 51-53.

Grief 2002

Nicholas Grief, 'Non-discrimination under the European Convention on Human Rights: a critique of the United Kingdom's refusal to sign and ratify Protocl 12', *European Law Review. Human Rights Survey* 2002, HR/3-HR/18.

Grundmann & Möslein 2002

Stefan Grundmann/Florian Möslein, 'Die Golden Shares Grundsatzentscheidungen des Europäischen Gerichtshofs', *BRK* 2002, 758-765.

GTE Commentary 1991

Hans von der Groeben, Jochen Thiesing & Claus-Dieter Ehlermann (eds), *Kommentar zum EWG-Vertrag*, 4th and revised edition, Baden-Baden: Nomos 1991.

GTE Commentary 1997

Hans von der Groeben, Jochen Thiesing & Claus-Dieter Ehlermann (eds), *Kommentar zum EU-/EG-Vertrag*, 5th revised edition, Baden-Baden: Nomos 1997.

Guild 1997

Elspeth Guild, 'EC Law and the Means to Combat Racism and Xenophobia', in: Alan Dashwood & Síofra O'Leary (eds), *The Principle of Equal Treatment. A Collection of Papers by the Centre for European Legal Studies (Cambridge)*, London/Dublin/Hong Kong: Sweet & Maxwell 1997, 189 –213.

Gundel 2001

Jörg Gundel, 'Die Rechtfertigung von faktisch diskriminierenden Eingriffen in die Grundfreiheiten des EGV', *JURA* 2001, 79-85.

Hailbronner, Klein, Magiera & Müller-Graff Commentary 1998

Kay Hailbronner, Eckart Klein, Siegfried Magiera & Peter-Christian Müller-Graff, *Handkommentar zum Vertrag über die Europäische Union (EUV/EGV)*, 7th additional delivery, Köln/Berlin/Bonn/München: Carl Heymanns Verlag 1998 (certain specific parts date from an earlier year).

Hakenberg 2000

Waltraud Hakenberg, *Grundzüge des Europäischen Gemeinschaftsrechts*, 2nd edition, München: Franz Vahlen 2000.

Hall 1995

Stephen Hall, *Nationality, Migration Rights and Citizenship of the Union*, Dordrecht/Boston/London: Martinus Nijhoff 1995.

Hanau & Preis 1988

Peter Hanau & Ulrich Preis, 'Zur mittelbaren Diskriminierung wegen des Geschlechts', *Zeitschrift für Arbeitsrecht* 1988, 177-207.

Handoll 1995

John Handoll, *Free movement of persons in the EU*, Chichester etc.: John Wiley 1995.

Harms 2000

Theo Harms, 'The Principle of Equality in Legal Reasoning', in: Pauline C. Westerman (ed), *Non-Discrimination and Diversity*, Den Haag: Boom Juridische Uitgevers 2000, 104-114.

Harrison 1996

Virginia Harrison, 'Using EC Law to Challenge Sexual Orientation Discrimination at Work', in: Tamara K. Hervey & David O. O'Keeffe (eds), *Sex Equality Law in the European Union*, Chichester/New York/Brisbane, Toronto/Singapore: John Wiley 1996, 267-280.

Hatzopoulos 1995

Vassilis Hatzopoulos, 'Fiscalité directe des Etats membres et "libertés personnelles" reconnues par le taité CE', *Revue du Marché Unique Européen* 1995 (4), 121-156.

Hatzopoulos 1996

Vassilis Hatzopoulos, (Case note on *Svensson and Gustavsson*), *CML Rev* 1996, 569-588.

Hausammann 2002

Christina Hausammann, *Menschenrechte – Impulse für die Gleichstellung von Frau und Mann in der Schweiz*, Bern: Eidgenössisches Büro für Gleichstellung von Mann und Frau und Basel/Geneva/Munich: Helbing & Lichtenhahn 2002.

Hauser 1996

Jean Hauser, (Case note on *P. v S.*), *Revue trimestrielle de droit civil* 1996, 579.

Heerma van Vos 1997

G.J.J. Heerma van Vos, (Case note on *P. v S.*), *Nederlands tijdschrift voor de mensenrechten/NJCM Bulletin* 1997, 284-286.

Heide 1999

Ingeborg Heide, 'Supranational action against sex discrimination: Equal pay and equal treatment in the European Union', *International Labour Review* 1999, 381-410.

Hein 1990

Werner Hein, 'Steuererstattungsanspruch und Freizügigkeit', *Europäische Zeitschrift für Wirtschaftsrecht* 1990, 346-347.

Heinze 1994

Eric Heinze, *Sexual Orientation: A Human Right*, Dordrecht/Boston/London: Martinus Nijhoff 1994.

Helfer 1990

Larry Helfer, (Case note on *Grant*), *American Journal of International Law* 1999, 200-205.

Hellebrckers 1991

J.H.C. Hellebrekers, 'Obstakels voor vrij verkeer van werknemers in de Nederlandse fiscale wetgeving', *Weekblad voor fiscaal recht* 1991, 795-800.

Hendriks 1998

Aart Hendriks, 'Lesbische partner uitgerangeerd door britse spoorweg-maatschappij', *Nederlands tijdschrift voor de mensenrechten/NJCM Bulletin* 1998, 834-847.

Hendriks 2000

Aart Hendriks, *Gelijke toegang tot de arbeid voor gehandicapten. Een grondrechtelijke en rechtsvergelijkende analyse*, Ph.D. thesis, Utrecht: Utrecht University 2000.

Hepple 1990

Bob Hepple, 'Discrimination and Equality of Opportunity – Northern Irish Lessons', *Oxford Journal of Legal Studies* 1990, 408-421.

Hepple 1994

Bob Hepple, 'Can direct discrimination be justified?', *Equal Opportunities Review* 1994, no. 5, 48.

Hepple 1996

Bob Hepple, 'Equality and Discrimination', in: Paul Davies, Antoine Lyon-Caen, Silvana Sciarra & Spiritis Simitis (eds), *European Community Labour Law. Principles and Perspectives. Liber Amicorum Lord Wedderburn of Charlton*, Oxford: Clarendon Press 1996, 237-259.

Hepple 1997

Bob Hepple, 'The Principle of Equal Treatment in Article 119 EC and the Possibilities for Reform', in: Alan Dashwood & Síofra O'Leary, *The Principle of Equal Treatment in E.C. Law*, London/Dublin/Hong Kong: Sweet & Maxwell 1997, 137-152.

Hepple, Choussey & Choudhury 2000

Bob Hepple, Mary Choussey & Tufyal Choudhury, *Equality: A New Framework. Report of the Independent Review of the Enforcement of UK Anti-Discrimination Legislation*, Oxford/Portland: Hart Publishing 2000.

Herdegen 2003

Matthias Herdegen, *Europarecht*, 5th edition, Munich: Verlag C.H. Beck 2003.

Hernu 2003

Rémy Hernu, *Principe d'égalité et principe de non-discrimination dans la jurisprudence de la Cour de Justice des Communautées européennes*, Paris Cedex: Librairie Générale de Droit et de Jurisprudence 2003.

Hervey 1991

Tamara Hervey, 'Justification for indirect sex discrimination in employment: European Community and United Kingdom Law compared', *International and Comparative Law Quarterly* 1991, 807-826.

Hervey 1996

Tamara K. Hervey, 'The Future for Sex Equality Law in the European Union', in: Tamara K. Hervey & David O. O'Keeffe (eds), *Sex Equality Law in the European Union*, Chichester: John Wiley 1996, 399-413.

Hervey 2002

Tamara K. Hervey, 'EC Law on Justifications for Sex Discrimination in Working Life', paper presented at the VII European Regional Congress of Labour Law and Social Security ("Labour Law Congress 2002"), held at Stockholm University, Sweden, see www.labourlaw2002.org (text on file with the present writer), 103-147.

Hervey & Shaw 1998

Tamara Hervey & Jo Shaw, 'Women, work and care: women's dual role and double burden in EC sex equality law', *Journal of European Social Policy* 1998, 43-63.

Heselhaus 2001

Sebastian Heselhaus, 'Rechtfertigung unmittelbar diskriminierender Eingriffe in die Warenverkehrsfreiheit', *EuZW* 2001, 645-650.

Hilson 1999

Chris Hilson, 'Discrimination in Community free movement law', *EL Rev* 1999, 445-462.

Hintersteininger 1999

Margrit Hintersteininger, *Binnenmarkt und Diskriminierungsverbot. Unter besonderer Berücksichtigung der Situation nicht-staatlicher Handlungseinheiten*, Berlin: Duncker & Humblot 1999.

Hinton 1999

Eric Hinton, 'Strengthening the Effectiveness of Community Law: Direct Effect, Article 5 EC, and the European Court of Justice', *NYU Journal of International Law & Politics* 1999, 307-348.

Holtmaat 1989

Rikki Holtmaat, 'The Power of Legal Concepts: The Development of a Feminist Theory of Law', *International Journal of the Sociology of Law* 1989, 481-502.

Holtmaat 1995

Rikki Holtmaat, (Case note on *Helmig*), *ILJ* 1995, 387-394.

Holtmaat 1996 (Alle dingen)

Rikki Holtmaat, 'Alle dingen die opwaarts gaan komen ergens samen', *Nemesis* 1996, 125-131.

Holtmaat 1996 (Deeltijdwerk)

Rikki Holtmaat, 'Deeltijdwerk, gelijkheid en gender', *Nemesis* 1996, 4-17.

Holtmaat 1999 (Eeuwige kwesties)

Rikki Holtmaat (ed), *Eeuwige kwesties. Honderd jaar vrouwen en recht in Nederland. Jubileumuitgave van Nemesis, tijdschrift over vrouwen en recht*, Deventer: W.E.J. Tjeenk Willink 1999.

Holtmaat 1999 (Overtime Payments)

Rikki Holtmaat, 'The Issue of Overtime Payments for Part-time Workers in the *Helmig* Case – Some Thoughts on Equality and Gender', in: Yota Kravaritou (ed), *The Regulation of Working Time in the European Union. Gender Approach/La réglementation du temps de travail dans l'Union européenne. Perspective selon le genre*, Bruxelles/Bern/Berlin/Frankfurt a.M./New York/Wien: Peter Lang 1999, 411-444.

Holtmaat 2001 (Uit de keuken)

Rikki Holtmaat, 'Uit de keuken van de Europese Unie: De gelijkebehandelingsrichtlijnen op grond van artikel 13 EG-Verdrag', in: Commissie Gelijke Behandeling & Titia Loenen (eds), *Gelijke behandeling: oordelen en commentaar 2000*, Deventer: Kluwer 2001, 105-134.

Holtmaat 2001 (Gender)

Rikki Holtmaat, 'Gender: An analytical concept that tackles the hidden structural bias of law', in: Verein Pro Fri (ed), *Recht Richtung Frauen*, Lachen/St. Gallen: 2001, 159-182.

Holtmaat 2002

Rikki Holtmaat, 'Het gelijkheidsbeginsel: van een vat vol dilemma's naar drie typen van gelijkerechtenwetgeving', in: M. Kroes, J.P. Loof & H.M.-Th.D. ten Napel (eds), *Gelijkheid en rechtvaardigheid. Staatsrechtelijke vraagstukken rondom ,minderheden'*, Deventer: Kluwer 2002, 161-175.

Holtmaat 2003 (CEDAW)

Rikki Holtmaat, 'European Women and the CEDAW-Convention. The way forward', in: AFFJ & EWLA (ed), *L'Egalité entre femmes et homes et la vie professionnelle. Le point sur les développments actuels en Europe*, Paris: Editions Dalloz 2003, 153-173.

Holtmaat 2003 (Stop de uitholling)

Rikki Holtmaat, 'Stop de uitholling van het discriminatiebegrip! Een herbezinning op het onderscheid tussen discriminatie en ongelijke behandeling', *NJB* 2003, 1266-1276.

Holtmaat 2004 (Seksuele intimidatie)

Rikki Holtmaat, '(Seksuele) Intimidatie en (on)gelijke behandeling: nieuwe normen, nieuwe praktijken?', in: Commissie Gelijke Behandeling & D.J.B. Wolff (eds), *Gelijke behandeling: oordelen en commentaar 2003*, Deventer: Kluwer 2004, 89-106.

Holtmaat 2004 (Towards Different Law)

Rikki Holtmaat, *Towards Different Law and Policy. The significance of Article 5a CEDAW for the elimination of structural gender discrimination*, Research undertaken for the Ministry of Social Affairs and Employment in the Netherlands; text available at http://www.rikkiholtmaat.nl/e_index1.html (see also http://home.szw.nl/navigatie/rubriek/dsp_rubriek.cfm?rubriek_id=5&subrubriek_id=1045&link_id=46384).

Holtmaat & Loenen 1997

Rikki Holtmaat & Titia Loenen (eds), *vrouw & recht*, Nijmegen: Ars Aequi Libri 1997.

Honeyball 2000

Simon Honeyball, 'Pregnancy and Sex Discrimination', *ILJ* 2000, 43-52.

Hoppe 2002

Tilman Hoppe, 'Europäischer Schutz vor sexueller Diskriminierung beim Zugang zur Arbeit', *ZEuP* 2002, 78-95.

Hoskins 1994

Catherine Hoskins, 'Gender issues in international relations: the case of the European Community', *Review of International Studies* 1994, 225-239.

House of Commons 2000

House of Commons, European Scrutiny Committee, *Commission Proposals to Combat Discrimination*, Session 1999-2000, 7th Report, xviii-xxix, London: The Stationary Office 2000.

House of Lords 2000 (EU proposals)

House of Lords, Select Committee on the European Union, *EU proposals to combat discrimination*, Session 1999-2000, 9th report, London: The Stationary Office 2000.

House of Lords 2000 (Framework Directive)

House of Lords, Select Committee on the European UnionN, *The EU Framework Directive on Discrimination*, Session 2000-01, 4th Report, London: The Stationary Office 2000.

Hovius 2000

Berend Hovius, 'Equality and the Canadian Charter of Rights and Freedoms', in: Pauline C. Westerman (ed), *Non-Discrimination and Diversity*, Den Haag: Boom Juridische Uitgevers 2000, 5-23.

Hufton & Kravaritou 1999

Olwen Hufton & Yota Kravaritou (eds.), *Gender and the Use of Time. Gender et Emploi du Temps*, The Hague/London/Boston: Kluwer 1999.

Huglo 1996

Jean-Guy Huglo, 'Liberté d'établissement et libre prestation des services (1er juillet 1995-1er juillet 1996)', *RDTE* 1996, 741-746.

Imbrechts 1986

Luc Imbrechts, 'L'égalité de rémuneration entre hommes et femmes', *RTDE* 1986, 231-242.

Iliopoulou & Toner 2002
    Anastasia Iliopoulou & Helen Toner, (Case note on *Grzelczyk*), *CML Rev* 2002, 610-620.

Jacobs 1994
    Lesley A. Jacobs, 'Equal Opportunity and Gender Disadvantage', *Canadian Journal of Law and Jurisprudence* 1994, 61-71.
Jacqmain 1994
    Jean Jaqmain, 'Pregnancy as Grounds for Dismissal', *ILJ* 1994, 355-359.
Jarass 1995
    Hans D. Jarass, 'Elemente einer Dogmatik der Grundfreiheiten', *Europarecht* 1995, 202-226.
Jarass 2000 (Elemente)
    Hans D. Jarass, 'Elemente einer Dogmatik der Grundfreiheiten II', *Europarecht* 2000, 705-723.
Jarass 2000 (Unified Approach)
    Hans D. Jarass, 'A Unified Approach to the Fundamental Freedoms', in: Mads Andenas & Wulf-Henning Roth (eds), *Services and Free Movement in EU Law*, Oxford: Oxford University Press 2000, 141-162.
Jeffrey 1998
    Mark Jeffrey, 'Not really going to work? Of the Directive on Part-Time Work, 'Atypical Work' and Attempts to Regulate It', *ILJ* 1998, 193-203.
Jessurun d'Oliveira 2003
    H.U. Jessurun d'Oliveira, 'Het Europese Hof activeert het Europese burgerschap', *NJB* 2003, 2238-2243.
Johnson & O'Keeffe 1994
    Esther Johnson & David O'Keeffe, 'From Discrimination to Obstacles to Free Movement: Recent Developments Concerning the Free Movement of Workers 1989-1994', *CML Rev* 1994, 1313-1346.
Jolls 2000
    Christine Jolls, 'Accommodation Mandates', *Stanford Law Review* 53 (2000), 223-306.
Jolls 2001
    Christine Jolls, 'Antidiscrimination and Accommodation', *Harvard Law Review* 115 (2001), 642-699.
Jones 2000
    Clifford A. Jones, 'Television Without Frontiers', in: Piet Eeckhout & Takis Tridimas (eds), *Yearbook of European Law* 19 (1999-2000), Oxford: Oxford University Press 2000, 299-345.
Julén 2001
    Jenny Julén, 'A Blessing or a Ban? About the Discrimination of Pregnant Job-Seekers', in: Ann Numhauser-Henning Ann (ed), *Legal Perspectives on Equal Treatment and Non-Discrimination*, The Hague: Kluwer Law International 2001, 169-204.
Junter-Loiseau & Tobler 1999
    Annie Junter-Loiseau & Christa Tobler, 'Rèconciliation of domestic and care work with paid work. Approaches in international legislation and policy instruments and in the scientific discourse', in: Olwen Hufton & Yota Kravaritou (eds.), *Gender and the Use of Time. Gender et Emploi du Temps*, The Hague/London/Boston: Kluwer 1999, 341-369.

Kaddous 2004

Christine Kaddous, 'Le droit communautaire et les partenariats de meme sexe', *Die Praxis des Familienrechts* 2004, 598-621.

Kägi-Diener 2001

Regula Kägi-Diener, 'Von Olympe de Gouges zum UN-Übereinkommen zur Beseitigung jeder Form von Diskriminierung der Frau: Entwicklungen im Recht der Gleichstellung', in: Verein Pro Fri (ed), *Recht Richtung Frauen*, Lachen/St. Gallen: 2001, 239-263.

Kaldellis 2001

Evangelos I. Kaldellis, 'Freedom of Establishment versus Freedom to Provide Services: An Evaluation of Case-law Developments in the Area of Indistinctly Applicable Rules', *Legal Issues of Economic Integration* 2001, 23-55.

Kapteyn & VerLoren van Themaat 1995

P.J.G. Kapteyn, P. VerLoren van Themaat, L.A. Geelhoed & C.W.A. Timmermans (eds), *Kapteyn/VerLoren van Themaat. Inleiding tot het recht van de Europese Gemeemschappen na Maastricht*, 5th, totally revised edition, Kluwer: Deventer 1995.

Kapteyn & VerLoren van Themaat 2003

P.J.G. Kapteyn, P. VerLoren van Themaat, L.A. Geelhoed, K.J.M. Mortelmans & C.W.A. Timmermans (eds), *Kapteyn/VerLoren van Themaat. Het recht van de Europese Unie en van de Europese Gemeemschappen*, 6th, totally revised edition, Kluwer: Deventer 2003.

Keeling & Shipwright 1995

Elizabeth Keeling & Adrian Shipwright, 'Some Taxing Problems Concerning Non-Discrimination and the EC Treaty', *EL Rev* 1995, 580-597.

Kenner 2003

Jeff Kenner, *EU Employment Law. From Rome to Amsterdam and Beyond*, Oxford/Portland (Oregon): Hart Publishing 2003.

Kentridge 1994

Janet Kentridge, 'Direct and indirect discrimination after *Enderby*', *Public Law* 1994, 198-206.

Keunen 1994

F.W.M. Keunen, 'Verordening 1612/68, art. 7 lid 2, Verordening 1408/71, art. 4, art. 18 lid 1', *Sociaal Maandblad arbeid* 1994, 238-240.

Keunen 2001

F.W.M. Keunen, *Schets van het Europees socialezekerheidsrecht. Europese coördinatieregels inzake sociale zekerheid*, Lelystad: Koninklijke Vermande 2001.

Khan 1994

Daniel-Erasmus Khan, (Case note on *Vander Elst*), *EuZW* 1994, 602-603.

Kiblböck 1995

Ingrid Kiblböck, (Case note on *Schumacker*), *EC Tax Review* 1995, 114-115.

Kilpatrick 1996

Claire Kilpatrick, 'How long is a piece of string? European regulation of the post-birth period', in: Tamara K. Hervey & David O. O'Keeffe (eds), *Sex Equality in the European Union*, Chichester/New York/Brisbane/Toronto/Singapore: John Wiley 1996, 81-96.

Kingreen 1999
Thorsten Kingreen, *Die Struktur der Grundfreiheiten des Europäischen Gemeinschaftsrechts*, Berlin: Duncker & Humblot 1999.

Kirsten 1990
Mathias Kirsten, 'Anforderungen an die Rechtfertigung einer mittelbaren Diskriminierung wegen des Geschlechts', *RdA* 1990, 282-286.

Kischel 1997
Uwe Kischel, 'Zur Dogmatik des Gleichheitssatzes in der Europäischen Union', *EuGRZ* 1997, 1-11.

Klett 2004
Kathrin Klett, 'Inspiration des Bundesgerichts durch den EuGH/das EU-Recht im Bereich der Gleichstellung der Geschlechter', in: Astrid Epiney & Ira von Danckelmann (eds), *Gleichstellung von Frauen und Männern in der Schweiz und der EU/L'égalité entre femmes et hommes en Suisse et dans l'UE*, Zurich/Basel/Geneva: Schulthess 2004, 133-152.

Knauff 2004
Matthias Knauff, 'Die Reform des europäischen Vergaberechts', *EuZW* 2004, 141-144.

Knobbe-Keuk 1995
Brigitte Knobbe-Keuk, 'Freizügigkeit und direkte Besteuerung', *EuZW* 1995, 167-169.

König 2004
Doris König, 'Die Diskriminierungsverbote im Übereinkommen der Vereinten Nationen zur Beseitigung jeder Form der Diskriminierung der Frau (CEDAW)', in: Doris König, Joachim Lange, Ursula Rust & Hanna Beate Schöpp-Schilling (eds), *Gleiches Recht – gleiche Realität? Welche Instrumente bieten Völkerrecht, Europarecht und nationals Recht für die Gleichstellung von Frauen?*, Rehburg-Loccum: Evangelische Akademie Loccum 2004, 21-36.

Körber 2000
Torsten Körber, 'Innerstaatliche Anwendung und Drittwirkung der Grundfreiheiten?', *Europarecht* 2000, 932-952.

Koggel 1994
Christine Christine, 'A Feminist View of Equality and Its Implications for Affirmative Action', *Canadian Journal of Law and Jurisprudence* 7 (1994), 43-59.

Kohnstamm 1988
Manuel Kohnstamm, 'De nationale Televisie voorziening en cultuurpolitieke argumenten', *Nederlands Juristenblad* 1988, 1267-1271.

Kok 1976
D.H. Kok, (Case note on *Coenen* and *van Binsbergen*), *SEW* 1976, 251-261.

Kokott 1990
Juliane Kokott, (Case note on *Bronzino* and *Gatto*), *American Journal of International Law* 1990, 926-929.

Kon 1981
Stephen Kon, 'Alleged discrimination in a procedure for the recovery of debts', *EL Rev* 1981, 363-368.

Koopmans 1975
Thijmen Koopmans, *Constitutional Protection of Equality*, Leiden: Sijthoff 1975.

Koukoulis-Spiliotopoulos 2001

Sophia Koukoulis-Spiliotopoulos, *From Formal to Substantive Gender Equality. The Proposed Amendment of Directive 76/207. Comments and Suggestions*, Athens/Komotini: Ant. N. Sakkoulas and Brussels: Bruylant 2001.

Kraus 2003

Dieter Kraus, 'Diplomas and the recognition of professional qualifications in the case law of the European Court of Justice', in: Mark Hoskins & William Robinson (eds), *A True European. Essays for Judge David Edward*, Oxford/Portland, Oregon: Hart Publishing 2003, 247-256.

Krause 2002

Hartmut Krause, 'Von "goldenen Aktien", dem VW-Gesetz und der Uebernahmerichtlinie', *NJW* 2002, 2747-2751.

Kravaritou 1994

Yota Kravaritou, 'Women and the Law: In Search of an Ever-Evasive Equality', in: Stephen Martin (ed), *The Construction of Europe. Essays in Honour of Emile Noël*, Dordrecht/Boston/London: Kluwer 1994, 227-238.

Krüger & Polakiewicz 2001

Hans Christian Krüger & Jörg Polakiewicz, 'Propositions pour la création d'un système cohérent de protection des droits de l'homme en Europe. La Convention européenne des droits de l'homme et la Charte des droit fondamentaux de l'Union européenne', *Revue universelle des droits de l'homme* 2001, no 14, 1-14.

Kyriazis 1990

Georgios Kyriazis, *Die Sozialpolitik der Europäischen Wirtschaftsgemeinschaft in bezug auf die Gleichberechtigung männlicher und weiblicher Erwerbstätiger*, Berlin: Duncker & Humblot 1990.

Lacey 1987

Nicola Lacey, 'Legislation Against Sex Discrimination: Questions from a Feminist Perspective', *Journal of Law and Society* 14 (1987) 411-421.

Lacey 1992

Nicola Lacey, 'From Individual to Group', in: Bob Hepple & Erika Szyszczak (eds), *Discrimination: The Limits of Law*, London: Mansell 1992, 99-123.

Landsmeer 2000

Arie Landsmeer, 'Capital Movements: On the Interpretation of Article 73b of the EC Treaty', *Legal Issues of Economic Integration* 2000, 195-200.

Langenfeld 1990

Christine Langenfeld, *Die Gleichbehandlung von Mann und Frau im Europäischen Gemeinschaftsrecht*, Baden-Baden: Nomos 1990.

Lanquetin 1996 (Egalité de chances)

Marie-Thérèse Lanquetin, 'De l'égalité des chances. Á propos de l'arrêt Kalanke, CJCE 17 octobre 1995', *Droit social* 1996, 494-501.

Lanquetin 1996 (La preuve)

Marie-Thérèse Lanquetin, 'La preuve de la discrimination: l'apport du droit communautaire', *Droit social* 1996, 494-501.

Lanquetin 1998
Marie-Thérèse Lanquetin, 'Discrimination à raison du sexe. Commentaire de la directive 97/80 du 15 décembre 1997 relative à la charge de la preuve dans les cas de discrimination à raison du sexe', *Droit social* 1998, 668-693.

Lauria 1998
Felicetta Lauria, *I Pubblici Appalti. Disciplina comunitaria e giurisprudenza italiana*, Milan: Giuffrè editore 1998.

Lawson 1993
Rick Lawson, (Case note on *Konstantinidis*), *CML Rev* 1993, 395-412.

Leader 1996
Sheldon Leader, 'Proportionality and the Justification of Discrimination', in: Janet Dine & Bob Watt (eds), *Discrimination Law. Concepts, Limitations and Justifications*, London/New York: Longman 1996, 110-120.

Léger Commentary 2000
Philippe Léger (ed), *Union Européenne. Communauté Européenne. Commentaire Article par article des traités UE et CE*, Bâle/Genève/Munich: Helbing & Lichtenhahn, Paris: Dalloz, Bruxelles: Bruylant 2000.

Lehner 2000
Moris Lehner, 'Limitation of the national power of taxation by the fundamental freedoms and non-discrimination clauses of the EC Treaty', *EC Tax Review* 2000, 5-15.

Lelakis 1991
Vassili Lelakis, 'La libre circulation des capitaux au sein de la Communauté', *Revue du Marché Unique Européen* 1991 (1), 47- 62.

Lenaerts 1991
Koen Lenaerts, 'L'égalité de traitement de droit communautaire. Une principe unique aux apparences multiples', *CDE* 1991, 3-41.

Lenaerts & Foubert 2001
Koen Lenaerts & Petra Foubert, 'Social Rights in the Case-Law of the European Court of Justice. The Impact of the Charter of Fundamental Rights of the European Union on Standing Case-Law', *Legal Issues of Economic Integration* 2001, 267-296.

Lenaerts & Nuffel 1995
Koen Lenaerts & Piet van Nuffel, *Europees Recht in hoofdlijnen*, Antwerpen/Apeldoorn: Maklu 1995.

Lenaerts & Nuffel 1999
Koen Lenaerts & Piet Nuffel, *Constitutional Law of the European Union*, London: Sweet & Maxwell 1999.

Lenz & Borchardt Commentary 2003
Carl Otto Lenz & Klaus-Dieter Borchardt (eds), *EU- und EG-Vertrag. Kommentar zu dem Vertrag über die Europäische Union und zu dem Vertrag über die Europäische Gemeinschaft, jeweils in der durch den Vertrag von Nizza geänderten Fassung*, 3rd edition, Basel/Genf/München: Helbing & Lichtenhahn; Wien: Ueberreuter; Köln: Bundesanzeiger 2003.

Lenz Commentary 1999

Carl Otto Lenz, *EG-Vertrag. Kommentar zu dem Vertrag zur Gründung der Europäischen Gemeinschaften, in der durch den Amsterdamer Vertrag geänderten Fassung*, Basel/Genf/München: Helbing & Lichtenhahn; Wien: Ueberreuter; Köln: Bundesanzeiger 1999.

Ley 1993

Katharina Ley, 'Illustion Gerechtigkeit? Ein Plädoyer für die Anerkennung', in: Kathrin Klett & Danielle Yersin (eds), *Die Gleichstellung von Frau und Mann als rechtspolitischer Auftrag. L'égalité entre hommes et femmes – un mandat politique pour le législateur. Festschrift für Margrith Bigler-Eggenberger*, Basel/Frankfurt: Helbing & Lichtenhahn 1993, 205-219.

Loenen 1992

Titia Loenen, *Verschil in Gelijkheid. De conceptualisering van het juridische gelijkheidsbeginsel met betrekking tot vrouwen en mannen in Nederland en de Verenigde Staten*, Zwolle: Tjeenk Willink 1992.

Loenen 1995 (Substantive equality)

Titia Loenen, 'Substantive equality as a right to inclusion: dilemma's and limits in law', *R & R* 1995, 194-203.

Loenen 1996 (Holtmaat en Helmig)

Titia Loenen, 'Holtmaat en *Helmig*, of: het trekken van verkeerde conclusies uit een verkeerd arrest', *Nemesis* 1996, 123-124.

Loenen 1996 (Inclusion)

Titia Loenen, 'In search of inclusion: A feminist perspective of women and international human rights law', in: 6. Schweizerische Feministische Juristinnentagung (ed), *Frauen und internationales Recht. Instrumente, Chancen, Perspektiven*, Bern: 6. Schweizerische Feministische Juristinnentagung 1996, 19-26.

Loenen 1998

Titia Loenen, *Het gelijkheidsbeginsel, Ars Aequi Cahiers 37*, Nijmegen: Ars Aequi Libri 1998.

Loenen 1999

Titia Loenen, ' Indirect Discrimination: Oscillating Between Containment and Revolution', in: Titia Loenen & Peter R. Rodrigues (eds), *Non-Discrimination Law: Comparative Perspectives*, The Hague/London/Boston: Kluwer Law International 1999, 195-211.

Loewisch 1994

Manfred Loewisch, 'Lektorenrechtsprechung des EuGH und Lehrfreiheit der Hochschulen', *Juristenzeitung* 1994, 293-294.

Loiseau 1995

Grégoire Loiseau, (Case note on *Konstantinidis*), *European Review of Private Law* 1995, 504-513.

Lombay 1996

Julian Lombay, (Case note on *Gebhard*), *CML Rev.* 1996, 1973-1987.

Luckhaus 1988

Linda Luckhaus, 'Sex discrimination in state social security schemes' (Case note on *Rinner-Kühn*), *EL Rev* 1988, 52-58.

Luijendijk 1999

J. Luijendijk, (Case note on *Bickel and Franz*), *SEW* 1999, 348-350.

Lundström 2001
Karin Lundström, 'Indirect Sex Discrimination in the European Court of Justice's Version', in: Ann Numhauser-Henning (ed), *Legal Perspectives on Equal Treatment and Non-Discrimination*, The Hague: Kluwer Law International 2001, 143-160.

Lutjens 1990
E. Lutjens, 'AOW-toeslag discriminerend?', *Nederlands tijdschrift voor de mensenrechten /NJCM Bulletin* 1990, 139-153.

Lyons 2001
Timothy Lyons, *EC Customs Law*, Oxford: Oxford University Press 2001.

MacKinnon 1979
Catharine MacKinnon, *Sexual Harassment of Working Women. A case of Sex Discrimination*, New Haven/London: Yale University Press 1979.

MacKinnon 1982
Catharine MacKinnon, 'Feminism, Marxism, Method and the State: An Agenda for Theory', *Signs* 1982, 515-544.

MacKinnon 1983
Catharine MacKinnon, 'Feminism, Marxism, Method and the State: Toward a Feminist Jurisprudence', *Signs* 1983, 635-658.

MacKinnon 1987
Catharine MacKinnon, *Feminism Unmodified. Discourses on Life and Law*, Cambridge/London: Harvard University Press 1987.

MacKinnon 1991
Catharine MacKinnon, 'Reflections on Sex Equality under Law', *The Yale Law Journal* 1991, 1281-1328.

MacKinnon 2001
Catharine A. MacKinnon, *Sex Equality*, University Casebook Series, New York: Foundation Press 2001.

Mahler 1997
R. Mahler, 'Indirecte discriminatie en vervoer', *NTER* 1997, 101-102.

Mahoney 1992
Kathleen E. Mahoney, 'The Constitutional Law of Equality in Canada', *New York University Journal of International Law and Politics* 1992, 759-793.

Mahoney 1994
Kathleen Mahoney, 'Canadian Approaches to Equality Rights and Gender Equity in the Courts', in: Rebecca J. Cook (ed), *Human Rights of Women. National and International Perspectives*, Philadelphia: University of Pennsylvania Press 1994, 437-461.

Malmstedt 2001
Matthias Malmstedt, 'From Employee to EU Citizen – A Development From Equal Treatment as a Means to Equal Treatment as a Goal?', in: Ann Numhauser-Henning Ann (ed), *Legal Perspectives on Equal Treatment and Non-Discrimination*, The Hague: Kluwer Law International 2001, 95-124.

Mancini & O'Leary 1999

G.F. Mancini/S. O'Leary, 'The new frontiers of sex equality in the European Union', *EL Rev* 1999, 331-353.

Manolkidis 1997

Sotirios Manolkidis, 'The Principle of Equality from a Comparative Constitutional Perspective: Lessons for the EU', in: Alan Dashwood & Síofra O'Leary, *The Principle of Equal Treatment in E.C. Law*, London/Dublin/Hong Kong: Sweet & Maxwell 1997, 80-104.

March Hunnings 1980

Neville March Hunnings, (Case note on *Debauve and Coditel*), *CML Rev* 1980, 464-469.

Marenco 1984

G. Marenco, 'Pour une interpretation traditionnelle de la notion de mesure d'effet équivalent à une restriction quantitative', *CDE* 1984, 292-364.

Martin 1993

Denis Martin, 'Reflexions sur le champ d'application matériel de l'article 48 du Traité CE (à la lumière de la jurisprudence récente de la Cour de justice)', *CDE* 1993, 555-596.

Martin 1994

Denis Martin, *La libre circulation des personnes dans l'Union Européenne*, Bruxelles: Bruylant 1994.

Martin 1998

D. Martin, '"Discriminations", "entraves" et "raisons impérieuses" dans le traité CE: trois concepts en quête d'identité', *CDE* 1998, 261-317 (first part) and 561-637 (second part).

Martín Jiménez 1999

Adolfo J. Martín Jiménez, *Towards Corporate Tax Harmonization in the European Community: an Institutional and Procedural Analysis*, London/The Hague/Boston: Kluwer Law International 1999.

Massaro 1976

Lorraine Massaro, 'The Nationality of Married Women and the Principle of Gender Equality in the European Economic Communities', *Columbia Journal of Transnational Law* 15 (1976) 514-537.

Mattera 1991

Mattera A., 'Les principes de "proportionnalité" et de la "reconnaissance mutuelle" dans la jurisprudence de la Cour en matière de libre circulation des personnes et des services: de l'arrêt "Thieffry" aux arrêts "Vlassoupoulou", "Mediawet" et "Dennemeyer"', *Revue du Marché Unique Européen* 1991 (4), 191-203.

Mattera 1993

A. Mattera, 'La libre circulation des travailleurs', *Revue du Marché Unique Européen* 1993 (4), 47-108.

Mavridis 1998

Prodromos Mavridis, 'L'Arrêt *Vougioukas*: une révolution discrète? Réflexions sur la mobilité et la protection sociale des agents publics en Europe', *CDE* 1998, 191-213.

McCrudden 1977

J.C. McCrudden, (Case note on *Price v Civil Service Commission and Society of Civil and Public Servants* [1977] I.R.L.R. 291(E.A.T.) and *Steel v. Union of Post Office Workers and General Post Office* [1977] I.R.L.R. 288 (E.A.T.), *Industrial Law Journal* 1977, 241-246.

McCrudden 1982

Christopher McCrudden, 'Institutional discrimination', *Oxford Journal of Legal Studies* 2 (1982) 303-367.

McCrudden 1985

Christopher McCrudden, 'Changing Notions of Discrimination', in: Stephen Guest & Alan Milne (eds), *Equality and Discrimination: Essays in Freedom and Justice*, Stuttgart: Franz Steiner 1985, 81-91.

McCrudden 2001

Christopher McCrudden, 'International and European Norms Regarding National Legal Remedies for Racial Inequality', in: Sandra Fredman (ed), *Discrimination and Human Rights. The Case of Racism*, Oxford: Oxford University Press 2001, 251-307.

McCrudden 2003

Christopher McCrudden, 'The New Concept of Equality', written version of a presentation given at the conference 'Fight Against Discrimination: The Race and Framework Employment Directives', held in Trier (Germany), 31 March – 1 April 2003, www.era.int/www/gen/f_15802_file.pdf (text on file with the present writer).

McCrudden 2004

McCrudden Christopher, 'Using public procurement to achieve social outcomes', *Natural Resources Forum* 28 (2004) 257-267.

McGinley 2000

Ann C. McGinley, '¡Viva la evolucion! Recognizing unconscious motive in Title VII', *Cornell Journal of Law and Public Policy* Winter 2000/2, 415-492.

McGlynn 2001

Clare McGlynn, 'Pregnancy Discrimination in EU Law', in: Ann Numhauser-Henning (ed), *Legal Perspectives on Equal Treatment and Non-Discrimination*, The Hague: Kluwer Law International 2001, 205-216, at 179.

McGolgan 2000

Aileen McGolgan, *Discrimination Law: Text, Cases and Materials*, Oxford/Portland: Hart Publishing 2000.

McInerny 2000

Siobhan McInerny, *'Equal treatment between persons irrespective of racial or ethnic origin: a comment'*, EL Rev 2000, 317-323.

McKean 1983

Warwick McKean, *Equality and discrimination under international law*, Oxford: Clarendon Press 1983.

McMahon 1990

Brian M.E. McMahon, (Case note on *Groener*), *CML Rev* 1990, 129-139.

Meenan 2003

Helen Meenan, 'Age Equality after the Employment Directive', *MJ* 2003, 9-38.

Mégret Commentary (various dates, as of 1972)

Mégret Commentary, *Le droit de la CEE*, Brussels: Editions de l'Université de Bruxelles, various dates of the individual volumes, as of 1972 (see indications in the references).

Meussen 1999

Gerard Meussen (ed), *The Principle of Equality in European Taxation*, The Hague/London/ Boston: Kluwer Law International 1999.

Meyer 2002

Michael Meyer, *Das Diskriminierungsverbot des Gemeinschaftsrechts als Grundsatznorm und Gleichheitsrecht*, Frankfurt am Main a.o.: Peter Lang 2002.

Möstl 2002

Markus Möstl, 'Grenzen der Rechtsangleichung im europäischen Binnenmarkt. Kompetenzielle, grundfreiheitliche und grundrechtliche Schranken des Gemeinschaftsgesetzgebers', *Europarecht* 2002, 318-350.

Moitinho de Almeida 1994

José Moitinho de Almeida, 'Les entraves non discriminatoires à la libre circulation des personnes; leur compatibilité avec les articles 48 et 52 du traité CE', in: *Festskrift til Ole Due*, Copenhague: G.E.C Gads Forlag 1994, 241-263.

Mohn 1990

Astrid Sybille Mohn, *Der Gleichheitssatz im Gemeinschaftsrecht. Differenzierungen im europäischen Gemeinschaftsrecht und ihre Vereinbarkeit mit dem Gleichheitssatz*, Kehl et al.: N.P.Engel Verlag 1990.

Moore 1994

Sarah Moore, 'Sex, pregnancy, and dismissal', *EL Rev* 1994, 653-660.

More 1993

Gillian C. More, '"Equal Treatment" of the sexes in European Community Law: what does "equal" mean?', *Feminist Legal Studies* 1993, 45-74.

More 1996

Gillian More, 'Equality of Treatment in European Community Law: The Limits of Market Equality', in: Ann Bottomley (ed), *Feminist Perspectives of the Foundational Subjects of Law*, London: Cavendish 1996, 261-278.

More 1999

Gillian More, 'The Principle of Equal Treatment: From Market Unifier to Fundamental Right?', in: Paul Craig & Gráinne de Búrca (eds), *The Evolution of EU Law*, Oxford: Oxford University Press 1999, 517-553.

Morris 1995

Andrew J. Morris, 'On The Normative Foundations of Indirect Discrimination Law: Understanding the Competing Models of Discrimination Law as Aristotelian Forms of Justice', *Oxford Journal of Legal Studies* 1995, 199-228.

Morse 1975

Geoffrey Morse, (Case note on *Van Binsbergen*), *EL Rev* 1975, 67-69.

Morse 1979

Geoffrey Morse, 'Provision of services: the professional supervision exception', *EL Rev* 1979, 375-377.

Mortelmans 1990

K.J.M. Mortelmans, (Case note on *Groener*), *Ars Aequi* 1990, 304-310.

Mortelmans 1997
K.J.M. Mortelmans, 'Excepties bij non-tarifaire intracommunitaire belemmeringen: assimilatie in het nieuwe EG-Verdrag?', *SEW* 1997, 182-190.

Mortelmans 1998
Kamiel Mortelmans, 'The Principle of Loyalty to the Community (Article 5 EC) and the Obligations of the Community Institutions', *MJ* 1998, 67-88.

Mortelmans 2002
K.J.M. Mortelmans, (Case note on the *Golden Shares* cases), *SEW* 2002, 341-347.

Müller 1992
Thomas Müller, 'Beschränkte Steuerpflicht und einige Aspekte des EG-Rechts', *Steuer und Wirtschaft* 1992, 157-169.

Mulder 1999
Louise Mulder, 'How Positive Can Equality Measures Be?', in: Titia Loenen & Peter R. Rodrigues (eds), *Non-Discrimination Law: Comparative Perspectives*, The Hague/London/Boston: Kluwer Law International 1999, 65-75.

Nachbaur 1991
Andreas Nachbaur, 'Art. 52 EWGV – Mehr als nur ein Diskriminierungsverbot?', *EuZW* 1991, 470-472.

Napoletano 1972
Guido Napoletano, 'Libera circolazione dei lavoratori e limiti al principio di non discriminazione', *Rivista di diritto internazionale* 1972, 693-700.

Nicolaysen 1978
Gert Nicolaysen, (Case note on *Thieffry*), *Europarecht* 1978, 288-289.

Nielsen 1990
Henrik Karl Nielsen, 'The concept of discrimination in ILO Convention NO. 111', *International and Comparative Law Quarterly* 1990, 827-856.

Nielsen 1992
Ruth Nielsen, (Case note a.o. on *Dekker*), *CML Rev* 1992, 160-169.

Norberg, Hökborg, Johansson, Eliasson & Dedichem Commentary 1993
Sven Norberg, Karin Hökborg, Martin Johansson, Dan Eliasson & Lucien Dedichem, *The European Economic Area. EEA Law. A Commentary on the EEA Agreement*, Stockholm: Fritzes 1993.

Norberg 2001
Per Norberg, 'Non-Discrimination as a Social and a Free Market Value', in: Ann Numhauser-Henning (ed), *Legal Perspectives on Equal Treatment and Non-Discrimination*, The Hague: Kluwer Law International 2001, 65-90.

Notaro 1998
N. Notaro, (Case note on *Safir*), *Revue du marché unique européen* 1998 (2), 268-269.

Novak 1997
Meinhard Novak, 'Ungleichbehandlung von ausländischen Produkten oder Dienstleistungen – Einheitliche Rechtfertigungstatbestände im EG-Vertrag', *Der Betrieb* 1997, 2589-2593.

Novak 1998
   Meinhard Novak, 'EG-Grundfreiheiten und Europäisches Sozialrecht', *EuZW* 1998, 366-369.
Novak 1999
   Meinhard Novak, 'EuGH: Gleichbehandlung bei der Gerichtssprache', *EuZW* 1999, 82-85.
Nowak & Schnitzler 2000
   Carsten Nowak & Jörg Schnitzler, 'Erweiterte Rechtfertigungsmöglichkeiten für mitgliedstaatliche Beschränkungen der EG-Grundfreiheiten', *EuZW* 2000, 627-631.
Numhauser-Henning 2001 (Swedish Sex Equality Law)
   Ann Numhauser-Henning, 'Swedish Sex Equality Law before the European Court of Justice', *ILJ* 2001, 121-126.
Numhauser-Henning 2001 (Introduction)
   Ann Numhauser-Henning, 'Introduction. Equal Treatment – A Normative Challenge', in: Ann Numhauser-Henning (ed), *Legal Perspectives on Equal Treatment and Non-Discrimination*, The Hague: Kluwer Law International 2001, 1-27.

Odendahl 2004
   Kerstin Odendahl, 'Die Berücksichtigung vergabefremder Kriterien im öffentlichen Auftragswesen. Rechtslage nach EG- und WTO-Recht', *EuZW* 2004, 647-652.
O'Donovan & Szyszczak 1988
   Katherine O'Donovan & Erika Szyszczak, *Equality and Sex Discrimination Law*, Oxford: Basil Blackwell 1988.
O'Hare 2001
   Ursula O'Hare, 'Enhancing European Equality Rights: A New Regional Framework', *MJ* 2001, 133-165.
Ohler 1997
   Christoph Ohler, *Die fiskalische Integration in der Europäischen Gemeinschaft*, Baden-Baden: Nomos 1997.
O'Leary 1997
   Síofra O'Leary, 'The Principle of Equal Treatment on Grounds of Nationality in Article 6 EC. A lucrative source of rights for Member State nationals?', in: Alan Dashwood & Síofra O'Leary (eds), *The Principle of Equal Treatment in E.C. Law*, London/Dublin/Hong Kong: Sweet & Maxwell 1997, 105-136.
O'Leary 1999
   Síofra Leary, 'The Free Movement of Persons and Services', in: Paul Craig & Gráinne de Búrca (eds), *The Evolution of EU Law*, Oxford: Oxford University Press 1999, 377-416.
O'Leary 2002
   Síofra Leary, *Employment Law at the European Court of Justice. Judicial Structures, Policies and Processes*, Oxford/Portland (Oregon): Hart Publishing 2002.
O'Leary & Fernández Martín 2002
   Síofra O'Leary & José Fernández Martín, 'Judicially-Created Exceptions to the Free Provision of Services', in: Mads Andenas & Wulf-Henning Roth (eds), *Services and Free Movement in EU Law*, Oxford: Oxford University Press 2002, 163-195.

Oliver 1999

Peter Oliver, 'Some further reflections on the scope of Articles 28-30 (ex 30-36) EC', *CML Rev* 1999, 783-806.

Oliver 2003

Peter Oliver, *Free movement of goods in the European Community Under Articles 28 to 30 of the EC Treaty*, 4th edition, London: Sweet & Maxwell 2003.

Oliver & Roth 2004

Peter Oliver & Wulf-Henning Roth, 'The internal market and the four freedoms', *CML Rev* 2004, 407-441.

Palermo 2001

Francesco Palermo, 'The Use of Minority Languages: Recent Developments in EC Law and Judgments of the EC', *MJ* 2001, 299-318.

Pannick 1985

David Pannick, *Sex Discrimination Law*, Oxford: Clarendon Press 1985.

Peers 1995

Steve Peers, 'Indirect rights for third-country service providers confirmed', *EL Rev* 1995, 303-309.

Peers 1997

Steve Peers, '"Social Advantages" and Discrimination in Employment: Case Law Confirmed and Clarified', *ELRev* 1997, 157-165.

Peers 2002

Steve Peers, 'Free Movement of Capital: Learning Lessons or Slipping on Spilt Milk', in: Catharine Barnard & Scott Joanne (eds), *The Law of the Single European Market. Unpacking the Premises*, Oxford/Portland, Oregon: Hart Publishing 2002, 332-349.

Pennings 2003

Frans Pennings, *Introduction to European Social Security Law*, 4th edition, Antwerp/Oxford/New York: Intersentia 2003.

Pernice 2003

Ingolf Pernice, 'Der verfassungsrechtliche Status der Unionsbürger im Vorfeld des Vertrages über eine Verfassung für Europa', in: Ninon Colneric, David Edward, Jean-Pierre Puissochet & Dámaso Ruiz-Jarabo Colomer (eds), *Une communauté de droit. Festschrift für Gil Carlos Rodriguez Iglesias*, Berlin: BWV Berliner Wissenschafts-Verlag 2003, 177-194.

Peter 1988

Gabriele Peter, *Frauendiskriminierung durch Teilzeitbeschäftigung, insbesondere bei betrieblichen Sozialleistungen und der Vergütung von Überstunden*, Frankfurt a.M./Bern/New York/Paris: Peter Lang 1988.

Peters 1996

Anne Peters, 'The Many Meanings of Equality and Positive Action in Favour of Women under European Community Law. A Conceptual Analysis', *European Law Journal* 1996, 177-196.

Peters 1999

Anne Peters, *Women, Quotas and Constitutions. A Comparative Study of Affirmative Action for Women under American, German, European Community and International Law*, The Hague/London/Boston: Kluwer Law International 1999.

Peters & Snellaers 2001

Cees Peters & Margreet Snellaers, 'Non-discrimination and tax law: structure and comparison of the various non-discrimination clauses', *EC Tax Review* 2001, 13-18.

Pfarr 1988

Heide M. Pfarr, 'Die mittelbare Diskriminierung von Frauen im Erwerbsleben – Chancen eines neuen Rechtsinstitutes', in: Ute Gerhard & Jutta Limbach (eds), *Rechtsalltag von Frauen*, Frankfurt am Main: Suhrkamp 1988, 33-45.

Pfarr & Bertelsmann 1989

Heide Pfarr & Klaus Bertelsmann, *Diskriminierung im Erwerbsleben. Ungleichbehandlungen von Frauen und Männern in der Bundesrepublik Deutschland*, Baden-Baden: Nomos 1989.

Pieter van der Mei 2002

Anne Pieter van der Mei, 'Cross-border Access to Health Care within the European Union: Some Reflections on *Geraerts-Smits and Peerbooms* and *Vanbraekel*', *MJ* 2002, 189-213.

Pijnacker Hordijk & Van der Bend 1999

E.H. Pijnacker Hordijk & G.W. van der Bend, *Aanbestedingsrecht*, 2nd edition, Den Haag: SDU Uitgevers 1999.

Pintens 1995

Walter Pintens, (Case note on *Konstantinidis*), *Zeitschrift für europäisches Privatrecht* 1995, 92-104.

Pirstner-Ebner 2004

Renate Pirstner-Ebner, 'Neue Gemeinschaftsentwicklungen im Bereich des Gender Mainstreaming', *EuZW* 2004, 205-209.

Piso 1998

Ingeborg Yvonne Piso, *De rechter klem tussen discriminatie en rechtvaardiging. Jurisprudentie over gelijke behandeling van mannen en vrouwen in de sociale zekerheid*, Den Haag: Sdu Uitgevers 1998.

Plender 1982

Richard Plender, 'Equal Pay for Men and Women: Two Recent Decisions of the European Court', *American Journal of Comparative Law* 1982, 627-653.

Plender 1995

Richard Plender, 'Equality and Non-Discrimination in the Law of the European Union', *Pace University School of Law International Law Review* Winter 1995, 57-80.

Plötscher 2003

Stefan Plötscher, *Der Begriff der Diskriminierung im Europäischen Gemeinschaftsrecht*, Berlin: Duncker & Humblot 2003.

Poiares Maduro 2000

Miguel Poiares Maduro, 'The scope of European Remedies: The Case of Purely Internal Situations and Reverse Discrimination', in: Claire Kilpatrick, Tonia Novitz & Paul Skidmore (eds), *The Future of Remedies in Europe*, Oxford: Hart Publishing 2000, 117-140.

Poma 1992
Cristina Poma, 'La libera circolazione dei professionisti e il riconoscimento dei titoli di studio', *Diritto comunitario e degli scambi internazionali* 1992, 669-676.

Powers 1996
Madison Powers, 'Forget about equality', *Kennedy Institute of Ethics Journal* 1996, 129-144.

Prechal 1985
Sacha Prechal, 'Gelijke behandeling in de rechtspraak van het Europese Hof van Justitie', *Nemesis* 1985, 167-176.

Prechal 1991
Sacha Prechal, (Case note on *Dekker*), *SEW* 1991, 665-669.

Prechal 1993
Sacha Prechal, 'Combatting indirect discrimination in Community Law context', *Legal Issues of European Integration* 1993, 81-97.

Prechal 2004
Sacha Prechal, 'Equality of treatment, non-discrimination and social policy: achievements in three themes', *CML Rev* 2004, 533-551.

Priebe 1984
Reinhard, 'Der Alkohol in der Rechtsprechung des Gerichts der Europäischen Gemeinschaften – oder: ein Beitrag zum Verständnis supranationaler Rechtsprechung', in: Dieter C. Umbach, Richard Urban, Roland Fritz, Horst-Eberhard Böttcher & Jochen von Bargen (eds), *Das wahre Verfassungsrecht. Zwischen Lust und Leistung*, Gedächtnisschrift für F.G. Nagelmann, Baden-Baden: Nomos, 1984, 147-159.

Puissochet 2002
Jean-Pierre Puissochet, 'Problems of interpretation by the European Court of Justice of Community legislation on equal treatment for men and women', *Amicus Curia* 2002, 19-24.

Quigley 1997
Conor Quigley, 'Equal Treatment, the Internal Market and Indirect Taxation', in: Alan Dashwood & Síofra O'Leary, *The Principle of Equal Treatment in E.C. Law*, London/Dublin/Hong Kong: Sweet & Maxwell 1997, 168-289.

Rating 1994
Stefan Rating, *Mittelbare Diskriminierung der Frau im Erwerbsleben nach europäischem Gemeinschaftsrecht. Richterrecht des EuGH und die Voraussetzungen seiner Rezeption am Beispiel Spaniens und der Bundesrepublik*, Baden-Baden: Nomos 1994.

Refaeil & Siegwart 1997
Nora Refaeil & Karine Siegwart, 'Das Konzept der mittelbaren Diskriminierung in europäischen und schweizerischen Recht', in: N. Refaeil, K. Siegwart, S. Strahm & E. Baumgarnter (eds), *Die Gleichbehandlung von Mann und Frau im europäischen und schweizerischen Recht. Ausgewählte Fragen*, Swiss Papers on European Integration 9, Bern: Stämpfli/Zürich: Schulthess 1997, 5-37.

Riegel 1978
Reinhard Riegel, 'Arbeitsplatzschutzgesetz und Europäisches Gemeinschaftsrecht', *Betriebs-Berater* 1978, 1422-1423.

Rodière 1989

Pierre Rodière, 'Droit social: famille et égalité de traitement', *RTDE* 1989, 297-312.

Rodière 1990

Pierre Rodière, (Case note on *Rush Portuguesa*), *RTDE* 1990, 635-640.

Rodière 1991

Pierre Rodière, 'Sur les effets directifs du droit (social) communautaire', *RTDE* 1991, 565-586.

Rodrigues Iglesias 2000

Gil Carlos Rodrigues Iglesias, 'Drinks in Luxembourg. Alcoholic Beverages and the Case Law of the European Court of Justice', in: David O'Keeffe (ed; associate editor: Antonio Bavasso), *Judicial Review in European Union Law. Liber amicorum in Honour of Lord Slynn of Hadley*, The Hague/London/Boston: Kluwer Law International 2000, 523-539.

Romanoli 1973

Umberto Romanoli, 'Il principio d'ugualianza sostanziale', *Rivista trimestriale di diritto e procedura civile* 1973, 1283-1330.

Rossi 2000

Matthias Rossi, 'Das Diskriminierungsverbot nach Art. 12 EGV', *Europarecht* 2000, 197-217.

Roth 1993 (Bachmann)

W.-H. Roth, (Case note on *Bachmann*), *CML Rev* 30 (1993) 387-395.

Roth 1993 (Kraus)

W.-H. Roth, (Case note on *Kraus*), *CML Rev* 30 (1993) 1251-1258.

Roth 1993 (Säger)

Wulf-Henning Roth, (Case note on *Säger*), *CML Rev.* 1993, 145-154.

Roth 1997

Wulf-Henning Roth, 'Die Niederlassungsfreiheit zwischen Beschränkungs- und Diskriminierungsverbot', in: Wolfgang Schön Wolfgang (ed), *Gedächtnisschrift für Brigitte Knobbe-Keuk*, Köln: Verlag Dr. Otto Schmidt 1997, 729-742.

Rott 2003

Rott P., 'Minimum harmonization for the completion of the internal market? The example of consumer sales law', *CML Rev* 2003, 1107-1135.

Ruge 2002

Reinhard Ruge, 'Goldene Aktien und das EG-Recht', *EuZW* 2002, 421-424, at 422

Rust 1996

Ursula Rust, 'Reach and Substance of the Principle of Equal Treatment in Social Security Law Under European Community and German Constitutional Law', *Cardozo Women's Law Journal* 1996, 427-449.

Rust 1997

Ursula Rust, 'Nadelöhr und Einschätzungsprärogative – die Rechtsprechung des Europäischen Gerichtshofes zur (un)mittelbaren Geschlechterdiskriminierung im Sozialrecht', *Streit* 1997, 147-154.

Safferling 2000

Christoph J.M. Safferling, (Case note on *Bickel and Franz*), *American Journal of International Law* 2000, 155-159.

Sanfilippo 1990

Luca Sanfilippo, 'Divieto di discriminazione e appalti pubblici di forniture', *Diritto comunitario e degli scambi internazionali* 1990, 419-423;

Schefer 2002

Markus Schefer, *Die Kerngehalte von Grundrechten. Geltung, Dogmatik, inhaltliche Ausgestaltung*, Berne: Stämpfli 2002.

Schermers 1975

Hein G. Schermers, (Case note on *Airola*), *Ars Aequi* 1975, 519-520.

Schiek 1992

Dagmar Schiek, *Nachtarbeitsverbot für Arbeiterinnen. Gleichberechtigung durch Deregulierung?*, Baden-Baden: Nomos 1992.

Schiek 1997

Dagmar Schiek, *Europäisches Arbeitsrecht*, Baden-Baden: Nomos 1997.

Schiek 2000

Dagmar Schiek, 'Acceptance of Non-Discrimination as a Principle of (Consumer) Contract Law – and Future Legislation on Art. 13 EC Treaty', in: Pauline C. Westerman C. (ed), *Non-Discrimination and Diversity*, Den Haag: Boom Juridische Uitgevers 2000, 27-41.

Schilling 1996

Theodor Schilling, 'Singularia non sunt extendenda. Die Auslegung der Ausnahme in der Rechtsprechung des EuGH', *Europarecht* 1996, 44-57.

Schimana 1978

Rudolf Schimana, 'Arbeitsplatzschutzgesetz und ausländische Arbeitnehmer', *Betriebs-Berater* 1978, 1017-1019.

Schindler 1957

Dietrich Schindler, *Gleichberechtigung von Individuen als Problem des Völkerrechts*, Habilitation University of Zurich, Winterthur: Verlag P. G. Keller 1957.

Schlosser 1995

Peter Schlosser, (Case note on *Mund & Fester*), *Zeitschrift für Europäisches Privatrecht* 1995, 253-257.

Schmidt 1995

Marlene Schmidt, *Teilzeitarbeit in Europa. Eine Analyse der gemeinschaftsrechtlichen Regelungsbestrebungen auf vergleichender Grundlage des englischen und des deutschen Rechts*, Baden-Baden: Nomos 1995.

Schmidt 1998

Marlene Schmidt, 'Die neue EG-Richtlinie zur Teilzeitarbeit', *NZA* 1998, 576-581.

Schneider 2003

Christian F. Schneider, 'Kapitalsverkehrsfreiheit für EWR-Bürger und Beschränkungen für den Grundstückserwerb', *European Law Reporter* 2003, 380-387.

Schneider 1996

Hartmut Schneider, 'Zum Funktionswandel der Grundfreiheiten des EGV und zu seinen Auswirkungen auf das nationale Recht', *Neue Justiz* 1996, 512-515.

Schockweiler 1991

Ferdinand Schockweiler, 'La portée du principe de non-discrimination de l'article 7 du traité C.E.E.', *Rivista di diritto Europeo* 1991, 3-24.

Schockweiler 1995

Ferdinand Schockweiler, (Case note on *Konstantinidis*), *European Review of Private Law* 1995, 496-503.

Schön 1997

Wolfgang Schön, 'Europäische Kapitalsverkehrsfreiheit und nationales Steuerrecht', in: Schön Wolfgang (ed), *Gedächtnisschrift für Brigitte Knobbe-Keuk*, Köln: Verlag Dr. Otto Schmidt 1997, 743-777.

Schroeder 1994

Werner Schroeder, 'Kein Glücksspiel ohne Grenzen', *Europäische Grundrechtezeitung* 1994, 373-380.

Schutte-Feenstra 2002

J.N. Schutte-Feenstra, (Case note on the *Golden Shares* cases), *Ondernemingsrecht* 2002, 273-276.

Schwander 1994

Ivo Schwander, (Case note on *Mund & Fester*), *AJP* 1994, 795-797.

Schwarze Commentary 2000

Jürgen Schwarze (ed), *EU-Kommentar*, Baden-Baden: Nomos 2000.

Schweitzer & Hummer 1996

Schweitzer Michael & Waldemar Hummer, *Europarecht. Das Recht der Europäischen Union – Das Recht der Europäischen Gemeinschaften (EGKS, EG, EAG) – mit Schwerpunkt EG*, 5th edition, Neuwied/Kriftel/Berlin: Luchterhand 1996.

Scovazzi 1979

Tullio Scovazzi, 'Le competenze degli Stati Membri della CEE in materia di conservazione delle risorse ittiche', *Diritto comunitario e degli scambi internazionali* 1979, 57-68.

Scott 2002

Joanne Scott, 'Mandatory or Imperative Requirements in the EU and the WTO', in: Catherine Barnard & Scott Joanne (eds), *The Law of the Single European Market. Unpacking the Premises*, Oxford/Portland, Oregon: Hart Publishing 2002, 269-293.

Sedler 1999

Robert A. Sedler, 'The Role of 'Intent' in Discrimination Analysis', in: Titia Loenen & Peter R. Rodrigues (eds), *Non-Discrimination Law: Comparative Perspectives*, The Hague/London/Boston: Kluwer Law International 1999, 91-103.

Seeland 1982

Rolf Seeland, 'Das Gleichberechtigungssystem in den USA und in den Mitgliedstaaten der EG unter besonderer Berücksichtigung des Verhältnisses von Männern und Frauen im Arbeitsleben', *ZvglRwiss* 1982, 286-319.

Selmi 1999

Michael Selmi, 'Indirect Discrimination: a Perspective from the United States', in: Titia Loenen & Peter R. Rodrigues (eds), *Non-Discrimination Law: Comparative Perspectives*, The Hague/London/Boston: Kluwer Law International 1999, 213-222.

Senden 1996

Linda Senden, 'Positive Action in the EU Put to the Test. A Negative Score?', *MJ* 1996, 146-164.

Sewandono 2001

I. Sewandono, 'De Rassenrichtlijn en de Algemene wet gelijke behandeling', *SEW* 2001, 218-226.

Shaw 1989

Josephine Shaw, 'Sick pay for cleaners' (Case note on *Rinner-Kühn*), *EL Rev* 1989, 428-434.

Shaw 1990

Josephine Shaw, 'The burden of proof and the legality of supplementary payments in equal pay cases', *EL Rev* 1990, 260-266.

Shaw 1991

Josephine Shaw, 'Pregnancy discrimination in sex discrimination', *EL Rev* 1991, 313-320.

Shaw 2001

Jo Shaw, 'Gender and the Court of Justice', in: Gráinne de Búrca & J.H.H. Weiler (eds), *The European Court of Justice*, Oxford: Oxford University Press 2001, 87-142.

Shrubshall 1987

Vivien Shrubsall, 'Article 119, Pensions and Part-time Workers', *ILJ* 1987, 52-54.

Shuibne 2002

Niamh Nic Shuibne, 'The free movement of goods and Article 28 EC: an evolving framework', *EL Rev* 2002, 408-425.

Sideek 1999

Mohamed Sideek, *European Community Law on the Free Movement of Capital and the EMU*, The Hague/Boston/London: Kluwer Law International and Stockholm: Norstedts Juridik 1999.

Sjerps 1994

Ine Sjerps, 'Het concept van indirecte discriminatie', in: T. van Vleuten (ed), *In concreto. Bijdragen over rechtsvorming gelijke behandeling*, Commissie Gelijke Behandeling van mannen en vrouwen bij de arbeid, Den Haag: Ministerie van SZW 1994, 87-98.

Sjerps 1999

Ine Sjerps, 'Effect and Justification: Or how to Establish a Prima Facie Case of Indirect Sex Discrimination', in: Titia Loenen & Peter R. Rodrigues (eds), *Non-Discrimination Law: Comparative Perspectives*, The Hague/London/Boston: Kluwer Law International 1999, 236-247.

Slot 1995 (CML Rev)

Piet Jan Slot, (Case note on *Corsica Ferries Italia*), *CML Rev.* 1995, 1287-1294.

Slot 1995 (SEW)

Piet Jan Slot, (Case note on *Corsica Ferries Italia*), *SEW* 1995, 63-65.

Smith 1994

Lesley Jane Smith, 'Postgraduate degrees, vocational training and reverse discrimination: the narrow divide', *EL Rev* 1994, 67-75.

Snaith 1981

Ian Snaith, 'Current survey. Free movement of workers and social security. Two more equal pay cases from the United Kingdom', *EL Rev* 1981, 193-198.

Snell 2002

Jukka Snell, *Goods and Services in EC Law. A Study of the Relationship Between the Freedoms*, Oxford: Oxford University Press 2002.

Snyder 1993 (Effectiveness)

Francis Snyder, 'The Effectiveness of European Community Law: Institutions, Processes, Tools and Techniques', *Modern Law Review* 1993, 19-54.

Snyder 1993 (The Community)

Francis Snyder (with the collaboration of Han Somsen and Henrik Duedahl Hoyer), 'The Community as Employer. Staff Regulations: an Aspect of European Community Law and its Relevance to Lesbians and Gay Men', in: WAALDIJK Kees/CLAPHAM Andrew (eds), *Homosexuality: A European Community Issue. Essays on Lesbian and Gay Rights in European Law and Policy*, Dordrecht: Martinus Nijhoff Publishers 1993, 247-260.

Sohrab 1994

Julia Adiba Sohrab, *Sexing the Benefit: Women, Social Security and Financial Independence in EC Equality Law*, Ph.D. thesis, Florence: European University Institute 1994.

Somek 2001

Alexander Somek, 'Equality and Constitutional Indeterminacy. An Interpretative Perspective on the European Economic Constitution', *European Public Law* 2001, 171-195.

Sommer 1998

Imke Sommer, *Zivile Rechte für Antigone. Zu den rechtstheoretischen Implikationen der Theorie von Luce Irigaray*, Baden-Baden: Nomos 1998.

Speyer 1991

Stefan Speyer, 'Anwendung der Cassis de Dijon-Doktrin und Spaltbarkeit reglementierter Tätigkeiten als neue Ettappen der Dienstleistungsfreiheit', *EuZW* 1991, 588-590.

Stadlmeier 1995

Sigmar Stadlmeier, "Contrary to what has previously been decided ...'. The search for the rule goes on', *Legal issues of European integration* 1995/2, 9-33.

Stample 2001

Michèle Stampe, *Das Verbot der indirekten Diskriminierung wegen des Geschlechts. Konzept/ Tatbestand/ Verfassungsrechtliche Zuordnung unter besonderer Berücksichtigung der amerikanischen und europäischen Rechtsentwicklung*, Zürich: Schulthess 2001.

Steen 1998

Steen I., 'Vergoeding van medische zorg over de grens: alleen bij toestemming vooraf ?', *NTER* 1998, 159-163.

Stein 1992

Torsten Stein, (Case note on *Vlassopoulou*), *CML Rev* 1992, 625-636.

Stein 1994

Torsten Stein, (Case note on *Schindler*), *EuZW* 1994, 315.

Steindorff 1965

Ernst Steindorff, *Der Gleichheitssatz im Wirtschaftsrecht des Gemeinsamen Marktes*, Berlin: Walter de Gruyter 1965.

Steindorff 1994

Ernst Steindorff, (Case note on *Allué II*), *Juristenzeitung* 1994, 95-98.

Steiner 1983

Josephine M. Steiner, 'Sex Discrimination under UK and EEC Law: Two Plus Four Equals One', *International and Comparative Law Quarterly* 1983, 399-423.

Steiner & Woods 2003
    Josephine Steiner & Lorna Woods, *Textbook on EC Law*, 8th edition, London: Blackstone 2003.
Steiner 1999
    Oliver Steiner, *Das Verbot der Diskriminierung aufgrund des Geschlechts im Erwerbsleben*, Basel/Genf/München: Helbing & Lichtenhahn 1999.
Steyger 1995
    Elies Steyger, (Case note on *Helmig*), *Nemesis* 1995 nr. 3, katern, 9-10.
Steyger 2002
    Elies Steyger, 'National Health Care Systems Under Fire (but not too heavily)', *Legal Issues of Economic Integration* 2002, 97-107.
Strauss 1998
    David Strauss, 'The Illusory Distinction between Equality of Opportunity and Equality of Result', in: Neil Devins & Davison M. Douglas (eds), *Redefining Equality*, New York/Oxford: Oxford University Press 1998, 51-64.
Streil 1975
    Jochen Streil, 'Grundrechtsverwirklichung am Beispiel des Grundsatzes der Gleichbehandlung von Mann und Frau', *EuGRZ* 1975, 321-323.
Streinz & Leible 2000
    Rudolf Streinz & Stefan Leible, 'Die unmittelbare Drittwirkung der Grundfreiheiten', *EuZW* 2000, 459-467.
Sulds & Israel 1999
    Jonathan L. Sulds & Jonathan L. Israel, 'Discrimination by Association', reprinted from the New York Law Journal of 28 July 1999, available at www.akingump.com/docs/publication/275.pdf.
Sundberg-Weitman 1977
    Brita Sundberg-Weitman, *Discrimination on Grounds of Nationality. Free Movement of Workers and Freedom of Establishment under the EEC Treaty*, Amsterdam/New York/Oxford: North-Holland Publishing Company 1977.
Szyszczak 1981
    Erika Szyszczak, 'Differences in pay for part-time work', *Modern Law Review* 1981, 672-682.
Szyszczak 1990
    Erika Szyszczak, 'Recent Cases. Equal Opportunities Law', *ILJ* 1990, 114-120.
Szyszczak 1992
    Erika Szyszczak, 'Race Discrimination: The Limits of Market Equality', in: Bob Hepple & Erika Szyszczak (eds), *Discrimination: the Limits of Law*, London: Mansell 1992, 125-147.
Szyszczak 1996
    Erica Szyszczak, 'Community Law on Pregnancy and Maternity', in: Tamara K. Hervey & David O. O'Keeffe (eds), *Sex Equality Law in the Euroepan Union*, Chichester: John Wiley 1996, 51-62.
Szyszczak 1997
    Erika Szyszczak, 'Building a European Constitutional Order: Prospects for a General Non-Discrimination Standard', in: Alan Dashwood & Síofra O'Leary (eds), *The Principle of Equal Treatment in E.C. Law*, London/Dublin/Hong Kong: Sweet & Maxwell 1997, 35-58.

Szyszczak 2002

Erika Szyszczak, 'Golden Shares and Market Governance', *Legal Issues of Economic Integration* 2002, 255-284.

Temmink 1995

H.A.G. Temmink, 'Minimumnormen in EG-richtlijnen', *SEW* 1995, 79-106.

Temmink 1998

H.A.G. Temmink, (Case note on *Decker* and *Kohll*), *TvC* 1998, 273-283.

Temple-Lang 1990

John Temple-Lang, 'Community Constitutional Law: Article 5 EEC Treaty', *CML Rev* 1990, 645-681.

Terra & Wattel 2001

Peter Wattel, *European Tax Law*, 3rd edition, Deventer: Fed 2001.

Thömmes 1997

Otmar Thömmes, 'Tatbestandsmässigkeit und Rechtfertigungen steuerlicher Diskriminierungen nach EG-Recht', in Wolfang Schön (ed), *Gedächtnisschrift für Brigitte Knobbe-Keuk*, Köln: Verlag Dr. Otto Schmidt 1997, 795-845.

Thömmes & Kiblböck 1993

Otmar Thömmes & Ingrid Kiblböck, 'The Tax Treatment of Non-Resident Taxpayers in the Light of the Most Recent Decision of the European Court of Justice', *EC Tax Review* 1993, 158-163.

Thümmel 1994

Roderich C. Thümmel, 'Der Arrestgrund der Auslandsvollstreckung im Fadenkreuz des Europäischen Rechts', *EuZW* 1994, 242-245.

Timmermans 1978

C.W.A. Timmermans, (Case note on *Sea Fisheries*), *SEW* 1978, 582-589.

Timmermans 1981

C.W.A. Timmermans, (Case note on *Debauve*), *SEW* 1981, 137-142.

Timmermans 1982

Christiaan Timmermans, 'Verboden discriminatie of (geboden) differentiatie', *SEW* 1982, 427-460.

Timmermans 1983

C.W.A. Timmermans, (Case note on *Seco*), *SEW* 1983, 314-319.

Timmermans 1989

C.W.A. Timmermans, (Case note on *Heylens*), *Ars Aequi* 1989, 288-291.

Timmermans 2003

Christiaan Timmermans, 'Lifting the Veil of Union Citizens' Rights', in: Ninon Colneric, David Edward, Jean-Pierre Puissochet & Dámaso Ruiz-Jarabo Colomer (eds), *Une communauté de droit. Festschrift für Gil Carlos Rodriguez Iglesias*, Berlin: BWV Berliner Wissenschafts-Verlag 2003, 195-206.

Tinnion 1977

John Tinnion, 'Charges having equivalent effect. Parafiscal charges in the national court', *EL Rev* 1977, 359-363.

Tizzano 1974

A. Tizzano, (case note on *Sotgiu*), *Foro italiano* 1974 IV210-211.

Tobler 1996

Christa Tobler, 'Harmonisierung im EG-Recht am Beispiel des Mutterschaftsurlaubes. Von einem Bermuda-Dreieck im EG-Recht', in: Francois Baur & Georges Baur (eds), *Aktuelle Rechtsfragen 1996. Liber amicorum zum sechzigsten Geburtstag von Theodor Bühler*, Zürich: Schulthess 1996, 127-148.

Tobler 1997

Christa Tobler, 'Quoten und das Verständnis der Rechtsgleichheit der Geschlechter im schweizerischen Verfassungsrecht, unter vergleichender Berücksichtigung der EuGH-Entscheidung *Kalanke*', in: Kathrin Arioli (ed), *Frauenförderung durch Quoten*, Basel/Frankfurt a.M.: Helbing & Lichtenhahn 1997, 49-134.

Tobler 1998

Christa Tobler, 'Zum Begriff der Diskriminierung aufgrund des Geschlechts', *Jus & News* 1998, 62-69.

Tobler 1999

Christa Tobler, '"Qui dit temps partiel, pense femmes" – Part-time Work in the Context of Indirect Discrimination', in: Yota Kravaritou (ed), 'The Regulation of Working Time in the European Union. Gender Approach', Bruxelles a.o.: P.I.E.-Peter Lang 1999, 383-410.

Tobler 2000 (Women's Clauses)

Christa Tobler, 'Encore: "Women's Clauses" in public procurement under Community law', *EL Rev* 2000, 618-631.

Tobler 2000 (Sex Equality Law)

Christa Tobler, 'Sex Equality Law under the Treaty of Amsterdam', *European Journal of Law Reform* 2000, 135-153.

Tobler 2001 (Same-Sex Couples)

Christa Tobler, 'Same-Sex Couples under the law of the EU', *AJP* 2001, 269-286.

Tobler 2001 (Parité)

Christa Tobler, 'Parité – trois syllabes magiques. Oder: Wie Frankreich zur Geschlechter-quote kam', in: Verein Pro Fri (ed), *Recht Richtung Frauen*, Lachen/St. Gallen: 2001, 199-223.

Tobler 2001 (Schnorbus)

Christa Tobler, (Case note on *Schnorbus*), *SEW* 2001, 238-240.

Tobler 2001 (Begriff der Ehe)

Christa Tobler, 'Der Begriff der Ehe im EG-Recht', *Die Praxis des Familienrechts* 2001, 479-498.

Tobler 2001 (Rechtvaardiging)

Christa Tobler, 'Rechtvaardiging van direct onderscheid in het EG-recht', *Nemesis* 2001, 121-127.

Tobler 2002 (Rechtsgelijkheid)

Christa Tobler, 'Rechtsgelijkheid en voorkeursmaatregelen in het EG-Recht', *Nederlands tijdschrift voor de mensenrechten/NJCM-Bulletin* 2002, 360-374.

Tobler 2002 (MacKinnon)

Christa Tobler, Book review on: Catharine A. MacKinnon, 'Sex Equality', University Casebook Series, New York: Foundation Press 2001, *The Modern Law Review* 2002, 960-962.

Tobler 2003

Christa Tobler, 'Positive action under the revised second equal treatment directive', in: AFFJ & EWLA (ed), *L'Egalité entre femmes et homes et la vie professionnelle. Le point sur les dévelopments actuels en Europe*, Paris: Editions Dalloz 2003, 59-92.

Tobler 2004

Christa Tobler, (Case note on Case E-1/02 *EFTA Surveillance Authority v Norway*), *CML Rev* 2004, 245-260.

Trakman 1994

Leon E. Trakman, 'Substantive Equality in Constitutional Jurisprudence: Meaning Within Meaning', *Canadian Journal of Law and Jurisprudence* 1994, 27-42.

Traversa 1991

Enrico Traversa, 'Jurisprudence communautaire en matière de politique sociale. Année 1990', *RTDE* 1991, 425-439.

Tridimas 1999

Takis Tridimas, *The General Principles of EC Law*, New York: Oxford University Press 1999.

Tridimas 2000

Takis Tridimas, 'Enforcing Community Rights in National Courts: Some Recent Developments', in: Claire Kilpatrick, Tonia Novitz & Paul Skidmore (eds), *The Future of Remedies in Europe*, Oxford: Hart Publishing 2000, 35-50.

UK Department of Trade and Industry 2002

UK Department of Trade and Industry, Consultation Document *Towards Equality and Diversity. Implementing the Employment and Race Directive*, published in spring 2002, available at http://www2.dti.gov.uk/er/equality/.

Usher 1998

John A. Usher, *General Principles of EC Law*, London/New York: Longman 1998.

Usher 2001

J.A. Usher, *EC Agricultural Law*, 2nd edition, Oxford: Oxford University Press 2001.

Van de Meent 1995

Gerrit W.A. van de Meent, *Overheidsbestedingen: De EG-rechtelijke context*, Ph.D. thesis, G.W.A. van de Meent: Hilversum 1995.

Van der Burgh 1998

F.H. van der Burgh, (Case note on *Kohll*), *AB Rechtspraak bestuursrecht* 1998 nr. 255, 1204-1211.

Van der Burgh 2001

F.H. van der Burgh, (Case note on *Geraerts-Smits and Peerbooms*), *AB Administratiefrechtelijke beslissingen* 2001 nr. 241, 1154-1168, at 1167.

Van der Mei 1998 (Decker)

A.P. van der Mei, 'Decker en Kohll: Op weg naar een vrij verkeer voor patiënten in de Europese Gemeenschap', *Sociaal recht* 1998, 187-196.

Van der Mei 1998 (Cross-Border Access)
A.P. van der Mei, 'Cross-Border Access to Medical Care within the European Union – Some Reflections on the Judgments in *Decker* and *Kohll*', *MJ* 1998, 277-297.

Van der Steen 2000
I. van der Steen, (Case note on *Dafeki*), *SEW* 2000, 31-35.

Van de Wetering 1996
G.C. van de Wetering, 'Bachmann gesneuveld, Lidstaten gekneveld, Europa de overwinnaar?', *Weekblad fiscaal recht* 1996, 98-104.

Van Empel 1993
M. van Empel, (Case note on *Säger*), *SEW* 1993, 668-670.

Van Gerven 1971
Walter van Gerven, 'Schets van een Belgisch Economisch Grondslagenrecht', *SEW* 1971, 404-428.

Van Gerven 1975
Walter van Gerven, 'Het economisch recht van de lid-staten van de Europese Gemeenschappen in een economische en monetaire unie', *SEW* 1975, 295-307.

Van Gerven 1977
Walter van Gerven, 'Contribution de l'arrêt Defrenne au developpement du droit communautaire', *CDE* 1977, 131-143.

Van Horzen 1993
F. van Horzen, 'De vaste inrichting in de gemeenschappelijke markt', *Weekblad voor fiscaal recht* 1993, 1875-1884

Vanistendael 1994
Frans Vanistendael, 'The limits to the new Community tax order', *CML Rev* 1994, 293-314.

Van Raad 1986
Cornelis van Raad, *Non-discrimination in International Tax Law*, Deventer: Kluwer 1986.

Van Raad 1995
Kees van Raad, 'The Impact of the EC Treaty's Fundamental Freedoms Provisions on EU Member States' Taxation in Border-Crossing Situations – Current State of Affairs', *EC Tax Review* 1995, 190-201.

Van Raad 2004
Kees van Raad, *2004/2005 Materials on International & EC Tax Law*, volume 2, 4th edition, Leiden: International Tax Center 2004.

Van Raepenbusch 1986
Sean van Raepenbusch, 'Les limites de la coordination communautaire des législations nationales en matière de sécurité sociale au regard du principe de l'égalité de traitement après l'arrêt Pinna', *CDE* 1986, 475-524.

Van Raepenbusch 1998
Sean van Raepenbusch, 'Le libre choix par les citoyens européens des produits médicaux et des prestataires de soins, conséquence du marché intérieur', *CDE* 1998, 683-697.

V.C. 1979
V.C., (Case note on *Sea Fisheries*), *Journal de droit international* 1979, 923-929, at 928.

Vegter 2000

Marlies Vegter, 'Zwangerschap en discriminatie. De pijnpunten van het gesloten stelsel van discriminatiegronden', *Nemesis* 2000, 118-125.

Veldman 1995

Albertine Veldman, *Effectuering van sociaal-economisch recht volgens de chaostheorie. Beleidsinstrumentering en rechtshandhaving van (supra)nationaal gelijke-behandelingsrecht (The Effectiveness of Social Economic Law According to the Chaos Theory. Policies and Enforcement of (Supra)National Equality Law)*, Ph.D. thesis, Utrecht: Utrecht University 1995.

Veldman 1996

Albertine Veldman, 'De bescheiden functie van het juridisch gelijkheidsbeginsel. Het fundamentele verschil tussen juridische leerstukken en wetenschappelijke concepten binnen vrouw en recht', *Nemesis* 1996, 31-38.

Veldman 1998

Albertine Veldman, 'Het homoseksuele paar, hun treinkaartjes en het recht', *Nemesis* 1998, 1-4.

Veldman 2001

Albertine Veldman, 'De nieuwe Europese arresten over voorkeursbeleid. Abrahamsson en Schnorbus', *Nemesis* 2001, 116-120.

Verhoosel 2002

Gaëtan Verhoosel, *National Treatment and WTO Dispute Settlement. Adjudicating the Boundaries of Regulatory Autonomy*, Oxford/Portland Oregon: Hart Publishing 2002.

VerLoren van Themaat 1977

P. VerLoren van Themaat, 'Nogmaals het Defrenne-arrest: een juiste sprongmutatie in de rechtspraak?', *SEW* 1977, 90-95.

Verschuur 1995

René Verschuur, (Case note on *Mund & Fester*), *European Review of Private Law* 1995, 613-648.

Vick 2001

Douglas W. Vick, 'Disparate effects and objective justification in sex discrimination law', *International Journal of Discrimination and the Law* 2001, 3-38.

Vierdag 1973

Eduard Vierdag, *The Concept of Discrimination in International Law*, Den Haag: Nijhoff 1973.

Vizkelety 1999

Béatrice Vizkelety, 'Adverse Effect Discrimination in Canada: Crossing the Rubicon from Formal to Substantive Equality', in: Titia Loenen & Peter R. Rodrigues (eds), *Non-Discrimination Law: Comparative Perspectives*, The Hague/London/Boston: Kluwer Law International 1999, 223-236.

Vogel-Polsky 1990

Eliane Vogel-Polsky, 'Unlawful Discrimination in Employment – International Law and Community Law: Their Interrelationship with Domestic Law', *Georgia Journal of International and Comparative Law* 1990, 3-12.

Vogel-Polsky 1998

Eliane Vogel-Polsky, 'La construction socio-sexuée du droit du travail en Belgique', in Yota Kravaritou (ed), *The Sex of Labour Law in Europe. Le Sexe du droit du travail en Europe*, The Hague/London/Boston: Kluwer Law International 1998, 31-51.

von Bahr 2003

Stig von Bahr, 'Le législateur, la Cour de justice et l'harmonisation des impôts directs', in: Ninon Colneric, David Edward, Jean-Pierre Puissochet & Dámaso Ruiz-Jarabo Colomer (eds), *Une communauté de droit. Festschrift für Gil Carlos Rodriguez Iglesias*, Berlin: BWV Berliner Wissenschafts-Verlag 2003, 433-442.

von der Groeben & Schwarze Commentary 2004

Hans von der Groeben & Jürgen Schwarze (eds), *Kommentar zum Vertrag über die Europäische Union und zur Gründung der Europäischen Gemeinschaft*, 6th edition, Baden-Baden: Nomos 2004.

von Leyden 1985

Wolfgang von Leyden, *Aristotle on equality and justice: his political argument*, London: Basingstoke 1985.

von Prondzynsky & Richards 1995

Ferdinand von Prondzynsky & Wendy Richards, 'Equal Opportunities in the Labour Market: Tackling Indirect Sex Discrimination', *European Public Law* 1995, 117-135.

von Toggenburg 2000

Gabriel von Toggenburg, 'Horizontale Drittwirkung der Personenfreizügigkeit vor dem Hintergrund der Südtiroler Autonomie', *European Law Reporter* 2000, 242-247.

Voogsgeerd 2000

Herman H. Voogsgeerd, 'The Approach of the EC Court of Justice Towards the Concept of Indirect Discrimination: A Unique Approach?', in: Pauline C. Westerman (ed), *Non-Discrimination and Diversity*, Den Haag: Boom Juridische Uitgevers 2000, 67-84.

Waaldijk 1997

Kees Waaldijk, 'Onderscheid wegens geschlachtsgelijkheid. Burgerlijke staat, sexuele gerichtheid of geslacht als grond?', *Nemesis* 1997, 117-120.

Waddington & Bell 2001

Lisa Waddington & Bell Mark Mark, 'More equal than others: distinguishing European Union Equality Directives', *CML Rev* 2001, 587-611.

Waddington & Hendriks 2002

Lisa Waddington & Aart Hendriks, 'The Expanding Concept of Employment Discrimination in Europe: From Direct and Indirect Discrimination to Reasonable Accommodation Discrimination', *The International Journal of Comparative Labour Law and Industrial Relations* 2002, 403-427.

Wägenbaur 1977

Rolf Wägenbaur, 'Das Thieffry-Urteil und das Niederlassungsrecht der Rechtsanwälte in den Europäischen Gemeinschaften', *EuGRZ* 1977, 260-262.

Waelbroeck 1983

M. Waelbroek, 'Mesures d'effet équivalent, discrimination formelle et matérielle dans la jurisprudence de la Cour de Justice', in: *Liber amicorum Frédéric Dumon*, Antwerpen: Kluwer Rechtswetenschappen 1983, 1329-1343.

Wathelet 2002

Melchior Wathelet, 'The Influence of Free Movement of Persons, Services and Capital on National Direct Taxation: Trends in the Case Law of the Court of Justice', in: P. Eeckhout & T. Tridimas (eds), *Yearbook of European Law 2001*, Oxford: Oxford University Press 2002, 1-33.

Watson 1989 (Equal treatment)

Philippa Watson, 'Equal treatment in the award of family allowances', *EL Rev* 1989, 346-351.

Watson 1989 (Free movement)

Philippa Watson, 'Free movement of workers: Recent cases', *EL Rev* 1989, 415-422.

Watson 1995

Philippa Watson, 'Equality of Treatment: A Variable Concept?', *ILJ* 1995, 33-48.

Wattel 1995

Peter J. Wattel, 'Taxing Non-Resident Employees: Coping with Schumacker', *European Taxation* 1995, 347-353.

Wattel 1996

Peter J. Wattel, 'The EC Court's attempts to reconcile the Treaty freedoms with international tax law', *CML Rev.* 1996, 223-254.

Wattel 1997

P.J. Wattel, 'Rechtvaardigingsgronden voor fiscale inbreuk op EG-Verdragsvrijheden', *SEW* 1997, 424-435.

Wattel 1999

P.J. Wattel, 'Het Safir-arrest: Fiscaal onderscheid tussen binnenlands en buitenlands afgesloten kapitaalverzekeringen', *NTER* 1999, 190-196.

Wattel 2004

P.J., Wattel 'Red Herrings in Direct Tax Cases before the ECJ', *Legal Issues of Economic Integration* 2004, 81-95.

Weatherill & Beaumont 1995

Stephen Weatherill & Paul Beaumont, *EC Law. The essential guide to the legal working of the European* Community), 2nd edition, London: Penguin 1995.

Weatherill & Beaumont 1999

Stephen Weatherill & Paul Beaumont, *EU Law. The essential guide to the legal workings of the European Union*, 3rd edition, London: Penguin 1999.

Weiler 2000

J.H.H. Weiler, *The EU, the WTO, and the NAFTA. Towards a Common Law of International Trade?*, Oxford: Oxford University Press 2000.

Weiss 1999

Wolfgang Weiss, 'Nationales Steuerrecht und Niederlassungsfreiheit. Von der Konvergenz der Grundfreiheiten als Beschränkungsverbote zur Auflösung der Differenzierung zwischen unterschiedslosen und unterschiedlichen Massnahmen', *EuZW* 1999, 493-498.

Wentholt 1990
Klaartje Wentholt, *Arbeid en Zorg*, Ph.D. thesis, Amsterdam: Amsterdam University 1990.

Wentholt 1996
Klaartje Wentholt, 'Equality and Gender: The (In)Compatibility of the Legal and the Feminist Debate', in: Yota Kravaritou (ed), *The Sex of Labour Law in Europe*, The Hague/London/Boston: Kluwer Law International 1996, 139-153.

Wentholt 2000
Klaartje Wentholt, 'The Dutch General Act on Equal Treatment', in: Pauline C. Westerman, *Non-Discrimination and Diversity*, Den Haag: Boom Juridische Uitgevers 2000, 43-66.

Wernsmann 1999
Rainer Wernsmann, 'Steuerliche Diskriminierungen und ihre Rechtfertigung durch die Kohärenz des nationalen Rechts – Zur Dogmatik der Schranken der Grundfreiheiten', *Europareacht* 1999, 754-775.

Westen 1982
Peter Westen, 'The Empty Idea of Equality', *Harvard Law Review* 1982, 537-596.

Westen 1981/82
Peter Westen, 'On "Confusing Ideas": Reply', *The Yale Law Journal* 91 (1981/82) 1153-1165.

Westen 1983 (The Meaning of Equality)
Peter Westen, 'The Meaning of Equality in Law, Science, Math, and Morals: A Reply', *Michigan Law Review* 81 (1983) 604-663.

Westen 1983 (To Lure the Tarantula)
Peter Westen, 'To Lure the Tarantula from Its Hole: A Response', *Columbia Law Review* 83 (1983), 1186-1208.

Westen 1990
Peter Westen, *Speaking of Equality. An Analysis of the Rhetorical Force of 'Equality' in Moral and Legal Discourse*, New Jersey: Princeton University Press 1990.

Westerman 2000
Pauline C. Westerman, 'The Principle of Equality as a Heuristic Device', in: Pauline C. Westerman (ed), *Non-Discrimination and Diversity*, Den Haag: Boom Juridische Uitgevers 2000, 115-124.

White 1994
Robin A. White, 'Equality in the Canteen', *El Rev* 1994, 308-313.

Whiteford 1997
Elaine Whiteford, *Adapting to Change: Occupational Pension Schemes, Women and Migrant Workers*, The Hague/London/Boston: Kluwer Law International 1997.

Whittle 1998
Richard Whittle, 'Disability Discrimination and the Amsterdam Treaty', *EL Rev* 1998, 50-58.

Whittle 2002
Richard Whittle, 'The Framework Directive for equal treatment in employment and occupation: an analysis from a disability rights perspective', *EL Rev* 2002, 303-326.

Whittle & Bell 2002
Richard Whittle & Mark Bell, 'Between social policy and Union citizenship: the Framework Directive on equal treatment in employment', *EL Rev* 2002, 677-691.

Williams 1994

David Williams, 'Freedom of establishment and double taxation agreements', *EL Rev* 1994, 313-319.

Winkel & van Borries 1978

K. Winkel & R. van Borries, (Case note on *Sea Fisheries* and the infringement procedure connected with it, Case 88/77 *Commission v Ireland* [1978] ECR 473), *CML Rev* 1978, 494-502.

Wintemute 1995

Robert Wintemute, *Sexual Orientation and Human Rights*, Oxford: Oxford University Press 1995.

Wintemute 1997

Robert Wintemute, 'Recognising New Kinds of Direct Sex Discrimination: Transsexualism, Sexual Orientation and Dress Codes', *The Modern Law Review* 1997, 334-359.

Wintemute 1998

Robert Wintemute, 'When is Pregnancy Discrimination Indirect Discrimination?', *ILJ* 1998, 23-36.

Winter 1991

Jan Winter, 'Public Procurement in the EEC', *CML Rev* 28 (1991) 741-782.

Winter 1998

Regine Winter, *Gleiches Entgelt für gleichwertige Arbeit. Ein Prinzip ohne Praxis*, Baden-Baden: Nomos 1998.

Wisskirchen 1994

Gerlind Wisskirchen, *Mittelbare Diskriminierung von Frauen im Erwerbsleben. Die Rechtsprechung des Bundesgerichts, des Europäischen Gerichtshofes und des U.S. Supreme Court*, Berlin: Duncker & Humblot 1994.

Witteveen 2000

Willem Witteveen, 'Over de vermeende olievlekwerking van het gelijkheidsbeginsel', in: Rikki Holtmaat (ed), *De Toekomst van Gelijkheid. De juridische en maatschappelijke inbedding van de gelijkebehandelingsnorm*, Deventer: Kluwer 2000, 179-192.

Wolff 2002

Alexander Wolff, (Case note on *Pokrzeptowicz-Meyer*), *Europäisches Wirtschafts- und Steuerrecht. Betriebs-Berater für Europarecht* 2002, 188-189.

Wouters 1994

Jan Wouters, 'The Case-Law of the European Court of Justice on Direct Taxes: Variations upon a Theme', *MJ* 1994, 179-220.

Wouters 1999

Jan Wouters, 'The principle of non-discrimination in European Community law', *EC Tax Review* 1999/2, 98-106.

Wouters 2001

Jan Wouters, 'Constitutional Limits of Differentiation: The Principle of Equality', in: Bruno de Witte, Dominik Hanf & Ellen Vos (eds), *The Many Faces of Differentiation in EU Law*, Antwerpen/Oxford/New York: Intersentia 2001, 301-345.

Wyatt 1975

Derrick Wyatt, 'The scope of "equal treatment" under Articles 7 and 12 of Regulation 1612/68', *EL Rev* 1975, 62/63.

Wyatt 1980

Derrick Wyatt, (Case note on *Macarthys*), *EL Rev* 1980, 374-380.

Wyatt 1981

Derrick Wyatt, 'Current survey. Contrasting cases on non-discrimination', *EL Rev* 1981, 42-51.

Wyatt 1986

Derrick Wyatt, (Case note on *Pinna I*), *CML Rev* 1986, 703-717.

Wyatt & Dashwood 2000

A.M. Arnull, A.A. Dashwood, M.G. Ross & D.A. Wyatt, *Wyatt & Dashwood's European Union Law*, 4th edition, London: Sweet & Maxwell 2000.

X 1978 (Steinike & Weinlig)

X, (Case note on *Steinike & Weinlig*), *Journal de droit international* 1978, 373-384.

X 1978 (Thieffry)

X, (Case note on *Thieffry*), *Journal du droit international* 1978, 957-964.

X 1981

X, (Case note on *van Wesemael*), *Journal du droit international* 1981, 154-157.

X 1988

X, (Case note on *Heylens*), *Journal du droit international* 1988, 517-518.

X 1990

X, (Case note on *Data-processing contracts*), *Foro italiano* 1990 IV 113.

X 1995

X, (Case note on *Corsica Ferries*), *Il Foro Italiano* 1995 IV 373-374.

X 1997

X, (Case note on *O'Flynn*), *Journal du droit international* 1997, 542-543.

Xuereb 2002

Peter G. Xuereb, 'The future of Europe: solidarity and constitutionalism. Towards a solidarity model', *EL Rev* 2002, 643-662.

Ysewijn 1997

J.L. Ysewijn, (Case note on *Gebhard*), *SEW* 1997, 24-28.

Zacher 2002

Hans F. Zacher, 'Wird es einen europäischen Sozialstaat geben?', *Europarecht* 2002, 147-164.

Zuleeg 1992

Manfred Zuleeg, 'Betrachtungen zum Gleichheitssatz im Europäischen Gemeinschaftsrecht', in: Jürgen R., Peter-Christian Müller-Graff & Manfreed Zuleeg (eds), *Europarecht – Energierecht – Wirtschaftrecht. Festschrift für Bodo Börner zum 70. Geburtstag*, Köln et al.: Carl Heymanns Verlag 1992, 473-483.

INDEX